Understanding Mughal India

Sixteenth to Eighteenth Centuries

Meena Bhargava

Orient BlackSwan

UNDERSTANDING MUGHAL INDIA: SIXTEENTH TO EIGHTEENTH CENTURIES

ORIENT BLACKSWAN PRIVATE LIMITED

Registered Office
3-6-752 Himayatnagar, Hyderabad 500 029, Telangana, India
e-mail: centraloffice@orientblackswan.com

Other Offices
Bengaluru, Bhopal, Chennai, Guwahati,
Hyderabad, Jaipur, Kolkata, Lucknow, Mumbai,
New Delhi, Noida, Patna, Visakhapatnam

First published by Orient Blackswan Private Limited in 2020

ISBN 978-93-5287-869-7

Typeset in
Adobe Garamond Pro 11.5/13.5
by Shine Graphics, Delhi 110 094

030541

Printed in India at
Glorious Printers, Delhi

Published by
Orient Blackswan Private Limited
3-6-752, Himayatnagar,
Hyderabad 500 029,
Telangana, India
e-mail: info@orientblackswan.com

Contents

Understanding Mughal India

Boxes

Images and Plates

Images

Plates (Between Chapters 1 and 2)

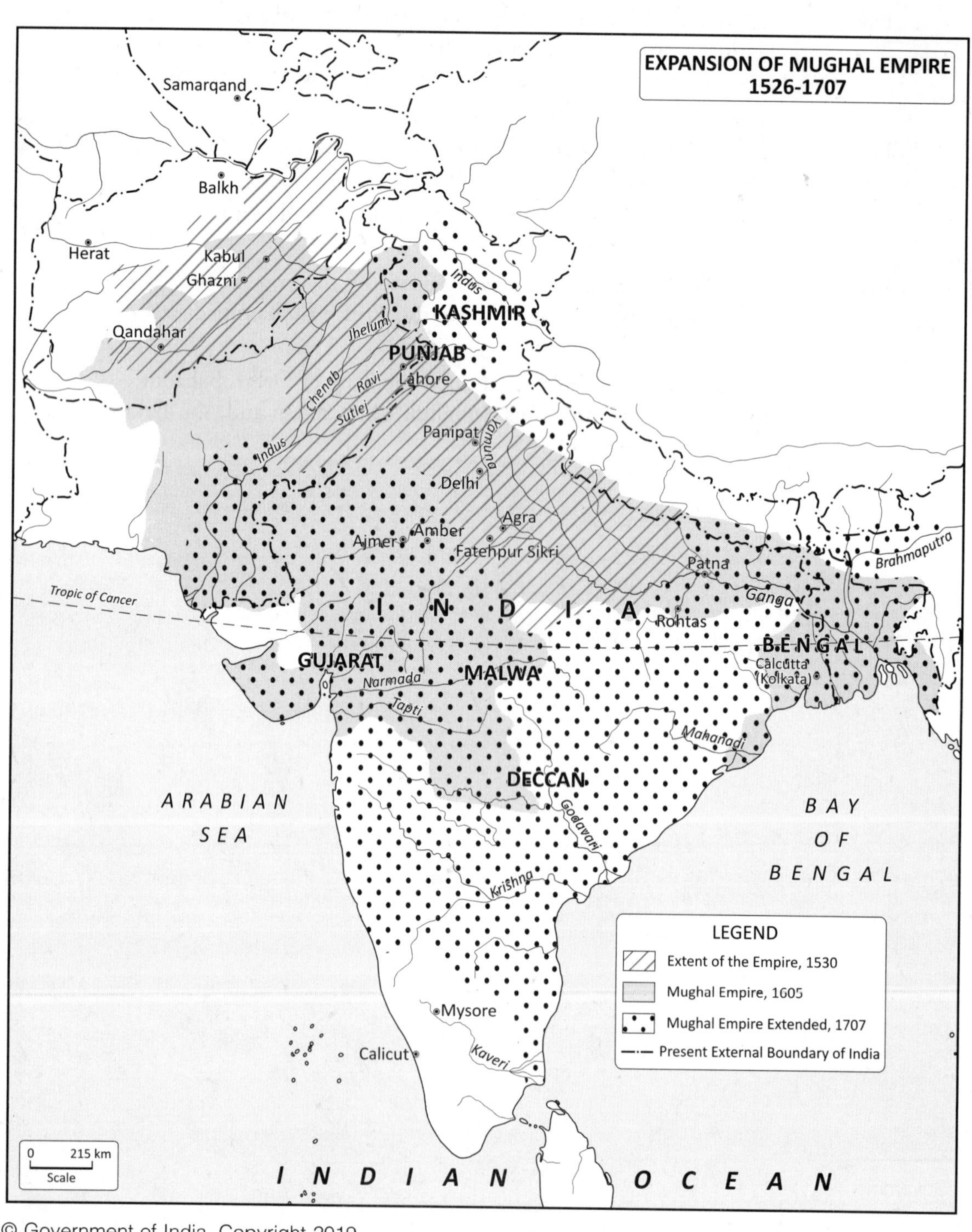
EXPANSION OF MUGHAL EMPIRE
1526-1707
Samarqand
Balkh
Herat
Kabul
Ghazni
Qandahar
Indus
KASHMIR
Jhelum
PUNJAB
Lahore
Chenab
Ravi
Sutlej
Panipat
Yamuna
Indus
Delhi
Agra
Ajmer
Amber
Fatehpur Sikri
Patna
Brahmaputra
Tropic of Cancer
Ganga
Rohtas
I N D I A
BENGAL
GUJARAT
MALWA
Calcutta
(Kolkata)
Narmada
Tapti
Mahanadi
DECCAN
ARABIAN
SEA
Godavari
BAY
OF
BENGAL
Krishna
LEGEND
Extent of the Empire, 1530
Mughal Empire, 1605
Mughal Empire Extended, 1707
Present External Boundary of India
Mysore
Calicut
Kaveri
0 215 km
Scale
INDIAN OCEAN

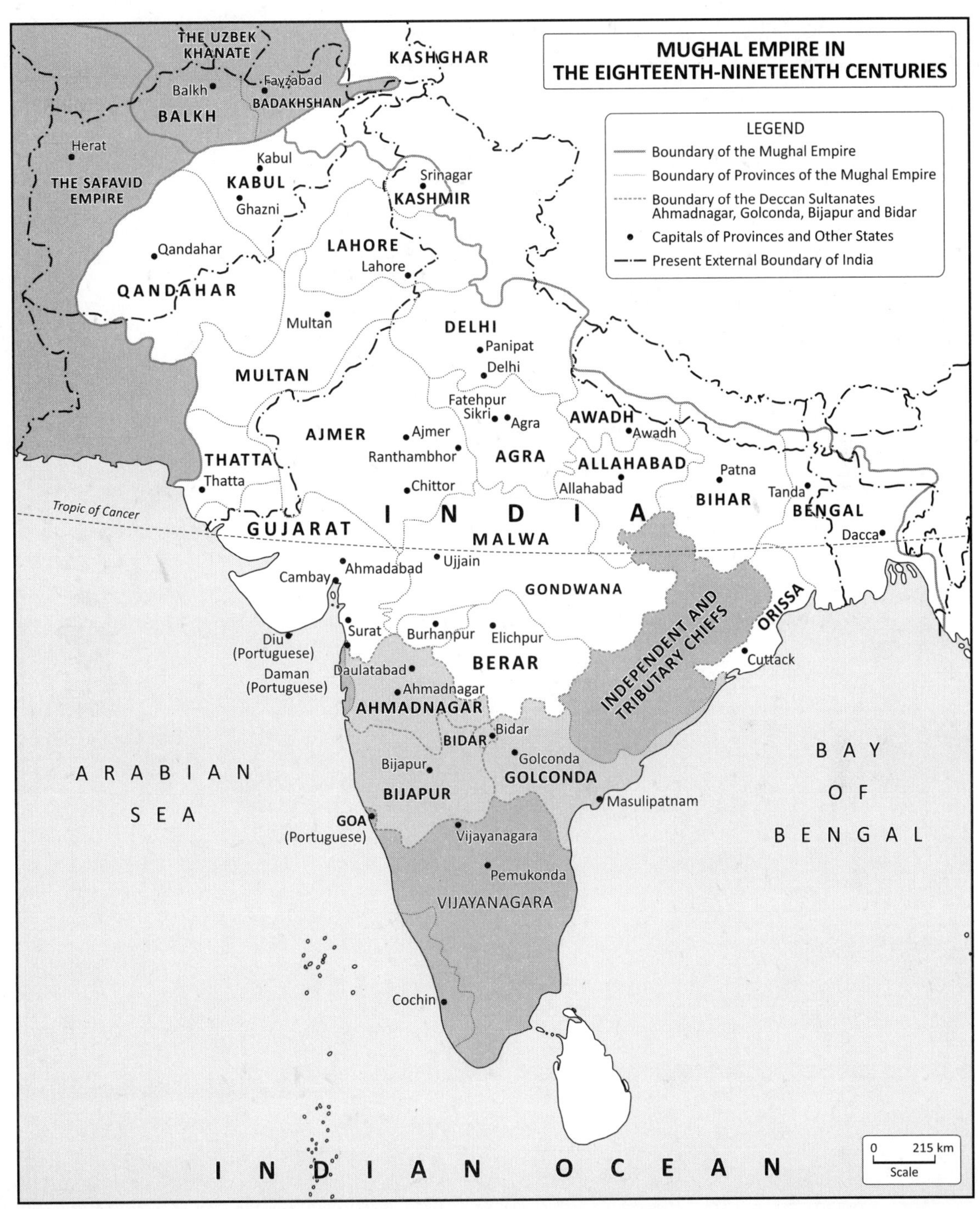

The external boundaries and coastlines of India agree with the Record/Master Copy certified by the Survey of India.

INTRODUCTION

This study is an attempt to understand the Mughal State in India, its idioms and institutions, and the regions that constituted it. Marked by social and economic dynamism and cultural vibrancy, it bound together persons of different ethno-racial, religious, and linguistic backgrounds, although 'Regional Centralization' (a term borrowed from Alam and Subrahmanyam 1998) remained its distinguishing feature, stimulated further in the eighteenth and early nineteenth centuries by the political and military expansion of the English East India Company. There has been some debate on the use of the term 'Mughal' as an incorrect description for Babur's dynasty. 'Mughal' is an Arabised transliteration of 'Moghol', the Persian term for Mongol, although Babur and his progeny had identified themselves as Timurids.

It is the 'misspelling of a misnomer', as Stephen Dale (1996) observed; he suggested that given the generalised use of the term 'Mughal' for South Asian Timurids, it would be worthwhile to adopt John Richards (2007 [1993]) formulation, with a modification of the spelling, and use the epithet 'Timurid-Mughuls' for Babur's dynasty. Notwithstanding the debate, the Mughal emperors, like a number of others in Central Asia and Iran, claimed to be the legitimate descendants of the great figure of the 'Lord of the Conjunction' (*Sahib-i-Qiran*), Amir Timur Guregen, asserted their right to the territories held by him, referred to themselves as

Box 1: The Mongols

The **Mongols** were originally from the steppe region of Central Asia and followed a nomadic way of life. Known to be fierce warriors and cavalry, the Mongol clans were united in 1206 by Temujin, later addressed as Genghiz (Chingiz Khan). Like Chingiz Khan, the Mongols were Tengerians and believed in Shamanist philosophy. Shamanism is a form of animism, which believed that everything has spiritual essence, including rocks, water, and plants, and that human beings were mere living spiritual creatures in a world of other spirits or forces or gods. The greatest spirits, the Shamanists believed, were Koke Mongke Tengri, the Eternal Blue Heaven, and Mother Earth. Although a Tengriist, Chingiz Khan was interested in all religions. In fact, many Mongols, despite their belief in Shamanism, were practitioners of other religions as well. Chingiz Khan followed a policy of religious tolerance and allowed freedom of worship, even as the Mongols embarked on a rigorous policy of conquests. Eastern Iran, Khwarazm, and Afghanistan felt the severe brunt of their campaigns. The Mongols first came to India when Chingiz Khan entered the western bank of the river Indus in CE 1221 in pursuit of the Sultan of Khwarazm, Jalal-ud-din Mingbarni.

By the mid-thirteenth century, the Mongols had become a menace in the entire Punjab region, up to Lahore and Dipalpur. It was Ala-ud-din Khalji, the Sultan of Delhi (1296–1316), who could successfully eliminate the constant Mongol threat. Many Mongols deserted their clans and several were taken prisoner. They were converted to Islam and recruited in the service of the Sultanate of Delhi as soldiers and military officers, thus casting tremendous influence on the political and military institutions of the Sultanate.

Silsilah-i Guregen or *Guregeniyya*, and exuded a deep sense of being a part of a tradition of Might and Power that characterised the Mongols.

Jahangir, for instance, was relentlessly obsessed with his dynastic lineage and urged the maintaining of Timurid political and cultural continuities, referring to Transoxiana (Turan) as his *vilayet-i marusi* (hereditary territories) and *mulk-i marusi* (ancestral domain). Abu'l Fazl, Akbar's biographer and a chronicler of the sixteenth century, traced Mughal ancestry back through Timur and Chingiz Khan to the mythical Mongol Queen, Alanqoa/Alanquwa, impregnated by divine light. Amongst her children, one of whom was an ancestor of Chingiz Khan's nine generations earlier, was also the progenitor of the Mughals. Her day of conception, Abu'l Fazl said, was *aghaz-i zuhur* or 'the beginning of the manifestation of his Majesty (Akbar)'.

Box 2: Timur

Timur (1334–1405) was born in the Barlas tribe of the Mongolid Turks. He established his rule at Samarqand in 1370. Subsequently, with the assistance of his Turko-Mongol corps of military officials, he expanded the extent of his empire that included the whole of Khwarazm and Turkistan, Persia and Mesopotamia. He further conquered the Ottoman territories in Anatolia and the entire region that extended up to the Sulaiman range in the east. In 1398, he crossed River Indus near Bannu and proceeded towards Delhi. Upon conquering Delhi in 1398, he set up his throne at Idgah and ordered the *Khutba* to be read in his name at *masjid-i jami* (*Quwwat-ul-Islam* mosque) and several other mosques of Delhi. The *Malfuzat-i Timuri* narrates extensively the stay of Timur in Delhi and describes his visits to the cities of Siri, Old Delhi (then Qil'a Rai Pithora), Jahanpanah, Firuzabad, and Firuz Shah Tughluq's palace, called *Jahan Numa* (now known as Kotla Firuz Shah). Timur's act of touring the cities of Delhi was later emulated by the Mughal emperors whenever they visited it, prior to its becoming the capital in the seventeenth century.

Such formulations evidently influenced traditions in art, visible in the painting (*c.* 1550–55) by Abd as-Samad, titled 'Princes of the House of Timur', that portrayed dynastic succession (see Plate 1).

The Mughal Empire, in other words, manifested that phase in the early modern period in which Mongol traditions of rule and empire, Central Asian ethnic heritage, and the cultural orientation of Persia were imbibed by indigenous South Asian culture, and introduced new patterns of power, patronage, and wealth. While it represented cross-cultural interaction and dynamism in almost all spheres, be it economy, technology, culture, social relations or aesthetics, it was not irreligious; but at the same time,

Box 3: Chingiz Khan

Chingiz Khan (1155–1227), the chief of the nomadic Mongol tribes, initiated Mongol invasions and conquests that took place throughout the thirteenth century, resulting in the vast Mongol Empire. His campaigns were against the Qara Khitai, Caucasus, Khwarazm, Western Xia, and Jin dynasties. By the time of his death in 1227, the Mongol Empire covered a large portion of Central Asia and China. During the reign of the Sultans of Delhi, cities in north India were flooded with immigrants from eastern Iran, Khurasan, Transoxiana, and Afghanistan, seeking refuge from the invasions of Chingiz Khan. He reached India in 1221 in search of the Sultan of Khwarazm, Jalal-ud-din Mingbarni. Iltutmish, the Sultan of Delhi at that time, succeeded in preventing direct conflict with Chingiz Khan by refusing Mingbarni asylum in Delhi. Iltutmish instead projected Delhi as the 'sanctuary of Islam' and a shelter against Chingiz Khan's holocaust.

it was far from being theocratic. Recognising the space for religious differences, it permitted exclusive modes of worship and was a testimony to social peace and composite culture, rather than communalism. It was, as some scholars have argued, a grandiose realm; one of the great early modern agrarian empires, the most powerful and richest the subcontinent had ever known—'a top-down enterprise' (Asher and Talbot 2008) that did not eliminate or merge the local societies that it ruled, but kept them together through the imposition of bureaucracy and administrative practices. The most glamorous of the Muslim superpowers of the early modern period, it shared its Turko-Mongol heritage with Uzbeks in Central Asia, Safavids in Persia, and the Ottomans in the Near and Middle East and the Balkans.

The core military and economic institutions of these early modern empires, argued Barbara Metcalf (2009), were not specifically 'Islamic', but shared characteristic patterns that were common across Asia. In fact, throughout Eurasia, this was an era of increased global contacts, demographic transformations and growth, and political power and authority. Many others like Ghalib and Muhammad Zaka'ullah, the proponents of Urdu and Persian nostalgic indigenous literature in the eighteenth–early nineteenth century, wrote in celebration of Mughal glory and splendour and high Mughal culture. Contemporaneous with these celebratory writings were the works of some British and other European scholars that re-investigated the Mughal institutions subsequent to the changing political developments in the nineteenth century. Historians and philologists like H. Blochmann surpassed William Jones in their understanding of the Mughal Empire and contributed to the publication of texts in Persian (*Bibliotheca Indica Series*), facilitating the positivistic history-writing of the early twentieth century. The magnificence and the festivity of the empire apart, for some it was a regime that engendered oppression, exploitation, and tyranny. The Mughal State has remained polarised, controversial, and complex vis-à-vis several such issues and debates, and occupies an important place in the historiography of early modern India.

THE ISSUE OF COMMUNITY IDENTITY

These characteristics notwithstanding, the question that arises is: Did the Mughal State symbolise 'Islamic Conquest', or was it proto-nationalist? The answer lies in contemporary sources. While the Indo-Islamic responses were assimilative and integrative, the Sanskrit sources from the eighth to the fourteenth centuries categorised the immigrants not as 'Muslims', but as *Turushka* (Turks) and *Yavana*, and referred to the Mughal emperors as *Dillipati*, *Dillisa* or *Dillisvara*. In fact, a few Sanskrit sources even described the *Yavana* rulers as pious and *dharmic*, protectors of *varnashrama dharma* whose texts, even in their own language, could provide corrections or improvements to the Sanskrit tradition of astronomical principles, that is, *siddhanta*s. The Telugu inscriptions of the fourteenth through the seventeenth centuries identified them by terms such as *ashvapati*, the lords of the horses, demonstrating that the Muslims were not a 'unique foreign category' as claimed by later ideologies, but assimilated as yet another ethnic group in diverse India. Islam and Muslim—or its Persian variant, Musalman—do not figure in these inscriptions; instead, they use ethnic labels—Turk or *Turushka*, Persian or *Parasika*, and Greek or *Yavana*.

Rayavacakamu, a Telugu narrative that situated itself in the reign of the king of the Vijayanagara kingdom, Krishna Deva Raya, characterised the rulers of the northern sultanates of Deccan—Bijapur, Ahmadnagar, and Golconda—as 'Turks' rather than as 'Muslims' while referring to their pernicious practices of punishment, suggesting that their code distinguished the 'civilised' from the 'barbaric' norms of justice, and identifying 'Turkish' rulers with the latter because of their fondness for wine and opium. This was further contrasted with the Brahmins who consumed a simple diet of rice, pulses (*sambhar*), and salt, indicating thus that the concerns were regional, geographical, linguistic, and pertaining to diet, rather than religious. Similarly, *Andhra Kamandakamu*, a *niti* book by Jakkaraju Venkatakavi, written in 1584 in the post-Krishna Deva Raya period in the Vijayanagara kingdom made no mention of the Muslims (either approvingly or disapprovingly), but referred to them as Turks or *Turakalu*, demonstrating that its interest lay not in religion but, like all other Telugu texts, was 'this-worldly' (*laukika*) or 'secular' in character. Inscriptions from other areas of the Indian subcontinent are likewise silent about the Islamic religion and Islamic affiliations of the Turks; the Rajputs, Brahmins, and other non-Muslims did not characterise the establishment of the Delhi Sultanate in the thirteenth century as 'Islamic Conquest' or 'Muslim Period', nor did the Mughals excite xenophobia or face the problem of being 'foreigners' ruling over an alien land, as anachronistically imagined during the colonial period. In fact, as Phillip Wagoner (1996) has argued in the context of the kingdom of Vijayanagara, the Turks, Telugus, Brahmins, and others interacted in the same social space. He has identified inscriptions that illustrate Turks in the service of the Vijayanagara kingdom, while the Brahmins were patronised by the Adil Shahi rulers of Bijapur, which had strong Persian connections.

Moreover, a mosque inscription from Vijayanagara talks of a mosque built by a *Shaivite* king and described as a *dharmsala* or a rest-house, ascertaining that while religious activities would be one of the many characteristics of a mosque, it could also serve as a rest-house for travellers. Cynthia Talbot (1995) observed that although, during the initial period of immigration, the Turks were described as *mleccha* (a term that can be traced to Vedic texts, meaning 'impure' and used to refer to non-Sanskrit speaking peoples often outside the caste hierarchy. Sanskrit literature frequently used the term to describe foreigners; in English, *mleccha* could be translated as barbarian, connoting a lack of culture and civilisation), it was also used for low castes and tribal communities. *Mleccha*, then, does not have a primary religious connotation. It is, as Romila Thapar (1989) has argued, 'a signal of social and cultural difference', a generic category into which all such social groups that did not adhere to Brahmanical norms were thrust. These varying terms with historical meanings thus suggest diverse perceptions rather than a monolithic view, and point to the fact that the determinants for judging a ruler were not his religion, but his ethnic or linguistic identities or his place of origin. Similarly, within early medieval Brahmanical discourse, B. D. Chattopadhyaya (1998) located an 'essential urge to legitimize' any ruling authority that was effective and responsible, as manifested in the case of the Tughluq Sultans as legitimate successors to the Tomaras and Cahamanas, or of the Mughal emperors as supporters of *Ramarajya* (the rule of Lord Rama).

This discussion evidently runs contrary to colonial polemics on religious identities. But the paradox remains: If the people of India did not perceive the immigrants as 'Muslims', then was there a 'Hindu' identity? To answer this, it is imperative to understand the notion of community in pre-colonial India and delve into the historical evolution of the concept of 'Hindu', a geographical feature at the outset. The notion of community, while present in pre-colonial times, was one of multiple communities identified by locality, language, caste, occupation, and sect; there was no idea of a uniform, religious community that could be identified as 'Hindu'. Arabic and Persian use of the term 'Hindu' denoted a variety of meanings, sometimes ethnic or geographic, but was used neither for a religion nor a culture. It referred to those who inhabited the Indian subcontinent, that is, the land across the Sindhu or the Indus river.

The early Muslim view of India shows a close parallel to the Western *Mirabilia Indiae* in the narrative of '*aja'ib al-Hind*'. *Al-Hind* was an Arab conception, a political-geographical identity, and 'Hindus' were those who resided in this region. It was the Muslims who first defined India as a civilisation, demarcated it conceptually, and delineated its boundaries. Gradually, and over a period of time, the term 'Hindu' was used for not only those who stayed in India, but also for those who practised a religion other than Islam or Christianity. This all-inclusive usage of the term 'Hindu', which included not only the Brahmins but also low castes, challenged the precepts of Brahmanism and surprised the different castes and sects who saw themselves as separate entities.

Observations such as these counter the polemical discussions of the nineteenth and twentieth century that hold that 'Hindu' and 'Muslim' were fixed categories; or that tend to differentiate the 'Hindu' or 'Muslim' elements in culture (when they may be neither or both); or that religion was the cause of all social conflicts; or that there were forced mass conversions during the period. Taking the case of Bengal and Punjab, Richard Eaton (1994) showed the redundancy of the term 'conversion' and urged for it to be dropped. He argued that what we call conversion was simply the appeal of esoteric mystical traditions and thus the allegiance of the people to the Sufi intermediaries. In Bengal, as in the subcontinent in general, Eaton (2001) reiterated, Islam and Islamic culture were integrated with indigenous culture and local societies, and by the eighteenth century, Islam in South Asia had, in several respects, become as utterly Indian as any other religion. If the actual history of religious exchange exemplifies that there have never been clearly defined groups labelled 'Hindu' and 'Muslim', then it is worthwhile to adopt a new vocabulary—*Islamicate* (coined by Marshall G. S. Hodgson) and *Indic*—and move beyond fixed categories, whether religious or ethnic, Hindu or Turk, in order to understand their plural identities in different historical contexts, transcending divisions. To illustrate this, the verse of a Qadiri poet, Bullhe Shah (1680–1758), may be considered, which reads:

Neither Arab am I nor man of Lahore;
Nor Indian from the town of Nagaur;
Neither Hindu am I nor Turk of Peshawar.

Both the terms *Islamicate* and *Indic* suggest 'a repertoire of language and behaviour, knowledge and power that define broad cosmologies of human existence'; neither denotes a 'simply bounded group self-defined as Muslim or Hindu' (Gilmartin and Lawrence 2002, 2). Labels such as Hindu and Muslim may have been used in colonial architectural styles, but they signified 'shared taste' and not religious exclusivity or isolation. There is thus a general consensus that it is questionable whether a Hindu or a Muslim identity existed in any meaningful sense prior to the nineteenth century. Investigations into the issue of community identities reveal that the notion of communal violence was a British construct, influenced by the orientalist assumption that religion was the fundamental division in Indian society. Given the criticism of the colonial sociology of knowledge and its emphasis on caste, many scholars have argued that pre-colonial society was too fragmented by sub-caste and local loyalties to have allowed larger allegiances to emerge. In this context may be mentioned the work of Benedict Anderson (1991), which has been particularly effective in generating the understanding that identities uniting large numbers of people could be achieved subsequent to attaining a certain technological level.

RE-READING THE ORIENTALIST DISCOURSE

Europeans, however, considered Islamic civilisation a 'wholly alien "other"' and 'a historic and cultural foil', in contrast to which they defined their own collective identity as a world civilisation and justified European domination over Islamic societies in the eighteenth–nineteenth century, by representing Islam as a 'static monolith', insusceptible to change and historical process. Narratives such as these necessitate a reflection on the orientalist view of Indian history and its prejudice against the pre-colonial period, in particular, the rule of the Delhi sultans and the Mughal emperors. It was alleged that Islamic history could be understood and interpreted on its own terms by the 'believers' alone, implying thus the study of theology and not history, and negating the fact that Islam, like Christendom, was also a historical phenomenon that interacted with people outside its fold and required the same critical tools, namely freedom from bias, and from preconceived assumptions and convictions. Affected by the orientalist view of history, the periodisation of Indian history—into Hindu, Muslim, and the British periods, almost like 'ontologically fixed epochal boundaries', essentialist and statist in nature—subsequent to the publication of James Mill's *The History of British India* in 1817, set aside the understanding of processes and evolutions in an extremely pluralistic Indian society.

It may be mentioned, though, that Sir William Jones (1746–94), founder-member of the first Indological institution, the Asiatic Society of Bengal (1784), had already propounded the idea of a Hindu and Muslim India, emphasised the necessity of studying Eastern languages and texts, and compared the 'golden age of India' with the classical periods of Greece and Rome. While European scholars of the eighteenth century defined Indian culture and the Sanskrit texts as ahistorical, Jones was convinced that some texts, even if they included the myths and legends of the Hindus, contained the core of a history. He believed that the *Purana*s, which contained a story of a flood (similar to Noah's flood), were proof of the *Bible* narrative. Dubbing Jones as an 'Orientalist', 'Anglicists' like Mill, and subsequently Lord Macaulay, advocated that Western knowledge in English should displace the Eastern, for India—especially 'Hindu' India—lacked a strong tradition of historical writing, and time for them was supposedly 'fuzzy', or even 'cyclical'. Inspired by his 'utilitarianism' and undeterred by any notions of racism and discrimination in his colonial form of knowledge, Mill defined the pre-colonial period in India not simply by the religion of the ruling dynasties; he also characterised it as lacking in any vision of science, rationality, and enlightenment until it was incorporated into the British Empire. Strongly pejorative, Mill introduced a new idiom for imperial control by articulating the theory of Oriental Despotism, implicit in which is a denial of a sense of history, alleging that the Indians, in relation to historical, cultural, and moral development, were far inferior even when compared to the primitive tribes of early Britain. His argument became seminal in suggesting that Indian society was static, marked by constancy and changelessness, 'befogged in timeless "tradition"'—opaque, distant, and inaccessible, until the British government introduced legislations heralding change, and thus the notion of history. Such assertions make his ideas both heuristically irrelevant and politically dangerous.

Mill's *History* or John Bentley's *A Historical View of the Hindu Astronomy* (1823) emphasised the superiority of European civilisation as compared to Indian antiquity and drained all representations of India from British historical scholarship—which were replaced by a much more overt linking of British understanding of Indian history and culture to their own Empire's civilising mission. For instance, any claims made by Indians to scientific knowledge was explained by Bentley as a relatively recent acquisition and borrowed from Europe; that the Indian texts could provide alternate systems of knowledge was hardly conceded, and neither was there an attempt at a discourse with Indian scholars on the wider context of the texts and their authors. This ideology of conflict over the status of Indian knowledge and the veracity of Brahmanical authority persisted into the nineteenth century. James Ballantyne, Principal of the Benares Sanskrit College, stressed on the propagation of Western knowledge and Christian ideas through indigenous media using Sanskrit and Hindi, although many of his students considered Hindi a 'vulgar tongue'. Although contemptuous of the intellectual culture of the *pandit*s, Ballantyne made it his personal project to improve the Sanskrit and Hindi dictionaries of the Serampore missionaries and advocated the rigorous application of the principles of Panini and classical grammarians, because the 'careful examination of their teaching systems would make it possible to build on layers of European knowledge onto the Indian substrata' (Bayly 1994, 8).

Lancelot Wilkinson, Assistant Resident at Bhopal, displayed a more intricate, complicated objective behind using the *Siddhantic* rationalist and observational traditions as a medium for transmitting Western scientific, mathematical, and cosmological ideas to Indians. It was not an attempt at seeking information, but was deeply implicated within Christian principles in the belief that since Christ's truth was essentially reasonable, the Indian system of philosophy and mode of reasoning could be attained by its implementation. An important trope of the nineteenth century—that India was the centre of 'decaying' knowledge—is evident in the observation of Lord Minto (1811), who lamented that Indian knowledge was in decay, that the number of the learned had diminished, and that the civilised world was confronted with 'the disuse or even loss of many valuable [Indian] books'.

Ideas of German romanticism reinforced religion and mysticism as aspects of Indian culture, averring that it lacked knowledge and that since caste was a major factor in Indian civil society, it overwhelmed the State; and without the State, there could be no history. Hegel, like Mill, attributed 'dreaming irrationality' to the Indian mind and talked of 'repellent characteristics, pervading every single feature of society' as one crossed the Indus, and that 'the Hindus have no history, no growth expanding into a veritable political condition' (Hegel 1956, 163; *cf* Hasan

2005, 86). Hegel's view of a stagnant pre-colonial India was shared by several orientalists, who asserted that the Hindus 'perfectly destitute of historical records, displayed every sign of being an irrational people ... and are gratified with the productions of the mythologists and poets' (Mill 1840–48, Vol. I, 114–15; *cf* Lal 2001, 103). Even Karl Marx was in accord with these proponents of imperialism, although his reasons lay not in stagnant religious beliefs but in the Asiatic Mode of Production, which depicted the Indian State as a strange 'hermaphrodite juxtaposing the unchanging, unstratified, communally landowning village societies and the absolute power of the oriental despot' (Kulke 1995, 3). Hypotheses such as these were in conjunction with the observations of Max Weber; for instance, 'Only in the West does science exist at a stage of development which we recognize to-day as valid', or 'rational chemistry has been absent from all areas of culture except the West', or that 'all Indian political thought was lacking in a systematic method comparable to that of Aristotle' (Pollock 2011, 2n). These emphasised the distinctness of Western rationality, technology, rights-bearing citizenship, aptitude for capitalism—in brief, Western modernity and, therefore, eventually the global conquest. Weber, nevertheless, was quick to add—and probably the first to acknowledge—that his ideas were provisional, presumably realising that these interpretations were based more on assumptions rather than an actual analysis of data.

The *locus classicus* for the colonial story, however, as Barbara Metcalf (2009) pointed out, was the highly judgmental work of Sir Henry M. Elliot and his colleague John Dowson, *History of India as Told by Its Own Historians*, first published in 1849 (as a compilation in eight volumes of translated selections from Persian and Arabic sources), which intended to tell the story of the Muslims in India, but instead became the story of the British. Elliot disabused the 'bombastic young *baboos* (English-educated gentry of Calcutta)' of the idea that the Mughal era was superior to British rule and reaffirmed that his publication was a reminder of the ineffable superiority of the British. With the advent of British rule, 'a more stirring and eventful era of India's History commences ...', and the 'colonial subjects had been delivered from oppression and granted the free gift of enlightened rule'. Critical of commentaries such as these, Metcalf asserted that the histories created in the colonial period 'are thus not academic'. Thomas Trautmann (2004), on the other hand, argued that the Orientalists' biased verdict towards pre-colonial India, particularly the ancient times, signified the clash of chronologies between the *Bible* and the ancient period of Indian history. The Orientalists just could not recognise and accept what they saw in India as comparable to their idea of constituted history. Orientalist scholars like James Mill, argued Richard Eaton (2001), indulged in 'armchair theorizing', with most of them never having visited India, dependent on normative textual material published in Europe and unaware of 'ground-level data' that may have better informed them about the people of whom they theorised.

PERIODISATION IN INDIAN HISTORY

James Mill's *History*, written to refute many of William Jones's ideas is, as Ronald Inden (2006) observed, a model text of utilitarianism, pre-Darwinian evolutionism, and a hegemonic narrative based on Indological discourse, even though Mill can hardly be hailed as the founder of Indology. Yet, he triumphed over the 'Orientalists', influenced the policies of the East India Company, and prevailed on it to adopt his 'utilitarian, positivist view', not only in the discipline of Indology but also in government practice. James Mill's formulation—Hindu, Muhammadan, and the British period—dominated the writing of Indian history much beyond the middle of the twentieth century. It was replaced by the terms Ancient–Medieval–Modern only around the turn of the twentieth century, when Stanley Lane-Poole used the European prism of history to study Indian history. Despite his efforts to transpose the European model onto Indian history, Lane-Poole failed to generate immediate response, evident from the works of Vincent A. Smith. Smith's imperialist, orientalist bias remained unshaken when he included selections from Mill's work in his volume *The Oxford History of India* (1919) and continued to use terms like 'Muslim Conquest', 'The Medieval Hindu Kingdoms' (for the period between the death of King Harsha in 647 CE and the 'Muslim Conquest'), 'India in the Muslim Period', and 'India in the British Period'.

Europeans and North Americans had produced many overlapping images of 'the Orient' or the 'East' as the 'Other' and created an identity for Orientalism by constructing compartments, viz., the 'East' (the Oriental) and the 'West' (the Occidental), and enforced a disjunction between the modern and medieval periods of history. In this concept, the medieval is portrayed as the 'adolescent' stage of modernity, compelled to be seen as the 'other' over time as it became memorialised and rigidly periodised. 'Medieval' appeared as a residual category, as something that was 'un-modern' and, as if in order to understand the 'medieval', it was first necessary to understand the 'modern'. The links and continuities between the medieval and modern periods were ignored and the practitioners of medieval history relegated to 'disciplinary exile'. The knowledge of the medieval was seen as redundant and useless for knowing the modern. Both periods were perceived as intellectually separate and isolated from each other. In the Indian context, where modernity was associated with colonialism and imperialism, the division between medieval and modern periods was even more rigid. British imperialism and colonialism were seen as the pioneers of change, whereas the medieval period was cast as archaic, encouraging constancy and devoid of history.

Suggestions such as these tend to insinuate that had India not witnessed colonialism, it would have remained deprived of modernity and enlightenment. However, if Indian society on the eve of the colonial period was medieval and feudal, then historical evolution was not completely alien to it, and neither was the hiatus between Indians and 'civilised Europeans' as wide and intense as has been suggested; to the contrary, the 'white man's mission' (Jha and Vanina 2009) itself was questionable. Critiquing the 'Orientalist discourse' and with a view to deconstructing it, Inden (2006) argued that it has produced facts on India by an 'episteme' (a way of knowing that implies a particular view) that has resulted in a hierarchic relationship between the 'knower' and the 'known', privileging the former and subordinating the knowledges of the 'known'. It is an 'artificial construct' contradicting the assumptions of the 'knower'—that her/his knowledge is natural and objective and beyond political debate.

The fondness for imperialist credentials espoused by the likes of James Mill, which continued to cast its shadow on the works of some twentieth-century British historians like Edward Thompson and G. T. Garrett (1934), who eulogised Britain's civilising mission and efforts at arbitration in the disputes between the supposedly homogenous blocs of Hindus and Muslims. Thompson (1925, 27–28) even asserted that 'Indians are not historians . . . they rarely show any critical ability . . . their most useful books . . . research and information exasperate with their repetitions and diffuseness and lose effect by their uncritical enthusiasms . . . So they are not likely to displace our account of our connection with India'. Such views stand averted, displaced, and confined to oblivion. Several South Asian scholars have rejected and challenged the rigid periodisation in Indian history and demonstrated interconnections and continuities between the pre-colonial/medieval and colonial/modern periods, notwithstanding the chronological markers in Indian history—Ancient, Early Medieval, Medieval, Early Modern, Modern—although not in the conventional, stereotyped way. They have been redefined to represent not merely a chronological phase but their specific attributes, cultural traits, and historical processes, implicitly rejecting the notion of the changelessness of Indian society, inextricably connected with the theories of Orientalism. As we entered the twentieth century, newer issues and concerns inspired by the Marxist framework, subaltern studies, anthropology, sociology, religious and literary studies, arts and aesthetics further eroded these boundaries.

Studies on medieval India created and strengthened a separate realm of research facilitating discussion on the possibilities of evolution within the medieval period. The term 'medieval' is now considered too conventional, one that can barely generate any systematic dialogue between medievalists in different parts of the globe, for it neither defines a social formation nor a stage of development. Contrary to the nationalist and feudalist historiography, B. D. Chattopadhyaya (2005) and Hermann Kulke (1995) provided an 'integrative' or 'processural' model that did not see the medieval State as a pre-given entity or a consequence of political fragmentation; instead, it was seen as having developed in a 'continuous process from below'. The focus of study thus shifted from dynastic, personality-based narratives to economy and society, and the structure, organisation, and formation of the regional State became fundamental historical concerns. The historiography on the Mughal State moved towards greater diversity and complexity, reflecting several methodologies—colonialist, nationalist, Marxist, regional dynamics that complicated the 'military-fiscalist' Marxist model (the Aligarh School), non-State centred histories of social communities, and the ethno-history of military labour markets.

With the emergence of new approaches and critiques, many scholars sought to situate the Mughal Empire within a larger global, trans-regional framework; understand the shared historical trajectories (including the shared Turko-Mongol heritage) with its contemporaneous empires—Safavid, Uzbek, and Ottoman; stressed on the South Asian mercantile connections in the Indian Ocean from 1500; and reinterpreted the eighteenth century as dynamic and vigorous. This heralded the unmistakable rise of a new social order as an *inqilab*—a world turned upside down. This pattern of studies, along with the vibrant historiography of south India, has demonstrated India's links to the realm of the Indian Ocean and 'Eurasia', but more importantly, to the wider global historical paradigms, and authenticated that narratives of social formation, state formation or state typology, and modes of production cannot be studied or evaluated in the tripartite framework of Ancient, Medieval, Modern. This further reiterated that history cannot be periodised; neither can it be held that India was excluded from the rest of the world and that it followed its own rigid norms until it became a part of the British Empire. In fact, the period from the thirteenth to the eighteenth centuries, argue Asher and Talbot (2008), marked the beginning and heralded the 'highly pluralistic human landscape' of modern South Asia. It thus makes a good deal of sense to categorise the sixteenth through the eighteenth centuries, or roughly the three or four centuries preceding British colonial rule, as 'Early Modern' rather than 'Mughal India' or 'Late Medieval India' or 'Late Pre-Colonial India', not only, as Sanjay Subrahmanyam (2005a, b) has argued, for reasons of justice to the history of that period, but also to have a different premise to understand the colonial intervention and situate South Asia in 'wider historical conjunctures' going beyond the narrow political and cultural dimensions of history, contextualise South Asian culture, civilisation, and society in a way to better understand the more specific unfolding of Indian history, and lessen the extent to which India is seen as exceptional, unique, exotic, and detached from world history.

Although it is important to differentiate between colonial modernity and that which existed prior to it in India or elsewhere, it cannot be argued that the period preceding colonialism was not a form of modernity. In fact, various elements of 'modernity' may be found in 'indigenous' cultural forms between the sixteenth and the eighteenth centuries, marked by global social, political, and technological transitions and profound continuities that linked the early modern and modern worlds. The notion of the 'Early Modern' has been a matter of dispute among scholars, both regionalists and generalists, for over the past decade with regard to its teleological connotation (although one cannot avoid this in any form of periodisation that is not mechanical, but argumentative), which must be resisted, observed Sheldon Pollock (2011, 3), and so refuse 'to assign the period between 1500 and 1800 any shared structure or content a priori, let alone to insist on finding in it western modernity in embryonic form'. He stressed the importance of historical synchronicity, in which there was no space for definitional consistency or conceptual symmetry. The period, he stipulated, constituted an entirely reasonable periodisation for intellectual history, and can be called 'Early Modern' in the sense of a 'threshold, where potentially different futures may have been arrested or retained only as *masala* for that dominant form' (ibid.). There is yet another recent suggestion to dispense with all categories of the division of historical time and conceptualise value-neutral categories, namely early, recent, contemporary, or a simple demarcation by millennia, centuries, and decades (Mukhia 2013).

Contrary to the Orientalist construction of Indian history, it is widely established that societies construct a past or many pasts, and communities relate themselves to the perceived past, for the past has a social function. It provides social identity, although its construction, form, and content might change with new definitions of identity. The past is a permanent dimension of human consciousness and a necessary component of institutions, values, and other patterns of society. Therefore, to believe that '"traditional society" is static and unchanging is a myth of vulgar social science' (Hobsbawm 1972, 5). In variance to the suggestion that India lacked a sense of history, the pre-colonial period was not a *tabula rasa*, but had its own indigenous traditions of historiography, the *itihas-purana* tradition that included not only the genealogical tables of kings and definite historical data, but also a philosophy of history.

Bana Bhatta's *Harshcharita*, a text written in the first half of the seventh century, and Kalhana's *Rajataringini*, a twelfth-century chronicle on Kashmir, both in Sanskrit, provide remarkable evidence of historical analysis and historiographical tradition. Emphasising the importance of historiographical methods, Kalhana stipulated the ascertainment of evidence and evaluating the truth, 'free from passion and hatred'.

The energy and dynamism of South Asian society and culture are further strengthened and diversified by multitudinous sources and texts demonstrating multilingual literacy—dynastic and regional histories, memoirs, biographies, biographical dictionaries, historical gazetteers, collections of historical letters and administrative documents—during the medieval–early modern period that reflect both historical consciousness and historical tradition and are a challenge to the psycho-historic method of investigation and analysis. The advent of *Pax Mughlana*, as Pollock called it, from the second half of the sixteenth century further intensified the intellectual inquiry. There is a large body of sources in Persian as well as in Hindi (literature on devotionalism, astrology, aesthetics, erotics, *ritikal* tradition), Sanskrit, and other vernacular languages—Marathi, Rajasthani, Bangla, Gurmukhi, Sindhi, *Braj Bhasha*, Telugu, Tamil, Urdu; European languages—English, French, Portuguese, Dutch; travellers' accounts; translations; and paintings and illustrations that embellish the manuscripts and architectural record of monuments. These sources/texts represent first-hand accounts of those who witnessed history in the making and provide a noteworthy insight into pre-colonial society in the way they discern the past and record it; facilitate understanding of the ideology and attempts at legitimacy and consolidation by the Mughals; and provide virtual interactions with and perceptions of the diverse facets of the rulers, whether as military commanders, administrators, statesmen, or patrons of arts and aesthetics and composite culture. As we scrutinise and ponder over these sources and ask relevant, intelligent questions, it helps to separate rhetoric from reality and reconstruct the history of the period more dispassionately. It may thus not be incongruous to suggest that historiography or the narrative interpretation of historical data rests at the core of our knowledge of the past; and that history is a pragmatic science that ought not to be marginalised by the legacies of orientalism and politics, but be written and read in a wide variety of ways so as to make sense of the past for the present. In this era of increasing global interdependence, histories are written that connect distinct, dissimilar contexts or surroundings, institutions that are not 'Western' or 'Eastern' (Dale 2002), and of engagement with other geographic areas in our disciplines that belies orientalist specificity (Khalidi 1995). Such history may also be produced in a political context, but to insist, like the post-modernist nationalist argument, that only belief matters is to deprive history of its proper perspective.

1

LITERARY TRENDS

Languages and the Scribes

HIGHLIGHTS

- Persian as a form of literary expression
- The making of Persian as the language of State and power
- Sanskrit, a language of the Classics
- Sanskrit and the role of Brahmins in the sixteenth and seventeenth centuries
- Relational dynamics between Sanskrit and the Vernaculars: Growth of *Braj Bhasha* and *Riti* literature
- Vernacular languages and literary traditions: *Khari Boli*, *Braj bhasha*, *Dakhani*, Hindavi, *Rekhta*, and *Riti*
- The role of the scribes: *Munshi*s and *Karanam*s

Learning, knowledge, and culture are closely associated with the power of language, particularly in the context of multilingual pre-colonial India, when several literary traditions and the pursuit of wisdom were carried out in various specific languages at different levels of society, including the highest echelons of power, with 'a marked diglossia between "classical" languages and the "vernaculars"' (Orsini 2011, 1). This entails a scrutiny, to begin with, of how Persian became the language of power during the medieval and early modern period—the language of not only the king and the court or the elite, but also that of the *mutasaddi*s (clerks), *munshi*s (scribes), and those holding minor official positions. Persian, seen synonymously with liberalism in the medieval Islamic world, made its mark in the northern parts of India as well as other regions, including the Deccan, between the twelfth and the nineteenth centuries as a language of political and cultural dialogue, adapting diverse religious and cultural traditions and creating a legacy for 'Indian style' Persian or Indian usage in Persian (*sabk-i Hind* or *isti'mal-i Hind*). However, while the texture of the Mughal Empire may have reflected the dominance of Persian language and diverse Persian literary compositions, it illustrated equally eminently the richness of Sanskrit and vernacular languages and their significance in the making of linguistic and literary patterns in pre-colonial India.

PERSIAN—LANGUAGE OF POWER

The evolution of Persian as a form of literary expression around the third quarter of the ninth century in the Islamic East ran parallel to India's developing contacts with new Persian culture with the assimilation of Sindh in the Saffarid kingdom by Ya'qub bin Abi Lais. That Persian had increasingly sharpened its profile during the eleventh century is apparent from at least one well-known example: the *Shahnama*, written by Firdausi and dedicated to Mahmud of Ghazni. Sultan Mahmud, along with his counterparts in Iran and Central Asia, had used Persian as his court language, which distinguished him from the rulers of Spain, Egypt, and Baghdad, who spoke Arabic. This once again coincided with the introduction of Persian in its full formal contours into India by Mahmud of Ghazni and his successors with the establishment of Ghaznavid power in Punjab in the eleventh century, making Punjab the first Indian spot to imbibe and inculcate the learning of Persian language and its literary traditions. With the coming of the Turks, Persian flourished even further, extending its boundaries. The Sultans of Delhi, from the thirteenth to the fifteenth centuries, promulgated Persian as the court language, patronised the Persian scribes, writers, and poets, including the Sufis, *'ulama*, and other men of distinction who had migrated from Central and South-central Asia following the imperialism of Chingiz Khan and Timur. The revenue grants (*imlak, auqaf, vaza'if, idrarat*) to these learned persons, primarily in the rural areas, facilitated the penetration of Persian into the countryside and small towns, contributing to the cultural integration of north India with the Perso-Islamic identity (in opposition to Arab culture) known as 'Ajam'.

Box 1.1: Amir Khusrau

Amir Khusrau (1254–1325) was one of the leading Persian poets of his time who contributed immensely to the emergence of a distinct Indian style in Persian literary traditions, Indian classical music, and folk culture. In fact, the *insha* tradition in India owes its origin to Amir Khusrau. His *Ijaz-i-Khusravi* provides a lot of information on the literary, cultural, and social history of the thirteenth and fourteenth centuries. Born into a family of Turkish emigrants who served the Delhi Sultans in the Gangetic Doab at Patiyali (near Etah in modern Uttar Pradesh), Amir Khusrau became a disciple of Shaikh Nizam ud-din Awliya at a young age. Commissioned by the Delhi Sultans—Balban to Mubarak Khalji—to write an account of their reigns, Amir Khusrau's narrative was mainly episodic, written to capture an occasion and in praise of his patron-Sultan.

His works include:

- *Qiran-us-Sadain*, written in the form of *ghazal* and relating the meeting between Sultan Kaiquabad and his father Bughra Khan;
- *Khazain ul-Futuh*, which describes the accession and conquests of Sultan Ala-ud-din Khalji;
- *Tughluqnama*, written to celebrate the enthronement and triumphs of Sultan Ghiyas-ud-din Tughluq;
- *Miftah ul-Futuh*, a versified narration of the military campaigns of Sultan Jalal-ud-din Khalji;
- *Nuh Sipihr*, an account of the reign of Sultan Qutb-ud-din Mubarak Khalji; and
- *Deval Rani-Khizr Khan Ishqia* (Love Story of Deval Rani and Khizr Khan).

During the period 1298–1300, which coincided with Ala-ud-din Khalji's reign, Khusrau completed his well-known romantic versified stories, namely *Matla' al-anwar*, *Shirin-Khusrau*, *Majnun-Laila*, *A'in-i Sikandari*, and *Hasht Bihisht*. Amir Khusrau passed away in Delhi in 1325 soon after the death of his preceptor, Shaikh Nizam ud-din Awliya.

Sufi *khanqahs* played a substantial role in encouraging the evolution of the Persian literary tradition and the spread of Persian to the people, cutting across religious affiliations. The *murids* (disciples, devotees) were inspired to learn Persian when they realised that the *malfuzat* (conversations), letters, and other writings of their Sufi *Pir* (master, spiritual guide) were in Persian. The Persian language used in the *malfuz* and the Sufi treatises was generally of the high literary register. Amir Khusrau and Amir Hasan Sijzi, disciples of the Chishti Sufi saint Nizam ud-din Awliya, further enriched the Persian language, while the writings of Hafiz Shirazi and Daulat Shah instilled an appreciation of Persian poetry and literary culture in north India and beyond, from Delhi to Shiraz and Isfahan.

By the fifteenth century, then, Persian had developed as a language of the State and a language for intellectual and religious discourse. It flourished as the language of the migrants from Persia and Central Asia, local converts to Islam, and also such Hindus who wished to pursue a career in State service. Sultan Sikandar Lodi's contribution in this context is worth mentioning. He initiated Persian learning amongst the Hindus, particularly the *Kayasthas*, *Khatris*, and the Brahmin scribes, by providing them access to the *madrasas*. The arrival and consolidation of Persian as a language in the Indian subcontinent coincided with the first complete Persian translation from Arabic of the animal fables from Sanskrit, the *Pancatantra*. This translation, titled *Kalilah va Dimnah*, was among the first works to introduce the Turko-Persians to Indian literary culture. Another Indian fable, *Tutinama*, was translated from Cintamani Bhatta's Sanskrit work, *Sukasaptati* (Seventy Tales of the Parrot), in the fourteenth century; *Hathayoga*, a work on bodily and spiritual discipline, was first translated into Arabic in Bengal and then into Persian early in the fourteenth century; Shaykh 'Abd al-Quddus Gangohi's *Rushd-namah* and Mir 'Abd al-Vahid Bilgrami's *Haqa'iq-i Hindi* added to indigenous representations in Persian literary style in the sixteenth century. This implied a gradual Indianisation of the Persian language. This development, although considered by some as a dilution of the purity of the Persian language, had begun to be identified by

Box 1.2: Amir Hasan Sijzi

Amir Hasan Sijzi (1254–1337) was a disciple of Chishti Sufi Shaikh Nizam ud-din Awliya, a noted poet, and a close associate of Amir Khusrau and Ziya-ud-din Barani, the two chroniclers of the Sultanate period. He began his career as a personal attendant of Prince Nasir-ud-din Mahmud, son of Sultan Balban. Later, he joined the service of Sultan Jalal-ud-din Khalji and subsequently rendered military service for Sultan Ala-ud-din Khalji at Lakhnauti and Deogir. Sijzi began the tradition of *malfuzat* or conversations of saints when he compiled the discourses of his *Pir* (teacher) Nizam ud-din Awliya and published them as *Fawa'id-ul-Fu'ad* in 1307. This became a kind of *dastur* (manual, guide) for the Sufis and other saints of different *silsilahs* (orders): Suhrawardi, Naqshbandi, Qadiri, Shattari. Prior to Sijzi's work, *malfuzat* was not considered a suitable style for narrating the conversations of a great *Pir*, the preferred modes of expression instead were *isharat* (treatises or mystical instructions) or *tazkirat* (literally, the book of 'memory'). *Fawa'id-ul-Fu'ad* focuses on the social and economic aspects of the Sultanate period and represents the Delhi of the Khalji period, that is, a Delhi that was full of hope and exuberance. The chronicle, divided into five parts, is a record of Nizam ud-din Awliya's discourses at 188 *majlis* (assembly) during the period 1308–22. On Nizam ud-din Awliya's demise in 1325, Sijzi migrated to Daulatabad, where he lived until his death in September 1337.

the mid-fifteenth century as *lahja-i Hindustaniyan* (Indian style), *Hindustaniyanah* (Indian), or *ravish* (style) of the people of Hindustan. It was a step towards the dissemination of the language and evolution of Persian lexicography in India.

Such factors heralded the extraordinary expansion and efflorescence of Persian literary culture under the Mughals, independent of their Chaghtai Turkic heritage and the fact that Turkic was their mother tongue. Also, Persian had not evolved as a prominent language in the court of the early Mughals. Babur was a renowned literati of the Turkic language; he recorded his memoir in the same language and was held next in eminence to 'Ali Shir Nava'i (d. 1526) in Turkic prose and poetry. Humayun, too, patronised Turkic and held frequent sessions of Turkic poetry at his court, regardless of his appreciation of Persian culture, customs, and traditions of the Safavid court that had inspired him during his exile in Persia. Bairam Khan, Akbar's tutor and *wakil-us sultanat*, added to the genre as a noted Turkic poet of the time. Turkic continued to be the personal spoken language of the Mughals till at least the end of the seventeenth century, although it could not develop as a literary language of the Mughal imperial court. Jahangir was effectively the last of the Mughals who could effortlessly write in Turkic; Shahjahan remained adamant about not learning the language while Aurangzeb, posted for brief tenures in Central Asia, could acquire sufficient professional knowledge of Turkic. The Sur Afghan rulers (1540–55) were not fluent in Persian, nor did they encourage it as a court language, despite their close connection with Persia. Hindavi was ordained a semi-official status during their rule and the decrees of the chancellery, if in Persian, were transcribed in Devanagri script, a practice earlier initiated by the Lodi Sultans.

Akbar's inheritance of Persophilia from his father gave a tremendous boost to the linguistic profile and literary sensibility of Persian. Fostering social, cultural, and intellectual links with Iran, the emperor projected his empire as *dar ul-aman* (abode of peace) and a retreat for the wise and the learned. This attracted a large number of Persian literati to India, begetting close contacts with Iran and the emergence of Persian as the first language of the king and the court in Mughal India. It was from his reign that Persian was formally recognised as the language of the government at all levels of society, making it not only the language of politics but also the language for cultural expression. A decree promulgating Persian as the official language was issued by Raja Todar Mal, Akbar's revenue minister. The departments of revenue and administration, Ghulam Husain Tabataba'i (1832) stated, were reorganised by the emperor's Iranian noble, Mir Fath-Ullah Shirazi, in accordance with the *zawabit* (special regulations) acquired by Raja Todar Mal from the *nawisindagan* (scribes) of Iran, known as *wilayat* then in popular parlance. Consequently, all official documents—*farmans* (imperial orders), *muchalka*, *tamassuk*, *qabuliyat* (bonds and acceptance letters)—were written in Persian by the village *chaudhari* (intermediary).

Several Hindu communities, particularly *Kayasthas* and *Khatris* in the Mughal administration, who had previously used Hindi or any of its vernacular forms as the official language, were obliged to attend *madrasas* to study the nuances of the Persian language, especially if they wished to join the imperial service as *muharrirs* and *munshis* (clerks, scribes, and secretaries) commensurable with the Iranians already in service. Persian thus became the most operative and pragmatic outfit of communication and a language of learning, knowledge, and high culture during the

Mughal period. It continued to be in reckoning till at least the early part of the nineteenth century. Siraj al-Din 'Ali Khan Arzu (1687–1756), a linguist and lexicographer of the Mughal Empire, observed that unlike Hindavi, which sustained diverse dialects in different regions and could not emerge as a uniform idiom even in north India, Persian acquired a wide expanse as a pan-Indian literary language and evolved as a political culture cutting across different religious and cultural identities of India.

The study of Persian language and literature, however, remained gendered and was a domain confined largely to men from the fifteenth to the eighteenth centuries. There were, though, a few women like Gulbadan Begum (sixteenth century), and Jahanara Begum and Zebunnisa (seventeenth century) who indulged themselves in Persian prose and poetry. The female voice was more prominent in vernacular literature, particularly in the sphere of devotional and erotic literature.

By the mid-nineteenth century, as the British government began to patronise vernacular languages and urged the learning and fluency of the English language, the importance of Persian began to wane. It lost even its distinct status as *zaban-i sh'ir*. Urdu instead became more widespread and emerged as the common language of India. The term Urdu is derived from the Turki word *Ordu*, meaning military camp. Urdu or Hindustani had evolved in the imperial military camp as *zuban-i Urdu-i mu'alla, zuban-i Urdu-i shahi*. A consequence of the Persianisation of Hindavi in the eighteenth century, Urdu strode ahead as a clear, specific language, a lingua franca, in the sixteenth and seventeenth centuries, using the Persian script, Hindi syntax, and Perso-Arabic vocabulary mixed with a few Hindi words. Francesca Orsini (2011) argued that as far as language definition was concerned, Hindi and Urdu were names for an array of north Indian vernacular dialects, which, from a layman's perspective, were simply called Hindavi (language of India) or Bhakha (the spoken language) to distinguish them from either Persian and Arabic, or Sanskrit and Prakrit. It is believed that it was Wali, a poet from the Deccan, who set the diction of Urdu in Delhi. From the late seventeenth century, Urdu had become the popular language of the harem and virtually the mother tongue of the Mughals, although Persian continued to be their official language. Some Urdu scholars like Jamil Jalibi (*Tarikh-i Adab-i Urdu*, 1989) have suggested that during Shahjahan's reign, it was mandatory for State officials to be proficient in Urdu. By the eighteenth century, Urdu had entrenched itself extensively in the literary arena. More significantly, Urdu poetry acquired dominance and flourished in the imperial court under the patronage of the Mughal Emperor, Muhammad Shah.

SANSKRIT—LANGUAGE OF THE CLASSICS

Sanskrit or *Hindi-yi Kitabi* had the potential of becoming the official language of the Mughal Empire, but it was identified as too sacred, too divine, a *devabani*, a *suryabani* (language of the gods, language of the sun), and an *akashbani* (language of the heaven or upper firmament), which no *mleccha* could be permitted to pollute by choosing it as a symbol of power. The word *Sanskrit* means 'perfected'. It was further defined to connote 'height of dignity'. Yet, despite its long tradition of scholarship, Sanskrit could never become a medium of everyday usage.

Such was its claim to perfection and divine status that no language could compete with it. It was not, observed Mirza Khan, the author of *Tuhfat al-Hind* and a court litterateur of Aurangzeb, a language of the masses or the ordinary; instead, it was a language in which books on various sciences and arts were composed.

Sanskrit was implicitly understood to be Brahmanical and the oldest literature, the *Veda* (*Veda* or *Vid* in Sanskrit means, 'to know'), that comprised orally transmitted texts of myth and ritual. It acquired a pan-Indic, hegemonic status in literary culture with its patronage as a classical language from 300 CE. Distinguishing itself from other trans-regional agencies of communication, it overwhelmed—rather, obscured—all other languages and literature, creating, as Sheldon Pollock (2006) has argued, a Sanskrit 'cosmopolis'—a world of political and religious knowledge and an exclusive idiom for most areas of science, systematic thought, and scholarship outside the Persianate cultural sphere. Seeking to understand the dynamics between science and language in pre-colonial India, Pollock (2011) observed that *science*, *systematic knowledge*, *scholarship*, *learning* (and also *rule* and *scripture*) can be translated by the Sanskrit word *sastra*. So, if *science*, whether as *jnana* in the sense of understanding or *sastra* in the sense of *system*, is viewed as *knowledge*, then science in the pre-colonial period could be manifested and transmitted *only* in Sanskrit. Such a relationship between Sanskrit—the 'correct' language—and the truth, or that Sanskrit was the only language that could enunciate reality and science, was expounded by Kumarila, an eminent scholar of *mimamsa* (discourse analysis and scriptural hermeneutics) in the seventh century, and Khandadeva, an expert and advocate of *mimamsa* in mid-seventeenth century Varanasi. Varanasi, Rosalind O'Hanlon (2011, 175) explained, had risen as an unrivalled centre for Sanskrit learning, 'a city of Siva and a destination for aspiring, hopeful Brahmin migrants' during the Mughal period.

Sanskrit sources are valuable and informative on the social history of interactions between *Haindavas* (Indians) and *Parasikas* (Persians) and the role of the Brahmins in the sixteenth and seventeenth centuries. The patronage of Brahmin scholars in the Mughal court began in the 1560s with the accession of Akbar and his territorial expansion into eastern India. Sanskrit scholars Mahapatra Krsnadasa of Orissa and Narasimha, first associated with the court of Gajapati Mukundadeva, were the earliest recipients of Mughal patronage. While some Brahmins learnt Persian and joined the imperial service, several others preferred to stay out of the imperial framework and remained rooted to the traditional Indian knowledge. Brahmin Sanskrit intellectuals, however, were actively engaged in the courts of Jahangir and Shahjahan, not only as preachers or educators on Indian tradition or as translators of Sanskrit works, but also as *jyotisaraja* (king among *jyotisas*) or astrologers of the Mughal emperors; in cases of expediency, they also served as strategists for political negotiations. The latter can be illustrated by the example of Kavindracarya Sarasvati, a Maharashtrian Brahmin based in Banares, engaged in both Sanskrit and vernacular writing. During his stay in the court of Shahjahan, he taught Sanskrit texts to members of the royal family; and to the imperial gathering, he presented melodies (*dhrupad*) in vernacular in praise of the emperor. He was esteemed in the Brahmin community for his efforts at persuading Shahjahan to remove the levy on Hindu pilgrims visiting Banares and Prayag. Kavindracarya was paid a substantial imperial stipend during Shahjahan's reign. It was stopped by Aurangzeb not for religious reasons, but in a bid to rival his elder brother, Dara Shukoh, who was held in high regard and applauded by Kavindracarya in his *Kavindrakalpalata* for his Sanskrit scholarship and learning, philosophical inclination, and for symbolising the knowledge of Brahmins (*brahmajnana*). Kavindracarya was later patronised by a Mughal notable, Danishmand Khan. Subsequently, he served as a cultural mediator and guide to Francois Bernier, the European traveller who visited India in the seventeenth century. Significantly, however, except for Kavindracarya, the Brahmin Sanskrit scholars remained hesitant to record their experiences at the Mughal court, even though their texts were replete with information on the patronage they received from the Mughals. In fact, Sanskrit texts rarely provided a glimpse of the cross-cultural currents that prevailed in the imperial court, or elucidated on the relationship between Brahmins and the Mughal emperors, or how the Mughal court patterns impacted the cultural, social, and religious life of the Brahmin community.

The Brahmins considered themselves *sista*, a community of the learned and disciplined, a class of religious ideologues who upheld *dharma*, but were also court poets, scribes, record-keepers, and ministers. Their monopoly over Sanskrit learning and the conviction that the language of Sanskrit scholars was superior—intellectually, culturally, and spiritually—created linguistic hierarchies, adversely affecting the literary prestige of vernacular languages, regardless of the *kavya* (literature) in vernacular. Vernaculars were characterised as 'corrupted' (*apabhrasta*) languages; their low status as compared to Sanskrit was attributed to the fact that they were merely *bhasa* (language) with no claim to divinity, and therefore distinction. These perceptions, many a time, were a source of ambivalence for the literary and scholarly potential of vernacular writings. Kavindracarya Sarasvati, for instance, spoke of *laj* (shame) at writing in the vernacular language: a sentiment expressed by several other vernacular *pandits* and poets of the time.

The Mughal period nevertheless represented a phase in which the relational dynamics between Sanskrit and the vernaculars were renegotiated. *Braj Bhasha* began to encroach upon the intellectual terrain, the *alankarasastra* or the knowledge system of literary science monopolised by Sanskrit scholars. It received patronage from regional kingdoms to create works on classical literary themes, different from those composed in Persian, the Mughal court language. This facilitated the genre *Ritigranth* (book of method), which dominated the period 1650–1850, popularly known as the *ritikal* (period of method or neoclassicism). *Braj Bhasha* could now challenge the exclusivity of Sanskrit and influence scholars like Jagannatha Panditaraja (d. 1670), patronised by different rulers, both Mughal and regional, namely Jahangir, Shahjahan, Jagat Singh of Udaipur, and Prana Narayana of Assam. Allison Busch (2011b) described him as the last great Sanskrit poet-intellectual with a new sensibility, before the vernaculars could rejuvenate their cultural status and co-exist with Sanskrit as trans-regional literary languages.

Riti literature grew as a cultural repertory in which both Hindus and Muslims could participate, providing a diversion from Persianate courtly traditions, while Sanskrit remained largely inaccessible except through some Persian translations. The initiative in this direction, which was politically significant and heralded religious liberalism, was taken by Akbar in 1575 when he established the *maktab khana* (bureau of translation) to sponsor the translation of Indian classics into Persian, thus facilitating the knowledge of Indian scriptures and local traditions to an audience that was largely familiar with Persian. Badauni, in addition to other courtiers, was actively engaged in the tasks of the *maktab khana*. *Mahabharata* was translated with the Persian title *Razmnama* or *The Book of War*, with emphasis on the martial nature of the epic, setting aside its religious and didactic content. In the introduction to *Razmnama*, Abu'l Fazl stressed the importance of commissioning translations of the sacred, holy books of both communities (*fariqain*), so that they could stay away from hostility, seek the truth, and amend vices. Other translations into Persian included *Ramayana*, *Atharvaveda*, *Singhasanbatisi*, *Pancatantra*, *Kathasaritsagara*, *Yoga Vasishtha*, and *Harivamsa* or Lineage of Krishna: an appendix to the *Mahabharata*. Bhaskaracharya's *Lilavati*—a classical Indian textbook on mathematics—was translated by Faizi; *Bhagavatha Purana* was translated by Todar Mal; and Abdul Rahim Khan-i Khanan translated Babur's memoirs from Turki into Persian. Later in the seventeenth century, Dara Shukoh pioneered the translation of metaphysical texts such as the Upanishads (*Sirr-i akbar*) and *Bhagvad Gita* under the title *Ab-i zindagi*, while a number of other texts related to Hindu religion, law, ethics, mathematics, medicine, astronomy, romance, moral fables, and music were translated into Persian, a process that continued into the eighteenth century. These translations were widely used beyond the imperial court. In Mughal India, in addition to the *'aqliya* (rational) and *naqliya* (traditional) categories of *'ulum* (Islamic sciences), there were also texts of *hikmat-i amali* (practical wisdom) that were included in the syllabi of the *madrasa*s.

If Sanskrit remained inaccessible to the larger community and could not become the official Mughal language, neither could Prakrit, nor could Hindavi. Prakrit was attested as *patal-bani*, the language of the underground and of snakes, that is, too low to be appropriated as the imperial language. Contrary to the perception, however, Prakrit represented 'common' or 'natural' dialect(s), of which Sanskrit was considered the grammatically

Box 1.3: Faizi

An intellectual, Persian poet, and scholar of the late sixteenth century, **Abu'l Faiz ibn Mubarak**, popularly known as **Faizi or Fayyazi**, was the son of Shaikh Mubarak and elder brother of Abu'l Fazl. One of the ***navaratnas*** of Akbar's court, he was a tutor for Akbar's sons—Salim, Murad, and Daniyal. In 1581, he was appointed ***sadr*** of Agra, Kalpi, and Kalinjar. Later, in 1588, Akbar anointed him ***Malik-us-Shu'ara*** (poet laureate) of his court. During his posting (1591–93) as a Mughal envoy in Khandesh and Ahmadnagar, Faizi wrote a series of reports on the political and cultural conditions of Deccan and contemporary Iran. His writings in Arabic language included ***Swati al-Ilham*** and ***Mawarid al-Kalam***. He translated Bhaskaracharya's Sanskrit work on mathematics, *Lilavati*, into Persian. His *Diwan* (collection of poems), which comprised ***qasidas***, ***ghazals***, ***ruba'is***, and elegies, was entitled ***Tabashir al-Subh***.

His major work included the retelling of the classical story of Nala and Damayanti, or Nal and Daman, in Persian language in the verse-narrative form known as ***masnavi***. This text demonstrates the religious liberal and tolerant credentials of Faizi and reflects his inclinations towards Chishti Sufi ideals and vocabulary. When Faizi was commissioned by Akbar to write a Persian version of the Indian story of Nala and Damayanti, he conceived it as one of the five *masnavi*s that he planned to write. Of these, however, he could complete only two before his premature death in 1595, namely the ***Nal-Daman*** text (completed in 1594, a year before his death) and the ***Markaz-i Adwar*** (The Centre of the Circle), which he finished in the last weeks before his death. The three other texts—***Sulaiman wa Bilqis, Haft Kishwar***, and ***Akbarnama***—were never completed, although the first was initiated as early as in 1589–90.

disciplined variety; Prakrit implied a literary language and was seldom seen as a spoken vernacular. Prakrit, in literature, was understood as a grammaticised dialect and was used in the early centuries of literacy, that is, *c.* 250 BCE–250 CE, for writing public inscriptions, until overwhelmed by Sanskrit. While Sanskrit was admitted as a single, unified register in literary theory, Prakrit was neither associated with nor restricted to any region. It was related to different regional varieties: Maharashtri (belonged to Maharashtra), Shauraseni or Sauraseni (related to Surasena or Mathura and its neighbourhood), Gaudi or Magadhi (while Gauda referred to Bengal, Magadha represented Bihar), and Lati (belonged to Lata, southern Gujarat), although for all practical purposes Prakrit became linked to Maharashtri, which ultimately emerged as the primary language of the Prakrit literary style.

VERNACULAR LANGUAGES

Vernacular languages and literature had remained vibrant in the regional states, even though, as compared to Hindavi, Persian enjoyed uniformity—in Amir Khusrau's words, 'throughout the length of four thousand *parasangs* of India'—as early as the fourteenth century. Hindavi, it is true, had not evolved a uniform idiom even as late as the eighteenth century, including in northern India. But it represented diverse forms of dialects. Siraj al-Din 'Ali Khan Arzu (d. 1756), an eighteenth century poet, writer, and lexicographer, mentioned Gwaliyari, Braj, Rajputi, Kashmiri, Haryanavi, Hindi, and Punjabi as different authentic forms of Hindavi, along with the dialects of Shahjahanabad (Delhi) and Akbarabad (Agra). Hindavi was, in fact, close in language and poetic form to *Braj Bhasha* (known by many names, including *Bhasha*, Hindi, and Gwaliyari, among others), rather than *Khari Boli*. The earliest use of *Khari Boli* in north India can be traced to the sixteenth century in the Mughal court, although there are some indications that it may have been promoted prior to this by the Sufis. This would suggest that the development of *Khari Boli* literature in north India ran parallel to the growth of *Dakhani* and *Gujri* in the southern part of India. Hindavi, thus, was not only identified as *Bhakha* (the spoken language) or the common vernacular language of north India, but had also enjoyed the status of literary language since the fourteenth century. It emerged as a popular medium of communication for the ordinary; but it was considered apt for romantic poetry and music by the Mughal Emperors and the Sufi poets, too, who widely appropriated Hindavi to spread Persian culture. Hindavi songs were sung along with Persian ones in Sufi *sama'* and other gatherings, despite the initial opposition of celebrated Sufi saints of Bengal such as Sharafuddin Maneri (1263–1381). *Bikat Kahani*—a poem—is the earliest extant literary text written in Hindavi in north India in the form of *masnavi*, comprising 325 *shi'r*s by Muhammad Afzal (popularly known as Afzal Gopal). Gesudaraz and later Anand Ram 'Mukhlis' described Hindavi as a language with emotional and sentimental appeal, melodious, tender, and clear, in which the feelings of romance or divine love could be expressed.

The development of independent Hindavi literature coincided with the popularity of *rekhta*. *Rekhta*, a Persian word (that meant poured, interspersed, mixed), had several technical connotations. It was part of musical terminology prior to the eighteenth century and also referred to a mode of writing, particularly poetry, written in a language that mixed lines, phrases, and vocabulary from Hindi and Persian (the reference to Persian included the Arabic vocabulary imbibed by Persian), in which the Hindavi component was generally *Khari Boli* and sometimes *Braj Bhasha*, or a mix of the two. *Rekhta* poetry in the Persian script was nurtured in Deccan and by the Sufis of north India. Sufis in Awadh, for instance, wrote in both Awadhi and Persian, and no Sufi except Shaikh 'Abdul Quddus Gangohi (1455–1538) used Hindavi as a form of literary expression in the north, because Persian was widely understood in the region. Patronised by the Mughal court in the sixteenth century, *rekhta* was further promoted by religious poets in the second half of the sixteenth century. The earliest collections of *rekhta* poems in the *Nagari* script were widely noticeable in the teachings of *Nirgun* bhakti saints, who contested and overshadowed the Hindu–Muslim division. Their use of mixed language, evident from the *Guru Granth Sahib*, is an indication that they were probably more comfortable with the use of *Khari Boli*.

Dadu Dayal's *Khari Boli muktaka*s (poems) can be considered the first examples of *Nagari rekhta*. Although Dadu used elements from different languages or dialects, he composed poems in Rajasthani, Gujarati, Braj, Punjabi, Persian, and Sindhi, and consciously applied the mixed language of the Mughals by interspersing Hindavi phrases with long Persian ones. His disciples, except Sundardas and Vajid (several works of the latter that fall in the *Nirgun* bhakti tradition are about *niti* [morals]), did not continue with his Hindavi–Persian hybridity or with *Khari Boli*; they evolved their own style, that is, *sadhukari bhasa*, that mixed vernacular languages and dialects. *Rekhta*, however, was increasingly used in the Persian, *Gurmukhi*, and *Nagari* scripts in the seventeenth–eighteenth centuries, rendering *Nagari rekhta* dominant over the region extending from Bihar to Rajasthan, despite the remarkable appeal of *Braj Bhasha riti* poetry in the eighteenth century. The blend of Hindavi and Persian that became common in the eighteenth century with Vali Aurangabadi was earlier illustrated in a poem by Chandar Bhan Brahman, *mir munshi* and *wazir* of Dara Shukoh.

Vernacular literature flourished from around the thirteenth–fourteenth centuries, imbibing several influences, namely the *bhakti* movement that used vernacular languages and the symbolism of erotic poetry to reach out to the local gentry; Sufi bilingual (Awadhi and Persian) romantic epics; and the belief in the supernatural powers of Sufi saints and *rishi*s. A form of mystical poetry known as *prema-akhyan*, or listening to *prema-kahani*, was composed in Awadhi or eastern Hindavi in pre-colonial fourteenth–sixteenth-century north India by Sufi Muslim poets who were Persian-speaking. This genre of *prema-akhyan* in Hindavi was influenced and introduced by these poets as a consequence of their cultural and religious interactions in the different provinces of Hindustan. These poems, defined as Sufi romances by scholars, are somewhat allegorical (*sanketatmak*), describing and equating human love and love for the divine; in other words, they express a mystic's desire for God. Widely known amongst both the literate and the common masses, these poems were written and performed from the fourteenth until the nineteenth century in Delhi, Jaunpur, and the eastern provinces of Bihar. Hindavi Sufi romances heralded a new Indian Islamic literary tradition and devotional culture in the local, regional languages.

So while this kind of Indian Islamic literary tradition indicated the indigenisation and assimilation of Islam in Indian culture, it also symbolised the elevation of Hindavi—a north

Indian vernacular, that is, *bhakha*—into a literary language. Amir Khusrau, for instance, known for his contributions to Indian music (*ghazal*) and Hindavi and Persian writings, wrote poetry in Hindavi to *Mahbub-i Ilahi* (Beloved of *Allah*), that is, Shaikh Nizam ud-din Awliya, his *Pir*. Some of the valuable works written in Hindavi in the genre of *prema-akhyan* include *Candayan* (1379) written by Maulana Daud, a disciple of Shaikh Zain ud-din Chishti, the successor of Shaikh Nizam ud-din Awliya; and *Mirigavati* (1503), composed at the court of Sultan Husain Shah Sharqi of Jaunpur by Qutban, disciple of Shaikh Buddhan Suhrawardi. The style of *Candayan* and *Mirigavati* was emulated by Malik Muhammad Jayasi, also a disciple of Shaikh Buddhan Suhrawardi, in several of his poems, the most significant of which was *Padmavat* (1540), written during the reign of Sher Shah. The text invoked the style of Persian *masnavi* or verse romances and explained the genre of *rasa* signifying *joga* or asceticism, *singara* or love, and *vira* or valour. Another work in the same genre was *Madhumalati* (1545) written by Mir Sayyid Manjhan Rajgiri, a Sufi of the Shattari order and disciple of Shaikh Muhammad Ghaus Gvaliyari (d. 1563). It was at the multilingual and multicultural court of Islam Shah Sur that Manjhan composed this text in Hindavi using Sufi symbols and Indic narrative in the form of a hybrid Sufi romance poem, which reflected on the lives of two lovers who shared the composite Indic–Islamic culture, where Muslim spiritual values and the Hindu gods could be invoked harmoniously and co-exist.

These texts indicate multilingualism because, while the Sufi authors of Hindavi *prema-akhyan* read Persian and understood the traditions of Persian *masnavi*, they chose not to use Arabic-Persian words in these poems. This trend reflected that while north India was not homogenous politically, it was well-connected both culturally and linguistically. It can, in fact, be described linguistically as 'multiple diglossia' (Orsini 2012). The texts were circulated in different scripts and formats to suit the context. This was especially facilitated by the absence of colophons in many manuscript copies. For instance, for use in the Sufi *khanqah*, they were produced in unornamented *nasta'liq*; for local Persianate elites, they were illustrated in *naskhi-diwani*; in unornamented *kaithi* or *devanagiri* script for storytellers; and illustrated in *kaithi* script for local Rajput and merchants elites. Tulsidas, the author of *Ramacharitmanas* (1575)—devotional literature on Rama (the *avatar* or incarnation of Vishnu) that derived its cues from the *Ramayana* of Valmiki, written in Sanskrit, and retellings of the epic in regional languages, particularly the Tamil version, that is, Kamban's *Ramayana*—chose to compose the text in Awadhi *chaupai* and *dohas*, probably under the influence of Awadhi Sufis.

In expounding the vernacularisation of literature in fifteenth-century pre-colonial India, Sheldon Pollock (1998) described the relationship between language, literature, and politics and between a 'High Language', that is, Sanskrit, and Indian vernaculars. He observed that in the Turkish and Afghan courts from the fourteenth to the sixteenth centuries, regional literary, musical, and aesthetic identities prevailed that fostered cosmopolitan vernacular languages. Francesca Orsini (2012) interpreted literary culture during the same period in north India as multilingual and multi-locational, which explained the social forces of the regions, notwithstanding their cultural and political diversity: Delhi (under the Lodi Sultans), Jaunpur, Malwa, and Gwalior. The Gwalior court under the Tomar dynasty in the fifteenth century was the earliest to develop and patronise *Braj Bhasha* poetry. By early sixteenth century, *Braj Bhasha* literature—songs, hagiographies, *prabhanda-kavya*, theoretical texts of theology and poetics (first in Sanskrit and then also in *Braj Bhasha*)—had emerged in Delhi during the reign of Sikandar Lodi. *Braj Bhasha* poetry, such as Mir 'Abd al-Vahid Bilgrami's *Haqa'iq-i Hind* (1566), contained *dhrupad* songs that were also used in Sufi '*sama* and showed significant strides at the regional courts of Deccan, Gujarat, and Jaunpur.

The religious and political developments throughout the sixteenth century thus facilitated the ascension of *Braj Bhasha*, which unfolded as a popular and a prominent vernacular amongst the *bhakti* saints and *bhakti* poets. Vaishnavas in north India appropriated the areas associated with the region of Braj and poets like Surdas and Tulsidas (known more popularly for his *Ramcharitmanas* in Awadhi) wrote literary works in the vernacular, focusing on the playful and romantic activities of Krishna (eighth *avatar* of Vishnu). Rajput and Mughal patronage under Akbar to the temples in Braj *mandal* (Vrindavan and Mathura) fostered greater interest in *Braj Bhasha*—the language of the region—transforming it from the language of *bhakti* or devotion to the court language. Although it could not surpass Persian, it had begun to overshadow Awadhi by the end of Akbar's reign. The importance of *Braj* poetry in the imperial court could not find a prime place in Abu'l Fazl's *Ain-i Akbari*, but there is sufficient evidence to suggest that poets like Gang were among the prominent literary persons in Akbar's court and that Akbar's courtier and revenue minister, Raja Todar Mal, and court poet Faizi were actively engaged in *Braj* poetry.

Braj Bhasha literature produced in regional courts and the Mughal imperial court came to be known as *riti* literature. Around the seventeenth century (*c.* 1600), at the Bundela court in Orchha and later in the other Rajput kingdoms, *riti* literature evolved in the form of *Braj Bhasha* poetry that dominated elite vernacular poetry in north India for the next three centuries. *Riti* means 'method' and refers specifically to the Sanskrit method. One of the most prevalent genres of *riti* literature that sums up the literary and intellectual profiles of *riti* authors, the *Ritigranth* (Book of Method), was designed to disseminate classical literary ideas in a vernacular medium. *Riti* literary culture flowed from the regions to the imperial centre, achieving remarkable trans-regional success in the seventeenth and eighteenth centuries with patronage from the Mughal emperors, who demonstrated an avid interest in Hindavi/*Braj* poetry. Aurangzeb's grandson, Prince Muhammad Rafi-ush-Shan, wrote poetry in Hindi under the pen-name 'Nyayi', while Emperor Farrukh Siyar patronised 'Abd-ur-Rahman 'Premi', a well-known *ritikal* poet. One of his nobles patronised Nawaz, a *Braj* poet, who rewrote *Shakuntala*, an adaptation of *Mahabharata* and drama-composition of Kalidasa. Nawaz was decorated with the coveted title of *kabishwar* or poet laureate by the emperor, a privilege that none of the poets in Persian language allegedly enjoyed at his court. Later, Shah Alam II (1761–1818) not only patronised, but also indulged in writing poetry in Hindi, using Nagari and Persian scripts.

To understand the *riti* writings and the variability of language practices within it, a few select authors may be considered to illustrate that a poet's literary language was influenced more by his individual choice rather than his birth, caste or community. Keshavdas Mishra, a learned Brahmin well-versed in Sanskrit literary theory and its intellectual trends, reputed as *acharya kavi* in the Hindi tradition, pioneered the *Braj Bhasha riti* tradition. He adopted a linguistic style that supported flexible rather than fixed language practices, and adapted to Persianate vocabulary when his patron Bir Singh Deo Bundela of Orchha entered into an alliance with the Mughals. His prominence coincided with the reign of Akbar that patronised *Braj* culture and *Braj Bhasha* literature in the Mughal court. Keshavdas represented a range of language profiles. His scholarly works *Rasikpriya* (1591) and *Kavipriya* (1601) were highly Sanskritised (although *Rasikpriya* made scattered use of vernacular terms) and explained the technical aspects of literary categories such as *nayikas*/*nayakas* (heroines/heroes), *rasas* (emotions, mood, temper), and *alankaras* (rhetorics), which formed the basis of the *Braj Ritigranth* genre. Persian-Arabic vocabulary crept in selectively into his last two works—*Virsimhdevcarit* (Deeds of Bir Singh), commissioned in 1607 at a time when his patron was politically aligned with Jahangir, and *Jahangirjascandrika* (Moonlight of the fame of Jahangir, 1612). The latter text, written partially in Sanskrit, eulogised Jahangir, Keshavdas's Indo-Muslim *nayaka*, as 'master of both faiths' (*duhum din kau sahib*). He may have chosen this style in emulation of the fact that Sanskrit, as compared to any other language, supposedly stood for perfection, moral conduct, and kingly authority.

Like Keshavdas, Chintamani Tripathi was a Brahmin, Sanskrit scholar, and a leading poet of the *riti* tradition, interested in the vernacular presentation of Sanskrit literary theory. His *Ritigranths*—*Kavikulakalpataru* (Wish-fulfilling Tree for the Brotherhood of Poets, *c.* 1670) and *Srngaramanjari* (Bouquet of Passion, *c.* 1666)—are examples of his acclaimed scholarship in Sanskrit. *Srngaramanjari*, a translation of a Telugu work by Akbar Shah (son of a preceptor to Golconda's Qutb Shahi Sultan, Abul Hasan 'Tanashah', r. 1672–87), exemplified his style of linguistic interactions. Unlike Keshavdas, Chintamani rarely used the Persian-Arabic vocabulary, although he adapted local linguistic usages (including Persian), qualifying himself as a cosmopolitan poet. He was patronised by several Hindu and Muslim rulers from the northern and Deccan states, where Persian had developed as the language of culture from the seventeenth to the nineteenth centuries.

Bhushan Tripathi, probably the brother of Chintamani Tripathi, was apparently the court poet of Shivaji, known for his *Sivarajabhusan* (Ornament to King Shivaji), the literary narrative of his patron, commissioned in 1673 on the occasion of Shivaji's coronation. Ostensibly, the text was a *Ritigranth*, albeit unusual in its presentation. Evading poetic theory and the portrayal of the romance of Krishna and Radha—a basic feature of *Braj* poetry—it focused instead on the conquests and triumphs of Shivaji, perhaps in an attempt to establish itself as a *prasasti*. His expression, often intense on Persian vocabulary, was generally hybrid—a mix of Sanskrit and Persian. Sanskrit was considered most appropriate to write a *prasasti*. It fulfilled the criterion of technical literary language for a *Ritigranth* and was a language that represented moral perfection for a king. Persian, on the other hand, was a language of power that exemplified seventeenth-century politics, in addition to being a language of communication for those not fluent in Hindi or *Khari Boli*.

The importance of the Hindi literary style and its various dialects as vernacular languages is clearly seen in the works of Abdul Rahim Khan-i Khanan, more popularly known as Rahim (1556–1627). Rahim and Keshavdas were contemporaries and shared a personal bond. This was apparent from

Keshavdas's introduction to *Jahangirjascandrika*, which he began with verses in eulogy of Rahim's family—his father Bairam Khan, Rahim himself, and his son Iraj Khan (see Image 1.1). Yet their language practices, influenced perhaps by their distinct cultural contexts, were different, especially in the selection and use of the Persian-Arabic vocabulary. Rahim was multilingual: his native language was Turki, he was well-versed in Persian, and he had mastered Sanskrit and Portuguese. His command over Sanskrit was excellent, and his two famous works on astrology included *Khetakautukam* and *Dwatrimshadyogavali*. As a Mughal courtier and administrator, Rahim was exposed to refined, sophisticated spoken Persian and Persian poetry and his default vernacular was Persianised *Khari Boli*. He translated Babur's memoirs from Turki to Persian, titled *Vaqi'at-i Baburi*; while he composed his poems in Sanskrit and Persian, the bulk of his literary work was in several dialects of Hindi—*Awadhi, Braj, Khari Boli*. His understanding of the technicalities of Hindi, Sanskrit, and Persian literary forms, his patronage of contemporary Persian poets, and his knowledge and learning of Indian mythology and Vaishnava *bhakti* indicated his multiculturalism and Mughal cosmopolitanism.

Image 1.1: Illustration from *Akbarnama* by Anant, *c.* 1590–95. It shows the young (4-year-old) Abdul Rahim Khan-i-Khana being received by Emperor Akbar

Source: https://commons.wikimedia.org/wiki/File:Young_Abdul_Rahim_Khan-i-Khana_being_received_by_Akbar,_*Akbarnama*.jpg.

Like Rahim, Sayyid Ghulam Nabi 'Raslin' Bilgrami (1699–1750) was a Mughal courtier and a recruit in the Mughal army. He was trained in Arabic and Persian languages, although his writings were the least Persianised as compared to the other *riti* authors mentioned above. He was known more for his poetry in *Braj Bhasha*, notwithstanding the fact that the Hindi dialect of Bilgram, the region he came from (now in Uttar Pradesh), was not *Braj Bhasha*. It appears that 'Raslin' had made a conscious choice to write in *Braj Bhasha* rather than *Awadhi*, influenced perhaps by the prevailing literary trend from the sixteenth to the eighteenth centuries in which *Braj Bhasha* dominated the cultural writings in most regions of the subcontinent, whether Mughal, Rajput or Dakhani. His *takhullas* 'Raslin' (meaning, 'absorbed in sentiments') was probably a way to convey his intense engagement with the *riti* themes. Some of his important works included a short *Nakh-sikh Angdarpan* (Mirror of the Body, 1737), a *Ritigranth* entitled *Rasprabodh* (Understanding of Sentiment, 1742), and several *mutafarriq* or *phutkal* (miscellaneous) verses that occasionally mixed *Braj Bhasha* with Persian-Arabic vocabulary.

A few decades before 'Raslin', Mirza Khan, a Mughal court intellectual during the reign of Aurangzeb, expounded the *Bhakha* in his *Tuhfatu'l Hind* (*c.* 1675), that is, *Bhasha* as *zaban-i ahl-i birj* (the language of the people of Braj, a region that he identified in close proximity to Mathura), and acclaimed the nuances of *Braj Bhasha*: its grammar, glossary, and literary theories. To make its linguistic profile more accessible and understandable, especially to the Persian-knowing audience, he translated *Braj* poetry, eroticism, and music.

Rekhta and *Braj Bhasha* were overwhelmed by Urdu in eighteenth-century Mughal Delhi, influenced by the preferences of the Persian-educated Hindu and Muslim elite for Urdu and Persian literature, as compared to local vernacular traditions. This may have been the reason for the neglect of Afzal Gopal's *Bikat Kahani*. Persianised Hindavi thus emerged as an important medium in mainstream *rekhta*. *Rekhta*, however, continued to use the grammatical forms of *Khari Boli* or *Braj Bhasha*, but from the eighteenth century, this style began to be associated with genres like *marsiya*s (represented use of aesthetic-emotional sensitivity by the Urdu poets, significantly different from that of *ghazals*) and *barahmasa*s (associated with folk poetry, practised by the poets of *Awadhi* epics, devotional and *riti* poets, and also Urdu poets from the fourteenth to the nineteenth centuries).

By the sixteenth century, Bengali had flourished as a vernacular language. In Bengal, while both Hindu and Muslim intellectuals wrote in the common language of the region, that is, Bengali, Persian and Arabic religious and secular texts, including poetry and prose, were translated into Bengali. Influenced by Bengali poets, who dedicated a large body of their works to Krishna, the eighth incarnation of Vishnu, the Muslim poet Saiyid Sultan composed a genealogy in Bengali called *Nabi Vamsha* ('Lineage of the Prophets of Islam'), which included Krishna. Not only did *Nabi Vamsha* inculcate interest in local traditions, but it also fostered harmony between the two sects, facilitating peaceful coexistence and simultaneous invocation of the Hindu deities and *Allah* or *Rasul Allah* (Prophet of God, that is, Muhammad) without any conflict.

Vernacular literature in Rajasthani provided a perspective on the Rajputs, their values and ideology, and their relations with the Mughals. The case histories of the Rathor Rajputs of Marwar in western Rajasthan are derived from documents: *pidhiavaliyam/vamsavaliyam* (genealogies), *khyat* (derived from the Sanskrit word *khyati*, meaning fame, renown, glory; as a form of literature, it concerned itself with clan histories), *bat* (inferred from the Sanskrit word *varta*, meaning account or narrative; in Rajasthani, it meant *kahani* or story and *lok-katha* or folk tale), and *vigat* (literally meaning 'gone away', 'departed', 'deceased', but in the literary sense, these are lists, descriptions, accounts, a sort of chronicle, and like *khyat*, clan histories) written in *dimgal bhasha* or western Rajasthani that dates from the mid-seventeenth century. These narratives are based on local oral traditions as well as written information. Mumhata Nainsi Jaimalot, *diwan* in the court of Maharaja Jaswant Singh (1638–78), was the most notable of all the literati officials, commissioned by the Maharaja himself to compile and write the *vigat* and the *khyat*. Nainsi and his brother Sundardas belonged to a group of administrators known as *mutasaddi* rather than *munshi*; his father Jaimal held important offices under Raja Gaj Singh (who preceded Raja Jaswant Singh).

Notwithstanding the post that he held, Nainsi's major sources were not *mutasaddi*s, *qanungo*s or *munshi*s, but *Bhat*s and *Charan*s, who maintained the genealogical records of major Rajput lineages in oral form. This explains Nainsi's conscious effort to write in a genealogical mode that adhered to the genealogical sources of legitimacy and clan-based structures of authority in Rajputana. The oldest extant *khyat* in Rajputana is *Nainsi ri khyat*, a collection of *batam* (tales) and *pidhiavali* (genealogies). His works from the 1660s are valuable for the details on castes, agricultural production, crop patterns, irrigation, and revenue assessment. His *Marvar ra Parganam ri Vigat* (completed 1664) is a detailed survey of seven *pargana*s granted by the Mughal emperor Shahjahan to Raja Jaswant Singh in 1640. One of his *khyat*, initiated in 1648 (which took a decade to be completed) and extremely valuable in its contents, included miscellaneous administrative, demographic, and economic information, in addition to the histories of all ruling *shakha*s (branches) of Rajputana till the middle of the seventeenth century. Valuable data on economic history, particularly of the eighteenth century, were obtained from *bahi*s, *chopanya*s, *haqiqat*s, *dastur*s, and *arhsatta*s.

The literary traditions in Marathi, the vernacular of western India, can be traced to the twelfth century—the vernacular millennium, as Sheldon Pollock (1998) characterised it. Stewart Gordon (2009) emphasised the importance of six kinds of Marathi literary genres:

- *The Rajatarangini* (The River of Kings);
- *Siva Bharata*, an epic poem commissioned by Shivaji close to his ascension;
- *Powada*, a bardic ballad genre, the roots of which can be traced to the mid-seventeenth century;
- court depositions, revenue appeals, tax projections; and
- *bakhar* literature, comprising a corpus of 200 major texts from the fifteenth to the early nineteenth centuries, mentioned by Vishwanath Kashinath Rajwade in his *Aitihasik Prastavana* (1928).

Rajaram Hervadkar, editor and analyst of the genre of *bakhar*, observed that the term *bakhar* originated by transposition from the Persian-Arabic word *akhbar*, used under the Mughals for news reports that were sent from one court to another by *waqi'anavis* or *wakil* (newsletter writer). Disagreeing with Hervadkar, Bapuji Sankpal, another eminent scholar, argued that the two terms—*bakhar* and *akhbar*—were in use simultaneously, and therefore one could not have emerged by metathesis from the other. Whatever the inception, *bakhar* had acquired a popular official space by the 1670s, when Shivaji ordered the preparation of a thematic Sanskrit lexicon to reduce the usage of *Yavani* (Islamic) words in governance and statecraft. *Bakhar*s, written in the cursive *modi* script, often in prose, were the first histories written by Brahmins in the late seventeenth–mid-eighteenth centuries that narrated the story of a family or a lineage, a politically important personality (whether a king or a minister), a significant event, battle or conflict, matters concerning rank, status, honour, inheritance, judicial cases, administrative inquests, and revenue appeals. *Bakhar*s were mostly written as hagiographies that reinforced local patriotism and regional pride; upheld Shivaji's coronation as a momentous happening; and revelled in their illustrious history. They were also linked to *kaiphiyata*, another set of texts (not very different in character from the *bakhar*s) that focused on a place. *Sabhasad Bakhar* and *91-Kalami Bakhar* were considered the most valuable among *bakhar* literature for their detailed narration of events—both heroic and tragic—in Maharashtra. Written in 1694 by Krishnaji Anant Sabhasad at a time when the Mughal–Maratha conflict was at its height, *Sabhasad* described itself as a *caritra* (biography), but in its concluding remarks characterised itself as a *bakhar*. Although *Sabhasad* provided information on land assessment, land grants like *mokasa* and *saranjam*, and other land rights, it was effectively a eulogy and glorification of Shivaji, ascribing divinity to him.

Peninsular south, as compared to the north, demonstrated greater vigour in the development of vernacular languages for a variety of reasons: rural Deccan was governed by local leaders who spoke the local dialect—Marathi, Kannada, Telugu—although they had imbibed the Islamicate culture of the Deccan courts and adopted Persian administrative and financial terminologies. Also, the indigenous people—warriors and Brahmins—had a greater involvement in the state system. Ibrahim 'Adil Shah of Bijapur, after his accession in 1536, entrusted important administrative and financial affairs to the Brahmins and proclaimed Hindavi (in this case, Marathi) as the official language; in the Barid Shahi Sultanate of Bidar (1503–1619), the inscriptions were in both Persian and Marathi; in Golconda, too, the administrative orders followed a bilingual format—Persian and Telugu, the language of the Andhra region. The Deccan Sultans nurtured not only Telugu and Marathi but also *Dakhani* (a mix of Persian and local languages, especially Marathi) to communicate with their people. Persian, however, remained dominant as the language for record-keeping. Sultan 'Ali Adil Shah II of Bijapur promoted *Dakhani* (*lughat-i khass-i khwesh*) and patronised writing and listening to poetry in *Dakhani*, thus facilitating mutual interaction and exchange not only in his court, but also with the masses.

The mingling of Indic-Islamicate traditions was significantly evident in the courts of two Deccan Sultans, Ibrahim Adil Shah II of Bijapur and Muhammad Quli Qutb Shah of Golconda, both known as patrons of culture. With an inclination towards mysticism and a passion for music, Ibrahim Adil Shah II, also known as Jagat Guru, authored a collection of *Dakhani* poems and songs known as *Kitab-i Nauras* or Book of Nine *Rasa*s. His text, informative on the different *rasa*s and *raga*s (melodic and rhythmic patterns), began with an invocation to Saraswati, the Hindu goddess of learning, followed by the praise of Prophet Muhammad and then the Sufi saint, Gesudaraz. Muhammad Quli Qutb Shah's *Kulliyat*, a collection of poems in *Dakhani*, was influenced by *bhakti* and other Indic poetic genres and addressed God in the feminine voice. Abdullah Qutb Shah instituted a special office to frame royal *farman*s in Telugu (*dabiri-yi* *faramin-i Hindvi*) and Abu al-Hasan Tana Shah, the last Qutb Shahi Sultan, issued *farmans* in Telugu, with a summary of it in Persian inscribed at the back of the order. Generally, however, the format for the royal edicts in Golconda was bilingual, while the administrative and revenue affairs at the local level were conducted in Telugu.

Dakhani was also the language of the folk literature of the Sufis of Bijapur of the Chishti order; their descendants were spread in other parts of Deccan as well. This literature, written in the seventeenth–eighteenth centuries in the form of short poems based on indigenous perceptions and imagery to propagate simple Sufi teachings, rather than complex mystical doctrines, was preserved as an oral tradition of *Dakhini*-speaking villagers in Deccan. Sufi folk poetry—*chakki-nama, charkha-nama, lun-nama, shadi-nama, suhag-nama, suhaila*—was sung by rural women while they performed household chores. Folk poetry with similar themes related to work at the spinning wheel and the grindstone were composed in Marathi and Kannada even before the influence of Islam was felt in Deccan. The Sufis of Bijapur adapted these popular local creations and substituted Marathi and Kannada with *Dakhani*.

In south India, Persian and Arabic had never been the dominant languages in intellectual discussions. A substantial body of literature that theorised politics from the fourteenth to the late eighteenth centuries was produced in vernacular languages: Telugu, Kannada, and Marathi. Telugu had emerged as a major literary language by *c.* 1300 in the southeastern part of peninsular India. The Telugu texts, argued Velcheru Narayana Rao and Sanjay Subrahmanyam (2013), were concerned with *niti* or politics or statecraft rather than *dharma* or religion, and were therefore mostly 'this-worldly' (*laukika*) or 'secular' in character. Writing *niti* texts in Telugu was actively pursued from the twelfth to the mid-fourteenth centuries, spanning the Kakatiya period in Andhra. Madiki Singana's *Sakala-niti-sammatamu*, an anthology of *niti* texts in Telugu, is particularly significant for emphasising the importance of *niti* as a subject in medieval Andhra and illustrating the distinct conceptual separation between *niti* and *dharma* practised by Telugu authors. This is apparent from the non-inclusion of even a single verse from the thirteenth-century Brahmanic *dharmashastra* prescriptive discourse, Ketana's *Vijnaneshvaramu*, a Telugu text based on the Sanskrit *mitakshara* commentary of Vijnaneshvara to the *Yajnavalkyasmriti*. Similarly, *Rayavacakamu* narrates the reign of Vijayanagara king Vira Narasimha in the early sixteenth century, who customarily listened to verses from different *niti* texts, including Canura's *Niti* (Canura is a distortion of Chanakya).

The Vijayanagara kingdom patronised literature in Sanskrit as well as Kannada and Telugu. Telugu had emerged as the prominent language of the ruling elite of the kingdom by the early sixteenth century, a process facilitated by a large number of warlords who were either from Andhra or had been in the service of the kingdom for a long time. Literary productions, including the genre of *niti*, were available for the sixteenth century and for the reigns of the Tuluva (Third) and Aravidu (Fourth) dynasties in Vijayanagara. One of the Tuluva rulers, Krishna Deva Raya, an accomplished scholar of Sanskrit and Telugu, is known for his work on *raja-niti*, *Amuktamalyada*, a Telugu devotional poem dedicated to Lord Vishnu, whom he addressed as a Telugu *Raya* (Telugu king). *Amuktamalyada*, a work of introspection-cum-political experience, is a revelation of Krishna Deva Raya's anxiety about being acceptable to his people; his self-perception as a Kannada *Raya*; his recommendations for the political management of the kingdom by the Brahmins, who were not associated with the class of warriors but were trained in military activities and were relatively detached from local entanglements. A political statesman, Krishna Deva Raya was aware that such a strategy would favour the king; he thus skillfully advocated it, hoping to resolve the potential discord between the king and the ministers. These conflicts were widely written about in treatises and chronicles by the *karanams*, who themselves were ministers. The *niti* of the kingdom, enunciated distinctly by Krishna Deva Raya, paved the way for the *niti* of small kingdoms established throughout Deccan by Aravidu Ramaraya's relatives and his extended family. The context of the writings changed with rampant family conspiracies, rivalries, wars, and opportunities for upward mobility. The *niti* texts, for instance, hailed the rise of the Nayakas, who had successfully set aside the refrain posed by complex, uncertain, and chaotic political conditions. *Andhra Kamandakamu* (1584), authored by Jakkaraju Venkatakavi, a courtier of Kondraju Venkataraju, a small king from the Aravidu family, described Venkataraju's efforts to restore the Ahobilam temple following its destruction by the Turks (*turakalu*); yet it abstained from referring to the Turks either approvingly or critically and focused simply on regional and secular (non-sectarian) features of *niti*. Although Venkatakavi claimed that his work was a translation of the Sanskrit text *Kamandakiya* or *Nitisara*, it included several *niti* statements not found in the original text and appeared more of an early modern *niti* text than a mere reiteration of the classical *niti* vision.

The Tanjavur Nayaka kings were known for their patronage of literature, particularly Sanskrit and regional literature in the genre of dance drama, known as *Yakshagana*. One *Yakshagana* on Raghunatha Nayaka (r. 1612–34) is significant for its portrayal of accountants speaking and bickering in the different local languages—Tamil, Telugu, and Kannada—reflecting thus the use of local vernacular languages in administration and the tension between the diverse constituents of the kingdom.

SCRIBES: *MUNSHIS* AND THE *KARANAMS*

The *munshis* in the north and the *karanams* in the south were a significant corps of professionals within a wider community of scribes in early modern India. They were the literati of the chancellery who produced systems of knowledge, ideas, and information and helped to disseminate them till at least the nineteenth century or the coming of the printing press. The technique of inscribing or writing as a social technology and social calibre was first initiated by the Mauryan king Asoka through his rock and pillar inscriptions. The roots of the scribal class during the period of our study lay in the socio-economic changes that led to the rising importance of written communications and record-keeping. Knowledge itself, C. A. Bayly (1996) observed, is a social formation and as people of knowledge, the scribes represented a distinct, active social segment that encountered a number of opportunities and challenges. Expertise in writing, book-keeping, and in the understanding of Mughal politics made them valuable. As writer and clerical cadre, these scribes formed a part of Mughal bureaucracy and emerged as a middle class, albeit distinguished by caste and religion, and depended for their success on royal patronage.

Image 1.2: Colophon Portrait from the *Khamsa of Nizami*, created for Akbar by Daulat, *c.* 1595–96. The portrait shows Daulat (left) and Abdul Rahim, a scribe, working on the book

Source: https://commons.wikimedia.org/wiki/File: Colophon_from_the_khamsa_of_Nizami_Bl_Or._MS_12208_f._325v.jpg.

Specific skills and training were mandatory for the scribes, which were provided within the family structure to ensure recruitment and the efficient discharge of duty while in employment. Pursuing the ethic of loyalty and inspired by Persian literary culture, a large section of the *munshi*s came from the two castes of Kayasthas and Khatris that were generally associated with clerical culture—correspondence, accountancy, information retrieval, and office; however, they also comprised Muslims and Brahmins. Keen on aggrandising their career opportunities, they had no hesitation in undertaking local migrations, thus making their social identities complex. As the Mughal Empire acquired eastern and southern territories, Kayastha, Khatri, and Muslim officials moved into Bengal, Orissa, Gujarat, and Deccan. The Kayastha community, remarked J. Duncan Derrett (1968), was the best example of a caste of indeterminate origin that had the capacity to turn an aptitude to advantage. The title 'Kayastha' is derived from the Sanskrit word *kaya*, that is, body, and can be translated as 'that lay near the body or *kaya*' and, therefore, those who stayed by the side of the master with unstinted loyalty. Over the years, the term Kayastha came to be used to refer to a series of regionally-based caste communities. In cultural terms, west India's Kayastha communities stood in sharp contrast to their northern counterparts and those in Bengal. In Bengal, like in north India, the scribes or those engaged in administrative work came usually from the Kayastha community, but they also came from other *jati*s (castes) like the Brahmins and the Vaishyas. In the Maratha region, to the contrary, the reach of the Kayasthas as a scribal class was not as strong; instead, it was the Brahmins that prevailed. With well-equipped scribal skills, they were seen as upholders of *dharmasastra*s and an authority on Sanskrit literary culture. The Brahmins also exercised a firm hold in the Bahmani and Vijayanagara kingdoms and the Deccan sultanates.

Image 1.3: Another version of the Colophon Portrait from the *Khamsa of Nizami*, created for Akbar by Daulat, *c.* 1595–96

Source: https://commons.wikimedia.org/wiki/File: Colophon_from_the_khamsa_of_Nizami_Bl_Or._MS_12208_f._325v.jpg.

The Mughal royal chancelleries prescribed a form of writing that was elaborately followed. The entire nobility was disciplined into nurturing and venerating the style of letter-writing, and creation and construction of documents and state papers, that is, *insha*, an important genre of the Indo-Persian literary tradition and political diplomacy. This meant that a large body of clerks existed with expertise in record-keeping, draftsmanship (*insha*), and accountancy (*siyaq*), and many more rushed to acquire the talent in recognition of the fact that the profession of *munshi* had, over generations, proved immensely lucrative. In several respects, thus, a *munshi* evolved as more than a secretary; he was also a diplomat and an expert in regulating social and political relations. The importance of a *munshi* was immediately connected to Mughal imperial policy and its use of Persian as the language of administration and culture. The royal *munshi*, placed at the helm of a hierarchy comprising clerks (*munims*) of commercial firms, individual landowners or the elite, and the ordinary writer of the bazaar, was an important figure who managed social communication and interaction. The commercial communities that preferred to hire the services of their family members to write the accounts or business letters in Bengali and Hindi could not overlook the necessity and value of Persian writers, especially if they had to correspond with local officials and verify the records of the *Qazi*. Linguistic and scriptural complexity and multiplicity enhanced the value of the scribes, whether at the government or at the private, local level.

To investigate the social identities of the *munshi*s, their attributes, the process of acculturation and the training they went through, as well as their contributions to the state, society, and culture of the subcontinent, a few narratives by the *munshi*s may be cited: commonly normative texts similar to 'Mirror of Princes' or, more suitably in this case, 'Mirror for Scribes', as suggested by Alam and Subrahmanyam (2004b), and a few autobiographical accounts. There were a number of Kayastha and Khatri *munshi*s who contributed substantially to Indo-Persian vocabulary, literature, and philology, and whose works were taught at *madrasas* as a part of the syllabi of Persian studies. It is not possible to discuss all of them, but a few may be mentioned as case studies.

Nigarnama-i Munshi, written during the reign of Aurangzeb by an anonymous author with the pen-names *Munshi* and *Malikzada*, described the kind of training and technical knowledge that a *munshi* ought to acquire in epistolary, accountancy, and financial management. A didactic text, *Nigarnama* comprised two *daftar*s (sections): an introduction to the features of *insha* and a description of the works of former eminent *munshi*s. A complement to *Nigarnama* is *Khulasat us-Siyaq*, written during the last years of Aurangzeb's reign by Indar Sen. Concerned primarily with financial management, the text focused on the importance of arithmetic formulae to aid the *munshi*s in *siyaq*. Describing the replacement of Hindavi by Persian in the department of *siyaq* during the reign of Akbar, it emphasised the language skills of the *munshi*s, in addition to details of the offices of *diwan-i a'la*, *khan-i saman*, and the *bakshi*. An earlier text from the reign of Jahangir, *Insha'-i Harkaran* written by Harkaran Das Kambuh of Multan, was an exemplar account by a first known Hindu *munshi*. It was later translated and served as an archetype for officials of the East India Company in the late eighteenth century grappling with the intricacies of Mughal administrative patterns.

Yet another of the secretarial elite, Chandar Bhan Brahman, considered second only to the *mir munshi* Shaikh Abu'l Fazl, was proud of his Brahmin identity and saw no conflict between his commitments to imperial service and his *dharmic* propriety. Known for his literary versatility and his writings on the administrative practices and political and intellectual culture in the seventeenth century, his perspective was somewhat different, perhaps influenced by the fact that he lived through the reigns of four Mughal emperors—born towards the end of Akbar's reign, he was a *munshi* for Jahangir, Shahjahan, and Aurangzeb. His prose, *Chahar Chaman*

('The Four Gardens'), was both a memoir of his service in the Mughal administration and a didactic manual for the *wazir*s or *dastur al-wizarat* along the lines of the Indo-Persian tradition of *nasihat-nama*s or 'advice-books'. Emphasising ethical behaviour (*akhlaq*), civility, humility, efficiency, mystical awareness (*ma'rifat*), religious tolerance, and public morality as necessary virtues in a *wazir*, he also provided an assessment of several Mughal *wazir*s and other administrative officials, many of whom he had worked with and known personally. *Chahar Chaman* was also valuable for providing information on courtly life and a description of the *Urdu-i mu'alla* (camp) in Delhi. Writing about provinces, people, architecture, commerce, and the fauna of Hindustan, he had special praise for Akbarabad (*dar al-khilafat*) and Lahore (*dar al-saltanat*), and showered even greater applause on the capital city of Shahjanahabad (*dar al-hukumat*) through his verse (wrongly attributed to Amir Khusrau):

> *agar firdaus bar ru-yi zamin ast*
> *hamin ast u hamin ast u hamin ast*
> (If there is paradise on earth
> It is here, it is here, it is here)

Chandar Bhan's letter to his son Khwaja Tej Bhan is equally significant for its advice on the making of an ideal, perfect *munshi*. A *munshi*, he observed, should undergo training in the Mughal system of norms or *akhlaq*, for it led to the acquisition of knowledge; read the works of history, *diwan*s, and *masnavi*s; learn the skills of *siyaq* and *nawisindagi* (scribal techniques), for a man who could combine good prose with accountancy 'is a bright light even among lights'; be discreet and virtuous; and above all, increase and improve his linguistic abilities.

Sections of Chandar Bhan's work was cited in *Khulasat-ut-Tawarikh* (Essence of Histories) by Sujan Rai Batalvi (or Bhandari), a *Khatri dabir* (secretary) to several nobles in the seventeenth century. Influenced by Abu'l Fazl and the Indo-Persian style of history-writing, Sujan Rai traced the history of India from the time of King Yudhishthira to 1696, the latter part of Aurangzeb's reign, and introduced elements (not given much importance earlier) of ethnography and analytical narration into history. His text, therefore, is a rich account of Hindustan, its topography, provincial boundaries, fauna, flora, people and their customs, handicrafts, revenue, and much more. His allusion to *Quranic* concepts, the *sulh-i kul* ideology of Akbar, and the esoteric Sufi language in the introductory text is extremely revealing but causes confusion about his identity, even though he referred to the social position of the Khatris. He predictably hoped to advance non-sectarianism and harmony. With this in view, he recommended the reading of books on *akhlaq*, *tasawwuf*, and history; history, he believed, not only inculcated spiritual ecstasy, but also removed ignorance and promoted knowledge and intelligence. His style was simple and straightforward and enhanced the readability of his works in the eighteenth century and thereafter.

Another text of the seventeenth century that reflected on the evolution of literati culture under the Mughals and the extraordinary role and training of the *munshi*s is a short autobiographical account, *Tazkirat al-Safar wa Tuhfat al-Zafar* (Account of Travels and the Gift of Success) by Nek Rai, a Kayastha *munshi* in the court of Aurangzeb. Written in highly embellished Persian, the text began with a eulogy of God and *qalam* (pen). Contrary to the title, the text did not delve into the theme of *safar* (travel), but concentrated on *sukhan* (speech) itself, probably to convey the 'constantly on the move' nature of a *munshi*'s job. The text was invaluable for its suggestion of four necessary constituents in a *munshi*'s education: unlike texts such as *Nigarnama-i Munshi*, he was completely silent on aspects of technical knowledge, although he himself must have learnt *siyaq* and finances while in Deccan. Like Chandar Bhan, his emphasis was on the essential reading of texts: history, *diwan*s, *masnavi*; also clear was his admiration and emulation of the style of *mir munshi*, Abu'l Fazl, who, by the seventeenth century, was revered for his views on ecumenical learning and religious pluralism and the importance that he attached to the Persian language and the secular Indo-Persian tradition to understand the world that surrounded him. These observations of Nek Rai may be read as his reflections on what it meant to be a *munshi* in the later Mughal period.

The *munshi*s had consistently evolved, beginning with the consolidation of Mughal rule in north India. They evolved their own templates of history-writing in the late seventeenth century and as their power increased in the early eighteenth century, they assumed different roles: scribe, historian (*arbab-i qalam* or 'lords of the pen'), militarist (*arbab-i saif* or 'lords of the sword'). The number of Kayasthas and Khatris increased in the middle rungs of the Mughal polity and so did the 'Persianised' Brahmins, who emulated Chandar Bhan Brahman. A *munshi* from the eighteenth century who exemplified a scribe's protean character was Nawal Rai, a Kayastha of the Saksena sub-caste belonging to the *qanungo* family of a village in Etawah. Employed as a *munshi* by Abu'l Mansur Khan Safdar Jang in a low cadre, he steadily rose to the position of a *bakshi* and then *na'ib subadar* of Awadh. Later, in 1743, he was elevated to the rank of deputy governor, Allahabad, with the title of *Raja* and then *Maharaja Bahadur* by Safdar Jang.

Rai Chaturman, a Saksena Kayastha and author of *Chahar Gulshan*, was yet another significant example of a *munshi* from the eighteenth century. He belonged to a family that had long been associated with Mughal service, and one of his kinsmen was a *peshkar* in Bengal. Chaturman served the imperial army in Deccan and later joined Ghazi-ud-Din Khan, *wazir al-mamalik* of Mughal Emperor Shahjahan II. His text, *Akhbar ul-Nawadir* or *Khulasat ul-Nawadir*, left incomplete by his death around 1759–60, was put together with an additional preface by his grandson, Rai Chandrabhan, in 1789–90. It comprised four sections, beginning with an account of the rulers of Hindustan from Yudhishthira to Shahjahan II; a description of the Sufis living in Delhi and its neighbourhood; and temples and fairs for the Hindus in north India and the provinces of the empire. In addition, he provided details on the southern provinces (*junubistan*) of the empire—Berar, Khandesh, Aurangabad, Bijapur, Hyderabad, and Bidar; information on the empire's communication networks starting from Shahjahanabad–Delhi; and concluded with a statement on Sufi and Hindu ascetic orders and saints like Guru Nanak, Ajit Singh, and Mata Sundari in Hindustan.

*Munshi*s continued to be invaluable to the *Nawab*s and the English East India Company, which conformed to the general practice of the Mughals of hiring *munshi*s to draft their letters. *Munshi*s also served as Persian language teachers for the officers of the Company, notwithstanding the frequent charges of incompetence against them. These complaints were perhaps motivated by the fact that only a few *munshi*s knew English, making the learner/pupil and the learned/teacher unintelligible to each other. Despite this, the *munshi*s emerged as prominent intermediaries by the late eighteenth century, who read and interpreted the Company's correspondence and helped the Company comprehend the traditions of knowledge and governance in the subcontinent. A *munshi* of importance in the late eighteenth century was Kishan Sahay, a Kayastha from Bihar in the service of Antoine Polier, a Franco-Swiss officer of the Company till the beginning of 1776. He was one of the *munshi*s involved in the preparation of *I'jaz-i Arsalani* (which contains about 2,000 letters of Polier; Arsalan Jang was Polier's Mughal title); he drafted most of the letters of the first volume of *I'jaz* and wrote a preface for it. Although *I'jaz* represented the eighteenth-century Persian *insha*, Polier and his *munshi*s did not incorporate all the features of *insha* in it. It is difficult to comment on Polier's knowledge of Persian, but it is certain that he surveyed these letters and advised Kishan Sahay to put them in a volume.

Another writer of interest from the same period is Prem Kishor 'Firaqi', grandson of Jugal Kishor, a *bhat* or bard by caste and liquor-seller by profession, who wrote a *roznamcha* (diary) of two months for the reign of Shah 'Alam II. Unlike his grandfather, 'Firaqi' wrote poetry in Persian and *rekhta*; was an accomplished calligrapher, especially in *khatt-i shikast*; and though he was a trained *tir-andaz* (archer), circumstances compelled him to seek employment as a *munshi*. He wrote several *masnavi*s, although none of these are extant; the only work that has survived from amongst his many is *Waqa'i-i 'Alamshahi*, written in Persian but with odd word combinations between Persian and Arabic and Persian and Indian vernaculars. In fact, his avid use of vernacular words is reflective of the changing times and growing vernacularisation during the late eighteenth century. 'Firaqi' rarely mentioned the East India Company in his works, paying no heed to the fact that *munshi*s of his generation were keen on employment with the Company either as translators or interpreters, or because they sought to introduce the British and/or the French to the affairs of the Mughal chancellery and *adab*. Some, of course, like Mirza Muhammad Hasan 'Qatil', author of *Haft Tamasha*, preferred to move to Lucknow or other regional centres, either for reasons of religion or availability of resources.

The equivalents of the *munshi*s in south India, the *karanams*, a politically and culturally important group of the Brahmin caste in Andhra, Karnataka, and Orissa, were professional accountants and record-keepers. In Andhra, they were mostly Niyogi Brahmins, who managed public affairs, as opposed to the Vaidikis, who were specialists in ritual texts and performances, although both wrote poetry and had made writing their profession. They were, however, not mere copyists or note-takers, but a literate community that used writing for communication and not merely for preservation or recording. Their rising social importance was for the fact that like the *munshi*s, they too were engaged in the diffusion of secular knowledge and cosmopolitanism, but primarily in the southern part of India (the *munshi*s, to the contrary, moved to all corners of the empire). Their value lay in their multilingualism, their calligraphic skill, their competence in reading different scripts, Sanskrit, and particularly Persian which, by the seventeenth century, had become the established official language and language of culture and religious pluralism. *Karanams* were not patronised by either the royal or any other patron, and neither was their work dedicated to gods. Their histories, which comprised diverse commentaries on subjects like *niti*, political philosophy, sexuality, and the concept of public space, generally exuded a sense of independence as compared to other contemporary writings.

Their writings often served as an ideal model for men of humble status who, by their shrewd, crafty style, moved up in the hierarchy and even became companions of the rulers—for instance, Niyogi Brahmins like Akkanna and Madanna in the 1600s and 1670s in the Sultanate of Golconda and Saluva Timma (popularly known as Appaji) in the early sixteenth century, mentioned eminently in *Rayavacakamu*, one of the important *karanam* histories in Telugu. In spite of the claim that this text provided descriptions of events beginning with the reign of Krishna Deva Raya in the early sixteenth century, Philip Wagoner (1996), in his translation and annotation of the text, argued that it belonged to the seventeenth century. The *karanams* have left behind a rich legacy of historical texts in addition to writing about themselves, their code of conduct and training. An anonymous text, probably of the eighteenth century, that codified their conduct was *Sumati Shatakamu*. While the book attached a greater significance to the role of a *karanamu* (minister) than to that of the king in maintaining discipline in the kingdom, it prescribed a pragmatic—rather, a cynical—outlook for the common masses, that is, women cannot be trusted; kings do not abide by their promises; money determines the loyalty of friends; in brief, no one helps, and one has to be dependent on oneself!

Plate 1: Princes of the House of Timur by Abd as-Samad, *c.* 1550–55. The painting shows a ruler (believed to be Humayun) seated in a garden pavilion, flanked by courtiers and nobles. Many of the figures were repainted to depict the succeeding Mughal emperors, creating a genealogical scene

Source: https://commons.wikimedia.org/wiki/File: Princes_of_the_House_of_Timur.jpg.

Plate 2: Illustrated pages from *Ain-i Akbari* by Abu'l Fazl

Source: https://commons.wikimedia.org/wiki/File: Ain-i-Akbari_(The_Chronicles_of_Emperor_Akbar),_Lahore_Pakistan, *c.* 1822.jpg.

Plate 3: Babur Supervising the Laying Out of the Garden of Fidelity (Illustration from *Baburnama*, 1530)

Source: https://commons.wikimedia.org/wiki/File:Babur supervising the laying out of fidelity_right_large.jpg.

Plate 4: Illustration from *Hamzanama*, commissioned by Emperor Akbar, shows the witch Anqarut in the disguise of a beautiful young woman tying King Malik Iraj to a tree, whom she hoped to seduce (*c.* 1562–77)

Source: https://commons.wikimedia.org/wiki/File:Hamzanama.jpg.

Plate 5: Scene from *Tutinama*, 1556–65, A Girl with a Parrot. The parrot addresses a woman called Khojasta to prevent her from committing any illicit affair while her husband (a merchant by the name of Maimunis) is away on business

Source: https://commons.wikimedia.org/wiki/File:Indischer_Maler_um_1580_001.jpg.

Plate 6: Akbar and Tansen visit Swami Haridas in Vrindavan. Swami Haridas is to the right, playing the lute; Akbar is to the left, dressed as a common man; Tansen is in the middle, listening to Haridas (Jaipur-Kishangarh mixed style, *c.* 1750)

Source: https://commons.wikimedia.org/wiki/File:Akbar and Tansen visit Haridas.jpg.

Plate 7: Emperor Jahangir weighs Prince Khurram (later crowned Shahjahan), *Tuzuk-i-Jahangiri*, 1610–15

Source: https://commons.wikimedia.org/wiki/File:Manohar._Emperor_Jahangir_Weighs_Prince_Khurram._Page_from_Tuzuk-i_Jahangiri._1610-1615,_British_Museum,_London.jpg.

Plate 8: Emperor Shahjahan standing on a Globe, artist, Hashim, seventeenth century

Source: https://commons.wikimedia.org/wiki/File:Shahjahan_on_globe_mid_17th_century.jpg.

Plate 9: Emperor Aurangzeb in *Darbar*, painted by Bichtr, *c.* 1660. Shaista Khan is standing to the left of Prince Muhammad Azam, third son of the emperor

Source: https://commons.wikimedia.org/wiki/File:Darbarscene.jpg.

Plate 10: Captain William Hodson captured the King of Delhi, Bahadur Shah II, and his three sons, Moghul, Khizr Sultan and Abu Bakr, during the Mutiny of 1857

Source: https://commons.wikimedia.org/wiki/File:'Capture_of_the_King_of_Delhi_by_Captain_Hodson'.jpg.

2

LITERARY TRENDS

Persian Compositions and Travelogues

HIGHLIGHTS

- Trends in medieval-early modern Indian historiography
- Genres of literature in Persian language
- *Malfuzat*, *Insha*, and other works
- Topographical works
- *Tarikh*/*Tawarikh* or General Histories
- Travelogues: European, Central, and West Asian

GENRES OF LITERATURE IN PERSIAN LANGUAGE

Medieval–Early Modern Indian historiography emulated a strict adherence to chronology influenced by the Arab-Islamic and Mongol-Persian traditions, in which the notion of historical periodisation was significantly absent except for a temporal break, with the *hijri* era as a centre point between the two periods—that is, before and after the rise of Islam in history and theology. The pre-Islamic phase was marked by *jahiliya* or ignorance and savagery, pre-literate culture, and the absence of articulate historical thought, while the Islamic era referred to the descent of the last prophet, Muhammad ibn Abdullah, whom God had chosen to reveal the ultimate truth and banish any remains of untruth, infidelity, and *kufr* (ingratitude and denial of God; subsequently, the term was used for anything incompatible with Islam) from the world before *hashr* or the Day of Judgement. This paradigm initiated Arab historians into conceptualising world history as a single unit, with exceptions in Iran and India in the subsequent centuries. In medieval India, all historians—ranging from orthodox historians like Ziya-ud-din Barani (fourteenth century) and Mulla Abdul Qadir Badauni (sixteenth century), to mildly 'liberal' Muslim historians like Shams-i Siraj 'Afif (fourteenth century), Nizam-ud-din Ahmad Bakshi (sixteenth century; d. 1594), Abdul Hamid Lahori (seventeenth century), and others (except Abu'l Fazl, who wrote universalist history)—accepted the *hijri* era and wrote the histories of Muslim dynasties in India, ignoring regions that existed prior to Islam (perhaps they saw them as a manifestation of *jahiliya*). Nevertheless, all made a valuable contribution to segregating history from theology and explained historical causation in relation to human or king's will, rather than divine will.

The Indo-Islamic traditions that developed and prospered between the eighth and the eighteenth century contributed to acclimatise Islam to the regional cultures of Hindustan. From seventh century onwards, Muslims in all parts of the world were involved in the process of cultural accommodation, adaptation, and assimilation, which transformed what had begun as an Arab cult into what is now a widely practised religion. Islamic history, in fact, can be seen as a 'venture' (a term borrowed from M. G. S. Hodgson [1975]) in which the people, without rejecting their local cultures, managed in many ways to blend into their lives a normative order as they believed to have been revealed in the *Quran* or the covenant of *Allah*, with which Prophet Muhammad bound together and organised the warring Arabs into a polity by arousing among them the need for unity. In effect, there were no established and sanctioned political institutions in Islamic polity. Religion preceded the State. Theoretically, the State had no independent existence. It was an instrument to fulfil religious obligations for it was not the State, but the *Quran* that was recognised as the ultimate source of law.

Box 2.1: *Ziya-ud-din Barani*

Ziya-ud-din Barani (1285–1357), a disciple of Shaikh Nizam ud-din Awliya, a scholar, and contemporary chronicler of the Delhi Sultanate, belonged to an aristocratic family of courtiers and had been in State service to the Mamluks, Khaljis, and the Tughluqs. He served as the *nadim* (courtier) and *muqarrab* (companion or aide) of Muhammad bin Tughluq for seventeen years. But with the accession of Firuz Shah Tughluq, he lost his position, his property was confiscated, and he was briefly imprisoned in the fort of Bhatnire, possibly on suspicion of being associated with Khwaja Jahan Ahmad bin Ayaz's conspiracy to raise one of the sons of Muhammad bin Tughlaq to the throne. Reduced to poverty, he spent the rest of his life at Ghiyaspur (a village near Delhi), the site of the *dargah* of Shaikh Nizam ud-din Awliya. It was here that he wrote *Tarikh-i-Firuzshahi*. He had not written anything before this work. In fact, when Barani wrote *Tarikh-i-Firuzshahi*, he was more than sixty years of age; he had no access to official records or notes or any library. He wrote solely from memory and did not follow a chronology like any historian would. But this style was deliberate. He wrote what he remembered, and he remembered what impressed him the most or what he thought was important in determining the history of the period.

Tarikh-i-Firuzshahi begins with the accession of Balban in 1266 and ends in the sixth year of Firuz Shah Tughluq's reign in 1357, covering a period of ninety-five years in the history of the Delhi Sultanate. Had it not been for Barani's *Tarikh-i-Firuzshahi*, the history of this period may have perhaps remained unsaid. His three political works, *Tarikh-i-Firuzshahi*, *Fatawa-i-Jahandari*, and *Hazratnama*, deal with the power struggle of the Sultans and talk about the philosophy and ideals of kingship and empire. Although he was conservative and orthodox and represented the *'Ulama*, he advocated *zawabit* (special regulations) to the Sultans and advised them to set aside the principles of *Sharia't* for State governance. In addition to these political chronicles, he wrote a biography of the Prophet, *Sana-i-Muhammadi*, for, as he claimed, spiritual fulfillment and atonement for his sins.

Islam became a crucial factor in the idea of medieval historiography and represented historical consciousness. The Arabic word for history, *tarikh*, appears to have had no pre-Islamic origin. It does not occur, said Franz Rosenthal (1952, 13; *cf* Mukhia 2010, 3–18), in the Quran or in the old *hadis* (traditions), but 'to all appearances, the word *tarikh* is mentioned in Arabic literature first together with the stories of the introduction of the Muslim era'. Rosenthal's perception was reaffirmed by Tarif Khalidi (1994), who observed that 'the Arabs learnt a new history when they acquired a new religion'. Traditions of Quran and *hadis* learning had given a pedagogical emphasis to their memorisation by a small 'literate' class. In pragmatic as well as in conceptual terms, among the Muslim religious groups, knowledge was believed to be located in persons rather than in books. Books were not considered independent sources of knowledge, but appendages to the personal pedagogical relationships through which knowledge was transferred. It was within this dimension that the *murids* (disciples) of the Prophet contributed to history writing by recording the *hadis* of the Prophet in *Mawazhi* literature.

Box 2.2: Etymology of the term 'Arab'

The term **Arab or 'Arab** has been used diversely or at least in five different ways as both noun and adjective. It was originally used to refer to the Bedouins—the nomads, and especially the camel nomads of Arabia. In fact, the customary term for them in Arabic was A'rab. 'Arab was also used for those who claimed descent from the Bedouins or identified culturally with the Bedouins—nomads or settled—or their language. Historically, the term 'Arab implied 'Muslim', especially because the early Muslims were Arabs. But jurists like Abu Yusuf provided a plural interpretation to the term 'Arab and defined it to refer to not only the Muslims, but also Christians and Jews. 'Arab was also used for all such people who spoke Arabic-derived dialects, irrespective of their connection to the Bedouins or Bedouin traditions or to Islam. Another usage of 'Arab was for all such individuals for whom the language of literacy was classical Arabic or Mudari, regardless of whether their local vernacular language was derived from Arabic or was completely unrelated to it. In other words, this terminology was used for persons who wrote in Arabic, but whose language was Persian or Spanish or Turkish or Kurdish. This would suggest that this practice was not applied for those people who possessed literacy only in Arabic—for example, the Somalis. Nevertheless, the phraseology was used for people among whom Arabic was at least the language for rituals.

Written in glorification of the Prophet, *Mawazhi* literature provided a methodology to the writing of history by developing a technique of *asnad/isnad* (sources). Every *hadi* had *asnad.* Ziya-ud-din Barani, the fourteenth-century chronicler, argued that *ilm-i-hadis* and *ilm-i-tarikh* were inseparable, that is, for the knowledge of *hadis*, knowledge of history was essential. This assertion led Peter Hardy to argue that Barani's historical approach was theologically conditioned. K. A. Nizami and P. K. Hitti, however, offered a different explanation. They observed that when medieval historians like Barani bracketed the study of history with the study of *hadis*, it was not influenced by the theological content of the latter but by its *usul-i-asnad* (methods of investigation and enquiry, acceptance and rejection; in brief, the principles of critique evolved by the scholars of *hadis*) which, as Hitti said, 'meets the essential requirements of modern historiography'. *Asnad* was important to verify information and establish the historical value and veracity of facts. It was in this context that the theologians encouraged the idea of universal history or the history of the community. But with the decline of the Abbasid *Khilafat* in the tenth century and the establishment of several independent Sultanates, the idea of universal history channelled into regional history. The *'ulama* and their modes of learning cast a significant influence on literate learning throughout the medieval–early modern period, with their institutions providing a basis for bureaucratic and clerical training in the Turkish Sultanates of Persia and north India.

Although history-writing developed within the framework of Islam, it neither indulged in theology nor grew as its offshoot, but unfolded gradually as the domain of the courtiers, who generally focused on the court and court-related activities like accession, battles, and administration, or wrote to celebrate occasions, that is, *fatah* or victory or conquest or opening of a new society and a quest to know about these societies. The best example of the latter would be the *Tarikh-ul-Hind* or *Kitab-ul-Hind* of Al-biruni.

Box 2.3: Abu Raihan Muhammad bin Al-biruni

Abu Raihan Muhammad bin Al-biruni (973–1048) was hailed as the first of the scientific Indologists. He came from the region of Khiva, Khwarazm, which was ruled by the Samanid dynasty of Transoxiana and Persia in the tenth–eleventh centuries. It is believed that because he was not born within the city but in a suburban area, he was named Al-biruni. Biruni is a Persian word that means 'of or belonging to the outside'. Al-biruni was in the court of Khwarazm when the latter was invaded and annexed by Mahmud of Ghazni in 1017. He was brought to Ghazni by Sultan Mahmud, where he continued to live till his death in 1048. Held in high esteem for his scholarly attainments and knowledge of astronomy and astrology, it was during his stay in Ghazni—a primary political and cultural centre of Islam visited by the Indians—that he developed his interest in India and the Indians. A linguist and a prolific writer, he was well-versed in Hebrew, Syriac, Greek, Sanskrit, Arabic, and Persian, although he mostly wrote in Arabic.

The bulk of Al-biruni's work is either lost or is unpublished. Two of his works—*Athar-ul-Baqiya* and *Kitab-ul-Hind*, popularly known as *Tarikh-ul-Hind*—are available in print, and the latter has been translated into English as *Alberuni's India*. *Tarikh-ul-Hind* is a valuable, exhaustive scholarly account of Indian society comprising eighty chapters, which provide details on philosophy, astronomy, science, alchemy, customs, festivals, food, dress, games, currency, weights and measures. Al-biruni's sociological insight is clearly reflected in his discussion of the caste system, civil and religious law, and iconography. Although he was reticent on political and economic matters, trade, industry, agriculture, art and architecture, he mentioned the importance of Somnath as a centre for sea-faring and trade activities and the significance of banning cow slaughter, indicating that cows were valuable for agricultural and domestic purposes. *Tarikh-ul-Hind* was written during the reign of Sultan Mahmud, but Al-biruni rarely mentioned him. In fact, he dedicated the book to Sultan Mas'ud, son of Mahmud.

Tarikh (plural, *tawarikh*) was one of the genres of Persian literature that had a mnemonic function; in addition, there were a range of others. These included:

- *tabaqat* or biographical books, intended to serve as moral models to be emulated;
- instructional literature that pertained to spiritual beliefs and conduct (broadly speaking, *isharat* literature), specifically the conversations of Sufi teachers, that is, *malfuzat*;
- *tazkirat* or a biographical compendium or the biographical encyclopedias of Sufis, *'ulama*, also literati and artists;
- *manaqib* or florid, panegyrical accounts in verse and prose;
- *adab* or didactic texts that prescribed ideal norms of conduct;
- *farmans*, *parwanas*, *arzdashts*, *nishans*, *bakhars* or royal orders;

- three distinct categories of Persian poetical literature—*ghazal*, *masnavi*, and *qasida*—and other documents.

With a variety such as this in medieval–early modern literature, there can be no uniform method of enquiry and interpretation.

Malfuzat

Malfuzat texts vary a great deal in style, form, and content. Seeing the world as a divine manifestation and interpreting it in terms of their transcendental predilections, they constitute a source of information on the life and thought of Sufis, *Pirs*, *Shaikhs* (venerated as saints) or *Awliya* (friends of God). *Fawa'id al-Fuad* of Amir Hasan Sijzi (completed in 1322 CE), a record of the conversations of Shaikh Nizam ud-din Awliya, was significant in the evolution of this genre. Barani described it as a manual of guidance for not only the mystics of Chishti *silsilah* (order) but also the saints of other *silsilahs*, namely Suhrawardi, Firdausi, Naqshbandi, Qadiri, and Shattari. Muslims were impressed by the historical anecdotes narrated in the *malfuzat* texts, which discussed the achievements of their *Shaikhs*. Historians like Carl Ernst and Bruce Lawrence have emphasised the stylistic form, content, and narrative intent of Sufi texts to understand their importance in constituting a *Shaikh*'s authority. The historical, didactic, and panegyric elements were all present and reconfigured within the *malfuzat* texts.

> **_Box 2.4:_ Ghazal, Masnavi, _and_ Qasida**
>
> ***Ghazal*** is a kind of amatory poem or ode, the roots of which can be traced to Arabic poetry. In *ghazal*, every verse is in the form of a self-contained, complete unit, both in thought and expression. It is a medium through which to manifest erotic sentiments, although it is also used by mystics to convey cosmic emotions. On a few occasions, the style of *ghazal* has been used by poets to communicate their discontent against the political and State authority of the times.
>
> ***Masnavi*** is a long versified narrative on any theme, historical or romantic. In the historical *masnavis*, the poets were obliged to concentrate on historical themes, although to suit their poetic needs they could digress; on some occasions, the *masnavi* became completely disconnected from the primary theme. However, they could not modify, rectify, contort or distort historical themes to fulfil their poetic urges. The romantic *masnavis* were generally based on the data derived from the social, political, and cultural institutions of the time. Amir Khusrau was engaged in the writing of both forms of *masnavis*. His *Qiran-u's-Sa'dain*, *Miftah-u'l-Futuh*, *Dewal Rani*, *Nuh Sipihr*, and *Tughluqnama* represent historical *masnavis*, while *The Khamsa: Matla'u'l-Anwar*, *Shirin Khusrau*, *A'ina-i-Sikandari*, *Majnun Laila*, and *Hasht Bihisht* are examples of romantic *masnavis*.
>
> ***Qasida*** is an ancient Arabic word and a form of writing poetry as an ode. The *qasidas* written in Persian followed the tradition of hyperbolism and exaggeration. The reigns of Akbar and the two Sultans of Delhi, Iltutmish and Ala-ud-din Khalji, were pre-eminent in the production of this style of poetic literature.

Prior to Sijzi's work, *malfuzat* was not considered a suitable style for narrating the discourses of a great teacher; instead, the preferred expression was the *isharat* (treatises on mystical instructions) or *tazkirat*, literally the book of 'memory' (*zakira*), to supplement or correct the 'failing recollections of its users', a genre of literature produced by the 'elite for other elites'. Written in Persian during the Mughal period, Indo-Persian *tazkirat* were translated into Urdu in the late Mughal and colonial period, accompanied by Urdu sequels and companion compositions in Punjabi, Sindhi, and Gujarati. *Tazkirat* are like 'memorative communications' that memorialise individuals and communicate their legacy to a new generation, projecting them as icons of urban Indo-Muslim collective identity. Stories or verses served as *aides-memoire*: whatever was important was committed to memory. Sufi *tazkirat*s, argued Gilmartin and Lawrence (2002, 11), 'appealed to Sufism as an overarching Islamicate model for the operation of charisma and legitimation of authority, yet their aim in doing so was to establish competitively the particular precedence and distinctiveness of their own orders, genealogies and places'.

Imperial political agendas were implicit within the *tazkirat*, which were often dedicated to political rulers. The *Nafa'is-u'l-Ma'asir* of 'Ala-u'd-daula Qazwini, compiled in 1565–66, is an important *tazkirat* that provides a brief narrative on the first three Mughal emperors—Babur, Humayun, Akbar—and biographical notices of the poets of the period. *Tazkirat*, a significant source for the study of imperial norms of masculinity, became prominent from the latter half of the seventeenth century as a valuable source for the study of social, cultural, and literary aspects. *Malfuzat* and *tazkirat* are read more carefully for their rhetorical significance. Although the narratives and the histories of these texts were very different from those of the *tawarikh*—obsessively engaged with the narration of rulers, their courts, and their capital—they were as effective in constructing history.

Insha

Insha literature, an evidence of Persian and Arabic influence on the Mughal Empire, was yet another literary trend, valuable for reconstructing the history of the period, particularly political history. Written documents had been used for diplomatic and commercial purposes by the Arabs even before the rise of Islam, although the situation changed with the emergence and expansion of Islam. *Insha*, an Arabic word that literally means 'creation' or 'construction', was used in the same sense in classical Arabic literature. Later, it came to signify prose composition, letters, documents (*rasa'il*), and State papers, as distinct from regular treatises and books. Subsequently, it was used as a synonym for *munsha'at*, the documents composed in accordance with certain prescribed norms that distinguished their form, style, and diction from ordinary prose. *Insha* could also include advice that read like an *akhlaq* text or a treatise on ethics, one that contained philosophical discussions on justice and social organisation and advised rulers on norms of comportment. The term *ilm-i insha* is used for refined prose writing, although in a strictly technical sense, it is applied only to the different forms of letters and documents. Some historians like Jurji Zaidan, the noted Arab literary historian, have made this distinction and observed that *insha* was concerned primarily with the expression of inner feelings, as against the exposition of learned sciences. This, in his opinion, was the main reason for the change and development in the style of *insha* as compared to other branches of literature.

The rise of *insha* as a distinct literary style can be traced to empires such as the Sassanids, which had evolved an elaborate system for the drafting of State papers. The *dabir* was the official responsible for drafting. Both Arabic and Persian were used as the language of the chancellery by the Ghaznavids and the Seljuqs in Central Asia, and it was during this period that, for the first time, *insha* in Persian was located. *Insha* emerged and developed as a literary form from the time of the Delhi Sultans—which witnessed an efflorescence of Persian language and literature with the coming of the emigrants from Central Asia—to the end of Akbar's reign. Representing a distinct genre in Arabic and Persian literature during the Sultanate and the Mughal period, it comprised original texts of documents from royal chancelleries, letters, and other kinds of documents by persons known for their excellence in style and writing, along with a large number of documents of different types created by the compiler himself.

The Timurid Khurasan and Central Asian tradition of Persian prose and *insha* writing flourished greatly under Mughal patronage. Several letters from Humayun to Shah Tahmasp during his sojourn in Persia, contrary to the ornate diplomatic correspondences of the Mughals, were written in simple, pragmatic style; so was his letter to an Afghan noble in 1554, possibly after the re-occupation of Delhi and Agra. More significant was the contribution of Abu'l Fazl to the Persian *insha* of the sixteenth century—*Maktubat-i Allami* or *Insha-i Abu'l Fazl*. He had a consciously contrived style of abstract thought and concepts, reflecting his pantheistic outlook in a consistent way. He wrote a letter or an official document of any kind with the objective of not only conveying the message, but also philosophising at an abstract level, using the message as a reference point. While these were complementary, Fazl used a distinct language and style to convey the two and avoided the use of such phrases, verses, and sayings that were inconsistent with the philosophy of the document. His style set the standard for *insha*, although his critics dismissed his writings as *bida'* (innovations).

The most voluminous *insha* collections comprise *Munsha'at-i Namakin* by Abu'l Qasim Khan Namakin dedicated to Akbar, which provided interesting information on the political, institutional, and cultural aspects of Akbar's reign. Several collections are available from the reign of Aurangzeb, including his own letters—*Adab-i Alamgiri* and *Kalimat-i Tayyabat*—compiled by Muhammad Sadiq and Inayatullah Khan, respectively. In the 1680s, Malikzada collected a number of diplomatic and historical documents in *Nigarnama-i-Munshi*. These are only a few examples of *insha* during the Mughal period; the list is endless. Several histories like the *Mirat-i-Ahmadi*, the history of the Mughal *suba* of Gujarat by Ali Muhammad Khan in 1759–60, were reconstructed with *insha* as their basic source.

Waqa'i, Akhbarat, Dastur-u'l-'Amal

Waqa'i or reports of the proceedings at the court in the *suba*s and the letters sent by the *waqa'inavi*s (writer of the reports) from the *suba*s to the centre, were sources used by Mughal court chroniclers for the construction of Mughal history. Official histories like the *Akbarnama* of Abu'l Fazl; the *Padshahnama* of Amin Qazwini, Abdul Hamid Lahori, and Waris; *Alamgirinama* of Muhammad Kazim; and Jahangir's memoirs derived their chronology and information on political, social, and economic matters of the State from the *waqa'i*.

*Akhbarat*s or news reports were sent by the nobles and *wakil*s to the imperial court and the *suba*s. But since they were not State-sponsored records, they, like the *waqa'i*, were not considered official documents. Yet the *Akhbarat*s, along with the *Dastur-u'l-'Amal*s or the revenue manuals, are a valuable source of information on the functioning of the Mughal administration.

Topographical Works

A large corpus of topographical work in verse and prose is yet another significant aspect of Persian literature. The authors of such works focused on flourishing centres of power, commerce, and culture at a given point in time in history, and used three interconnected literary topoi to explain Indian society, for instance, its flora and fauna, architecture of particular cities, the *bazaars* and tradesmen. These topoi became a valuable part of a variety of verse and prose texts, like *masnavi*, *tazkirat*, *tarikh*, and travelogues. Amir Khusrau was the earliest Indo-Persian author to combine the three topoi in his works during the Delhi Sultanate. The next phase of Indo-Persian writing on buildings and cities that occurred in the sixteenth–seventeenth century, especially during the reigns of Akbar and Shahjahan, was marked by literary innovation and aesthetic independence, although they remained within a defined system of poetics. The poets invoked the 'metaphoric language of love' and their favourite literary topos—*shahrashub* or *shahrangiz* (city disturber, that is, someone who invigorates or animates a city by his beauty)—to describe the relationship between cities and their residents. This genre was frequently used in Indo-Persian writings when the Mughal emperors and Deccani rulers began constructing and redesigning new cities. These patterns were evident in the memoirs of Babur, the *Baburnama*, Abu'l Fazl's *Ain-i Akbari*, Muhammad 'Arif Qandahari's *Tarikh-i Akbari*, Asaf Khan Ja'far Beg's *Tarikh-i Alfi*, and Asad Beg Qazwini's *Waqa'i-i Asad Beg*. Qazwini's chronicle is significant for its description of the newly constructed city of Nauraspur while on a visit to the court of Ibrahim 'Adilshah at Bijapur in 1603–06.

Haft Iqlim (Seven Climes), completed in 1594 by Iranian émigré Amin Ahmad Razi, belonged to the same genre, but was written like a *tazkira* of the world. In each clime, the author talked about the major cities, their architecture, and the biographies of the accomplished ones, especially those who practised Persian poetry. For instance, Delhi's magnificence, its architecture, and the close association of the Sufis to the city figured in the third clime, while the city of Ahmadabad, the centre of literati patronised by the Mughal general 'Abdur Rahim Khan-i Khanan, was described in the second clime. *Saqinamah* (Book of the Saqi), the work of Nur ud-Din Muhammad Zuhuri, related to the seventeenth century and provided a panoramic view of a new city (*shahr-i naw*) built on the outskirts of Ahmadnagar. With the construction of Shahjahanabad, the poets wrote copiously on the architectural vision and achievements of Shahjahan. The emperor's *munshi* Chandar Bhan 'Brahman', in his *Chahar Chaman* (Four Meadows), wrote in praise of the capital city of Shahjahanabad (*dar al-hukumat*; see Ch. 1). He similarly wrote about the imperial cities of Akbarabad (*dar ul-khilafat*) and Lahore (*dar ul-saltanat*), even as he glossed over the other provinces cursorily.

Tarikh/Tawarikh

Tarikh or *tawarikh* (plural) were general histories or court chronicles that had the objective of recording 'dates' (as the name evinces), but more effectively were a commemorative venture that had made historiography focal to book-writing at the court. With the evolution and strengthening of the institution of monarchy and the concept of the divine theory of kingship, *tarikh* were commissioned by rulers; they were to be written by courtiers to record collective memory with a bent towards eulogy, sycophancy, and glorification of the monarch. This pattern was influenced by the chronicle of the Seljuq Empire, the *Siyasatnama* or the 'Mirror for Princes' authored by Nizam ul-Mulk, which not only acclaimed and extolled the kings, but also advised them on rules of governance. The genre of the 'Mirror for Princes' is widely noticed in Indo-Islamic texts of the time, from the Sultanate of Delhi to the Mughals, including regional Sultanates like Deccan. These texts, often written in Persian, were at times influenced by Indic models such as the *Pancatantra*, also known as *Kalila wa Dimna* in its translated version. They were also affected by the non-theological perspective on kingship that had emerged in the Islamic world as a consequence of the Mongol conquests; this perspective was used to instruct the Muslim *wazirs*, who were expected to advise the *kafir* rulers and princes on matters of governance without raising any controversial theological issues. This genre was expansive: it included the cultural refinement of the ruler and imparted core values on politics and political mannerisms to the rulers. The best examples of this style of writing are the *tawarikh* of Ziya-ud-din Barani and Abu'l Fazl, both of whom eulogised but also counselled their respective patrons and rulers.

Tarikh were written as a long narrative of human experience which began either with Adam, the first Prophet, or Muhammad, the last Prophet, and ended in the lifetime of the respective chroniclers with an extraordinary commendation of their patrons. Two traditions of historiography—Arab and Persian—determined the nature and character of historical writing during the medieval period. The Arab tradition goes back to the ninth-century historian Yaqubi, author of the first surviving work in this genre, and to Rashid al-Din, the Mongol-Persian historian of the early fourteenth century. It was rooted in democratic principles and considered history to be the biographies of nations—that is, while the narrative was chronological, it focused upon the political, social, economic, cultural, and military aspects of the period. Historians writing under this tradition did not dedicate their work to either kings or nobles.

The Persian tradition, on the other hand, advocated by al-Tabari (in which he located the impact of Persian national historiography even though, prior to the thirteenth century, most works on Iran's history were generally written in Arabic), was influenced by monarchical institutions. It was a biography of kings and the governing class, with rarely a reference to other sections of society. For the historians of this tradition, dedications were necessary to enhance the value of their writings. The Arab tradition dominated medieval historiography till the tenth century until the emergence and strengthening of the Persian Renaissance and Persian tradition of history-writing. Struck by the Persian tradition, the Sultans of the Ghaznavid Empire and the Sultanate of Delhi urged their court chroniclers to write in the Persian tradition, that is, in praise and glory of the Sultan.

A valuable, anonymous, untitled Arabic work, now known as the *Chachnama*, pioneered the Arab tradition of history-writing in India. Translated into Persian by Ali bin Hamid Kufi in 1216–17, the text comprises two parts: an account of the Brahman dynasty of Sind preceding the Arab conquest and a narrative of the Arab conquest, 710–14. By the sixteenth century, however, India had evolved a Perso-Islamic tradition of writing history, the tone and standard of which were set by the chroniclers of the thirteenth–fourteenth century, namely Hasan Nizami, Minhaj-us-Siraj Juzjani, and Ziya-ud-din Barani. It was under such influences and the Mongol style of history writing that the historians of the Mughal period evolved patterns of historiography, even as they approached history somewhat differently, in their own way.

Driven by the objective of creating an imperial narrative and affirming the legitimacy of Mughal dynastic rule, the chroniclers of the Mughal period not only used written records as *asnad/isnad*, but also based their comprehensive historical documentation on memory and hearsay. Babur, the first Mughal Emperor, allegedly depended on his memory, but also consulted his *roznamcha* (diaries) for writing his autobiography, *Baburnama*, which reflects his unrelenting, courageous scramble for power. Written in an annalistic style, *Baburnama* comprises three parts:

- the life and career of Babur in Farghana and Transoxiana (1494–1503);
- Kabul (1504–25); and
- Hindustan (1526–29).

The memoir is valuable for details on the bureaucracy or the nobility, civil and military matters, physiography, climate, society and economy, and the emperor's personal affairs and ambitions. But whatever the discussion, it revolved around and remained focused on the emperor, his court, power, and prestige. Reflecting on the oscillations in his political career, Babur contrasted the phases of defeat, exile, and powerlessness with those of victory, status, and power and described these cycles as an interchange

Box 2.5: Sadr-ud-din Hasan Nizami and Minhaj-us-Siraj Juzjani

Sadr-ud-din Hasan Nizami came to India from Khurasan in search of work just before the assassination of Sultan Muiz-ud-din Muhammad bin Sam at Damyak in 1206. At Nishapur, his home town, he had encountered political turmoil. On the advice of his *pir*, Muhammad Kufi, who lived in the shrine of Imam Raza (the eighth-century Shi'i Imam) at Mashhad, he came to India. Before this, however, he went to Ghazna. He moved to India when he heard about Qutb-ud-din Aibak's patronage to the learned and the scholarly. Ascending the throne at Lahore in 1206, Aibak had issued a *farman* commanding that the history of his reign and achievements be written, emulating the Persian tradition of historiography. Hasan Nizami was urged to write the *fatah* and glories of Muhammad bin Sam and Aibak in this tradition. Although he wrote in Persian, Hasan Nizami believed that histories could only be written in the Arab tradition. He wrote the first official history of the Delhi Sultanate, *Taj-u'l Ma'asir*, which began with the battle of Tarain of 1191 and stretched up to 1229, the year that Iltutmish applied to the *Khalifa* for investiture.

Minhaj-us-Siraj Juzjani belonged to Ghor. His father was a *Qazi* in the Ghorid army. His other relatives too were professionally linked to the Ghorid and Ghaznavid ruling families. It was perhaps these family connections and patronage that provided him with training in diplomacy and prepared him for his journey to India. When he came to India in 1227, he was inducted into the service of Iltutmish as *Ihtisab* (censor of public morals), a post that he continued to hold for ten years. He later became the *Qazi* and *Khatib* during Iltutmish's reign. He distinguished himself from the *'ulama* by accepting a woman as Sultan and standing in support of Raziya Sultan. It was these political experiences and understanding that led him to write the *Tabaqat-i-Nasiri*. This chronicle, which began the trend of dynastic history in the *tabaqat* (literally meaning 'layers') genre, is dedicated to Sultan Nasir-ud-din Mahmud. Juzjani's account ended in 1260, although he continued to live till the accession of Balban in 1265. His approach to history was global. He presented *Tabaqat-i-Nasiri* as a connected account of Muslim dynasties of Persia and Central Asia and their relation with the Abbasid *Khalifa*s. He provided such details of these regions as were necessary to appraise the ideas and institutions as they influenced and developed in India of that time.

between *fatrat*, a powerless interregnum, and *fursat* or leisure; he characterised the inordinate in his political destiny as *qazaqliq*, or like a political vagabond or in exile without a throne; and *istiqlal*, or the exercise of sovereignty. Profoundly different in style and content from Timurid historical works like the *Zafarnama* ('Book of Victory') of Sharaf-ud-din 'Sharaf' Yazdi and other Timurid court histories such as Khvandamir's *Habib al-Siyar*, Babur wrote in Chaghatai-Turkish (translated later into Persian on Akbar's order by 'Abdul Rahim Khan-i Khanan) rather than the ubiquitous court Persian. Yazdi and Khvandamir wrote in Persian and used allusive, metaphorical language that distinguished court-patronised historical literature.

Babur's autobiography discreetly delineates the glory of his ancestral links, with a subtle bend towards his Timurid descent without negating his Chingizid legacy. His rivalry with his Uzbek clansmen entailed that he aggressively assert his Timurid identity. For a while, his direct descendants had continued to call themselves 'Chaghatai princes (*salātīn-i-Chaghata*)' or the 'lineage of Timur (*khāndān-i Tīmuriyya*)', and disliked the epithet 'Mughal' or 'Mogor' which the Europeans had used for them from the sixteenth century. As is evident from certain didactic passages, it appears that Babur's memoir had a two-fold purpose: to validate his right to rule and create an advice-literature or *nasihat namah* for his sons and future Timurid kings, but most importantly, to develop a 'canonical narrative' of Mughal origins. Yet, many sections of the *Baburnama* display scarce connection with the dynastic history and genealogy of the Timurids. Some sections look similar to treatises on geography and natural history, while others seem to be premised on the memoirs of poets. On some occasions, it resembled the accounts of European travellers, like Alexander Burnes' *Travels into Bokhara*.

Babur also contributed to the metre of Persian poetry, *Hanafi* law, and other themes, which, along with his autobiography, are known to be important works of Chaghatai-Turkish literature. He even invented his own form of writing, the *khatt-i baburi*. Babur was atypically modern for his times, particularly for conveying so convincingly a sense of his own individuality. The narration of his life in the *Baburnama* is supplemented in some instances by *Tarikh-i Rashidi*, written in the court of 'Abdul Rashid Khan of Yarkhand (r. 1533–60) by Muhammad Haydar Dughlat (1545–46). The text, in addition, is also a remarkable account of Dughlat's own personal history and the political and cultural intricacies of Central Asia and Afghanistan.

Humayun did not write his own memoir but he, too, guarded his Timurid and Chingizid heritage and closely emulated the ways of his ancestors, evident from the several histories of his time, one of them being *Qanun-i Humayuni* by Khvandamir. He was commissioned by Humayun to write an account of his reign, heralding official history-writing and marking a shift away from the personal, autobiographical genre of Babur. Khvandamir's memoir is, as he told us, an eyewitness account of the rules and ordinances of Humayun's reign, accompanied by descriptions of court festivities and buildings erected by the *Padshah*. In an attempt to encapsulate the structure of the State, steeped in the 'Circle of Justice', he introduced Humayun as one of those rulers who, 'having extended the shadow of their protection did not permit the Sun of injustice to blaze upon the wanderers in the desert of disappointment' (Darling 2002, 8). He was comparable to just rulers like Solomon and Alexander the Great, 'a *Nushirvan*' (of his time) and one 'who shut the gate of tyranny' (ibid.).

Ali Anooshahr (2008), however, described Khvandamir's work as more of a catalogue of the emperor's regulations, 'curious toys and his wardrobe, than a continuous narrative'. In 1587, Mehtar Jauhar Aftabchi, Humayun's barely literate ewer bearer, relied on his memory to put together the memoir *Tazkirat-ul-Vaqi'at*, also known as *Tarikh-i Humayun* and *Humayun Shahi*. Composed in a 'shaky and rustic' Persian, the text is a contemporary and candid account of the life and times of the second Mughal emperor, revised subsequently by Ilahdad Faizi Sirhindi (who was in the process of writing the history of Akbar's reign), who presented it in a more sophisticated style to Akbar in 1590. Another addition to the corpus was *Tazkireh-i Humayun va Akbar* by Bayazid Bayat, a native of Tabriz, who later joined the Mughal army under Humayun. Completed in 1590–91, the text covers the history of the reigns of Humayun and Akbar from 1542–91. Bayat narrated that he could neither read nor write; as he spoke while working in the kitchen, Abu'l Fazl's scribe recorded his words.

The narratives of Bayat and Aftabchi, argued Anooshahr (ibid.), are a significant reflection on the gender roles appropriate to a warrior king, especially regarding the categories of violence, that is, exerting violence, resisting, enduring and restraining violence, and the politics of sexuality, which included self-control, marriage, and conquest. To illustrate these, both chroniclers constantly compared Humayun with his rivals, like his brother Mirza Kamran and the Afghan chief Sher Shah, and demonstrated that the emperor failed to fulfil these roles sufficiently. Babur had used the term '*mardana*' ('manly') to describe the brave soldiers and military commanders, for masculinity or manliness implied not only inflicting violence on one's enemy, but also demonstrating the courage and ability to withstand pain and hardships. Bayat thus praised several *amirs* (nobles) of Humayun's period for showing 'utmost manliness and leadership' by continuing to fight despite sustaining acute injuries from swords and maces. The Afghan historian Abdullah, in his *Tarikh-i Daudi*, also commented on the warrior king qualities of Sher Shah, who endured violence and hardships, thus setting an example of perseverance and persistence for his men during his march in full armour to Bengal.

The two biographies—by Aftabchi and Bayat—were a response to Akbar's orders in 1587 to the 'servants of the state' and 'old members of the Mughal family' to pen down their personal memories of Babur and Humayun so as to affirm the legitimacy of the dynasty and construct the official imperial past. It was in the same context that Gulbadan Banu Begum (Babur's daughter) wrote the biography of Humayun, *Ahval-i Humayun Padishah*. Although she was barely eight years old when Babur died, she gave a vivid, dramatic account of extraordinary, momentous events from the reign of Babur to that of Akbar. In contrast to Babur's memoir that narrated the emperor's life, her account of his death and the life of Humayun expressed the tension between the bonds of family and kingship and described the transfer of power to Humayun as an act of human and divine will, blessed by the elders of the household (of whom she was one) as witnesses. The original *Ahval-i Humayun*, it is conjectured, contained an account up to the twenty-second regnal year of Akbar's reign. This view is guided by a note in the manuscript in Shahjahan's handwriting, although scholars have been unable to provide adequate reasons for the disappearance of the last portion of Gulbadan's text. Contrary to official writings, she talked of the processes and mechanisms in the making of monarchy and the formalisation of the empire: the empire she wrote about was not institutionalised like the one presented in the *Akbarnama*.

Gulbadan's writing was significantly different from that of Aftabchi or Bayat or any other courtier of the time. She chose a different genre—*ahval*, meaning conditions, state, circumstances, or situations. There are a few questions, though, that remain unanswered in Gulbadan's writing—for instance, which language she chose to write in, whether she wrote the memoir herself or dictated it to a scribe, or whether she favoured Turki or Persian. Turkish was the native language of Gulbadan and her husband Khizr Khwaja Khan, a Chaghatai Mughal, an *amir-ul-umara* under Humayun. Regardless of these complexities, the fact that she was chosen to write the memoir bestows recognition upon her as a 'learned' person. Moreover, the Persian verse attributed to her and mentioned in the work of Mir Mahdi Shirazi is evidence of her knowledge of the language. Maulana Shibli in his *Maqalat-i Shibli* described Gulbadan's text as 'unaffected and spontaneous', considerably superior to *Tuzuk-i Jahangiri* and *Ruqqat-i Alamgiri* in its unique spontaneity, cogent and terse expression, and colloquial diction.

It appears that Abbas Khan Sarwani's *Tuhfa-i Akbarshahi* was also written on Akbar's orders, but with the intent of memorialising the Sur rulers (1540–56). Athar Ali (2006c), however, pointed to the uncertainty of whether it had been written as a collective for Abu'l Fazl, or earlier. Sarwani's *Tarikh-i Sher Shahi* also reads like a 'creative' and a foundation text for understanding the development of the notion of *zabt* under Akbar. While it depicted Sher Shah's management of *jagir* and a pattern of land revenue assessment and collection, it could have been, observed Peter Hardy (1993, 70), more than a record, perhaps a pedagogic exercise to train Akbar to combine justice with financial efficiency; or perhaps, as Alam and Subrahmanyam (1998) suggested, the purpose may have been to project his family's former patron 'as a sort of proto-Akbar'.

Mughal historiography continued to flourish, with many more biographies and autobiographies. Akbar commissioned a number of histories, their illustrations, and translations to record his reign, the splendour and legacy of his ancestors, and the grandeur of the empire. His pursuit of these productions with great alacrity in his *atelier*, his supervision of the collection of works to commemorate the first two Mughal emperors and to correct the perceived flaws from his memory are evidence of not only the extent to which he could influence some of the narratives prepared by his historians, but also his fondness for literary works. Milo Beach (2012) suggested that the emperor had 24,000 books in his library at the time of his death in 1605, and learnt significant portions of the poetry of Hafiz and Rumi despite being an *ummi* (illiterate, as *Sura* 7:15 of the Quran defines it). No detail escaped him, commented Jesuit Jeronimo (Jerome) Xavier, and though 'he did not know how to read or write he knew everything', a portrayal completely at variance with the European imagination of an Oriental despot.

Akbar believed, as his biographer Abu'l Fazl confirmed, that his unlettered status was marked with divinity, for all prophets were illiterate and it was incumbent upon all parents to allow one of their sons to follow them. Akbar possessed, Fazl said, *'ilm laduni*, that is, knowledge directly from God. Moreover, many Sufi saints were deemed to be *ummi* by their disciples, despite being the authors of several works in Arabic, Persian, and other languages. It is perhaps in this sense that the word *ummi* ought to be interpreted. That the emperor held literary abilities and literary works in high esteem, notwithstanding his genealogical and imperial concerns, is manifested by his composition of a few Persian verses and a note in clear Arabic letters, his remarkable memory for poetry and dates, his fondness for having books read to him, frequently those written in Persian, and above all, his fostering of literary wisdom in the court.

Tarikh-i Khandan-i Timuriyya, an unfinished and anonymous chronicle, was initiated in the 1580s to emphasise the Timurid aspects of Akbar's legacy. This work later caught the attention of Shahjahan, who was eager to reassert his heritage at the time of territorial expansion in Central Asia. Another chronicle valuable for understanding the evolution of Akbar's ideology is *Tarikh-i Alfi*, commissioned by him in 1581–82, to be written severally by authors under State patronage. It was eventually written by Mulla Ahmad Thattawi (murdered in 1585) and Asaf Khan Ja'far Beg Qazvini to commemorate the approaching end of the first millennium of the Islamic calendar (in 1591–92). Unlike *Tarikh-i Khandan-i Timuriyya*, the chronicle began not with Timur but with the *rihlat*, that is, the death of Prophet Muhammad, until the reign of Akbar, although it was abandoned subsequently and *Akbarnama* pursued as the official chronicle. *Tarikh-i Alfi* is a dialogical text with a new view of territoriality that pioneered the concept of Hindustan as a political and cultural unit under the Mughals, thus setting the pace for the later historicisation of Hindustan (in the works of Nizam-ud-din Ahmad Bakshi, Badauni, and Firishta) as an independent political and cultural unit different from the rest of the Islamic world.

It is in this context that Athar Ali (2006c) observed that the historical unity of India first appeared not in British colonial historiography, but in late sixteenth-century Indo-Islamic chronicles. As the Mughals occupied northern Indian Sultanates in the sixteenth century, they devised a new notion of Hindustan to emphasise the changed political context. Ja'far Beg Qazvini described Akbar's empire after a temporary fragmentation of territorial unity under Humayun as *savad-i a'zam Hindustan* (*savad*, in medieval Arabic terminology, is defined as a large region and a community of people) and *iqlim-i Hindustan* (the clime/region of Hindustan). He characterised Akbar as a superb, immortal monarch who, while similar in some ways to his contemporaries—Shah Tahmasp of Iran and Sultan Suleyman of the Ottoman Empire—went much beyond them, outshone his predecessors, and could be compared to none except the Sultan of Kashmir, Zayn al-'Abidin (r. 1420–72 CE), who embodied the same virtues as Akbar (he abolished *jizya*, protected Hindu customs and traditions, commissioned the translation of Sanskrit books into Persian, and above all, 'possessed magical, miraculous powers of prophecy'). These descriptions appear puzzling as, on the other hand, the chronicle depicted Akbar within the framework of Islam as a seeker of truth, upholder of tradition, and *Badshah-i Islam*, who transcended partisan and sectarian bickering, sought to resolve conflicts between Shi'is and Sunnis, and ensured that '*kafirs* are shouldering the burdens of Islam' (Rizvi 1975). It is probable that Akbar may have preferred to be portrayed this way in India and to his competitors—the rulers of the Safavid, Ottoman, and Uzbek states, particularly the latter—but by the 1590s, when the threat of the Uzbeks receded, Akbar may have felt more secure internationally and may have decided to abandon *Tarikh-i Alfi* in favour of Abu'l Fazl's formulations regarding syncretism and radicalism.

The chronicles continued to be State-oriented and eulogised their patron, that is, the monarch, but they also held *asnad*, eyewitness accounts, official news reports, and memoirs valuable for reconstructing history. If they came across an event with multiple versions, they invoked the principle of rationality, as Nizam-ud-din Ahmad Bakshi supposedly did to understand the death of Sultan Ghiyas-ud-din Tughluq. Nizam-ud-din had served Akbar as *bakshi* for the Mughal *suba* of Gujarat in 1585, and then for the entire empire in 1593. In his Preface to *Tabaqat-i Akbari* (1594), written at his own initiative, Nizam-ud-din claimed that his chronicle was the first history of India based on at least twenty-nine works to produce authentic information. In his account of the death of Sultan Ghiyas-ud-din Tughluq, he quoted both Barani's *Tarikh-i Firozshahi* and Isami's *Futuh-us Salatin*. He was sceptical of both, and pointed towards the irrationality of the explanation of Ghiyas-ud-din Tughluq's death as accidental. He questioned the veracity of *Futuh-us Salatin*, alleging that it was compiled twenty-six years after the demise of Ghiyas-ud-din Tughluq, ignoring the fact that the works of both Barani and Isami were near contemporary. In fact, *Futuh* (1351) was completed six years before *Tarikh-i Firozshahi* (1357).

Although Nizam-ud-din disappointed by his inaccurate chronology, his major strength lay in his ethical use of *asnad*. Unlike Khafi Khan and others, he acknowledged the sources that he consulted to assemble the facts on the period prior to the sixteenth century. Like Abu'l Fazl, he talked about the sacrosanct, divine aura that surrounded Akbar and impacted his empire. With regard to the emperor's religious views, he was cautious, perhaps because of his official position. He did not criticise them, but remained silent on the religious controversies of the time. He was perhaps deeply concerned and hoped that the tide would be stemmed. It was probably anxieties such as these that explain his relationship with Badauni, who is said to have referred to *Tabaqat-i Akbari* to derive the data for his *Muntakhab-ut Tawarikh*. In contrast to his contemporaries, Nizam-ud-din conceived of Hindustan as a geographical, political entity and as a state rather than a regnal unit, first under the Sultans of Delhi and then under the Mughals. This description is a clue to the fact that Nizam-ud-din was among the original authors of *Tarikh-i Alfi*, for it is in this text that the idea of Hindustan as a pan South Asian political state, alongside Rum and Iran, was developed and the concept of a new imperial India conceived.

Ahval-i Asad Beg (formally known as *Nushka-i Ahval-i Asad Beg*) was written as a memoir by Asad Beg Qazwini, who held the title of Peshrau Khan. He was in the service of Abu'l Fazl for seventeen years and after Fazl's assassination, he was hired by Akbar and then Jahangir. The text, written during Jahangir's reign, provides information on the transition period (from Akbar to Jahangir), that is, 1601 to roughly 1606. It is valuable for its diplomatic description of Abu'l Fazl's murder by Bir Singh Deo Bundela in connivance with Prince Salim near Sironj in the forty-seventh regnal year of Akbar, and the chastisement of the Bundela chief by the Mughal army. It also provides information on Asad Beg's deputation to the court of the Sultan of Bijapur, Ibrahim Adil Shah II, and Asad Beg's success as an envoy (*hajib*), returning with *peshkash* (including the daughter of the Sultan of Bijapur as a bride for Prince Daniyal). Narrating the etiquette and life in the court of Bijapur, Asad Beg described the elite culture of the Mughals and the Deccan region, and the Mughal responses to the practice of smoking tobacco. From the text, it appears that Asad Beg's main concern was to stress upon the special favour or treatment (*tarbiyat*) at the hands of Akbar. While he mentioned the increase in his *mansab* rank and the *tankhwah*, he was more emphatic about his intimate relationship with Akbar and the *shast-i muridi* that he had received from him in 1603 as a member of *tauhid-i ilahi* before being sent to Bijapur. However, even as a member of *tauhid-i ilahi*, he made no comment on Akbar's religious views. His account is significant for its details on Bijapur and the nature of political alliances during the shift of power from Akbar to Jahangir.

Haji Muhammad 'Arif Qandahari's *Tarikh-i Akbari*, also known as *Tarikh-i Arif Qandahari*, can be considered a transitional text written in a rhetorical style in admiration of Akbar before Abu'l Fazl wrote a profuse eulogy of the emperor. The text is valuable for its narrative on Akbar's conquest of Gujarat and the construction of Fatehpuri Sikri as the capital city (*dar al-khilafat*) in 1563–64, the diversity of Akbar's empire, the incorporation of the Indian Muslims and non-Muslims in imperial service, and occasional mention of some Rajput nobles. He otherwise refrained from providing actual instances of imperial patronage or induction of the Rajputs into the nobility since 1560, or the emperor's marriage with Rajput princesses, or the participation of non-Muslims in religious discussions in the *ibadatkhana*. Although he completed his work in 1580, he made no reference to Akbar's *sulh-i kul* or *tauhid-i ilahi*. In fact, he spoke of Akbar's orthodox religious leanings and praised his religious conversations with the *'ulama*.

In this intense period of chronicling and history-writing, in 1589, Akbar commissioned Abu'l Fazl, his close associate and confidante, to write the official history of his reign. Abu'l Fazl informs that it took him seven years to complete the work, during which time he prepared several tentative drafts but found them consistently unworthy in style and disposition and therefore incessantly modified them. Being a perfectionist, he apparently drafted the *Akbarnama* five times. Not impressed by his creativity, he was on the verge of a sixth revision when he was compelled to close it upon the insistence of the emperor and formally present it to him on 21 March 1595.

It is evident from Nizam-ud-din Ahmad Bakshi's *Tabaqat-i Akbari* (completed in 1593) that earlier versions of the *Akbarnama*, including *Ain-i Akbari*, were made available to the contemporary scholars and chroniclers of the imperial court as early as 1592, the year in which he himself referred to the *Akbarnama* in his historical composition. For narrative and partly for style, the model text for *Akbarnama*, like for any other Timurid chronicle, was Sharaf-ud-din Ali Yazdi's *Zafarnama*, a history of Timur written in 1424–25 that used official records as *asnad*. *Akbarnama*, however, went beyond it, basing itself on a large repository of archival material. The specially commissioned memoirs of courtiers, servants, and family members at Akbar's court, cited above, were made available to Fazl in addition to his privileged access to the contents of the imperial records office—reports, *yad-dasht* (memoranda), *farmans*, and other such documents. Fazl visualised the *Akbarnama* and the *Ain-i Akbari* as a single *magnum opus*: the separation of the first two *daftars* (volumes), *Akbarnama* from the third *daftar*, *Ain-i Akbari*, referred to as *daftar-i akhir* or *jild-i akhir* or the last volume by its author (See Plate 2), is now treated as a separate book, which in effect is the contribution of the later editors and translators of the text. The chronicle has dominated Mughal historiography for successive generations, projecting 'imperial images as imperial realities', and is considered by many as a 'foundational' source not only for its

Image 2.1: Abu'l Fazl presenting the *Akbarnama* to Emperor Akbar

Source: https://commons.wikimedia.org/wiki/File: Abul Fazl Presenting *Akbarnama*.jpg.

alleged accuracy and objectivity, but also for being an official compilation that provided details on issues related to administrative, agrarian, and institutional aspects. Some have regarded the work as representing rationalism, tolerance, complete absence of religious fanaticism, and secular vision, while others like Peter Hardy (1985) viewed the *Akbarnama* as 'a personal puff for a pal'. For some, Abu'l Fazl was both a name and a legend in Mughal historiographical literature for promoting concepts and perspectives of history and skillfully combining the Arab and Persian traditions of history-writing.

To assess Abu'l Fazl as an official historian, a scholar, and an important source for Akbar's reign, it is necessary to study his ideas and philosophy and the extent to which these influenced his approach to history. Abu'l Fazl was brought up in an intellectual, liberal environment, being the son of Shaikh Mubarak (1505–93), a Sufi scholar of the time. Trained in orthodox theology at Nagaur and Ahmadabad, Mubarak subsequently turned to Sufism and *ishraq*, the philosophy of illuminated wisdom of Shihab ud-Din Suhrawardi Maqtul (1155–91) and *wahdat-ul wujud* (unity of being) of Ibn al-'Arabi (1165–1240). For these reasons and also for his admiration of the *wilayat* (the greatness and mystic status) of Saiyid Muhammad of Jaunpur (1443–1505), the founder of the *mahdavi* movement in India, who was denounced by the orthodoxy, Mubarak's family faced religious persecution at the hands of the *'ulama*. The two thought patterns and the attitude of the *'ulama* had a tremendous impact on the religious and political outlook of Abu'l Fazl. In 1574, Akbar extended royal patronage to both Shaikh Mubarak and Abu'l Fazl. It is said that on being invited for the courtier's position, Abu'l Fazl went through an inner conflict—he 'looked upon external circumstances as destructive of inwardness and limitation as opposed to absoluteness' (*Akbarnama* III, 118; *cf* Nizami 1995, 21). His intellectual and spiritual leanings and his desire to reach the ultimate truth convinced him of the futility of a courtier's life. Allegedly, it was on Shaikh Mubarak's persuasion that Abu'l Fazl joined the imperial service, and thenceforth contributed to the most formative years in Akbar's reign.

Abu'l Fazl's learning and rationality impressed Akbar, especially during the religious discussions and debates in the *Ibadatkhana* that strengthened the critical and analytical ambience of the imperial court, subjecting the *'ulama* to challenges on issues of reason and tolerance. A follower of *ishraq* tradition and *wahdat-ul wujud*, Fazl denounced *taqlid* or blind fanaticism, rejected the formalities of religion (prayer and invocation), emphasised the spiritual content in religion, *sulh-i kul* (universal concord) and *'aql* (rationality), and appealed to the tradition of the philosophers (*filasafa*) and the scientists (*hukama*). He claimed to have written for the 'elect' few who understood his language of reason rather than for the majority of the 'illiterate' (the reference may have been to the *'ulama*). Asserting a definite philosophy of history in his writings based on *asnad*, an analytical and rational recording of individual experiences and achievements, he rejected the orthodox view that history enlightened only the 'believers'. Abu'l Fazl displayed an intellectual temperament and an interest in philosophical speculation, indicating that the philosopher and the Sufi in Fazl outdid the historian and that ethical and moralising elements dominated historical analysis.

However, despite this philosophical or scientific temper (*mushrib*), his espousal of rationalism seemed strange and not in consonance with his critique of the irrational behaviour of the *'ulama* when he described the 'holy manifestations' preceding the birth of Akbar. Abu'l Fazl wrote that a light emanated from Hamida Banu's face before Akbar was born; divine light or *farr-i izadi* surrounded and permeated him, and even when the child Akbar was at play, his movements were like divine gestures through which he secretly influenced the course of events in the world. Fazl virtually immortalised the emperor, drawing upon Sufi and *ishraqi* theories of divine illumination of kingship, and thus presented him as an ideal, inclusive, benevolent ruler, an extant personification of, as Rosalind O'Hanlon (2007a) observed, 'masculine virtues and exemplar for his servants'. Such contradictions point towards Fazl's theoretical imperfection, which perhaps he could never come to grips with and therefore made no attempt to resolve it. Instead, he accepted that recording the achievements of an ideal ruler like Akbar was worship for him and that veneration for the emperor amounted to adoration, which may be considered his weakness. He stipulated that his fault was one of rhetorical adulation rather than sycophancy.

Abu'l Fazl formulated a powerful dynastic ideology in the *Akbarnama*, glorifying Akbar as the 'king of manifestation and reality' (Lal 2001, 942), 'the living embodiment of the empire', and the 'focus for the direct personal devotion of the imperial nobility' (O'Hanlon 2007a, 889). *Akbarnama* traces Mughal history from Babur to 1602 (Akbar's reign), in which the persistent focus was on Akbar as the centre of all things, the leader of *din-u-dunya* (religion and realm) with magical powers (*karamat*), who did not need to seek any legitimacy. Such extraordinary representations of Akbar—both spiritual and political—make the *Akbarnama* read like a panegyric account, an encomium of his reign and as if virtually co-authored by the emperor. Not only did Akbar keenly pursue and evaluate his biography to see how he was being presented, but the eulogistic details of Fazl also matched the emperor's ambitions. It seems that Fazl wove Akbar's 'unspoken wishes' into the matrix of a philosophic system. It appears, thus, that even if Akbar partially contributed to the creation of his official image, as if he was being seen the way he wanted to be seen, the *Akbarnama* should be read, as Kumkum Sangari (2000, 83) argued, as 'an intersection between hagiography, biography and autobiography, providing a continuum between Akbar, the court, some contemporary perception and hagiographic inscription'. *Ain-i Akbari*, the statistical account of the *suba*s (provinces) of the empire that provides territorial, fiscal, and ethnographic data, even though idealised, stands in stark contrast to the hagiographic style of the *Akbarnama*. It indicates Fazl's skill in interpreting and arranging data of different categories—prices, salaries, revenue rates—and giving comprehensive information on the organisation of the empire and administration, ranging from institutionalised establishments like the imperial household, army, mint, amusements, etiquette, astronomy, medicinal and philosophical ideas; and details on animals, particularly the *cheetah* (leopard)—its hunting, training, co-habitation, and diet.

Recognising the importance of such information and regulations for the empire and signifying the value of official archives and the establishment of a quasi-bureaucratic State, *Akbarnama* and *Ain-i Akbari* were a means to convey the authority of Akbar to imperial officials and the court. Fazl's strategy was to establish that both the imperial regulations of the *Ain* and history, as exemplified in the *Akbarnama*, were 'philosophy teaching by example'; as the *Ain* stated, it was 'a lesson book for the instruction of mankind' and a 'moral treatise for the teaching of subjects in the right conduct of life' (O'Hanlon 2007a, 897). These references have been seen as incidental to serious contemporary political history, but in fact they had an important pragmatic purpose and were significant in the formation of imperial service and in projecting the emperor as divinely ordained, *insan-i kamil* (perfect man), and a *mujtahid* (spiritual guide or one who can or has the right to interpret the law) who possessed *buland iqbal* (good fortune).

Akbarnama and *Ain-i Akbari* unfold a complex theory of sovereignty and relate the importance of a strong and righteous ruler who could protect the four worldly 'essences'—access to wealth, life, honour, and religion. Fazl further explicated that only a rare ruler could fulfil these obligations because most rulers were not under the shadow of *farr-i izadi* or divine light communicated directly by God to kings. Without this benediction, no monarch could be a perfect king. But Akbar, he insisted, was an exception. Attributing to Akbar the concept of *farr*, or divine glory, derived from the ancient Iranian concept of *khwarena*, the 'divinely sanctioned kingship', Abu'l Fazl stated that royalty was a light emanating from God—it was a ray from the sun that illuminated the universe. This theory of illumination, derived from the Persian neo-platonic philosophy of Shihab-ud-din Suhrawardi Maqtul, suggested that all life was given existence by the continuous illumination, almost blinding, from the East of the Light of Lights or God. All men possessed a divine spark, but only the highest three grades of men were the true theosophists or masters of the age: men such as Suhrawardi himself, Plato and, in Abu'l Fazl's interpretation, Akbar. A chain of dazzling angels revealed God's illumination to man; above these angels was Angel Gabriel, identified with the true spirit of Prophet Muhammad.

Invoking this theory, Fazl averred that a combination of divine illumination and virtuosity enabled Akbar to achieve *sulh-i kul*. He did not refer to his monarch in conventional terms, that is, *Zill-i ilahi* or 'God's shadow', but called him *paziranda-i farr-i izidi*, a recipient of divine light, possessor of illumined wisdom, and the reflector of the light received. But all worldly sovereigns, stipulated Fazl, did not receive such light. It was only the just and enlightened ruler who could receive God's light and possess the title of *Padshah*, for it was only the enlightened one who could distinguish between the 'godly ruler' (*farmanfarma-i haqiqi*) and the self-seeking authority (*peshi-ju-i khwud-kam*). While 'godly rule' was marked by peace, harmony, justice, and longevity, the reign of the selfish monarch was characterised by cruelty, theft, terror, and was short-lived. For Fazl, Akbar fulfilled the parameters of a just, enlightened, 'godly' rule. He possessed a large and courageous heart, paternal love and tolerance towards his subjects (*pidari*); he bestowed on them the title of *farzand* (son) if the need was to show favour; he believed in God, but rejected *taqlid* and religious differences, fulfilling Fazl's fundamental social outlook that all men formed one brotherhood and that there was a basic cultural identity between Hindus and Muslims.

Taking his cues from Nasir-ud-din Tusi's *Akhlaq-i Nasiri*, a work of ethics composed in Persian in 1235, the emperor, Fazl observed, maintained harmony among the four classes of mankind: *ahl-i qalam* ('men of pen', or the learned); *ahl-i saif* ('men of sword', or warriors), men of negotiation (merchants, traders, tax-collectors), and men of husbandry (farmers, agricultural labourers). His monarch thus had the wisdom to understand the spirit of the age, and that made him a perfect monarch. Presupposing the evil nature of man—corruption, selfishness, greed, and lust—Abu'l Fazl located the basis of sovereignty in the needs of the social order and talked of the necessity of a monarch, envisioned as benevolent, sacred, sublime, but despotic all the same (like Thomas Hobbes's *Leviathan*), assisted by four sets of 'state servants'—nobles; assistants of victory, revenue-collectors, in charge of income and expenditure; companions of the king or wise learned men in the court; and *khansama* or household servants—with complete, absolute, autocratic control over them. His vision and justification of monarchy were somewhat similar to that mentioned in the *Mahabharata*. In this text, Bhishma, the warrior-sage, traced the origins of kingship and talked of Prithu, the seventh in the generation of rulers, endowed with divine, supreme invincible powers, who successfully restored calm and stability and put an end to the confused, anarchic order of the time. Abu'l Fazl's monarch, Akbar, also possessed such awesome qualities and by his omnipresence, brought concord and compassion in the empire and constructed a Hindustan that could stand out in the world.

Analysing Abu'l Fazl's writings and trying to ascertain why he wrote the way he did for Akbar, S. A. A. Rizvi argued that this was a period when hopes and fears were aroused in the popular Muslim mind by the approaching Islamic millennium, and Fazl probably felt that disputes amongst the religious leaders could be effectively handled if unsurpassable, prophetic, supernatural powers were claimed for the emperor—a status above the ordinary rulers. Nevertheless, it was his obsession with Akbar that attracted several critics, many of whom accused Fazl of sycophancy, of concealing the truth about the emperor, of being the *mujtahid* of Akbar's 'new religion' *tauhid-i ilahi*, promoting apostasy and heresy in the empire.

Abu'l Fazl's major critic was his contemporary Mulla Abdul Qadir Badauni, who possessed diverse qualifications as a theologian, scholar, and historian. Like Fazl and Faizi (Akbar's poet-laureate and Fazl's brother), he too was a student of Shaikh Mubarak, trained in a liberal, Sufi, intellectual environment, and shared royal patronage with them when Akbar invited him to the court around 1574, a time that coincided with the emperor's search for *aql* (reason) and denunciation of *taqlid*. Badauni immediately found favour with Akbar for his literary and scholarly abilities, and more significantly for subordinating and challenging the *'ulama* during the early phase of discussions in the *ibadatkhana*, although Badauni himself belonged to the section of the orthodoxy.

If the beginnings were cordial, what made the relationship suspect? Perhaps Badauni's peculiar attitude towards Abu'l Fazl and the *'ulama*—his scorn for the *'ulama* when with Fazl, and criticism of the latter when in the company of the *'ulama*—undermined his usefulness to Akbar. Also, by 1578–79, the situation had changed radically in Akbar's empire. Badauni could no longer accept the 'revolution in laws and in manners' and was convinced that the *'ulama*—the only section that he considered righteous—were being persecuted and the *shari'at* diluted. While several others in the court did not raise their voices against the maligning of the 'true religion', either for fear, greed, ambition, reward, recognition or ignorance, he presented his own version, in justification of Islam, in his *Muntakhab ut-Tawarikh* ('Choice of Histories') against what he believed was the travesty of truth in the *Akbarnama*. The latter part of the *Muntakhab*, on which scholarly opinions are largely based, is particularly critical of and negative about Akbar's reign, which has led a few scholars to censure Badauni as 'the thwarted and choleric orthodox opponent' of Fazl, a 'fundamentalist *mullah*', 'narrow-minded Sunni', 'crabbed and bigoted' (Anooshahr 2006, 276), who rigidly upheld religious orthodoxy and produced a 'notoriously vituperative history' (O'Hanlon 2007a, 910).

The other view, to the contrary, holds that however diametrically opposed or subversive the text might be, the *Muntakhab* is a valuable counterpoint and counterbalance to the hyperbole of Fazl's *Akbarnama*, and elucidated social details that had found no place in Fazl's exalted history. Many aspects of Akbar's religious experimentation, and the subsequent unrest and social tension during his reign, might have remained hidden 'under the blandishments of the master stylist, Abul Fazl' had it not been for the *Muntakhab*, despite its many rough edges. Nevertheless, *Muntakhab* cannot be the only criterion; Badauni's other academic and intellectual achievement, *Najat al-Rashid*, a voluminous text that he himself described as *ujalah* (hastily produced), *risalah* (treatise), and *jaridah* (volume, register), further explicated and supplemented his postulates. The book has been variously described by some, like Blochmann, as a theological, mystical and polemical work, and a commentary on Sufism, ethics, and the *mahdavi* movement. The contents, however, reveal that it is basically a Hanafi treatise (theological treatise) that delves neither into Sufism nor ethics (Badauni had intended to write a separate book on ethics, *ilm-i akhlaq*, but could never do it), but talks instead about the sins, crimes, offences, and misdemeanours—both mortal (*kabirah* [plural *kabair*]) and venal (*saghirah* [plural *saghair*])—that Islam had forbidden. The text is introduced with an emphasis on *taubah* (repentance), the pathway to piety and correct religious life, without which divine forgiveness could not be obtained, while the *khatimah* (conclusion) elaborates on the right ways of expressing repentance, the necessity of avoiding the inherent 'wickedness' of the world, and achieving spirituality.

Reading the two texts, written almost contemporaneously, permits cross-referencing and brings out several aspects of Badauni as a historian and thinker. Evaluating Badauni in the context of the rise of absolutism and in a religious-social milieu that saw the millenarian *mahdavi* movement in sixteenth-century Eurasia, Ali Anooshahr (2006) commented on his contributions to intellectual and cultural history during the Mughal period. Badauni apparently stood staunchly against royal autocracy and the divine right to rule. Refusing to subscribe to the imperial ideology constructed by Abu'l Fazl, he launched a scathing attack on the latter's claim to divinity or near-divinity for Akbar, not sparing even the eminent *'ulama* of the past if they practised religious pretensions. He often echoed Akbar's liberal leanings in his conciliatory gestures towards the Hindus, even as he propagated Sunni Islam. In upholding these ideas, Badauni demonstrated his sympathies for the egalitarian, socially dynamic, millenarian *mahdavi* movement prevalent in the fifteenth–sixteenth centuries, notwithstanding his profound engagement with the tradition of Islamic political thought. The influence of these diverse thoughts make his writings complex and complicated. *Muntakhab ut-Tawarikh* exemplifies this style and Badauni's maverick overtones.

Emulating Nizam-ud-din Ahmad Bakshi, Badauni chose Abd al-Hayy Gardizi's *Zayn al-Akhbar* ('Adornment of Historical Reports') as a source rather than Abu Nasr al-'Utbi's *Yamini*. The latter account, written in Arabic around 1020, was the earliest surviving example of dynastic history in Islamic historiography and glorified Sultan Mahmud's campaigns in the Indian subcontinent, while Gardizi's narrative was more of a personal reminiscence that reflected an inclusive and conciliatory attitude towards the local people. This indicates that like Nizam-ud-din Ahmad Bakshi, Badauni too presumed that an Islamic rule and monarchy would be inclusive and incorporate the local people. Again like Nizam-ud-din Ahmad, he began his description in Volume I of the *Muntakhab* with Subuktgin and his son Sultan Mahmud, whom he credited with establishing, strengthening, and stabilising Muslim kingship in Hindustan. Badauni, like other contemporary historians (except Abu'l Fazl), assumed that the 'Muslim' conquest of India was the dividing line of historical periodisation and scarcely referred to any event or phenomenon prior to it, thus reiterating the *jahiliya*-Islam dichotomy. The first volume is a formal political history written chronologically up to the reign of Humayun. While he described the accessions, wars, rebellions, and expeditions during the rule of these monarchs, he neither expressed nostalgia nor did he glorify them or set them as examples of 'orthodoxy' versus Akbar.

The second volume is quite distinct from the first in form, substance, and treatment. It covered the first forty years of Akbar's reign in order of chronology. However paradoxical it may seem, a close reading of the volumes indicates that Badauni had many ideas and attitudes in common with Akbar and, like Nizam-ud-din Ahmad Bakshi, identified himself with India and its past, its rulers and its people. The third volume of the *Muntakhab* is in the form of memorative communications or *tazkirat*, or short biographical sketches of *mashaikh* and the *'ulama* and also the *hakims* (physicians) and poets during Akbar's period. Exuding freshness in contrast to a similar section in the *Ain-i Akbari*, the part on saintly biographies illustrated spiritual efforts outside the imperial court. Badauni held those *shaikh*s in high esteem who were trained in the traditional religious sciences of Sunni Islam yet also pursued mysticism, for example, Shaikh Nizam-ud-din Ambethi, Shaikh Daud of Chati, Shaikh Abd al-Haqq Muhaddith Dihlawi, among many others. Describing the saints as 'holy men', he talked of their magnanimity, sophisticated ancestry, their consistent pursuit of learning, and calm composure. Badauni excluded the nobles of Akbar's court from the *tazkirat*, probably because Nizam-ud-din Ahmad Bakshi had written about them in his *Tabaqat-i Akbari*, or perhaps, more significantly, because he did not want to write about these 'fallen', 'corrupted' men.

Prompted by Nizam-ud-din Ahmad Bakshi's *Tabaqat-i Akbari* and yet subverting it through subtle, profuse editing, Badauni wrote the *Muntakhab* clandestinely, probably in 1595–96, as a counterpoise to Abu'l Fazl's panegyrist, imperial account, *Akbarnama*. Not beholden to the imperial ideology that upheld the 'celestial exaltation of the king' or the 'heresies' and *bida* ('innovations') as advocated by Abu'l Fazl and Akbar, he was sceptical of the *mahzarnama* or the decree of 1579 that had given the emperor exclusive power of *ijtihad* or religious reasoning and decision-making and pronounced him the *kar-giya* or a 'just ruler', *mujtahid* or the spiritual guide and interpreter of law. In this context, both Nizam-ud-din and Badauni, especially the latter, sensed a *coup* by Shaikh Mubarak and Abu'l Fazl, who forced the leading *'ulama* to sign the document. Despite his bitterness and hostility towards Akbar, he did not abandon the imperial service, nor did Akbar dismiss him; instead, in recognition of Badauni's versatility and accomplishments, the emperor engaged him in the intellectual activities of the *maktab khana* (Bureau of Translation) and in the translation of Indian classics, including the *Ramayana*, *Mahabharata*, and *Singhasanbatisi*, into Persian. His contribution to the compilation of *Tarikh-i Alfi* was also invaluable.

However, his decision to impose secrecy over his work provoked his passions even further, putting him under intense emotional stress. Perhaps he had no alternative but to vent his apprehensions and feelings surreptitiously, for he needed the salary given to him as *Imam* of Wednesday prayers at the court and for his activities in the *maktab khana*. He did not expect official patronage or reward for his book, nor did he intend to dedicate it to any ruler or noble. He may have hoped for historical redress and expiation for his 'sins' in the court of Akbar and salvation as a reward, as opposed to the reward of royal patronage sought by his peers. Written in a plain, simple style, interesting yet disconcerting with a splash of ridicule and satire, the *Muntakhab* was not publicised till the reign of Jahangir. The latter, upon discovery of the text, punished Badauni's children and ordered all copies of the book to be searched out and burnt; it survived, nevertheless, to act as a corrective and supplement to Abu'l Fazl's *Akbarnama* and *Ain-i Akbari*.

Inheriting a deep sense of history-writing and archives, Jahangir pursued the literary precedent laid by his predecessors, albeit with a difference. He chose to move away from the tradition of chronicle-writing and emulated his great-grandfather, Babur, to write his memoirs, *Tuzuk-i Jahangiri* or *Jahangirnama*, in Persian, interspersed with Turkish, Hindustani, and Kashmiri words, indicating the evolution from Chaghatai-Turkish to Persian and demonstrating his diverse linguistic abilities. Written in a simple, informal, fluent style, the memoir is evidence of Jahangir's intellectual complexity, his knowledge of classical Persian authors like Firdausi, Nizami Ganjavi, Sa'di, and Hafiz, and his understanding of Hindustani poetry and its imagery. Somewhat similar in orientation to *Baburnama*, the *Jahangirnama* too followed a chronological, annalistic style concentrating on the attributes of kingship (although unlike Babur, Jahangir focused on the royal dispensation of justice and a divine mandate to rule rather than military triumphs and loyal nobility). The memoir carves an interrelated self-representation of Jahangir as a monarch, naturalist, an aesthete, and a collector. An objective, coherent, and perhaps the only official account of the period, *Tuzuk* reflects on the emperor's views on politics and religious and social issues; reveals his scientific mind and urge to enhance knowledge by patronising ethnological, zoological, and botanical experiments; his spiritual life and his meetings with the Sufis and *yogis* like Gosain Jadrup; and his personal life, including his addiction to narcotics and drugs (although it is significantly silent on his relationship with Nurjahan). Jahangir ordered the distribution of the fascicule of his memoirs to his officials in the thirteenth year of his reign, with the first copy given to his eldest son and successor, Shahjahan.

To fulfil Jahangir's wish to send his memoirs to different parts of the world to serve as an advice on kingship, the *Jahangirnama* was translated into Ottoman Turkish in the eighteenth century in Istanbul at the court of Sultan Mustafa III. It is noteworthy that the *Tuzuk* did not end in the thirteenth year of Jahangir's reign but carried on through his nineteenth regnal year, when the emperor, weakened by his illness, nominated Mu'tamad Khan, his court chronicler, to continue the task of recording the subsequent events of his reign. Yet another account of Jahangir's period is a text by 'Abdus Sattar Qasim Lahori, *Majalis-i Jahangiri* (Assemblies of

Jahangir), which describes the night-time sessions and conversations presided over by Jahangir from 1608–11, attended by the imperial high cadre officials, dignitaries, and poets from Iran and Central Asia, and religious elite comprising Brahmin, *'ulama*, Jesuit, and Jewish scholars. The text discussed Mughal politics and culture in the early seventeenth century and demonstrated Jahangir's interest in a number of issues ranging from kingship, religion (particularly Christianity), literature, to poetry and music. The Jesuit priest Jeronimo Xavier described it as a 'holy and pure mirror in which one deals with the life and marvellous doctrine of Our Lord Jesus Christ' (Alam and Subrahmanyam 2011, 267). Representing the literary traditions of *munazara* (disputation) and *malfuzat*, *Majalis* is a dialogical work, perhaps more cosmopolitan than any other contemporary Mughal chronicle, exhibiting a vast linguistic dimension and providing a good sense of the courtly intellectual milieu.

Three years after Jahangir's demise, Mu'tamad Khan wrote a panegyric account, *Iqbalnama-i Jahangiri* (based largely on *Tuzuk*) in three volumes, the last of which described Jahangir's reign. Another work composed during this phase, *Ma'asir-i Jahangiri* by Kamgar Husaini, is a shorter version of Jahangir's memoirs. Both these non-commissioned histories provide a continuous narrative from 1622–27 and reflect on aspects ignored or partially mentioned in the *Jahangirnama*, namely the rebellions of Salim and Khurram and the politics of Nurjahan that had isolated Jahangir. These works were presumably intended to win the patronage of Shahjahan, and yet it is not certain whether they were presented to him. Nevertheless, they had a tremendous influence on the historiography of Shahjahan's reign and the chronicles commissioned by him, particularly *Padshahnama* (1638) of Muhammad Amin Qazwini. Based on official records, Qazwini's *Padshahnama* covers the first ten years of Shahjahan's reign and describes the deep involvement of the emperor in the creation of official court history, reminiscent of his forefather, Timur. Qazwini allegedly predicted that the Taj Mahal would be 'a masterpiece for ages to come', increasing 'the amazement of all humanity'. When Shahjahan decided to shift from the solar to the lunar calendar for dating events, he hired Abdul Hamid Lahori to rewrite the history of the first ten years of his reign. Describing Shahjahan as 'that pride of the Guregen (Mongol) dynasty', Lahori composed a detailed account of the political, social, and cultural life of the twenty lunar years of Shahjahan's reign under the title *Padshahnama*. Allegedly, when he presented a few passages of the work to Shahjahan, he was rewarded with gold equal to his weight, and Rs 3,000. It was under the same title (*Padshahnama*) that the account of the third decade, including a list of the *shaikh*s, scholars, and poets who flourished during the period, was prepared by Lahori's student, Muhammad Waris. Added to these were the works of Muhammad Salih Kambu and Sadiq Khan, entitled *Amal-i Salih* and *Shahjahannama*, respectively.

Continuing the tradition of official histories, Aurangzeb enlisted Muhammad Kazim, a courtier with access to the state archives, to write the history of the first ten years of his reign, the *Alamgirnama*. Like the other official histories—*Akbarnama* and the *Padshahnamas*—*Alamgirnama* too depended for its documentation on *waqa'i* or reports of the proceedings at the court and events in the *suba*s, information provided by the *waqa'inavi*s from the *suba*s to *bakshi-ul-mamalik*, a central minister. Emulating Shahjahan, Aurangzeb insisted on scrutinising the chronicle and rejecting all such details that were not acceptable to him. In the thirty-second year (1668) of his reign, Aurangzeb stopped any further writing of official court histories, although he ordered the codification of laws, *Fatawa-i Alamgiri*, a compilation in Arabic explaining the four Sunni legal schools on facets of civil and personal law. *Fatawa-i Alamgiri*, influenced by Hanafi jurisprudence, together with the emperor's *farmans* to Muhammad Hashim and Rasikdas, was perhaps the first attempt to impose explicitly defined legal norms over the *subas* under Mughal rule.

Notwithstanding the ban, Muhammad Saqi Mustai'd Khan continued to write secretly throughout his forty years of stay at Aurangzeb's court. His *Ma'asir-i Alamgiri*, ostensibly an official history of Aurangzeb's reign, is in two parts: the first is an abridgement of *Alamgirnama* and the second is a history of the last forty years of Aurangzeb's reign, written after the emperor's death at the persuasion of Inayatullah Khan, *wazir* of Aurangzeb's son and successor, Bahadur Shah, but more importantly, a loyalist of Aurangzeb (*murid-i khass-i Alamgiri*). Yet another chronicle of Aurangzeb's period is *Mir'at al-'Alam* by Muhammad Bakhtawar Khan, contemporary of Muhammad Kazim. Bakhtawar Khan had joined Aurangzeb's service as his personal assistant in 1654 during the war of succession and continued to hold the same post for thirteen years after Aurangzeb's coronation. His proximity to the emperor and privileged position at the court provided him access to the details written in the *Mir'at al-'Alam*, although Bakhtawar Khan claimed that the large material was derived and processed from *Alamgirnama*. *Mir'at* began the narrative with the history of the universe and ended with Aurangzeb's reign. The account comprised seven chapters and several sub-chapters, and Bakhtawar Khan named each chapter *ara'ish* (adornment). The first section of the seventh *ara'ish* contains the history of Aurangzeb from the war of succession to his accession; the second part is a discussion of Aurangzeb's personality traits, his descendants, the extent of his empire, data on *subas*, and the revenue collected. The next part is a depiction of the ethos and intellectual and cultural life beyond the imperial court, written like a *tazkirat* and providing details on the learned men who lived during his time—the *'ulama* from the reign of Akbar to Aurangzeb, calligraphers from Ibn-i Muqlah to Aurangzeb's period, and a few selected poets.

In addition, a few notable non-commissioned, private histories for Aurangzeb's reign include Abu'l Fazl Mamuri's untitled history, almost entirely incorporated in Khafi Khan's *Muntakhab al-Lubab* (1731; although Khafi Khan concealed this fact); Bhimsen's *Nuskha-i Dilkusha* (1709) that adopted Mamuri's candour, insight, and critical approach; and an anonymous history, *Tarikh-i Shivaji* (1777), an assessment of Shivaji based on Marathi *bakhar* (narration).

The declining Mughal court in the eighteenth century sought to legitimise its authority by patronising histories such as *Tazkira-i Chaghatay* and *Tarikh-i Chaghatay*, which emphasised the Chingizid lineage of the dynasty. *Tazkira-i Chaghatay* of Muhammad Hadi Kamwar Khan narrated the history of the Mongols, emphasised the significance of the direct Chingizi descent of the Mughals, and ended the account in 1724, the seventh year of the reign of Muhammad Shah. *Tarikh-i Chaghatay*, on the other hand, written by Muhammad Shafi Tehrani, began with the establishment of the Mughal Empire and covered the entire Mughal period till the reign of Muhammad Shah, focusing particularly on the withdrawal of Nadir Shah from Hindustan in 1739. Interestingly, it referred to an imperial order after Nadir Shah's departure that forbade historians from recording the events of Muhammad Shah's reign, reminding that 'at present the record cannot be a pleasant one'. Shafi's account deserves special recognition for the mention of the imperial order: a valuable reminder of the process of control and manipulation of dynastic regnal histories begun in the sixteenth century by the Mughal emperors, which continued still.

TRAVELOGUES

Adding to the literary trends of the period are the travelogues that form a significant segment of the historiography of the early modern period. The discussion here focuses on a few European and Central Asian travellers, who visited the Mughal court during the sixteenth–seventeenth centuries. European writings on South Asia in this period were earlier considered important for understanding facts on prices, wages, temperatures, travel time from Surat to Burhanpur, or the way a *hundi* (bill of exchange) operated in the Mughal Empire. This approach, Ashin Das Gupta (1979, 315) argued, brought 'the world of the Indian Ocean ... into its own, and within it, the history of trade (became) ascendant over politics'. Later, however, the discourse of the Europeans was found to be problematic in the way they represented the Asian mercantile communities, polities or societies. Their interest, it appeared, lay in the self-representation and analysis of European societies vis-à-vis the Asian ones. Keen to record the impressions of their itinerary and the places that they visited, more perhaps for their compatriots than the Indian audience, the travel accounts nevertheless serve as an important conduit to understand the society and economy of the time and the lives of the people. They do not shy away from details about the emperor, his personal life, and the imperial court, and inevitably go beyond descriptions of the king and his court. In fact, the encounter between the European and his 'Other' represents a chronology and a series of events rather than a mere simple moment. Travellers' accounts may not necessarily be free from bias and misunderstandings, primarily for reasons of linguistic ignorance or language insufficiency and their oriental outlook, especially the European ones; yet they can be considered a valuable source of information that complement the genre of Persian literature.

The European travellers had arrived in India as traders from the fifteenth century. The Portuguese, as Abul Qasim 'Firishta' narrated in his *Gulshan-i Ibrahimi*, had initiated efforts to consolidate their position on the west coast in 1495, taking advantage of the political weakness of the Deccan kingdoms. It was, as Sanjay Subrahmanyam (2005d) called it, the first Indian perception of 'Europeans without Europe'. The Persian and Arabic chronicles in the sixteenth century and even later had described the Europeans as 'religious bigot, devious, untrustworthy and slippery', who could go to any extent to achieve their missionary ends; but there was another image as well: Europeans as purveyors of the 'strange and wonderful (*aja'ib-o-ghara'ib* and *adbhuta*)'. Badauni and Asad Beg Qazwini illustrated this through examples from Akbar's court, with the emperor sending his representatives to Goa to the Portuguese authorities to get these 'strange objects'. These included musical instruments like *arghanun*, birds and creatures from the New World, and tobacco. Badauni remarked rather condescendingly, 'because the emperor (Akbar) was so pleased, the Europeans kept coming at every moment in red and yellow colours, and went from one extravagance to another . . . .'

These dealings acquired a religious dimension with the presence of the First Jesuit Mission in the *Ibadatkhana* in 1580 for religious discussions with members of other religions, as well as the *'ulama* and Shi'i scholars. Two years before the arrival of the First Jesuit Mission, Akbar had despatched an envoy to Goa asking the Portuguese to send priests to his court 'with the chief books of the Law and the Gospel'. This further inspired the Portuguese zeal for political and missionary activity. The Jesuits, who may be considered the earliest European travellers at the Mughal court, served as a channel of communication between the Portuguese at Goa and the Mughal court, especially since the *Estado da India* and the Mughals maintained no formal diplomatic ties. (*Estado da India* in the sixteenth century did not suggest a geographically demarcated space but territories, establishments, goods, people, and collective interests controlled by the Portuguese Crown in the Indian Ocean and adjacent seas or rivers, from the Cape of Good Hope to Japan).

Interestingly, none of the three priests—Antonio Monserrate, a Catalonian (and official chronicler of the mission), Rodolfo Acquaviva, an Italian, and Francisco Henriques, a Muslim convert from Ormuz, fluent in Persian language—sent as part of the First Jesuit Mission were ethnically Portuguese but came from three different cultural worlds, brought together by the all-encompassing political and ecclesiastical authority of the Portuguese. Carrying with them a number of gifts for the emperor—an atlas that comprised a collection of uniform map sheets, considered the first true modern atlas and summary of sixteenth-century cartography, sent by the Archbishop of Goa; the gold copy of the *Royal Polyglot* (in Hebrew, Chaldee, Latin, and Greek), printed in 1569–72 for Philip II of Spain; and a copy of *The Lives of the Apostles* in Persian—they had hoped to achieve evangelisation. Akbar reciprocated the gifts by registering his second son, Murad, as a student of Monserrate, for instructions in Portuguese language and Christian moral and ethical values. Misunderstanding Akbar's liberal, eclectic mind and fascination for Christianity (overlooking the same sensitivity towards all other religions), Monserrate accused him of apostasy and optimistically anticipated the emperor's conversion, or at least that of some of his courtiers. But the Jesuits soon realised the futility of the dialogical process and wanted to return to Goa—which the emperor did not allow, giving the impression that his interest in Christianity had not abated. The Second Jesuit Mission stayed briefly at Akbar's court in 1591.

Yet again, at the invitation of the emperor, the Third Jesuit Mission arrived in 1595, heralding the continuous presence of Jesuits in the Mughal court till the eighteenth century. Notwithstanding the missionary endeavours of the Jesuits, if Akbar continued to invite them and interact with them, the reason lay not in his religious inquisitiveness but his commercial strategy: to trade through the ports of Bengal and Gujarat so that, even as he held a dialogue with the Jesuits, the ports could be protected from Portuguese onslaughts. Consequently, the commercial rapport with the Portuguese could lead to the integration of the Mughal economy in the maritime space of the Indian Ocean.

Jesuit Father Du Jarric's (Third Jesuit Mission) *Histoire* is a valuable account that reproduced and summarised the letters of Jesuit priests written prior to 1610. C. H. Payne translated *Histoire*, but confined himself to the portions that related to Akbar's reign. Du Jarric and Monserrate described Akbar's fondness for European dresses, particularly a black velvet dress stitched in

Image 2.2: Jesuits at Akbar's Court, an illustration from *Akbarnama* by Narsingh, *c.* 1605. The painting depicts a scene from a religious assembly held by Akbar in the *Ibadatkhana*. The two men dressed in black are Jesuit missionaries, Rodolfo Acquaviva and Francisco Henriques

Source: https://commons.wikimedia.org/wiki/File: Jesuits_at_Akbar's_Court.jpg.

the Portuguese style and worn on private occasions; the emperor's personality, his melancholic disposition and mental depression, to overcome which he engaged himself in a variety of amusements, like watching the *mast* elephants fight or camels, buffaloes or rams butting each other with their horns, or even cock fights. Abu'l Fazl, however, interpreted Akbar's depression differently, associating it with the emperor's spiritual awakening and enlightenment. Monserrate was the author of many works, but his most popular writing, *Commentarius*, is an account of his stay at the court of Akbar in 1580–82. He provided extensive details of the cities that he visited and the routes that he followed; Akbar's religious beliefs, his political and military skills, the heterogeneity of the emperor's vast army, the order and discipline in the imperial court, and the military camps 'made in the traditional Mongol style'. Monserrate expressed his astonishment at the 'cheapness of grains amongst so great a multitude'; forms of address, titles, and circumscribed speech adopted in the court; some details on the common people, their religious beliefs, superstitions, and celebration of festivals.

A Jesuit document, namely a letter written by Jeronimo (Jerome) Xavier from Lahore to the Provincial of the Society of Jesus at Goa on 25 September 1606, nearly a year after the death of Akbar, is an important source for the period 1605–06 concerning the death of Akbar and succession of Jahangir that supplemented *Tuzuk-i Jahangiri* (or *Jahangirnama*). Xavier, present in Agra in the last months of Akbar's life and the first few months of Jahangir's reign, wrote a laudatory obituary of Akbar but more importantly, expressed his concerns and anxiety at the nature of the transition under Jahangir. Contrary to the Jesuit belief that Jahangir was a crypto-Christian and would convert to Christianity, the emperor had sought the support and indulgence of the *'ulama*. The Jesuit vision of Jahangir was initially less complimentary, fearing that he might not be as favourably disposed towards them as Akbar, but their opinion changed by 1607–08. Xavier is supposed to have remarked, 'the King is now not as much of a Moor as he showed himself at the start …'.

The reigns of Shahjahan and Aurangzeb, too, aroused negative emotions in the Jesuit mind. The Jesuits who lived in Agra described Shahjahan as 'tyrannous' and 'cruel' with a 'natural aversion for the *Padres* and all the *firangis*', and referred to him pejoratively as 'Sultao Corromo', while Aurangzeb's accession was seen as the beginning of difficult times for the Christians, ending the eclecticism of Akbar and Jahangir. The Jesuits perhaps believed that had they succeeded in converting Jahangir, it would have resulted in a dramatic mass conversion in India, although this was never the situation. The Mughal emperors in the sixteenth and early seventeenth century were simply inquisitive about European culture, whether it was their paintings, clocks or firearms, and thus welcomed them to their courts as 'minor interlocutors'.

Europeans had thronged Indian shores for over two centuries before the arrival of Sir Thomas Roe. Roe was despatched as an ambassador to the Mughal court by James I and the London directors of the English East India Company in 1615 in the hope of negotiating a formal trade treaty. He was preceded by William Hawkins (1603–13), who impressed Jahangir during his stay at Agra from early 1609 to November 1611 with his linguistic abilities and knowledge of Turkish, holding conversations and narrations without an interpreter. He provided details on the personal life of Jahangir, including the jewels that he wore and possessed, the emperor's daily routine, behaviour and norms of the imperial court, the nobility, the common people and their religious beliefs, customs, and superstitions—even though he could barely stabilise the commercial position of the Company in Gujarat.

Other English travellers who visited parts of northern and western India included Ralph Fitch (1583–91), John Mildenhall (1599–1606), William Finch (1608–11), Nicholas Withington (1612–16), and Thomas Coryat (1612–17). The proposal to send an ambassador to the Mughal court was floated by Thomas Aldworth, a Company factor from Ahmadabad, in November 1613 so as to establish the prominence of the Company in trade vis-à-vis the rivals: the Dutch and the Portuguese. Given the not-too-encouraging experiences of Hawkins, the Company decided to send Thomas Roe as an envoy to India. Roe was described as a person 'of a pregnant understanding, well spoken, learned, industrious and of a comelie personage'. Deeply immersed, both ritually and emotionally, in the late sixteenth–early seventeenth century English courtly life and its European connections, Roe had enjoyed the distinction of being the Esquire of the Body to Queen Elizabeth, was knighted by James I in 1603, shared a close relationship with the King's children, Henry and Elizabeth, was acquainted with Sir Walter Raleigh, and belonged to a commercial family of Kent that dominated global trade in the sixteenth century.

As the first English ambassador to the Mughal court, Roe led an embassy to the court of Jahangir during the years 1615–19. Presenting himself to Jahangir at Ajmer in January 1616, he accompanied the imperial court to Mandu and Ahmadabad, of which he provided an interesting account, narrating the splendour and festivity at the imperial camp and Jahangir's departure ceremony. His chaplain, Edward Terry, on the other hand, described the royal camp as '*ambulans respublica*', that is, a walking republic that took almost twelve hours to cross any one place. In addition, Roe provided a vivid description of the personal attributes of Jahangir, his sons Khurram and Khusrau, the emperor's religious tolerance, his emulation of Akbar's religious sentiments, the influence of Nurjahan on the emperor and his court, and the emperor's incessant addiction to alcohol and opium. More significantly, although Roe held the English painters in high esteem, he presented Jahangir as a connoisseur of art, fascinated by European paintings and European techniques. It was, in fact, from the reign of Jahangir that Mughal portraiture acquired symbolic imagery. Elaborating on the Mughal interest in cartography, Roe mentioned his gift of Mercator's last edition of the maps of the world that he presented to Jahangir in September 1617 and the emperor's curiosity about Mercator's atlas (which he subsequently returned to Roe). Ebba Koch (2012) argued that the presence of globes and maps in the allegories of Jahangir is a reflection of the understanding of geography and European cartographic techniques, and the way they could be implemented in Mughal art. Regardless of the vivid descriptions that Roe provided, he oscillated in his views on Mughal court culture. He could not overcome his prejudices and oriental outlook and found the Mughal court culture 'theatrical', was unhappy with the Mughal State in general and Jahangir in particular, whom he felt did not pay enough obeisance to the envoys in his court. But then Roe also talked about the courtesies extended to him by the emperor, the *khilat* and the gifts that he received from him, the invitation to the *ghusl khana* (emperor's consultation room or tent) and court coterie, and his cordial relationship with the emperor, especially as his drinking partner.

Notwithstanding these encounters, Roe remained arrogant and boastful, at times dubious, unconvinced, and dissatisfied; he regarded his embassy to Jahangir unsuccessful, especially because he had failed to contract a trade treaty with the Mughals (for which he held Asaf Khan responsible). Roe sought the emperor's leave at Ahmadabad in August 1618 and returned to London in 1619 after four months of residence in Surat. It is difficult to ascertain the truth of Roe's narrative in the absence of any other commentary on his work, except for some observations made by Edward Terry. Terry, however, cannot be treated as an independent voice for two reasons: he had accompanied Roe as his chaplain and was his close associate; moreover, both depended on the same interpreter.

Other European travellers who reflected on the Mughal Empire as the 'other' and shared the prejudices and biases of Thomas Roe included the French physician Francois Bernier, the French goldsmith and gemologist Jean Baptiste Tavernier, and the Venetian physician, Niccolo Manucci. Bernier's text, *Travels in the Mughal Empire, A.D. 1656–1668*, considered an important source on oriental despotism by intellectuals from Montesquieu to Marx, was partly disputed by his eighteenth-century compatriot, Anquetil du Perron. Serving as a physician in the Mughal court for eight years to finance his stay in India, Bernier travelled widely—Delhi, Agra, Lahore, Kashmir, Bengal (accompanied by Tavernier), Masulipatam, and Golconda—before leaving India in 1667, visiting Persia on his way to Paris and thus fulfilling his desire, as he noted in his account, to 'see the world' and 'record history'. He arrived in India at a time when Shahjahan's sons were engaged in a war of succession: an event that he recorded vividly, cautioning against fratricidal wars and centrifugal tendencies at the centre. Bernier's statement, anticipated earlier by the Dutch merchant Francisco Pelsaert (1590–1630) in his *Remonstrantie*, that 'the empire of the Great Mogol comprehends several nations over which he is not absolute master', supports the description of the Mughal Empire as a vast 'galactic' assembly exercising complicated authority, rather than as a centralised State. Speaking of the 'execrable tyranny' of the *jagirdar*s caused by the frequent transfer of their *jagir*s, Bernier was the first to expound the significance of the Mughal assignment system and its implications. He argued that this pattern of transfers had a disastrous impact on the *jagirdar*s, who felt deprived and had no incentive to improve the land or its production. Instead, they appropriated large amounts for themselves, leaving the land and agricultural production completely depleted and exhausted, with no concern for the peasants. His proposition regarding the 'crisis' influenced the writings of imperialist and Marxist historians like W. H. Moreland and Irfan Habib, respectively.

It is pertinent to point out, however, that Bernier's commentary—evident from his observations in a letter written in the late 1660s to Jean Baptiste Colbert, the finance minister of France's King Louis XIV—was addressed to correspondents in France and had a rhetorical purpose. A member of the French landed gentry, Bernier probably wished to criticise revenue farming as a principle—a practice then prevalent in France—and instead advocate an indispensable, urgent need for security of private property in land. Believing that such security was absent in India, he identified that absence as a serious drawback in Mughal India, one that he did not wish to see replicated in France. Using the Mughal Empire as an example, Bernier may have hoped to influence Colbert's revenue policies and warn of the consequences if certain despotic and tyrannical policies were followed. In addition, he provided details on the accession of Aurangzeb, the pomp, splendour, and wealth of the imperial court, its rituals of power, *nazr* and *peshkash*, geography and economy, including trade, commerce, land systems, and land rights.

Together with Bernier, Jean Chardin, and Jean de Thevenot, Jean Baptiste Tavernier was yet another celebrated French traveller who visited Asia in the seventeenth century. It is believed that, as compared to the first three, Tavernier was less inclined towards philosophical speculation and faced the contempt of intellectuals like Voltaire, while Montesquieu relied on him for information on oriental despotism. Under the influence of his geographer father, Tavernier had inherited the passion to know places and visit foreign countries; yet the descriptions of his travels are brief. His account is not like his 'life history': the events of his early childhood are completely missing and so are the years 1633–38 when he was not travelling; the actual period in which some of his adventures took place are mentioned casually, with a virtual absence of chronology and the dates scattered through his works. Tavernier made six voyages to Asia in a span of forty years, of which his second voyage was to Bengal, from 1638–43; the third was via the eastern Mediterranean to Surat and Deccan between 1643–49. He visited Deccan again during his fourth voyage from 1651–55; his sixth and final voyage, which began in November 1666, took him to north India and the Mughal imperial court. By the time Tavernier returned to France in late 1668, he had accumulated substantial wealth through his trade in jewels, precious stones, and textiles.

During his voyages, Tavernier took exhaustive notes on the administration, religion, customs, trade, commerce, weights, measures, currency, and prices of the country that he passed through, hoping that the latter details in particular would motivate some to trade with the regions described. It is suggested that his description of Mughal politics was derived from Bernier's account or from their conversations when they travelled together to Bengal. The information gathered was collated and compiled into two quarto volumes—the first one on Turkey and Persia and the second on India and the islands in its vicinity—published in 1676, translated into English in 1677 and later in German and Dutch, followed by several reprints and new editions. Engaged in buying and selling diamonds and precious stones during his visit to India, Tavernier mooted his work to be read like a treatise interspersed with anecdotes, rather than as a story of adventures. Visiting India at the time of Shahjahan's imprisonment by Aurangzeb, Tavernier's *Travels in India* is the only account (with no other contemporary evidence) that ascribed to Shahjahan the desire, turned down by Aurangzeb, to build a replica of the Taj Mahal in black marble as his mausoleum on the opposite bank of the river Yamuna, connected with that of Mumtaz Mahal by a bridge. Unsympathetic to the treatment meted out to Shahjahan, Tavernier provided an excursus on Sultan Bulaqi (Dawar Baksh, son of Khusrau) in the context of the war of succession (1657–58) to illustrate a moral connection between crime and punishment. He depicted the imprisonment of Shahjahan by Aurangzeb as a punishment in return for the injustice meted out by Shahjahan when he pronounced the execution of his nephew Bulaqi, three decades earlier. His observations, however, are not dissimilar to other European accounts. Tavernier shares their oriental bias when he views seventeenth-century India through the prism of caste, *sati*, idolatry, and the temple-chariot of Jagannath. Describing the *chaturvarna* system or the four castes—Brahmins, Rajputs or Khatris, Banias, Sudras—he added artisans as the fifth caste and then talked of the untouchables as 'alacors', a term derived probably from the Persian *halal-khwor*.

Fellow traveller and contemporary of Bernier and Tavernier, Niccolo Manucci, who arrived in Surat in January 1654, was also driven by the imaginative impressions (especially his visits to the harem as a physician to examine the ailing—or those feigning illness, as he believed—women of the royal household) of what he witnessed during his visit to India. In the early part of his journey to India, he enlisted himself in the service of Dara Shukoh as an artilleryman. A witness to the war of succession between Shahjahan's sons, he described Dara's army as 'not very war-like; they were butchers, barbers, blacksmiths, carpenters, tailors and such like'. Critical of Aurangzeb's behaviour during the war of succession, Manucci narrated how Aurangzeb blockaded his retreat and his attempt to gallop out of Agra after the defeat of Dara. Following Dara's death, Manucci sought the patronage of Shah 'Alam, who employed him as a physician, notwithstanding his informal and unrecognisable qualifications as a doctor; as his compatriot Legrenzi observed, Manucci 'lacked letters as well as a knowledge of the [medical] art'. Manucci attempted several times, in vain, to leave Mughal India for the Portuguese territories—Goa, Daman, Bassein, and Bandra. It was, however, only in 1686 after seriously considering his return to Europe that he finally decided to leave the Mughal domain and live in the British and French territories of Madras and Pondicherry, respectively, where he spent the last three decades of his life, chronicling his thirty years in Mughal service for an audience that he believed was European, whether in Europe or in India.

Writing about his experiences and observations in the voluminous text, *Storia do Mogor*, Manucci stated that he wrote it 'for the benefit of voyagers, merchants and missionaries' because those who preceded him were neither well-informed of, nor well-versed in, the greatness, wealth, power, and politics of the Mughal Empire. In stating this, he was particularly critical of Bernier, probably because of a rivalry based on two reasons—Manucci's doubtful claim to be a doctor as opposed to Bernier's reputation as a doctor, and the fact that his narrative could compete with neither Bernier's nor Tavernier's in the European market. His work was translated into English by William Irvine in 1907, but it was never published in the original. To establish the authenticity of his text and convey that he understood Mughal politics and religion like the local people, Manucci used Persian citations and commissioned copies of Mughal miniatures, painted by Indian artists in the Madras region, which rarely corresponded to the prototype and often reflected Manucci's disregard for Indian religion and society. Analysing the text and the illustrations that accompanied it, Sanjay Subrahmanyam (2005b, 17) observed that it was 'very much a hybrid text, a product of a multiple series of *metissages* across European cultures, between Indian and European elements, and between Persian and vernacular textual and representational traditions'. Not too kind in his opinion of India and Indians, Manucci found Mughal polity distasteful and declared it 'impossible to live amongst people so barbarous and enemies of every sort of justice and reason'. Yet his decision to stay back in India, despite twice contemplating a return to Europe (in 1711 and 1715–16) makes him, as Subrahmanyam (2008, 67) stated, something of an 'enigma'.

The accounts of European travellers and their perception of India as the 'other' provide an interesting contrast with the individual experiences of Central and West Asian travellers who visited India between 1400 and 1800. The latter shared the Persophone culture of the elites of early modern India; however, this did not prevent them from presenting India as the 'other'—sometimes exotic (*'aja'ib*), at other times foreign, annoying, barbaric, and embarrassingly seductive—except when its characteristics were found to be similar to other parts of the Islamic world. These travellers, who came over a span of one-and-a-half centuries beginning from the 1550s, included:

- The Ottoman admiral Seydi 'Ali Re'is, who sojourned in India in the 1550s, was surprised by his own itinerary, and metaphorically embodied an unfortunate voyager;
- The poet Mutribi from Samarqand, who came to Jahangir's court in the late 1620s;
- Mahmud Wali, who had set out from Balkh in 1625 to witness the splendour and marvel of India, and travelled widely in India after escaping shipwreck on the coast of Orissa. He also spent some time in the Mughal imperial service;
- Ashraf Mazandarani, a poet from Iran who migrated to India in the 1650s during Aurangzeb's reign. The emperor hired him as a tutor for his daughter, but Mazandarani could never adjust to the environment of Hindustan or get rid of his homesickness;
- Mufid, a traveller from Iran who came in the 1670s, only to be disillusioned and disappointed by the reception he received at the royal court;
- Hazin, a poet from Isfahan, visited in the 1720s in search of career opportunities, but was appalled by the discomforts, which he attributed to the bad climate.

Of these, the focus here is on Seydi 'Ali Re'is and Mutribi. The accounts of both can be cited as examples of embassy-accounts, like those of the European, Chinese or Arab voyagers. Seydi 'Ali's narrative was high on diplomatic content, and Mutribi's was court-oriented.

Seydi 'Ali Re'is was appointed admiral by the Grand Vizier Rustem Pasha in November 1553 in response to the suggestion of the Governor of Jiddah, Selman Re'is, that trade in the Red Sea should be seized by occupying the strategic ports in the western Indian Ocean. Seydi 'Ali Re'is was an exceptional rather than a reluctant traveller, who did not anticipate the journey that he was compelled to endure; it was inflicted on him by 'brute circumstance'. After a series of mishaps, being stranded in storms and tempests (*tufan*), and shipwrecked off the coast of Gujarat subsequent to the unsuccessful naval attack on the Portuguese in the Persian Gulf that diminished his fleet, he reached Delhi in October 1555 to present himself to the Mughal Emperor Humayun, who was in the process of re-consolidating his rule over northern India. He remained in Delhi for three months, becoming a witness to the events leading to the death of Humayun and accession of Akbar in early 1556. Seydi 'Ali described vividly the court ceremonies on his arrival at Delhi, the award of *khilat* and gift of money by Humayun; his attendance at the council of the emperor in the late evening as per the custom of the imperial court, where he presented gifts to the emperor and wrote chronograms in celebration of the emperor's re-conquest of Hindustan. He elucidated his intense relationship with Humayun, with whom he had become 'virtually inseparable, by day or by night', the emperor's insistence upon teaching him the skills of using astronomical tables, the calendar for solar and lunar eclipses, the astrolabe, and the treatise on the equinoctial cycle.

The emperor was so impressed, related Seydi 'Ali, that he asked him to stay in the Mughal court for at least a year. But when he explained that had it not been for the turbulent weather conditions, he would not even have touched the shores of India, and that his actual mission was to ensure the liberation of Gujarat from the *kafirs*, that is, the Portuguese, the emperor relented, but urged him to stay till *birishkal* (winter rains), teach him the astronomical science in three months, and only then would he be allowed *rukhsat* (leave to depart). Seydi 'Ali regales his readers with his earnest efforts to meet the emperor's deadline and write *ghazals* (odes) and eulogistic chronograms that made Humayun refer to him as the 'second Mir 'Ali Sher Nawa'i' (the fifteenth-century Turkish poet from Herat). The emperor finally loaded him with extraordinary gifts and permitted him to leave. But destiny, observed Seydi 'Ali, intervened differently. On a Friday, at the time of evening prayer, as Humayun hurried down the stairs, he had a fatal fall, causing anxiety and commotion, especially since his heir Akbar and the *Khan-i-Khanan* were not present. Seydi 'Ali claimed that invoking a similar experience in the Ottoman, he advised that the death of the emperor be concealed till Akbar arrived. He, however, left for Lahore even before Humayun's death was made public but returned briefly in February 1556 to meet Akbar and his regent Bairam Khan. Subsequently, he left for Samarqand via Lahore and Kabul.

These details, interspersed with accounts of the misfortunes of his journey, are contained in his text *Mirat al-Mamalik* (*The Mirror of Kingdoms*), a title chosen over his earlier intended *Book of Torments*. Probably written for the Sultan of Ottoman as the primary audience to justify his disastrous expedition and its adversities, the text can be cited as an example of a 'closed' or self-centred travel account that ignored the 'unfamiliar' and sought reassurance from the 'familiar'. Seydi 'Ali's strategy seemed to have worked for he faced no severities from the Sultan; instead, he continued to enjoy his favour till his death in Istanbul in January 1563.

Mutribi al-Asamm al-Samarqandi, a visitor to the court of Jahangir in Lahore in 1627, was a significant variant, or rather, an 'indigenous counterpart', to the Oxonian Thomas Roe. Mutribi could converse with the emperor in Persian, a language in which both were fluent (although Jahangir also knew Turkish, Arabic, *Braj Bhasha*, and a bit of Portuguese), while Roe had to completely rely on the interpreters, a fact he was discreet about and which may have affected his dealings with the emperor. Initially, Mutribi's interaction with Jahangir was through a certain Khwaja Fakhr-al-Din Husain, son of Maulana Khwaja Khan Diwan. Within a few months, as Mutribi introspected upon and recollected his conversations with the emperor, he wrote them in a form of court literature, conscious that the Mughal emperor would be one of its readers. This had a two-fold impact: Mutribi could not criticise the emperor even if he wished to like Thomas Roe; and second, whatever he wrote was under surveillance, constantly evaluated and verified by the other courtiers. His work, *Khatirat-i Mutribi Samarqandi*, may not technically qualify as a travel account, particularly in the absence of the mention of itinerary or the paths traversed. It is a 'chatty, personal' memoir of twenty-four conversations and meetings, described as *waqi'a* (happenings), between him and Jahangir. He reported that in the course of the conversations,

Jahangir constantly verified the veracity of his statements; yet he developed a close relationship with the emperor, who bestowed several favours on him. He also managed to keep the emperor impressed with his anecdotes and with the information that he was completing a text, *Nuskha-yi Ziba-yi Jahangir*, in honour of the emperor. When the text was presented, Jahangir was so delighted that he offered Mutribi four gifts, on condition that he would not give them together but one after the other: money for his expenses; a *khilat*; a horse and saddle; and a slave to serve him.

When Mutribi narrated the conversations, the text was transmuted into a travel text with two travellers within—Mutribi himself and the emperor. As Mutribi compared the two cultures (Central Asia and Hindustan) and provided an eyewitness (*bayan*) account of the affairs in Transoxiana, he transformed Jahangir into an 'armchair traveller'. Further, with the exposition of the *aja'ib* or wonders of Hindustan, for example, a magical (*tilism*) book gifted to him by Jahangir, Mutribi represents the biases and opinions of Jahangir. Later, Mutribi presented the book to the King of Turan as a token of marvel from Hindustan. Unlike Roe, however, he made no comparison between the two political systems, nor did he express any feeling of humiliation in the Mughal court or in the company of the emperor.

Mutribi's *Khatirat* was contemporaneous with several other historical writings—Jahangir's memoir, *Tuzuk-i Jahangiri*, Mu'tamad Khan's *Iqbalnama-i Jahangiri*, Asad Beg's *Ahwal-i Asad Beg*—and yet it stood apart. The text began with a brief introduction as he prepared for twenty-four conversations between himself and Jahangir; he praised God and the Prophet, and emphasised thanksgiving and patience, in particular thanksgiving to God for giving him the privilege of the company of a great ruler like Jahangir.

The texts of Seydi 'Ali and Mutribi are significant because they bring out the similarities and differences between the imperial systems of the Ottomans, Safavids, Mughals, and Shaibinids, whether it be in the form of sovereignty or the Persianate norms that determined diplomatic interactions. This sense of difference and yet familiarity that the Central Asian and West Asian travellers encountered upon their arrival in India made their experiences different from that of the European travellers, who often faced linguistic challenges and failed to understand the Mughal institutions. So while travellers like Seydi 'Ali and Mutribi could arrive in a strange environment and yet settle with ease, European ambassadors like Thomas Roe and others were prone to dismiss the Mughal court as 'a stage for tawdry theatre and unbridled cruelty'.

3

CONTEXTS AND MILIEUS OF POWER AND AUTHORITY

HIGHLIGHTS

- Iranian migrants in the Deccan Sultanate and the Mughal court
- Afghan diaspora: Lodis and Surs
- Sher Shah: Political, social, and cultural contributions
- Evolution of kingship and polity under the early Timurids
- Bairam Khan and Mirza Hakim as contenders to power
- Transformation of Timurid polity under Akbar
- Legitimacy and authority: Rituals, traditions, and customs
- Norms of governance: Legislation and jurisprudence—*akhlaq* and *shari'a*

MIGRANT COMMUNITIES AND ETHNIC GROUPS: IRANIANS AND THE AFGHANS

A constant stream of migrations from West and Central Asia of 'warrior elites' perhaps best explains the nuances of power under the Mughals, as well as the formation of the Delhi Sultanate. The migrants generally followed the practice of first settling on the north-western frontier of the Delhi Sultanate, and then moving to the centre at an opportune moment. They envisioned India, particularly the northern zone, as a centre of refuge, an escape from the central Islamic lands and the constant threat of Mongol invasions. It is due to these migrations that the Delhi Sultanate could retain its Central Asian links; adopt, adapt, and assimilate Persianised Sassanid traditions; retain Turko-Mongol characteristics and Turkish dialects; and also, quite considerably, continue the rituals regarding succession and burial. In fact, Iranian influence was fairly evident as Islam expanded into the Indian subcontinent from the fourteenth century. It is alleged that Sultan Firuz Shah Tughluq had sent empty ships to Hurmuz and other ports to bring back the 'precious human cargo' comprising soldiers, administrators, traders, and artists from the Persian Gulf into India. Jean Aubin (1988; *cf* Subrahmanyam 1992a, 342) argued that 'while neither theologians and jurists nor traders from Arab-speaking lands were absent, this enterprise of military and spiritual conquest is essentially due to Iranian Islam, which was to transform Indo-Muslim civilization into a civilization of Persian culture'.

Both talent and precious metals flowed from the Persian Gulf into India in the latter half of the fifteenth century to the Deccan Sultanate of Bahmani. Muhammad Qasim Firishta wrote that Ahmad Shah Bahmani (r. 1422–36) imported from the Iranian city of Kirman a number of disciples of the Sufi saint Shah Nimatullah. Another migrant of repute during the reign of Ahmad Shah was Khalaf Hasan, a merchant from Basra, who had settled in Deccan and traded extensively with Iran. He was subsequently given the title of *malik ut-tujjar* by the Bahmani Sultan. Later, in the fifteenth century, the same title was given to Khwaja Mahmud Gawan, a *wazir* in the Bahmani Sultanate. Gawan was a migrant to Deccan and had been educated in Cairo and Syria; one of his brothers, Ahmad, practised trade in Egypt while Ahmad's son was settled in Mecca. Gawan's own son, Abdullah, worked as his father's trade agent between Deccan and Iran. This indicates that those who migrated to the Bahmani Sultanate did not break their ties, but persistently continued their links with their original homes. For this reason, perhaps, prominent Iranians like Mahmud Gawan were described in the literary works on Deccan as *afaqi* (distant) or *ghair mulki* (foreign), as opposed to *dakhni* or Deccani (sons of the soil). This sort of distinction was evident from the mid-fifteenth century when foreigners became dominant in the nobility and the civil bureaucracy, leading to the exclusion of the Deccanis who began losing their social and political status. Two other reasons for their exclusion could have been, first, the language: while the *afaqi*s preferred the Persian language, the *dakhni*s chose to stay with their own dialect, a mix of Marathi and Kannada; and second, the sectarian aspect, that is, while the *dakhni*s were Sunnis, the *afaqi*s were Shi'is.

The Sultanates that succeeded the Bahmani kingdom in the late fifteenth and early sixteenth century continued to maintain links with Iran. Rafi-ud-din Shirazi observed that Yusuf Adil Shah (r. 1490–1510), the founder of the Bijapur Sultanate, was brought to Deccan by an Iranian merchant, Khwaja Zain-al Abidin Simnani; the Qutb Shahs of Golconda also claimed Iranian descent. The founder of the Qutb Shahi dynasty, Quli Qutb Shah, had fled Hamadan for India in 1478. In fact, Bijapur, Golconda, and Ahmadnagar continued to maintain contacts with Iran in the sixteenth century and encouraged the migration of the learned, the warriors, administrators, and merchants from Iran. During the reign of Sultan Ibrahim Adil Shah, a number of important posts were monopolised by the Iranians in Bijapur, and in case a Marathi Brahmin was appointed, he was obliged to learn and incorporate the Persian language in the functioning of the administration, especially the revenue department. The Nizam Shahs of Ahmadnagar also encouraged Iranian migration and maintained correspondence with the Safavid rulers in the mid-sixteenth century. Bijapur and Ahmadnagar could not, however, sustain the migration from Iran beyond the late sixteenth century, but Iranian influence maintained its hold over Golconda even in the seventeenth century. Amongst the prominent migrants to Golconda was Sayyid Kamal-ud-din Husain Ardistani (also known as Mustafa Khan Ardistani), appointed the *peshwa* by Sultan Ibrahim Qutb Shah. Subsequently, he shifted to Bijapur where he was again appointed the *peshwa* by Sultan Ali Adil Shah, a post that he retained till his assassination in the early 1580s. Another well-known Iranian migrant who came to Golconda in 1581 and stayed until his death around 1625 was Mir Muhammad Mu'min, who was known for his remarkable, fluent understanding of Persian poetry and served as the *peshwa* and *mir jumla* in the courts of Muhammad Quli Qutb Shah and Muhammad Qutb Shah.

The Iranian migration was, however, not confined to Deccan alone. Many Iranians held important positions in the Mughal nobility as well in the sixteenth and seventeenth centuries, and several left their imprint on the political and cultural life of the Mughals, whether in the sphere of Persian poetry, historiography, epistolary, or transmission of traditional and/or mystical Islam. A few well-known Iranian migrants during the 1560s comprised Mir Abdul Latif Qazwini, his son Ghiyas-ud-din Naqib Khan, and also Shams-ud-din Khwafi. Some others who flourished in the eighteenth century included Mir Muhammad Amin Nishapuri (popularly known as Burhan-ul-mulk), who succeeded in establishing the rule of his dynasty in Awadh, which ruled for almost 136 years. From 1740–57, a Shi'i family originating partially from Khurasan is known to have controlled the Mughal *suba* of Bengal. In addition, as the migration of the Iranis became increasingly limited to Awadh and Bengal in the early eighteenth century, Bengal acquired a large number of *Tajik*s from Surat and many merchants of Iranian origin dominated the region of Bengal during this period.

Understanding migrations into India, it appears that at least in the case of Iranian communities, both *imarat* and *tijarat* (state-building and trade) were of crucial significance. While the travellers from Isfahan and Istanbul found a familiar environment in the Mughal territories, they also saw it as a land of wonder (*'aja'ib*) and enormous wealth that offered better opportunities to poets, artists, calligraphers, and litterateurs, and an escape from the rigid religiosity of Safavid Persia. In his letter to the Safavid *wazir* in the late 1640s, Mir Muhammad Sayyid Ardistani cited several reasons for the migration to India, namely:

- for a better livelihood;
- to remit money to aged and infirm members of the family who had stayed back in Iran; and
- to get rid of the *zulum* (atrocities) of the Persian *shaikh ul-Islam* on the property of the orphans and the poor.

Ardistani had migrated to Deccan from Isfahan in the early 1620s. In Deccan, he invested in jewel trading and used the profits from the diamond trade to enter the administration of Golconda through revenue farming. In the 1630s, he rose from a petty financial official to local governor to *sar-i-khail* of the entire Sultanate, and in the 1640s, he was appointed the *mir jumla*. From the mid-1640s to the mid-1650s he was engaged in extensive maritime trade from the Red Sea and Basra to Makassar, and his fleet of over ten ships sailed under the protection of Portuguese, Dutch, and English passports. Ardistani later shifted from the service of the Sultan of Golconda to Mughal service in 1654–55.

The Afghan diaspora, an essential element of the pre-colonial State in South Asia, is of substantial relevance in the understanding of the vicissitudes of the Mughal Empire. It was in this diaspora that distinctive aspects of the Afghans' sense of historical identity took a definite form. Apart from the term 'Afghan' or a more conventional 'Aughan', there were the Indianised names of Pathan and Rohila (also spelt as Rohilla). The title Pathan was generally used for the eastern Afghan Pakhtun, whereas in the eighteenth century, Pathan indicated a person of genuine Pathan or Afghan descent; Rohilla developed as a nomenclature during the seventeenth century for people who had migrated from Roh, a site corresponding roughly with the mountainous terrain of the eastern Hindu Kush and Sulaiman range. Subsequently, in the seventeenth century itself, Roh was used as a more specific geographical term for the territory extending from Swat and Bajaur in the north to Sibi and Bhakkar in Sind, and from Hasan Abdal in the east to Kabul and Qandahar in the west. From the eighteenth century, there was yet another mutation: Rohilla emerged as an identity for all Indo-Afghans who had settled in Rohilkhand, or all such individuals in the service of a Rohilla chief. It is difficult, as is apparent, to provide a precise ethnic or geographical definition to the designations 'Afghan' or 'Afghanistan', the meaning of which, as Jos Gommans (1995) has argued, was conditioned by the time and place of the context in which they were used. For instance, the term 'Afghan' represented a more open category of peoples in 1500 than it did in 1800, indicating that it was a fluid category susceptible to the fluctuations of the historical process.

The evolution of the historical consciousness of the Afghans was influenced by their experiences of migration to Hindustan and their confrontation with social, religious, and political institutions, including cosmopolitan and imperial ones, which were considerably different from their own, and which had an impact on the social basis of their widely dispersed tribal bands. The phase of Afghan political supremacy in north India under the Lodi and the Sur dynasties during the fifteenth–sixteenth centuries manifested a protracted period of migration that had begun as early as 1200, seeking military service or agricultural or pastoral lands. Even as the Afghans migrated to India in search of *naukari* or *chakari* (service) and, if possible, a *wilayat* to ensure protection of the dignity and honour of the clan and the tribe, they remained organised as war-bands, ready to migrate with their family, tents, and flocks to whichever camp their chiefs would decide upon. The Pashtuns, in particular, came in search of commerce and a military career; in fact, their primary centres of political and cultural strength lay in the subcontinent. These factors apart, it was trade in horses, a major profitable business enterprise, that induced the Afghans to migrate and constituted them into a significant trading diaspora. Their value was further enhanced by their expertise, experience with, and access to war horses. Many of the Indo-Afghan rulers, including the Lodi and Sur Sultans, the eighteenth-century chiefs of Rohilkhand and Kasur, had begun their careers in Hindustan as horse traders and developed their territorial frontiers along the trade routes to Central Asia. For the people of Roh, India was the land of wealth and economic gains, and for them, it was the *eastward ho* that appealed to their sense of opportunity. In other words, trade incentives and commercial vitality determined Afghan migrations, evidently acknowledged in the Rohilla classic *Khulasat ul-Ansab*, which discussed the lure of Indian wealth by referring to *qismat-abkhwur* (share of fortune), thus nullifying the official Afghan accounts that claimed *jihad* against the *kuffar* of Hind as the primary objective of migration.

The Lodi and the Sur rulers patronised the migrant warriors and adopted such migration strategies as facilitated Afghan settlements in northern India (particularly in Punjab), and later in Deccan. Additionally, what is worth noting, as commented upon by *Waqi'at-i-Mushtaqi* of Shaikh Rizqullah Mushtaqi (1581) and *Tarikh-i-Sher Shahi* of Ahmad Yadgar (1572–76), is the extensive integration of the Afghans into the Indian social and religious systems during the Lodi and the Sur period, facilitated by their connections with the Sufi saints and transcending all kinship and ethnic ties. It is evident from *wajh i-ma'ash* and *wajh i-amlak* land grants that while the Afghan notables owed allegiance to their exclusive saints, they also patronised the non-Afghan Sufis and their shrines, particularly the saints of the Chishti Sufi orders during the Lodi and Sur rule. Sikandar Lodi, for instance, patronised a number of Sufi saints, including the immigrant Syrian Qadiri Sufi, Muhammad Ghaws, who had settled in Uchch and lived there until his death in 1517. The most important amongst the numerous non-Afghan Sufis who enjoyed patronage from the courts of the Lodis and Surs was Abdul Quddus Gangohi (d. 1537). Dattu Sarwani (1546–47), an Afghan soldier and a notable who penned an autobiographical account of his association with several Sufi saints, was one of the prominent disciples of Gangohi. Sher Shah, too, is supposed to have made a pilgrimage to the shrine of Moin-ud-din Chishti at Ajmer after defeating Humayun. Moreover, the Afghan diaspora could connect with other social groups with ease, supported by the decision of their leaders to patronise Persian rather than Pashto as the language of the court and wider communication.

Notwithstanding the agricultural and commercial wealth that inspired the Afghan diaspora, it was military service that proved worthwhile in providing the Afghans access to power and status, and an incentive to the Lodis to exploit the fragmented politics of northern India. Early sixteenth-century India was a witness to a number of regional states, comprising the principality of Kashmir, the Langah kingdom of Multan (southern Punjab), and the kingdom of Sind under the Jams. Punjab, with its capital at Lahore, was a *suba* (province) of the Lodi kingdom, the foundation of which was laid after Bahlol Lodi, a descendant of the Afghan-Khalji confederation, displaced the Sayyid dynasty in 1451. It is alleged that Bahlol Lodi's elevation to the throne was connected to the blessings of the Chishti saints. Mushtaqi described the pre-ordained good fortune of Bahlol Lodi and observed that the destiny of great men was always decided by 'higher powers'. He referred to the bestowal of kingship on Bahlol Lodi by a *majzub*

Box 3.1: Shaikh Rizqullah Mushtaqi

Shaikh Rizqullah Mushtaqi was a Sufi and belonged to the Shattari order of Sufism. A scholar, poet, and a linguist with knowledge of Arabic, Persian, and Hindavi, his work represents the transitional phase between the Delhi Sultanate and the Mughal period. He led the prayers for Lodi nobles but spent most of his time in understanding history, collecting historical anecdotes, and telling stories. Equipped with requisite knowledge of the period (fifteenth and early sixteenth-century north India), Mushtaqi's text, *Waqi'at-i-Mushtaqi*, could have been a complete historical account within a chronological framework; however, he preferred to focus on historical events and incidents that related to the Lodi Sultans, early Mughal emperors, scholars, and saints of the time, as well as some provincial rulers.

In his Introduction to *Waqi'at*, Mushtaqi explains how it came to be written. He states that he used to narrate stories to friends who often took notes, and then many began urging him to write. It is alleged that Shaikh Farid Bukhari was a major force in persuading Mushtaqi to compile and record his reminiscences or *waqi'at*. *Waqi'at-i-Mushtaqi* can, in a way, be considered as belonging to the genre of *malfuzat*, but in political terms, it stands between the reigns of the Afghans and the Mughals and represents two different political understandings and views, that is, political rationalism and the mystical and mysterious powers of a Sufi. Mushtaqi wrote about the Afghans at a time when Afghan rule was over and appeared to be irreversible. He thus recounted with admiration the events of the reigns of the Lodis and the Surs, and stressed on their *akhlaq* (ethics, character) to demonstrate that no one, neither kings nor even the Shaikhs, existed any longer with such morals.

(a saintly person who had renounced the world) and narrated the nocturnal encounter of Bahlol Lodi at the grave of Qutb ud-Din Bakhtiyar Kaki in Delhi. While praying there, Bahlol Lodi saw a mysterious figure appear from the world of the unseen (*mardi az ghayb*), probably the saint himself, who handed him a *chubi* (wooden stick) and assured him of his assistance in the campaign and control of northern India. Having said this, Mushtaqi cited anecdotes and linked Bahlol Lodi's emergence to power to his political and military abilities, thus demonstrating the two fundamental interpretations of the world: political rationalism and mysterious elements.

Nizam-ud-din Ahmad Bakshi and Sujan Rai Bhandari, too, alluded to Bahlol Lodi's religiosity, his engagement with the *faqir*s (holy men), the learned and the wise, his piety, his abiding loyalty to the laws of the Prophet, and his commitment to justice and equality. Eulogising and commending Bahlol Lodi's usurpation of the throne from his rival Sayyid Alauddin Alam Shah, Ahmad Yadgar described the latter as incapable and unfit to rule because of his 'pathetic weakness (*zabunbakht*), serene countenance and nature and a bashful constitution'. These traits, Yadgar averred, rendered the Sayyid Sultan redundant and weak in his determination for vengeance (*intiqam*), which proved contrary to the rule of kingship. Bahlol Lodi governed as a *primus inter pares*, declared his empire to be a sort of confederation of tribes, and proclaimed to the chieftains of Afghanistan that he would share all his possessions with them, except the sovereignty of India. This inspired the Afghans to descend to the plains 'like ants and locusts' to be in the service of Bahlol Lodi, as Abbas Khan Sarwani commented in his *Tarikh-i-Sher Shahi*, even as he traced the origin of Afghan immigration into northern India. Bahlol Lodi won the support of his Afghan kinsmen by rewarding them with *iqta*s (territorial assignments).

Consequently, the steady flow of the Afghans into Hindustan continued, but so did the problems of legitimacy and authority. The Afghan aristocracy of the Lodi period remained ambivalent towards the Sultan, unwilling to accept the concept of indivisible monarchy. But the unperturbed Lodi Sultans continued the trend and made efforts to strengthen and consolidate kingship. They invoked tribal lineages and customs for conquest and mobilisation; and once that was achieved, they set aside the tribal customary practices and asserted their sovereignty by appropriating the diverse traditions and symbols of power that were used earlier by the Sultans of Delhi, namely *khutba*, issuing *sikka*s in their own name, collecting revenue, using architecture as a visual representation of royal authority, and, under compelling circumstances, even rejecting the injunctions of the *sharia't* in matters of governance, especially if it concerned the non-Muslims.

The second Lodi Sultan, Sikandar Lodi (1489–1517) did exactly that. Mushtaqi described him as one known for his leanings towards Sufis, supernatural powers, commitment to *dervish*es, and as blessed by Sufi Shaikh Sama-ud-din. However, he was also a political realist who upheld the traditions of kingship, discreetly asserted royal authority without outraging aristocratic sentiments, succeeded in abating the internecine conflicts amongst the Afghans (Afghan immigrants comprised a large section of the ruling group in the Lodi Sultanate, although there was a considerable group of non-Afghans as well), and extended his territory from the Indus to Bihar with his capital located at the newly-founded city of Agra. Sikandar Lodi's son and successor, Ibrahim Lodi (1517–26), the last sultan of the dynasty (1517–26), assayed a more vigorous role for himself as the Sultan. Affirming his powers, he purged any thought of equality or clannish affinity from the minds of his nobles and treated them as subordinates rather than as compatriots, thus intensifying factional hostilities amongst his Afghan *amirs*, who turned recalcitrant by either declaring their independence to affirm their inherited customs and rights, or sought the support of rulers like Babur in Kabul. Such dissensions caused Babur to raid western Punjab in 1520, occupy Lahore in 1524, and march upon Delhi to defeat Ibrahim Lodi in the battle of Panipat in 1526 (see Image 3.1). Later, Babur curbed the remnants of the Afghan opposition in the battle of Ghaghara in 1529. These battles, as Babur narrated in his autobiography, were inspired by his *mulkgirliq* or imperial ambitions fuelled by his Timurid identity, although this aspect would presumably have had a bare impact on the determination of his multiethnic army.

These triumphs of Babur, however, did not herald the end of Afghan rule in Hindustan. Undeterred, Sultan Mahmud Lodi raised a fresh Afghan army in Bihar. Although Humayun succeeded in routing Mahmud Lodi's army, he could hardly prevent the revival of Afghan power in the east under Sher Khan Sur, whose grandfather had migrated from Afghanistan in pursuit of a military career and later served the Lodis in Punjab. In recognition of Sher Khan's military credits, Babur had recruited him as a soldier during the battle of Ghaghara in 1529. Subsequently, around 1532, Sher Khan proclaimed himself master of Bihar and continued to escalate his power by conquering Bengal in 1536 and defeating Humayun at Chausa and Kanauj in 1539 and 1540, respectively. Later, he crowned himself and adopted the title of Sher Shah, followed by the occupation of Agra, Delhi, and Lahore. To consolidate his power and authority and build legitimacy, Sher Shah patronised not just the Sur clan that lived in Hindustan or those that had migrated from Roh, but the entire Afghan *qaum* (clan), which he successfully mobilised by insisting on the abandonment of the principle of clan loyalties. He believed that clan divisions were not only *fazul* (impertinent), but unnecessary *himaqat* (stupidity). Consequently, the entire Afghan population, whether Batini, Sarbini or Gharghashti, were united as 'brothers' and motivated to defeat and drive out the Mughals.

Afghan historians like 'Abdullah and Ahmad Yadgar have showered laurels on Sher Shah for his valour, masculinity, and warrior-like qualities, while Humayun was ridiculed as a 'pleasure-seeker' (*ayyash*), 'comfort-loving' (*faraghatdust*), and a 'delicate king' (*padshahilatif*). The Mughal emperor's overzealous forbearance and magnanimity towards his brother Kamran were read as his weakness, which cast a shadow on his masculinity. His failure to avenge his defeat and his lack of the aggression and fortitude exemplified by Sher Shah, Kamran, and Babur had a detrimental effect on Humayun's image as a king, even though the emperor personified clemency. Sher Shah, on the other hand, was acclaimed by Sarwani, 'Abdullah, and Harawi as an ideal ruler for his welfare measures, charity, *madad-i ma'ash* grants (revenue-free land grants), justice and, above all, for embodying Afghan unity, restoring and improving the state system from what it had been under the Lodis. Ni'matullah stated that Sher Shah received kingship on account of his personal piety and in accordance with Muslim cosmology, which considered kingship a divine bestowal. In his *Tarikh-i-Khan-i-Jahani wa Makhzan-i-Afghani*, he provided an elaborate description of a dream that Sher Shah had on the eve of the battle of Chausa. Sher Shah, as Ni'matullah believed, dreamt that both he and Humayun were summoned by the Prophet, who informed

Image 3.1: Scene from the First Battle of Panipat, 1526. Illustration taken from Babur's autobiography, *Baburnama*

Source: https://commons.wikimedia.org/wiki/File: The_battle_of_Panipat_and_the_death_of_Sultan_Ibrahim_the _last_of_the_Lodi_Sultans_of_Delhi.jpg.

Humayun of the conferment of kingship upon Sher Shah, and then took away the royal crown from Humayun and gave it to Sher Shah, with the instruction to practice justice (*adl-wa-insaf*) amongst his people. Through this narration, Ni'matullah probably wished to reiterate that the *'ulama* and the Sufis had begun to desert the Mughals.

While studying Sher Shah's administration, it is imperative to investigate whether his power base differed institutionally from that of the Lodis. Dirk Kolff (1990) argued that at the outset, his reign presented a new departure in north Indian history. Sher Shah transformed the segmented aristocratic military polity and entered the 'military labour market'—which generated socio-religious identities—to raise an army that comprised not only Afghans but also diverse communities of north India (including the agrarian-based troopers), cutting across ethnic identities such as Turks, *Shaikhzada*s, and Rajputs, whose loyalty he ensured through a regular salary and consistent discipline. To maintain order and stability in cavalry, he instituted the practice of *dagh* or branding of horses, and *chehra* or *hulia* or descriptive rolls of the soldiers (introduced earlier by Alauddin Khalji in the fourteenth century). Sher Shah ordered the branding of horses and inspection of the rolls of soldiers in his presence before their monthly pay was announced, or monthly emoluments were fixed for the new recruits. This was done to preclude any distinction (*farq*) between the rights of the nobles and the soldiers and prevent the nobles, as under Ibrahim Lodi, from dismissing the soldiers or depriving them of their dues, or even appropriating large sums once they (nobles) had acquired *iqta'* and were elevated to the position of *muqata* (revenue farmer).

To facilitate regular payments to the army, maintain military discipline, and ascertain the fidelity of soldiers, Sher Shah introduced innovations in land revenue administration and sought to systematise land revenue assessment and collection by introducing the 3 *rai'* (crop rate) system. This entailed the measurement of the land under cultivation; division of the cultivated area into three categories—good, middling, bad; calculation of the total produce of these three categories of land to obtain an average of the total produce, and fixing one-third of the average produce as the State's share. The 3 *rai'* system, defined as *zabt* under Sher Shah, was further evolved by Akbar and his revenue minister Raja Todar Mal to synchronise the crop rates with the local variations. Regardless of the 3 *rai'* system, no uniform system of assessment prevailed under Sher Shah. Distinct local methods were applied according to regional customary practices like *batai*, or sharing of crops between the peasants and the State, and *nasaq*. *Batai* was practised in three ways:

(*i*) *Khet batai*, or fixing of the share while the crop was still standing in the fields;
(*ii*) *Rasi batai*, that is, when the share was fixed after the harvest; and
(*iii*) *Lang batai*, or determining the shares after the crop was removed from its chaff.

The exact meaning of *nasaq* was not clear under Sher Shah, but if the sixteenth-century definition as formulated by Abu'l Fazl is applied, it would mean the fixing of revenue on the basis of the previous year's estimate of the average yield. Sher Shah recognised *kharaj* (land revenue) as the main source of income and preferred its payment in cash, although it could also be paid in kind, especially in areas under *batai* or some specific areas under *nasaq*.

Further, he reformed the currency system by introducing a new silver *tanka*, thus standardising the silver-based monetary unit called *rupiya*, which acquired greater eminence by the close of the sixteenth century. Another major development in Sher Shah's period was a network of roads around a great arterial road cutting across the centre of the Sur territory, later known as the 'Grand Trunk Road' linking Sonargaon in Bengal to Agra, Delhi, and Lahore. His objectives in fostering road-building activities were many, ranging from its military usefulness to its commercial importance, to improving connections between the Sur territories (especially the Ganga–Yamuna Doab region) and the trade routes extending into Central and West Asia via Kabul and Qandahar (it was Babur who, in the late 1520s, had conceived of the idea to establish a road link from Agra to Kabul). The construction of roads with *dakchauki*s (posts) and *sarai*s (inns) was evidence not just of his public welfare schemes to control highway robberies, but more importantly, was an attempt to ensure State control over the regions, facilitate rapid and secure movement of the army for campaigns, increase trade and commerce, and prevent petty chiefs from harassing the merchants.

In addition to the road network, Sher Shah's major building enterprise, his patronage of architectural projects—mosques, forts, and tombs, in particular the *Purana Qila* in Delhi; *Qila-i Kuhna Masjid* inside the *Purana Qila*; his own enormous octagonal tomb in the midst of an artificial lake in Sasaram, a visual allusion to the abundant waters of paradise described in the Quran, with a particular Quranic verse carved on the tomb's interior prayer niche; and the tombs of his father and grandfather in Sasaram and Narnaul, respectively—is no less valuable. The territorial divisions of Sher Shah's empire and their organisation have aroused much debate amongst historians, although the primary sources have been considerably quiet on the issue. Yet it cannot be denied that Sher Shah was engaged in constant experimentation in different regions and at various levels of his empire. Notwithstanding the idealised portrayal of his rule by contemporary sources, with Sarwani almost depicting him as 'proto-Akbar', he was indeed a key factor in anticipating several institutions that developed under the Mughals, for which Akbar has invariably held the credit.

Islam Shah succeeded in maintaining the administrative rigour of his father, but could barely contain the recalcitrance of the Afghan nobles that led to intense internal conflict after his death, providing Humayun the opportunity to defeat Sikandar Sur (Islam Shah's son) and recover his empire in 1555, thus ending the cosmopolitan diversions of Afghan culture and displacing a dominant ethnic group in north India. The Afghans, consequently, were compelled to redefine themselves by resorting to either rebellion or accommodation, or serving the Mughal State and competing with the Irani, Turani, and Rajputs for power and influence in the imperial system.

There were a few instances of Afghan resistance against the Mughals, but in general most Afghans co-operated with them in establishing a stable imperial and commercial network. The Yusufzais, along with the mercantile tribes in the Peshawar region, had allied with the Mughals in 1530 to oust the Dilazak Afghans along the Khyber route. Several local Afghans had joined Mughal service and received potential *jagir*s in lieu of a cash salary across the river Indus. For example, following the migration of the Yusufzais, the Muhammadzai-Khweshgi Afghans moved into Hashtnagar. The Khweshgis, generally known as horse traders, had provided horses and mercenaries to both Babur and Humayun and supported them against the resistance and challenges of the Surs. In return for their service, the Khweshgis were assigned *jagir*s in Kasur and appointed *faujdar*s of Lakhi jungle, a region associated with horse-breeding and comprising a large grazing area where horses from Central Asia could rest and revive themselves before being despatched further into the Indian peninsula. Many other Afghan tribes were assigned the task of guarding the passes through the mountain ranges of the northwest. For instance, the Afridi Afghans were asked to guard the Khyber Pass and the Khalils were assigned the task of shielding the road between Attock and Khyber. These tribes were thus transformed into imperial customs officials, who could levy transit duties and facilitate their incorporation into the Mughal imperial service.

Yet there were a few Afghan groups and individuals like Bayazid Ansari, the founder of the millenarian Raushaniyya movement, who undermined the Afghan political establishment. Ansari was not an Afghan but a Barki, whose parents had moved from Waziristan to Punjab. Along with his father, he was engaged in the horse trade between India and Central Asia; and as a merchant, he often complained against the oppressive levies imposed by the Mughal government. But by the first half of the seventeenth century, in an attempt to negotiate with the Raushaniyyas, the Mughal emperors invited its leaders to join the imperial service as *mansabdar*s and promised them *jagir*s in north India. It was felt that the spiritual disposition and political leadership of the Raushaniyyas could attract members from the tribal Raushaniyya community of Roh to join the Mughal service. The Raushaniyya movement lost its millenarian and mystical appeal by the latter half of the seventeenth century; yet it retained its power to recruit Afghan mercenaries for the Mughal Empire. Many of these recruits were Bangash Pathans who later established their own principality in Farrukhabad. In the late seventeenth century, with the expansion in trade relations, the Afghan merchants and mercenaries were further motivated to supply horses and military labour to India. Their talent for handling horses not only proved rewarding, but also served as an incentive to migrate from their homeland and make India their permanent home.

KINGSHIP AND POLITY: EVOLUTION AND TRANSFORMATION, 1526–75

To understand the transition from Afghan-style sovereignty to Mughal sovereignty, it is pertinent to raise the issue of the Mughals' exclusive claim to sovereign status while other members of the lineage were excluded from it. Nevertheless, the succession strife continued to exist, although the number of claimants to the throne was narrowed down by the insistence on direct descent. These issues of ideological significance are a matter of curiosity, especially since the Mughals traced their ancestry to Timur and Chingiz Khan, both of whom stood for notions of shared political sovereignty and distribution of appanage among the male descendants of the royal family. Nevertheless, the Timurid-Chingizi ideology of inheritance was fraught with an inherent problem of succession that was unique to not only Turko-Mongol or Central Asian steppe societies, but was also noticed throughout the Middle East. In fact, even when pastoral nomadic tribes developed into sedentary societies, established states, and enforced complex bureaucratic administrative patterns, succession conflicts continued. Succession rivalries affected all Turkic empires initially, entailing a distinct handling of it by the Ottomans, Safavids, Uzbeks, and the Timurid-Mughals.

Babur was a progeny of Chingiz Khan's second son, Chaghatai, a ruler of western Central Asian territories, the region where Timur subsequently rose to power. Babur was descended on his father's side from Timur through Abu Sai'd of Herat, while his maternal grandfather was Yunus Khan of Tashkent, Great Khan of the Mongols, and thirteenth in the line of descent from Chingiz Khan. Succeeding his father to the throne of the small Central Asian principality of Farghana at the age of eleven, Babur adapted the contemporary Central Asian steppe tradition that encouraged all male members of the wider Chaghatai and Timurid families (from whom the Mughals claimed descent) to stake their claims to political sovereignty, and provided further incentives to members of the royal clan to compete for power even more aggressively and fiercely. By the late fifteenth century, Babur found himself involved in a scramble for power along with the other Chaghatais and Timurids, who also claimed descent, however nominal, from Chingiz Khan, for the territories in Central Asia. Encountering several disappointments and defeats, Babur moved to Kabul, which he confiscated from his uncle in 1504.

In 1507–08, subsequent to the Uzbek capture of Herat, Babur assumed the title of *Padshah*, claiming to be the sole surviving Timurid to rule a kingdom and thus setting aside the much favoured and commonly used title of *Mirza* (a ruler's son) in Central Asia in those times. (It may be worth noting that Timur himself never used any title higher than *amir*, although Timur's successor Shah Rukh had adopted the lofty Turkish titles of *Padshah* and *Sultan-ul Azam*.) Generally, till Babur, Timurid rulers of Central Asia did not assume the title of *Khaqaan* (Khan of Khans), which implied that they continued to acknowledge the special status of the Khans of Mughulistan even after rejecting their formal overlordship. Babur became the first Timurid prince to take on the supreme Mongol title of *Khaqaan*. Contemptuous of the 'Mughals' settled in Central Asia, Babur preferred to address his maternal uncles, the Khans of Kashghar and Khotan, as 'Chaghatai Khans' rather than 'Mughal'. (The term 'Mughal' was used for the nomadic tribes of Mughulistan, suggesting a hierarchical division—'Mughal' and 'Turk'—among the people of Mughulistan.)

Emulating the norms of patriarchy as enforced in Central Asia to determine social and dynastic identity, Babur described himself as a Timurid and a Turk and used the two expressions to ascertain the features of his lineage. Yet for him, his matrilineal identity was as important. His inner coterie and commanding military officials comprised both Timurids and Chaghatai Mongols. He further sealed his links with the Mongols by negotiating the marriages of two of his daughters with Chaghatai Mongols prior to his death in 1530. Irrespective of these connections, Babur apparently despaired at the idea of shared sovereignty and its inherent weakness, sufficiently evident from his memoirs, wherein he twice alluded to the lines from Sa'di's *Gulistan*: *'Dah darwish dar gilimi bakhuspanad, ve du padshah dar iqlimi nakunjanad!'* ('Ten poor men may sleep under one blanket, but two kings cannot fit into one clime!'). Despite his realisation of the latent tensions present in the distribution and sharing of territories amongst his royal sons,

Babur was adamant about continuing the traditional Timurid-Chingizi principle of partitioning the empire. The degree of autonomy that he intended for his sons as provincial governors was not known to anyone, including Humayun, whom he had nominated as his successor, thus initiating an unwritten law of primogeniture for his dynasty. The ambiguities in political succession and the complexities of the related custom of distributing appanage amongst the male members of the royal family became even more overwhelming over the years, when any son, brother or nephew could participate in the contest for power and challenge the rights of the eldest son as the nominated heir.

Court intrigues, competition, rivalries, and sometimes even violence within the royal family did not seem disconcerting enough for the Mughals, or perhaps were not sufficiently efficacious to prompt them into instituting a code of succession. One reason for this could have been their abiding interest in and loyalty to the unspoken norm derived from Islamic law and Turko-Mongol ideas, which pledged an equal share to all sons in their father's patrimony and equal right to all males of the ruling family to ascend the throne. These patterns were particularly dominant during the early Timurid rule prior to 1556, a period when Mughal rule appeared more like a 'corporate-style clan dynasty' inspired by Central Asian patterns, with Babur as a fundamentally steppe clan leader, albeit a victorious one.

It was not just Babur who claimed a Turkish identity; even the nobles who accompanied him comprised Turkish-speaking Turanis. In fact, the Chaghatais of Farghana were predominantly Turkish-speaking. Babur, whose mother tongue was Turkish, was unaware of the 'Mughal' dialect and therefore characterised his Central Asian nobles and soldiers as Turks. He perhaps also did so with the objective of separating them from the 'local' soldiers of Bhira. The Turkish-speaking Turanis were of Mongol descent but had abandoned the Mongol language and a few Mongol social norms in support of the Turkish language and Central Asian customs. So the status and character of the Timurid royalty and its connections with the nobility continued to be determined by traditions formulated under the early Mongol *Khaqaan*s, referred to as *Yasa-i Chingizi, Yasa-i Chaghatai, Tura-i Chingizi*, and *Tura-i Chaghatai*. This indicates that Mongol patterns had a remarkable impact not only in Kashghar and other parts of Mughulistan, but also on the Timurids of Transoxiana.

Babur observed in his autobiography that while *Tura-i Chingizi* was a major instrument in governing the nomads of Mughulistan, it barely had any influence on the Turkishised Muslim 'Mughals' settled in Central Asia. Yet it was the latter who recognised *Yasa-i Chingizi, Yasa-i Chaghatai, Tura-i Chingizi*, and *Tura-i Chaghatai* as the primary source of tradition. In this context, it may be averred that Babur's assumption of the title of *Khaqaan* in 1526 and 1527 and the proclamation of himself as *ghazi* (registered on the coins along with *Khaqaan*) in 1527 were attempts by the Timurids to revive certain Chingizi institutions that had been relegated to the background since the time of Timur.

The Chingizi traditions of kingship that gave a tribal character to Mongol polity and were strongly influential in the Timurid state till Babur's reign overruled any form of absolutism comparable to Turkish monarchy, despite the belief in the divinity of the sovereign. The principle enforced in Chingiz Khan's empire was that the empire belonged not to the ruler but to the ruling family, implying that all those who descended from Chingiz Khan were a part of the royal lineage and thus shared sovereignty. Also, as per the Mongol code, a king (at least theoretically) was dependent on the support of the nobles since his elevation to the throne was determined by the princes and high officials from amongst the descendants of Chingiz Khan. Moreover, as sanctioned by the *Tura*, a large section of the nobility enjoyed hereditary rights. For instance, the descendants of the three mythical figures—Bukhu Khatagi, Bukhatu Salji, and Bodaunchar—who were divinely ordained and owed their birth to supernatural dispensation, had a special status. The progeny of three of Chingiz Khan's lieutenants also held hereditary privileges and so did the nobles who claimed ancestry from Chingiz Khan. The rights of none of these categories could be withheld or curtailed by the king without violating the Mongol code. Significantly, nobles from all these groups formed a large part of Babur's nobility.

Even as Babur's nobility remained strongly clannish and attached to its privileges, Babur aspired for more power and authority; the two developed contradictions, making their co-existence problematic and leading to military and administrative hardships. Babur could maintain some semblance of control and authority probably because a large section of the nobility that served him in Hindustan were elevated from ordinary ranks and positioned as *amir*s by the emperor. Thus, irrespective of their attachment to their lineage, they remained loyal to Babur. During his four-year stint as emperor, none of these nobles contested Babur's authority or took advantage of his informal behaviour at the convivial, *ma'jun* parties; resistance came from the Indian chiefs, the Afghans, and the Shaikhzadas (popularly known as Indian Muslims) who had joined his retinue after the victory at Panipat. What is even more noteworthy is Babur's success in overpowering the political ambitions of all other clans and focusing imperial attention on his sons. That is, even while adhering to *Tura*, he heralded a transition for the Timurids, as argued by Munis Faruqui (2012), from 'royal descent group' to 'stem dynasty', a succession practice that continued through Humayun's reign, reaching its culmination under Akbar when it was firmly established that the legitimate claimants for the imperial throne were only the direct male descendants of the emperor. It was perhaps for this reason that, despite the machinations of Babur's close aides, it was Humayun and not Babur's brother-in-law and loyalist, Mahdi Khwaja, who ascended the throne after the emperor's death.

The difficulties for the Mughals compounded under Humayun when he invoked strategies that articulated an ideology in defence of an all-powerful monarch, distinct from being 'first amongst equals' and with invulnerable authority and intolerance to dissent and impudence. In other words, he patronised a theory that was in complete contrast to Babur's steppe-inspired vision of empire, which was rigidly Timurid in character with Turks and Mongols wielding predominant political power. While Babur had recruited Shaikhzadas to his army, they were kept isolated from his inner coterie. Attempting a new dispensation of sovereignty and a new doctrine of political organisation, Humayun grouped those subordinate to the sovereign into three categories:

- men of *daulat* (fortune), comprising his brothers, other relatives, military and civil officials, and soldiers;

- men of *saadat* (happiness), that is, the *'ulama*, Sufis, and poets; and
- men of *murad* (hope), or the artists, singers, and musicians.

Although he did not live long enough to see any effective transformation, his strategies hardly impressed the nobility, who rarely showed him the kind of regard they had exhibited for Babur. Nor could Humayun inspire the loyalty of his brothers—Mirza Kamran, Mirza 'Askari, Mirza Hindal—and their supporters. His inability to mobilise was probably affected by the fact that he had barely spent three years at the imperial court between 1519 and 1530. Supported by only a few Turani nobles with hardly any social or cultural base in India, Humayun found it difficult to retain his imperial hegemony and was in constant contention with the Afghans, of whom there were allegedly 800,000 families in India (as stated by *Afzal ut-Tawarikh*, an anonymous seventeenth-century Persian chronicle). In fact, from the time of his accession in 1530, Humayun had encountered obstructions, disobedience, and disrespect, at the forefront of which was his brother Mirza Kamran.

As early as 1531, Kamran occupied Punjab in defiance of Humayun's orders, replaced the military officials loyal to the emperor, and resisted the payment of revenue to the imperial treasury. He further bolstered his political ambitions by becoming a devotee of the *Naqshbandi Tariqa* (like his father), securing their support. In 1541, he declared himself the king of Afghanistan and had the *khutba* read in his name. Kamran's growing power resulted in two centres of power, one at Lahore and the other at Agra, although there was no formal division of sovereignty. The conflict between Humayun and Kamran triggered resistance from 'Askari and Hindal, who attempted to seize their autonomy in Gujarat and Agra, respectively. The scramble for power by Humayun's brother affected the attitude of the nobility, which wavered in its loyalty between Humayun and Kamran on the issue of the distribution of *jagir*s. By 1545, as the nobles came to realise the increasing shortage of *jagir*s in Kamran's territories, they began deserting him in favour of Humayun.

Political adversities notwithstanding, Humayun sought to resuscitate his power by initiating the process of strengthening his empire to rid it of the warring and extensive clan system. He began by appeasing the Shaikhzadas to counter the Central Asian nobles and developed ties with individuals like Shaikh Bahlul, a valuable member of the India-based Shattari Sufi order who, by the late 1530s, had emerged as Humayun's ardent supporter and political and religious advisor. Later, the emperor appointed an Indian Muslim cleric, Shaikh Gadai Kambo, as *sadr-us-sudur* (chief of religious endowments) and inducted a large number of Persian Shi'ite nobles into the Mughal nobility. Between 1540 and 1552, the emperor manoeuvered to oust Kamran, weakened his control over Qandahar, and seized Kabul with the support of Shah Tahmasp I of Safavid Iran. To further counter Kamran and consolidate his own position, he revived his relations with the *Naqshbandi*s by confirming their *waqf* (revenue-free charitable grants). Having disabled Kamran's *Naqshbandi* roots, Humayun focused on eliminating his brother and his supporters, particularly Yadgar Nasir Mirza (a first cousin) and Mirza 'Askari, the two who had colluded with Kamran against Humayun. Yadgar Mirza was executed in 1546; 'Askari was ordered into exile in 1550; and Kamran was defeated, captured, blinded, and sent off to Mecca in 1553, where he died in 1557.

By the end of his reign, Humayun had succeeded in sapping the energy of the surviving Mirzas, deprived them of their privileges, and subordinated them to the ranks of the imperial nobility, thus rendering them worthless as potential candidates for the throne. With this, he hoped for the smooth succession of his son, Akbar. However, but for the ill-timed demise of Humayun, Akbar's accession may not have been as easy. The small cadre of nobles who returned to India with Humayun in 1555 comprised a number of Persian Shi'ite nobles, with many holding important offices like that of *mir bakhshi*, *mir munshi*, *diwan*, and *mir saman*. They were willing to accept an invincible *Padshah* according to the Persian imperial tradition, but a significant majority of Turanis (53 per cent of the total), mostly Chaghatai-Turkish in the upper echelons, trained in Central Asian norms of egalitarianism and shared sovereignty, were aware that Mirza Muhammad Hakim, Humayun's infant son, offered a legitimate alternative to Akbar. It was because of apprehensions such as these that Humayun's unexpected death was kept a secret till Akbar returned to the imperial court from his provincial posting in Punjab. While Akbar was accepted as the legitimate heir by the court nobility, he could not escape the constant threats to his power, whether from Afghan and Rajput coalitions beyond the court, or his infant half-brother Mirza Hakim, or Mirza Abu'l Qasim, son of Mirza Kamran, or the subsequent joint rebellions of Mirza Sharaf-ud-Din Husain Ahrari (married to Akbar's half-sister) and Shah Abu'l Ma'ali between 1562 and 1564. There was also the resistance by the Mirzas in 1566 and the north India-based rebellion of 1580–81. Mirza Hakim was alleged to be the key mastermind in the latter revolts.

The first phase of Akbar's reign (1556–60), marked by the tutelage of Bairam Khan as his *ataliq* (regent), was in effect a period of factional tussle and contradiction between the attempts at centralisation by the expanding State and the dominant sections of the nobility comprising Chaghatai and other groups of Turani origin, who were keen to preserve their autonomy and traditional privileges. When Bairam Khan was appointed the *wakil-us-sultanat*, there were many other nobles—Tardi Beg, Munim Beg Khan, Khizr Khan, Khwaja Jalaluddin Mahmud, Khwaja Muazzam, and even Shah Abu'l Ma'ali, a severe critic of Bairam Khan—who could claim the *wikalat* on grounds of long service, blood relationship or past association with Akbar. They accepted Bairam Khan as the regent but with limitations, hoping to share power with him or at least till the Afghan power under the leadership of Hemu was crushed (see Image 3.2). Bairam Khan, on the other hand, was in a dilemma: he wanted to exercise *de facto* sovereign powers and curtail the independence of the nobles, and yet he needed their support to sustain his authority. Anticipating challenges to his power, he began by eliminating all those nobles who could pose a threat to him. This included the dismissal and imprisonment of Shah Abu'l Ma'ali, which met with little opposition since he was unpopular amongst the nobles. In addition, he transferred nobles like Munim Beg Khan (whom he did not trust, yet sought their support) to Kabul so as to restrict their presence in the imperial court; charged Tardi Beg with treachery for the defeat in the battle of Tughlaqabad, and ordered his execution without the consent of Akbar.

To consolidate his position, Bairam Khan prevented those whom he considered rivals, like Munim Beg Khan and Khwaja Jalaluddin Mahmud, from accessing the emperor and appointed his favourites to the primary administrative posts: Pir Muhammad Khan as his personal *wakil*,

Image 3.2: The defeat of Hemu at the Second Battle of Panipat, a painting from the 1590s by Kankar from the *Akbarnama*

Source: https://commons.wikimedia.org/wiki/File:The_defeat_of_Hemu,_*Akbarnama*.jpg.

Khwaja Aminuddin as the *bakshi*, and Shaikh Gadai as the *sadr*. His authoritarianism declined with the arrival of Hamida Banu Begum (Akbar's mother) and Mahamanga (Akbar's foster mother) from Kabul in 1557, compelling him to share power with the other leading nobles. They also forced him to include Akbar actively in all decisions pertaining to administration. As protests increased against his autarchy, Bairam Khan attempted a *coup* in 1559, replaced Pir Muhammad Khan with Muhammad Khan Sistani as his personal *wakil*, gave additional powers to Shaikh Gadai, and granted promotions to low-ranking officials irrespective of merit and/or essential qualifications. Engrossed in manipulations and obsessed with power, Bairam Khan miscalculated the political shrewdness of Akbar. Taking the regent by surprise, the emperor dismissed him in early 1560 and deprived him of all his loyalists, who either declared their loyalty to the emperor or remained neutral.

When Akbar formally assumed the throne, he was still not in a position to abandon fervid vigil against threats to his power. From the early 1560s until the mid-1580s, there were persistent efforts from varied sections to replace Akbar with his half-brother Mirza Hakim. Akbar, however, constantly countered his rivals by either co-opting them (like Mirza Sulaiman of Badakhshan in 1575) or ordering their imprisonment (for instance, that of Muzaffar Husain Mirza in 1577), or even disposing them by directing the death penalty (for example, against Mirza Abu'l Qasim in the mid-1560s, and Ibrahim Husain Mirza and Muhammad Husain Mirza in 1573). Although Akbar was initially protective of Mirza Hakim despite their acute rivalry, the subsequent decades took a different turn until Mirza Hakim's death in 1585, indicating that notwithstanding Humayun's efforts, Mughal succession had yet to gain a strong foothold. Virtually a sovereign ruler of Kabul, Mirza Hakim was tutored according to his father's instructions in the 'manners and customs of Hindustan' and introduced to *ahl-i Hind* (Hindustanis). Portraying himself as different from Akbar, he promoted himself as the guardian of Chaghatai-Timurid political and religious ideals vis-à-vis Akbar's 'Hindustani' image; claimed to be the true heir of Mughal familial traditions; maintained close relations with the rulers of Turan and in particular with Abdullah Khan Uzbek; proclaimed himself a *ghazi* and a devotee of *Naqshbandi Tariqa* like Babur; maintained his grandfather Babur's tomb in Kabul; and demonstrated his eagerness to consolidate orthodoxy by forging an alliance with the Sunni Shah of Persia, Shah Ismail II, who ruled briefly from 1576–77.

In 1570–71 Mirza Hakim attacked the Raushaniyya, a Muslim revivalist and millenarian movement with a strong base amongst the Afghans in the eastern part of his kingdom, and like Babur, attempted to disperse the Afghans and set them against one other. He attracted the attention of those resistant to Akbar and received an invitation to north India in 1566, and then again in 1581, to carry out a massive revolt and dethrone Akbar. His challenges, which kept the empire on edge, proved anticlimactic, primarily owing to his limited influence on Akbar's Indian nobility (although he had significant support amongst the Turani nobles of Akbar's court). On his demise, Akbar incorporated Kabul into the Mughal Empire in 1585 and imprisoned Mirza Hakim's young sons, Kaikobad and Afrasiyab, in India, indicating thus his resolve to end the system of granting appanages to princes. The emperor further weakened the base of Mirza Hakim's loyalists and reconstituted them under his authority to ensure that his sons emerged as the strongest focus of power in the empire. Akbar consolidated his strategic plans into action in 1585 when he granted his sons imperial ranks directly subordinate only to the emperor, that is, himself.

With the impelling need to reconstruct the ideology of the empire, Akbar set out to transform the basic character of Timurid polity. Determined to broaden the base of the Mughal nobility and mark a shift from owing allegiance to merely the Turanis, Akbar inducted two new elements into imperial service—Rajputs and *Shaikhzadas*—and fostered a remarkable increase in the number of Persians, especially in the higher grades. From 1562, central administrative departments were dominated by Iranis, Rajputs and *Shaikhzadas*. Allegedly, of the forty provincial governors (*subadars*), eleven were Iranis, who also monopolised posts like *wazir* and *mir bakhshi*. The Persians had earned extraordinary promotions during the period 1562–67 as a reward for supporting the emperor in curbing the rebellion of the Turani nobles. This affected the significance and strength of the Turanis and led to the erosion of Chaghatai traditions and customs upheld fervently by Babur in particular. This further led to Akbar's alienation from the Turani nobility and the growing conflict between Turanis and Persians, which often assumed a sectarian bias for most Persians followed Shi'ism as opposed to the Turanis, who were Sunnis. Beginning in 1565, such developments had a long-term impact. In the same year, the appointment of a military commander sent against Ali Quli Khan, who, despite his Persian background had led the rebellion of the Uzbeks, was resisted on racial grounds. Later, Mirza Aziz Koka persistently accused Jahangir of favouring the Persians and the *Shaikhzadas*. Such obstructions and accusations were noticed till at least the reign of Farukh Siyar.

The Turani nobles were further estranged by Akbar's administrative measures, which included his decision to discourage clan groups within the nobility and end the concentration of *jagirs* belonging to the same clan of nobles in a region. For instance, subsequent to curbing the Uzbeks in 1567, the *jagirs* of the members of Atka Khail were transferred from Punjab and dispersed throughout the empire, despite their loyalty to the emperor. This provoked the Turani nobles for they were primarily the only clan group to hold contiguous *jagirs*—Uzbeks in the east and Malwa, Mirzas around Sambhal, Qaqshals in Kara-Manikpur, and Atka Khail in Punjab. Any attempt to disperse them was viewed as a way of disintegrating and weakening them. But here again, the responses varied. Not all Turani clans had a large clan base, nor were all as well-knit as the Uzbeks and the Mirzas. Such reactions were explicit in the attitude of nobles like Munim Beg Khan, who showed no defiance but generally remained unaffected by the growing tension, working wherever feasible to reach a reconciliation. The Persians remained indifferent to the emperor's decision to break the continuity of *jagirs*. They had come from the Safavid territories and joined Mughal service under Humayun in minor positions. As yet they had no substantial foundation; they depended on royal patronage and looked for opportunities to be useful to the king. In fact, except for the brief uprising of Asaf Khan in 1565–66, there were no protests by the Persians; to the contrary, they lent their services to the emperor to suppress the Turani rebellions during 1562–67. The *Shaikhzadas* and the Rajputs, too, confident of their strong local roots, showed no anxiety at the dispersal of *jagirs*. They were excluded from the imperial order, given their fresh recruitment and Akbar's possible keenness to cultivate their support.

The Turani nobles were further alienated by other administrative strategies to revitalise Akbar's government. As a step towards the restoration and enhancement of revenue, the emperor ordered the assessment of the revenue arrears of *jagirs* in different *subas* and *wilayats* under the control of the *hakims* (military commanders), most of whom were Turanis. The *jama* (revenue assessed) of these *jagirs*, formerly assigned under Bairam Khan, was written off arbitrarily, causing bankruptcy in the central treasury around 1561. Moreover, in an attempt to systematise the administration, like Humayun in 1533–34, Akbar implemented the separation of routine administration from military functions, excluding the upper echelon of the nobility, mostly Turanis, from the central government and replacing them by professionally competent persons who had risen to distinction not because of their heredity or roots in the nobility, but because of their expertise, merit, and zeal to implement the emperor's decisions. The new cadres of officials appointed to the central departments were mostly *Shaikhzadas* and Rajputs. They included Todar Mal, Abu'l Fazl, Faizi, Birbal, Fathullah Shirazi, Khwaja Shah Mansur, Parmanand, and many others who, notwithstanding their low ranks, acquired importance at the court. The Turanis and the Persians, on the other hand, who held prominent positions were generally deputed to command the frontier provinces like Bengal, Gujarat, and Thatta, especially if they disagreed with the introduction of *dagh* (branding of horses), which placed constraints on them.

For this reason—and perhaps also deprived of their lucrative central imperial postings—the nobles revolted in Bengal in 1580. Among them were Turanis, a few *Shaikhzadas*, Rajputs, and a considerable number of such Persians who had been promoted to high ranks during 1560–67. Akbar crushed these rebellions with the support of the Indian nobles and thus transformed the character of the Mughal nobility. He succeeded in weakening the Chaghatai traditions, curtailed the power and privileges of the Turani nobility, and integrated Indian Muslims and non-Muslims into his administration. The latter comprised

- Barhas and *Shaikhzadas*, primarily with military and service descent;
- Rajput chieftains;
- *Kayasths* and *Khatris*: the caste-based scribal class;
- Indian Muslim clerics;
- Chishti Sufi saints; and
- the Hindu priestly order.

Lest it indicates that centralisation was successfully achieved, it is pertinent to observe that as the empire embraced multiethnicity and diversity, it also moved towards greater complexity, engendered decentralising tendencies and a multi-pronged socio-economic, cultural system in which the resistance and rebellions of the nobility became a prominent feature. Moreover, a close reading of Abu'l Fazl's *Ain-i Akbari* illustrates that despite an elaborate and largely uniform bureaucracy, centralisation was rather slack, perhaps even suspect.

Akbar attempted to reshape Timurid dynastic ideology to reinforce his own legitimacy and that of his progeny, fully aware that it might pre-empt challenges from his Timurid compatriots and even the *'ulama*. The panacea for such apprehensions was provided by his ideologue, Abu'l

Fazl, who defined a theory of sovereignty for the emperor as 'divinely ordained' and with an 'illuminated right to rule' the 'ordinary mortals with lesser qualities', which could overcome threats of conquest, coup or secession. He projected Akbar as a *mujtahid* (interpreter of the *Shari'a*) who surpassed the knowledge of the Sufi *pirs* (teachers) and the charisma of the *mahdi* (saviour). By devising an illuminationist theory of *farr-i izadi* (divine light) and creating a royal cult that resembled the early relationship between the Safavid ruler and the *qizilbash* (their Turkmen tribal followers), Fazl emphasised the personal qualities of the emperor and the concept of single sovereignty rather than a shared one, thus claiming invincibility and invulnerability for Akbar. Such ideas reflected a kingship that facilitated a flexible interpretation of the *Shari'a*, suitable to preserving social harmony particularly in circumstances when population statistics showed Muslims to be in a minority.

FORMULATION OF POWER: RITUALS AND TRADITIONS

Formal legitimacy for the Timurids was initiated in April 1370 when Amir Timur (the *Sahib-i-Qiran*), firmly ensconced on the throne of Samarqand, placed the 'crown of world conquest' on his head and subsequently, in over three decades, ensured his recognition as a true Muslim by getting the *khutba* read in his name from the pulpits of Mecca, Medina, and other public mosques. Emboldened by this act and tracing his dynastic genealogy to Timur, Babur assumed legitimacy and authority for his descendants. The Timurid legacy remained the decisive axis of orientation for the self-determination of the dynasty, even when the empire had reached its apogee. The interest in the political adventure and achievements of the dynasty was not merely symbolic but continued to inspire the Mughals as late as the seventeenth century, with Shahjahan claiming to be the 'second *Sahib-i-Qiran*'.

By the thirteenth century—rather, before the establishment of the Delhi Sultanate in north India—several complexities regarding Islamic royal power and kingship were resolved in Arabia and Persia and a generally accepted normative structure was laid down for a Sunni Muslim king, namely the source of ultimate authority, the codification of the *Shari'a*, the relationship of the *'ulama* to the king, the norms adopted after the decline of the *khalifa*'s (caliph) temporal power, and the specific duties of a Sultan. These idioms were largely emulated by the Sultans of Delhi, evident in their practice of continuing to acknowledge the spiritual authority of the *khalifa*, even though his importance had waned after the destruction of the *khilafat* in 1258. Additionally, the title and the investiture provided by the *khalifa* had become mere symbols of tradition and redundant ornamentation, losing their significance and glamour. The Mughals, however, made a complete break with the custom by not even pretending to acknowledge the *khalifa*, thus emancipating the Mughal State from subservience and bondage to the church, a pattern perceptible from the reigns of Babur and Humayun.

Apropos monarchy were the issues of legitimacy, legal, constitutional, and fundamental roots of sovereignty. In accordance with the Islamic primer, the kingdom belonged to the *millat* (brotherhood), which decided who the ruler would be. There was no law of succession in Islamic polity; traditions and conventions were the dictum and dynastic turmoil a frequent feature.

Rebellion acquired a logical and rightful assent, that is, those who could exercise force and capture the throne were accepted as legitimate rulers (or at least, such was the situation during the Delhi Sultanate). The Mughals effected a change in the pattern of succession, notwithstanding the ensuing confusion. Sovereignty was pronounced the exclusive prerogative of the imperial family, but not without invoking the Mongol custom of dividing the heritage between children and kinsmen. Family became the source of stability and the empire's durability but also the cause of its fragility; no law of primogeniture or theory of kingship was formulated in the real sense, and a scramble for power, court intrigues, and civil rebellions persisted throughout the Mughal period. The Mughal emperors may have succeeded in exalting the empire and the imperial court to splendid heights, but early in their reign they were confronted with the urgent need to shield against tenuous filial bonds.

However, far from weakening the roots of the empire, the political struggle for power within the royal family, argued Munis Faruqui (2012), helped to spread, deepen, and mobilise Mughal power. Understanding the psychological uncertainties that accompanied 'hyper-competitive', 'open-ended' imperial succession politics, each prince who saw himself as a potential emperor with an exposure, training, and education similar to that of the other princes realised the necessity of creating a network of support, building alliances, and outmanoeuvring their male relatives, for it was through their own achievements that they could thrive and attain the throne. The jurists and rulers engaged to protect and raise the prestige of the crown, sustain the imperial system, and legitimise the institution of monarchy, the remarkable feature of which was that it was directly 'tied to the ubiquity of dread' realised that simple reverence and universal desire for a monarch were not sufficient to resolve the problem of authority. Legitimacy of power was imperative. In other words, law was often interpreted according to the interests of the emperor or the powerful stakeholder, political ethics notwithstanding; and this was applicable uniformly to almost all Mughal emperors.

Pragmatism, political rationality, and formalisation of power entailed rituals, customs, and traditions to bolster legitimacy and authority. Mughal sovereignty, in the words of F.W. Buckler (Pearson 1985; *cf* Mukhia 2005, 15–16), was a 'corporate kingship' in which the nobles were 'members' rather than 'servants', similar to the concept of 'court society' and court sociability that Norbert Elias (1983) had applied to study the medieval French monarchy. The imperial court under the Mughals emerged as an arena of activity and knowledge, a complex agency of rule, and an extension of the king's household. It acquired importance as a sociological locale and court culture and reflected a complex set of practices that were formative and constitutive of political life. The coronation ceremony, in this context, was an important occasion. Austere and often spartan, the rite was followed by the acclaim, approval, and personal homage of the nobility and the *'ulama* to the sovereign, accompanied by a presentation of *nazr* and/or *peshkash*. *Nazr*, derived from the Arabic word *nadhr*, or vow, was customarily presented in person and implied an oath of allegiance, whereas *peshkash* could be sent to the ruler and did not necessarily require the personal appearance of the giver. Creating loyalty and acceptance through *nazr* and *peshkash*, the new sovereign reciprocated the gesture by bestowing *khila't* or a robe of honour on regional rulers, nobles, and several others in an attempt to sustain his legitimacy and consolidate authority.

The royal ceremony, known as *khil'at* or *khil'a* in Arabic and *sar-upa* in Persian, can be traced to the early period of the Abbasids in Baghdad. The *khalifa* is known to have presented his old garment or any other belonging to someone who, by this means became (if he was not one already) a dependant. Through this act, the *khalifa*, a divine figure and the *amir-al mu'minin*, allegedly passed on his *baraka* or inner essence or radiance to the recipients. The recipient could be a kinsman, an administrator, military official or a courtier rewarded for his services; men of learning and wisdom, that is, religious persons; literati or musicians. There is a representation of Mahmud of Ghazni that can be traced to 999 CE, wearing a silk robe of honour that he had received from the *Khalifa* of Baghdad. Although *khil'at* had originated in the court of Abbasid *Khalifa*, it did not become denominational but is known to have prevailed in almost all parts of India since the tenth century, whether in the court of the Sultans of Delhi, regional kingdoms (like Gujarat, Rajputana, Vijayanagara), or the Mughal emperors, for whom *khil'at* had acquired a major significance as a symbol of legitimacy.

An instance can be cited from Gujarat in 1526 as an example, when Sultan Bahadur Shah, upon ascending the throne after defeating Imadul Mulk, lavishly distributed wealth, gave *khil'at*s, titles, and assignments to the nobles, enormously enhanced the stipend of the soldiers and granted them one year's wages (*'ulufa*) in advance. Such profusion attracted several others, whether from Rajputana or Deccan, to become his *mulaziman-i-khas* or privileged servants. The custom was subsequently adopted by the Marathas, Mysore (under Tipu Sultan), and even the English East India Company, who also regarded *khil'at* as an important determinant in defining their relationship with the Mughal emperors. *Khil'at* could be awarded not only to men but also to women, children (at the birth of a nephew, Mahmud of Ghazni is said to have sent both mother and child robes of honour), and slaves (who tended to be *mamluk*s and/or eunuchs). By the fourteenth century, the tradition of *khil'at* was extensively adopted by the Sufi orders, with the *murid*s (disciples) keen to receive the robe of their *murshid* (spiritual leader) or the *Shaikh* to deepen their piety and knowledge.

As descendants of Chingiz Khan and Timur, the Mughals were well-accustomed to the practice of *khil'at*. Emulating Timur who had distributed robes of honour to his kinsmen, *amir*s, men of learning, and diplomats subsequent to his victory over the Ottoman Sultan Bayazid Yilderim in 1402, Babur sought to reinforce his authority by the frequent gifting of robes of honour. Following his triumph at Khanua, Chanderi, and Gwalior, Babur organised an extravagant *durbar* at Agra in 1528–29 to distribute *khil'at* to all those who supported him—his kinsmen and religious elite—and to those whose support he looked forward to, that is, his potential rivals. This assembly, as narrated by Babur in his *Tuzuk-i Baburi*, displayed a remarkable public political bonding, festivity, and gift-giving, attended by representatives from Shaibanid and Safavid kingdoms, Indian *raja*s or their *wakil*s, Babur's Chaghatai and Timurid kinsmen, and other notables. *Khil'at*s were also given to those appointed as governors of provinces, who were expected to take an oath of loyalty; for instance, his son-in-law Muhammad Zaman Mirza and sons of his maternal uncle Kichik Khan—Esan Temur Sultan and Tokhta Buqa Sultan—as well as several Afghans formerly in the service of the Lodis or the Sultan of Bengal.

More interestingly, Babur also related the significance of the *khil'at* that was given to kinsmen as an assurance of their fidelity. In this context, he mentioned the support of his mother's brothers, Mahmud Khan of Tashkent and Ahmad Khan of Aqsu (referred to in the *Tuzuk-i Baburi* as Ulugh Khan and Kichik Khan, respectively). In 1502–03, Kichik Khan allegedly greeted Babur in the customary 'Mughal' style and presented him with a range of apparels equivalent to robes of honour: the *bas-ayaq* (Turki term for a robe of honour of several pieces, similar to the Persian *sar-upa*). Babur narrated that these strategies and tactics subordinated him completely to his powerful relative.

Khil'at acquired a diverse character under the Mughal emperors as an act of political bonding, a relationship of fealty that confirmed personal ties between the emperor and his officers, symbolising patronage and protection, clientage and service, an extraordinary act of favour and/or recognition of some exceptional service to the empire. *Khil'at* defined imperial munificence and extravagance that became the basis of political relations and buttressed sovereignty. In the *khil'at* ceremony—a public ceremony with full audience—in which the receiver's special status was acknowledged, the most valuable was a garment or set of garments worn personally by the emperor (*malbus-i khas*). If the emperor did not give the clothes or belongings taken off his body, he touched it with his palm or it was brushed across his shoulder before being handed over, to infuse it with his *baraka*. Receiving the *khil'at* was considered an honour, but it was equally an acknowledgement of the subordination by the receiver to the emperor, replicated in a number of court ceremonies such as *kurnish* and *taslim*—two customs that were an expression of the receiver's loyalty and submission and a reminder that he owed his elevation to his subordination. It gave the receiver, as Harbans Mukhia (2005) suggested, his *raison d'être*.

The symbols of legitimacy that bolstered the authority of the new emperor included the *khutba*—the sermon read by the *'ulama* in the name of the emperor during the Friday *namaz* (prayer service) in mosques throughout the realm; and the *sikka* (coins) minted in the name of the emperor, bearing his titles, and date and place of accession. The Mughal coin, especially the silver rupee that weighed about 11 grams, was a testimony to the continued sophistication and standard of the imperial coin. The quality and quantity of the imperial coinage devised under Akbar was maintained by the imperial mints located throughout the empire. As the empire expanded, so did the circulation of the rupee and its copper and gold counterparts. The other prominent symbols of the emperor's authority included the yak tails of Turko-Mongol kingship, the throne and other symbolic adornments of Persian kings, the umbrella, drums, peacock fans, as well as the emblems of Indian rulers. An imperial ritual that reinforced the authority of the emperor and demonstrated the loyalty of the people was the *jharokha*, a practice initiated by Akbar emulating the Rajput royal custom. Customarily, the emperor appeared on a balcony in the early morning, to be seen by the people as a reassurance of his well-being. It was a ceremony where people could pay their obeisance and, if need be, tender petitions. *Jharokha* perpetuated the Persian tradition that expected the king to be accessible to his subjects to redress their grievances, and resembled the military audiences held by the Turkish Sultans of Central Asia. The Mughal emperors could thus symbolise and assert their authority by weaving together different cultural strands.

NORMS OF GOVERNANCE: *AKHLAQ* AND *SHARI'A*

Tura-i Chingezi or *Yasa-i Chingezi* (Code of Chingiz Khan) was held in high esteem by the Mughals and guarded zealously as their Central Asian heritage. Jahangir often cited the *Tura* in his memoirs to uphold the importance of kinship ties, promote the notion of respect for the old and the senior, and demonstrate how regard for the elders informed a normative imperial hierarchy. A similar predisposition to order, stability, and obedience to the ruler was enunciated in *akhlaq* literature—a corpus of ethical thinking—that inspired the Mughal emperors and served as advice literature. *Akhlaq-i Padshahan*—an anonymous text commissioned by an unnamed prince and completed in 1645—provided an imposing panorama of the powers and duties of a king. The king, it observed, was obliged to maintain order in the universe, protect all living beings, uphold truth and justice, and reward the deserving. The king, in other words, was not a mere political figurehead but the one who maintained social harmony and justice, was primary to ensuring the daily existence of his subjects, and whose influence and significance extended beyond the political to the cosmological. *Akhlaq-i Padshahan* further observed that the king's laws and the *shari'a* 'are like two sons born from the womb of the same mother, like two rings on the same finger', and obedience to one entailed obedience to the other. Therefore, any form of disorder, strife or rebellion had to be necessarily severely punished.

Norms of legitimate rule and attributes of kingship, as perceived in the fourteenth and fifteenth-century Islamic world, emphasised *'adalet* (justice, that is, reward and punishment by the ruler for good and evil deeds) and the 'theme of the ruler as shepherd of his people'. This thinking about the primary responsibilities of medieval and early modern Muslim rulers, derived from pre-Islamic Sassanid Persia, particularly from the kingly practices of legendary Iranian ruler Khusrau I Anushirvan (531–579 CE), and the Islamic literary genre of advice to kings or 'mirrors for princes' widely influenced the monarchs and people in the Islamic world. The ancient Iranian text, *Mirror for Princes*, translated into Arabic during the tenure of the Abbasid dynasty, inspired a new genre of ethics, that is, *akhlaq*, which became popular throughout the Persianised world. Emulating the model of kingship of the pre-Islamic kingdom of Sassanid Persia, *akhlaq* focused on the celebration of the achievements of monarchy and asserted that kings had to be judged differently for they were divinely anointed and answerable only to God. With such a philosophical mandate, the later Abbasid rulers posed as 'deputies' of God, a practice followed subsequently by the Turk Sultans of Central Asia and the Sultans of Delhi in the thirteenth century, particularly Iltutmish and Balban, who claimed descent from an ancient line of Turanian kings and described themselves as 'shadows of God on earth'. In this context, it becomes imperative to consider the impact of the *akhlaq* tradition and its relation with Mughal political ideals and administrative norms.

Akhlaq represented a genre of writing in medieval Persian literature that comprised philosophical discussions on justice, ethical and moral codes, and an advisory to princes on norms of comportment and ways to achieve a stable social order interspersed with *Quranic* verses and traditions of the Prophet relevant to universal human values. Many of these texts also contained discourses on family, household (*tadbir-i manzil*), politics, and state organisation (*siyasat, mamlikatdari*).

Akhlaq often displayed features of *insha*; in fact, the two significantly overlapped. A treatise on *akhlaq* could contain correspondence manuals or copies of correspondences while *insha* could hold copies of advice that read like an *akhlaq* text; the best example was the autobiographical and *akhlaqi* constituents in the writings of Chandar Bhan Brahman. The influence of Greek and Persian ethical virtues was notable on these otherwise medieval Muslim intellectual texts, particularly in the chapters on statecraft, as pointed out by Muzaffar Alam (2000, 67) and Christopher Bayly (1998, 13–17). While Bayly suggested that *akhlaq* understood the science of good government in concrete terms and not as an abstract science, Alam talked of *akhlaq* literature as the best example of appropriation of non-Islamic—and, in some instances, (strictly juristically) even anti-Islamic—ideas, demonstrated in the expositions on the norms of governance (*jahandari*, *mamlikatdari*), politics (*siyasat*), and the concepts or meanings of religion (*din*), *shari'a* and justice (*'adl*). In its expressions on political organisation, *akhlaq* literature emphasised on cooperation to be achieved through justice (*'adl*) in accordance with a law shielded and promoted by a king who ought to control with affection and favours (*rafat-o-imtinan*), and not by insistence on command and obedience (*amr-o-imtisal*). Non-juristic in nature, the *akhlaq* texts do not concern themselves with notions of *kufr* (infidelity) or the *zimma*. *Shari'a*, in these texts, also connoted a non-juridical concept of Islamic law, although there was a reiteration of the *Quranic* verse on the oneness of God, who sent prophets to different communities with *shari'a* to suit the different circumstances.

Nevertheless, to legitimise their political behaviour and resolve problems that related to the compatibility of the *shari'a* with their political decisions, the Muslim rulers of India resorted to *shari'a*. In 1579, for instance, Akbar was compelled to seek the approval of the *'ulama* for a politically compliant interpretation of the *shari'a*. Towards the end of Akbar's reign and subsequently in the Mughal rule of the seventeenth and eighteenth centuries, the *shari'a* no longer remained a focal point in political discourse. *Shari'a*, however, held a significant place in medieval Islamic political formations. Several historians have understood it only in its juristic sense and have overlooked the importance and implications of the varieties of its use in non-juridical literature. The impression that *shari'a* is rigid and resistant to change is based on the conviction that there was no scope for innovations in *shari'a* after the first centuries of Islam, that is, it was 'the closure of the gate of *ijtihad*', a view pioneered by Joseph Schacht's (1964) understanding of the history of Islamic law. To the contrary, it has now been argued that *shari'a* was reinterpreted gradually to accommodate to a changing political order; so any emphasis on its rigidity and bigotry implied the loss of an important context.

It is pertinent to note that even in juristic terms, *shari'a* was, and continues to have, a measure of flexibility and it recognises and legitimises diversity within Islamic schools. Also, while the jurists regarded a non-*shari'a* act as an offence, they tolerated it and suggested its expiation (*kaffara*). The general agreement between the Muslim jurists and clergies over the significance of diversity (*ikhtilaf*) in the readings of the prophetic traditions led to the emergence of more than one school in jurisprudence (*fiqh*) and scholasticism (*kalam*). This can be exemplified by the institution of *fatwa*, which created a space for interpretation and the enforcement of a juristic position in different situations.

The Muslim philosophers and intellectuals used the term *shari'a* in their earlier politico-cultural writings to express dissent, but their work over the years was integrated into a larger body of Islamic literature. Thus, like the *shari'a* of the jurists, the *shari'a* of these philosophers and intellectuals is equally important for the understanding of pre-modern Muslim politics. When *shari'a* is used only in the juridical sense, the emphasis is on its uncompromising fixed meaning as applied by the theologians. Consequently, the legitimacy or illegitimacy of a political act tends to be explained by its criteria in the light of religion, that is, as either religious or irreligious. However, notwithstanding the importance of *shari'a* in medieval Indian Muslim politics, it did not have the same meaning in every context but implied varying political meanings in India. Using the evidence from *Fatawa-i Jahandari* of Ziya-ud-din Barani, whose writings represented *adab*, a literary style that had originated in the first Arabic translations and adaptations of Greek and Iranian texts and had a fairly extensive impact on the political and intellectual history of Islam, particularly Perso-Turkic, Muzaffar Alam has argued that state legislation or *zawabit* was seen as totally opposed to the *shari'a*. Yet, for political pragmatism state legislation was approved.

Barani attempted to resolve the conflict between the demands of *shari'a* and the problems of governance in his time. He discussed the close connection between *dindari* (looking to the faith) and *jahandari* (concern with the world), considered the two inseparable, and observed that their combination created and sustained ideal conditions for the promotion of Islam. For Barani, therefore, the changing times necessitated a secular intervention of legislation for the preservation of the Muslim community. In *akhlaq* literature, to the contrary, there was no such compromise. For it, state legislation was not necessarily opposed to *shari'a*; in fact, here the distinction between 'secular' and *shari'a* regulations merged. *Shari'a* in these texts is redefined, partly to denote a kind of protest against an overly legalistic approach and also to provide a philosophical, non-sectarian and humane solution to the emergent problems that India's Muslim society encountered. Alam argued that these two traditions of writing—*adab* and *akhlaq*—have often been categorised indiscriminately under the term 'mirrors for princes' without considering that the two are disparate. Each ascribed a different meaning to *shari'a*; while one upheld the theological context, the other was a complete divergence from the theological or orthodox approach.

The fusion of Islamic, pre-Islamic, and Hellenic cultures resulted in a compilation of a number of treatises that laid down norms of governance. Abu'l Hasan al-Mawardi's (974–1058) *al-Ahkam al-Sultaniya* pioneered this style. He asserted that the prime authority was vested in the *Khalifa*, that only a member of the Quraysh tribe (the tribe to which Prophet Muhammad belonged) could rise to the position of a *Khalifa* or the *imam*, and that he had to be necessarily obeyed. A contrarian opinion, however, was articulated by Nizam ul-Mulk Tusi, a prominent theorist of the eleventh century, who wrote the *Siyasatnama* or *Siyar al-Muluk* during the reign of Malik Shah Saljuq (1072–92). He emphasised an invincible, all-mighty centre, ignored the standing of the *Khalifa*, and in fact, referred to him as a mere pension-holder. Al-Ghazzali, a Sunni theologian-saint (1058–1111), nevertheless argued for a new relationship between the *Khalifa* and the Sultan and a compromise between pragmatism and theory in his *Nasihat al-Muluk*, written for another Saljuq Sultan, Sanjar bin Malik Shah (1105–18). His affirmation of the ordinary duties of the king for reasons of political expediency and Nizam ul-Mulk's encomium of the Persian kings as exemplars influenced the political theory of the first few Sultans of Delhi. In this context may be mentioned Fakhr-i Mudabbir's *Adab al-Harb-i wash-Shuja'a* and Ziya-ud-din Barani's *Fatawa-i Jahandari*, as well as Saiyid 'Ali Hamadani's *Zakhirat al-Muluk* (although the latter is largely concerned with the history of the Muslims in Kashmir). Some of these treatises, from Mawardi to Barani and Hamadani, encased in the same tradition, not only influenced the making of Indo-Persian norms of governance but also facilitated the understanding of the evolution of the theory and practice of governance.

Distinct from these traditions was *akhlaq* or *akhlaqiyat*, which represented a non-juristic articulation of power and its enforcement, a prescription for good conduct, ethics and urbanity that exerted a powerful influence on the Mughal Empire. Its prototype, *Akhlaq-i Nasiri*, normative in character, highly idealistic and theoretically sound, is a Persian treatise of the thirteenth century composed by Khwaja Nasir ud-Din Tusi at the instance of the Ismaili ruler, Nasir-ud-din 'Abdur Rahim bin Abi Mansur, *wali* of Quhistan. Tusi's work was a remarkable blending of Greek philosophical and scientific tradition with his own 'Islamic' view of man and society. His first discourse was a summary of Ibn Miskawaih's *Tahzib*. To this he added two new discussions based on the philosophical writings of Farabi and Ibn Sina on the management of household and family (*tadbir-i manzil*) and politics (*siyasat-i mudun*) to impart practical knowledge (*hikmat-i 'amali*). In Tusi's *akhlaq* tradition, while *din* (religion) had an important place in the State, *din* and *shari'a* did not have a similar connotation. They were solicited to exemplify universal human ideals. The *akhlaqi* discussion in the text was entirely different from a book on jurisprudence, even if the language appeared the same at first instance. The familiar 'religious' language was chosen deliberately for quick acceptance of views—a strategy invoked by the medieval intelligentsia to 'Islamicise' a non-Islamic tradition. Tusi's *akhlaq* was intended to serve as an advisory manual for the thirteenth-century rulers of Iran. Subsequently, with the Mongol invasion of West Asia, Tusi wrote a new Preface to his text without changing the content and presented it as a manual for kingship to the non-Muslim Mongol rulers. Devised for non-Muslim rulers, Tusi's treatise could not advocate strict legalist adherence to Islamic norms, but it counselled for ideal kingship, paternalistic benevolence, justice, harmony amongst diverse ethnic groups, and benevolent kindness (*ihsan*). It was perhaps for these reasons—or perhaps as a legacy of Babur—that Nasirean ethics appealed to the Mughal emperors, who ruled over multiethnic groups of people.

Babur had inherited Nasirean ethics from the Timurids of Herat subsequent to their eradication by the Shaibanids. The last of the great Timurids, Sultan Husain Bayqara (r. 1470–1506) of Herat, had, despite being a Sunni, rejected the idea of his government being based on rigid Sunni Islamic norms and had instead sought Tusi's political philosophy that resulted in two versions—*Akhlaq-i Muhsini* by Husain Wa'iz al-Kashifi and *Dastur al-Wizarat* by Qazi Ikhtiyar al-Din Hasan al-Husaini. Following the collapse of Timurid power, when al-Husaini, the chief *qazi* of Herat, moved to Kabul, he was allegedly so impressed by Babur's views on diverse sciences and governance in the course of his discussions that he wrote a treatise (this treatise was the same as *Dastur al-Wizarat*, which he had written for Prince Husain Mirza), which he decided to name *Akhlaq-i Humayuni* (the *Humayuni* or auspicious ethics) since it carried the ethical ideals of Babur. Didactic in nature, even as the treatise evaluated the character of Babur, al-Husaini hoped that Babur would use it as an ethical and political guide and pass it on to his descendants.

Several *akhlaqi* digests entered Mughal political culture in different versions and recensions, including Ikhtiyar al-Husaini's *akhlaq* that had a tremendous influence on the religious and political views of the Mughals. Yet *Akhlaq-i Nasiri* of Tusi had a preferred and authoritative role. The influence of Nasirean *akhlaq*, Alam (2004) argued, reinforced by the impact of Persian poetry and Sufic thought, was so immense on Mughal governance that the *shari'a* had become synonymous with *namus-i ilahi* (divine law), the objective of which was to ensure harmony between communities, non-interference in their personal beliefs and counterpoise conflicts. The norms of behaviour proclaimed in Tusi's *Akhlaq*, internalised universally in all Persian-speaking countries, were reiterated by Abu'l Fazl in *Ain-i Akbari* in the chapter 'On Etiquette' under the section 'Regulations about standing and sitting' (*Ain-i istadah wa nishast*), which emphasised the necessity of maintaining the sanctity of ranks at the court with the king as the centre-point who determined the course of actions. He listed *Akhlaq-i Nasiri* amongst the five most important works in Akbar's library; it was read aloud to him almost every day and influenced his administrative philosophy greatly. The text was not only prescribed as a part of the curriculum in the *madrasa*s, but the emperor also ordered it as necessary reading and instruction for his nobles, for modulating their personal and official conduct and obligations. In the latter segment of the 1580s of Akbar's reign, Tusi's work was chosen singularly for copying and elaborate illustration in the imperial library, where books were kept, copied, gilded, illustrated, and bound. Subsequently, Chandar Bhan Brahman, the chief *munshi* of Shahjahan, in his letter of advice to his son urged him to necessarily read Tusi's *Akhlaq* and also its later interpretation, *Akhlaq-i Jalali* by Jalal ud-Din Dawwani, and Sa'di's *Gulistan* and *Bustan* for their invaluable relevance in defining the Mughal cultural code. He further averred that the wisdom derived from this select literature would facilitate young men to 'earn their capital and be blessed with the fortunes of knowledge and good moral conduct'.

Akhlaq-i Jahangiri by Nur-ud-din Qazi al-Khaqani is the first major text on *akhlaq* compiled under the Mughals, completed and dedicated to Jahangir in 1622. The author, a *qazi* of Lahore, an *alim*, a jurist, and an émigré from Herat, was a grandson of Hasan 'Ali bin Ashraf al-Munshi al-Khaqani, the chief secretary of Akbar's half-brother Mirza Hakim, the ruler of Kabul. But more importantly, he was the author of *Akhlaq-i Hakimi*, a text that he dedicated to his patron and that represented the orthodox view of kingship prevalent in the court of Mirza Hakim. *Akhlaq-i Jahangiri*, written to counsel the rulers in general and Jahangir in particular on norms of governance, was an expanded and enlarged edition of *Akhlaq-i Hakimi*, although it differed in some contexts. For instance, Al-Munshi al-Khaqani's preface, which stipulated the importance of the life and teachings of the Prophet in moulding human culture and ethical values, was dropped in *Akhlaq-i Jahangiri*; instead, a chapter was added on justice. Like Tusi, Qazi al-Khaqani stressed the importance of justice in matters of governance and asserted that a non-Muslim, just ruler was better than an unjust Muslim ruler. Reflecting on the themes related to good behaviour, courage, patience, bravery, and generosity, he pointed towards the effective value of consultation and abiding by one's promise. His religious and juridical background impacted the form and content of the *akhlaq* that he generally wrote in the form of anecdotes or didactic narrative, and was similar in style to *Akhlaq-i Jalali*, a significant part of the curriculum during this period. *Akhlaq-i Jahangiri*, though a commentary on political thought, rarely concerned itself with the analysis or interpretation of political philosophy; it was more of an intermediate connect between the juridical and philosophical works.

Akhlaq-i Hakimi and *Akhlaq-i Jahangiri*, with their predominantly legal and juristic content, often counteracted the effect of Nasirean ethics. Similar was the tone of *Risala-i Muhammad Sa'id* and *Wajib al-Hifz* by Hafiz Muhammad Sa'id and 'Aqil Khan, written in 1690 and 1693, respectively, during the reign of Aurangzeb. Mir Ahmad 'Ali Khan's *Akhlaq-i Muhammad Shahi*, written in 1721 under the patronage of a Mughal *wazir*, Amin ud-Daulah, was closer in style to Hamadani's *Zakhirat* than Tusi's *Akhlaq*. Although he applauded *'aql* (reason) and held it in high esteem, he displayed an overt obsession with the concern for Islam and Muslims. Neither was Dawwani's *Akhlaq-i Jalali* the same as Tusi's digest. Even al-Husaini's *Akhlaq-i Humayuni* exaggerated the importance of *Shari'a-i Islamia* or rights of Muslims (*huquq-i ahi-i Islam*) and, unlike Tusi, concluded with an appeal to the monarchs to pursue the *Shari'a* of Muhammad and strengthen the community of Ahmad. Tusi's *Akhlaq*, considered more ascetic in spirit, had to also contend with works classified as heroic renditions, like *Zafarnama*, *Shahnama* of Firdausi, and *Chengiznama*, which Abu'l Fazl had advised Abdul Rahim Khan-i Khanan to read when the latter was on the verge of embarking on the conquest of Qandahar in the 1590s.

4

TOWARDS CONSOLIDATION

Legitimacy, Power, Authority

HIGHLIGHTS

- Conquest and territorial expansion
- Use of gunpowder and military technology
- Towards a multiethnic empire: Reconstituting power and authority
- New imperial idiom: The *mansab*s
- *Jagir*, *jagirdar*, and the complexities
- Revenue assessment and collection

CONQUEST, TERRITORY, MILITARY TECHNOLOGY

Conquest, warfare, and territorial expansion were an integral part of Mughal empire-building. Johan Huizinga, Dutch Indologist and historian, argued that pre-modern warfare had a certain element of game in it, which, through its competitiveness and playfulness and also through its shared rules and conventions, facilitated the coming together of different parts of society. While Mughal warfare, observed Jos Gommans (2002), bridged various inner frontiers of empire, the socio-economic and cultural aspects of warfare were significant in connecting the different regions and peoples of the empire to each other. Theoretically, the empire appeared unlimited. Practically, however, the Mughal army faced operational and logistical challenges that stranded the territorial expansion at different inner frontiers throughout the imperial high roads. It is this system of high roads, elaborated Gommans, connecting the outer and inner frontiers of the empire that formed the basis of Mughal State formation. Conquest, in his opinion, implied the extension of the Mughal high roads, that is, moving the *termini* or boundary of the empire along the radiating axes from *madhyadesha* (middle country) to *uttarapatha* (north), *dakshinapatha* (south), *aparantapatha* (west), and *pracya* (east).

Mughal expansion began in Kabul and moved along the *longue duree* pattern of these Indian limits. In fact, from its inception in the 1520s to the early eighteenth century, the history of the Mughal State was one of extension in all directions beginning from its core, viz., the Ganga-Yamuna Doab region, to the southern regions. An important element in the legitimating of power and authority, conquest in the Mughal period was a complex event, dependent on several factors in which force or military power may have been primary; but equally significant were political alliances, control over the military labour market, forms of communication and information. Conquest entailed sovereignty, not only over territories but also over people. In other words, territorial expansionism was generally preceded, accompanied, and followed by widespread political alliances and negotiations percolating down to the varied social groups—religious elite, petty merchants, local gentry, tribal lineage groups, warrior clans, common urban dwellers—and not confined to merely the elite or the upper strata of society. Conquest imbued sovereignty with a political dynamism at a time when loyalties were tenuous and transient, marked by uncertainties of alliance and conflict. Dirk Kolff (1990) argued that while an integrated military labour market had developed, it continued to waver in its alliances with the rulers despite its significant role in all conquests and expansionism. No political power could claim monopoly over the military market, which looked for a patron competent to provide a steady and stable income and livelihood. In other words, the relations of the military labour market with their employers were defined by traditions of *naukari* (service), rather than loyalty to any particular dynasty. The Mughals co-opted many from this pool, a large section of which comprised Indian peasants enrolled in military service as professional soldiers, skilled with weapons, whose loyalty rested more with their masters, kin, and clan than with the empire. This necessitated the incorporation of their leaders in imperial service. The process of expansion was the process of incorporation.

Conquest constituted its own process of legitimation through much of the ancient, medieval, and early modern world, or at least till the coming of colonialism. Colonialism changed the meaning of conquest, implying the governance of a territory and its people on behalf of, and primarily to serve the economic interests of, a community inhabiting a distant land. This notion of conquest stood in sharp contrast with conquest in the medieval and early modern centuries when the conqueror either returned to his original territory with a large plunder or stayed back in the vanquished territory, assimilating in it his identity and that of his group or clan to such an extent that it became inseparable from the acquired territory. In India of the medieval and early modern times, rulers sought to legitimate the conquest of territories in their own considered ways. Sultan Mahmud of Ghazni, for instance, combined plunder with religious zeal. Barani, the political theorist of the Sultans of Delhi in the fourteenth century, envisioned both conquest of territory and governance as 'an exercise of terror by the king and a manifestation of the king's virility' (Mukhia 2005, 50). Babur's claim to the conquest of territories in India derived from his Timurid descent and his conviction that it belonged to his ancestor, a Turk (although India had never been under direct Timurid rule). He asserted that this was why he saw the region of Hindustan as his own and ordered his soldiers to refrain from harassing the local people during military expeditions, for he deemed them to be his subjects already and therefore entitled to protection. In his efforts towards political outreach, Babur attempted to patronise the Afghans and the Indian Muslims, was anxious for a political settlement with the Sisodia clan of Rana Sangha following their defeat at the battle of Khanua in 1527, and sought interaction with other powerful non-Muslim landholding groups, including the Baghelas of Bhatta, Bachgotis of Awadh, and Purbias of Malwa.

Humayun too attempted to forge alliances, but his politics rarely touched the lower social base beyond the nobility, warriors, and chieftains. This perhaps explains why, despite having occupied Gujarat, he failed to retain it; on the other hand, he faced several other bitter experiences with his rivals and resistance from the zamindars, merchants, petty officials, peasants, and tribal warrior clans. This adequately demonstrates that for a successful conquest, the support of the wider local society, and not merely that of the upper crust, was a necessary factor, suggesting thus that persistent engagement and involvement with the local constituents of the society was a preliminary requirement for conquest. This remained a major feature under Akbar and his successors. For Akbar, in fact, as Abu'l Fazl observed, conquest meant establishing peace and justice, and shielding the people of a territory from the oppressions of the existing ruler.

Defining Akbar's imperialism and his success in the expansionary campaigns, Abu'l Fazl suggested that it was Akbar's desire to extend his rule beyond the 'Mughal homeland', visit Prayag, visit the eastern territory, root out rebellion and then go to Deccan, which had been longing for a 'just ruler'. To quote Abu'l Fazl, 'the sole idea of the *Shahinshah* was to clear the territory of Ahmadnagar of the weeds and rubbish of rebellion, and then to prevail over Bijapur, Golconda and Bidar, so that the rulers of these places should make binding treaties of obedience' (*Akbarnama* III; *cf* Chandra 2003, 448n). From there, Abu'l Fazl narrated, Akbar planned to move to Turan and Badakhshan and by his policies enable the 'various classes of mankind to experience the joys of concord'. The objective of Akbar's territorial expansionism, as Abu'l Fazl alleged, was not simply imperialism but strategic, motivated by administrative consolidation and that which demonstrated the emperor's tolerance. Abu'l Fazl enumerated a variety of reasons to explain Akbar's expansion into regional kingdoms—Malwa, the Gond kingdom of Garh Katanga, Gujarat, Khandesh, Kashmir, Sind or Thatta: if the regional rulers failed to acknowledge the paramountcy of the emperor and did not submit to him, or to save the people from the oppression of the regional rulers; or simply his desire to implement justice and *sulh-i kul* (peaceful co-existence).

The victories of Akbar, Fazl reiterated, were a result of '*Shahinshah*'s fortune' and divine intervention or 'celestial aid' in favour of the emperor, rather than the daring courage and military abilities of the military commanders. Bestowing immortal and divine attributes on Akbar, he insisted that service to Akbar was *neku-bandgi* (excellent worship) while opposition to him was *sarkashi* (recalcitrance) and *bad gauhari* (wickedness). It was therefore necessary, said Fazl, to 'chastise the stiff-necked ones', render the *mutamarridan* (stubborn), *mufsidan* (pernicious), and *fitna-andozan* (seditious) to obedience (*bandgi*), and particularly hail those who acknowledged Akbar's authority and fought for him as *mujahidin* (warriors or fighters), *mujahidan-i ikhlas* (sincere or loyal fighters) or *mujahidan-i daulat* (fighters for the empire), because according to the theory of sovereignty this was the 'greatest and choicest form of worship' (*ibadat-i kubra* or *ibadat-i guzida*) for the emperor. Moreover, the emperor's expansionist strategies were essential because Akbar embodied spiritual and temporal power.

After the early 1590s when Sind was captured and the resistance of the Sultans of Gujarat overpowered, the western territory remained largely stable. The campaigns to the east came to an end only in the 1660s with the fall of Chittagong. North and northwest continued to be potential areas for expansion up to the reign of Shahjahan, when the latter led an expedition to Balkh, albeit unsuccessfully. Subsequent to the consolidation of their conquests in Bengal, Gujarat, and the northern and northwestern frontier, the Mughal emperors focused on Deccan and then Karnataka.

Contrary, however, to Abu'l Fazl's honorific narration, an evaluation and understanding of the process of 'regional centralisation' indicates that even while the Mughal emperors, including Akbar, carried out their plans of expansion and attempted to integrate the regions within the empire with the objective of achieving centralisation, the regions remained unwavering in their resistance to the Mughal State. Critiquing Fazl, scholars like Ahsan Raza Khan (2010) have argued that Fazl first decided the intent and then fabricated the reason to justify the means adopted to achieve it. Often, the reason fell apart and it became apparent that the expansion was inspired by material gain, as in the case of Malwa, Gondwana, and Sind, and military strategies were adopted to break the *nakhwat* and *gharur* (haughtiness and pride) of the local chieftains (*raja*s, *rana*s, *rao*s, zamindars) who did not accept Akbar's authority (*niyayishgari na-karde*). Rejecting Fazl's claim that *sulh-i kul* inspired Akbar's imperialism, Khan argued that it played no role in such decisions for, as Fazl tells us, even if no offence was committed by a ruler against Akbar, he was still subjugated. *Sulh-i kul*, Khan suggested, has therefore to be seen as confined to the sphere of religion, which was a significant—although only one—aspect in the political theory of the State. As a pragmatic statesman, Akbar responded to the situation irrespective of his personal convictions.

Conquests, then, for the Mughals—particularly the first three emperors—signified the ability to mobilise resources for further expansion and consolidation, occupying not only the important and large cities of the western and central Indo-Gangetic region, that is, Lahore, Delhi and Agra, but also the countryside. Control over cities and countryside was imperative to ascertain political order and stability, and more notably the collection of agrarian revenue from these territories. Emphasising the import of the issue, Jahangir, in his memoir *Tuzuk-i Jahangiri*, observed that 'territory and forces' or agrarian revenue and manpower were most valuable in politics. Manpower facilitated the formation and consolidation of the State, that is, the military workforce, and the income of the State that was distributed amongst them. The territorial extent of the Mughal State varied vastly in the beginning of the eighteenth century as compared to the early sixteenth century, with Aurangzeb controlling a large realm that extended into southern India and virtually stretched from the borders of Myanmar to Central Asia. As the territory expanded through the seventeenth century, the Mughals came to be linked, argued Alam and Subrahmanyam (1998), with the only 'sovereign idea' and the only true source of sovereignty in the Indian subcontinent. This point is exemplified by the fact that although the Marathas enjoyed greater *de facto* power as compared to the Mughal military force in the eighteenth century, they continued to operate behind a Mughal façade, as did the English East India Company in Bengal and Hindustan after 1765.

That the Mughals traversed diverse regimes during the seventeenth century is illustrated by Gommans (2002). He cited the three major campaigns at the far ends of the imperial high roads: the most eastern, the most northern, and the most southern, that is:

- the successful conquest of eastern Bengal (1608–13);
- the disappointing, unaccomplished campaign in Balkh (1645–48); and
- the interminable siege of Gingee (1689–97).

These campaigns explain how and to what extent the different geographical settings determined the outer frontiers of the empire. Notwithstanding the closely bound phenomena of success and failure, expansion and contraction, these conquests facilitated not only the outward expansion of the empire but also fostered the inward encroachments of the Marathas, the Afghans, and the European companies. The Mughals had established their dominance in Bengal by 1612 and made Dhaka the provincial capital, which had acquired a new physical topography ranging from palaces to forts, roads to canals. Developing as a cosmopolitan provincial capital, it held a major attraction for people and resources from different segments of the Mughal Empire and the Dutch and English Companies. By the early eighteenth century, as Bengal flourished, its governors asserted their autonomy and de facto power; subsequently, it evolved as the foci of a new imperial system stimulated by the efforts of the English East India Company.

The western frontier, particularly Balkh, was of special significance for the Mughals, both politically and emotionally. Ousted by the Uzbeks from their homeland in Turan, as stated by Abdul Hamid Lahori in his *Padshahnama*, to 'inhospitable, uncivilized and heathen' Hindustan, the Mughals were affected by the loss of their hereditary kingdom of Samarqand and had always dreamt of recovering it, a dream that nevertheless remained distant. Like Bengal, the location of Balkh as a frontier province had inspired the urge for independence amongst the Afghan tribes by the beginning of the eighteenth century, paving the way for Afghan imperialism under the Durranis. Gingee, on the southern frontier, the most strategically located fort in the Carnatic, had aroused conflict between different Maratha, Sidi, Nawayat, and Deccani Muslim groups from 1649. Politics, however, changed with the capture of Gingee by the Mughals in 1698, shifting the front once again towards Maharashtra. Aurangzeb had achieved remarkable success in seizing fort after fort, but with his death in 1707, the Mughals lost control over the *dakshinapatha* crossroads in Central Deccan. Instead, the Marathas consolidated a new state structure that incorporated large parts of northern and western India; to its east, an erstwhile *subadar* of the Mughal Empire, Chin Qilch Khan alias Nizam-ul Mulk, established the Asaf Jahi dynasty in Hyderabad; Arcot emerged as the regional capital ruled by the Nawayats; and the Walajahis played a valuable role in the rise of Madras as the new imperial centre of the south. These examples are evidence of the ways in which regional centralisation was stirred by the military changes in the latter half of the eighteenth century and the way the infantry facilitated the colonial conquests of the British.

Conquests and territorial acquisitions by the Mughals demonstrated impressive military development. To understand whether this can be attributed to their centralised, well-equipped army and military superiority as suggested by some historians, it is imperative to evaluate the role of military technology, that is, the issue of gunpowder and firearms or artillery and whether it steered Mughal invincibility. Or were there other reasons for the submission of the regional chieftains?

In its initial phase, military historiography was replete with information on military events, that is, when and which battles were fought and who were involved, but there were rarely any details on how these battles and sieges took place or the tactics or logistics of the war and weaponry. William Irvine heralded the work on military history through his book, *The Army of the Indian Moghuls: Its Organization and Administration* (1998 [1903]), and Jadunath Sarkar's *Military History of India* (1970 [1960]) pioneered the methodology of studying battles to understand the nature of warfare, wherein he attributed Babur's success in the battles of Panipat and Khanua to his skilful use of artillery and musketry in open contests. Later historians such as Marshall G. S. Hodgson (*The Venture of Islam*, Vol. 3, 1974) and William H. McNeill (*The Pursuit of Power*, 1982) argued that it was artillery that gave the Mughals—as well as the contemporary Ottoman and Safavid empires—military superiority. Hodgson expounded the theory of 'gunpowder empires' to describe the three Asian empires and argued that it was the effective use of cannon and diffusion of firearms, especially siege artillery, that made the Mughals invincible, facilitating the centralisation of the empire.

Following the hypothesis of Russian scholar V. V. Bartold, Hodgson and McNeill attributed the political success of the three empires—Mughal, Ottoman, and Safavid—to the use of artillery to occupy stone fortresses. Although he found the gunpowder hypothesis inadequate, Douglas Streusand (2001, 2011) conceded that it did explain the significance of military superiority, and observed that the 'gunpowder empires' meant 'empires of the gunpowder era' and not 'empires created by gunpowder weapons'. He argued that the Mughals neither produced nor employed firearms in as sophisticated a manner as the Europeans or the Ottomans. Unlike the Ottomans, the Mughals did not engage in the manufacture of gunpowder but purchased it on the open market. Moreover, if gunpowder was produced internally, it was invariably of inferior quality. The Mughals, Streusand asserted, lagged behind European military technology in the late seventeenth and early eighteenth century when flintlock muskets supplanted matchlocks and cast-iron artillery became the standard form (while the Mughals produced and worked with only matchlocks and brass and bronze guns). Others like Irfan Habib argued that it was not artillery but cavalry that made the Mughals invincible. Artillery, he said, was never successful against really strong forts; the strength lay in their cavalry or mounted archers in a battle in the open field, and in rapid movements.

Iqtidar Alam Khan (2004), however, observed that even though gunpowder (*barud* or *barut*) was known in India as early as the thirteenth century, it was under the Mughals from the sixteenth century that it acquired a significant form in warfare. It was introduced in India as the Sultans of Delhi (although there is very little evidence to support their use of firearms or cannons) came into contact with the Mongols, who had earlier learnt the use of it from the Chinese. The first use of gunpowder, Khan said, was during the reign of Firuz Shah Tughluq but for the display of pyrotechnics or *atishbazi*; gunpowder as a military device was used in some regional states like

Malwa in the fifteenth century in the form of *hawa'i* or *ban* or *tir-i harra'i*. As the new skills and concepts poured in from Europe and the Ottoman Empire, firearms reached India in the beginning of the sixteenth century. These influences and ideas, Khan argued, came with the arrival of the Portuguese at Calicut in 1498 and Babur's occupation of Delhi and Agra in 1526.

Jos Gommans, whose publications have brought ecological and geographical factors to the forefront of historical analysis in the context of Indian warfare, disagreed with Iqtidar Alam Khan's assertion that firearms were known to India in the fifteenth century. He argued that South Asia experienced a 'cavalry revolution' with the intrusion of Turkish mounted archers between 1000–1200 CE, and that since most forts were located on inaccessible hill tops and inside forests, the *trace italienne* sort of thing was redundant to the needs of the fort builders. Gommans, along with Dirk Kolff (2001), further added that gun-carriages in pre-colonial India were deplorable and lacked in the manufacture of cast-iron guns—an obstacle to the mass production of standardised guns—probably because the blast furnace and finery with water-powered hammer were unknown in India at that time (although it had appeared in West Europe during the fifteenth century). Notwithstanding the observations of Gommans and Kolff, Richard Eaton (2012) asserted that gunpowder was known to India, particularly western India, even before the coming of *Estado da India* or the establishment of Portuguese power in the region:

- In 1472, for instance, Bahmani engineers had deployed explosive mines to besiege the fort of Belgaum, an ally of the Vijayanagara kingdom;
- Gaspar Correia, Albuquerque's secretary and a chronicler of the *Esatdo*, recorded that in 1502, Portuguese naval squadrons were bombarded from the hill top overlooking the port of Bhatkal;
- Firishta noted in his *Tarikh-i Firishta* that gunners and rocketeers were employed by Sultan Ahmad Nizam Shah of Ahmadnagar in the military expedition against Khandesh in 1504; and
- In the civil strife in Bijapur in 1510, Firishta spoke of the use of *tufangi* (matchlock-men) and large cannons to blow up the citadel's walls.

More importantly, Albuquerque's son observed that when his father took possession of Goa in 1510, Bijapur used artillery fire against him. Later in the same year, after first losing and then recapturing the city, Albuquerque seized almost 100 large guns (*bombardas*) and an equally large quantity of smaller artillery, many of which were locally manufactured. When the Portuguese occupied Goa in 1513, they found that Bijapur had already established its own munitions plant in the city. It appears that Turkish gunners and gunsmiths had settled in Bijapur subsequent to the Mamluk and Gujarati naval engagements with the Portuguese off the coast of Konkan and Gujarat, and the battle of Chaul in 1508. These Turks brought with them the Ottoman gun technology to the Goa arsenal. Albuquerque was so impressed with Goa's gun-making tradition that he sent samples of city-manufactured heavy cannon to the king of Portugal and reported that the matchlocks manufactured by Goa gunsmiths could easily compete with those made in Bohemia. With the realisation that Goa gunsmiths could produce high quality iron cannons and matchlocks, Albuquerque initiated the 'Indo-Portuguese' tradition of matchlocks, that is, a combination of the German and Bohemian gun-making traditions brought to India by the Portuguese with the Turkish gun-making traditions already existent in Goa.

Despite such stirring developments, the absence of major battles meant that none of these could be put to use before 1520 in Deccan or anywhere in the interior. It was in 1520 in the battle of Raichur between the Bahmani and Vijayanagara kingdoms that cannons were used extensively by Bahmani (although minimally by Vijayanagara). Six years later, in April 1526 in the First Battle of Panipat, Babur deployed field cannons and matchlocks in addition to mounted archers to defeat Ibrahim Lodi. While the First Battle of Panipat, observed Eaton, has sometimes been hailed as the beginning of India's 'Gunpowder Age', the battle of Raichur has often been ignored, probably because the side (Bijapur) with more firearms lost. In Panipat, however, the winning side was also the firepower side.

Image 4.1: Illustration from Hutchinson, *Story of the Nations*, depicts field guns introduced by Babur in the First Battle of Panipat, 1526

Source: https://commons.wikimedia.org/wiki/File:Babur_introduced_field_guns_at_panipat_1526.Jpg.

Babur, equipped with light artillery pieces and matchlocks and lightly armed mounted archers trained in *taulqama* (tactic used by the highly mobile mounted archers of the arid regions that had caused his defeat at the hands of Uzbek chief Shaibani Khan in the battle of Sar-i Pul in 1501, the value of which he deeply understood), demonstrated decisive military superiority, which caught the Afghans and the Rajputs unawares in the battles that he fought during the years 1526–30. In the First Battle of Panipat and the battle of Khanua, Babur replicated the wagon *laager* tactics used by the Ottomans against the Safavids in the battle of Chaldiran in 1514. The battlefield at Panipat was arranged under the supervision of the Ottoman gunner Ustad Ali Quli in the *Rumi* style (wagon *laager* tactics), with the artillery and gun-armed infantry at the centre and mounted archers on the wings. Around 700 carts, procured earlier, were arranged in a row along the front of the army, joined together by ropes of raw hide with five or six mantelets fixed between every row, behind which the *tufangchi*s and *topchi*s could take shelter and fire from hidden positions. Such protection for the gunners was necessary especially because the matchlocks were primitive and slow-firing, and needed to be reloaded after every shot.

In Turkish, this technique was known as *taburjangi*. Since the tactic was essentially defensive, it was imperative for the skirmishers to provoke the enemy and lure it out of its camp. They could inflict heavy losses and were successful to some extent against the Afghans, but did not perform so well against the Rajputs.

The technology of firearms was introduced to Babur by two Ottoman professionals, Mustafa Rumi and Ustad Ali Quli. *Baburnama* mentioned several types of firearms:

- *Tufang* or handguns, possibly some kind of matchlocks similar to those developed in Europe in the middle of the fifteenth century. They were long harquebus or arquebus, the gunpowder of which had to be ignited with a lighted match; this is perhaps why they were named matchlock. The *tufangchis* or *topchis* (matchlock-men) under Babur were generally from the infantry. It appears that Babur had acquired Turkish matchlocks sometime before 1519.

Image 4.2: Officer of the Mughal Army with a large matchlock, *c.* 1585

Source: https://en.wikipedia.org/wiki/Mughal_Weapons.

Image 4.3: A Mughal infantryman, *c.* 1850

Source: https://commons.wikimedia.org/wiki/File:A_Mughal_Infantryman.jpg.

- By the first quarter of the sixteenth century, a firearm of European origin had reached Central Asia and travelled to India under the name *fo-lang-chi chhung*, a contemporary Chinese firearm. This could have been the *firingi* (literally meaning Frankish) mentioned in the *Baburnama* in the context of the siege of Bajaur (the garrison of which was unfamiliar with the firearms used by Babur) in 1519. *Firingi* was translated by William Erskine in his *Memoirs of Zehir-ed-din Muhammed Baber, Emperor of Hindustan* (1826) as a swivel gun, invented actually in the eighteenth century in Asia and not in Europe as the name *firingi* would suggest. It was used for the first time in India by Ahmad Shah Abdali in the Third Battle of Panipat in 1761. Iqtidar Alam Khan, however, differed and observed that a *firingi* was a kind of small field cannon from which *shaturnal* (*shatur* means camel; it therefore means guns mounted on the back of the camels) was later developed.

- *Baburnama* also discussed the use of *qazan* or *kazan* and *zarb zan*. *Qazan/kazan* were brass/bronze mortars, with long barrels that could strike high angle fire; they could fire stone balls in a parabolic path, with the projectiles aimed to fall on the rear ranks of the enemy formation. *Zarb zan* were brass/bronze light field cannons with a long barrel and a funnel-shaped mouth that were mounted on baggage carts (*araba)* in the battles. They shot stones in a straight path up to a distance of 1,600 paces to strike an opponent charging from the front. Both *qazan/kazan* and *zarb zan* were extremely heavy guns and required at least 400–500 men to haul them, although they could be conveniently drawn by elephants.

Babur's tactics and strategies in the wars had provided enormous military prestige to the Mughals, although of course it did not deter Sher Shah from challenging Humayun, under whom the number of *tufang*s, *qazans/kazan*s and *zarb zan*s continued to be high, with at least 5,000 *tufangchi*s in employment. Sher Shah's army, as described by Mirza Haidar Dughlat in his *Tarikh-i Rashidi*, was already quite large in size, characterised by *deg* (mortars) and *zarb zan*s, yet he continuously mobilised resources to enhance the number of heavy and light cannons. If Abbas Khan Sarwani (*Tarikh-i Sher Shahi*) is to be believed, Sher Shah apparently requisitioned the entire available copper in the market for making *deg* during the siege of Raisen in Malwa in 1543. Although Sher Shah's *zarb zan*s reflected a new appearance influenced by European concepts and designs of light cannons brought by the Portuguese to Bengal, he sought, Dughlat observed, to incorporate the features of Mughal *zarb zan*s used in the battle of Kanauj, with which the Afghans were not familiar. This is evident from the surviving pieces manufactured by Saiyid Ahmad Rumi at Sonargaon during the period 1541–43. Islam Shah shifted from light artillery to heavy mortars with the objective of overwhelming his adversaries, especially when he heard of Humayun's retreat to Hindustan in 1553. The mortars that he used, observed Nizam-ud-din Ahmad Bakshi (*Tabaqat-i Akbari*), were so heavy that bullocks had to be mobilised for dragging them, or else 1,000–2,000 foot soldiers had to be deployed for dragging each mortar.

In the Second Battle of Panipat, the Mughals neither used *taburjangi* nor were they equipped with superior artillery. The Afghan forces under Hemu used elephants as a 'shock-action' to break the Mughal cavalry; the Mughals responded by retreating behind the ravines which the elephants could not cross, facilitating the Mughal mounted archers to use firepower successfully and establish victory over the Afghans. This combination of artillery and mounted archers ended the system of elephant-based warfare from the reign of Akbar (although Jahangir was supposed to have maintained about 12,000 elephants). With the increase in firing artillery and handguns and with improved musketry in the seventeenth century, elephants became less valuable as weapons and more significant as command vehicles, apparent from their use in this capacity during the war between Shahjahan's sons. Having lost their military role by the seventeenth century, the elephants nevertheless served as 'high platforms' from which the commanding generals could watch, and be watched from, the battle scene—a consequence of the shift towards a warhorse economy and gunpowder weaponry.

However, at the siege of Chittor in 1567 and in the battle of Haldighati in 1576, both the Mughals and the Sisodia Rajputs had elephants but neither had artillery, although the Mughal force could boast of some musketeers. The battle fought between Sisodia cavalry and elephants on the one hand and the Mughal combination of fire and 'shock-action' using elephants on the other resulted in the triumph of Mughal archers and musketeers. The dissemination of musket-related skills in Mughal India was probably made possible by the training provided in the Mughal Empire and other regional states to personnel recruited from communities that specialised in foot-archery. In the Mughal army, archers and musketeers were perceived to have identical roles in battles, that is, assisting the cavalry by shooting missiles at the enemy camp from discreetly selected vantage points.

Image 4.4: Illustration from Indian and Himalayan Art, Kota, Rajasthan, depicts an elephant in battle, *c.* 1750–70

Source: https://commons.wikimedia.org/wiki/File:Elephant_in_Battle.jpg.

With Akbar began the rejuvenation of the Mughal artillery, significantly so with the realisation that Islam Shah's heavy mortars were almost redundant, with no tactical advantage. While they could operate in occasional sieges, they were hardly of any use in military encounters. For this reason, perhaps, heavy mortars were excluded from the 'stirrup artillery' of Akbar, that is, the stock of artillery that accompanied him. Nevertheless, the number of heavy mortars in Akbar's artillery continued to be considerable, although he rarely used them in military operations because of their tactical disadvantages. The fifty large cannons of Islam Shah captured by Akbar during the Second Battle of Panipat from Hemu were stationed at Agra and never used in any military campaigns. They were, as Nizam-ud-din Ahmad Bakshi observed, not only difficult to transport and prone to accidents, but their slow movement also hampered the pace and speed of the army. Moreover, they had an inaccurate aim, consumed large amounts of gunpowder, and if there were no fixed installations during the siege, the mortars proved superfluous. However, their value was enhanced if they were directed at fixed targets: for instance, in 1570, during Akbar's assault on Ranthambor, the mortars performed effectively when carried to the top of a hill overlooking the fort.

Manucci, a gunner of Dara Shukoh, claimed that he had noticed pre-Mughal guns, made of 'excellent metal', that is, hardened copper and/or brass, captured by Akbar during his military campaigns in different parts of Hindustan. Although he did not mention wrought-iron guns in this context, they were put to greater use and regained their popularity in the seventeenth century. Akbar ensured the continuance of the trend set by Babur of spending on the production of guns for battles from the central treasury. The manufacture of firearms was done in the imperial household, a pattern that continued into later times. The documents of Aurangzeb's reign substantiate that all matters related to artillery, however minor, were decided by the *buyutat* (central department of the household). Akbar inherited a large range of artillery—*tufang*, *top*, *deg*, *zarb zan*. But marking a transition from Babur's time, he did not use category-specific terms either on the basis of the size of a cannon or by the weight of its shot or that of the projectile that it threw. Notwithstanding this, Abu'l Fazl classified the artillery into three kinds:

- heavy mortars (*kaman-ha-i buzurg*) that threw projectiles (shots) weighing 12 *mans* (roughly 248 kg or 664 pounds) or more. These required several thousand bullocks and elephants to drag them;
- artillery used for sieges and naval attacks (*paikar-i qila wa awaiza-i kashti*). These always accompanied the king in the battles;
- a variety of light cannons such as *narnal* and *gajnal* (guns drawn or borne on the back of an elephant). These were kept in the *subas* for deployment in the forts.

Image 4.5: Elephants pushing canons drawn by bullocks, eighteenth century

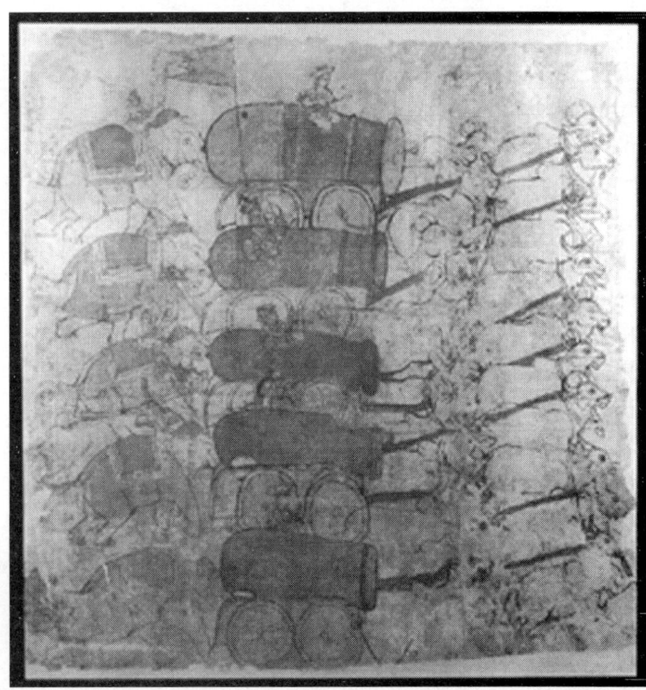

Source: https://commons.wikimedia.org/wiki/File:Elephants_pushing_canons_drawn_by_bullocks.Jpg.

Later improvements and innovations in the design of the light cannons led to the production of *shaturnal* and *jzail* (*shaturnal* was probably a developed form of *narnal*, handled by a single man), that were added to the artillery in the seventeenth century. *Zamburaks* (same as *shaturnal*) as well as *huqqa* (a sort of grenade) bombs were used by Golconda to resist the Mughal siege in December 1686.

Akbar introduced the system of *sabat* (approach trench) and excavating mines in 1567–68 to avoid the long siege of Chittor. The *sabat* or trench, with the excavated soil forming walls above ground level, was beyond the gun or bow range of the fortresses, wide enough for at least ten men to ride abreast, and deep enough to protect a man on an elephant. At Ranthambor too in 1569, the need was felt for a *sabat*, without which the fort would have remained impenetrable. The *sabat* was thus constructed, which facilitated the movement of the mortars to the top of the hill overlooking the fort (although, as Abu'l Fazl stated in his *Akbarnama*, 400 oxen were required to pull the mortars and 700 men emplaced them). The projectile or the fireball that these mortars threw weighed 60 *mans* (roughly 140 kg or 3,098 pounds), which succeeded in breaching the walls of the fort. *Sabat* were also used during the siege operations in Bijapur in 1685, to which the garrison of Bijapur responded with repeated attacks to destroy the Mughal trenches, opposing the Mughal army with musket fire, cannon shots, and rockets. The fort was ultimately captured in September 1686.

Heaping praise upon the developments in the arsenal, Abu'l Fazl eloquently characterised gunpowder artillery or *top* in the *Ain-i Akbari* as 'a wonderful lock [*qufl-i shiqarf*] for securing the august edifice of royalty [*iqbal sara-i jahanbani*] and a key [*kulid-i dilkusha*] to the door of conquest [*darwaza-i kishwarsitani*]'. He was emphatic in his assertion that as compared to the Mughal Empire, it was in *Rumistan* and not in *Rum* that gunpowder artillery was found in greater abundance. Fazl perhaps wanted to indicate, as Iqtidar Alam Khan observed, that it was not only the Turkish core of the Ottoman Empire comprising Anatolia and Thrace (*Rum* proper of the Persian and Arabic texts), but also territories like Syria, Palestine, Egypt, and the Maghrib, conquered by the Ottomans in the early sixteenth century, that were quite ahead in the technology of gunpowder artillery. Such a statement implicitly supports the fact that Mughal artillery was superior to that of the Safavids of Persia and the Shaibanids of Central Asia. These articulations of Abu'l Fazl, Khan further elaborated, cannot be dismissed as mere rhetoric for they significantly point towards the strengthening of centralisation, expansion, and consolidation. Having said this, Khan suggested that along with the efficient deployment of firearms by the Mughals, there was a rapid diffusion of these weapons among the nobles, zamindars, local chieftains, and peasants. This implied that the local groups gradually gained strength and acquired the capability to face the challenges of Mughal expeditions and conquests. This, then, would indicate that the artillery provided only a marginal edge to the Mughals over their rivals in the empire.

Douglas Strcusand, however, pointed to the 'paucity of battles' in the Mughal Empire because, except for a few, in most conquests the Mughals displayed their military strength and followed the tactic of limited engagements to check out the military preparedness of their opponents. By 1575, in Rajputana, Punjab, Gangetic Plains, Orissa, Malwa, and others, Akbar's military campaigns that led to territorial acquisitions did not involve prolonged siege operations; instead, in most cases they were open battles without the mortars. In the next phase of Akbar's conquests, which began in 1585 with the annexation of Kabul (1585), Kashmir (1586), Sind (1591), Qandahar (1594), Khandesh (1600), Ahmadnagar and Berar (1601), the heavy mortars were sparsely used, owing to the difficulty of transportation. McNeill attributed the 'precarious' nature of Mughal control in Deccan later in the seventeenth century to the difficulty of moving siege guns overland over

Image 4.6: Illustration from *Akbarnama*, 1568, depicts bullocks dragging siege guns up the hill during Akbar's attack on Ranthambor, Rajasthan

Source: https://commons.wikimedia.org/wiki/File:Bullocks_dragging_siege-guns_up_hill_during the_ attack _on_Ranthambor.jpg.

Image 4.7: Illustration from *Akbarnama* by Miskina, *c.* 1590–95, depicts an explosion of a mine during the siege of Chittor, Rajasthan

Source: https://commons.wikimedia.org/wiki/File:1567 -A_mine_explodes_during_the_siege_of_Chittor_left_*Akbarnama*-large.jpg.

Image 4.8: Illustration from *Ain-i Akbari* by Abu'l Fazl showcasing weapons used in India at that time

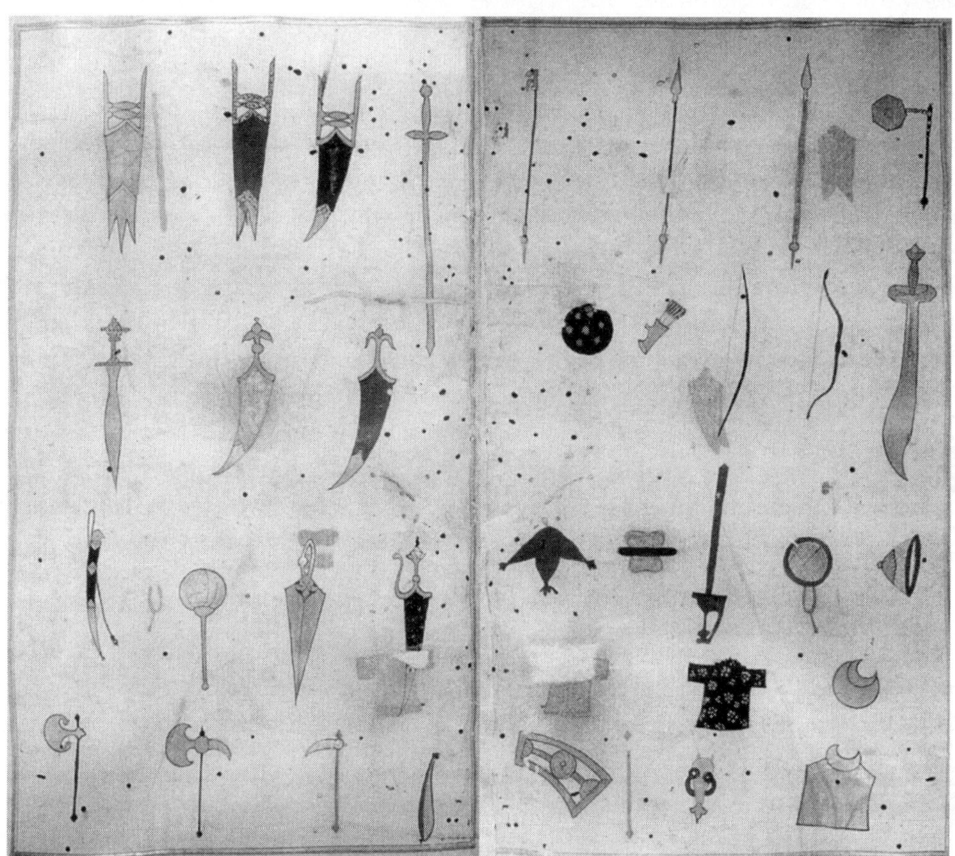

Source: https://commons.wikimedia.org/wiki/File:Ain-i Akbari_Weaponry.jpg.

long distances. In other instances, notwithstanding the role of the military, conquests depended on political bargaining and negotiations with the conquered. Mughal sovereignty in Kalinjar and Gujarat, for instance, was established with the support and approval of the local power holders. The Raja of Kalinjar surrendered the fort, submitted to Mughal forces, and offered to pay the *peshkash*; Akbar, in return, granted him a *jagir* at Arail in Allahabad, in addition to the raja's kingdom. In Gujarat, on the eve of Akbar's conquest, the Sultan's authority was eroded by local rebellions, giving the emperor an opportunity to mediate, to which there was no resistance. In fact, the merchants and residents of Cambay welcomed Akbar's authority.

So it was not merely the military strength of the emperor but the political alliances as well that facilitated his triumphs. Dirk Kolff, however, completely dismissed the military superiority of the Mughals (Gommans and Kolff 2001). He argued that the expansion of the Mughal Empire was the product of their espionage, their intelligence system, and their wealth, which generated support and determined their relationship with the nobility and the local elite. Setting aside the importance and the role of the mounted archers in the Mughal army, Kolff suggested that the prominence of archers in Persian chronicles was the result of a cultural preference for the gentleman-warrior and the ethos of chivalry.

NOBILITY: ITS ETHNIC AND POLITICAL IDENTITY

Notwithstanding the debate and differences of opinion on the military calibre and supremacy of the Mughals, it is pertinent to suggest that while the mounted archers, cavalry and artillery had an important role in facilitating territorial expansion, the process of consolidation necessarily entailed political bargaining and negotiations with the nobility and the local chieftains. In fact, for sovereignty to be firmly established, political alliances, recognition of ethnic and political identities, and the incorporation of these into imperial service were inevitable, although many a time the empowerment of the local social groups could undermine sovereignty. The Mughal emperors attempted to reconcile the zamindars by offering them concessions in the payment of land revenue and evolving the *zabt* system; inducting the regional chieftains and their kin as *mansabdar*s and absorbing their kingdoms as *suba*s of the empire and yet granting them, especially the Rajputs, autonomy, provided they accepted Mughal sovereignty. The Afghans, who had resisted and opposed the Mughals on several occasions, rarely joined the Mughal imperial service, but the Rajputs and *Shaikhzada*s did. However, their relationship with the Mughal emperors remained tenuous. They had joined the imperial service to counter certain political exigencies and as long as the Mughal emperors could fulfil their expectations, they remained loyal; otherwise, they reverted to their family and kin groups with which they had strong ties. None of the Mughal emperors succeeded in creating a chasm between the local chiefs and their family and kin. This adversely affected the process of centralisation.

Akbar initiated the process to reconstitute the authority and ideology of the empire by setting aside the rhetorical allegiance of Babur to Timurid polity, curtailed the privileges of the Turani nobility, and weakened the Chaghatai practices and norms. Remaining steadfast to the imperial vision of his father, who had sought a broad-based empire in which the 'Hindustanis' had a stake, Akbar was determined to build an empire premised on the integrated support of the Indian Muslims and non-Muslims that acknowledged and transcended India's diversity, a multiethnic empire in which narrow sectarian or ethnic appeals could find no place. Abu'l Fazl, his political advisor, generated the intellectual scaffolding required to move the Mughal Empire away from its Central Asian and exclusively Muslim roots. To achieve this, Fazl

- affirmed the multicultural, multireligious character of the Mughal Empire and prescribed an innovative framework by stressing on heterogeneity, cohesiveness, spiritual well-being;
- advocated that India had been a home for famous prophets, saints, Sufi *silsilah*s and many Muslim kings; and
- advised an exchange of literary, philosophical, religious, and scientific ideas between the Hindu and the Muslim elite.

The Mughal nobility under Babur, which was primarily Turani or Central Asian in nature, underwent a first change under Humayun when a few Irani Shi'ite nobles, including Bairam

Khan, were inducted as a counterweight to Turani or Central Asian Uzbeks. Akbar brought a further transformation by minimising the dependence on Turani nobles, strengthened the enlistment of the Iranis or the Persians, and recruited 'new men' (*Shaikhzadas* and Rajputs) with Indian backgrounds, thus setting aside the significance of racial, religious, and Central Asian origins. By 1580, the nobility looked distinctly diverse, heterogeneous, and non-sectarian, with the Persians numbering forty-seven, Chaghatai and Uzbek Turanis forty-eight, *Shaikhzadas* forty-four (that is, 16 per cent of the enlarged nobility), and Rajputs (with a few non-Rajput Hindus) forty-three. With a composition such as this, some, like Mirza Hakim, felt confident enough to generate a rebellion against Akbar, hoping that the Iranis and Turanis would switch their loyalty towards him, while the *Shaikhzadas*, Afghans and Rajputs could be easily crushed. Even if not to the extent that Mirza Hakim expected, factional strife and conflicts were present largely between the Shi'i Iranis and Sunni Turanis, which often assumed the shape of religious controversy. Amongst the *Shaikhzadas*, the Afghans were the most numerous, but because of their continuous resistance, it was not considered feasible to recruit them. Other *Shaikhzada* clans like the Saiyids of Barha, referred to as 'brave warriors', and the Kambus, who had lived in north India for long, were favoured. The ancestors of the Saiyids of Barha claimed descent from Prophet Muhammad, had migrated from Iraq during the thirteenth century, and settled in Sirhind near Delhi. From Sirhind, they proliferated in and inhabited several villages and regions in north India. Known for their valour, martial qualities, and loyalty, the Saiyids mustered their relatives for service under Akbar and his successors but began to lose their prominence in the later years of Aurangzeb's reign. That was probably because the Saiyids of Barha allegedly supported Dara Shukoh. The Kashmiris were assigned important positions, with Inayatullah Kashmiri emerging as Aurangzeb's favourite noble.

The Rajputs, an important section of Akbar's nobility, showed, as discussed by Lahori and Waris in the *Padshah Nama* (Beach and Koch 1997), a substantial increase during the rule of Shahjahan, which improved further during the early years of Aurangzeb's reign. During Shahjahan's period, there was no Rajput officer who held the *mansab* rank of 7,000, but Aurangzeb promoted Mirza Raja Jai Singh and Raja Jaswant Singh to the rank of 7,000 *zat*/7,000 *sawar*, appointed Jai Singh as the Viceroy of Deccan in 1665, and posted Jaswant Singh twice as the Governor of Gujarat, in 1659–61 and 1670–72, while he continued to serve as the *thanadar* of Jamrud until his death in 1678. The appointment of the two Rajput officials to high administrative positions is particularly significant in view of the fact that after Raja Man Singh's recall from Bengal in 1606, no Rajput except Jaswant Singh (posted to Malwa in 1658) was allocated an important assignment in a province. If the number of Rajput nobles declined during the second phase of Aurangzeb's reign (1679–1707), it was neither because of his religious orthodoxy nor was it affected by the Rathor rebellion; instead, it appears to have been influenced by Aurangzeb's engagement in the Deccan wars. *Waqi'at-i Ajmer*, in fact, provides an elaborate description of the Rajput officials who joined the Mughal army along with their contingents during this period. Yet, the number of Rajput officers showed a decline in 1679–1707, 12.6 per cent compared to the proportionate number of Rajputs in 1658–78, which was 14.6 per cent. Calculating the proportionate figures, Athar Ali (1997) suggested that the reduction was not only in the number of Rajputs but the entire non-Deccani elements, and amongst the non-Deccanis, the number of Rajputs was the highest, that is, 17.6 per cent in 1679–1707 as compared to 16.6 per cent in 1658–78, thus allaying allegations of special discrimination against the Rajputs after 1678, as argued by Jadunath Sarkar (1972). The restraint in the allotment of *jagir*s to the Rajputs outside their *watan* was a venture to accommodate the newly recruited Deccani nobles, who very largely comprised the Marathas. This seems to be the most appropriate explanation, especially in view of the fact that instead of being humiliated, the Rajputs were given a status higher than other non-Muslims and those in the imperial service were exempted from *jizya*. More importantly, notwithstanding the limitation on the allotment of *jagir*s and promotions, Rajput officers like Ram Singh Hara, Dalpat Rao Bundela, and Jai Singh continued to serve the Mughal army in Deccan along with their contingents. *Kayastha*s and *Khatri*s, who served as accountants and clerks, were also recruited in the imperial service (though in the lower cadre), and a few of them rose to high ranks, like Raja Raghunath, the *Diwan-i Wizarat* during Aurangzeb's reign.

In the seventeenth century, particularly during the reign of Jahangir, *hakims*, that is, professionals and wrestlers, were inducted in the nobility. Their recruitment heralded the emergence of the 'lobbyists' or those who could canvass with the emperor for entry into imperial service. The 'lobbyists' generally comprised Irani, Turani, and *khanazad*s (descendants of the nobles). The number of Iranis (also known as Khurasanis and Iraqis, who comprised Persian-speaking people from Herat to Baghdad, that is, present-day Iran and the Persian-speaking parts of Afghanistan and Iraq) and Turanis remained more or less equal in this period, although there was a disproportionate increase in the number of Iranis as against the Turanis, whose numbers faced a decline. It was alleged by Mirza Aziz Koka that while Jahangir was hostile to the Chaghatais (Turanis), he showered unprecedented favours on the Khurasanis (Iranis) and the *Shaikhzada*s. Another reason for the shrinking numbers of Turanis could have been the waning power of the Central Asian Uzbek kingdom (much earlier than the Safavids), or it could be that the Turanis, especially the Badakhshis, were considered 'uncultured and boorish' in India. That the reduced strength of the Turanis was consistent is evident from the figures provided by Athar Ali (1997) for Aurangzeb's reign: in 1658–78, there were sixty-seven Turani *mansabdar*s in the rank of 1,000 and above out of 486, but in 1679–1707, they stood at a mere seventy-two out of 575.

Compared to the Turanis, the Iranis could perhaps partly maintain their position because of their influx into the Deccan kingdoms. Most of Jahangir's important ministers—three *wakil*s, six *diwan*s, all his *mir bakhshi*s and *mir samans*—were Iranis. This remarkable increase in the number and importance of the Iranis may have been due to the influence of Nurjahan and her family, all of whom were of Irani origin. Her father, Khwaja Ghiyas-ud-din Muhammad (popularly known as I'timad-ud-daula), had migrated to India in the sixteenth century and had risen from the *mansab* rank of 700 *zat* in the early seventeenth century to the rank of 7,000 *zat*/7,000 *sawar* in 1621, and held the position of *subadar* of Lahore. The patronising trend towards the Iranis continued later in the seventeenth century under Shahjahan and Aurangzeb. Although Shahjahan emphasised the Central Asian Timurid roots of his dynasty, he continued the pattern of allotting important financial positions like *diwan* and *mir bakhshi* to the Iranis. When Ardistani, a migrant from Isfahan, shifted to the Mughal service from Golconda in 1654–55, Shahjahan granted him a *mansab* of 6,000 *zat*/6,000 *sawar*, appointed him chief *diwan*, and conferred upon him the title of Mu'azzam Khan. In 1660, Aurangzeb appointed him *subadar* of Bengal, where he also engaged in foreign trade and trading accounts till his death in 1663. Apart from Ardistani, Mirza Abu Talib or Shayasta Khan (son of Asaf Khan), another Irani, was an ardent supporter of Aurangzeb. Further, as reported by Khafi Khan, Aurangzeb had tremendous faith in the abilities of the nobles from Khawaf (Khurasan), who received promotions and reached prominence 'never seen in the histories of previous rulers'. Both Bernier and Tavernier appeared to agree with Khafi Khan's statement when they suggested that the 'greater part' of Aurangzeb's nobility consisted of Persians, or that the Persians held the 'highest posts' during his reign.

Afghans, who were discouraged and excluded from recruitment in the sixteenth century, showed a distinct improvement in their status in the nobility with the accession of Jahangir. At the beginning of his reign, one of the most powerful and influential nobles at the Mughal court was Khan-i Jahan Lodi. Despite this, Lodi could not be prevented from organising the revolt of his loyalists during the early years of Shahjahan's reign with the support of Nizamshahi Sultan of Ahmadnagar, to express the widespread resentment of the Afghans against the Mughal Empire. Although the rebellion was ultimately crushed, it was significant for its appeal to not only the Afghans in the interior of the empire, but also the tribal leaders in the northwest frontier. Except for a brief lull, there was again a considerable increase in the number of Afghans from 1678, that is, the latter part of Aurangzeb's reign, probably because of their extensive recruitment in the Bijapur kingdom. However, irrespective of the imperial offices that they held, the Afghans remained assertive and inclined towards rebellion, often threatening the internal cohesion of the nobility.

Later in the seventeenth century, as Aurangzeb expanded into Deccan, the Deccanis—Bijapuris, Haiderabadis, and Marathas—were added to the nobility. An official document issued during the eleventh year of his reign defined Deccanis as those nobles, whether of Indian or foreign origin, who were in the service of Bijapur or Golconda prior to their recruitment in the Mughal nobility. This definition technically excluded the Marathas, although by birth they were Deccani and counted and designated so by contemporary writers. From 1681 when Aurangzeb embarked on the virtual annexation of Deccan, the Deccanis were extensively recruited in the Mughal service; they were either compelled to surrender their fortresses and districts or absorbed into the Mughal nobility subsequent to the conquest of Bijapur and Golconda. Jahangir had understood the value of Maratha support with the defeat of Malik Ambar in 1616. Both Shahjahan and Aurangzeb, keen on Deccan conquest, also attempted to strengthen the alliance with the Marathas, although Aurangzeb could not conciliate Shivaji with the *mansab* of 5,000 *zat*/5,000 *sawar*. In his last years, Aurangzeb granted Shahu, Shivaji's grandson, a *mansab* of 7,000 *zat*/7,000 *sawar* that placed him amongst the highest nobles of the empire, even if in a titular sense. But generally, the Marathas could not be reconciled by the grant of *mansab*s. They continued their aggrandising activities and the ravage of Mughal territories, thus rendering themselves an undependable ally.

What is noticeable, however, is that the Marathas, along with the Rajputs, formed a large majority of Aurangzeb's Hindu nobility. While the position of the Hindu nobles declined slightly during the first phase of Aurangzeb's reign, there was a remarkable proportionate improvement in their numbers during the last twenty-nine years of his rule as compared to the reigns of Shahjahan or the earlier Mughal emperors. The increase in their number was caused by the influx of the Marathas who outnumbered the Rajputs during this period. As they became the largest section from amongst the Deccanis in the high ranks, it led to the reduction in the numbers of not only the Rajputs but also the Saiyids of Barha, Turanis, and Iranis. The Afghans, earlier in the service of Bijapur, also improved their position. The investigation into the political and ethnic identities of the nobles reveals that while talent may have been one of the criteria, family and clan were often the deciding factors in their recruitment, making the *khanazads* a significant section of the Mughal imperial service.

NEW IMPERIAL IDIOM: THE *MANSAB*

To control and dominate the diverse, heterogeneous nobility that had a factional, conflict-ridden disposition, Akbar, in 1572–73, initiated the process of defining his ruling elite and bureaucratising it by bringing it under a single imperial service directly subordinate to him through the grant of *mansabs*. Later, Jahangir, Shahjahan and Aurangzeb widened the base of the Mughal Empire by granting *mansabs* liberally to the chiefs of different regions, their complexities notwithstanding. Primarily a mechanism of military organisation or a military rank, *mansab* represented social status and the recipients' order of precedence or position in society or public service, that is, rank in a general sense. A fundamental aspect of the programme of political consolidation, the *mansabdari* system was not an innovation of Akbar but a combination of Timurid and Indo-Muslim conceptions. Akbar followed the precedent of Humayun's tripartite division of society—men of *daulat* (fortune), men of *saadat* (happiness), men of *murad* (hope)—and assigned numerical ranks to his sons in 1577, recognising them as officers and delegates on behalf of the emperor rather than as fellow sovereigns. The classification of princes as *mansabdars* and their appointment as *subadars* and military commanders put an end to the system of appanage and collective sovereignty. Mirza Muhammad Hakim was perhaps the only exception who continued to rule Kabul until his death in 1585.

The precursors to and the evolution of the *mansabdari* system are complex, but the use of numerical ranks to define the status and income of officers reflected the Turko-Mongol practice of decimal military organisation recommended by Chingiz Khan and Timur. In their army, the lowest unit of command was 10; then came 100, 1,000, and 10,000. A unit of 10,000 was generally called a *tuman* and its commander a *khan*. Timur subsequently introduced the ranks from 1,000 to 12,000, reserving the ranks of 7,000 to 12,000 for his sons. Even before the Mughals introduced the system, the cavalry of the Delhi Sultans, as Barani described it (although it is considered erroneous and a 'suppositious calculation' by Athar Ali), was modelled on the decimal system, with officers appointed to command 10, 100, 1,000, 10,000, 100,000 *sawars*, designated as *sar-i khail*, *sipahsalar*, *amir*, *malik*, and *khan*, respectively. Akbar may have followed the procedure of decimals in army organisation, but the system that he instituted was at variance in certain respects. He gave *mansabs* to both civil and military officials, emphatic in his assertion that not merely heredity or family but merit and service to the State would be the criteria for appointment as *mansabdars*, and that they would be directly subordinate to the king. The pay scales of the *mansabdars* were minutely planned and they were paid either in *naqd* or *jagirs*.

Mansab by itself did not constitute any office. Far from a rigid command structure, it was an indication of imperial hierarchy that denoted unequal distribution of imperial honour and dual ranks, represented by *zat* or the original rank of a *mansabdar* indicating his status and personal salary, and *sawar* or an additional rank that signified his military obligations to the State and maintenance of cavalry. In assigning dual ranks, Akbar followed the principle of *dah-bishti*, that is, 10–20, by which a *mansabdar* of the *zat* rank of 10 was required to maintain 20 *sawars*. In addition to *dah-bishti*, the emperor also devised other norms like *do-aspah* or a noble having two horses, *yek-aspah* or a noble with one horse, *nim-aspah* or one horse for two nobles. The nominal rank was limited to the *zat* rank to determine the hierarchical position of a *mansabdar*, but to ensure that he maintained the contingents in accordance with the salary or income granted to him, the *sawar* rank was instituted, which was either equal to or less than the *zat* rank. Abu'l Fazl suggested that the monthly grants to a *mansabdar* could vary according to his *sawars*. For instance, a *mansabdar* who was expected to maintain as many *sawars* as his *zat* rank was placed in the first category of that rank, whereas if his *sawars* were one-half or more, he was put in the second category. If he maintained less than one-half the contingent, then he was assigned the third category. In other words, there were three categories in every *mansab* although there was no rigidity; shifts could be made to meet the exigencies. Akbar's objective in introducing double ranks (*zat* and *sawar*) was to ensure that the *mansabdars* maintained the number of horses and horsemen required of him for imperial service. To affirm that they did not evade the military obligations, Akbar implemented *dagh* or branding of horses with the imperial seal, and *chehra* or *hulia* or descriptive rolls of the *mansabdars*. Each *mansabdar* was expected to present his contingent for muster, until which time he was paid only a proportion of his estimated salary; full pay was given only after he presented his men for inspection. In case of default or delay in bringing his *sawars* for muster, he was penalised and one-tenth of his *jagir* was withheld.

Akbar established the ranks of *mansabdars* from *dahbashi* or commander of ten to *dah-hazari* or commander of 10,000. *Panch-hazari* or the rank of 5,000 was fixed as the highest for an ordinary noble under Akbar. Ranks above 5,000 were reserved for his sons, although exceptions were made in the case of Mirza Aziz Koka and Raja Man Singh, who were honoured with the rank of 7,000. The limit of granting the rank of 7,000 to nobles other than the royal princes was generally retained till the reign of Aurangzeb, although both Shahjahan and Aurangzeb assigned *mansabs* of 7,000 to Rajput rajas Jaswant Singh and Jai Singh. During Aurangzeb's reign, there were at least fifty-one *panch-hazaris* or in the rank above in the first twenty years, while in Shahjahan's entire rule there were only forty-nine such *mansabdars*. The increase may have been because of the new appointments and promotions that Aurangzeb made during and after the succession struggle to consolidate his position. This indicates that the emperor was a decisive factor in the appointment of a *mansabdar* and in determining his status, position, promotion or demotion. *Mansabdars* could be appointed on the advice of the royal princes, powerful, influential nobles of the empire, *subadars* and military commanders, but whoever was the proponent had to stand surety (*zamin*) for the *mansabdar* and the rule was rigorously enforced.

Mashrut or conditional ranks and *inam* were also granted to the *mansabdars*. *Mashrut* rank was given for the additional services that a *mansabdar* performed at a particular post and was usually added to his existing *zat* and *sawar* ranks. For example, if a *mansabdar* was assigned an additional charge as a *faujdar* of an area, he was allotted an additional *sawar* rank of 100, his *mansab* was conditionally increased so that he could employ 100 *sawars*, and a *jagir* was bestowed on him to meet the additional salary of this rank. Once the specially allocated job was achieved, the *mashrut mansab* and *jagir* were resumed; however, if in some instances the conditional was transformed into unconditional, it was considered a promotion and a favour to the *mansabdar*. *Inam* represented additional pay or *jagir* not against any rank, but as supplementary to the amount paid against *mansabs* and without any obligation. However, whatever the form of appointment, the *mansabdars* did not possess hereditary rights and their posts were transferable. In fact, as per the rule, he could not retain the same land assignment throughout his tenure of office, rendering his relationship to land as not one of landlord–tenant, but as that of cash-nexus.

To understand the implications of the conditions of service, it is pertinent to assess escheat that formed a significant and formidable part of the *mansabdari* system. *Ain-i Akbari* is discreet and does not elaborate much on the working of escheat, but the European travellers have left a detailed account of it. Purchas was the earliest to comment on it. They suggested that under escheat, the death of a noble was a call for the resumption of his property by the emperor who, after deducting a portion for himself, restored it to the noble's heir at his pleasure and discretion. The practice of escheat during the reigns of Akbar and Shahjahan was not quite contrary to the reports of the European travellers, but there were slight variations in the case of a few like Munim Beg Khan, Abu'l Fazl, and Ali Mardan Khan. When these nobles died, the emperor did not confiscate their entire property but took only the *mutalaba* (amount borrowed by the deceased noble from the imperial treasury) or a little more before disposing it to their heirs. Aurangzeb is said to have revised the system remarkably by his *farman* of 1666 to the provincial *diwans*, which provided different options of operating the escheat in the event of the death of a noble:

- If a noble died without a legal heir and without any debt to the State, his property was deposited in the *bait-ul mal*;
- If he died in debt in similar circumstances, then, after collecting the State dues, the noble's property was sent to the *bait-ul mal*;
- If the noble had heirs but owed an amount to the State, his property was seized within three days of his death, the *mutalaba* was deducted if the property exceeded it, and the rest was delivered to the heir. But if the debt exceeded the total property of the dead noble, then the entire property was attached;
- If the noble had heirs and he had no *mutalaba* in his name, then the whole property was restored to the heir.

The *farman* of 1666 was further reinforced by another order in 1691 which stipulated that the property of such deceased nobles would not be confiscated whose sons were in the imperial service, for they could be asked to reimburse the *mutalaba* contracted by their late fathers. There are a number of examples from the reign of Aurangzeb that confirm that the emperor's orders were implemented and that he claimed only the *mutalaba* of the dead noble, but there are also instances from which it is not quite clear whether the confiscation of the dead noble's property was to merely recover the *mutalaba* or to enforce the right of escheat.

The *mansabdari* system as it evolved and developed is variously interpreted by historians. While Percival Spear (1970) described the *mansabdar*s as 'elite within elite' and '*lal purdahris*', Stephen Blake (1995) preferred to define the Mughal Empire as a 'patrimonial bureaucratic empire'. Douglas Streusand (2001) argued that the *mansabdari* system was a political compromise that indicated a gap between the theory of service at pleasure and service for security of status in which the *mansabdar*'s own self-perception was influenced by his caste and clan identity, although the relationship between the *mansabdar* and the emperor was defined by the latter's perception of sovereignty. A *mansabdar* could thus be transformed into a slave but, unlike military slaves and *naukar*s, he could not lose his physical identity, that is, his caste and clan identity. John F. Richards (2010) pointed to the ways in which the *mansabdari* system emulated the terminology of Islamic corporate military service. The term *bandah* or slave, he said, helped to shape the expectation, style, and intensity of relationship between the imperial master and his servants.

From the master-slave connection between the emperor and his elite, there developed two bonds: first, that of 'disciple' for the person chosen by the emperor, and second, the familial hereditary service which, by early 1600, had become increasingly significant. *Khanazads*—both Hindus and Muslims—belonged to this category, a group that had proved its devotion, reliability, and capability over four centuries. The bonds of hereditary, familial service and discipleship were sustained through formal audience and interviews at fixed hours in the emperor's *ghusal khana* (consultation room). During public assemblies in the *Diwan-i-Aam* (audience hall) of palaces or camps, the emperor and his *mansabdar*s enacted formal rituals of authority and subordination. Richards argued that by the early seventeenth century, the diverse Mughal elite had become a corporate body of paid officers, whose status and posting were determined by the emperor, although the Rajputs, Afghans, and the Shaikhzadas retained hereditary links with their 'patrimonial domains' or *watan-jagir*s and turned to these lands whenever the necessity arose. Akbar used various methods to balance the varied ethnic groups and subordinate individual and group identities to keep pace with rapid territorial expansion and guard the dignity of the emperor by building upon his personal appeal. Richards established an image of the emperor as an embodiment of the empire, implying that to challenge or destroy the emperor's person was to challenge or destroy the imperial system, for they were identical. These tactics, Richards reiterated, may have been evolved to achieve centralisation and formulate imperial authority, but the kin and clan loyalties and sentiments of localism and parochialism remained strong, making the task of centralisation difficult for the Mughal emperors, including Akbar.

The basic principles, framework, and organisation of the *mansabdari* system as initiated by Akbar were retained in the seventeenth century, barring a few changes introduced during the period. Jahangir announced the *du-aspa sih-aspa* rank, which was theoretically considered a part of *sawar* rank with the stipulation that the obligation of *du-aspa sih-aspa* was double the obligation of the *barawurdi* (ordinary) rank. The pay, therefore, of the *du-aspa sih-aspa* also had to be double that of the *barawurdi*. But the *du-aspa sih-aspa* could never exceed the *sawar* rank of a noble. This implied that if a noble was placed in the *sawar* rank of 4,000, then 1,000 were made *du-aspa sih-aspa* and 3,000 remained *barawurdi*. The pay and obligations for *barawurdi* were on the same scale as fixed, whereas for *du-aspa sih-aspa* both were doubled. Effectively, it meant that the pay and obligations of a noble in the *sawar* rank of 4,000, of which 1,000 were *du-aspa sih-aspa*, the *sawar* rank would be 5,000. This suggests that whenever the emperor wanted to favour a noble or wanted him to maintain a larger contingent without increasing his *zat* rank, he granted him a *du-aspa sih-aspa* rank. The earliest instance of *du-aspa sih-aspa* was noticed in the tenth regnal year of Jahangir when, to honour Mahabat Khan at his appointment in Deccan, the emperor made 1,700 *sawars* of his *sawar* rank *du-aspa sih-aspa*. The grants of *du-aspa sih-aspa* were, however, fewer under Jahangir than under Shahjahan and Aurangzeb, a phase that witnessed their substantial increase.

Shahjahan introduced the institution of *mahwar* or month-scales to deal with the socio-economic crisis evident in the financial administration, that is, a growing gap between *jama'* and *hasil* or a gap between revenue required for assignment to the *mansabdars* and its availability. *Jama'* of a *jagir* in all circumstances had to be equal to the pay-claim of a *mansabdar* because *hasil* formed the income of a *mansabdar*. But by Shahjahan's reign it was realised that when a *mansabdar* was allotted a *jagir*, the *jama'* of which was theoretically equal to his annual *talab* (salary-claim), it yielded, in actuality, only one-half or one-fourth of his claim. The *jagirs* of most *mansabdars* in Deccan met not more than four-monthly or sometimes even less of a *mansabdar's* claim, although the situation was a little better in the northern parts of India. To reduce the gap between *jama'* and *hasil*, Shahjahan introduced *mahwars* and the rule of one-third, one-fourth, one-fifth. The purpose was to scale down the total pay due on a *mansabdar's* rank while retaining the ranks as they were; with the reduction of the pay on the ranks, the obligations of the *mansabdars* were also reduced. That is, under different circumstances, the commanders had to maintain one-third, one-fourth or one-fifth of the number of the contingents on his rank. In the twenty-seventh year of his reign, Shahjahan issued a *farman* that *tankhwah-i naqdi* or cash-salaries of a *mansabdar* should not be fixed above *ashtmah* or eight-monthly, and below four-monthly. An exception was made only in the case of the two highest nobles of the empire and the royal princes, who received their pay on the scale of ten-monthly. By the twenty-first year of Aurangzeb's reign, the scale was reduced from *ashtmah* to *shashtmah* (six-monthly).

The substantial reduction in the scales of pay that took place on *zat* ranks in the seventeenth century led to a debate between W. H. Moreland (1936) and Irfan Habib (1967). Moreland was the first to understand not only the essential features of *mansab* but also the changes in the mechanism of its organisation. While Irfan Habib agreed that changes occurred, he differed with Moreland on the timing and the kind of changes that took place. On the issue of when the reductions in the scales of pay of the *mansabdars* occurred, Habib disagreed with Moreland and argued that the reductions in the scales of pay on *zat* ranks happened sometime between 1618 and 1630, and that there was no evidence to suggest that these reductions were announced by Shahjahan. Exemplifying his point, he argued that the pay for *sawar* rank was calculated on a complex basis until 1595 and could not be compared to the rates of pay subsequently. The permanent standard rate of pay on *sawar* rank was established during the early years of Jahangir; its reduction from 9,600 *dams* per annum to 8,800 *dams* per annum took place not after Shahjahan's accession but in 1615–16, and Shahjahan further reduced it from 8,800 *dams* to 8,000 *dams* per annum. Also, the additional rate permitted for *du-aspah sih-aspah* rank was lower under Jahangir than under Shahjahan. So, in Habib's view, no scaling down of the size of the contingents can be proved in terms of the pay sanctioned; although the scaling down of pay in relation to the *mansabs* happened, it occurred not during the early years of Shahjahan's reign but in the early years of Jahangir's rule.

Satish Chandra (1982), on the other hand, argued that the number of *sawars* a *mansabdar* maintained was reduced proportionately, including the contingent needed for the collection of land revenue. This diminished his ability to collect land revenue without the intervention of a *faujdar*. To meet the requirements of the *mansabdars*—the numbers of whom had grown remarkably between 1605 and 1621: the *zat* ranks held in 1605 exceeded the figures of 1595, almost doubled by 1620, and increased by one-third in 1637—and keep the level of land revenue high, both Shahjahan and Aurangzeb expanded the *khalisa*, that is, from one-ninth under Jahangir, it grew to one-fifth under Aurangzeb. While Habib considered the extension of *khalisa* an instance of 'deliberate policy' and not mere coincidence, Alam and Subrahmanyam (1998) regarded it as an 'abortive attempt' at redefining the relative role and powers of the imperial household towards the *amirs* and the *jagirdars*. Satish Chandra, however, argued that the increase in *khalisa* did not imply a decrease in *paibaqi* or land reserved for assignment as *jagirs* to the *mansabdars*; the problem lay in the demarcation of *khalisa*. While the *mansabdars* were assigned *zortalab* (less developed or disturbed areas that did not pay revenue unless force was used) areas, the imperial *mutassadis* (clerks) demanded *sair-hasil* (productive and manageable) *khalisa jagirs*. If some *jagirs* were found to be *wiran* (waste) with virtually nil realisation, the *mutassadis* insisted on the payment of *khurak-i dawwab* (fodder for animals).

The practice of *khurak-i dawwab* was applied to all nobles, unless specifically exempted. It began as a mandatory tradition, mentioned in *Ain-i Akbari* (although it does not use the term), to maintain and feed elephants, horses, camels, and carts for the emperor's establishment, the numbers of which were regulated according to the *zat* rank of a *mansabdar*. The term *khurak-i dawwab* was first defined as fodder for animals in a manual of Aurangzeb's reign, which also laid down the number of animals, horses and elephants in particular, that were to be fed by *mansabdars* of each rank. By the reign of Shahjahan, it had become common practice to deduct the cost of *khurak* or *rasad-i khurak* from the *talab* or salary of the *mansabdar*. Aurangzeb, however, assigned the *jagir* for full salary and then demanded the *khurak* in kind or cash from the *mansabdars*; if they resisted, *sazawals* or imperial messengers were deputed to counter the resistance and collect it coercively. Realising the growing resentment of the *mansabdars*, Aurangzeb, in the forty-sixth year of his reign, abolished the *khurak* for the elephants; later, the *mansabdars* were freed from paying for the feed of other animals as well.

The aim of the *mansabdari* system as envisioned by the Mughal emperors was to effect centralisation, but it failed to do so. The nobles were dependent for their power and position on the emperor who appointed them; they had no hereditary lands that they could consolidate or bequeath, and all their resources were under the surveillance of the State. In actuality, they were the salaried civil and military officials to whom power was delegated at the emperor's discretion. The nobility, nevertheless, had its tensions. The principle of payment of salaries in *jagirs* and the frequent transfer of *jagirs* prevented them from building a personal base even as it strengthened the imperial organisation. On several occasions, the nobles resisted the implementation of the rule of transfers which remained unenforced in the seventeenth century, giving rise to *jagir-i mahal-i watan* (permanent estates). These long-term *jagir* holdings, Muzaffar Alam argued, further strengthened the nobility, leading to the realignment of different constituents that facilitated carving out independent kingdoms for themselves.

JAGIR, JAGIRDAR AND THE COMPLEXITIES

Jagir or land revenue assignment to the *mansabdars* in lieu of cash salary was the most established form of payment, notwithstanding the payment in *naqd* to some, who were referred to as *naqdi mansabdars* (those paid in *jagirs* were known as *jagirdars*). *Iqta* (the term used under the Sultans of Delhi) and *tuyul* were widely known synonyms for *jagir*, although not so commonly used in Mughal India. In Arabic, *jagir* was called *iqta*. *Jagir* is a compound of two Persian words and should technically be spelt as *jai-gir*, literally meaning one who holds or occupies a place. *Bahar-i 'Ajam*, a Persian dictionary completed in India in 1739–40, defined *jagir* or *jaigir* or *tuyul* as a tract of land which kings conferred upon *umara'* (nobles) and *mansabdars* in lieu of a monthly salary, so that they could appropriate the *mahsul* (revenue) from whatever was produced on that land through cultivation. *Khalisa* or *khalisa-i sharifa* or emperor's revenue domain, which comprised territories and sources of revenue reserved for the imperial treasury, covered a large portion of the empire; yet the greater part, that is, no less than four-fifths of the revenue of the empire, was allocated as *jagirs*. So, when *jagirs* were assigned in lieu of salary to a *mansabdar* for his *zat* and *sawar* rank, they were known as *jagir-i tankhwah* or *tankhwah-i jagir*. The principle in the allotment of a *jagir* was that since it was granted in lieu of cash salary to a noble, its yield in net revenue (that is, gross revenue, less cost of collection) necessarily had to equal the salary entitlement of a *mansabdar*. In other words, the *jama'* prepared for each unit of territory, the village, and especially the *pargana* or *mahal* had to be closely approximated to the *hasil* or actual collection that formed the income of a *mansabdar*. Abu'l Fazl observed that one of the objectives of Akbar's revenue organisation was to prepare such a *jama'*.

Akbar had inherited *jama'* figures known as *jama'-i raqami* prepared for each village (including for the reign of Babur), but they were found to be highly inflated and arbitrarily increased. He thus attempted a revision in 1566–67 on the basis of information from the *qanungos*; nevertheless, barring marginal improvement in the revised *jama'*, the balance between *jama'* and *hasil* could not be achieved. Later, in 1574–75, Akbar resumed all *jagirs* except those held in Bengal, Bihar, and Gujarat, fixed permanent local cash rates for the different crops, and prepared a new *jama'* for purposes of assignment largely for the *zabti* provinces. For the rest of the *subas*, constant repeated attempts were made to reach an accurate *jama'*. In the seventeenth century, *jama'*, known as *jama'-i dami* or *jama'dami*, was stated in *dams* for purposes of assignment and calculated at a fixed ratio of 40 *dams* to a rupee. This implied that the *jamadami* of the *pargana* or the village assigned as *jagir* to a noble had to be exactly equal to his pay. Practically, as in the early years of Akbar's reign, the *jama'dami* figures rarely matched the *hasil*; in fact, it seldom amounted to the full value of the *jama'*, as was the case in some *jagirs*, where the actual receipt was eight-monthly, seven-monthly or six-monthly. It therefore became imperative to compare the paper value of the *jama'* with the *hasil* and make the changes accordingly.

Shahjahan attempted to resolve the issue through *mahwars* or month scales, as discussed above. But generally, the *jagirdars* had to deal themselves with the fluctuations in the revenue receipts. If a *jagirdar* resisted the inflated nature of the *jama'dami*, he was granted a reduction in it, known as *takhfif-i dami*; cash payment was made from the imperial treasury to keep the *jama'dami* equal to his pay or an additional *jagir* was granted with a *jama'* of an equivalent amount. To the contrary, if the *hasil* was found to be in excess of the *jama'dami* or the month-ratio sanctioned for the *jagirdar*, the difference was recovered from the *mansabdar* or added to his *mutalaba*.

Jagirs were not hereditary and could not devolve from father to son, although the emperor could reward the good services of a *jagirdar* by inducting his son into the imperial service and conferring a *jagir* on him. *Jagir* was a means of payment for the services rendered by a noble; it therefore lasted only as long as the noble was in service. This implied that a *jagir* did not provide any right on land, and neither could a *jagirdar* claim any hereditary territorial position. All *jagirs* except *watan-jagirs* and few *al-tamgha* or *altun-tamgha* (these were first granted by Jahangir to allow every noble to have his native place under a permanent assignment) were subject to *taghaiyur* or transfer. The *jagirs* were frequently transferred; generally no assignment was held by the same person for more than three or four years, probably to prevent him from developing local associations or becoming a local potentate. The *jagirdars*, then, were the bureaucrats of the Mughal Empire, strictly an official class whose economic and social status depended on the emperor's discretion. Akbar initiated the practice of transfers in 1568 when he dislodged the nobles of the Atka family from their *jagirs* in Punjab. The periodic transfers that continued rigorously even later caused inconvenience and complications for the *jagirdar*. For instance, in implementing transfers, it was assumed that except for Bengal and Orissa the *kharif* and *rabi* crops were of equal value everywhere, when actually this was not the case. The assignee therefore encountered heavy losses if he was transferred mid-season, that is, if a *jagirdar* held a *jagir* during the *kharif* harvest in one place and during *rabi* harvest in another, and if neither happened to be important crops in the respective territories, the *jagirdar* stood to lose. A sudden transfer could pose problems, especially if the *jagirdar* was unable to collect the full revenue owed to him. In some cases, the assignee was obliged to collect the *baqaya* (previous year's arrears of revenue) and send them to the previous assignee.

Moreover, in most cases, the transfers of *jagir*s were conflict-prone and rarely free from discord. Despite the meticulous rules framed by the State, the implementation of orders was often delayed, resulting in the *jagirdar* collecting the revenue to which another was entitled. Sometimes the *jagirdar*s could use violence or physical force against each other, especially if one received the transfer orders while the other did not. He could, of course, make a pay-claim if he remained without a *jagir* between his transfer and the next assignment. But by the later years of Aurangzeb's reign, no such pleas were entertained for the intervening period; in practice, thus, the *talab* for the gap years between changeover of assignments was rarely met.

The *jagirdar*, as official of the State, was authorised to collect sanctioned land revenue (*mal-i wajibi*) and all other claims of the State (*huquq-i diwani*) within the territorial limits of his *jagir*. He was also expected to implement the agrarian plans of the State, that is, improve, expand, and bring new lands under cultivation, provide for irrigation facilities, and promote *jins-i kamil* (high-grade crops) against the low-grade ones. These financial and administrative obligations of a *jagirdar* entailed interaction with the zamindars, a heterogeneous group of people organised on caste, clan, and tribal basis, who worked in close conjunction with the peasants, possessed territorial rights and military contingents or *ulus* or *jama'iyat* of their own. The arrogance of the zamindars, derived from their political, social, and military strength, had made them resistant to the payment of land revenue from the time of the Sultans of Delhi. Like the Sultanate of Delhi, the Mughal State, too, sought to limit the prerogatives and perquisites of the zamindars and attempted to integrate them into the central administrative system by granting *mansab*s and offering them responsibility for the local land revenue system and maintenance of law and order. For these reasons, collection of land revenue from the zamindars was fraught with complications that often led to conflict between the *jagirdar*s and the zamindars, especially because both considered the land a source of power and wealth.

Equally significant in a village society were the *khud-kasht* (self-cultivators), a privileged section of cultivators drawn from one caste or clan, considered owners of the land that they cultivated with hereditary rights, and who could not be evicted as long as they paid the land revenue. In such circumstances, the Mughal emperors attempted to assert their power by instituting a system of inspection and checks and balances through the *jagirdari* system in order to prevent the monopolisation of power in one class or encroachment of one class into another. This led to the gradual development of what Satish Chandra called a triad or a triangular or tripolar relationship between the central government represented by the *jagirdar*, the zamindar, and the cultivators, among whom the *khud-kasht* predominated. This was the basis, Chandra said, of Mughal stability, which lasted as long as the central government could convince the zamindars and the cultivators that it was beneficial to be under the banner of the Mughal State and look to it for redressal of grievances rather than resist or challenge it. The *pargana* administration and the *faujdari* system contributed to sustaining this relationship. The *faujdar*s were expected to furnish not only military support to the *jagirdar* in collecting his share of land revenue, but also provide protection against the exactions of the *jagirdar*, his *gumashta*s (agents), and the zamindars.

A valuable role in this system of checks and balances was played by *waqi'a navi*s, who watched over both the *jagirdar* and the zamindar. This system, argued Satish Chandra, was a defence mechanism against the corruption and abuse of power and authority at various levels. But the social balance in the Mughal State was very fragile and could be disturbed on several occasions: effects of struggle for power at the centre, factionalism and discontentment amongst the nobles, challenges by regional chieftains, increase in the power of the zamindars or weakening of the position of *khud-kashts*, tensions at the village or local level around caste, religion or ethnic ties, or large-scale local migrations.

The tripolar relationship, as argued by Satish Chandra (1982), was further investigated by Muzaffar Alam (2013 [1986]), who added a fourth dimension in the form of *madad-i ma'ash* holders and a large number of indigenous elements such as *Shaikhzadas* in Awadh and *Khatris* in Punjab. These classes, dependent for their finances on imperial funds, also contributed to defining the nature of the struggle for control over resources during this period. In other words, not only the small group of nobles but also the zamindars, the village and *qasba*-based *madad-i ma'ash* holders, and a number of lower-level officials from different regional and local communities were integrated into the framework of the empire. The stability of the empire depended on the balancing of these diverse elements. However, despite its projection as a coordinating agency between different communities and the indigenous socio-political systems at various levels, the empire could not obliterate or override the *mansabdar*'s attachment to his kin, clan or caste. Political integration in Mughal India had inherent defects. It was conditional and relied on the harmonious interaction of the interests and political activities of social groups.

REVENUE: ASSESSMENT AND APPROPRIATION

The Mughal State, seen in fiscal-economic terms and characterised as primarily an agrarian economy by a group of economic historians, derived its major finances from land revenue or *mal* or *kharaj*, which accounted for the larger part of agricultural surplus and formed the bulk of the State income. This structure has been termed the Mughal 'agrarian system' by Irfan Habib and several others, although Muzaffar Alam and Sanjay Subrahmanyam prefer to define it as the 'fiscal system'. To consolidate and formalise its power and authority, it was imperative for the Mughal State to not only regulate revenue from agricultural produce—whether through assessment, appropriation or extraction of surplus from the peasants—but also establish control over all spheres of revenue. In this context, it would be appropriate to comment on and analyse the cesses levied on the peasants, which would be valuable in calculating the total demand upon a village as well as the demand per *bigha* in different areas. Other than *kharaj*, there were other taxes known as *wujuhat* that included *jihat*, which were imposed to obtain the remuneration of officials associated with the assessment and collection of revenue and fixed as a particular percentage of it. Connected to *kharaj*, *jihat* was assimilated into it as *mal-o-jihat*, giving *jihat* an appearance of allowances paid out of the gross tax collected. The other rural taxes were grouped under *sair-jihat*, considered an important source of income, charged on almost every article—sale of cloth, oil, grain, food items, medicines, horses, camels, and others (various trades, market and transit dues, fees of officials); in brief, all taxes other than land revenue or *kharaj* or *mal*. In addition, certain levies and exactions that did not form a part of the *jama'* were imposed by the zamindars and officials personally and were collectively called *furu'at*, *ikhrajat* or *abwab* and *hububat*. The taxes levied under these categories varied from one region to another; nevertheless, it appears that the total amount collected under the miscellaneous items aggregated to approximately 25 per cent of the land revenue.

In addition to the tax on land under cultivation in a village, two other major taxable items included cattle and orchards. *Ain-i Akbari* suggested that if a cultivator kept a land under pasture that could otherwise have been *kharaji* (yielded land revenue), he had to pay a tax of 6 *dams* per buffalo and 3 *dams* per cow or bullock. No tax was, however, imposed on the *gaushalas* or places where the cows lived to serve a charitable or religious purpose. Abu'l Fazl mentioned *gau shumari* or tax on cows as one of the exactions remitted by Akbar, a practice emulated by Jahangir that continued till 1634. *Kah-charai* or pastoral levy, similar to *ghasmari* in western Rajasthan, described in a *hasbu-l hukm*, was implemented by all Mughal emperors on herds grazing in public pastures. Jahangir wrote in the *Tuzuk-i Jahangiri* with great aplomb the remission of taxes on orchards, a custom noticed also under Akbar. So, while no *sardarakhti* or levy on trees was made under Akbar and Jahangir, Aurangzeb nullified the exemption and ordered a charge of one-fifth for the Hindus and one-sixth for the Muslims, except in cases where the orchards yielded no profit or had graves.

Jizya or poll tax on the non-Muslims added to the magnitude of rural taxation. It was abolished by Akbar in 1564 for pragmatic and strategic reasons—to not only assert political sovereignty, but also because it smacked of discrimination and was regressive and economically unviable. It was later re-imposed by Aurangzeb in 1679 to resurrect his power and authority. *Jizya* had no fixed rate but it was generally computed at never more than 4 per cent of the *jama'* or total assessed revenue, and was expected to be collected by *umana'* or a separate organisation of collectors. Nonetheless, given its retrogressive nature, *jizya* was a heavy imposition even at its lowest rate, equal to about a month's wages of an unskilled urban labourer.

Revenue derived from sources beyond *kharaj*, *wujuhat*, and other taxes included custom duties, mines and mints. Custom duties formed a substantial income from the port towns. Akbar had fixed them at the rate of 2.5 per cent and it continued to be so till the end of Shahjahan's reign. Aurangzeb changed the rate by collecting 5 per cent from Hindus and 2.5 per cent from Muslims; the latter were exempted from it in 1667, a privilege they continued to enjoy till 1682. Thevenot, a European traveller to India in 1666, added that Aurangzeb fixed yet another rate for the Christians, that of 4 per cent. Mines yielded some income, probably from the fee collected from merchants who were permitted to dig and work out the mines on payment to the State. The amount of income that the State could have derived from mints can be speculated from the observation of Manucci, another foreign traveller, who stated that the Mughal government received Rs 11 lakh as profit from the new coins struck at one of the mints located in Surat.

The above-mentioned taxes may have been valuable as State income, but a proper evaluation of agrarian relations and agrarian income entails a discussion on *kharaj* or land revenue—its nature, assessment, and appropriation—claimed by the State as a share of the actual produce. The British understood *kharaj* as the property vested in the government of 'ten-elevenths of the net rental of the country', whereas European travellers of the sixteenth and seventeenth centuries, including Bernier and Tavernier, described the king as the 'owner of all land' for, in their opinion, he appropriated the 'rent of the soil'. These postulates were rejected by an eighteenth-century jurist who argued that *kharaj* in India often exceeded one-half of the produce and was not similar to the *kharaj* sanctioned by Islamic law or as laid down by the *shari'at*, which prescribed one-half as the maximum rate. Technically speaking, *kharaj* in the Mughal economy was not a rent or a land tax. It was a tax on the crop, its actual produce; completely dissimilar to the land revenue of the British, which was a standard rate fixed in cash applied to a particular area of land, irrespective of whether it was cultivated or what was cultivated. So, *mal* or *kharaj* or land revenue in the Mughal State can be best defined as a claim of the State to a share of the actual produce. Irfan Habib has suggested that the predominant feature of the Mughal agrarian system was the transfer from the peasant of his surplus produce, exacted in the form of land revenue. However, there is no way of determining the average size of the surplus produce as a part of the total produce; it must have varied from one piece of land to the other owing to differences in the productivity of soil and the climatic and social conditions that laid down the minimum levels of subsistence.

Recognising the significance of land revenue as substantial income, Akbar initiated the tradition of making its assessment and prescribed methods of assessment and collection—a process continued by subsequent Mughal emperors with few adjustments. In an attempt to reorganise the territories and ordain a system of assessment by which an accurate estimate of the crop could be achieved, Akbar's officials came into contact with a variety of geographical conditions and local customary methods of assessment, which made it difficult to implement a single method of assessment. So even when a major portion of the empire was brought under *zabti*, other customary methods of assessment continued in their respective localities. The systematisation of land revenue necessitated two levels of arrangement: *tashkhis* or assessment and *tahsil* or actual collection. In this process, *jama* indicated the amount assessed or receipts and *hasil* stood for the amount collected. Keeping in view the different agricultural seasons, assessment was made separately for the harvest of *kharif* (autumn) and *rabi* (spring) crops. On the assessment of revenue, the authorities issued a written document called *patta*, *qaul* or *qaul-qarar* stating the amount or the rate of revenue demand. In acknowledgement, the assessee gave his *qabuliyat* or assent to the demand imposed upon him, specifying the time and mode of payment. The Mughal State generally fixed the State demand in cash and insisted on payment in the same mode. Payment in kind was permitted, but only as a concession in times of calamity or if the crop had failed, or in recognition of a local regional customary practice.

Several methods of assessment were noticed in the Mughal Empire. One of them, not strictly a method of assessment but collection, was crop-sharing, known as *ghalla-bakshi* in Persian and *batai* and *bhaoli* in Hindi. *Ain-i Akbari* enumerated three ways of working this system:

- *Batai* or sharing of crop according to the *qarar-dad* or agreement on the threshing ground in the presence of both parties;

- *Khet batai* or sharing of the crop while it was still standing, or division of the field;
- *Lang batai* or sharing of the crop after it was cut and stacked in heaps.

In *lang batai*, the peasant probably piled the crop in equal heaps, which were then collected by the revenue collector proportionate to the share of the State. The Mughal documents described *ghalla-bakshi* as the most favoured method of collection by both peasants and the State; the peasants preferred it for it allowed them to share the risks of the season with the authorities while the State could, in case of dubious assessment, check the productivity level of a village. This method could also generate profits if the grain fetched a high market price. But the State remained apprehensive of the escalating costs as reported by Abu'l Fazl and later Aurangzeb when *ghalla-bakshi* was introduced in Deccan, in case it had to hire security guards to control misappropriation and curb dishonesty.

Hast-o-bud was a method of assessment in which the assessor inspected the village and, on considering the good and bad lands, made an estimate of the total produce, on the basis of which he determined the revenue. Yet another method was to simply count the ploughs, assess the revenue, and apply the rates fixed according to the localities. Neither practice was free from blemish: in the first, the integrity of the assessor was the primary requisite, and in the second, there was no equipoise in revenue demand. To counter these failings, *kankut* or *danabandi* was introduced, in which the *kan* or grain was not shared; instead, a *kut* or an estimate was made by first measuring the land either by a *jarib* (rope) or by pacing; then an estimate of the crop-rate or the yield of each crop per unit of area was made and applied to the whole area under a particular crop. If the assessor could not calculate the crop-rate on the basis of mere observation, he took sample cuttings from three plots of high, medium, and low productivity and made the estimate accordingly. An important characteristic of *kankut*, as Abu'l Fazl observed, was that the demand was not fixed in cash but in kind, that is, first an assessment of the full crop was made on the basis of crop-rates, from which the peasant's share was deducted and the rest (that represented the revenue) was commuted into cash by applying a schedule of prices for the different crops. Although *kankut*, based upon the actual produce of the harvest, appeared similar to *batai*, it was more accurate and less costly for it required no shield on the reaping and threshing ground. However, one of the prerequisites of operating *kankut* was the integrity of the assessor, the sole determinant of the crop-rate. The government had often felt constrained to divest him of his power.

These considerations may have induced Sher Shah to make alterations in *kankut* between 1540–45 through his 3 *rai'* or crop-rate system, that is, instead of fixing a *rai'* or rate at each harvest, a standard schedule of rates was prepared and applied, irrespective of the actual harvest, to lands under continuous cultivation (*polaj*) that were rarely left fallow (*parauti*). The *rai'* was prepared on the basis of three categories of land—good, medium, and low productivity—and the average of these was calculated to attain a general rate of the produce, one-third of which was claimed as the State share, that is, land revenue. The evolution of the 3 *rai'* system as described in the *Ain* modified *kankut* and transformed it into *zabt* under Sher Shah and Islam Shah. *Zabt*, characterised synonymously with *jarib* or *amal-i-jarib*, was a distinct mode of assessment in its own right and stood for measurement and assessment based on it. Under *zabt*, land under cultivation was measured; revenue was fixed in cash and the payment too was made in cash. The revenue assessor under the system was no longer concerned with the actual harvest; he had to simply measure the land sown with each crop, determine the standard schedule of *rai'*, and tell the revenue payer in advance the amount that he had to pay. In case the crop failed at harvest, an allowance was made by declaring the sown area *nabud* or crop-less or destroyed, but it could not be more than 12.5 per cent of the total area. Remission in payment of tax was also granted with arrears to be paid in the next harvest season.

During the early years of his reign, Akbar accepted and sanctioned throughout his empire not only the *rai'*, but also the proportion assigned as State share that he had inherited from the Sur administration. Abu'l Fazl, however, does not tell us whether the 3 *rai'* system was applied to only Delhi and Agra or the whole of Hindustan, that is, the territory from Lahore to Awadh, although the latter seems to be the case. It is apparent from the figures provided in the *Ain* that the annual *dasturu-l 'amal*s or *dastur*s or cash-rates for the various crops (the rate in kind did not express the revenue demand and therefore had to be commuted into cash-rates) in the *zabti* provinces (except Ajmer and Bihar) were largely common for each crop, with either no or marginal change in the *dastur*s from one year to the next in the early years of Akbar's reign. These rates were hardly related to local productivity or price fluctuations, causing divergence between the actual revenue-paying capacity of the peasants of an area and the *jama'* at which the area was assigned to the *jagirdar*s. Fazl further added that the *jama'* could often be increased to meet the salary claims of the *jagirdar*s. To improve the system, Akbar ordered the reporting of prices annually from every region of the empire from the eleventh year of his reign (1566–67); Muzaffar Khan and Todar Mal obtained the local area and revenue statistics (*taqsim*s) of the areas from the *qanungo*s; and an attempt was made to make the revenue rates realistic either by varying local *rai'*s or by commuting the *rai'*s into *dastur*s at local prices, or by both means. The *dastur*s showed large local variations from 1565–66, that is, the differences between the rates of different provinces and dissimilarity between the rates of each province in different years became remarkably noticeable. This practice resulted in new local crop rates and price schedules that were drawn up separately every year for each locality.

Even as the government prepared to enforce the *dastur*s to determine the revenue demand upon the peasants, there was rising dissatisfaction with the annual commutation of *rai'* into *dastur*s. Further, with the expansion of the empire, delays were noticed in sending local price reports to the court and receiving the sanctioned revenue rates. Consequently, the peasants complained of appropriation of revenue larger than the sanctioned amount during the intervening period and the *jagirdar*s expressed their discontentment at the unfulfilled payment of balances of revenue caused by the delayed information on ratified rates. To remedy these grievances, Irfan Habib argued that Akbar devised new revenue rates in 1574–75. Information for each locality was collected for a period of ten years, that is, 1570–71 to 1580–81, or *hal-i dahsala* on production, prices, and the area cultivated. Based on this, the revenue rates were fixed in cash for each crop, dispensing with the practice of commuting *rai'* into cash rates at the current price. To implement the system successfully, *pargana*s in each *suba* that were homogenous in yield were grouped together into revenue circles and a separate schedule of *dasturu'l 'amals* was prepared for various crops. These approved cash-rates were applied every year with only such changes or adjustments that were deemed necessary by the government from time to time. This was the *Ain-i dahsala* or the ten-year schedule or *zabt* in its final form, as Habib argued. It was called so based on the information of ten years preceding 1580–81. It was not a decennial system or a ten-year settlement, neither was it a permanent settlement, for the State gave no guarantee for its immutability.

Zabt entailed the classification of land on the basis of continuity of cultivation:

- *Polaj* or land cultivated every year;
- *Parauti* or land left fallow for some time;
- *Chachar* or land that remained fallow for three or four years;
- *Banjar* or land that remained uncultivated for five or more years.

To expand and improve cultivation, Akbar ordered lower rates of revenue for the latter three categories of land and charged the full sanctioned rate only when they reached the *polaj* level. *Zabt*, as Habib and many others observed, simplified the process of assessment and demonstrated some obvious merits from the administration's point of view. Measurements could be rechecked and fixed *dasturs* prevented abuse of power by the local revenue officials; more significantly, the standing *dasturs* could, to a certain extent, control the fluctuating annual revenue demand. But *zabt* had its limitations: fixed *dasturs* implied that there was rarely a direct relation between the revenue rates and the actual harvest in any year. So if the crops failed, relief was provided not by sanctioning low revenue rates but by declaring a part of the measured land as *nabud* on the recommendation of revenue officials who, after inspecting the standing crops, fixed not more than 12.5 per cent of the measured area as *nabud* in infertile regions if the monsoons were abundant there, and/or 15 per cent in the jungle and desert areas. *Zabt* could be implemented only where the soil was homogenous; otherwise, in case of seasonal variations, the peasants had to bear the risks of uncertainty. It was an expensive method of assessment for it required the maintenance of officials who measured the land, and had to be paid a cess of one *dam* per *bigha* called *zabitana*.

Notwithstanding these constraints, *zabt* largely continued along similar lines during the seventeenth century. It was established, as Habib (1999 [1963]) averred, in the entire region from Indus to Ghaghra, and was further extended into Deccan by Murshid Quli Khan in the later years of Shahjahan's reign. Alam and Subrahmanyam (1998) have questioned the constancy and steadiness in the principles for taxation and the unremitting centralisation suggested by Irfan Habib. They argued that a close reading of *Ain-i Akbari* reveals a different proportion between *zabt* 'regulation' territories and the rest of the empire. To ascertain the extent of the area under *zabt*, the data on *arazi* (taxable land) at the end of Akbar's reign, they said, needs to be reviewed; and if no such data is available for certain *subas*, it not only suggests the non-existence or non-implementation of the system, but it also becomes imperative to categorise them as 'non-regulation' territories. This further confirmed the postulate, also conceded by *Ain-i Akbari*, that by 1600 or by the close of Akbar's rule, assessment in several provinces was based on methods other than *zabt*. Even where the territories were under *zabt* or under 'regulation', there was not enough clarity except in the provinces of Allahabad, Awadh, Agra, Delhi, Lahore, and Multan, where it evidently functioned. Bihar and Malwa were partially under *zabt* while in Gujarat, assessment was largely based on *nasaq*. The *suba* of Ajmer, ruled by the chieftains, probably relied on their customary methods of assessment. Alam and Subrahmanyam observed that, in other words, the whole scenario of uniformity and centralisation appears 'suspect'.

Habib, however, stated that *zabt-i harsala* or annual measurement implemented till the thirteenth regnal year of Akbar or 1568–69 had led to major expenditure and misappropriation of funds by the revenue officials. It was, therefore, replaced by *nasaq*. *Nasaq* literally means 'good order, administration', but *Bahar-i 'Ajam* described it as *band-o-bast* in the sense of a fixed tax demand. Abu'l Fazl referred to it several times in *Ain-i Akbari*, but did not define it distinctly. Irrespective of the indefiniteness, if Fazl's information on *nasaq* is put together, it reveals it to be a system in which the whole or part of the assessment was not prepared annually but the assessment derived previously was repeated year after year, following the procedure of initial assessment in the region—whether area figures, *dasturu'l 'amals*, *ghalla-bakshi*, or counting the number of ploughs. It could be modified only under certain circumstances if the peasants demanded fresh *paimaish* (measurement). *Ain* clearly specified, for instance, that Berar had continued with its long-held customary practice of *nasaq*, disregarding completely the changes brought about by the Mughals in land revenue organisation. Similarly, in Mughal Deccan, *nasaq* was based on counting the number of ploughs in a village, irrespective of the land under cultivation or the extent of the actual harvest. In Bengal, too, *nasaq* was the mode of revenue assessment; *ghalla-bakshi* was never the rule here and measurement was an exception, although Abu'l Fazl was rather ambiguous on it. It appears that revenue assessment in Bengal based on *nasaq* was made on the zamindars, who then calculated the revenue rates to be paid by the peasants according to the local standards, one of which happened to be measurement. The narrative on Kashmir is elaborate and clear on the method of assessment and Abu'l Fazl characterised it as *nasaqi-i ghallabaksh*, with crop-sharing as its basis but different from the general practice of crop-sharing, that is, the quantity of produce collected as revenue remained fixed or persistent from one year to the other. Habib upheld *nasaq* as 'a handmaid of other methods' and not as an independent means of assessment, sometimes subordinate to *zabt* and at other times to *ghalla-bakshi*. But whatever it may have been, the diverse character of *nasaq* cannot be doubted, nor the fact that it continued to prevail in regions as a long-held customary practice of assessment, making it difficult to disagree with Alam and Subrahmanyam who stated that while several regions were brought under *zabt*, local standards of assessment continued to be followed in many others, rendering centralisation a distant possibility.

Village, not the peasant, was the basic unit of assessment, although Aurangzeb's *farman* to Rasikdas had prescribed *asamiwar* (individual cultivator) assessment. The Mughal State preferred *asamiwar* rather than *sarbasta* or collective assessment for the entire village, for the latter could result in an uneven distribution of *jama'* among the peasants by revenue officials like the *chaudhuri* or the *qanungo*. The *amin* or the assessor fixed the assessment on the village and left the shares of the peasants to be decided by the headmen; the *diwan* was expected to ensure that the *jama'* of the village conformed to its capacity and that it (*jama'*) was not oppressive when distributed among the peasants by the *chaudhuri*, *muqaddam* or *patwari*. The *amalguzar* (revenue collector), on the other hand, was supposed to give a written document or *patta* to individual peasants and get his *qabuliyat* in return. Yet another important official in land revenue organisation was the *bitikchi* or accountant, responsible for recording the name of each peasant along with that of his ancestor, the crop cultivated by him, and the *'jama* assessed upon it; he then calculated the total of the individual assessments to show the revenue (*mahsul*) of the village.

In accordance with Aurangzeb's *farman* to Rasikdas, the *'jama* of each village was fixed after an *asamiwar* assessment. Similarly, the *farman* stipulated that in case of a natural calamity, the *amin* was expected to stay away from granting lump sum remissions and not allow *chaudhuri*s, *qanungo*s, *muqaddam*s, and *patwari*s to make distributions among the peasants; instead, he was required to inspect the individual fields and appraise the amount of remissions for each individual peasant. Once revenue collection had concluded, the *bitikchi* was entrusted the task of checking the *sarkhat*s, that is, receipts or memoranda, given by the *muqaddam*s and *patwari*s to the peasants to ascertain that the collections had conformed to the assessments. The government ordered the occasional scrutiny of *kaghaz-i kham* (village accounts) to discern instances of misappropriation (if any). In case more than the specified amount was collected, it was supposed to be reimbursed and adjusted against the balance of revenue to be paid by individual peasants. Irfan Habib doubted whether these regulations were implemented in practice and suggested that the *asamiwar* entries in official assessment documents were either fictitious, or duplicated from the report of the village accountants or village headmen.

Land revenue was paid in cash from as early as the thirteenth century. In Mughal north India, the revenue demand was stated in cash under *zabt* and *nasaq*. In *ghalla-bakshi* and *kankut*, the demand was fixed in kind in relation to the produce, but it was then commuted into cash at market prices, the form in which revenue was collected from the peasants. Payment in kind was allowed in certain regions or if the peasant was unwilling to pay in cash in case he found the demand too burdensome. Whatever the case, payment of land revenue, argued Irfan Habib on the basis of the evidence of Abbas Khan Sarwani, was rigidly enforced. Non-payment was considered equivalent to rebellion, and could result in not only the eviction of the peasant from the land, but also severe punishments like imprisonment and torture of the village headman, massacre of adult male inhabitants of the village, and enslavement of the women and children.

Regardless of these diktats, there appeared to be a certain flexibility in the rules for payment of *kharaj*, keeping in view the local customs and practices and local agrarian conditions. Moreover, the volume of land revenue fluctuated constantly, influenced by the variations in agricultural production that depended on a number of natural phenomena. In such circumstances, the Mughal State made provisions for relief in case of harvest failure. One such measure, as mentioned in Aurangzeb's *farman* to Rasikdas, stated that land revenue could be paid over a period of time in *kist*s or instalments of four to six. In the case of *ghalla-bakshi* and *kankut*, the State was an equal partner in the increase or the risks of the actual produce, even if the rates in kind were commuted into *dasturu'l 'amal*s at market prices, whereas under *zabt* and *nasaq*, crop failure was provided for by declaring a part of the assessed area as *nabud. Taqavi* (literally meaning 'strength-giving') or loans, as described in *Ain-i Akbari*, were granted to 'empty-handed peasants' to facilitate cultivation and purchase of bullocks and seeds. *Taqavi* were distributed through the *chaudhuris* or *deshmukhs* and *muqaddams* or *patels* who also stood surety for their repayment; *taqavi* could also be given by the *muqaddams* or *patels* on their own account. Although Abu'l Fazl advised the gradual payment of *taqavi*, the order of Todar Mal and the manuals of the seventeenth century reveal that the general practice was to recover the loan at the first harvest, failing which it certainly had to be reclaimed in the next one of the same year. Concessions were, however, granted in the form of permitting repayment through annual instalments or adding the arrears from *taqavi* to the *sanwat-baqi* or the arrears (already existent) of the peasant. There is no evidence of interest being charged on *taqavi* loans, although it could be that the *chaudhuris* and *muqaddams*, who served as surety, exacted a commission from them. If a peasant died or fled the field, *taqavi* was expected to be repaid by his sureties or the revenue officials who had stood the guarantee, but in case the peasant was in extreme distress, though present on the field, his loan was completely written off as per the *farman* of Aurangzeb's reign.

In view of the disparate arrangements for revenue assessment, the Mughal government laid down norms for collecting land revenue from the peasants. The general instructions, evident from the revenue literature of Aurangzeb's reign as also the account of Abu'l Fazl, was that the amount of land revenue should in no case exceed one-half of the produce. This command was probably inspired by its regard for the *Shari'at*, which prescribed this as the maximum limit for *kharaj*. However, the share of the crop taken from peasants under crop-sharing and *kankut* varied according to the crop and the locality; the norm generally was one-half of the total produce from the less fertile regions and a substantially greater amount from the more fertile zones. Under *zabt*, the rate of *kharaj* varied from one-third of the produce to one-half. Habib (1999 [1963]) argued that from the beginning, the revenue demand had been fixed at such a high rate that it left little scope for further increase. To calculate the tax burden on the peasants, if *kharaj* was considered along with the other cesses imposed, it showed heavy risks and an encroachment on the peasant's subsistence, particularly if no expedient relief was granted to him. These complexities and variations in the revenue demand indicated a tenuous relationship between revenue assessment and agrarian production, as observed by Alam and Subrahmanyam, (1998) necessitating discreet evaluation.

5

ECONOMY AND SOCIETY

HIGHLIGHTS

- Agrarian property in land: Debate on the village community
- *Ra'iyat* (peasants) in rural society
- The role of the zamindars
- Patterns of crop production and agrarian technology
- The notion of 'agrarian environment'
- Rural-urban interlinkages, urban growth, artisans, trade
- Potentialities of capitalism in Mughal economy

The process of consolidation and integration entails the study of economy and society, agrarian and commercial trends. Legitimacy, power, and dominance in a traditional agrarian society was closely associated with unquestioned authority over resources—land, labour, capital—in other words, production and the market. Land is the basic premise of existential and evolutionary patterns of society and the interrelationship between land and human beings forms the basic element of agrarianism. Georges Duby (1988) had argued that whatever the nature of the inhabitants, whether bishop or king or trader, they are first and foremost 'countrymen' whose lives are dominated by the cycles of agriculture and agricultural seasons. Agriculture, an activity of vital importance for economic growth and commercial investment, impressed the Mughal emperors to stimulate production, appropriate land, and intensify land use. However, no understanding of agrarian relations or any rural society can be considered complete without reflection on one of the key elements of environment, that is, forests, or the importance of forestry for people or the distinct ways in which the people who used forests sought to define them or organise their relations with it. In other words, the contributions of the sedentary communities were not isolated from or exclusive of the tribal communities in the creation of economy and society and its consolidation.

Landed property rights regulate land use and manifest deep social anxieties in every society. Land rights were equally significant, extraordinarily complex and layered in every region of Mughal India. Some rights were made and enforced by the State, some by local custom and habit, and some by both agencies. Whatever the mode, it would be an over-simplification to suggest that each fiscal right-holder enjoyed exclusive proprietary rights independent of each other. To understand these facets, it would be apt to analyse the dynamics of economic life and the system of relations of production.

THE ISSUE OF AGRARIAN PROPERTY IN LAND: THE VILLAGE COMMUNITY

The proprietary rights in agrarian land and the nature of land tenures in Mughal India were a source of dilemma for officials of the English East India Company from the latter half of the eighteenth century. Debating the issue of agrarian property, Company officials were in a quandary as to who owned the land, the State or the zamindars, even as they completely ignored the importance of the peasants. The Company considered the aspect from three dimensions: the rights and privileges of the State; position and status of the zamindars and other assignees; and the rights of the different categories of peasants. Influenced by European travellers like Bernier, Tavernier, Manucci, Fryer, and others who visited India during the sixteenth and seventeenth centuries and who unanimously opined that the king in India possessed proprietary rights in land, the Company asserted its right of ownership over land as an inheritance from the Mughals. However, H. H. Wilson and Maxime Kovalevsky, critical of this principle formulated by James Mill, argued that such a custom was sanctioned neither by ancient Indian law nor Islamic law. Moreover, no claim to this effect was found to have been made in the Mughal official documents.

It was only in the eighteenth century that the king's right to ownership of land was asserted emphatically by Tek Chand 'Bahar' in his dictionary, *Bahar-i Ajam*. He alleged that the term *kharaj* signified land tax and when the king claimed a share of it, it was because of his *milkiyat* (ownership) of the land. Similarly, the European travellers affirmed the proprietary rights of the king, for the share of the produce that he received was so large that it approximated to rent rather than tax. Their stipulation was influenced by their misconception of the *jagir* system, or rather, their ignorance of how it worked. Convinced that the *jagirdar*s were the counterparts of the lords in Western Europe, who by the sixteenth century had acquired ownership rights over their manors and fiefs, the European travellers observed that if the *jagirdar*s were transferred frequently by the Mughal emperor from one territory to the other, then it was the king and not the *jagirdar* who possessed ownership rights.

In theory, the king appeared to be the proprietor of the *banjar* or *jungle* lands when he assigned them to the *ra'iyat* (peasants) or the zamindars for agrarian development or expanding cultivation. Yet, in pragmatic terms, the king possessed no proprietary rights in any absolute sense for all such allotments were accompanied by a clear title to the land recognising the cultivator's proprietary, hereditary rights. In case such lands became waste or were left uncultivated, they reverted back to the State, and the king could then, as observed by *Qazi* Muhammad A'la in his *Risala Ahkam-i Arazi* (*c.* 1700), expel the earlier ones and settle another *qaum* or caste (in an ordinary village, the bulk of the peasant population was identified by their *qaum*) on the same conditions. *Ain-i Akbari*, in its chapter on *Rowai Rozi* (means of subsistence), described the proprietary rights of a pioneer cultivator who cleared the land, brought it under cultivation, and kept it in constant cultivation. The State merely claimed a fixed share of the produce rather than the title to the land and, as has been variously argued, the stability of the Mughal State depended on its ability to appropriate a large part of the surplus beget by the agrarian society.

The village community played a pivotal role in the functioning of what has been called the Mughal 'agrarian system', which was constituted by the production of agricultural surplus, its appropriation by the zamindars and the State, and its distribution amongst the sections of the governing class comprising *jagirdars*, *madad-i ma'ash* holders, and others. Reviewing the position and rights of the zamindars and peasants in the village community, the European scholars had remained vexed by its peculiar congruities. To them, villages defined traditional India. In an attempt to understand rural society, villages were seen as systems of production and as objects of economic analysis. Recognising that the village community was an important factor in the evolution of Indian rural society, they viewed it according to a skewed understanding. They chose to characterise the village community as either the 'necessary adjunct of oriental despotism and superstition' or 'petty village republics' representative of 'archaic society' and as 'absolute proprietors'. Such ideas were represented by the likes of James Mill (1975, 127), who described the villages 'as not only a sort of small republic but to have enjoyed to a great degree the community of goods'. Expressing similar views on the formation and nature of the village community, John S. Mill and Henry Maine (1990, 99) argued that 'the village community was not co-extensive with the cultivating inhabitants of the village . . . the property in land resided not in the individual *ryot* but in the village communities'. Thomas Munro's descriptions were also the same. In 1806, he wrote that 'every village with its twelve *ayangadees* (village officials) was a kind of a little republic with *potail* (headman) at the head of it . . . and India is a mass of such republics'. Baden Powell (1892) believed that the village communities were created either by the multiplication of the descendants of chiefs or petty princes who obtained the villages by conquest or grant within late historic times; if this was the case, he argued, it was connected with archaic society. Powell saw the principle of joint inheritance and the custom of sharing, of pre-emption, and other means of excluding strangers as derived from the aboriginal tribal idea in which the family and not the individual was the owner of the property.

Contrary to such representations, scholarly research on Indian villages has established that they were neither 'petty village republics' nor 'archaic'. The villages were not isolated; they had links with cities and other villages; and were not particularly 'united in everyday matters'. It was oriental misconception that represented pre-colonial India as despotic, decadent, and deformed by de-contextualised versions of caste or the village community as the sole (and autonomous) basis of Indian society. The village community was in effect the community of proprietors in a village, especially where the village happened to be a *bhayyachara* village or a village of coparcenaries. It does not mean that there was a village commune or village community that owned the land on behalf of all its members. In essence, village community was a corporate body which the peasants formed for collective action outside the sphere of production. There is no evidence of the collective or communal ownership of land or a periodic distribution and redistribution of land among the peasants.

The documents of the sixteenth century, in particular Abu'l Fazl's *Ain-i Akbari*, described the peasant's permanent title and hereditary occupancy rights over the land that he tilled, and the inviolability and salability of these rights. The *farman*s of the seventeenth century further reinforced the position and rights of the peasants—a fact evident from the *farman* of Aurangzeb to Muhammad Hashim, which used the terms *malik* and *arbab-i-zamin* for the peasants. Similar evidence on the occupancy rights of cultivators, or the fact that they could not be evicted as long as they fulfilled the obligation to cultivate the land that they laid their claim upon or paid land revenue for regularly, are also abundantly recorded in the documents of the late eighteenth–early nineteenth centuries. So while the peasant's right to the land was his individual right, there were a number of claimants—zamindars, peasants, artisans, agricultural labourers, and others—to the share of the produce and it was collectively used, a practice alien to the capitalist idea of exclusive control and of the right to use or abuse. But the individual peasant production, argued Irfan Habib, could never be egalitarian: the resources of the peasants of different categories varied and the extension of market relations and usury and the retrogressive land tax intensified the differentiation within the peasantry. Nevertheless, the two essentials of the village community—its stratified nature and the peasant as the fulcrum, crucial to agricultural production—co-existed with the organisation of the village as a 'community', a network of caste divisions and customary service or barter relationships. Significant to the village community, peasants notwithstanding, were the tribal people and their persistent efforts in the socio-economic processes contributing to the stabilisation of agrarian society, serving the interests of the 'agrarian system'. The tribal populations, as Chetan Singh averred (2010, 2017), were not incongruous to rural society; in fact, the village communities of Mughal India lived in reasonable proximity to the tribal societies.

The village, argued Irfan Habib, had few demands on outsiders beyond its limits; it generally catered to the needs of its inhabitants from within itself, and therefore in that context, it was a self-sufficient unit. The close settlement of peasant households and the fact that peasant migrants moved together as a whole for better protection reinforced the feature of the collective organisation of peasants, within the framework of clan and caste. Specific social factors, he observed, that marked the bases of the village community, that is, the caste system, its hereditary division of labour, and a hierarchical system of caste dominance and caste co-operation, had its economic aspect, in the sense that all villagers were linked together as traditional customers to particular village artisans providing customary shares out of their harvests so as to get certain services from the craft workers. It is pertinent to note, however, that the emphasis on village self-sufficiency has been rather misleading, conveying the impression that village society was a 'closed' society based on some kind of natural economy, when, to the contrary, seventeenth-century India witnessed the growth of towns, a national market in certain types of commodities, growing involvement of India in the international market, growth of commodity production, particularly in coastal areas, and consequently, the increasing penetration of money in village economies.

The growth of money economy and accumulation of money capital aroused a controversial debate yet again when some pointed towards the disintegration of the village community in the eighteenth century due to increasing property inequalities, spread of commodity-money relations, erosion of the position of hereditary landholders, and the growth of a feudalising elite. In this context, it is worthwhile to comment that eighteenth-century India was not sunk in some primeval 'Asiatic' stagnation. It had exports and commercial centres; its problem perhaps was the small-scale nature of most internal markets, which were 'largely a cluster of village economies'.

RURAL SOCIETY: PEASANTRY AND AGRICULTURAL LABOURERS

Rural society represented the finest knowledge of local tradition, custom, and law in which the zamindars may have enjoyed the 'superior' right to land, but the one who understood deeply the nuances of land, put it to effective use, and improved and expanded its potentiality were the *ra'iyat*. The *ra'iyat* formed a significant section of the holders of land and its produce, and 'wielded customary dominion over the soil'. Categorised on the basis of their rent and occupancy and seasonal rent-paying rights, the Mughal documents defined two main parameters of cultivators—*khud-kasht* and *pahi-kasht*. The Regulation of 1795, too, recognised the two classes as *pahi-kasht* and *chapparband*. Wilson described the *pahi-kasht* as 'a migratory or non-resident cultivator, who cultivates land in a village to which he does not belong by birth or hereditary claim and holds his land either for a stipulated term or at pleasure of some member or members of the proprietary body', as opposed to the *chapparband*, who was defined as 'a resident cultivator'. Inequalities and differences existed between the two sets of cultivators, but the disparities varied from slight to large, particularly in the frontier regions. The exclusivity of the two classes could not be firmly established and the balance of advantage or disadvantage of the status of *khud-kasht* and *pahi-kasht* varied in different historical conjunctures. The term *muzarian* or *muzara* occurred frequently in Mughal documents alongside *ri'aya* and *ra'iyat*, which could mean both a peasant proprietor and a tenant cultivator, but more specifically a cultivating peasant or one who derived his subsistence from cultivation. *Muqarari Ri'aya* was a tenant cultivator or a cultivator for the lease period.

Khud-kasht

Khud-kasht is the Persian version of *thani* (in Sanskrit, *sthanika*) or resident cultivator. They were occupancy tenants whose names were entered in the *patwari* records and in the *jama-bandi* of the village, with the fields that they cultivated, known and marked on the village map. The *khud-kasht*s were also known as *bhomia* or *thikana* or *gaveti* or *gharu-hala* in Rajasthan and *mirasdar* or *mirasi* or *thalwahik* in Deccan. The origins of *khud-kasht* rights were variegated. They were cultivators who owned the lands that they cultivated along with oxen and other means of cultivation, successfully expanded cultivation and improved agricultural productivity in the region, and inhabited a village or a zamindari for a sustained period, in which they possessed a house. In other words, they were primary cultivators who held hereditary occupancy rights in the land that they cultivated, with rights to alienate, sell, transfer, and bequeath their land. Their labour was either in the form of self-cultivation or family labour or hired labour (*majur*s), and sometimes even sharecropping. The *khud-kasht*s could not be ejected from the land as long as they paid the land revenue. In fact, they may have rarely felt dispossessed. Aurangzeb's *farman* to Muhammad Hashim referred to the *khud-kasht* as *malik-i-zamin*, who possessed the right to reclaim their land even after a long gap (which could be thirty years) upon clearing the arrears that they may have owed to the State.

As a primary cultivator, the *khud-kasht*s enjoyed several privileges. They paid land revenue at a concessional rate or on the basis fixed by local customs. Theoretically, it could not be increased, but in practice it depended upon the bargaining power of the *khud-kasht*, the nature of the government, and the availability of land. In some instances, evident from different regions, the land revenue could be raised to one-half. Their other prerogatives included exemption, partially or wholly, from taxes paid to the *patil*s, such as tax on marriages, festivals, or any other celebration. They were not obliged to pay any house tax if they had only one habitation in the village. But they were not excused from certain village expenses, which varied from one region to the other, such as *gaon kharch* or taxes imposed to meet the different expenditures of the villages, such as maintenance of temples or costs of maintenance of the village officials. The *khud-kasht* was considered a valued right not only because of its economic benefits, but also because of the social status that it conferred. They formed the governing body of the village commune, its *bhadralok* or the elite of the village community, and participated in its governance, enjoying several perquisites.

There was, however, no unanimity amongst East India Company officials on the role and position of *khud-kasht*s in the village. The issue was whether these cultivators possessed legal title to the land. Were they landowners or tenants? Many Company officials were inclined to believe that the zamindars were the sole owners of the land. In their attempt to understand existing social institutions, their dilemma was quite apparent. Warren Hastings, in a note of November 1776, had observed that of the two *'riatta'*, the more valuable were those who resided in one fixed spot, built houses for themselves, or inherited them from their ancestors. While the Ameen Account of 1778 described the *khud-kasht*s as inhabitants of the village in which they cultivated the land, John Shore, in 1789, characterised them as such cultivators who acquired a right of possession in the soil by long occupancy and could not be removed; but they could still not sell or mortgage the land and, therefore, in that sense their right was distinct from the right of property. However, *khud-kasht* rights had a different connotation by 1815, closer to the *khud-kasht* of the Mughal period, exemplified by Elphinstone's comment after the conquest of the Peshwa's territory in the same year. He explained the *mirasi* and *mirasdari* (another term for *khud-kasht*) rights as hereditary, saleable, and transferable; they could not be evicted as long as they paid the 'fixed land tax' and, if removed, they could reclaim their territories on paying the dues to the government. Similarly, William Bentinck in his minute on land settlement in 1832 described the *khud-kasht* as 'hereditary *raiyat*' in the villages, who were found all over India and had a proprietary title to the lands cultivated by them. The *khud-kasht* rights largely retained the character and ingredients of the earlier period throughout the eighteenth and early nineteenth centuries. The Company was committed to confirm *khud-kasht* rights if they could be verified, and their validity established on the basis of *farman*s of the previous regime.

Pahi-kasht

Contrary to the *khud-kasht*, who had their homes in the same *pargana* or village where they cultivated the land, the *pahi-kasht*, according to a mid-eighteenth century text, had their homes in villages different from the one where they carried out cultivation. *Pahi* is derived from the old Hindi lexical *pakhi*, from the Sanskrit word *paksh*, meaning 'side'; the Persian term was *pai* which meant 'foot, low' and suggested a class of subordinate cultivators. S. W. Fallon, in his dictionary, defined the term *pahi* as 'non-resident cultivator' and used alternative forms like *pahi-asami*, *pai-kasht*, and *pahi-kasht*. There was some variation in nomenclature in Maharashtra, where they were known as *upari*, *gutkuli* or *kulwar*. While the opinions of the Company were conflicting on the *khud-kasht*s, there appeared to be a sort of consensus on the characterisation of *pahi-kasht*s. Warren Hastings referred to them as 'vagrant *riatts*' who rented the lands in a village they did not reside in. They were the tenants-at-will, declared the Ameen Accounts, who had 'accidental and temporary interest in the soil that they cultivated' and were more of the 'nature of annual or transit tenants'. An official report of 1812 classified them as those who 'cultivated lands belonging to a village where they do not reside'. Commenting on the nature of *pahi-kasht* tenure in the eighteenth-century Mughal *sarkar* of Gorakhpur, Buchanan-Hamilton declared that having no attachment to the land or knowing that they would move, the *pahi-kasht*s did not maintain 'comfortable abodes' like the *khud-kasht*s; the 'hovels' which they maintained were 'wretched'.

The *pahi-kasht*s, then, were such cultivators who volunteered as 'outsiders' to cultivate lands in villages or zamindaris different from their own caste, clan, and tribal settlements. This implies that even if he lived elsewhere but cultivated in a zamindari or a region that shared his tribal, clan, and caste configurations, he would not be considered a *pahi* but a *ra'iyat* or *ra'iyat-giri*, that is, tenant-cultivator or one who did not own the land that he cultivated. Distinct from the *khud-kasht*, the *pahi-kasht* were not obliged to stay on and cultivate the land. They generally took annual leases for cultivation, possessed no permanent rights of occupancy, and paid rent on the basis of the *patta*, which defined the terms of the lease. These cultivators, argued C. A. Bayly (2012 [1983]), provided a shifting population of agrarian servants and specialists, whose movements in response to political change could rapidly transform an area from high cultivation to wilderness, and vice versa.

The *pahi*s could be divided into two categories: One, who tilled the *khud-kasht* lands belonging to *patil*s and *inam* lands held by the zamindars or *madad-i ma'ash* holders. In some regions, the zamindars were prevented by social and caste taboos from cultivating the land themselves. But this rarely caused a problem, for there were a number of landless cultivators during the period, willing to offer their services to the zamindars. These cultivators worked on a *pahi-kasht* tenure. They were free to retain their lands as long as they wished, provided they paid the land revenue regularly, or else they were allotted a small-sized land for their maintenance in return for cultivating the zamindari lands. *Pahi*s of this category did not own agricultural implements: ploughs, bullocks, and seeds were furnished to them or rented by the zamindars, *muqaddam*s, *mahajan*s, or any other 'superior' land right holder of the village. Being without land and agricultural accessories, the *pahi*s remained mobile and eager to move from one area to another in search of better terms. They were generally assessed on the basis of *batai*, received one-fourth of the produce exclusive of the maintenance of implements, purchase of cattle, and so on, as opposed to the *khud-kasht*s or *mirasdar*s, on whom the assessment was made on fixed rates derived often (though not always) from the measurement of the land under cultivation.

The second category of *pahi*s, who possessed their own ploughs and bullocks, was hired by the *patil*s and *muqaddam*s to cultivate cultivable wastelands or repopulate, wholly or partially, a village that had been deserted due to man-made or natural calamities. These lands were granted on lease for settlement by a *patta* to the *patil*s and *muqaddam*s at a concessional rate, with the land revenue fixed at one-third of the produce for three years. To cultivate and settle these lands, the *patil*s and *muqaddam*s in turn hired the *pahi-kasht*s at the rate of one-third of the produce for the current year (the rate of one-third was fixed for extending cultivation on *banjar* or cultivable wastelands, whereas the normal rate of two-fifth was charged for *polaj* or fertile lands). *Pahi*s of this class, who generally came from the neighbouring villages, were allowed to make their own *chapparbandi* (huts) in the villages. They invariably brought their own ploughs for cultivation. The village documents of eastern Rajasthan, for instance, are replete with caste-wise information on the *pahi*s and the number of ploughs held by different castes. This indicates that although the upper castes owned more ploughs and land, the *pahi*s of this type came from both the upper and lower castes.

Those *pahi-kasht*s who possessed their own tools and implements were invaluable in facilitating the development and expansion of village society. The *muqaddam*s or *patil*s obliged to bring fresh lands under cultivation offered attractive terms to *pahi*s to cultivate new lands, or those abandoned by the *khud-kasht*s. These could either be in the form of a *qaul* or lease or an *istawah* or *muqta*. Under *qaul*, a progressive rate was fixed, which implied that the *pahi-kasht* was expected to pay a normal rate only during the third or fourth year. *Istawah* or *muqta*, specifically intended for the clearing of wastelands, gave the *pahi*s an incentive to pay a nominal rent. *Istawah* could be granted to both *khud-kasht*s and *pahi-kasht*s. It was a long contract, at the end of which the cultivator was supposed to pay a full rate of revenue. This was one of the ways by which a *pahi-kasht* could acquire *khud-kasht* rights. A *pahi* could also acquire a *khud-kasht* right by paying a *nazrana* or a fixed sum of money, or if his holding was not disturbed for sixty or even 100 years. Generally, however, they were not evicted if they paid the land revenue regularly, but while they could bequeath, they could not sell or transfer their lands.

Two other forms of tenant rights found in the village society included *muqarari riaya* and *muzarian* or *muzara*. *Muqarari riaya* was a lease cultivator with hereditary ownership rights and the right to sell, transfer, and mortgage the land during the lease period. To extend or improve cultivation and promote agrarian development, he gave out lands on *ijara* or contract on a purely temporary lease to tenants known as *muzarian* or *muzara*, but only after reserving a holding for his personal cultivation. However, the ultimate responsibility for payment of land revenue to the State was vested in only the *muqarari riaya*, regardless of whether he cultivated the land himself or gave it on *ijara* to the *muzarian*. He was subject to assessment even if the land was not brought under cultivation. In case the *muqarari riaya* failed to cultivate the land or deserted it, the State could make a provisional arrangement with an *ijaradar* or a *muzarian* for cultivation of the land. The *muzarian*, too, possessed a hereditary title to the land during the lease period. In the land cultivated by the *muzarian*, ownership was split between the *muqarari riaya* who, as landlord, took responsibility for payment of land revenue to the State, and the *muzarian*, who was expected to not only maintain cultivation but also develop the land. The *muzarian* could retain hereditary rights as long as he kept the land under constant cultivation and paid the land revenue regularly. In addition, as specified in the lease *patta*, he was also entitled to a fixed share in the produce.

The *muzarian* were valuable cultivating tenants to whom waste arable lands could also be leased by the zamindars or *muqaddam*s on easy revenue terms, that is, the *muzarian* could pay land revenue at a concessional rate for a period ranging from three to ten years, by which time he was expected to render the land cultivable or reach it to a *polaj* (fertile) level. Thereafter, he was obliged to pay normal rates of revenue. Such *muzarian*, along with the *pahi-kasht*, played a significant role in settling abandoned villages or wastelands. These *muzarian* could gradually acquire hereditary, proprietary rights—though not the right to sell and mortgage—and could enhance their social status if they made their own *chhappar*s (huts) in the villages, allotted to them for cultivation. In course of time, they could be recognised as a *gaveti* or a *khud-kasht*. Patterns such as these confirm that a *ra'iyat* with a periodical lease could not be deprived of his hereditary right to the land or be dispossessed as long as he paid the land revenue regularly and kept the land under constant cultivation.

Other forms of labour in rural society included *sanjhadar*s (sharecroppers) and agricultural labourers referred to in the Mughal documents as *majur*s, *hali*s, and *vasidar*s. Under the *sanjha* tenure, the *ra'iyat* cultivated *khud-kasht* lands on the basis of *batai*, that is, if a *khud-kasht* had a substantial landholding that he could not cultivate with only family labour, he resorted to *sanjhadari*. Many small-holding *ra'iyat* offered to work as *sanjhadar* to supplement their income. *Sanjha* tenure can be defined as cultivation in partnership, in which the land was owned by the landholder but the inputs or costs of production were shared by both partners. It is difficult to determine the percentage of produce shared between the *sanjhadar*s, that is, *khud-kasht* and the *ra'iyat*, but it can be easily conjectured that the proprietor of the land must have claimed an extra share of the produce. *Majur*s were those cultivators who had their own lands, yet the income from their holdings was insufficient for subsistence. This compelled them to labour on zamindari lands and get *majuri* (wages) either in *naqd* (cash) or in the form of a share of the produce that could supplement the earnings from their lands. *Hali*s and *vasidar*s were landless, solely dependent on the wages that they received from their labour. Rarely paid in *naqd*, they were either given a fraction of the produce or allotted a piece of land for subsistence cultivation.

By the late eighteenth–early nineteenth century, *hali*s and *vasidar*s had risen to become ploughmen in some regions of *suba* Awadh. An example may be cited from one of them, namely the *sarkar* of Gorakhpur, where three kinds of such ploughmen were noticed. The first category comprised the seasonal labourers, employed for both ploughing and sowing, who stayed in the region through the season (of ploughing and sowing), which lasted for about five months. Their allowances, paid in cash or kind or sometimes in both, were often meagre and insufficient to meet their subsistence. There were also labourers or ploughmen who resided here through the year, tied down by *sewak* or *bhot*, that is, advances, which they found difficult to liquidate. However, to keep up the motivation of the labourers and attract them on to the fields, occasional advances as high as Rs 50 with no interest were made to the category of labourers known as *pariya*s or *pariwala*s. They were expected to plough and sow the fields of their masters in the given season, while for the rest of the year they could weed, water, and reap their own lands. Then there were the *harwaha*s, who had no lands of their own and worked on the fields of the landlords for the whole year. In lieu of their services, they were paid a daily allowance in grain sufficient to feed a small family. Their share, nevertheless, varied between one-sixth and one-seventh of the total produce of the land which they cultivated.

THE DOMAIN OF THE ZAMINDARS

The interpretations of the term zamindar with regard to what it signified during the Mughal period are varied, especially given the absence of any definition or description of its essence in the histories or records of the sixteenth–seventeenth centuries, including *Ain-i Akbari*. W. H. Moreland (1995 [1929]) and Parmatama Saran (1974 [1941]) suggested that a zamindar of the Mughal times was a 'vassal chief', and found it a complete 'absurdity' to believe that they could be found in all parts of the empire. Irfan Habib (1999 [1963]) refuted the two and observed that the word zamindar is a Persian compound, literally meaning 'one who holds the *zamin* (land) or controls it'.

Irfan Habib reiterated that while there is no doubt that the term zamindar was used for the chiefs in Mughal India, its application was not limited to just that. Misunderstandings about the term, he said, were probably caused by Blochmann's misrepresentation of the statistical information in his translation of *Ain-i Akbari* when he dropped original tables and column headings that explained the castes of the zamindars or *bumi* (an alternative word that Abu'l Fazl used for zamindars; *bumi* was derived from the Persian word *bum*, meaning 'earth, land'). Other alternative terms used for zamindar included *satarahi* and *biswi* or *bis'i* in Awadh, *bhumia* in Rajasthan, and *malik* or *malkiyat* or *milkiyat* in records and documents of the seventeenth–eighteenth centuries. Anand Ram Mukhlis, an official in the imperial court, wrote in 1745 that a zamindar etymologically (*dar asl*) meant a person who was the master of the land (*sahib-i zamin*), and who signified a *malik* (proprietor) of the land of a village or township and carried out cultivation.

Box 5.1: Origin of the term 'Zamindar'

Unknown in Persia, the origins of the term 'zamindar' lay in India. An early fourteenth-century lexicon used the term to represent a *marzban*, that is, an overseer or *shahna* of a territory; a fourteenth-century chronicler, Isami, designated the zamindars as holders of *iqta*' or territorial assignment or *zabit-i zamin*, that is, controller of a territory, whereas his contemporaries Barani and 'Afif regarded the zamindars as chiefs found 'outside as well as inside the Sultanate'. By mid-fourteenth century, there appeared to be greater clarity in the usage of the term when Firuz Shah Tughluq, in 1353, referred to the *muqaddaman* or headmen as landholders appointed by the government (*mafrozian*) and landowners (*malikan*) as zamindars.

Inadequate and scanty discussion on the nature of zamindari rights in indigenous accounts kept the Company officials guessing and in conflict over the recognition of these rights. Understanding, regulating and, if necessary, modifying the existing system to simplify and secure land rights at every level to encourage capital investment, officials like James Grant combated the prevailing idea that the zamindars were proprietors and encouraged the notion that they were 'originally no more than officers of collection, holding property by temptation and connivance'. He asserted that instead of the zamindars, the 'sovereign ruler throughout Hindustan was the virtual proprietor of the soil'. Others like John Shore were willing to confirm the zamindars as hereditary proprietors of the soil, a provision that he considered 'just and necessary for their subsistence' and supported by 'usage and fact'. Many of the Company officials were swayed by the idea that zamindars were the sole owners of the land and claimed that the zamindars, in whom they had vested many privileges, were in fact the creation of the Company.

Notwithstanding the controversies that may have erupted around the meaning of the term zamindar, it has by now been authenticated that zamindars were the predominant and perhaps the most influential amongst the groups holding rights to land and its produce. Within their stipulated zamindari estates, the zamindars held legal proprietary rights over nearly all cultivated lands and vast tracts of *banjar* or wastelands or uncultivated *jungle* and grasslands. The origins of their power and resources, though, were independent of the Mughal State. But as they integrated into the empire, they grew in strength and influence, emerging as an important political and economic constituent of the Mughal State. As they aligned with and were absorbed into the Mughal system and the State became increasingly dependent on them, the zamindars enhanced their position by acquiring additional rights over their territories and those in its vicinity. 'Zamindar' was a generic term, ascribed in Mughal India to describe the rural magnates, superior to the peasantry. This by no means made them a congruous group. As hereditary 'local potentates' they were the leaders of the local communities, distinctly divided amongst themselves along caste, clan, and territorial lines, constantly apprehensive and in conflict with each other, perpetually on guard against threats and encroachment by the others. Crucial for political, economic, and cultural reasons, the assimilation of the zamindars in the empire was limited and negative. The relation of the zamindars with the State depended on the strength or weakness of their local community and the area that they controlled, with their power usually identified with territories. Confident of their political and economic indispensability, they often competed with the Mughal State, land revenue assignees or the *jagirdars*, other land right-holders like the *madad-i ma'ash* holders, the peasantry, and with each other (zamindar *vs.* zamindar) over the appropriation of surplus produce. Their persistent resistance to the payment of land revenue to the State rendered several localities *zortalab* (payment when force was used) or *zamindaran-i zortalab*. Contrary to the centralisation that the Mughal State may have expected them to achieve, the zamindars as local chieftains represented separatist, localist, and parochial trends. Yet, they could not be eliminated. Constituting the local, political, and administrative elites, the incorporation of localities and rural communities into the empire rested on them.

The zamindars, a dominant rural class, were mostly recognised as the virtual rulers of the region. *Ain-i Akbari*, the sale deeds, administrative records and papers of the sixteenth and seventeenth centuries are explicit in their assertion that the zamindars were found in all *subas* of the empire. In fact, there was hardly a *pargana* in the Mughal Empire without a zamindar and yet their influence did not necessarily engulf the entire rural society. There were peasants, too, particularly the *khud-kashts*, who were *maliks* (owners) possessing unassailable hereditary, proprietary rights. The distinction between the two—zamindars and the *ra'iyat*—was perhaps delineated by the size of the area held by a zamindar, emphasising that the area under a zamindari usually comprised a village or a certain fractional part of it, and seldom a few *bighas* or units of area. An important feature of the zamindari right was its uneven development, that is, within the same district some villages could be fully zamindari while others could be peasant-held or *ra'iyati*, with no recognisable persons as zamindars. But the limits between the two were not fixed. Peasants of a village, if they so desired, could sell their rights or force could be used to create a zamindari right. The Mughal State could also supplant zamindars and appoint new zamindars over peasant-held villages; in some instances, new villages could be settled without the intervention of zamindars.

Whatever the case, the status of zamindars and the nature of their rights were influenced by the extent of the dominance of their caste, clan, and kin network. Zamindars of a locality often belonged to the same caste. In fact, it was certain caste, clan and kin groups that dominated zamindari rights in most *parganas*. To extend their base and enforce their claims over large tracts, the zamindars relied on the unstinted support and loyalty of their caste-men, kinsmen, and clansmen, and maintained their own *ulus* (armed contingents; *ulus* was derived from the Mongols, meaning 'armed' tribes) and *qil'achas* or *garhis* (small forts). An exhaustive account of the castes of zamindars and their cavalry and infantry organised in different *parganas* is given in *Ain-i Akbari* in its chapter, 'Account of the Twelve *Subas*'. It was a normal custom for the zamindars to build *qil'achas*, the symbols of their armed power, to protect their possessions. The State, too, accepted it as a legitimate practice—unless, of course, the *qil'achas* began to be used for defiance against the State.

Distinctly prominent in local village life, the zamindars emerged as a remarkably valuable institution—politically, economically, even militarily—for the Mughal State. Notwithstanding their defiance in the payment of land revenue and turbulent and refractory activities, the State depended on them for land survey, cultivation, assessment and collection of revenue, and a variety of administrative functions. Many of them were also inducted as *mansabdars*. The zamindars in the empire represented a variety of interests, ranging from *malguzars* to *khidmatguzars*, including the rajas who exercised autonomous power over the territories under their jurisdiction. To investigate the intricate nuances of the class of zamindars and understand their role and functions, S. Nurul Hasan divided them into three categories:

- *malguzars* or primary zamindars;
- *khidmatguzars* or intermediary zamindars; and
- autonomous chieftains.

These categories, however, were not exclusive, but generally overlapped.

*Malguzar*s or primary zamindars were the holders of proprietary, hereditary, alienable rights over agricultural and habitational lands. They acquired these rights upon assuring the Mughal State that they would bring forests and wastelands under cultivation, maintain and extend cultivation, and pay the *kharaj* or *mal* regularly on terms fixed by the State. The *malguzar*s could either cultivate the land themselves, that is, *khud-kasht*, or with the help of family labour or hired labour and also, if the need be, the proprietors of other villages. To extend cultivation, the *malguzar*s often gave their lands on lease to the tenants, who were bound by the *patta* to pay *kharaj* regularly at the rates fixed. The tenants were provided security of tenure and hereditary rights during the lease; in case of non-payment, the tenant was not divested of his landholding rights but arrears were realised through different means. Given the land-man ratio and in view of the shortage of cultivators, it was considered prudent to restrain the tenants on land and compel them to cultivate all arable lands. Several sale deeds of the sixteenth century pertain to the *malguzari* rights of the primary zamindars. To protect the rights of these zamindars and maintain a proper record of claims, the Mughal State urged the registration of transfer and sale deeds at the court of the *qazi*s.

The *malguzar*s were so called because it was on them that the land revenue was assessed by the State. They were expected to collect *kharaj* from the peasants and give the Mughal State and its assignees their share; assist in the maintenance of law and order; and in certain circumstances, even provide troop support to the State. A reckoned perquisite of the *malguzar*s was *malikana*, a *haqq* (right) of a zamindar in recognition of him being the *malik* (owner) of the land. The zamindars, however, did not enjoy this fiscal claim if they were the revenue payers; they were instead given an allowance called *nankar*. *Malikana*, in other words, was not granted to such zamindars who held and cultivated their own lands and paid revenue to the State; it was also not given to those zamindars who, at their own discretion, farmed or leased their land or a part of their land to the *ra'iyat* or any other landholder for purposes of cultivation. *Malikana* or any other allowance could not be claimed by the *malguzar*s from these grantees without the approval of the government. Yet, when the State converted the zamindar land into *sir*, imposing direct assessment and collection on the peasants, bypassing the zamindars, the latter were given *malikana* to recompense their lost income. As Asiya Siddiqi (1973) observed, *malikana* was an allowance paid in recognition of proprietary and *malguzari* right 'when the exercise of the right had itself ceased'.

Malikana could be given both in the form of revenue-free land at a percentage of the total revenue-paying land or in *naqd*, which amounted to 10 per cent of the total revenue collected. The zamindar's proprietary right, his *haqq-i milkiyat*, entitled him to levy a number of *abwab*s and *furu'at*s (cess or taxes) in addition to a share in the produce of agricultural land. These included:

- *jalkar* and *bankar* or levies on water and forest produce;
- tanks, channels, *talab* (inundated land), wells, orchards, trees, wild rice, *jungles*;

- in some regions, a house tax (*khana-shumari*), a poll tax on men (*dastar-shumari* or tax on turbans), tax on marriage and birth, and a tax on craft professions called *muhtarifa*.

A zamindar was both a *malguzar* and a *khidmatguzar*. If a zamindar functioned as a *khidmatguzar*, it was his intermediary right or a right to *khidmat* or service. Amongst the *khidmatguzars* were included *muqaddam*, *chaudhuri*, *qanungo*, *deshmukh*, *desai*, *deshpande*, and *ta'alluqdars* (a generic term), which emerged in the second half of the seventeenth century. The *khidmatguzars* apportioned multiple roles and mostly enjoyed hereditary rights (although, in a few cases, there were short-term contracts). They entered into a contract with the government for the realisation of revenue of a given territory. This practice virtually brought the entire jurisdiction of the country under them. The *khidmatguzars* were also expected to prepare details of revenue assessment for the State, facilitate expansion of cultivation, assist in the maintenance of law and order and, if expedient, fulfil the State's requirement for a contingent. In recognition of their *khidmat*, the zamindars were paid an allowance known as *nankar*, either in the form of revenue-free lands or as a deduction from the revenue paid (in cash) equivalent to the standard rate of 10 per cent of the revenue demand; in some provinces, though, it varied and amounted to 5 per cent.

Malguzari and *khidmatguzari* rights were extended to the autonomous chieftains even as they continued to exercise 'sovereign' or 'state' powers in their own regions. To curtail the widespread resistances of chieftains to pay regular tribute, prevalent from the days of the Delhi Sultans, Akbar initiated the process of establishing links between the chieftains and the Mughal State by absorbing them in the imperial service, granting *mansabs* and allotting lucrative *jagirs*, the revenue of which far exceeded their hereditary kingdoms. He further asserted the principle of 'paramountcy', which was later continued by his successors. This implied that the position and status of the chieftains depended on the discretion of the emperor rather than on their own inherent rights. Only those chieftains were designated as rajas who were given this title by the Mughal emperor, and their hereditary domains were in turn granted and treated as *watan jagirs*. More importantly, the Mughals succeeded in securing the military services of even such chieftains who did not hold *mansabs*. Theoretically, therefore, the autonomous chieftains were reduced to the status of *jagirdars* and zamindars and subjected to imperial revenue regulations, while in reality they continued to enjoy hereditary rights over their territories and their *watan jagirs* remained immune to transfers, unlike that of the other *jagirdars*. Like the zamindars, they were expected to pay land revenue assessed on the basis of actual production, instead of the tribute that they may have paid earlier. But it is difficult to estimate whether this was achieved, for many of the chieftains continued to pay tribute on an irregular basis, known as *peshkash*. To determine the *peshkash*, the Mughal State obtained from the chieftains figures on the area under cultivation, the crop pattern, and the revenue collected from their vassals or their zamindars. Such processes, intended to bring the regions in line with the Mughal pattern, hardly succeeded. Instead, it aroused resistance from the chieftains against the extra imperial pressure on their economy.

Notwithstanding their significant role, the *khidmatguzars* and *malguzars* remained turbulent and resistant, constantly in conflict with each other and the State to enhance their rights and appropriate a greater share of revenue. On several occasions, invoking caste and clan prejudices, the *malguzars* capitalised on peasant grievances and organised and led their revolts against the exactions of the State and refused to pay the revenue, creating *zamindaran-i-zortalab*. The extent of their mobilisation was, however, limited; it could not transcend their caste and community loyalties. Many a time, the resistance of the zamindars was not against the State; the conflict was among the different zamindar groups that adversely affected their relations with the rural society, corroding the basis of Mughal power. The *ijaradars* (contractors) and *ta'alluqdars*, contrary to their assignments, often skipped detailed figures of assessment and paid only the stipulated amount, that is, whereas the actual revenue that they collected continued to increase, the gross revenue paid to the State remained constant, while the balance was appropriated by them. The *khidmatguzars* often consolidated their position at the expense of the State by arrogating to themselves the State's right to dispose of uncultivated wastelands. Bypassing the *malguzars*, they seldom gave them the *malikana*, affecting adversely the status of these zamindars.

To assert their authority, the *khidmatguzars* could even create a class of sub-proprietors known as *birtias*. *Birt* (derived from the Sanskrit term *vritti* or *britti*, that is, maintenance or means of subsistence) were also granted by the Mughal emperors as an incentive for cultivating the land. During the lease, the *birtias* were required to cultivate the land and make annual payments, that is, *malikana*, at the rate of 10 per cent to the zamindars and *jama* of the assigned villages to the government. Normally the *birtia* could hold his land as long as he paid the annual *jama* and *malikana*. Regardless, the *khidmatguzars* denied the *birtias* the privilege of entering into direct engagement with the government, reasserted their ownership rights and emphasised the status of the *birtias* as leaseholders or tenants. By the end of the seventeenth century, the *khidmatguzars* often sought to acquire hereditary, territorial rights or become chieftains and their rebellions became even more organised. Wielding enormous political and economic power, they emerged as chieftains and as local strongholds, leading to the growth of regional power.

AGRICULTURAL PRODUCTION AND TECHNOLOGY

The appropriation of revenue by the land right holders should be no cause for alarm or seen as a bleak picture of the Mughal economy or evidence of falling cultivation or declining production. A note of caution is needed while using revenue figures as a criterion for ascertaining the level of production or revenue yield, particularly if the revenue is intercepted by intermediaries or the political elite, and the assessed revenue does not reach the State treasury. The process of clearing, cultivating and expanding production continued to gather impetus throughout the sixteenth to the eighteenth centuries, making similar inroads, with perhaps a few brief interruptions, into the nineteenth century as well. Any kind of agricultural activity required substantial inputs of capital, seed, implements, and ploughs. Individual cultivators generally had support in the form of *taqavi* from the zamindars, *muqaddams*, and others to meet the costs of production. The involvement of landholders in the capital investment in land is indicative of their high-powered status in rural society and the easy availability of capital. It also reflects extensive production with more and more *bighas* brought under cultivation and the corresponding role of the *khud-kasht*, *pahi-kasht*, and the *ra'iyat* in escalating agrarian growth and economic stability.

Indian topography and ecology, which affected productivity and soil conditions, were complex in their potential. The geomorphology of the rivers of the subcontinent had a tremendous bearing on agricultural production. Most rivers developed a main channel sufficient to contain the volume of the flow that occurred annually; adjoining the main channel was a well-defined flood plain which was inundated at irregular intervals, depending on variable precipitation. These periodic inundations characterised natural phenomena that left their indelible mark through time, both on the land and in the use of it. Largely perennial, the rivers had a fertilising impact and enhanced the productivity of the soil by the alluvium which they carried. Soils in India varied in content, but were largely alluvial and productive. Even those areas that were not cultivated or remained *banjar* for long possessed cultivable soil and held the promise of good yield. Rains, generally copious and reliable, influenced the nature and volume of production. While there were some occasional dry years, monsoons generally were less prone to failure. A monsoon-determined economy, cultivation invariably followed the rain-pattern.

An important feature of Indian agriculture was the harvest of two—in some regions, three—crops annually. Mostly the lands were 'single-cropped' or *yak-fasla*, implying that they were sown either for the *rabi* (spring) or *kharif* (autumn) harvest; but some areas were 'double-cropped' or *do-fasla*, that is, sown with crops of both harvests one after another. In *yak-fasla* regions, land was left fallow for almost half a year and the same crop as the previous one could be cultivated again. In variance with the 'single-cropped' areas, it was mandatory for the cultivator of *do-fasla* land to adopt a two-crop cycle, especially because the crops of the two harvests were different. Significantly, the peasant was aware of the technique of crop-rotation and won accolades for his knowledge from the nineteenth-century English reports, particularly from south India and Awadh. The peasant, it appears, carefully opted for certain specific crops that fertilised and enriched the soil. *Rabi* was grown on *yak-fasla* land without irrigation and usually returned produce larger in quantity in proportion to the outlay. The principal *rabi* crop was wheat. *Kharif*, nourished by rainwater, did not require artificial irrigation but entailed a good deal of weeding to clear the grass that grew after the rains. Rice was the main produce of the season. Other food crops included barley, millet, *jowar*, *bajra*, maize, *chana*, pulses, and *jins-i kamil* or *jins-i ala*, that is, high-grade remunerative cash crops, namely cotton, sugarcane, oilseeds, indigo, opium. There was no evidence of depletion of soil or decline in fertility with the cultivation of cash crops. Food crops remained prosperous. A symmetry and balance was maintained between crops by organising their distribution on the lands best suited to them.

Tobacco cultivation was introduced in the seventeenth century, probably during the reign of Jahangir. *Ain-i Akbari* does not mention it, although there are references to an envoy from Bijapur presenting *hookah* (*chilim*) to Akbar. Jahangir, however, had prohibited the cultivation to stop addiction, but its production was revived under Shahjahan. Among the fibre-yielding crops, jute was probably grown, but it was not an important crop. Sann-hemp was instead cultivated widely for fibre till Aurangzeb completely eradicated it by his *farman* of 1659. From then, it was scarce in most parts of India. Sericulture and lac-culture were also known to the

Mughals. Coffee was imported from Arabia and Abyssinia. Its production was not acclimatised to India till the eighteenth century; some coffee cultivated in southern Maharashtra was of a crude variety. The cultivation of tea was not known throughout the Mughal period. Amongst spices, pepper was commercially the most important. Long pepper and round pepper were considerably expensive, while capsicum and chilli were introduced in the eighteenth century. Betel leaf or *pan* was grown in most parts of India. Its consumption was so high that its production was never enough to meet the demand. The cultivation of saffron, a commercial item, was mainly confined to Kashmir. Most of the vegetables known today were cultivated during the Mughal period; sweet potatoes and ordinary potatoes were experimented with successfully in the eighteenth century. Yet another characteristic of agriculture during the period was fruit cultivation. This included melon, pineapple, papaya, guava, cashew-nuts, oranges, and mangoes.

It was the Mughal fondness for Central Asian fruits that inspired them to introduce innovations in horticultural techniques. To develop the culture of Central Asian and Persian fruits, the Mughal emperors imported seeds and gardeners and even borrowed the technique of grafting from these regions. Although grafting was known to India from ancient times, it was the extensive application of the Central Asian style of grafting that yielded significant results and improved the quality of fruits. Emulating the Central Asian and Persian horticultural traditions, the Mughal emperors did not merely use the simple principle of grafting but promoted the implementation of its different methods—tongue grafting, side, crown, deft, saddle and root grafting, veneering, in-arching and inlaying—to apply the technique effectively and efficiently. It is difficult to ascertain which practice of grafting was most successful. There are suggestions of simple propagation by seeds, although it is also conjectured that when in-arching was applied, grafting produced better results. Chroniclers of the seventeenth century like Abdul Hamid Lahori (*Padshahnama*), Sadiq Khan (*Shahjahannama*), and also Jahangir (*Tuzuk-i Jahangiri*) have upheld the significance of grafting. Jahangir narrated that sweet cherry was brought to Kashmir from Kabul and propagated by means of grafting. Using the same technique, mulberry and apricots were made more productive in Kashmir. Recounting the widespread use of grafting under Shahjahan, Lahori and Sadiq Khan spoke of the value of grafting in improving the quality of three types of oranges: *sangtara*, *kaurla* and *narangi*.

The technique of grafting was just one example of the peasant's adaptation of technology. Conscious of the changes and the changing demands of the economy, the peasant persistently exhibited understanding and the ability to imbibe new technologies and accommodate them. Agricultural practices, tools and implements of the Indian peasant appeared no different than that of his counterpart in Europe, given of course the difference in crops and climate. Although the implements of an Indian peasant had a greater percentage of wood as compared to iron, it did not tarnish their utility. All tools, irrespective of the extent of wood in it, used iron screws, hinges, clasps, etc., and operated on mechanical principles such as pin-drum gearing and parallel-worm. The Indian plough, made of wood, normally had an iron tooth in the ploughshare and did not appear unusual to the Europeans who visited India at this time. While Terry described the Indian plough as a 'foot plough', a kind used in England, Fryer found nothing peculiar in it except that the coulters were 'unarmed mostly, iron being scarce, but they have hard wood which will turn the light ground'. Fryer's observation could, however, only be applied to the coastal belt for the soils in the interior were diverse in nature, ranging from light and sandy to dry and hard soils. The light and sandy soils could be handled without heavy iron coulter, but the use of iron teeth was indispensable for negotiating the dry, hard soils. Considering that the ploughshare had a small amount of iron, it was hardly prohibitive. Notwithstanding the scarcity of iron, its mining and manufacturing was widespread and its price in terms of wheat was not more than twice the price in 1914. Compared to the European plough, the Indian plough had a greater efficiency of traction; the harness in the Indian plough was fixed to the hump of the oxen as opposed to the horns of the beast in Europe.

Adapting to the soil conditions, the peasant used a seed-drill and practised dibbling, particularly in cotton cultivation. Dibbling required digging the ground with a *mekh* or peg, sowing the cotton seed and then covering it with earth; this process made the crop more productive. To maintain the fertility of the soil, bone manure was not commonly used, although exceptional value was attached to fish manure. It is alleged that it was applied to sugarcane fields in Gujarat and coconut palms in Konkan. Crop rotation was popularly used to retain and revive the fertility of the soil. Rice was generally transplanted in 'regular furrows'. Fields were primarily open fields, with no hedges or resemblance to the enclosures of Europe, except in Gujarat, where thorn bush hedges—a local peculiarity—were noticed to protect the fields.

An important aspect of agriculture was artificial irrigation to supplement the monsoons. Wells, tanks, and canals served as a major source. Wells could be both masonry (*pucca*) and non-masonry (*kutcha*), depending on the financial resources of the peasantry. It is observed that the number of wells relative to the cultivated area was substantially large in the seventeenth century, probably because the water table was closer to the surface. Tanks or reservoirs, a primary source of irrigation in Deccan, Central India, and Assam, can be dated between the fifth and the thirteenth centuries. Tanks were created by embankments from which canals of relatively short length were carved out to carry the water for agricultural purposes. Tavernier described the region of Golconda 'full' of tanks, which were made by building dams 'sometimes half a league long' with the objective of enclosing the water in natural depressions so that it could be channelled into the fields subsequent to the rains. Buchanan, in his *Journey from Madras* (1800–01), provided a survey of the pre-colonial system of south Indian dams or anicuts, tanks and canals. While natural inundation canals were widely used, canal or 'long canals' built from undammed rivers, traversing fairly long paths, were known since the fourteenth century. Inspired by the canal technology of Central Asia, such canals were mostly laid out by the Mughal emperors and the Mughal nobility, although the technique of canal-digging can be traced to the reign of Ghiyas-ud-din Tughluq, perhaps the first Sultan of Delhi to initiate the digging of canals for the promotion of agriculture. Firuz Shah Tughluq added to the process by creating the biggest network of canals known in India until the nineteenth century. Two large canals cut by Firuz Shah Tughluq included the *Rajab-wah* and the *Ulugh-khani*, stretching from river Yamuna to Hissar. These canals, which had begun to silt by the sixteenth century, were repaired under Akbar to facilitate the distribution of water from the canals during the cultivation season. Subsequently, Shahjahan ordered it to be reopened from its mouth at Khizrabad.

Later, to cater to the needs of Shahjahanabad, Shahjahan commissioned the excavation of a new channel known as *Nahr-i Bihisht* or *Nahr-i Faiz*, roughly 30 *kurohs* or 78 miles in length. Another canal known as *Shah Nahr*, less than 100 miles long, took off from river Ravi to rejoin it at Lahore. *Qanat* or *kariz* or the underground water channel was yet another technique used during the period. Bernier wrote that the *qanats* were most noticeable in the Indus basin: river Indus raised its bed to a much higher level than that of the surrounding plains, so that it was easy to use the supply in its mainstream as well as inundation channels for irrigating the fields. The local practice therefore was to cut the *qanat* from either the river or canals or, as Bernier said, set up 'Persian Wheels' to lift the water from the river.

Different mechanisms were used for lifting water from the wells and tanks into the fields or channelising water from the canals. The simplest device that a peasant used for raising water from the wells or tanks or canals was a *dhenkli* or a wooden scoop that worked on a lever principle, was manually operated, and could be used where water was close to the surface or for small plots primarily used by vegetable growers. It could generally irrigate 11 *mundees* (a little less than half a *kutcha bigha* or 860 square yards). Another water-lifting device was *charas*, in which the water was raised either in earthen pots, that is, *ghuras*, or in a leather bucket attached to a rope drawn over a pulley wheel by oxen. The system of water-lifting improved from the thirteenth–fourteenth centuries when the peasant resorted to the extensive use of *noria*, also known as *araghatta* or *ghatiyantra*. The ancient Indian *noria* or *araghatta* functioned on the basis of a string of pots fixed close to its rims; at a later stage, it used a rope-chain that facilitated it to reach water at some depth. Later, a little before the sixteenth century, crucial additions were made to the *noria*. Equipped with a pin-drum gearing, it worked on a combination of pin-drum gearing and belt, rotated by draught animals. This method of operating the *araghatta* was often described as the wood-and-earthen pot ancestor of the modern metallic Persian wheel or the *saqiya*.

The technology of the Persian wheel or *saqiya* was probably imported to India from Central Asia and Persia in the thirteenth–fourteenth centuries. In terms of the prevalent standards of technological development, it enabled the effective application of animal power and was most efficacious in areas where the water table lay at an intermediate level, ranging roughly from 5–10 metres from the surface. By the sixteenth century, it was accepted as a significant mode of raising water, particularly in the Indus, trans-Yamuna region, and Rajasthan. Yet, it had its limitations. The wooden gearing could not be used as efficiently in areas where the water table was high, like in the eastern parts of India or the Gangetic basin. In these regions, it could not compete with *charas*, although it was a better alternative for its ability to sustain a continuous flow of water. *Saqiya* could somewhat replace *charas* only by the latter half of the nineteenth century, when it was cast out of iron and transformed into a metallic machine. Some valuable accounts on the Persian wheel in India are provided in Babur's *Baburnama*, Sujan Rai Bhandari's *Khulasat-ut Tawarikh* (1695), and Munhta Nainsi's *Vigat* (1660), which suggested that 17 per cent of the wells in *pargana* Merta in Marwar had Persian wheels.

The technique of parallel-worm, Joseph Needham argued, subsequently established the rolling mill. It was applied in the cotton gin and sugar mills, irrespective of the limitations that it caused in the sugar mills, especially with regard to the crushing of sugarcane. The first limitation, Irfan

Habib suggested, was the mortar and pestle mill. Ideally, mortar was expected to be made of stone but because of its expense, it was replaced by wood, which rendered the crushing of cane difficult. Sugarcane, therefore, had to be cut into small pieces prior to the process of milling. This limitation, however, did not undermine the importance of the technique, neither was it a barrier to its usage in most parts of India, including the Gangetic Plains, Orissa, Bengal, Central India, and Rajasthan. In the second device of milling, which also used the method of parallel-worm, two vertical wooden rollers were used that moved in opposite directions: one of the rollers was rotated by oxen, which drove around the roller; the main roller moved the other through the ridges on its upper part fitting into the grooves of the other. The canes were crushed by being thrust between the rollers. One of the major deficiencies of the second device was that rollers could only be mounted vertically as long as gearing was not introduced to the appliance. This limited the number of canes that could be crushed at a time. The technique improved only in the 1830s in Punjab when wooden horizontal rollers with gears were used. They continued to be used till the 1880s, when further changes were experimented with and introduced. These technologies were used even in the ordinary peasant communities of Gujarat and Deccan and tribal areas like Chhattisgarh.

Agricultural technology also demonstrated evidence of the utilisation of non-human resources of power like water and wind. The concepts of both the water-mill and the windmill, introduced into India from Central Asia and Iran roughly around the fourth century, became widespread in India by the eleventh century. Both the mills, mounted horizontally, required no gearing. Water-mills were installed in Deccan by the seventh century and put to more extensive use by the sixteenth century. The undulating nature of the Deccan plateau suited the horizontal character of the water-mills. One of the best-known examples of a water-mill in Deccan is Malik Ambar's water-mill at Aurangabad. Water-mills were commonly used in Kashmir, the Himalayan region, and northwest Punjab. They were scantily used or were virtually non-existent in the north Indian plains, probably owing to the nature of the rivers in this region that were affected by constant seasonal fluctuations, making it difficult for the water to flow with sufficient force. The technical ingenuity in the use of water power was observed in the Hazara district en route to Kashmir from Delhi, a route frequently used by the Mughal emperors. Here, in addition to the conventional corn-grinding mill, a water-driven wooden trip-hammer, *pekoh*, was used for milling rice. The wheel in this case was vertical, marking a significant departure from the horizontal water-mill. This device allegedly came from China.

The technology of the windmill was suited to a region where the winds were strong and blew constantly in one direction, and where water as an alternative source of power was not available. A windmill or *asia-i bad*, installed at Ahmadabad, was locally known as *hawa-chakki* and operated through the movement of the wind and rotation of the curtains. By 1761, only the millstone remained; the time of its original installation, however, is not known.

The variety of agricultural technologies used by the peasants demonstrates their willingness to adapt to, accommodate, and adopt technical devices that provided them incentives to expand cultivation and experiment with new crops. New crops enhanced productivity. Patterns of production could change in response to, or as a reaction to, market stimuli. The peasants felt empowered to respond to the commercialisation of agriculture as the acreage under cash crops increased, the value of cash crops grew, and their marketability extended, but without any simultaneous decline in the acreage under food grains. With increased cultivation, investments in agriculture continued to grow.

AGRARIAN ENVIRONMENT

Agricultural dynamism, expanding cultivation, and diversified production—if these marked the process of economic expansion in Mughal India, should it be conjectured that human interventions into nature were successful? Or that with increased output, land was 'upgraded'? Or with reduced biodiversity and biomass, land was 'degraded', or that all changes in the environment caused 'irretrievable damage'? Opinions differ on it. But whatever it may be, agriculture cannot be seen exclusive of the other elements of the environment, although it has long been assumed that the prosperity of the Mughal State depended on its agrarian base. It was not, in fact, upon the settled villages and revenue-yielding lands alone that the stability of the Mughal society rested; there was much that lay beyond the agrarian economy. The Mughal ruling class did not possess absolute monopoly over geographical space and/or natural resources, even if they fell within the political confines of the empire. Ecological diversity—a mix of production, forests and grasslands—prevailed in the empire, fostering a variety of socio-economic systems that necessitated interconnectedness and mutuality with other social organisms that used the environment in diverse ways during the sixteenth and the seventeenth centuries. This, then, implies that to remove forests and pastures from the purview of agrarian history and banish the study of farms and agricultural fields from environmental history is not only problematic, but also conceptually unacceptable. The notion of 'agrarian environment' underscores this fact. To study the 'agrarian' and the 'environment' in isolation and within their self-imposed constraints is, argued Neeladri Bhattacharya (1998), 'as if these histories were not connected, as if environment did not impinge on the agrarian world'. It is requisite that the separation of the agrarian and the environment as independent domains or choosing between an agrarian or an environmental perspective be considered a misrepresentation of the interwoven dynamics between the agrarian and the environmental world. It is vital to remove the rift between the environmental and the agrarian, argue for a more nuanced and dialectical relationship between the two, and urge upon, as suggested by Daniel Esty and Marian Chertow (1997, 45), 'an *ecologicalism* that recognizes the inherent interdependence of all life-systems'. Agrarian environments have to be understood as part of a biophysical and social environment; urban and the non-urban; arable and non-arable; and areas that are integrally connected to the realm of agriculture and environment and their allied social-economic relations.

The broad definition of agrarian environment is an essential prerequisite because a variety of specialised kinds of production are knitted in a tight web in agrarian environments, urging the need for a term that can encapsulate different specialists even as their situations are considered separately. The importance of agrarian environments can be further demonstrated by focusing on landscapes of social power and bringing together the various dimensions of agriculture.

Agrarian history is not just a local matter. It is replete with examples of ecological interventions, whereby nature has been altered and landscapes modified to fulfil the expectations of the people. Agriculture was and continues to be the single most important means by which mankind has changed the lands and the ecosystems. It represents a major element of ecological transformation in human history for no occupation other than farming alters the land so much. New cultivation occurred at the frontiers of settlement when the pioneer settlers intruded upon the remote lands inhabited by shifting cultivators, hunter-gatherers, and pastoralists. Agrarianism includes not only farming but also animal husbandry, pastoralism, fishing, and harvesting the forest. It can thus be defined as a major source that produces organic material for human use, of which animal and forest products are an evidence.

There is no contest over the fact that constant changes occur in landscapes and many cause degradation, but then, it is equally important to concede that the term degradation is a matter of perception and is likely to be diversely used. For instance, sedentary cultivation and grazing are considered negative activities that may invariably lead to the erosion of the soil. Grazing is reckoned to be perilous to a forest because, as the sheep and the cattle eat the seedlings of trees, they may damage their reproductive potential. Yet, grass formed and continues to form the basis of the Indian peasant economy. The pastoralists may not consider the replacement of forests by grasslands as degradation, even though the hooves of a large number of cattle driven into a forest to graze may make the ground hard, compacted and dry, rendering it less conducive for seeds to germinate or plants to grow. Similarly, farmers may not perceive the replacement of forests by agricultural lands as degradation, despite the adverse changes in the soil and micro-climate, and the logging that may restrain new plant growth. Moreover, farmers often prefer agriculture and the development of cultivation in the proximity or within the ambit of a forested area so as to benefit from the springs or a high water-table, or less eroded soil or even the new soil produced by the decayed leaf litter in these areas. In several regions, the debris of burnt forest waste was considered a particularly good medium for seed growth. An abundant supply of such waste was well-suited for agriculture—a feature commonly noticed in the forest tracts and *banjar* lands (uncultivated and/or barren lands).

The congeniality and harmony between the agrarian and the environmental are evident in the fact that while agriculture developed, leading to a sedentary lifestyle, forests remained a way of life for many of its inhabitants. In this context, it is important to understand the people's experiences of ecological pressures and their responses to the changes over time. Forests were utilised as bases for social, economic, and political initiatives. The zamindars possessed proprietary, hereditary rights over the forests within their jurisdiction. For them, the forests were a way of life and not mere timber with a capital value. Being the sole practitioner of timber rights, they generally did not consent to the cutting of trees; and if they did, they took the entire responsibility of whether timber was to be cut for trade and which trees were to be cut. There was nothing rigid in the 'forest line'. Lands were reclaimed and agro-forestry, pastoralism and settlements could overwhelm the forests. There was constant fluctuation and fluidity between forests and cultivation, with shifting boundaries between the *jungle* and the arable. The Sultans of Delhi, for instance, had transformed spaces—deserted lands and *jungles* of thorn and scrub—into settled areas through the thirteenth century. Similar connections between forests and military campaigns and the creation of settlements were noticed during the Mughal period as well. The Mughal emperors encouraged reclamation of forests by granting *nankari* rights to the landholders. Fath Ullah Shirazi's observation on revenue matters for Akbar's period substantiates the point: 'The fluctuations of civilization are apparent to everyone. If in a village some land falls out of cultivation one endeavours to increase cultivation elsewhere.' From the reign of Shahjahan, the Mughal army was accompanied by *tabarzan* (woodcutters) and ploughmen to clear the land to make way for the army and establish new zamindaris. Asserting their political power, the zamindars and the *jagirdars*, too, hired professional woodcutters to clear the *jungles* and settle new villages.

Although several areas were reclaimed, many continued to be forest lands or were rejuvenated or replanted with trees. The forest trees were intermixed with mango plantations that helped preserve moisture in the warm climate, and all such trees that yielded timber and forage, reeds, thorns, wild rose trees, and a variety of grass. Some tracts were used as *dhab* lands (pasture grounds), especially during cold and hot weather. Large parts of the forest were home to large mammals, ungulates, and carnivores, especially lions and tigers, cheetahs and leopards, hyenas and wolves, elephants, and wild ants. However, irrespective of whether the forests were dense or subjected to the incursions of wild animals that made passage through them dangerous and difficult, there was nothing to deter local people from defining their relationship with the forests. They were conscious of the commercial and strategic advantages of the forests and shared a strong affinity with them. It was their home, a shelter, a way of life and sustenance and if their activities caused any harm, they were so mild as to have little impact on the environment. They held the forests as eternal and valuable for moisture, fodder, and firewood; and if they decided to exploit them for profit, it was either on their own or through merchants and traders. It was beyond their imagination that human beings could destroy this massive expanse of vegetation.

So while it would be prudent to consider the impact of human activity on the fauna and the flora that may have fairly changed the ecosystem, it would be equally pertinent to observe that nature's ability to reconcile competing human interests is not limitless, nor are all humans equally culpable of exploiting nature. In this context may be mentioned the nomadic pastoralists who are often cited as predatory to the sedentary agricultural societies; yet the two major forms of subsistence—pastoralism and agriculture—are neither totally separated nor fixed, but interchangeable and interactive. Ibn Khaldun, the Arabic historian of the fourteenth century, for instance, emphasised the importance of a dynamic interaction between the sedentary and the nomadic peoples to analyse the process of state formation. On some occasions, specialised herding was made possible only by a symbiotic relationship with agriculture. In a situation where pastoral-nomadism thrives, a movement towards sedentarisation was possible, like it was in the case of early modern Punjab, where the growth of commercialised agriculture under the Mughals encouraged and facilitated the absorption of pastoral people into the agrarian system. The contribution of the sedentary communities, on the other hand, to the creation and consolidation of economy and society cannot be seen as isolated or exclusive of the tribal communities. In fact, there are several instances of interdependence between tribal and sedentary life; one such example were the village communities of Mughal India that were at a reasonable proximity to tribal societies. There was continued participation of tribal populations in the socio-economic processes and the stabilisation of agrarian society and certain other social formations, although in many cases sedentarised communities relied considerably on pastoralism.

The lives of the peasants and pastoralists were inextricably entwined. Their involvement in the mutual exchange of products was accompanied simultaneously with the scramble for encroachment on each other's space: agriculturists treaded on the grazing grounds of the pastoralists and the herdsmen who wandered on the fringes of productive areas re-appropriated the abandoned fields and habitations. There are incalculable examples from several regions that demonstrate the close relationship between tribal-pastoralism and sedentary-commercialised society, and so intricately linked were its economic interests that any shift in the structure of any one of these societies would not leave the other unaffected. This implies that if tribal-pastoral populations were integral to agrarian society, then ignoring them would mean risking an incomplete understanding of the agrarian system of Mughal India, an understanding that need not be confined to the Mughal period alone. In some instances, however, the reverse was evident with cultivators taking to pastoralism; in yet other circumstances, *jhum* cultivators moved to settled cultivation and settled cultivators escaped to the forests. On several occasions forests served as 'hideouts' and provided a haven for such peasants and zamindars who escaped to the jungles to resist and avoid payment of taxes to the Mughal State. Sujan Rai described the Lakhi jungle near the channels of the rivers Sutlej and Beas as an area of refuge for the recalcitrant in the late sixteenth century (1595–96), while *Tuzuk-i Jahangiri* informs that during the reign of Jahangir, villagers in the vicinity of Mathura fled to the jungles on the other bank of the river Yamuna to resist payment of land revenue. Forests also served as an asylum for the seriously ill and convalescents of infectious diseases, particularly smallpox, rampant in the eighteenth century in several regions; the infected persons were removed from their homes and sent to the forest until the disease was eradicated from the village.

Community locations, thus, were rarely fixed during the early modern period when desertions and migrations could happen in response to climatic or political factors (*asmani wa sultani*), resulting in situations where wanderers might settle and the settled wander, forests be cleared and forests be grown. In other words, the shift from one form of livelihood to another was neither unilinear nor complete, nor did they exist in an isolated, exclusive, pure form.

URBANISM, ARTISANS, TRADE

Rural–urban economies in early modern India during the seventeenth and eighteenth centuries ought to be seen not as two distinct but as active constituents of the integrated Mughal economy, as opposed to the opinions of scholars who have argued for a 'forced nature of the integration' between the rural and the urban. They have suggested that the commercial interaction between town and village in Mughal India was determined by the State's ability to unilaterally extract and consume the surplus produced by the peasants, and that despite a flourishing internal trade, the villages remained unaffected. Irfan Habib finds it difficult to see how an inner village market or capitalistic characteristics could have arisen from any internal development in the village community in its 'classic form', especially in view of the individual peasant production and economic stratification that existed within the peasantry. Conversely, it can be argued that the relations between towns and villages were not so narrow; a town invariably organised a village existing around it through a number of political, symbolic, and commercial networks. Seventeenth-century Punjab, for instance, influenced by the political, administrative, and economic measures of Akbar, enjoyed a high degree of urbanisation, with many of its manufacturing and commercially important towns situated amidst the prosperously cultivated areas in the villages, illustrating thus that an urban centre required an agricultural hinterland, and that the two were connected.

The concept of a village as a 'closed, custom-based social and economic unit', 'essentially self-sufficient in its own consumption needs', and related to it the imperialist notion of a weak exchange economy, stagnant manufacturing and primitive technology that resulted in low productivity, adversely affecting development and growth, runs into difficulty with evidences that reveal the fulfillment of the demands of the rural elite for urban manufactured merchandise like cloth, jewellery, and items of weaponry, including swords, spears, knives, and guns. In addition, the silver and gold hoarded by the rural elite and their purchase of precious metals and imported horses indicates an increasing urban craft production. The expenditure on such goods by the zamindars and *muqaddams* was quite substantial, although there were exceptions and all may not have spent the same percentage on urban manufactures. Similarly, demand from the towns for several wares, ranging from the finest to the coarsest of cloths or food items or even weapons, including guns, which may be considered a part of the commodity composition of urban demand, were either manufactured in villages or, as C. A. Bayly (2012 [1983]) observed, produced in regions that were in the proximity of towns—a space between the villages and the towns—the rural–urban zones or areas of expanding intermediate economies in early modern India. What is worth noticing is a growing urban economy that narrowed the gap between rural–urban through several channels. Although the pre-colonial economy had initially developed as a subsistence economy, the peasants could respond to the growing urban consumer demand by raising agricultural production and shifting to *jins-i-kamil* or high value cash crops like indigo, cotton, sugar, opium, tobacco, and maize. Increased production of cash crops led to the growth of a money economy and replaced the barter system with a cash nexus or *naqd* payment. The rural–urban hiatus was further restricted by encouraging occupational specialisation through rural manufactures and developing semi-urban/semi-rural (rur-urban) localities and economic spheres between towns and villages, creating an economic hierarchy between the city and its rural hinterlands—a peculiarly early modern phenomenon, ascribed to an expanding urban economy.

The rapidly growing cash economy facilitated the local landlords and the rural elite to accumulate resources. One sign of new wealth was the emergence of several small towns known as *qasbas* into which the riches from the villages poured increasingly, making them the centres of production and exchange: markets, moneylending, and the grain trade. As intermediate and secondary urban centres between large, affluent cities, the *qasbas* developed as 'feeder towns', functioning as economic mechanisms that connected the cities with rural commodity hinterlands and guided the flow of supplies from the villages to the towns. These rural–urban interlinkages assisted by the *qasba*s helped in fulfilling the demands of the urban upper class as well as the ruling elite. To mobilise the resources from the agricultural hinterlands and meet the requirements for urban goods, new cities were established and the existing ones stimulated and expanded. Cities were indicators of economic growth and social change. As urban centres, they were not static, but their importance and meaning kept changing according to the transformations in the larger socio-economic processes within which they were located. Some have argued that Akbar initiated the process of 'poliscracy' (polis in Greek means town) when he built towns in the proximity of primary resource-yielding locations. He established several towns, including the imperial cities of Agra, Fatehpur Sikri, and Lahore. Agra had risen as a political centre, but over time developed into a vibrant economic hub of north India, continuing to be so even after the shift of the power base to Delhi. The city had pockets of both affluence and poverty, but its economic activities provided ample opportunities for interaction between professional groups comprising merchants, financiers, artisans, scribes, artists, and others that generated different social groups and institutions. Agra continued to be the intermittent power base for Jahangir, Shahjahan, and Aurangzeb before Delhi acquired the status of political authority.

While Delhi represented several processes and mechanisms by which power was inscribed into its cityscape, its urban dynamism was connected to its spatial and morphological evolution. In addition to its political power and authority, Delhi characterised different spectacles—economic power centre, military encampment, social and cultural centre, its religion and religiosity, language and literature. All these features contributed to making Delhi tremendously urbane and cosmopolitan. Towns that emerged in the north of Delhi, Punjab, Multan, and Sind during the sixteenth century were connected to each other through road and riverine routes. This entire area was linked to India's eastern and western seashores on the one hand and to Central Asia and Persia on the other through Kabul and Qandahar. The region around the routes had flourishing commercial and manufacturing centres that encouraged growth in the neighbouring countryside as well as urban centres in Punjab and its vicinity. Lahore, identified as the provincial headquarters in the sixteenth century, expanded under Jahangir, Shahjahan, and during the early years of Aurangzeb. It grew as a centre for manufacturing shawls and particularly the mixed silk and woollen textile. Along with Agra, Lahore became the chief market for indigo. Towns like Banares, which had arisen for reasons of religion and pilgrimage, were radically transformed into economic centres and core axes of banking and mercantile activities. Other politically important urban centres included Daulatabad, Gulbarga, Gaur, Bijapur, and Golconda, while Jaunpur, Burhanpur, Multan, Patna, Ahmadabad, Ujjain, Ajmer, and Allahabad, situated on the nodal points of the major trade routes, evolved as major commercial urban centres. Surat, Broach, Cambay, Chittagong, Satgaon, Buttor (Betor-Howrah), Calicut, and Cochin were some of the important port-cities that contributed to energetic maritime trade, transforming the nature of the coastal areas and their hinterlands. All sections of people of these megacities—affluent and not so affluent—portrayed a high demand for urban goods like ornaments and jewellery and, depending on the economic status of the consumer, the demand could vary from gold, silver, copper, ivory, sea-shells, bell-metals, and tin.

However, any observation on demand and productivity necessitates an assessment of the patterns of consumption, social habits, and customary traditions. No generalisations can be made. Regional variations in the demand for urban commodities, whether ornaments, clothing, furniture or utensils, cannot be taken to represent the condition—poverty, starvation and misery—of the masses. The inconstancy in requirements could be a sign of the minimal patterns of consumption. To determine the rate of demand in any pre-industrial society, not just in pre-colonial India, it is importunate to evaluate the needs for three consumer products—food, clothing, and housing. All regions invariably reflected the demand for manufactured food items like oil, butter, ghee, salt and sugar; the bazaar rates and circulation of these commodities indicated the market's potential for fulfilling the requirements of all classes of society. In addition, these goods formed a valuable part of interregional trade, thus challenging the notion of self-sufficiency.

Contrary to the assumption that loincloth was the customary clothing in India, Mughal miniature paintings provide evidences of simple, tailored clothing that illustrate a demand for manufactured clothing. Similarly, the demand for food and clothing indicated the existence of rural markets for manufactured items, although some of their needs were in variance with the urban markets. The rural markets, in some instances, could reflect a demand for subsistence-oriented production; its requirement for housing and domestic utensils could be meagre, especially if mud houses and bamboo houses with thatched roofs predominated and the utensils were largely of earthenware. In juxtaposition were the housing needs of the rich mercantile class and the middle-income group/middle class, which presented a substantial demand for building skills and construction material. Mortar, lime, and cement were extensively used in Mughal India and so were stone, brick, timber, and bamboo as building material. In places like Surat, which were largely inhabited by rich traders, there were carvings in relief on teak embellished with enamel and lacquer, while in Delhi the upper-class gentry lived in imposing buildings with large enclosures, although the bureaucracy occupied houses which, as Bernier described, 'had a tolerable appearance and were airy and pleasant'. In Lahore, Banares, Cambay, and Sironj, the traders and artisans lived in multi-storied houses of stone and brick; in Malwa and Agra, too, there were lofty stone houses and in Bengal, expensive, good quality bamboo was used as building material. The demand for furniture in wood was limited, although mats, carpets, pillows covered with silk brocade, bedsteads decorated with brass plates, jugs, metal pots, and mirrors were found in all upper and middle-class houses.

The variegated public demand was an indicator of the growing urbanism and urban manufacture. Equally esteemed in determining urbanism was the private demand, that is, the demand of the imperial household that led to the considerable production and manufacture of fine, luxury and decorative items—silk, brocade, muslin, jewels of precious metals and stones like pearls, gold, silver, diamonds, carpets, decorative mirrors, weaponry, perfumes, wine, etc. It also boosted the demand for building material, building skills, equipments for houses, elephants, and transports like palanquins, carts and boats. Both public and private demand—varied and expansive in its disposition—stimulated the economy and the interregional and coastal trade.

It can be seen on the basis of demand, the nature of expenditure, and population statistics that a large urban sector existed in the sixteenth–seventeenth centuries. At least 15 per cent of the total population lived in towns, totalling the urban population to roughly twenty million for the entire subcontinent. These estimates clearly support the view that a sizeable middle class existed in Mughal India, comprising lower ranks of the bureaucracy, professionals like *hakim*s, doctors and surgeons, architects, artists, scholars and scribes, and holders of *madad-i ma'ash* or *suyurghal* lands. In addition were the commercial and financial groups—*saudagar*s, *mahajan*s, *sarraf*s (*shroff*s), *dalal*s—who contributed significantly to the growth of monetisation, exchange economy, and interregional trade. Pelsaert referred to several artisanal crafts and service occupations—weaver, tailor, barber, carpenter, metalworker, mason, stone-cutter, oil-presser, carpet-maker, paper manufacturer—the clientele of which included the middle class. The middle class formed a proportionately large market for comfort and luxury items and, as the Mughal Empire consolidated, this group evolved as an important sector and claimed an increasing share of the resources of the empire.

Artisans made valuable contributions to the ascension of trade and commerce and the expansion of markets. They remained central to the complex interrelationship between groups and communities engaged in commercial transactions and manufacture. Integration and coordination between merchants, markets and artisans made the latter inevitably dominant in the commercial economy.

Heredity played an important role in determining the artisan's choice of trade. The family was developed as a unit and the production was done at the artisan's own household, using his own tools and equipments and with the help of family labour. The 'paterfamilias' or the master craftsman provided the necessary training in skills to his family members. But this was hardly a limitation, for while the general characteristic of artisanal production was uniform family-based production, modifications could be made depending on the nature of the demand and the type of commodity to be produced. To meet the merchant demand, artisans were urged to work in the *karkhana*s or workshops of their employers. The Dutch East India Company and English East India Company both adopted this system in their silk factories, particularly in Bengal. Artisans who consented to work in the *karkhana*s were given the option of bringing their own tools, but were not allowed the comfort of their homes for work or the use of family labour.

Each artisan developed a specialised skill as per the norms of his caste. Commenting on the close association between the artisan's skills and his caste, Babur observed that for every *jami* or caste, the profession was fixed, and the occupation of the father determined the son's choice. Bernier, in concurrence, observed that an artisan, whether embroiderer, goldsmith or physician, trained their sons in the respective skills and exhorted them to follow the same. To maintain the tradition and retain the monopoly over the skills of their caste, marriages too were not permitted outside one's own caste or trade or profession. In Coromandel, for example, caste was primary to the community organisation of weavers. In seventeenth-century northern Coromandel in the villages of Golepallam and Gondawaron, most weavers came from high castes like *saliwaar*s, *kykelwaar*s and *deerewaar*s, with hardly any from the low castes or outcastes. The head weaver or caste headman, known as *carredar*, was entitled to collect a certain fee on each piece of cloth produced under his supervision, a right given to him by the weavers as a kind of insurance. Other weaver castes that dominated south India in the seventeenth century included the *kaikkolar* in Tamil Nadu and *devanga* in Andhra and Karnataka regions, while the *saliwaar* were noted in the English East India Company record of 1694 as 'ancient inhabitants' of the Tamil country, engaged in the production of coarse and fine unbleached neck cloths. *Janrawaars* was a mobile weaver caste that had migrated from the Andhra region to Tamil Nadu in search of better economic opportunities. In addition to these traditional castes of weavers, the specialist weavers formed new castes like *pattunulkarar* in Madurai, the *caingaloon* weavers, who wove cloth specifically for the Malay Archipelago, the *mambaloom* 'painters' distinguished in the production of painted chintz, and the *mooree* weavers, mostly Muslims, who developed superior cotton cloth, used as a base for chintz-making. In a few north Indian cities like Delhi, Agra, and Lahore, a large number of artisans engaged in dyeing and weaving were Muslims, while a majority of wage labourers took to building construction.

Castes functioned like guilds that controlled competition, production, investments, profits, and even the preservation and transmission of skills within the caste. Max Weber (1958), however, had a different opinion. He felt that caste specialisations generated a negative impact and resulted in a low level of craft technology and segregation of skills, raising barriers between one craft and another, thus making the diffusion of techniques difficult. The artisan in such circumstances, he argued, remained content to adopt family devices and rejected or ignored the craft technologies of other castes, even if they looked more promising, and resisted any change unless approved by his caste peers. Arguing conversely, Morris D. Morris (1967) and Irfan Habib (1978) observed that caste was not an obstacle to the artisan's mobility; nor was he hesitant to adopt a technique if it profited his craft and was within the confines of his caste traditions or rituals. Morris went a step further to suggest that there were no restraints on the artisan's interregional movement within India, although they were prohibited from overseas migration. Considering the distance that they covered between regions, which could sometimes be as distant as England or Spain, the artisans, he stipulated, encountered no restrictions on their mobility. Several instances indeed confirm that caste was not a problem in the progression of the artisans. Castes could change their profession, especially if professions other than their own were commercially more advantageous and profitable. To consolidate the change, a segment of the caste—or sometimes the whole caste—asserted origins different from their traditional ones, and refrained from marrying members of their customary craft. Eighteenth-century Maharashtra, for example, is replete with examples of castes of tailors who took to dyeing, some of whom segregated completely to pursue indigo-dyeing. Such cases were many and demonstrate that notwithstanding the caste system, there was no scarcity of labour. Neither was household production a limitation. It did not prevent the artisan from becoming a commodity producer or meeting the specifications or varying demands of the merchants. To meet the requirements for specific commodities, castes proliferated and each artisan caste worked to improve and expand the minute processes and production of these commodities.

The bulk of rural manufacture was produced by hereditary artisan castes linked to dominant agricultural castes by traditional ties of patron-client relationships. Their earnings largely came from the hereditary fixed share of the produce, supplemented by grants of revenue-free lands or cash payments. The reciprocity in production and distribution of commodities at the village level was called the *jajmani* system. *Jajmani* prevailed despite its subsistence-oriented character because it was one of the valuable systems that ensured support during famines. There are references to the adversities encountered by those who had abandoned the *jajmani* system and taken to merely producing for the urban market, as happened in Surat during the famine of 1630. Changes, however, occurred in the working of the *jajmani* system during the seventeenth century; payments could now be made both in cash and kind for additional work, or on a piece-work basis. This pattern co-existed with the practice of granting fixed shares of produce or revenue-free lands to the artisan families. But whatever the basis of the relationship with the village community, the rural artisans produced for wider markets, too, more actively perhaps from the mid-eighteenth century, when they detached themselves from the *jajmani* system and produced for long and medium-distance trade.

Textiles formed a major portion of artisan production, although, as S. Arasaratnam (1990) argued, trade in textiles before the intervention of the Europeans in the textile market had remained erratic, seasonal, and highly unpredictable; there was a certain amount of overlap between artisan and agrarian activity. Many weavers took to weaving in their leisure hours whereas others opted out of spinning and weaving, depending on the market stimulus and the seasonal demand outside the villages. But with the increasing demand for better quality production by the English East India Company, the weavers switched to regular hours of work on the loom. Understanding the new and ever-rising demands of the market and keen to fulfil them, sometimes the weaver's entire family—men, women, and children—was involved in the various tasks related to weaving. The weaver's decision to shift from subsistence to increased specialisation and the use of capital was vital. As they moved into full-time weaving, they became conscious of the overhead expenses concerning loom, thread, and other raw materials, the perquisites to pay labour and the needs of their family. Conscious of the frequent changes in the market demand, they became aware that the Company, and thereby the merchants, influenced by European markets, could change its specifications of weave, dye and bleach. In view of these considerations, the weavers insisted on capital advances or credit before the actual returns. They remained adamant about not undertaking any particular specialisation unless the merchants provided the initial capital inputs and guaranteed purchase of the output. The weaver therefore became 'a man of credit or dependent heavily on available sources of credit'. Relying on the system of advances that either partly met the cost of production or provided the raw material, the weavers acquired the ability to work in different market conditions. With regular supplies of credit or capital advance, concessions in the prices of raw material and promises of further investments by the Company, the weavers of Gorakhpur, for instance, shifted from manufacturing narrow cloth or white cotton cloth of a coarse variety called *gaji* and *garha* to good quality cloth like *sahan* and *sallam*.

The advances could be procured either from the buyers or the middlemen; in some cases, advances could be given in grain. The system of advances and procurement of commodities led to the evolution of the *dadni* system. Under this system, commodities were procured either through spot purchase or advance. Spot purchases could be made both in the major markets and small urban markets. Both the small traders and big merchants hired *dalal*s or agents to procure a part of their supplies through spot purchase directly from the producers. An advance contract was necessary to supplement the capital of the artisans, which was considered inadequate for an expanding market. Beginning from the latter half of the seventeenth century, commodities for long-distance trade were procured by advance contract. *Dadni* was a kind of guarantee to the weavers, who were hesitant to change their looms in accordance with the specifications of the Company, fearing that if the Company rejected the product despite the modifications, they might suffer. Despite the *dadni* system, there was also a lurking apprehension amongst artisans of being reduced to wage-earners, in case the merchants decided to provide them the raw material but paid them on a daily basis. Notwithstanding the complexities, *dadni* transformed the artisanal production to a market-oriented production, stimulated by both inland and foreign trade. With the growth of markets, the artisan settled in and around the commercial *emporia*, that is, centres of export along the coast or European factory towns like Madras and Calcutta which had affluent consumers.

The artisanal production succeeded in expanding the urban sector. Production improved and increased with enhanced investments by merchants, nobles, and members of the imperial family. Thriving trades in agrarian commodities and Indian manufactured items, in particular textiles, developed. The Indian trading community, widespread over the Indian subcontinent, was a heterogeneous group that considered itself the allies of the rulers. It comprised the *seth*, *bohra* or *modi*, who specialised in long-distance, interregional trade, while the *beopari* or *banik* were engaged in local, retail trade. In addition to retailing goods, the *beopari*s, with the assistance of their own agents in the villages and towns, purchased food-grains and cash crops. The *banjara*s, yet another mercantile community known as 'pack-bullock traders' or 'roving grain traders', were categorised by some as a case of 'peddling trade organized on a massive scale'. Generally small traders (although some could come from peasant families), they were carriers of a variety of merchandise, particularly grain. Often hired by others to carry commodities to distant places, the *banjara*s were not merely carriers; they were in themselves merchants who bought grain at cheap rates and sold it at profitable prices. For instance, they imported almost the entire salt in Gorakhpur from western India. The *banjara*s moved in caravans over long distances with oxen and bullocks owned by them, laden with food-grains, pulses, ghee, salt, and others, while the more expensive goods such as textiles, silks, and other luxury items were carried on camels or mules or carts. Known in north India as grain-dealers and for their trade in salt, the *banjara*s were recognised as an established feature of the Deccan cotton trade, not only of the textile industry but also of the general exchange economy of northern Coromandel and Deccan. Allegedly, they owned the cotton they brought from Deccan, which they sold to purchase salt from the coastal salt pans to support their return trip to Deccan. The trading enterprises of the *banjara*s were not limited to the confines of Hindustan but spread to Central Asia, Afghanistan, Persia, Multan, Quetta, and Khyber as well. The trading activities of the Lohanis, a *banjara* tribe, which extended beyond India, may be mentioned in this context. They carried merchandise from India to Kabul and then bought and sold it in Ghazni, a pattern that continued into the early nineteenth century. With changes in and the growth of the Indian economy, the *banjara*s were subordinated as traders by merchant groups and lost their indispensability as carriers and suppliers by the end of the mid-nineteenth century. Their conventional form of traditional exchange was marginalised further with the widening of the railway network by the end of the nineteenth century.

Inland trade through *banjaras* was sometimes found to be more expensive as compared to boat traffic and coastal trade along the seashore. Foodstuffs and textiles were the most important items of interregional trade during the period. Bengal dominated the export of sugar and rice, delicate muslin and silk, while Coromandel as a centre for textile production had a brisk trade with Gujarat, both along the coast and across Deccan. Gujarat was the entry point for foreign goods and also exported fine textiles and *patola* silk to north India, with Burhanpur and Agra as the nodal points of trade. Lahore was the core of handicraft production and the distribution centre for shawls, carpets, and other luxury products of Kashmir. Punjab and Sind had close trade ties with Kabul and Qandahar, Delhi and Agra, and their goods were usually sailed down the river Indus.

The seventeenth century witnessed the growing involvement of the Mughal nobility and emperors in trade. Their attitude towards trade can be best illustrated by an analysis of the extensive Iranian influence on the Mughal court in the first half of the seventeenth century. The 'state mercantilism' advocated in Iran by Shah 'Abbas had apparently struck the Mughal emperors to such an extent that it led them to emulate the Iranian tradition of combining *imarat* and *tijarat* (statecraft and trade). Close links between trade and politics in Central Asia may have also affected the Mughals. Evidence from Central Asia reveals that royal instructions were sent to the local officials to exhort the merchants of neighbouring regions to trade in the Uzbek lands, for trade and traders were seen as a source of peace and happiness for society. The royal orders in Central Asia were issued in pursuance of such *Quranic* verses and traditions of the Prophet that stressed on the importance of trade in Islam, leading to the belief that one way of serving the cause of religion was through the promotion of trade and traders. It is in this context that the participation of the Mughal ruling elite—rulers and the nobility—needs to be assessed.

Asaf Khan, Shahjahan's father-in-law, was known for his dynamic role in the sea-borne trade of ports like Hugli and Surat, and the contacts that he maintained with the Portuguese at Goa. In Sind, during the 1640s, advances were made from the State funds and the mint by the *shahbandar* of Lahori *Bandar* and the *diwan* of the *suba* to the merchants of the region. Like in Sind, the Mughals, as of 1630, attempted to control maritime trade in Bengal. This necessitated weakening the power of the Portuguese traders, especially those settled in Hugli and Chittagong. The Mughals achieved this through military campaigns in the beginning of the 1630s, although they were not as successful in reducing the influence of the Arakanese over trade in eastern Bengal. Princes Dara, Aurangzeb, and Murad busied themselves with commerce in the ports of the Red Sea and Persian Gulf like Kung and Mokha through Thatta and Lahori *Bandar* around the 1640s. Surat emerged as an important centre for trade in the 1640s and 1650s, for both the emperors and the nobles. Both Akbar and Jahangir owned shipping. More importantly, the two women of Jahangir's reign—his mother Maryam-uz-Zamani and wife Nurjahan—were engaged in domestic and international trade, although it was Shahjahan who strengthened the interest and involvement in maritime trade. On the advice of the *mutasaddi* of Surat in the beginning of the

1650s, Shahjahan ordered the construction of half-a-dozen ships in Gujarat, to be used for trade with *Bandar* 'Abbas and Mokha, and virtually monopolised the freight carriage market on these routes till 1663, when the ships were sold off to private merchants. In addition, Shahjahan had his *karkhanas* in Burhanpur, like Dara and Jahanara. While Aurangzeb as a prince attempted to construct his own port at Sind, his grandson Azim-al-Shan was charged for *sauda-i-khas* or monopolistic control over business in Chittagong and Dacca. Unlike in Surat and Sind, the initiative for trade in Bengal was taken by the nobles. Chief amongst them were Mir Jumla, Shayasta Khan, and several others, mentioned in the Mughal documents as *tijarat-pisha* and *tajir-zadeh*, that is, merchants or belonging to the family of merchants.

The royal family and the nobles were engaged in a small percentage of the total commerce. It was the traders and merchants, as 'part of a homogenous business culture', along with the *sarrafs* and *dalals*, who formed a significant segment of the Indian economy. Caste distinctions overlapped the specialisation and professionalism of these groups. *Khatris*, principally a business community and the main carriers of India's overland trade beyond its northwest borders and Central Asia, dominated the upper echelons of commerce, and were closely linked to State service, holding petty to high ranks. Originally from Punjab, as a leading local trading community, they prided themselves as those who combined *imarat* and *tijarat*. Their increased strength in the administration as well as trade exemplified that the destiny of merchants in Mughal India was tied to those of the ruling elites. That the traders were the allies of the ruling family is evident from developments in eighteenth-century Punjab. When Punjab was shaken by rural rebellions, it was the *Khatri* traders who stood in support of the Mughal State and helped in suppressing the peasant revolt. Starting from the eighteenth century, they made way for the Afghans in trade with Central Asia, while a few *Khatri* families migrated to the east and others to the south of Multan, where in Shikarpur they maintained their trade. Many others moved to the upper Indus region and gradually regained their original position, sometimes as allies of the Afghans and at others as their subordinates. The other mercantile communities included the Hindu and Jain Gujarati merchants and Muslims, mostly Bohras; the Oswals, Maheshwaris, and Agarwals of Rajasthan, also known as Marwaris (the Marwaris further spread to Maharashtra and Bengal in the eighteenth century); the Chettis on Coromandel Coast and Muslim merchants of Malabar of both Indian and Arab origin.

Interregional trade was facilitated by complex networks linking wholesalers with merchants and the local and regional levels through *gumashtas* (agents) and *dalals* (commission agents). The movement of goods from the first half of the seventeenth century was made possible by the growing use of a system of bankers to transfer revenue to the centre from the provinces, leading to the coordination of the fiscal order with commercial and financial networks—an issue that generated wide scholarly debate. Karen Leonard (2014) analysed the organisation and volume of economic activities of the great indigenous banking firms and their participation in politics during the Mughal and early colonial period. She used the term 'great firm' to describe a business firm engaged in a variety of enterprises, with several branches, often based on one 'household'. The banking firms, she argued, were crucial to the financial functioning of both the central government and individual *mansabdars*/*jagirdars*, zamindars and *talluqdars*, all of whom directly depended upon them. When the 'great firms', the 'indispensable allies' of the Mughal State, began diverting both credit and trade from the Mughal centre to regional powers, the empire began to unravel. Between 1650 and 1750, said Leonard, the banking firms' growing engagement in revenue collection at the regional and local levels surpassed their provision of credit to the central government. Consequently, the empire's central structure suffered, even as many banking firms and merchants witnessed expansion and diversification.

While not in agreement with Leonard, John F. Richards (1981) nevertheless acknowledged that various private banking firms may have contributed significantly to the restructuring of the imperial system by regional states in the eighteenth century, and that these firms may have grown in power and importance owing to their close association with European trading companies. However, he insisted that there was no available evidence to indicate that these 'great firms' played a similar role for the Mughal imperial system in the sixteenth and seventeenth centuries. In the seventeenth century, Richards argued, there may have been occasional cases of merchants with enormous wealth, but even the wealthiest of these men were not direct participants in the imperial system, much less 'indispensable allies of the Mughal state'. Their services were limited and dispensable. Private bankers or moneychangers did not control or manage imperial treasuries and mints. Nor did private entrepreneurs collect imperial revenues. Rather, in large commercial centres, Mughal emperors imposed limits on indigenous markets by formally sanctioning traders or headmen for such specialised markets and by recruiting an officer from the local commercial community to collect urban taxes, alongside imperial officials. Richards' proposition of 'centralization through state power', which implied that the fiscal integration under Aurangzeb was mediated by the Mughal treasury and the great households rather than by bankers, has left many unconvinced. There appears to be far more evidence on the use of the characteristic credit institution or *hundi* or bill of exchange for fiscal transfers than what Richards suggested. *Hundi*s, instead of cash, were the standard form of payment in most commercial transactions. In long-distance trade, it not only fulfilled the expanding demand for credit, but also reduced the risks of transporting cash to distant places. *Hundi* promised payment at the end of a specified period (usually two months or less) at a particular place, and allowed a discount which included interest, *bima* (insurance), and expenses incurred during the transmission of money. It was a process in which everyone, from the *subadar* and *mutassadi* to the Dutch Company, participated. They were a channel for investment generally managed by *sarrafs* or *shroffs*, the professional moneychangers, who also acted as commercial bankers, supplying large credits. Several wealthy merchants like Virji Vora of Surat facilitated the smooth functioning of commerce by financing the English East India Company and setting up banking houses in different parts of India, as well as in West Asia and Southeast Asia.

The emerging importance of the Europeans reduced the control of Indian merchants over the seas. The Mughals had tried to regain their decisive status in maritime trade in Sind during the seventeenth century, but failed to achieve the desirable domination (although they could withhold Thatta). India, however, could retain its sea trade with Persia and the neighbouring regions through the Armenians, who, as trading partners of the Europeans, were preeminent in Persia and India in the seventeenth century. By the agreement of 1688 with the English, the Armenians managed to strengthen their trade share in India and, as they became the chief carriers of European commodities from India to Persia, they also consented to abandon the export of Indian goods by the land route and instead use Company-owned ships to transport them. The English, too, stood to gain from this understanding. They could now pursue their interests, taking advantage of the Armenian familiarity with the local language, customs, and political authorities.

The European corporate enterprises—the Portuguese *Estado da India* and *Casa da India* in the sixteenth century, and the Dutch, English, and French East India Companies in the seventeenth and eighteenth centuries—were the major agencies preponderant in the Euro-Asian commercial network. Some amount of Euro-Asian trade was also conducted by private European traders, although generally, in terms of the volume of trade, the Portuguese private traders were of greatest import. The Dutch East India Company was the only European corporate enterprise engaged in a significant way in the intra-Asian trade, while the rest were predominantly private traders—the Portuguese, the Dutch (VOC), the French and, most importantly, the English, who were allowed to participate in trade on a private basis even as they continued to be in the service of the Company. These traders, whether corporate or private, operating in the sphere of the Indian Ocean–South China Sea, shared a diversified relationship amongst themselves as well as with the Indian maritime merchants involved in intra-Asian trade. There were a few important and unexpected areas of cooperation between individual Portuguese traders on the one hand, and individual Asian and non-Portuguese European traders and European corporate enterprises, on the other. This pattern changed when the English East India Company acquired political authority in several parts of the Indian subcontinent during the latter half of the eighteenth century. The English Company as well as its servants engaged in trade on a private account, often invoking their coercive authority vis-à-vis the rival European corporate enterprises, private European traders, and the Indian merchants engaged in intra-Asian trade.

DEBATING POTENTIALITIES OF CAPITALIST DEVELOPMENT IN MUGHAL ECONOMY

A major controversy that has kept historians divided is whether the surplus produced in Mughal India and the pattern of distribution generated growth, and whether the economy possessed potentialities of capitalist development and capitalist order. Providing a rather grim picture of India's pre-colonial economy, W. H. Moreland (1993 [1920], 1992 [1923]) had argued that there was little possibility of capitalist development in medieval and early modern India without foreign intervention. He described the villages as 'self-sufficient' and 'petty republics' where production—whether agricultural or non-agricultural—was primarily for local consumption, which had no concern with outside demand nor felt the need to import commodities from outside. But ironically, while talking of production at the household level and for local consumption, he observed that the cotton production at the village level was a mark of high industrialism. Contradicting his own argument and yet not letting go of his imperialist bias, Moreland stipulated that the technique and technology of production were so primitive and undeveloped that they could hardly be compared with contemporary Europe. The extent of its backwardness was such, he said, that they could only contribute to local consumption and showed no signs of capitalist development. Also, while the workforce in India was large, it was no indicator of rapid growth or high performance, for the bulk of it was a 'consuming class', incapable of generating wealth. For Moreland, a large 'consuming class' was representative of economic backwardness and an exploitative society. His verdict, thus, was that per capita increase in national income became a possibility only with the coming of the British, with the rise in investments, production, and subsequently, capitalist development.

Morris D. Morris (1963) agreed with Moreland that there was scarce possibility of capitalist development in pre-colonial India without foreign intervention, although his arguments were based on different convictions. Commenting on the nature of capitalism, he observed that capitalism implied accumulation of capital and accumulation could be made possible not by production, but by a certain margin of surplus, that is, the amount left after meeting the cost of subsistence of the producers. So, if per capita production was low, the surplus could not reach the minimum level and thus hindered accumulation. This, Morris said, was the case in Mughal India. While it witnessed growth and development of production, it did not necessarily lead to accumulation of capital, and thus, despite the potential, there was no capitalist development in the period preceding colonial rule.

The arguments of Pavlov (2016 [1964]) and Chicherov (1971 [1965]) were opposed to that of Moreland and Morris. They spoke of the growing crisis of feudalism in the eighteenth century, with the possibility of an indigenous growth of capitalism in India. They argued that by the eighteenth century, the *mahajan*s, as moneylenders and credit facilitators, had emerged as the new feudal elite that replaced the *khud-kasht* in the villages; thus, by controlling the relations of production and mode of production, the *mahajan*s contributed to the collapse of the village community. In addition, the two observed that weavers outside the villages had increased their artisanal production and could meet the consumer demands of not only the villages, but also the distant markets, further accelerating the break-up of the village community. They asserted that this phenomenon of artisanal production could have led to capitalist development, and that no foreign intervention was required for the growth of capitalism in India.

Irfan Habib's (2001c) assessment of the potentialities of capitalist development in pre-colonial India lies within a Marxist framework, although ironically it is also closer to Moreland's arguments. Habib defined the village community as a closed, custom-based social and economic unit and as a collective organisation of peasants within the structure of caste and clan, in which peasants undertook agricultural production while artisans too produced to fulfil the needs of the peasants. The artisans were paid by the peasants according to customary norms, either by a share of the produce or revenue-free land or *naqd*. These features, Habib argued, clearly established that villages were self-sufficient and catered to their own needs. Emphasising an individualistic mode of production and the economic stratification of the peasantry, he completely rejected any indications of potentialities of capitalistic development in the villages or the village markets. The mechanism of the payment of land revenue—in cash or commutation of kind in cash according to market prices—resulted in an enormous drain of wealth from the villages. After making allowances to the ruling class—*jagirdars*, zamindars, *madad-i ma'ash* holders—the total net produce lost annually by the villages without any return amounted to a large portion, varying from one-third to one-fourth to half. Thus, the land revenue pattern, Habib asserted, was regressive, especially on the peasants, and monetisation was the major cause of stratification of the peasantry and poverty among the poor peasants. But then, the subversion of peasant economy may or may not pave the way for capitalistic or semi-capitalistic farming, as illustrated by Pavlov (2016 [1964]) and K. F. Ashrafyan (1965), who argued that zamindari rights in pre-colonial India contained 'seeds of capitalist private property'. Disagreeing with the Soviet view, Habib emphatically suggested that the subversion of peasant economy led to the decline of rural economy and agrarian exploitation, rather than an increase in agrarian investment; so in no way could such subversion lead to a semi-capitalistic form of agriculture in pre-colonial India.

In the urban sector, Habib (2001a) acknowledged that the demands of the imperial household, *jagirdars*, and zamindars resulted in increased production and investments by both the ruling dynasty and the nobility; the artisanal production had a multiplier effect and expanded the urban sector; moreover, a high proportion of the urban population was employed in individual crafts and the output per head was also considerable. But having said this, Habib added that in Mughal India, the manufactures required per head were of low value, and hence the productivity per capita was also low. This implied that low productivity led to a small surplus and therefore less capital accumulation. So in Mughal India, because of the different kinds of investment, there was considerable growth of merchant capital; however, as Marx observed, merchant capital on its own did not result in industrial capitalism. Alluding to Marx, Habib argued that the development of capital as merchant capital was an independent process and did not necessarily lead to the production of capital or capital development, which occurred independently through a social mode of production. In other words, merchant capital was inversely posed to the general economic development.

Analysing the potentialities of capitalistic development, Habib averred that both agricultural and urban production were governed by the market. In the agrarian sphere, the *khud-kasht* was the potential capitalist farmer, possessing an individual unit with absolute property rights on it—whether habitational, cultivating, sale or mortgage—and the privilege to hire labour, and yet he could not emerge as a capitalist owing to certain limitations. In craft production, too, merchant capital was enormous and controlled the artisans through the *dadni* and the 'putting out' system. Yet manufacturing never went beyond commodity production. In other words, the Mughal economy could never develop beyond merchant capital and, although it was a highly monetised economy, it was the domestic industry that predominated. Habib elucidated that the Mughal economy rested largely on agrarian exploitation and thus no rural market existed for urban crafts; the money economy in the villages came from the transfer of surplus from the rural to the urban, and when a crisis occurred in agriculture, the entire structure was affected. In the eighteenth century, the large market supported by the Mughal State was completely destroyed, resulting in the collapse of merchant capital; so, despite the potentialities, the Mughal economy could not develop into capitalism.

There is, however, no consensus on Habib's interpretation. Scholars have argued that the economy of the eighteenth century retained its vibrancy and continued to exploit the potentialities it had imbibed from the earlier Mughal centuries, namely the sixteenth and the seventeenth. Holden Furber and P. J. Marshall have argued that the East India Company trade and private European trade that emerged in the eighteenth century grew and developed by adopting and linking themselves to the existing trade and market economy in Bengal, implying thus that despite the weakening of the centre in the early eighteenth century, the economy retained its metre and could function without its active involvement. This authenticates that the pattern of merchant capital since the sixteenth century was such that the collapse of the centre could not hinder its growth. Similarly, Ashin Das Gupta, in his discussion of trade in Malabar and Surat, and the role of European traders and India in the Indian Ocean trade in the eighteenth century clearly demonstrated that these developments were made possible by the continuing commerce and political responses to it on the eastern and western coasts. Notwithstanding the changes in state formation from the mid-eighteenth century, the basis of socio-economic development remained the same as in the earlier period. C. A. Bayly noticed the growth of the merchant class as a homogeneous body, which, despite modifications, remained the crux of trade and commerce and dominated political life. The institution of the merchants affected the character and development of towns, leading to urban solidarity. Urbanism and the growth of mercantile activity were stimulated by the constant foreign demand that penetrated through Bengal, raising considerably the commercial production and export of Bengal in the eighteenth century, making trade generally prosperous.

Sanjay Subrahmanyam and Bayly have suggested the existence of great merchant corporations with vast resources, influence, and a well-developed culture of book-keeping and subcontinental credit. In this context, they have pointed to the important role of 'portfolio capitalists' or merchants 'able to straddle the worlds of commerce and political participation' in the Mughal system. These large-scale entrepreneurs utilised not only their own capital but also that of small-scale operators, who served as conduits for indirect investment. In northern India, great merchant families emerged and established their importance over the first half of the eighteenth century. For instance, the enterprise started by the Marwari merchants Manikchand and Fatehchand in Bengal, later called the house of Jagat Seth, was the most conspicuous amongst a series of significant networks of Gujaratis, Multanis, and Agarwals. These networks had developed over generations. In addition, there were the Banares Agarwals and the Kashmiri Mul.

The period also coincided with the dominance of Gujarati merchants in Bengal external trade, particularly after the *mansabdar*s withdrew. Evidence from Banares and Bengal also reveals the deep involvement of merchant capital in the conduct of revenue farms and other enterprises controlled by larger 'portfolio capitalists' and the State. Belonging to the military and administrative organisation, 'portfolio capitalists' of the early eighteenth century, generally Muslims and *Kayastha*s, were willing to perform functions that the great merchant families were either unable or were unwilling to perform. Unlike the great merchants, these men had access to and control over the military labour market; hence they could engage in political matters without relenting on their credit. Noting that such men 'commanded the state in matters of revenue',

Subrahmanyam and Bayly (1990) have argued that perhaps such great houses were already firmly placed in the administration of the *jagirs* of the *mansabdars* even before the beginning of the eighteenth century, and that the disintegration of the Mughal system in the early eighteenth century empowered them still further. This would suggest that merchant capital and 'portfolio capitalists' had begun to intervene in agricultural production and to control labour and trade, a process that facilitated the emergence of many 'new' zamindars of the eighteenth century. Merchant capital, in this way, contributed significantly to State and military finance, which later led to the rise of the English East India Company.

6

RELIGION AND STATE

HIGHLIGHTS

- Religious plurality and co-existence in Mughal India
- Akbar's religious ideas and *sulh-i kul*
- Religious tolerance and plurality reinforced by Jahangir, Shahjahan, Aurangzeb
- Millenarian movements; syncretism of Dara Shukoh
- Bhakti devotionalism
- Women *bhakta*s and their defiance of patriarchal social norms

Religion, or the role of religion in medieval and early modern India, has been a complex issue arousing controversial, conflictive debate. Often linked to religious disputes, destruction of prayer-houses, and brutality towards the 'other', what has emerged are the threatening communal trends of the recent past, casting an ugly spell on the secular texture of India. And all these have been justified on the grounds of taking revenge on India's historical past. This should inevitably lead to the question: Were Muslims inherently iconoclastic? Several scholars have asked this question, and the answers have been to the contrary. Certainly, there are examples in history of looting, pillaging and desecration of temples, but the analysis of these actions have persistently directed towards the realm of politics, identifying these as tools to assert political sovereignty, irrespective of whether the rulers were Muslim or Hindu. This, of course, is not a justification of invoking religion for the sake of politics. But it is also not prudent to isolate Muslims as iconoclasts or to hold them responsible for temple desecration in the historical past. It is truly unhistorical. To put these issues in proper perspective, the attempt would be to explore the relationship between religion, society, and politics and evaluate the religious ideas, reactions, and responses that marked the period.

While Akbar was considered the most transformative of all rulers, who consolidated the Mughal Empire and devised cultural and political reforms to reach out to diverse regional, religious, and linguistic communities, the inheritance of his father's tolerant philosophical and cosmological concepts were irrefutably his valuable assets. Humayun, in fact, deserves far greater credit than has been conceded to him for initiating the tone of transition and anticipating the ideological orientation under his successors. It is correct that Akbar pioneered social, political, religious, and cultural liberalism, but the fact remains that if these were sustained through the Mughal rule, it is an evidence of the continued efforts and practices—cosmopolitanism and pluralism—of Jahangir and Shahjahan. Aurangzeb may have shown a variation in his intellectual and ideological leanings, but he was no different from the others in political calculability or comprehension of political exigencies; in fact, he was fairly catholic in his dealings with the public.

The fifteenth to the eighteenth centuries had yet other characteristics: a variety of religious interactions, unfolding of Sufi ideology and *Bhakti* devotionalism, as well as millenarian movements that had wide cultural, social, and political consequences. The Islamic world during the years 1591–92 hovered around the expectation of a re-ordering of the known world through the mediation of a *mujaddid* ('Renewer').

AKBAR'S RELIGIOUS IDEAS AND *SULH-I KUL*

The processes of consolidation and empire-building under Akbar were strengthened not only through territorial expansion and administrative reforms, but also his firm and discreet handling of India's multiethnic, multiracial, multireligious, and multilinguistic identity. Keen to communicate and strike a rapport with India's diversity and heterogeneity, Akbar's efforts were focused on achieving cultural synthesis and institutionalised pluralism that later developed into *sulh-i kul* or 'absolute peace' or 'peaceful coexistence'. The contention is: Was *sulh-i kul* just a Sufi idea or was it a pragmatic move to attain political and social cohesion and cultural and religious liberalism? These variants can be best explained by examining the evolution of Akbar's religious ideas and his reactions and response to the different cultural and religious influences that may have contributed to shaping his personality. Tracing the development of Akbar's worldview from his accession in 1556 to his death in 1605 and assessing his ideas and ideology, two issues can be raised:

- the influence of his personal world outlook on his religious policy; and
- the response of the different sections of society, including the *'ulama*, to his religious views and the reforms adopted by him.

These questions, Iqtidar Alam Khan argued, even as he reconsidered the position taken by Athar Ali (1983) in his article 'Akbar and Islam', were important to be reckoned with in view of the claims of Badauni, the Jesuit fathers, and Shaikh Ahmad Sirhindi that Akbar had become an apostate and ceased to be a Muslim after 1581, and that it was his hostility to Islam that had made him tolerant towards the non-Muslims.

The impressions on Akbar as he moved into adolescence were many. Akbar's personality evolved under several liberal influences, like that of two Irani Shi'is—Bairam Khan and Abdul Latif Qazvini—and Sunni Turani, Munim Beg Khan; all of them were above sectarian bias and their impact on Akbar was considerable. His mother, Hamida Banu Begum, was allegedly a Shi'i with a liberal outlook—a fact contested by Iqtidar Alam Khan on the basis of an incident of 1546 when the Begum's brother, Muazzam Beg, assassinated Humayun's Iranian Shi'i *wazir*,

Khwaja Sultan Rushdi. This act, averred Iqtidar Alam Khan, could only be that of a Sunni bigot. Notwithstanding this, the cultural ethos of the Timurids continued to have an overarching impact on the Mughal court till the early years of Akbar's reign. It is asserted that Timur respected all religions and that Chingiz Khan, as *Yasa-i Chingezi* indicated, had abandoned bigotry and the practice of following any one faith or preferring one religion over the other. Akbar imbibed these values and inherited religious tolerance and innovative political ideology from Humayun, who had inducted in his nobility Irani Shi'i nobles without perpetrating any Shi'i–Sunni conflict and set aside Timurid–Chingizi notions of collective political sovereignty—because unless that prevailed, the expansion of power could not be a possibility.

In addition, Akbar was affected by his father's pre-Islamic Iranian concepts of kingship, solar symbolism or the close link between the sun and the king, natural science and philosophy, including astronomy, astrology, cosmology and Sufism. And yet, at his accession, Akbar could not outgrow the Sunni effect of being surrounded by his tutor, Mir Abdul Latif, *sadr* Abdun Nabi, and *mufti* Abdullah Sultanpuri, although some semblance of liberalism could be maintained by his *wakil-us-sultanat*, Bairam Khan. This phase coincided with the emperor's intolerance towards the *Mahdavis* and the Shi'is and the erosion of Timurid–Chingizi features.

Akbar succeeded in liberating the State from orthodoxy beginning 1562 when he married the Rajput princesses, made grants to the temples, celebrated Hindu festivals at the imperial court, and abolished the pilgrimage tax and *jizya* in 1563 and 1564, respectively. The abolition of the two taxes, as Irfan Habib argued, was necessitated by economic reasons. The importance of *jizya* was subsidiary with its rate never fixed, or at the most fixed at 4 per cent of the *jama*; moreover, it was discriminatory and extremely regressive even at its lowest rate, equal to one month's wage of an unskilled urban labourer. Iqtidar Alam Khan (1968, 1978), however, attributed the abolition of *jizya* to political reasons and linked it to the emperor's keen desire to win the support of the Rajputs to suppress the rebellion of the Turani nobles. Akbar's politics, however, went even beyond that: to secure the support of the *'ulama* that had become increasingly critical of the emperor's announcements and condemned him as a heretic. In this regard, Iqtidar Khan mentioned the *fathnama* issued by Akbar in 1568 subsequent to the conquest of Chittor, couched in orthodox language and sent to the *muhtasib* of Bilgram, *Qazi* Abdus Samad, in which Akbar declared his victory at Chittor as the victory of Islam over the *kafirs*. Such a *fathnama*, Iqtidar Khan reiterated, was not repeated, demonstrating the emperor's pragmatic strategy that reinforced his policy of inclusiveness, which had stabilised his position with the Rajputs by 1568. Substantiating his argument concerning political expediency, Khan observed that to further pacify the *'ulama*, Akbar re-imposed *jizya* in 1575 but repealed it again in 1580 when he failed to establish himself as *Badshah-i Islam*. This stipulation led Khan into conflict with S. R. Sharma (2001 [1940]), who argued that *jizya* was in fact never re-imposed; instead, the *farman* was sought to be repeated every ten years, which made it appear as if it was re-imposed in 1575. Shireen Moosvi (2007) concurred that *jizya* was re-imposed in 1575 but the reasons, she asserted, were not political as proposed by Iqtidar Khan. The re-imposition, she reiterated, was influenced by two representatives of the *'ulama*, Abdun Nabi and Makhdum ul-Mulk, and Akbar's own commitment to implement the *Shari'at*. But as the emperor's views evolved, *jizya* was withdrawn in 1580. Moosvi asserted that the abolition of the pilgrimage tax and *jizya* were a part of a pattern maintained throughout the 1560s–70s. Unlike Iqtidar Alam Khan, she argued that Akbar's tolerance of Hinduism at the beginning of the 1560s cannot be read as a mere attempt to placate the Rajputs, and neither can his military campaign in Chittor be seen as a reversal of an orthodox approach; in fact, the conciliatory overtures towards the Hindus did not require him to challenge the *'ulama*. In agreement with Badauni's hypothesis, she observed that in the years preceding the discussions in the *ibadatkhana*, Akbar behaved like an ordinary believer and followed tradition and custom, exemplifying an attitude that could accommodate Timurid culture as well as tolerance towards Hindus, and also promulgate the *fathnama* on the capture of Chittor.

The liberal and inclusive aspects of Akbar's reign are further illustrated by the several grants that he made to temples, information on which is widely available in the Vrindavan documents. Beginning in 1565, Akbar

- declared a grant of *inam* land to the Chaitanya priest Gopaldas;
- in 1568, he issued a *farman* delegating the *adhikar* (right/management) of the Madan Mohan and Govind Dev temples to Jiv Gosain;
- in 1572, by yet another *farman*, Akbar granted revenue-free land for the maintenance of the *Shri Nathji* temple at Gokul;
- Visvesvara temple in Banaras and a location for the meetings of the Brahmin *pandit* assemblies were rebuilt on Akbar's instructions around the 1570s–80s under the leadership of Narayanabhatta of the Bhatta family.
- In 1565, Akbar visited Guru Amardas and made a land grant to his successor Guru Ramdas, on which, much later, the city of Amritsar was established. The city emerged as a religious centre for the Sikhs, more vitally on the completion of the construction of the Golden Temple in 1601.
- In 1598, Akbar is known to have visited Guru Arjan, the author of *Adi Granth*, the holy book of the Sikhs.

Akbar came under Sufi influence, particularly that of the Chishtis, from 1571, although 'Abd al-Rahman Chishti in his *Mir'at al-Asrar* traced the Chishti influence on Akbar to 1556 when he ascended to power with the spiritual blessings of Khwaja Mu'in ud-din Chishti. The latter, 'Abd al-Rahman observed, was no ordinary saint (*wali*) but a prophet (*nabi*), especially in the absence of a 'proper prophet' in India, who bestowed his blessings not only upon Akbar but also upon his entire progeny to rule the country. The Khwaja, 'Abd al-Rahman reiterated, provided leadership and guidance to such religious or military leaders who contributed to the strengthening and consolidation of Islam in India. Akbar, he recounted, returned his debt through his sincere devotion to the Khwaja, visited his shrine, built a mosque, and organised the town of Ajmer. Expressing his loyalty and regard to the Khwaja, the emperor granted allowances to the Khwaja's descendants and appointed a *mutawali* (functionary) to maintain the shrine and take care of the pilgrims visiting it. Imbibing the Sufi doctrines of *fana* and *wahadat-ul-wujud*,

Akbar acquired an eclectic, questioning temperament and an inquisitive disposition with a Sufi bent of mind.

Commenting on the evolution of Akbar's personality and his commitment to *sulh-i kul*, Jesuit Father Monserrate made a rather complex remark—that Akbar had acquired 'a somewhat morose disposition' and calmed his mind by watching sports like hunting, and witnessing *mast* elephants or elephant fights. In a somewhat similar but modified expression, Abu'l Fazl observed that Akbar had gone through fits and depression before 1578, after which there was no evidence of such emotional upheavals, indicating the development of a new worldview in Akbar. Fazl preferred to call these moments 'spiritual experiences'. Annemarie Schimmel (2005), in agreement, observed that the mystical experiences of Akbar which some may have classified as 'an epileptic seizure' were certainly a *jadhba*, a spiritual 'calling' of a kind not uncommon among mystics.

To fulfil his eclectic, enquiring mind, the emperor, Abu'l Fazl stated, established the *ibadatkhana* at Fatehpur Sikri in 1575 as a pan-Islamic—rather, a pan-Sunni—assembly to which initially only the *'ulama* were invited, and discussions held on the philosophy of different religions in addition to the Prophet's *hadis* and *fiqhs*. Badauni, however, gave different reasons for the initiation of the *ibadatkhana*. He observed that by the early 1570s, Akbar had become increasingly conscious of divine intervention in his personal and kingly life, of being saved and showered with success; and he therefore decided to isolate himself in a cell called the *ibadatkhana* (place of worship) to meditate. Intensely inclined to serve religion, the emperor, Badauni observed, decided to consult the theologians on how he could implement the dictates of God, that is, the *shari'at*, but as the discussion proceeded, the emperor was completely disillusioned by the bitter controversy between the scholars on Islamic theology. What ensued was restrictive and disappointing for the orthodoxy, including Badauni. The in-fighting amongst the *'ulama* on several theological issues compelled Akbar to invite Shi'i scholars to join the assembly, aggravating the discord even further. Disappointed by the disputes and rigid stands of the two sects, Akbar opened the *ibadatkhana* to non-Muslims comprising Hindus, Jains, Jews, Zoroastrians, Jesuits, and Christians, giving the orthodoxy yet another opportunity to accuse the emperor of heresy and surrender to the *kafirs*.

Controversies notwithstanding, what was significant were the discussions that crystallised Akbar's religious ideas. In the *ibadatkhana*, Akbar was exposed to *sukhnan-i hikmat* or philosophical discourses by Shaikh Mubarak and his two sons, Faizi and Abu'l Fazl. He found these discourses *dil-awez* and *dilruba* (enchanting). Deeply impressed by these dialogues, he raised questions, sparing not even Islamic theology and Islamic jurisprudence (*fiqhs*), which alienated the *'ulama* even more. Badauni observed that in the context of these discussions, Shaikh Mubarak sought clarifications on the position of *Imam-i Adl* and *Mujtahid* that led to the proclamation of *mahzarnama* or, as Vincent Smith called it, an 'infallibility decree' in 1579. Badauni, critical of the *mahzarnama*, informed that the entire content was written by Shaikh Mubarak, forgetting perhaps that the *'ulama*, including himself, Abdun Nabi, and Abdullah Sultanpuri, had sanctioned the decree and declared Akbar as *Amir-ul-Mominin* (head of the orthodox Muslims) and *Badshah-i Islam*. Abu'l Fazl was quiet on the issue and showed no concern for the titles. He referred to the order only to suit his theory of sovereignty and to confirm that the emperor was a mere arbitrator between the orthodoxy and other religions in case of dispute.

Analysing the *mahzarnama*, Saiyid Nurul Hasan raised several issues on its nature and content, even as he took exception with Vincent Smith on its definition as an 'infallibility decree'. He refuted Smith's allegation that the document had made the emperor 'infallible' or that Akbar emulated the papacy; instead, Nurul Hasan argued, the *mahzarnama* reinforced legal validity for a variety of reasons. It declared Akbar the *Khalifa* of the time; *Khalifa* was higher than a *mujtahid* and *Khilafat* was essentially an Islamic concept. *mahzarnama*, Nurul Hasan asserted, had accorded Akbar the right of *ijtihad* and empowered him to arbitrate in case of a dispute amongst the *mujtahids*. More importantly, even as a *mujtahid* Akbar could promulgate only such decrees that did not go against *nass* (explicit statements of the Quran and the *hadis*). Reflecting on yet another aspect of *mahzarnama*, Nurul Hasan suggested that through this order, Akbar attempted to challenge the legal supremacy of the Ottoman Sultan, in whose name *Khutba* was read in Mecca and Medina: a fact on the basis of which the Ottoman Sultan had claimed the loyalty of all Muslims throughout the world. Influenced by political competition and economic and political rivalry in sixteenth-century Asian politics, Akbar was unwilling to allow his Muslim subjects to owe allegiance to anyone but himself, and certainly not to a rival Sultan. Through the *mahzarnama*, Nurul Hasan argued, Akbar wanted to project his idea of universal kingship and the liberal spirit that prevailed in sixteenth-century India. While the Uzbeks, the Ottoman Sultan, and the Shah of Persia had upheld the Hanafi law and Shi'ism, respectively, Akbar wanted to convey that in India there was growing unity between Hindus and Muslims, Shi'is and Sunnis, that he was the follower of *Din Panah*, and that the Mughal Empire was not the monopoly of any one sect and/or one school of law or one group of *mullahs*. The *mahzarnama*, Nurul Hasan emphasised, was an enunciation of the religious policy of the Mughal emperors vis-à-vis the rigid theological thinking of the Uzbeks, the Ottoman, and the Safavid Sultans. It released the Mughal Empire from sectarianism, making it attractive to intellectual and liberal individuals throughout the Islamic world. The decree, Nurul Hasan observed, exemplified the Mughal idea of sovereignty and its imperialism. The Mughal Empire had expanded rapidly and incorporated into itself diverse religious views and cultures that had facilitated its emergence as a 'culture' state. In such circumstances, it was imperative for Akbar to achieve cohesion and uniformity and not depend on any one religious law or any one *mujtahid*, especially because all of them had disappointed him by their disputatious behaviour. On each issue, Badauni stated, there arose such bitter controversy that it was impossible to resolve them and Akbar was compelled to devise his own criterion 'of the good of the inhabitants of the world' prior to announcing any judgement. Muhammad Ghausi Shattari, a Sufi critic who wrote in 1613 (*Gulzar-i Abrar*), shared Badauni's views (although perhaps he had no access to his work) about Akbar's disillusionment with Muslim theology caused by the contentious debates and rigid disputes between the *'ulama*, which induced the emperor to take recourse to mysticism and introduce esoteric precepts into the material world—something which no Sufi had earlier considered or countenanced. This may have implied a rejection of Muslim orthodoxy. But Nurul Hasan argued that it was a discreet political strategy adopted by Akbar to construct an empire disguised in Islamic terminology that would be acceptable to most of his subjects, including the nobles.

It was therefore not surprising that Akbar turned to spirituality and mysticism and ideas within Sufi thought that bypassed the *shari'at* and established a direct relationship with God. He rejected *faqihan-i taqlidi* (blind faith in traditions) and adopted a new concept of Islam which would help to fight *nafs-i ammara* or worldly desires and overcome the limits demarcating different religions (*kesh'ha*). Influenced by Shihab-ud-din Maqtul's 'illuminationist' theory that held aloft the position of the 'elect of God', and Ibn al-Arabi's notions of *insan-i kamil* (perfect man) and *wahadat-ul-wujud* (unity of being), Akbar acquired a new worldview, identified with *sulh-i kul*. The higher form of it was *muhabbat-i kul* (absolute love), or when the transcendental unity was completely recognised. But for those who could not reach it, the path of *sulh-i kul* or tolerance of all diversity was prescribed. The notion of *sulh-i kul*, as formulated by Akbar and Abu'l Fazl, was elevated from a mystic notion of *fana* to one that would bring plural harmony, for social conflict in sixteenth-century India, Fazl observed, was due to the prevalence of *taqlidi* and an absence of *sulh-i kul*. Akbar related so closely with *sulh-i kul* from 1581 that he rejected all such religious philosophies—whether Hinduism or Islam—that were ritualistic, formal, and divisive. He emphasised the futility of prayers but stressed on cultivating the self through a preceptor. Being a sovereign, Akbar posed as the preceptor, the *insan-i kamil* of Islamic mysticism, and stressed that *sulh-i kul* implied that worldly realities (including religion) were illusory. Consequently, all differences—as indeed religious differences—were insignificant. Therefore, all faiths ought to be tolerated to obtain mutual harmony, and a 'Perfect' human being was necessary to guide mankind to God. In other words, the attempt was to rationalise Akbar's claim to high spiritual status, insinuating that it is only the 'Just Sovereign' who could be a 'Perfect Man' and 'God's Vicegerent' for people of all faiths.

Even as Akbar's socio-religious outlook based on *sulh-i kul* made the *'ulama* critical of him, 'Abd al-Rahman Chishti in his *Mir'at al-Asrar* lent his support to the Mughal politics of *sulh-i kul*. He argued that the 'divine epiphanies', of which the Sufis were the first receivers, could reach the common man only through the intervention of the king of the time because it is only the rulers who, as leaders of the people (*muqtada-i 'alam*), could transmit the divine bounty (*faiz*) facilitated through their contact with the Sufis. Abu'l Fazl similarly expounded the emperor's ideas and ideology and asserted that Akbar believed in God, although he followed the Sufi way of worship that is different from the prayer ritual of the Muslims and Hindus. He believed that each individual's act of worship was influenced by the limitations of his own *ilm*. God was *be-surat* (formless) and could be grasped only by *chira-dasti-i-khyal* (mind), so all those who used *suri-paristish* (physical action in prayers) to reach the *be-surat* were the 'unawakened ones', because worship of the *be-surat* could only be achieved through the efforts of the mind and heart. In other words, for Akbar, real worship of God could be performed only if one possessed *raushan-dil-i-nur-dasti* (an illuminated heart that loves light).

The importance attached to light—its formless identity similar to that of a *be-surat* God—is illustrated by the two chapters of *Ain-i Akbari* (*Ain-i Rahnamuni* and *Ain-i Iradat Gazinin*) that exalt the sun, the source of light. It was in this context that Abu'l Fazl described sovereignty as *farr-i izadi* or divine light, and talked of the close relationship between the divine sovereign and temporal sovereign, emphasising thus that the real worship of God could be accomplished by the sovereign if he was just and like a 'father for humanity'; for the subjects, on the other hand, unstinted loyalty and obedience to the sovereign was a mark of true worship of the divinity. As a sovereign and as one sanctioned by God, Akbar saw himself in direct relationship with God and independent of any religion. He identified God with the Universe, emphasised his belief in pantheism, considered *din* as illusory as *dunya*, condemned religious rituals as *taqlid* and advocated *aql*, for it was *taqlid* which separated religions and differentiated them on the basis of religious beliefs and ceremonies. In expressing such ideas, he felt restrained by neither Islamic law nor Hinduism. It was within such specifications that Akbar's philosophy of *Tauhid-i-Ilahi* (divine monotheism), wrongly translated by Blochmann as *Din-i-Ilahi* (divine faith), ought to be interpreted. To propagate his philosophy of *sulh-i kul*, Akbar used the terminology of sufi *silsilahs*, referred to his followers as *iradat-i-gazinin* or *murid*, and presented himself as the *murshid* or spiritual guide. Exemplifying Akbar's beliefs, Jahangir narrated in his *Tuzuk-i Jahangiri* that only those who believed in *sulh-i kul* were admitted as his father's *murids*, and that Akbar did not encourage sycophancy nor allowed propagandists to surround him. Commenting on Akbar's espousal of the principle of *sulh-i kul* and religious tolerance, the author of *Dabistan-i Mazahib* (1653) hailed it as an instance of remarkable political foresight—to build a nobility that could accommodate diverse religious communities so that no one group could dominate. Some have also seen it as an attempt to strengthen the number of Rajputs and Iranis (mostly Shi'is) in the nobility, which otherwise was predominantly Sunni.

Akbar promulgated *Din-i-Ilahi* (actual name *Tauhid-i-Ilahi*) in 1582. Some have criticised it for being uncertain and undefined. But, as substantiated by the writings of Abu'l Fazl, Badauni, and the author of *Dabistan-i Mazahib*, the definition was not required because it was not a new religion: it had no book, no priests, no ceremonies, and practically no religious beliefs. Nor was it a mystic order. Of the ten virtues of *Din-i-Ilahi*, nine were derived from the Quran. It was, in fact, a synthesis of different religious philosophies. Badauni, however, made a few controversial statements, moving from alleging that Muslims were not allowed the membership of *Din-i-Ilahi* while all privileges were conferred on the *kafirs*, to saying that several Muslims were converted to *Din-i-Ilahi*. None of these observations appear convincing, particularly in view of the list of eighteen members of *Din-i-Ilahi*, all of whom were Muslims (except one, that is, Birbal). Abu'l Fazl interpreted *Din-i-Ilahi* differently, perhaps in a more mystic sense combined with political pragmatism to justify its promulgation. He argued that all religions had a common source and that man and God were one in the mystic sense according to the notion of pantheism; but people were unaware of the 'truth' and how to worship the 'truth', therefore they looked to the king for advice because of his high position and expected him to be their *murshid*. Fazl reiterated that the king alone could fulfil the expectations of the people and bring harmony: it was in this regard that *Din-i-Ilahi* was inevitable. Conceding to Akbar his vision and yet reinforcing his concept of sovereignty, Fazl observed that *Din-i-Ilahi* was inspired by the emperor's eclectic and enquiring mind, and to investigate the philosophy of different religions. The two issues were intertwined and could not be separated because the emperor could never hope to bring harmony in his plural empire without bridging the religious differences.

The *'ulama*, nevertheless, was convinced that Akbar's social ethics, his decrees, and institutions had a blasphemous impact on society. They thus denounced them as *bida'* (innovations) and accused the emperor of apostasy and heresy and persecution of Muslim theologians, whom they presented as *shahid*—an accusation hardly supported by the list of *shahid*s, for it did not establish whether the issue was religious. The orthodoxy also objected to Akbar's use of the term *Ahmadi Kesh* for Islam, which literally meant Muhammadan doctrine in its English translation. Whatever his terminology or beliefs, on doctrinal grounds Akbar could not be opposed. Most of Akbar's *Ain* had an Islamic background; some had precedents in the acts of the *Khalifa*s and the Sultans who preceded him, others were allowed by the *Shari'at* for reasons of State, while many were entailed by the social and economic conditions of the empire. Such changes, significantly, were permissible if the large number of the ruled were non-Muslims. So the reasons that may have upset the orthodoxy are a matter of conjecture.

S. A. A. Rizvi's observation that Akbar was hostile only to the Sunni orthodoxy had little basis. Akbar was firm in disallowing the monopoly of the State to either the Sunnis or the Shi'is. But this did not mean that Islam was endangered during Akbar's period; it was *taqlid* that was at a risk. Finding it difficult to agree with Badauni and his ilk, Iqtidar Alam Khan suggested that the *'ulama* was perhaps perturbed not by the emperor's tolerance of the Hindus, but his attempt to rid them of the status of *dhimmi*s or *zimmi*s by making them equal partners or sharers of power in the administration. Athar Ali argued that for Badauni, any decline in the power of the *'ulama* appeared to be the decline of Islam. Badauni was apparently disillusioned by the restrictive policy and curtailment of *suyurghal* grants or financial patronage to the *'ulama*, mosques, and the *madrasa*s. His criticism of Akbar may have been stimulated by his personal bias, even as the orthodoxy felt alienated by the emperor's eclecticism and liberal tendencies. Similarly, Shaikh Ahmad Sirhindi portrayed Akbar as a heretic and a serious threat to Islam. The millenarianism (*tajdid-i alf-i sani*) in the writings of Sirhindi and his disciples probably revolved around Akbar's hopes of being a millenarian leader and his 'anti-Islamic politics'. Contrary to Sirhindi's characterisation of Akbar as a 'defiler of Islam', 'Abd al-Rahman Chishti used the epithet *rahima-hu-Allah*, routinely used for a saint and meaning 'May God bless him'.

Iqtidar Alam Khan further observed that the *'ulama* was perhaps particularly upset during the decade 1591–1601 when Akbar ordered the closure of all mosques, prohibited *namaz*, and abolished the maintenance of *khatib*s, *muezzin*s, and *imam*s. Yet again Khan quoted a *farman* which declared that Akbar did so because whenever he found a person performing *namaz*, he considered it pertinent to give him *nasihat* (admonition) and guide him towards *rah-i aql* (path of reason). Nevertheless, the emperor refrained from exercising any compulsion; nor did he forcibly forbid the practice of rituals, apprehending that it would go against the spirit of *sulh-i kul*. Akbar's attitude, Khan remarked, underwent a change from 1601. He did not discourage *namaz* in congregation; more importantly, he himself practised 'external as well as spiritual austerities in the worship of God' to silence the *rasmiyan-i rozgar* (ritualists of the age). So when he died in 1605, there was no discontentment amongst the Muslims in general and the *'ulama* in particular, who felt that despite his *bida'*, Akbar had, after all, remained a Muslim king.

RELIGIOUS TOLERANCE AND PLURALITY REINFORCED IN THE SEVENTEENTH CENTURY

The social and religious tolerance of the Mughals did not end in 1605 as some may have us believe, but continued to be remarkably influential even in the global context. That this phenomenal Mughal spirit made a striking impression on persons like Thomas Roe, who had mixed feelings for India—more critical than favourable—was evident when he narrated his experiences and the moments spent at Jahangir's court in his speech in the British Parliament in 1641, almost two decades after his return from India. He commended the economic pluralism of the Mughals and proposed its emulation in England so that it could improve its global commercial competitiveness. Almost four decades later, Giles Shute, a Catholic pamphleteer, made a similar observation on Mughal pluralism, stating that the religious and cultural tolerance of the Mughals was not just a moral virtue, but augured well for business, too. Making a plea for greater religious tolerance and a liberal political philosophy in England through his pamphlet 'A New Test in Lieu of the Old One' (1688), Shute made this proposal, noteworthy for its timing, when Aurangzeb was in power—an emperor singly slandered rather unfairly as an intolerant, orthodox Muslim ruler of the subcontinent. This of course did not mean that there were no religious tensions in seventeenth-century India. But it certainly implied that Akbar's views on *sulh-i kul* and his approach to handling India's diversity had not ceased to exist following his death. It continued to be invoked by his successors, albeit with some departures, couched in political pragmatism rather than bigotry, including during the reign of Aurangzeb. Moreover, the Mughals imbibed the traditions of *adab* and *akhlaq* (political and ethical theory) that urged the rulers to concentrate on *'adl* (justice) rather than impose their religion on the people—a disposition sanctioned by the Quran that stood against any compulsions in religion.

Epithets such as 'fanatic', 'bigot' or 'communalist', used by some imperialist historians, are not only controversial, but also questionable for Jahangir. Though a faithful Muslim who expressed his belief in the effectiveness of *du'a* (prayers), Jahangir refrained from making the precepts of Islam the basis of his State policy or invoking Islamicate principles to appease the *'ulama*. Writing in praise of Akbar's liberal and tolerant policies in his *Tuzuk-i Jahangiri*, Jahangir continued his father's policy of harmony and peace. Critical of the sectarian and rigid attitude of contemporary States like those of the Safavids, Ottomans, and the Uzbeks, he observed that all religions could coexist in his father's domain without any strife or altercation, and that while the Sunnis and Shi'is could worship in the same mosque without any conflict, so could the Franks and the Jews in the same church. Jahangir's assessment may appear a bit exaggerated and idealistic, but it does capture the spirit of the Mughal court. Jahangir continued to use Akbar's imagery of sun and light when he adopted the title *Nur al-Din*, 'Light of the Faith'. He gave two reasons, explicitly mentioned in the *Tuzuk-i Jahangiri*, for assuming this title. Neither was influenced by Islam; the first emphasised his regard for the sun—a significant aspect of Akbar's religious ideas—and the second was apparently inspired by his desire for a title similar in meaning to that of his father's, namely *Nur* (light, illumination), to follow *Jalal* (splendour, glory). Imitating Akbar, he perpetuated the practice of encouraging 'spiritual disciples', a relationship, Barbara Metcalf (2009) observed, symbolised by their 'shared practice of ear piercing and wearing pearl earrings'. In his devotion to Khwaja Mu'in ud-din Chishti, Jahangir exceeded Akbar by not only perpetuating the grants in an increased form to the shrine, but also visiting it regularly. The multicultural, multireligious atmosphere of Jahangir's court was further illustrated, in addition to his memoirs, by the text *Majalis-i Jahangiri*, which described the night sessions initiated by the emperor at his court between 1608–11 to discuss religious, historical, and scientific subjects in the presence of connoisseurs of religion, including Brahmins, *'ulama*, Jews, and Jesuits, apart from his imperial elite, to fulfil his multifaceted curiosity for knowledge.

Jahangir's frequent encounters and dialogues with a *sanyasi* yogi, Gosa'in Jadrup, deserve recognition for his liberal, non-communal policy. Impressed, as he wrote in the *Tuzuk-i Jahangiri*, by Jadrup's 'unusual grace, lofty understanding, exalted nature and a heart free from the attainments of world', Jahangir expressed his great veneration for the yogi's Vedic learning and spiritual knowledge. Although Jadrup was known in Akbar's court, too, it was Jahangir who visited him several times and held conversations related to not only religious and metaphysical matters, but significantly also on State affairs. It is alleged that Jahangir sought the yogi's advice on a relatively important financial subject, that is, the change in the official weight measure or *ser*. A *ser* during Akbar's reign was equal to 30 *dams*, which Jahangir wanted raised to 36 *dams*. Allegedly, Jadrup guided the emperor on the matter, quoting the Vedas as the authority that prescribed 36 *dams* per *ser*. Jahangir was not the only Muslim of his reign to establish contact with Jadrup; the yogi attracted the allegiance of a large section of the nobility and intellectuals. Mu'tamad Khan, a courtier during the reigns of Jahangir and Shahjahan, wrote in appreciation of Jadrup's Sufi-Vedantic learning in his chronicle, *Iqbalnama-i Jahangiri*. Other examples of Jahangir's cosmopolitanism included his long contact with Siddhichandra, a Jain monk and literati in Akbar's court, known for his discourse with Jahangir and Nurjahan on the Jain sadhu's vow of celibacy. In deference to the Jain community of Agra, who observed sacred fasts, Jahangir in 1610 banned the slaughter of all animals throughout the Mughal Empire for twelve days. This proclamation of the emperor was memorialised by Ustad Salivahana in two of his paintings. The serenity of Jahangir's reign was ironically broken by his order of execution of Guru Arjun Dev. Allegedly, the execution of the Guru was prompted not by any religious but political considerations; the Guru's meeting with Prince Khurram at the time of the latter's revolt apparently aroused suspicion of his involvement in the rebellion against the emperor. There was, however, no evidence of harassment or persecution of the Guru's followers by the emperor.

Shahjahan was described by a few scholars as an orthodox Muslim ruler who revoked the policies of Akbar and Jahangir and revived Islamic political culture; however, to the contrary, there are literary works such as *Kavindrakalpalata* that praised the emperor for his liberal outlook, spiritual ecumenicalism, and the *dharmic* justness of his rule. The narrative of this *Braj* literature was further compounded by the political and cultural developments of the period. The steady rise in the number of Rajput *mansabdars*, Shahjahan's participation in Hindu festivals like Holi, and the renewal of several grants to temples can be read as his continued commitment to *sulh-i kul*. The Vrindavan documents of the period suggested that Shahjahan renewed the grants of the Madan Mohan temple and its affiliate temples. It was asserted that when a local official objected to the ringing of the bell in the temple, Shahjahan issued a *farman* condemning the stringency of the official and described the worship of the deity as *'ibadat-i ilahi* (divine worship), a term unusual for a Muslim ruler. The grants for the temple of Vrindavan and the Govind Dev temple were also confirmed, and management of the temple was transferred to the rulers of Amber. Significantly, it was during Shahjahan's period that Hindu Vedantic philosophy made inroads into the empire through his son, Dara Shukoh. Moreover, the emperor, as a keen student of Hindustani music, patronised several *dhrupad* composers like Lal Khan (a relative of Tansen) and his sons Khushhal and Vishram, and rewarded Darang Khan in 1636 with silver equal to his weight.

Trained by a Sufi, Shahjahan was a follower of *ahl-i sunna wa jama'a* and reached a high level of *tasawwuf* in his own right. While in Agra, he visited Shaikh Sufi (a disciple of Shaikh Nizam-ud-din of Amethi, an eminent Chishti saint of Awadh in the sixteenth century) to learn about Sufi texts and expositions of the *Quran* and the *hadis*. As with Akbar and Jahangir, 'Abd al-Rahman Chishti used the epithet *Rahima-hu-Allah* for Shahjahan and described his relations with the Shi'is and non-Muslims as a reflection of the emperor's unbiased approach towards any faith or sect. In fact, he represented Shahjahan as a follower of *mashrab* of *sulh-i kul*, the path of peace with all who did not leave the path of balance (*i'tidal*) and thus avoided divine wrath. As 'Abd al-Rahman Chishti analysed Shahjahan's personality, he was convinced that the emperor would spend the last years of his life as an ascetic (*tarikin*), equivalent to a spiritual opportunity given to him by God to achieve supreme goodness, spend his days worshipping *Allah*, recite the *Quran*, and study the exegesis of the *Quran* and the *hadis*.

In his adherence to the 'orthodox' versus 'liberal' binary, Aurangzeb stands alone, discredited for his beliefs. There is no denying that of all the Mughal emperors, he was the most theologically inclined. His interest in the *Shari'a* inspired him to compile, under the auspices of the State, an exhaustive collection in Arabic, *Fatawa'-i 'Alamgiri*, to explain the four Sunni legal schools on every aspect of civil and personal law. For Aurangzeb, piety was his avocation. Every year he completed a *chilla* (a long meditation retreat) and spent time copying the Quran and sewing caps—tasks that he considered holy and humbling. His commitment to improving Muslim education and culture was evidently demonstrated in the latter part of his reign in 1691 when he provided patronage to an important *'ulama* family of Lucknow, known by the name of the place they resided in, that is, *Firingi Mahal*, which subsequently grew as a centre for Muslim education. The *'ulama*, impressed by Aurangzeb's knowledge of Islamic jurisprudence and his compliance to the tenets of Islam, appropriated him as the 'defender of the faith' at the time of his accession. Reading this event narrowly, many historians have presented Aurangzeb as an orthodox Sunni Muslim, committed to the purification and promotion of Islam at the cost of political expediencies. In this regard, it is germane to reiterate that his orthodoxy and firm convictions were a matter of personal faith that did not interfere with the political or religious contours of the empire. Muhammad Bakhtawar Khan's *Mir'at-i 'Alam* may be seen as a testimony to this.

While it stressed the personal piety and religiosity of Aurangzeb, it exuded a spirit of optimism as it captured the ethos of the reign, portraying the emperor as the strongest of all rulers who was not particularly close to the *'ulama*, nor were the latter unduly powerful in influencing the emperor's policy decisions.

Yet histories have excoriated Aurangzeb for his bigotry and intolerance. This needs to be questioned. It is necessary to separate rhetoric from reality and reconstruct the reign dispassionately. Contrary to the interpretations of Jadunath Sarkar and Shri Ram Sharma who had argued that Aurangzeb's orthodox Islamic politico-religious ideology was responsible for the restraint of many cultural manifestations, including music, Katherine Brown (2007) found it 'mythical' and problematic to agree with the notion of the 'burial of music' or the banning of it by Aurangzeb from 1668–69 until his death in 1707. The bias of the historians, Brown argued, was perhaps influenced by their uncritical reading of Manucci and Khafi Khan who, through their writings, had transformed music into 'an elegy for freedom and tolerance crushed in the relentless grip of a bigoted despot'. Historians seemed to have overlooked Aurangzeb's acceptance of and inclination towards music in the earlier part of his reign, beginning 1658. There are evidences of male and female musicians and dancers who performed at the anniversary celebrations of Aurangzeb's coronation. Like his father, the emperor patronised *dhrupad* and is known to have rewarded his foremost *kalawant* (musician), Khushhal Khan, by bestowing upon him a sum of Rs 7,000. Manucci described a feast in Aurangzeb's war camp in 1658 where music was played the whole night following the 'common practice in Hindustan', and provided details of the dance and music sessions in Aurangzeb's harem (which of course he preferred to interpret as the 'hypocrisy' of the emperor), while Tavernier, writing in 1665, talked of the mesmerising effect of the music performed in Aurangzeb's presence at his daily *darbar*. Bernier noted that the emperor allowed Shahjahan to maintain his female musicians and dancers till the latter's death in 1666. In addition, both Naqshbandi and the Chishti Sufis in Delhi continued to practice *sama* throughout Aurangzeb's reign. Both Bakhtawar Khan and Faqirullah mentioned Aurangzeb as not only an exponent of music, but also as one who widely appreciated and enjoyed music. Faqirullah further added to the information by reciting the names of Aurangzeb's favourite singers and instrumentalists in his musical treatise, *Rag Darpan*, written in 1666. More importantly, Aurangzeb's sister Jahanara, daughter Zebunnissa, and his third son, Muhammad A'zam, were renowned patrons of music of the period. So if Aurangzeb decided to abstain from music in the latter part of his reign, it was a private matter, observed Brown, to fulfil his religious conscience and personal piety, but which had no adverse impact on music outside the imperial court, nor was it translated into public policy.

Significantly, Ras Baras Khan's (the son of Khushhal Khan) *Shams al-Aswat* provided testimony that notwithstanding Aurangzeb's personal commitments, music was perpetuated in his reign in some form or the other. Some *kalawant*s like Ras Baras Khan himself continued to be patronised and were not restricted from performing; moreover, Aurangzeb continued to encourage theoretical discourse on music even as late as 1698. Music continued to be patronised in Delhi, in the war camps of Aurangzeb in Deccan, and the regional courts, which interestingly challenge the notion of the Mughal State as centralised and confirm that the cultural life of India was hardly influenced by the choices of the emperor. If such was the ambience of Aurangzeb's reign, should one not hazard a conjecture that perhaps, like his predecessors, he too was committed to the ideology of *sulh-i kul*, irrespective of his personal religious views?

That Aurangzeb's orthodoxy and his dedication to his beliefs was personal rather than a matter for political interference is evident in his reactions and responses during the war of succession of 1658, a quadrangular conflict between Dara, Shuja, Aurangzeb, and Murad. Throughout the struggle, Aurangzeb was concerned about Dara's political manoeuvres (Image 6.1). Their individual feelings and religious outlook—which stood in sharp contrast—remained confined to the personal level. Aurangzeb referred to Dara as *mushrik* (heretic) while Dara called Aurangzeb *kotah pyjama* (narrow pants), a symbolic attribute of orthodoxy. Both attempted to rally public opinion, but never on religious grounds. In fact, the support that largely came for Aurangzeb was from the Rajputs, notably Rana Raj Singh of Mewar, Raja Jai Singh Kachwaha of Amber, and later, Maharaja Jaswant Singh of Marwar. In this context may be related an interesting *nishan* that Aurangzeb sent to Rana Raj Singh of Mewar, condemning such kings who practised intolerance that could become the cause of dispute, conflict, and harm to the people, and could 'devastate the prosperous creations of God and destroy the foundations of the God-created fabric'. Such attitudes of kings, Aurangzeb ordained, deserve 'to be rejected and cast off'. This document from the Udaipur records is a clear revelation of what Aurangzeb intended as his public policy. It further confirmed that Aurangzeb, in the struggle for succession, did not raise the cry of *jihad* or Islam in danger, nor did he promulgate a new religious policy contrary to that of his predecessors; neither did Dara claim to be the champion of liberal forces. The issue was not religious or ideological, or whether orthodoxy would triumph or liberalism. It was a question of personal vested interest, political in nature but free from religious connotations, that is: Who would be the emperor of India, Dara or Aurangzeb? It is in such a context that Aurangzeb deserves to be assessed.

Image 6.1: The Battle of Samugarh, *c.* 1658

Source: https://commons.wikimedia.org/wiki/File:The_Battle_of_Samugarh.jpg.

Debating Aurangzeb's leanings—religious orthodoxy or political pragmatism—one needs to ask: Did Aurangzeb really intend, as Jadunath Sarkar suggested, the establishment of *dar-ul-Islam* or a truly Islamic State in India, the conversion of the entire population to Islam, and the annihilation of dissenters? Or, as Ishtiyaq

Husain Qureshi argued, was it rigid adherence to the *shari'a* and undoing the damage caused by Akbar; or the triumph of Muslim theology, as Shri Ram Sharma asserted? If this was really the case, then the emperor's personal valour, military skills, and single-minded commitment to achieving territorial expansion and consolidation would stand negated. The biased ideological portrayal of the emperor, regardless of historical accuracy, makes it difficult to explain the increase in the number of Rajput *mansabdar*s in Aurangzeb's administration as compared to Akbar's period, and their rise from 24 per cent under Shahjahan to 33 per cent in 1689. Nor can Raghunath Ray Kayastha's dominance as *diwan-i kul* be understood rationally. Raghunath Ray not only supported Aurangzeb but also participated in several expeditions of the period. Aurangzeb honoured him with the title of *Raja* and when Raghunath Ray died in 1664, the emperor, in his obituary written in *Ruqa'at-i Alamgiri*, remembered him as the greatest administrator he had ever known.

Athar Ali set aside several doubts when he focused on the politics of the circumstances—the illegal imprisonment of his father and the execution of his brothers—in which Aurangzeb ascended to power. It was not a question of religious beliefs but the political situation which compelled him to pose as the defender of Islam to seek the support of the *'ulama* and emphasise his image as *Shah-i Islam*. However, whatever the promulgations at his accession, Aurangzeb made no radical departures in governance as practised by his predecessors. Neither did he woo the *'ulama*. He dismissed the chief *Qazi* who opposed his accession on ethical and legal grounds, that is, the *khutba* could not be read in the name of the son if the father was alive, and appointed another one, *Qazi* Abdul Wahab, who diluted the objection by elucidating that the frail health of Shahjahan had rendered him too feeble to govern. He thus rescinded all legal obstacles to the *khutba* being read in Aurangzeb's name. This would not have been the emperor's response had he been looking for the support of the *'ulama*. To the contrary, it was the *'ulama* that depended on the emperor for political favours. The decision of *Qazi* Abdul Wahab was juridically significant for it established that the law during the period was interpreted as per the interests of the emperor. Legitimacy, in other words, rested not so much on the correctness of the legal decision as on the capability of the man who wielded power, in this case Aurangzeb.

All of Aurangzeb's actions and responses suggest not his religious tyranny but his political acumen, which led him to often acknowledge and commend the valour and loyalty of his non-Muslim nobles. Yet certain aspects of his reign concerning temples, the re-imposition of *jizya*, and his relations with the Rajputs and Marathas in the latter part of his reign have remained shrouded in controversy. With regard to temples, Jadunath Sarkar and Shri Ram Sharma argued that the destruction of the sacred places of non-Muslims was fundamental to Islam and it was but natural that Aurangzeb, being an orthodox Muslim, ordered the general destruction of temples. S. R. Sharma went a step further and complicated the issue by observing that the temples that were expected to collapse within a decade still stood strong, and so were attacked in 1679. This alleged statement, however, failed to provide a reasonable explanation as to how a large number of temples built prior to 1669 still existed in different parts of the empire. Ironically, as opposed to the opinions expressed by the two historians, no copy of any such order has been found and nor has any contemporary chronicler referred to it—except Saqi Musta'id

Khan, who wrote at least six years subsequent to Aurangzeb's death. So, before embarking on any impression regarding the temple policy of the emperor, it would be apposite to ponder on Abul Hasan's *farman* decreed in 1659 and sent to the *subadar*s with the intention of allaying the fears of the Hindus at Banaras, who were being persecuted for practising their religious customs. The *farman* strictly prohibited any disturbance or interference in the performance of religious rites and rituals by Hindus or the temple *pujari*s. It further reiterated that according to the *shari'at*, while no ancient temples could be destroyed, no new ones could be built without the prior permission of the State.

This order nowhere reflected Aurangzeb's iconoclastic intent. To the contrary, there are well-documented evidences of Aurangzeb's patronage of various Hindu religious institutions, namely temples, *math*s, grants to Brahmins and *pujaris*:

- Land grants were renewed to the temples at Mathura, Banaras, Gaya, Gauhati, and others, while the emperor is known to have donated *ghee* for the *navadeep* in a few temples, including the Mahabateshwar temple at Agra;
- Gifts were offered to the Sikh *gurudwara* at Dehradun;
- *Madad-i ma'ash* grants, as listed in the Rajasthan documents, were continued to a *math* of Nathpanthi yogis in *pargana* Didwana, *sarkar* Nagor;
- Grants were also made to Ganesh Bharti *faqir* and his successors in *pargana* Siwana with the instructions that the *faqir* should not be disturbed so he could 'pray for this *sultanat*'.
- The Vrindavan document of 1704 referred to a *parwana* which sanctioned the rights of Chaitanya *gosain*s who had founded Vrindavan and established pilgrimages in Braj *Bhumi*, and recognised the right of Brajanand Gosain to receive a fee from the followers of the sect on account of *kharj sadir o warid*, that is, expenses on guests and travellers from each village. In effect, it was a government levy for the benefit of Brajanand Gosain and his Vaishnavite followers.

From the above description, Aurangzeb's patronage to temples appears without doubt. And yet some temples were attacked, while others were spared. This aberration in the emperor's attitude can be explained by only one rationale: it was not iconoclasm, but reprisal for rebellion or political misconduct or disloyalty to the emperor. This exposition can be applied to understand the attack on the Vishwanath temple at Kashi, the Keshav Dev temple at Mathura, and several prominent temples in Rajasthan. In 1669, during a zamindar revolt in Banaras, it was suspected that some of them had assisted Shivaji in his escape from imperial detention. It was also believed that Shivaji's escape was initially facilitated by Jai Singh, the great-grandson of Raja Man Singh, who had built the Vishwanath temple. It was against this background that Aurangzeb ordered the destruction of that temple in September 1669. Around the same time, in a Jat rebellion that had erupted in the neighbouring regions of Mathura, a patron of the local congregational mosque was killed, leading to Aurangzeb's order in 1670 to attack the Keshav Dev temple at Mathura. Temples in Marwar and Mewar were also attacked following the death of Maharaja

Jaswant Singh to reprimand and crush the Rathor rebellion and the development of a Sisodia–Rathor alliance. These included temples in Khandela patronised by rebel chieftains; temples in Jodhpur maintained by a former supporter of Dara Shukoh; and the royal temples in Udaipur and Chittor patronised by Rana Raj Singh after the Rana entered into an alliance with the Rathors that signalled the withdrawal of loyalty to the Mughal State. It may be observed that the Rathor rebellion was not a reaction or a protest against the re-imposition of *jizya*. Instead, this re-imposition, as Abu'l Fazl Ma'muri observed in the context of the suppression of the Satnami revolt and prior to the emperor's expedition to Ajmer, was meant for 'the affliction of the rebellious unbelievers'.

Politics seemed to have assumed a different format after 1687 when Aurangzeb occupied the Maratha territory and the southern region up to Jinji; the temples of the area, with a few exceptions, were left undisturbed. The selective attacks with no uniform pattern were clearly an attempt to enforce paramountcy and a pragmatic ideology to secure the empire—a strategy that displayed an interplay of religion and politics, a practice not unusual in medieval times, but certainly not an act that can be emulated in modern times.

Another controversial issue of Aurangzeb's reign was the re-imposition of *jizya* in 1679, ostensibly because it was considered *wajib* (compulsory) by the *shari'at*. If this was so, why did Aurangzeb wait for twenty-two years after his accession to reinforce his orthodoxy? The reason lay in political exigency, a decision meant to counter and curb the Rathor rebellion rather than his desire to follow the injunctions of the *shari'at* or implement religious orthodoxy. Nevertheless, many contemporary chroniclers have portrayed the act as one motivated by religious considerations. Musta'id Khan wrote that the aim of the 'religious emperor' was to spread the law of Islam and overthrow the practices of the *zimmis*. In agreement with Musta'id Khan, Isardas (Ishwardas) and Ali Muhammad Khan emphasised the role of the *'ulama*, who urged the levy of *jizya* as necessary and compulsory according to the *shari'at*. Whatever be the case, these scholars still do not explain why Aurangzeb, an expert in Islamic jurisprudence, should have taken more than two decades to implement orthodoxy. Manucci, a foreign traveller, and the English Factory Records, particularly those emanating from the office of the Deputy Governor at Bombay, ascribed economic reasons, that is, the growing gap between *jama* and *hasil* and expenditure on military expeditions from 1676, to explain the introduction of *jizya*. It could be true that expenses had exceeded the income by the thirteenth year of Aurangzeb's reign, but it is difficult to say whether *jizya* had economic viability, especially in view of the evidence of *Nigar Nama-i Munshi*, which stated that the rate and amount of *jizya* usually fluctuated and was generally never more than 4 per cent of the *jama*. Satish Chandra conceded that any economic importance that *jizya* could have had was for *khairat* or charity. The amount collected as *jizya* was put in a separate treasury called *khazana-i jizya*, from which payments were made to the *yaumiyadar*s or cash stipend-holders, thereby relieving the pressure on the main treasury. But to say that by imposing *jizya* Aurangzeb sought the conversion of non-Muslims to Islam or distinguished *dar-ul Islam* (land of Islam, or where *shari'at* prevailed) from *dar-ul harb* (land of the infidels), as Abu'l Fazl Ma'muri and Khafi Khan argued, is hardly tenable on the basis of historical facts. It neither altered the character of the Mughal State or mobilised popular Muslim opinion on wars against the Deccan states, nor did it mean the abandonment of alliance with the Rajputs or other indigenous ruling classes, or the beginning of an anti-Hindu policy as some would have us believe. That the reason behind the re-institution of *jizya* was political was further reinforced when it was remitted in Deccan in 1704 to handle war and famine in the region; or it could be that Aurangzeb, the strategist, considered the suspension of *jizya* necessary so as to negotiate with the Marathas by agreeing to Shivaji's concept of *swarajya* and the grant of *sardesmukhi* (not *chauth*, perhaps) in Deccan.

To understand exactly how Aurangzeb's religious policy evolved in the post-*jizya* phase, that is, 1680–1707, Satish Chandra suggested that the period be studied in two parts: up to the conquest of Bijapur and Golconda in 1687, and from 1687 till Aurangzeb's death in 1707. In the first phase, Aurangzeb had hoped to appeal to the religious sentiments of the Sultans of Deccan to create a wedge between them and the Marathas, but by the second phase he had realised the futility of such an attempt. The second phase illustrated the political dimensions of the re-imposition of *jizya*, its withdrawal in 1704, the policy towards temples and, more significantly, the emperor's transformed attitude towards the Marathas. He may have treated Shivaji as 'a petty *bhumia*' when the latter visited Agra in 1666, but by the second phase he had improved upon his policy towards the Marathas. Many from the families of Shivaji and other Maratha zamindars were inducted as *mansabdars* in the imperial service, leading to the Marathas making up half the Hindu office-holders and a sixth of the total *mansabdars*. Along with the Rajputs, the Marathas held high *mansabs* of 7,000 *zat*/7,000 *sawar*. Contrary to Jadunath Sarkar's proposal, the emperor made no attempt to effect conversions. *Jizya*, as cited above, was suspended in 1704 for the duration of the Mughal–Maratha war, but with no possibility of the war ending, *jizya* was virtually abandoned. The reversal of the deed of 1679 that began in the latter part of Aurangzeb's reign was subsequently consolidated by his successors—Bahadur Shah, Jahandar Shah, Farrukh Siyar—who not only abolished *jizya* but, allegedly from 1712 with the accession of Jahandar Shah, the celebration of the Hindu festivals of Dussehra, Diwali, Holi, and Basant Panchami also became a part of court celebrations.

Interestingly, the latter part of Aurangzeb's reign was also a valuable reflection of his views on state, statecraft, and sovereignty, which came through in his letters to Shahjahan written after the latter's imprisonment. In his advice to his sons and grandsons, collected in the *Kalmat-i-Taiyyabat*, Aurangzeb appeared to echo Abu'l Fazl when he emphasised the concept of justice as the highest ideal, the duties of the sovereign, and other worldly tasks, upholding them as 'truly religious', rather than stressing on defending the faith or punishing the irreligious or persecuting the infidels. While speaking of the concept of sovereignty, Aurangzeb often referred approvingly to the reigns of Akbar and Shahjahan, portraying his own policies as being in consonance with theirs, probably with the intent of seeking legitimisation for his actions. Several examples from Aurangzeb's reign convey that he could be fairly liberal and all-inclusive if it suited his purpose. For this reason, perhaps, some of the contemporary saints were not at all happy with Aurangzeb being called *zinda pir*, while others like the Chishti saint Shaikh Kalimullah accused Aurangzeb of hypocrisy and presumptuousness in trying to combine *sultanat* or worldly rule with *faqiri*.

MILLENARIANISM, ORTHODOXY, SYNCRETISM

Millenarian movements with wide cultural, social, and political consequences were a phenomena of the early modern period (roughly from the fifteenth to the seventeenth centuries) that united the world and interlinked global processes. These movements have often been characterised as rebellion, resistance, and a desperate attempt by threatened groups to rejuvenate themselves and produce their own prophets. It may be pertinent to consider two random examples of millenarianism from non-Indian societies to broaden our understanding of millenarianism. Writing about Europe, Norman Cohn (1961, xii) had argued that 'between the close of the eleventh century to the first half of the sixteenth it repeatedly happened in Europe that the desire of the poor to improve the material conditions of their lives became transfused with phantasies of a new Paradise on earth'. Jonathan Spence (1996, xx), on the other hand, defined millenarianism in the context of the nineteenth-century Taiping kingdom in China as 'a pattern of belief that promised the possibility of a final world in which there would be "cosmos without chaos", a world of "making wonderful" without imperfections, an eternal peace beyond history, a changeless realm ruled by an unchallenged god'. Spence further added that teachers and prophets anticipated that prior to the attainment of this new world, there would be a final doom-laden battle between the two forces, which would bring misery and agony, but subsequently good would triumph and evil would be driven from the earth.

It is in this context that the concept of 'connected histories' (Subrahmanyam 1997, 2010) can be invoked to understand millenarianism in the Indian subcontinent. Subrahmanyam talked of interlinked millenarian political movements that accompanied the process of European expansion, at times providing them with crucial ideological inputs. He characterised political millenarianism—a less explored global and early modern phenomenon—as a dominating ideology, 'as a building-block of empire and fuel for imperial ambition'. Commenting on a millenarian connection that existed over a large part of the Old World in the sixteenth century, and which formed the background for discussions between Albuquerque and Galvao or Akbar and Monserrate, Subrahmanyam observed that the sixteenth century witnessed the emergence of a new set of material conditions within which millenarianism could grow and spread as a current that embraced a large geographical space. As a phenomenon, it had specific, unique local manifestations.

In India, a notable millenarian movement—that of the *Mahdavi* sect—can be traced to the end of the fifteenth century to Sayyid Muhammad Jaunpuri (1443–1505), born in the Sharqi Sultanate of Jaunpur. After the capture of Jaunpur by the Lodi Sultans, Sayyid Muhammad left the city, believing the event to be an indicator of a troubled, problem-laden future. He set out for *hajj* in 1495–96 and declared himself *Imam Mahdi* (the 'guided one' or the 'directed one' or the one who is fit to guide or direct others) upon his return to India. *Mahdavi* sources described a number of miracles and incidents that accompanied the birth of Sayyid Muhammad, which was reminiscent of the birth of Prophet Muhammad, and attributed divine revelations to him, anointing him as *Imam Mahdi*. The genesis of the *Mahdavi* movement lay in a popular tradition that predicted the appearance of a *Mahdi*, presumably a man from the family of the Prophet, hence a member of the Quraysh or Quraish clan—a notion generally accepted by the Muslims and related by a fourteenth-century historian and philosopher, Ibn-i Khaldun, in his *Muqaddimah* and a canonical Persian text, *Rauzat al-A'imma*. The idea of a *Mahdi* gained great popularity and nurtured mystical hopes as the Islamic millennium drew closer. *Alims* of Mecca and Medina wrote *fatwa*s in support of the prophecy and observed that the Prophet would not remain in his grave for more than 1,000 years. In India, a few before Sayyid Muhammad had claimed to be the *Mahdi* during the reign of Sultan Firuz Shah Tughluq. One such pretender was a man called Rukn who claimed to be endowed with spiritual knowledge and called himself *Mahdi i-Akhir uz-Zaman* (*Mahdi* of the last days). An unconvinced Firuz Shah Tughluq had ordered his execution, along with that of his disciples and followers.

Sayyid Muhammad of Jaunpur, as the *Mahdi i-Akhir uz-Zaman*,

- preached strict adherence to asceticism and the purity of Islam;
- fostered a brotherhood of *Mahdavi*s who would depend entirely upon God for their sustenance; and
- sought to remove the distinctions that existed between the four *mazahib* (schools of jurisprudence), that is, they would not confine themselves to any single code of jurisprudence but devote themselves to the principles preached and practised by Prophet Muhammad.

To propagate his austere faith, Sayyid Muhammad established *da'ira*s or centres, distinct from the sufi *khanqah*s, and motivated his supporters to follow an egalitarian style of living based on *futuh* or gifts from the laity. Even as he instructed the strict following of the prescribed mode of life and worship, he was critical of the *'ulama*, whom he condemned as *'ulama-i-su* or worldly minded *'ulama*. His puritanism garnered considerable respect for *Mahdavi*s in western India, particularly in the Sultanate of Gujarat and the Deccan kingdoms. In fact, the hagiographers of Sayyid Muhammad suggested that he had almost converted Sultan Mahmud Begarha of Gujarat to *Mahdism*. Such trends, however, could not mollify the *'ulama*, who were agitated by the claims of the *Mahdavi*s. Sayyid Muhammad died in Farah in Baluchistan, where his tomb became a pilgrim centre. The movement continued for a few more decades before vanishing, except for an Afghan following in northern India.

The next landmark in the millenarian calendar coincided with the year 1552–53, which revolved around Shaikh 'Abdullah Niyazi, an Afghan, who was once a Chishti but later became a devotee of Sayyid Muhammad Jaunpuri and his disciple Shaikh 'Ala'i ibn Hasan Bayanwi (or Bangali), who, as Badauni reported, was originally faithful to the orthodox Hanafi school. Posing as *Mahdi*, Shaikh 'Ala'i advocated asceticism in Bayana near Agra, where he had settled on his return from *hajj*. Setting an example of austerity for his disciples, he practised self-mortification and humility and abandoned the *madad-i ma'ash* grants sanctioned to him by the State. It was his reproach of Islam Shah Sur as un-Islamic that earned him the wrath of court theologians, who initially deported him to Deccan and later beat him to death in 1550. Shaikh 'Abdullah Niyazi was also meted brutal treatment and compelled to change his views on the approaching millennium. Commenting on the indignities inflicted on Shaikh 'Ala'i, Badauni narrated that as catastrophe struck the Surs, many feared, as they had after the death of Sayyid Muhammad Jaunpuri, that the Day of Judgement (*qiyamat*) had arrived. Within months of the Shaikh's demise, the death of Islam Shah and two other Sultans—Burhan Nizam Shah of Deccan and Sultan Mahmud III of Gujarat—lent credence to rumours of divine wrath that influenced many theologians of the Sur court, including Shaikh Mubarak Nagauri and other ideologues of Akbar, into believing it to be the truth.

A movement of a similar nature that coincided with Akbar's reign, the *Raushaniyya*, was led by Bayazid Raushan, the *pir-i raushan* (the resplendent or illustrious master), although his opponents referred to him as *pir-i tarik* (master of darkness). Born in Jalandhar, Punjab, Bayazid belonged to a Pashtun tribal family settled in Waziristan. Several theoretical speculations were made to understand the origin of his ideas. A few connected them to a form of Pashtun national consciousness (the political dynamics of which seemed to have alarmed Akbar), while others defined the *Raushaniyya* movement as rooted in Sufism. Many others believed that the movement was probably influenced by the *Isma'ilis*. But whatever it may have been, Bayazid claimed to have received a divine call and God's message (*ilham*) and thus asserted his right as *Mahdi*. He exhorted the Sufi path and urged the pursuance of eight steps:

- *shari'at,* the law revealed by God;
- *tariqat* (the way);
- *haqiqat* (truth), which in Sufism meant the final step, but for the *Raushaniyya*s, implied contemplation of God;
- *ma'rifat*, a concept that the *Raushaniyya*s related to pantheism or seeing God everywhere (although the Sufis understood it as intuitive knowledge or gnosis);
- *qurbat*, or nearness or knowing God;
- *wuslat*, or connection or renunciation of worldly material pleasure;
- *tauhid* or unity; but contrary to orthodox Islam, which interpreted it as consciousness of the oneness of God, the Sufis saw it as unification of the self with God;
- The eighth step, *sukunat* or stillness, was formulated by the *Raushaniyya*s to mean the power to radiate godliness.

Through this discourse, Bayazid led his followers into the practice of silent *dhikr* (recollection, especially repetition of the names of God and religious formulae) and reprimanded those who defied him, avowing that defying him was equivalent to defying God and therefore all such people should be treated as unbelievers. Tension arose between the mystical Islamic elements of the movement and the tribal ethic of the Pashtuns, who possessed a more conventional Islamic bent. These problems were further aggravated by his arrogant pretensions. The growing influence of the movement perturbed Akbar, who considered it strategically inappropriate for his empire and deputed Raja Man Singh to lead an expedition to the northwest border region to crush it. By 1575, Bayazid was dead, but his son Jalala continued to dominate a large area. The power of the sect declined when Bayazid's last successor, Abdul Qadir, surrendered to the Mughals in the early years of Shahjahan's reign.

In the midst of these millenarian activities, the last decade of the millennium (especially the approach of 1581) was anxiously awaited. Badauni narrated the happenings of these years and observed that in 1578–79, some courtiers of Akbar recognised him as the *sahib-i zaman* (Master of the Age), who could remove the differences between the seventy-two Islamic sects and the Hindus. Later, an Iranian migrant, Sharif-i Amuli of the *Nuqtawi* sect, on the basis of the writings of Mahmud Paskhwani, the founder of the sect, suggested that in 1581 someone would appear to save the world from lies and corruption, apparently implying that Akbar was the 'chosen' one for the task. Badauni was harshly critical of *Nuqtawi* ideas not only because they seemed to have influenced Akbar's *sulh-i kul*, but also because of their close proximity to the Sufi and Shi'i concepts. In addition, Badauni was provoked by the declarations of Mahmud Paskhwani, who had rejected Islamic rituals and beliefs and stated that there were many prophets, and more significantly, claimed to be the promised *Mahdi*, who would overthrow the Arab and Arabic hegemony of the first nine centuries and establish the superiority of the Persians. Not impressed by Badauni's severe observations, Akbar granted Sharif-i Amuli, considered the *mujaddid* ('renewer', 'reviver' or 'renovator') by his followers, a *mansab* of 1,000 *zat* when he fled to his court from Iran to escape the persecution of Shah Tahmasp. Later, his *mansab* was raised to 2,500 *zat* by Jahangir. It was alleged that Akbar, after the conquest of Gujarat, initiated a dialogue with some of the *Mahdavi*s staying in Gujarat (such as Miyan Mustafa Bandagi), whom he invited to the *Ibadatkhana* to participate in religious discussions. The millenarian trend was further reinforced when Khwaja Maulana Shirazi brought out a pamphlet attributed to the *Sharif*s of Mecca, stating that the earth would last for 7,000 years, at the end of which the *Mahdi* would appear, marking the end of the Islamic millennium.

The year 1581 was marked by considerable political and social turmoil, when Akbar issued the *mahzarnama* and was declared the *mujtahid* and an arbitrator on matters of religious dispute by the *'ulama*, in addition to his role of *khatib* to lead the Friday prayers. Badauni, not happy with the decree (although he was a party to it as a member of the *'ulama*), stipulated that Akbar had initially hesitated to answer the queries of 'some shameless and ill-starred wretches' at his court as to why he could not produce any evidence like Shah Isma'il I to prove his divinity. Akbar later virtually declared himself the Caliph of the eastern Sunni domains through the *mahzarnama* and established a position equal to that of the Ottoman Sultans. The year 1581 (during the campaign in Afghanistan) was also when Akbar became curious about matters related to the millennium and the Day of the Last Judgement, that is, when it would occur and whether Christ would be the Judge. Anxious to understand the theological differences and similarities between heterodox Islam and the Jesuit version of Christianity, he raised these questions before Catalan Jesuit Antonio Monserrate (then on a mission to his court). Monserrate explained that the Day of the Last Judgement was a divine mystery that could be represented by wars and rebellions, the fall of kingdoms and nations, invasions, devastations and conquests of nation by nation and kingdom by kingdom. Not convinced by Monserrate's reply, Akbar further queried the presence of Muhammad in the Gospel, to which Monserrate averred that since Muhammad was a false prophet, there was no reference to him in the Gospel. Astonished at Monserrate's assertion, Akbar allegedly commented, 'Surely Muhammad cannot be he who is to appear at the end of the world as the adversary of all mankind (that is he whom the Muslims call *Dijal*)', referring to the idea of *masih al-dajjal*, the Anti-Christ, mentioned in some Islamic legends 'as riding on an ass at the End of Time'. This verbal exchange was recorded discreetly in Monserrate's *Mongoliecae Legationis Commentarius*. Otherwise, the decade 1581–91 was considerably calm with no claims or counter-claims on the issue of the millennium, although in Deccan, a *Mahdavi* coalition led by a nondescript individual, Jamal Khan, and his Afghan supporters briefly captured Ahmadnagar in 1590. Accused of sedition and rebellion, they were later ousted by a Nizam Shahi prince with Mughal support.

Popular perceptions of and expectations from the millenarian movements persisted for a while. In the years 1591–92, there was hope and optimism about reordering the world through the mediation of a *mujaddid* in pursuance of a tradition ascribed to Prophet Muhammad—that 'God will, on the eve of every century, raise a person in this *Ummat* who will renew the religion'. The idea of the *mujaddid*, expected to bring radical reform to the world, did not replace but paralleled the notion rooted in Islamic history of *Imam Mahdi*. Millenarianism was thus a political strategy in the sixteenth century that engulfed not only the Mediterranean, but also further east. At times, it was used to build a State as with Shah Isma'il I or to consolidate a phase of rapid geographical expansion as with Sultan Selim, while at other times like in India, it was used to challenge the State in significant ways. In this context may be mentioned the *Naqshbandi*s, who had come to India with the Mughals. As royal *pir*s in Central Asia, they shared a close relationship with the Chaghatais and, to some extent, with the early Timurid rulers in India. They continued to be privileged in the ruling circles until the first few years of Akbar's reign, but beyond that made little mark as notable Sufi *Shaikh*s. From the mid-1570s, Akbar had distanced himself from the pattern of early Timurid Islamic kingship, which corroded Chaghatai power and influence and the kind of relationship that the early Timurids had shared with the nobility and the *Naqshbandi* Sufi lineage. Akbar had by now evolved a universal kingship with invincible, paramount power for the emperor and established a new capital at Fatehpur Sikri, built in deference to the place's association with saint Salim Chishti. But Akbar was clear that it was not the place or the saint, but the emperor who had to be glorified and applauded as the centre of authority in the new Timurid polity in India. This characteristic of the Akbari dispensation of power conflicted with *Naqshbandi* notions of power and authority, politics and kingship. Nevertheless, Mughal politics in relation to the Sufis continued, in one way or the other, to be dominated by the *Naqshbandi*s during the late sixteenth–early seventeenth centuries.

Khwaja Baqi-Billah (d. 1603), a prominent member of the *Naqshbandi* order, succeeded in restoring its ascendancy during the period. Critiquing the Chishti understanding of *tasawwuf*, Baqi-Billah discarded the Chishti understanding of *tauhid* and their practice of *sama'*, dismissed as heretic (*zandaqa*) and stupidity (*ablahi*, *safahat*) the approbation of unbelief (*kufr*) and the emphasis on the basic unity between a believer and a non-believer or infidel. He urged that the primary function of the *salik* (sufi path) was to follow the *shari'at*, which was the reality (*haqiqa)* of gnosis (*ma'rifa*). These criticisms became even more acute under Shaikh Ahmad Sirhindi, known to be one of the best Indian Sufis and religious thinkers. The *salik*'s efforts, he observed, were nullified if his vision (*kashf*) digressed from the Quran and the *Sunna* (the tradition of the Prophet). There was no pardon, he further reiterated, for evading the rulings of the law (*ahkam-i fiqhiya*) in all matters obligatory (*fara'iz*) or desirable (*mustahabbat*); one who observed the law without fail (*multazim-i sharia*) possessed real knowledge (*ma'rifa*), whereas one who did not (*mudahin-i sharia*) was deprived of it (*az ma'rifat bi-nasib ast*). So the more one observed the law, the greater his share in gnosis. Sirhindi insisted that if a person chose a sufi path, his foremost duty was total compliance with one of the *ahi-i sunna wa jama'a* and regard for the *shari'at* obligations as given in *fiqh* (Islamic jurisprudence). The Sufi knowledge, he declared, was third in priority, prescribing thus that the school of Abu Hanifa was the ideal *mazhab* (religious jurisprudential school). Sirhindi, earnest in his commitment to the revival of the *Sunna*, persuaded his disciples of the significance of *hadis* as a source of guidance and provided a personal example by emulating the *Sunna* of the Prophet.

Notwithstanding his insistence on rigorous obedience to the *shari'at*, he stepped outside the traditional realm by declaring that Islam needed a *mujaddid* with extraordinary powers after every millennium, and that later God would ordain a *qayyum* (maintainer). It is in this regard that he assumed the title of *mujaddid-i alf-i sani* ('Renewer of the Second Millennium') and proclaimed himself the founder of the *mujaddidi* branch of the order that eventually spread his ideology to his disciples far beyond the Indian subcontinent, to nearly the entire Islamic East. In the dominant Muslim mind in South Asia, this was hailed as Sirhindi's major role, regardless of *tasawwuf*. Several modern scholars like Yohanan Friedmann (2001 [1971]) have projected Sirhindi as one who was a Sufi and not a jurist (*faqih*) interested in legalistic matters; he did not issue legal opinions (*fatwas*), nor did he write systematically on points of law. 'Sirhindi was a Sufi,' Friedmann asserted, 'and must be assessed as such.'

The struggle between *sunna* and *bid'a* (innovations), an integral part of the dynamics of Islamic history and tradition, engaged Sirhindi in his role as *mujaddid-i alf-i sani*, pledged to reinstate the *shari'at* to its rightful place. To achieve his mission, Sirhindi spelled out the roles of centennial and millennial *mujaddids*. A *mujaddid*, according to Sirhindi, ensured the resurgence of the *shari'at*; he was chosen by the community and belonged to the class of *'ulama*, who in Islam were similar to the prophets of Bani Isra'il. The *mujaddid* of the second millennium, he proclaimed, was both an Islamic scholar well-versed in knowledge (*'alim-i rasikh*) and a Sufi, the master of gnosis (*'arif-i tamm al-marifat*); he was like a determined, firm, unwavering messenger (*payghambar-i ulu al-azm*). As a millennial *mujaddid*, Sirhindi claimed that it was his divine task to restore the piety of the *shari'at* and rid the polity and civil society of the *bid'a* introduced during previous centuries. He distanced himself from free-thinking mystics and theologians and developed the concept of *wahadat-ul-shuhud* (unity of appearance) to counter Ibn al-'Arabi's notion of *wahadat-ul-wujud* (unity of existence or unity of being), which Sirhindi dismissed as a mere mystical experience. He was particularly distressed by the politico-religious interventions of Akbar, which he considered heretical: the emperor's similar concerns for Sunni Muslims, Hindus, and Shi'is, and the fact that the emperor was acknowledged as the Prophet and given divine attributes. He accused the Shi'is of being the 'promoters of false religion' who engendered trouble for Muslims even in India, calling them a 'plague in India' and the 'cause of schism and depravity in the whole world'. It was to counter these developments that

Sirhindi favoured the accession of Jahangir. His disciple Murtaza Khan was nominated to gather support for Jahangir in the Council of Nobles convened by Khan-i-Azam at the time of Akbar's death, and Shaikh Farid extracted from Jahangir the promise to defend Islam in return for the support of the nobles.

Trained as an *'alim*, Sirhindi understood the significance of *'ulama* as a class, but was disappointed by their failure to exert influence. He deplored the apathy and lack of action of the contemporary *'ulama* against *bid'a* (innovations), categorically stating that the *shari'at* could not be subjected to abrogation (*naskh*) and change. His resolve to eradicate *bid'a* left a deep imprint on the followers of the *Naqshbandiyyah Mujaddidiyyah* order in India and elsewhere. It was in these circumstances that Sirhindi wrote two brochures—'Proofs of Prophecy' (*Isbat-un-Nubuwwah*) and 'Refutation of the Shias' (*Risala Radd-i-Rawafiz*)—that explained his thoughts. Sirhindi's ideas were also communicated through his *Maktubat-i-Imam Rabbani*, which contained almost 534 letters and were arranged in three volumes. Although some of these works were quite polemical in nature, they were valuable for expounding Sirhindi's ideas and his contribution to Islamic mystical thought and the growth of the *Naqshbandi* order. Sirhindi's main concern was to establish the supremacy of the *shari'at* in Muslim States. The *shari'at*, he averred, had to be interpreted by the Sunni *'ulama* on the basis of *kitab* (book), *sunna* (tradition) and *ijma-i-ummat* (consensus of the community), and thus warned against the rational justification of religious laws for that implied the denial of greatness to the Prophet. His tirade against the *kafirs*—both Hindus and Shi'is—was violent. He wanted to translate his religious hatred of them into politics, believing that all States ruled by Muslims were Islamic States. But his theory was radically different from and clashed with that of the Mughal State, devised by Akbar and then continued by his successors, which rejected the monopoly of any one religion or race or group. Sirhindi disapproved of the non-sectarian common concerns of the 'Muslim' State, rejected the idea of 'infidels' issuing orders of '*kufr*' in the 'land of Islam', and considered such a State 'helpless and degraded'. He recommended the imposition of *jizya* for the subjugation and humiliation of non-Muslims, and suggested that non-Muslims be divested of their positions in the administration. His criticism of Hindu and Shi'i nobles, particularly the Persians, garnered support for him from amongst the nobility, creating a large following for him. Such assertions alarmed Jahangir. Apprehensive about Sirhindi becoming a potential threat to his power, the emperor decided to intervene when Sirhindi's vilification of Akbar, Nurjahan, Asaf Khan, and Itmad-ud-daulah became even more severe and harsh.

The contradictions in Sirhindi's preaching undermined the significance of his reforms and mysticism. His claim to be a *mujaddid* and *qayyum* on the basis of mystic revelation and inspiration, even as he was critical of saints like Mansur and Bayazid for their ideas which he believed had originated from a state of *sukr* (mystic intoxication) and were irreconcilable with the *shari'at*, agitated not only the Sunni orthodoxy but also moderate theologians like the *Qadiri* scholar 'Abdu'l Haqq. The protests against Sirhindi, especially when he asserted his superiority over Abu Bakr, the first Caliph, compelled Jahangir to summon him to the court in 1619. Sirhindi denied the charges, but was imprisoned by Jahangir. There are conflicting views on Sirhindi's imprisonment. I. H. Qureshi (1962) noticed an inconsistency in Jahangir's attitude towards religious personalities. He argued that while Jahangir was deferential towards Shaikh 'Abdu'l Haqq and others, he did not hesitate to imprison Sirhindi, although posterity credited him with the reversal of Akbar's eclectic, liberal policies, which reached 'political culmination with the ascendancy of Aurangzeb to the throne'. Friedmann (2001 [1971]) dismissed this view and observed that Sirhindi had no decisive influence on Mughal State policies. Contemporary sources, however, made a different assessment and suggested that Jahangir had no kind words for Sirhindi; he neither acknowledged his erudition nor approved his religious activism, but considered him a *shaiyad* (impostor) and imprisoned him. The *Naqshbandi* records took yet another view and observed that Jahangir had imprisoned Sirhindi because the latter had refused to perform *sijda* to the emperor.

Interestingly, Jahangir made no mention of the incident in his memoirs. The *Naqshbandi* records further stated that Jahangir had apologised to the *Shaikh*, promised to implement *shari'at*, introduce *jizya*, reconstruct desecrated mosques, sanction cow slaughter, suppress heresy and *bid'a*, abolish *sijda*, and appoint *Qazi*s to supervise these practices. But there is no contemporary account, including the *Tuzuk-i Jahangiri*, to confirm that Jahangir expressed regret or promised to comply with Sirhindi's demands. So if Sirhindi was released after a brief spell of imprisonment, it could have either been to ingratiate Sunni opinion during that troubled phase in Jahangir's reign or, as some have interpreted, it may have been to commend the elevation of Shaikh Sirhindi as the spiritual leader of pan-Islamic thought.

The spiritual life of India in the mid-seventeenth century was enveloped in complexities. On the one hand was the tradition of Akbar's eclecticism and on the other, the orthodoxy of Shaikh Ahmad Sirhindi. In these circumstances, Akbar's eclecticism took the form of intellectualised syncretism represented by Dara Shukoh, whose interest extended from Muslim mysticism to Hindu Vedantic philosophy, with a focus on finding a common mystical language between Hinduism and Islam. Aziz Ahmad (1999) argued that Dara and Aurangzeb represented a polarised tension between 'esoteric heterodoxy' and 'conformist orthodoxy'. It was through them that Muslim *ijma* (consensus), which had acquired some knowledge of both exoteric and esoteric Hinduism, had to decide whether to merge syncretically with Hinduism or preserve its identity through reorientation towards orthodoxy or formalism.

Dara Shukoh was an orthodox mystic of the *Qadiriyyah* order, influenced by the ideas of Ibn al 'Arabi and a disciple of *Qadiri* Sufis Miyan Mir (d. 1635) of Lahore, who had an ascetic bent and had spurned the material world and advocated tolerance, and Mulla Shah Badkhshi (d. 1661). Badkhshi, in particular, hailed Dara as a Sufi and described him as *sahib-qiran-i dil* (ruler of the realm of heart). Opinions on Dara are polarised. His rabid detractors charged him with heresy and argued that his intellectualism was completely misguided and posed an existential threat to Islam. *'Alamgirnama* (*c.* 1680s) may be quoted in this regard. It recorded that 'Dara Shukoh in his later years did not restrict himself to free thinking and heretical notions, which he had adopted in the name of *tasawwuf* but showed an inclination for the religion of the Hindus ...'. Thus, *'Alamgirnama* observed that the foundations of Islamic faith were endangered and the precepts of Islam 'would be changed for the absurdity of infidelity'. Milder versions of these sentiments were found in the works of Shibli Nomani, I. H. Qureshi, Aziz Ahmad, and others. His supporters saw him as a tragic figure who could not abide by his promise of greater Hindu–Muslim understanding, and nationalist historians eulogised him as one who aimed at a common nationality and synthesis of the different elements of the country. Rajeev Kinra (2009) suggested yet another alternative to Dara's liberal or heretical religious views. He argued that some disliked him for completely non-sectarian reasons, either because of personal enmity or Dara's 'narcissistic arrogance', which made him unsuitable for the throne. Kinra further added that over the centuries, such opinions have been drowned by the 'good Muslim, bad Muslim' polemics surrounding Dara.

Dara's spiritual quest, his engagement with the *Upanishads*, and his efforts to understand the nature of *tauhid* were preceded by his writings of around the 1640s that focused on doctrinal or hagiographical studies of the established canons of sufism. The major literary impact on Dara was that of Nur al-Din Abd al-Rahman Jami, a Persian poet, scholar, and author of mystical sufi literature during this period. Dara's *Sakinat al-awliya* (a Sufi hagiography written in 1642) and *Tariqat al-haqiqat* (a doctrinal work written around 1648–49) were influenced by Jami's *Nafahat al-uns* and *Lawa'ih*, respectively. In *Sakinat al-awliya*, Dara described his own unique spiritual visions of having been chosen by God for 'greatness' and condemned the performance of miracles as part of spiritual pursuit, while in *Tariqat al-haqiqat*, he demonstrated his growing belief that Islam and Hinduism both spoke the same ultimate truth. Convinced that God was omnipresent and omniscient, Dara stated that both Vedantic Hinduism and Islam echoed a similar divine scheme. He could thus associate with both Muslim Sufis like Muhib-ullah and Lisan-Allah Rustaki and Hindu mystics like Jagannath Misra and Babalal Vairagi to gratify his spiritual curiosity. Over the next six years, Dara manifested a growing interest in Vedantic philosophy and mystical ideas and concentrated on the Persian translation of several Vedantic texts and syncretic interpretation of Hindu scriptures. Identifying Hindu mysticism with Islamic mysticism, he argued that the path of gnosis (*ma'rifat*) was identical in both Sufi Islam and Vedantic Hinduism. He translated *Yogavasishtha* into Persian (the earlier translation, known as *Tuhfat al-Majalis*, was done by Sharif Qutb-i Jahani), which discussed the Hindu god Rama's search for spiritual liberation even as he continued to fulfil his worldly obligations. Later, Dara translated the *Bhagavad Gita* into Persian. His engagement with these scriptures convinced him further of the spiritual and lexicographical affinities between Islam and Vedantic Hinduism, and that they were distinct in name only. He related all this in his *Majma 'al-bahrayn*, completed in 1655–56. He trusted that certain Hindu texts could be a commentary (*tafsir*) on the *Quran* and the entire body of monotheistic religious texts, and provide insights into 'divine oneness' or the 'boundless ocean'. In 1657 he translated, in association with Brahmin scholars from Banaras, fifty-two *Upanishads* (considered the oldest and acknowledged by Hindus as possessing *shruti* or divine origins) into Persian, called it *Sirr-i akbar* (The Great Secret), and affirmed that *Upanishads* were in principle the textual source of monotheism.

In his succinctly written introduction to *Sirr-i akbar*, Dara described his spiritual quest, which began in 1641, to explain the secrets of God's Oneness and turned to the *Quran* in search of *kalam-i ilahi* (God's word) to overcome his doubts. He found the *Quran marmuz* (enigmatic) and tried to understand it through other monotheistic texts; in this regard, he distinctly mentioned the Old and New Testaments. He realised that these were as mysterious, but so poorly translated that they were barely intelligible (*matlub ma'lum nagirdid*). Disillusioned by the enigma and the mysteries of the Quran and Biblical texts, Dara was amazed by his discovery of the widely prevalent monism and monotheism in India and the divinely ordained scriptures, the *Vedas* and Upanishads. The *Vedas*, he asserted, were revealed to the 'Hindu Prophet' Brahma, who was none other than Prophet Adam (mentioned in the Book of Genesis; also in the New Testament and the *Quran*) in disguise, with a different nomenclature. So all those mysteries, he urged, that may have remained unexplained in the *Quran* could be elucidated through the *Upanishads*, for these were the 'concealed scripture' (*kitab-i maknun*), a 'treasure of Divine Oneness' (*ganj-i tauhid*), and provided the answers he could not find in either the *Quran* or the Biblical texts—'unknown things became known and incomprehensible things became comprehensible'.

It was on the hypothesis that the *Upanishads* were the source of all scriptures and monotheism that Dara built his syncretism. His identification of the *Upanishads* with the essence of Islam was more elaborate in *Majma 'al-bahrayn*, a work that dealt with syncretic 'lexique technique', that is, a collection of pseudo-lexicographical correspondences between Sufi and Upanishadic cosmologies, esoteric beliefs and practices. The personal equations in Dara's syncretic technique were intriguing, but significant. He identified Michael (an archangel in Jewish, Christian, and Islamic teachings) with Vishnu; Israphael (the 'Dark Lord' associated with anger and annoyance, who then emerged as a 'grand evil') with Mahadeva/Shiva; Adam with Brahma; and Gabriel (an angel, a messenger of God mentioned in both the Old and the New Testaments. In Islam, Gabriel is identified with Jibrail, an angel who brought the divine message to different prophets, including Muhammad) with Manu. Dara also talked about similarities between the Sufi concept of *ishq* (love) and the Hindu notion of *maya* (illusion) and compared the Sufi belief in *ruh-i azam* (complete soul of Muhammad), that is, *Haqiqat-i Muhammadiyyah*, with the Hindu concept of *Hiranyagarbha* (identified with the golden womb or creator deity, the *Upanishad* called it the 'soul of the Universe', that is, Brahma).

Most Muslims of the time rejected Dara Shukoh's conclusions and accused him of heresy and apostasy, which Aurangzeb cited as a reason for his execution. Regardless, Dara exemplified his unstinted commitment to Islam, urged that he had never forsaken Islam but that instead, his engagement with the *Quran* had become even more intense with the pursuit to reach the truth of monotheism. Religious scholars have found it hard to accept Dara's versions. Historians like Aziz Ahmad (1999) have considered them 'far-fetched and erroneous'. He argued that even if Dara's syncretism was liberal, it sounded hollow, lacked scientific and metaphysical premise, and appeared hypothetical. Dara, Ahmad alleged, believed in the Nietzschean concept of recurrence of history under the influence of Hindu theories of reincarnation, and talked of magic and superstition that had an effect on his metaphysical speculation and strategy. Manucci expressed a contrarian view to which some have consented, that is, Dara had no fixed religion and that he praised every religion. Dara was also connected with heretical (*bi-shar*) Sufism, as represented by Sarmad. It is believed that Sarmad was Armenian or Jewish by origin, had studied in Shiraz under Mulla Sadra (d. 1640), a renowned Muslim philosopher, but practised Sufi bohemianism and walked around naked in a state of ecstasy, preferring the company of 'mad mystics'.

Sarmad's quatrains, *ruba'iyat*, are gloomy and melancholic, although he claimed to have felt a special affinity with the mystic al-Hallaj, who was executed in Baghdad in 922. Like his mentor, Sarmad too was executed in 1661 by Aurangzeb on charges of obscene heterodoxy; many doubt it, though, and wonder whether anti-Semitism was really the reason for his execution. Walter J. Fischel (1951) had attempted to unravel Sarmad's Jewish roots and influences and prove that he had not completely dissociated himself from his inherited tradition. Several, however, have attributed Sarmad's persecution to his close relationship with Dara and argued that the reasons were political rather than religious. On Dara's execution, the Muslim perception was evidently not very clear; however, the common people of Delhi were shocked at his fate and the Hindu intellectual elite, as represented by the Bengali poet Dvija Ram in the late eighteenth century, lamented Dara's destiny.

Dara could perhaps not adequately explain himself owing to the sudden illness of Shahjahan and his defeat and capture by Aurangzeb in 1659. Although the introduction to *Sirr-i akbar* did not exhibit Dara's political interests, what emerged, as Munis Faruqui observed, was 'a potent princely self portrait' that compelled one to regard Dara as a man of 'rare intelligence, wisdom, discernment, courage, tenacity and conviction', who even without military and administrative expertise could have provided 'spiritual wisdom and gravitas' to the Mughal Empire. But *Sirr-i akbar* had controversial ideas that could have antagonised Muslim political and religious opinion, and yet it did not matter, as Rajeev Kinra argued, for much before the 1650s Dara had alienated many, except probably his supporters. His convictions and perceptions died with him, leaving his life 'encrusted in all sorts of myth'.

Despite their sharp differences, both *wujudi*s and *shuhudi*s strongly denounced the *'ulama* for their hypocrisy and attachment to the material world. The eighteenth century, in fact, witnessed a renewed emphasis on scriptural orthodoxy, which guided the beliefs and practices of the time. It was in these circumstances that Shah Waliullah (1703–62), considered to have been the greatest theological thinker of the period, who presided over a seminary in Delhi, attempted to remove sectarian controversies by introducing a new ethical moral code and reconciling the *shari'at* with the sufi path (*tariqa*). While denouncing many of the practices inherited from Hindus as un-Islamic, he conceded that the 'essence of all religions was the same and all of them enjoined a similar code'. Keen to end the dispute over Ibn al-'Arabi's theory of *wahdat-ul-wujud*, Shah Waliullah endeavoured to reconcile *wujudi* and *shuhudi* doctrines and proclaimed that *wahdat-ul-wujud* was as valid as *wahdat-ul-shuhud*. Earlier, Mirza Mazhar Jan-i-Jahan, a Sufi *naqshbandi* poet, had reinforced Dara's conclusions, that is, that the *Veda*s and *Upanishad*s were the revealed books, and therefore Hindus could not be identified with the *kafir*s of Arabia. He said there was little difference between idol worship and *tasawwar-i-shaikh* or concentration on the mental image of the preceptor. Shah Waliullah wrote several spiritual and legal tracts through which he articulated that Muslims rigidly followed the divine messages enshrined in the *Quran* and renounced all kinds of syncretic practices. In his basic ideology, there was no space for the poor or non-Muslims. His best-known work, *Hujjatullah al-baligha*, was based on this conception and extensively expounded the forms of worship, family life, and norms of social interaction detailed in the *shari'at*. His son, Shah Abdul 'Aziz (1746–1824), a prolific writer, continued his father's mission, polemicised against the Shi'ites, insisted on rigorous adherence to the *shari'at*, and dedicated himself to the purification and reform of the Islamic religion.

BHAKTI DEVOTIONALISM

Multiculturalism and multireligiosity were the vital components of the Mughal State that can be well-appreciated by exploring the relationship between religion, society, and politics during this period. The sixteenth to the eighteenth centuries were marked by significant historical changes in the religious culture of India. The period witnessed a considerable strengthening of popular devotional cultures within Islamic as well as 'Hindu' religious spheres. The affiliations of the Mughal rulers became increasingly inclined towards Sufi orders and 'heterodox' Sufi mystics that were less rigidly attached to Islamic religious law. From the reign of Akbar, Khwaja Muin ud-din Chishti and Shaikh Salim Chishti virtually emerged as the patron saints of the Mughals. The liberal and non-sectarian outlook of Akbar and his concept of *sulh-i kul* were widely endorsed by the *Chishti* and *Qadiri* Sufis. Interaction between the Sufi and Hindu *bhakti* saints was pursued persistently by the *Chishtiyya* and *Qadiriyya silsilah*s. In this context may be mentioned the association of Jahangir with Jadrup Gosain and of Dara with Mullah Shah, Shaikh Muhib-ullah, Miyan Mir, the wandering mystics and the Hindu saint Babalal Vairagi, and others. Aurangzeb was considerably more interested in *fiqh* than mysticism, but it is believed that he venerated the Sufi saints, especially the *wujudi*s, and invariably paid his regards whenever he passed by the mausoleum of any. More importantly, he did not discourage the interaction of his sons, Muazzam and Azam, his daughter Zebunissa, and his sister Jahanara with the Sufis. Zebunissa and Jahanara are known to have patronised liberal Sufis, and engaged in dialogues and exchanges with the Hindus or those accomplished in Hindu philosophy and Hindi poetry. The Sufis steadfastly pursued their liberal ideas, with many of them continuing to write *masnavi*s in Hindi.

There was a somewhat analogous development in the 'Hindu' religion, represented by sectarian movements of *bhakti* devotionalism that challenged both the religious and mundane hierarchy, questioned the right of the Brahmin priestly elite as mediators between themselves and gods, and developed their own ideologies and literatures to communicate their union with the divine as they proliferated across north India. Regional kingdoms hoped to benefit from their links with the multiple *bhakti* sects, 'whose desire to directly embrace the gods could be diverted to supporting the latter's earthly protectors'. The evolution of the *bhakti* movement with its multifaceted tendencies that influenced India at different times and impacted religious doctrines, rituals, and values can be understood in the context of theological differences that, as David Lorenzen (1996) has argued, are not simply the outcome of 'historical accidents ... but symptomatic and expressive of differences in social identities'. Religions, he observed, are communities of persons who follow or claim to follow common systems of beliefs and practices, and thus define the group's identity, its membership, and ideology. It was such social and political purport that added to the import of the *bhakti* movement. The *bhakti* movement characterised itself differently in different regions and represented a force opposed to the notions of a centralised State. It became closely associated with the growth of regional languages or dialects, devotional music, dance, art and aesthetics.

Bhakti is a generic term, although its academic interpretation has differed widely from the understanding of a common man. The latter would grasp *bhakti* as religious devotion regardless of its different manifestations, which occurred as a result of different practices and beliefs, whereas the academic argument saw it as a specific religious discipline, defined as a belief and an attachment to a personal God, and therefore an emotional religious cult rather than the path of *jnana*. Scholars like Irfan Habib have described *bhakti* as monotheism, as opposed to the monism (a metaphysical theory, according to which reality is conceived as consisting of only one basic substance) of Hindu thought. He has argued that although the popular monotheistic movement of north India from the mid-fifteenth to the mid-seventeenth century, represented by Kabir and Nanak, picked their ideas from both Hinduism and Islam, it did not explain why they selected certain ideas, denied allegiance to others, and rejected a large number of the basic elements of both religious systems. In fact, Habib argued, this point has often been missed in the anxiety to portray the monotheists as prophets of Hindu–Muslim unity. It is probable that what Abu'l Fazl said about Kabir was true of all monotheists. He was simply a *muwahhia* or a monotheist who had abandoned the traditional, conventional customs, and as the monotheists realised the truth about the unity of God, they questioned the 'lesser beliefs' and rejected the importance of both idol worship and *Kaba*. Their conception of God was rarely that of a mystic; it differed from *Bhakti* or Sufism. God for them was not—except occasionally—'the playful lover' of *bhakti* saints or the 'beloved' of Muslim mysticism; God was a 'strict and just master' who expected man to perform the given task. J. S. Grewal's idea of equality in Sikhism can be located in the same context. Grewal discussed the genesis of the notion of equality in Sikhism as he talked of Guru Nanak's view of his contemporary society (late fifteenth and early sixteenth century), his critical reaction to inequality in social institutions and social structures, that is, the oppression of the *raiyat* by the *muqaddams* and the injustice and insubordination practised by the rulers. He further exemplified Guru Nanak's attempt to create equality through the Sikh *Panths* and achieve the consolidation of an ideal Sikh social order through the order of the *Khalsa* under the Sikh *Gurus* by the early eighteenth century. Nanak's social order comprised *khatris*, generally traders and government officials, *Jat* peasantry, artisans, craftsmen, and also Brahmins. But all castes were bound together by common loyalty to their *Guru*, formed a local *sangat*, and worshipped and dined together.

For Satish Chandra (1996), the *bhakti* movement cannot be categorised as a mass movement for it made no direct attempt to improve or change the living conditions of the masses, although some effect may have been felt indirectly. He observed that the purpose of this movement was individual salvation and mystical union with God. Similarly, it could not be called a single movement with a single focus despite its broad doctrinal understanding, which emphasised devotion as a means of attaining salvation or proximity to God, but through the advice and support of a Guru. Regardless of the broad doctrinal understanding, there were variations in the nature of the relationship of a devotee with God, the attitude towards scriptures and traditional faith, and also towards society and the State. Krishna Sharma (1987, 2006), on the other hand, held the interpretations of the English and European Indologists responsible for misrepresenting *bhakti* and the *bhakti* movement, and understanding *bhakti* as Krishna-*bhakti* and Vaishnavism. Sharma was critical of their description of *bhakti* as a specific religious tradition that represented a staunch belief in a personal God, because an explanation of *bhakti* as monotheism at variance with the monism of Hinduism was a misrepresentation of the character of Hindu monotheism. These opinions, Sharma stipulated, delimited the general meaning of *bhakti* and wrongly portrayed it as similar to Western monotheism. In Hinduism, she reiterated, faith in one God did not necessarily mean belief in one Personal God. *Bhakti* was neither a cult nor a doctrine, nor did it signify any specific religious mode or belief or an integrated phenomenon. The followers of *bhakti* saints formed separate sects but, broadly speaking, they shared common convictions. In a somewhat similar manner, Lorenzen (1996) argued that all Sikhs and Hindus could be called followers of *bhakti* because their major style of worship was *bhakti* or devotion towards a divine being. Although their way of rendering this devotion and conceptualising the object of devotion varied remarkably, all expressions of *bhakti* shared common historical roots. More significantly, he observed, the roots of the *bhakti* sects and their ideology were influenced by two Sanskrit texts—the *Bhagavad Gita* and *Bhagvata Purana*—which gave them a common heritage and all its manifestations 'a family resemblance', which was not shared by other religions of India like Christianity and Islam, in which devotion to a divine being plays a central role.

From the latter part of the fifteenth century, the *bhakti* movement in north India was represented through two streams: *nirguna* (without attributes) and *saguna* (with attributes). The division, Lorenzen observed, was due to a theological difference in conceptualising the nature of the divine being, *viz.*, the object of worship. Krishna Sharma, on the other hand, suggested that the distinction between *nirguna* and *saguna bhakti* did not imply any essential difference between the two from the point of view of religion; they were used distinctly to indicate the qualitative difference that existed between the two in terms of the different concepts and ideologies associated with them. Some like John Hawley (1988) acknowledged the differences between the *pantha*s, yet emphasised the similarities arising out of their same historical roots and averred that 'we are talking about a single family of saints ... the family of *bhakti*'. The *nirguna* tradition was considerably more influential over north India, but remained a 'subordinate, minority tradition subject to the hegemony of the *saguna* tradition', as Lorenzen argued. Other ancient 'orthodox' traditions such as Vedic recitation and sacrifice, philosophic and yogic enlightenment, and *tantrism* continued to prevail, but none of them emerged as primary religious concerns except for a few practitioners, and even these were often syncretically combined with the traditions of *saguna bhakti*. Those who followed *nirguna bhakti* were fewer and worshipped a divine being, who remained 'unmanifest' and 'non-anthropomorphic'. The thought of *nirguna bhakta*s was more in accordance with Sankara's concept of *Advaita Vedanta* than the thinking of *Vaishnava Acharya*s. Sharma observed that Ramanujam, Nimbarka, Madhava, and Vallabhacharya ought to be understood as the *Vaishnava Acharya*s who initiated *Vaishnava Vedanta*, rather than be seen as the pioneers of any doctrine of *bhakti*.

The genesis of *nirguna bhakti* led by Kabir represented the trend that emerged from the combination of *astika* and *nastika* traditions. Kabir's thought, Sharma suggested, was based on monistic ideas and an impersonal concept of God, which was a part of the *astika* tradition from the time of the *Upanishads*. But his rejection and questioning of established religious norms reflected the influence of the *nastika* tradition and the importance of reason in his conception. Kabir based his ideas not on any particular scripture or doctrine but on mysticism, and regarded personal spiritual experience as the final truth. For him, the philosophical controversies surrounding the *dvaita* (dualistic) and *advaita* (non-dualistic) explanation of the Ultimate Reality were irrelevant. It was his adaptation of the unorthodox spirit of the *nastika*s that stimulated him to attack the caste system, idol worship, and ritualism. Also, his rejection of Sanskrit and use of vernacular language and vernacular dialect for communication was in accordance with the *nastika* tradition. Kabir preceded *nirguna bhakta*s such as Nanak, Dadu, Raidas, and Dhanna, the followers of whom formed separate sects even though, broadly speaking, they shared common beliefs and the movement that they led emerged into a new popular cult, *viz.*, *nirguna pantha*. Although *nirguna* literature guided the devotee to the worship of a formless, universal God, this God assumed partial embodiment in the Name of God and in the *bani* (collective words) and the person of the *Guru* and saints. This was particularly so in the case of Sikhism, in which the *bani* of the *Guru* and saints took the physical form of a Holy Book: the *Adi Granth* or *Guru Granth Sahib*.

Dadu Dayal (1544–1603), a low-caste cotton carder, was a spiritual descendant of Kabir. Like Kabir, he used a number of vernacular languages—*Khari Boli*, Rajasthani, Punjabi, and Gujarati—and Persian for easy communication, and preached in large parts of northern India. Dadu's verses are preserved in two traditions: *maghazia* (oral) and *kagazia* (written). A significant concept of Dadu's *Granthavali* was the concept of *Guru*, whom he saw as an important intermediary between God and man and as a spiritual guide who assisted man in attaining *nirvana*. He therefore urged complete and personal loyalty to the *Guru*. As opposed to *nirguna bhakta*s, the followers of *saguna bhakti* were large in numbers. Belief in a highly personalised God or worship of anthropomorphic manifestations of the divine being like Vishnu, his *avatar*s (incarnations) Rama and Krishna, Shiva, *Shakti* or the Goddess, close associates of these gods or their family members represented *saguna bhakti*. For instance, the *bhakti* of Chaitanya upheld Krishna *bhakti* above all forms of religious devotion and represented *saguna bhakti*. Shiva was worshipped in the semi-iconic form of a *linga* and *Shakti* was often invoked as Durga or *Mahisamardini*, the killer of the buffalo demon.

The *Bhakti* movement can be traced to the *Bhagavad Gita*, ascribed to the fifth century when it acquired its final form, and to the Tamil *Alvar*s, with whom the emotional, ecstatic form of *bhakti* originated and who laid the foundations for the emergence of the cult of Rama-*bhakti*. Later, the message of *bhakti* was spread in virtually all directions of the subcontinent—the west, north, and towards the east in Bengal.

- Ramanujam wrote devotional poems in the early twelfth century and inspired the spread of devotional *Vaishnavism* among the masses;
- Basava advocated *tantric* practices and temple rituals to foster the anti-Brahmin *lingayat* movement;

- through the *varkari* movement Namadeva, a saint from Maharashtra, promoted the idea that even the most humble or those engaged in mundane tasks could acquire the highest form of spirituality;
- Vallabhacharya created awareness of the importance of Krishna-*bhakti* during the late fourteenth–early fifteenth centuries; and
- Ramdasa popularised the worship of Vishnu in his *avatar* as Rama.

Shaivism was particularly strong in the Tamil country, patronised by the Cholas between the ninth and the thirteenth centuries.

Bhakti, an intense form of devotionalism that had cut across south India between the seventh and the twelfth centuries, became popular across north India, primarily in the Indo-Gangetic plain, from the fifteenth to the early sixteenth century. This was probably because the works concerned with *bhakti* were written in Sanskrit—a language understood primarily by the Brahmins—and therefore lacked mass support. It is believed that the ideas of *bhakti* travelled from south to north India through the efforts of Ramananda, who lived in Kashi around the last quarter of the fourteenth and the first half of the fifteenth century. He opened the path of *bhakti* to all irrespective of caste, and reversed the practice of his *Guru*, Ramanujam. It has often been asked: Did Ramananda reverse the traditions of his *Guru* to counter the *Nathpanthi*s, who accepted members of all castes? Whatever the reason, the evidence indicates that no one individual can be credited with the spread of *bhakti* in north India. Links with the north were further established by the *varkari* saints of Maharashtra and the growth of *Sahajayana* in Orissa and eastern India. Satish Chandra argued that the close connection between the south and the north was maintained by the tradition of *digvijaya*, that is, travel and discussion or *shastrartha* in different parts of India. However, despite this connection, there was a gap of at least 500 years between the popularity of *bhakti* in north and south India. In the south, the *bhakti* movement had reached its climax by the tenth century.

So, in the period preceding the sixteenth century, the focus of worship was on Shiva (for instance, the allegiance of the Sisodias of Mewar to *Eklingji*), but the situation changed from the early sixteenth century when devotion to Vishnu became widespread, leading to the *Vaishnavite* movement. The fundamental principle of this movement was the doctrine of incarnation with the Vedic God Vishnu at its centre, and love and worship of the incarnations of Vishnu. For its protagonists, Vishnu was the supreme deity and the other two gods of the 'trinity', Brahma and Mahesh (Shiva), were seen as deities created by him. The only way to liberation, they believed, was 'loving devotion' (*bhakti*) to Rama and Sita, or Krishna and Radha. Rama and Krishna were the last two *avatar*s of Vishnu, and Sita and Radha their respective consorts. The Vaishnavite movement thus had two forms: one devoted to the worship of Krishna that promoted the idea of reaching a state of ecstasy through *bhajan* and *kirtan* and the symbolic sexual union with God to achieve the ideal relationship between God and *jiva* (living embodiment), irrespective of caste, race, religion or status. The other form was dedicated to the worship of Rama.

The rise of the worship of *avatar* Rama, Sheldon Pollock (1993) argued, was a response of the Hindu community to the rule of the Turks, Afghans, and Mughals, and represented the search for a cohesive antagonistic identity. Devotion to Rama combined love with norms of social propriety and a stern ethical code of life. Tulsidasa, the chief exponent of Rama-*bhakti*, emphasised the divinity of Rama in his *Ramacharitmanas* (1575) and stressed the importance of social and political stability to achieve the proper performance of religious duties. He believed that people in general were evil and wicked, which necessitated political, religious and social control, and the maintenance of a reformed caste system so that people could not transgress their prescribed obligations. Such discipline and order entailed a just, discreet (*niti-nipuna*) ruler assisted by *sajjan* (well-behaved) administrators. But even they needed guidance, which could come only from a learned *Guru* committed to public welfare, who could attract a number of selfless devotees irrespective of their caste or status. Tulsidasa thus prepared the ground for wider cooperation with the Mughal State, which reciprocated by giving land grants to the centres of *bhakti* at Mathura, Vrindavan, and several others. *Ramacharitmanas*, written in Awadhi language, was derived to some extent from the *Ramayana*, written in Sanskrit by Valmiki, and retellings of the epic in regional languages, in particular the Tamil Rama story composed by Kamban. *Ramacharitmanas*, however, was more reverential towards Rama as compared to the *Ramayana*, with his divine attributes eclipsing his human character. Tulsidasa represented a fundamentalist or traditionalist approach by emphatically basing his teachings on the scriptures that had to be venerated and regarded as the fundamental principles of religion. By his *saguna bhakti* and his ecstatic love and devotion for Rama, Tulsidasa revived and strengthened the tradition of image worship, encouraging deference to and worship of a deity, thus reaffirming the tradition of reincarnation. The most prominent centres of *Vaishnava bhakti* were Mathura and Vrindavan, although these centres also represented the cult of Rama. A large majority of temples in these places were, however, dedicated to Krishna and Radha.

Gaudiya Vaishnavism was a mystical movement led by saint Chaitanya (1486–1533), who had renounced the world in 1510 at the age of twenty-four to become a wandering ascetic. The movement got its name from Gaur (Gaud), the sixteenth-century capital of the independent Sultanate of Bengal. *Gaudiya Vaishnavism*, dedicated to the worship of Krishna, the incarnation of Vishnu, was distinguished by its Bengali roots from other contemporary developments in north India such as the *Pushti Margi*s, *Nimbarki*s, and *Radha Vallabhi*s. The *Radha Vallabhi*s, for instance, gave Radha priority over Krishna and worshipped her as a supreme deity for her power to bring bliss to mankind, including Krishna. *Gaudiya Vaishnavism* as a theological system was evolved by Chaitanya's *bhakti* movement that originated in the Brahmanical society of Navadvipa and Shantipur. The sectarian character of *Gaudiya Vaishnavism* became obvious in the sixteenth century as it came to be disseminated by different groups: *mahants*, *gopals*, *upgopals*, and other *Vaishnava*s in Bengal and Utkala. Chaitanya propagated that no religion was higher than Krishna *bhakti* for, as an incarnation of Vishnu, Krishna possessed certain unparalleled characteristics, supernatural charm, and a remarkable power to destroy demons and tyrants. The movement that swept Bengal in the east and Vrindavan in north India was marked by a frenzy of passionate songs, dance, and ecstatic devotion. A unique combination of *bhakti*, ecstasy, congregational chanting, and dramatic performances marked the collective rejoicing, singing, and dancing in the *namakirtan*s, which were open to all regardless of caste distinctions, thus representing liberation from the priestly class and the iniquities of the caste system.

The movement initiated by Chaitanya was further formulated and developed by the *Gosvamins* of Vrindavan. For the *Gosvamins*, *bhakti* signified the intensification of devotion to such an extent that the devotee could experience a personal relationship with God. This relationship was mythical, and therefore indescribable. *Bhakti* could be either *vaidhi*, that is, 'regular', or *raganuga*, that is, 'devotion in consonance with passionate love'. Devotion in the form of passionate love for God, it was believed, led to the fullest absorption of the self in Him, but it was not carnal love. Krishna was regarded as the transcendental *rasika* for *rasa* itself was located in Krishna. In *Gaudiya Vaishnava* theology, Krishna in his human form was the Supreme Being; his adolescence was everlasting and everything associated with him was the essence of pure bliss. Krishna was considered *sat* (absolute existence), *chit* (absolute consciousness), and *ananda* (absolute bliss). He possessed *svarupashakti* (sentient power), *mayashakti* (non-sentient power), and *jivashakti* (marginal power); the third power in particular made life and the process of living a continuous reality. *Gaudiya Vaishnavas* did not yearn or pine for fusion with God; for them, the love of God was the fundamental focus of life. *Priti* or attachment to God was then the essential concept of *Gaudiya Vaishnavism* that purported love, affection, regard, which was unconditional, unqualified, and unambiguous. It believed that Krishna lived eternally in Vrindavan, making it the highest representation of heaven and an eternal abode of God from where love flowed infinitely to its devotees. For the *Vaishnavas*, Vrindavan emerged as the centre of pilgrimage with the construction of temples of Radha-Madan Mohan, Govind Deva and Gopinath. The temples of Vrindavan and *Gaudiya Vaishnavism* gained even greater popularity with the patronage of Akbar and Raja Man Singh.

The *rasa mandala*, Krishna's circular dance with the *gopis* or cow-herding women of Vrindavan, became distinctive in the visual and literary expressions of the *Gaudiya Vaishnava* religious community in the sixteenth–seventeenth centuries. The *Gaudiya* community venerated the *rasa* dance as the essence of Krishna's numerous *lilas* or playful acts and brought the relationship of Radha and Krishna into the *mandala* to emphasise Radha's deep, passionate love for Krishna, an insignia of selfless love to which the worshipper aspired. One of the oldest surviving *Gaudiya* temples, the Shyam Ray temple at Vishnupur in Bengal, had circular dance forms or roundels. The Shyam Ray temple version of the dance incorporated the figure of Radha at the centre of the *mandala* with Krishna. The importance given to Radha redefined the *rasa mandala* as a typically *Gaudiya* construct that distinguished it from other Krishna-worshipping groups in sixteenth-century north India. This dance form offered the worshipper a point of entry into the cosmic dance and direct access to Krishna, the object of desire.

In *Gaudiya Vaishnavism*, the 'feminisation' of worship was foregrounded since the essential nature of men was that of a *gopi*. 'Femaleness', argued Kumkum Sangari (2006), can be adopted by men to derive spiritual advantage once gender is extended into the metaphysical realm; also, the female voice epitomised the essence of devotion and the path of *bhakti*. Several male *bhaktas*, therefore, used the voice of a woman, wife or bride with sensuous desire or yearning. Mirabai's Krishna *bhakti* exemplified this context. She did not invent the language of passion, desire, and intensity for Krishna. Her *bhakti* was shaped, said Sangari, within prescriptive Brahmanical texts and the female devotional voice as it developed in the earlier and contemporary compositions of male *bhakta*s. It was conditioned within the overlapping contradictory configuration of the patriarchal assumptions of the medieval Rajput state, injustices within the family and kinship groups, injustices done to her because she was a woman. Despite elements of an *advaitic nirguna bhakti* in her *bhajan*s, she pined for union with God to realise the identity of the individual soul with God. Filled with sensuous yearning, Mirabai's *bhakti* could establish an irregular relation between a woman's duty and a woman's desire. Sexuality and desire, observed Sangari, were embedded and expressed within an ensemble of gender and class relations. For Mirabai, Krishna was the object of devotion and worship, her beloved, bridegroom, husband-lover, master, protector, king, and God, whereas she was the devotee, the eternal virgin, the bride, wife-beloved separated from the husband-lover, the servant, maid-servant and slave. Subordination was vested with symbolic power and became a metaphor for transcendence in Mirabai's *bhakti*. Caste and gender subordination acquired special significance in some strands of *Vaishnavism*, with Krishna being represented as one who was captivated and spellbound by the devotion of the lowest and the subservient, that is, women and Sudras. Social and patriarchal subjection formalised the path to salvation. Mirabai's metaphors were devised in this contradictory space for subordination. Her devotion characterised transgression and a reformulation of patriarchal ideologies in the face of resistance to Sudras and women. In popular imagination through legend and her songs, she was seen as a saint, a mystic, a devotee of Krishna, a *virahini* who abandoned the world for God, and as a rebel against the patriarchal system and oppression of women.

The *Vallabha Sampradaya* evolved in the sixteenth century with the establishment of the worship of Krishna at Gokul by Vallabhacharya (1479–1531). It is alleged that during one of his travels in the late fifteenth century, Vallabhacharya dreamt that he had to revive the memory of *Shri Govardhanadhar* and establish his cult (*seva*). Vallabhacharya proceeded to Govardhan, recovered the image (*svarupa*) of Krishna holding the mountain Govardhan to provide shelter to the cowherds and their cows from the rain, and began the *seva* of Shri Govardhananathji. With Vallabhacharya's approval, a merchant from Ambala built a temple and around 1520, Shri Nathji was installed in the temple on Govardhan Hill. The Vallabhas considered the worship in this temple the most real and actual dedication to God.

Vallabhacharya, known for his exposition of Indian philosophy, was amongst the esteemed *acharyas* of *Vaishnavism*, who propounded the philosophy of *shuddhadvaita* or non-dualism. For him, the only existing entity was *Parbrahman* Shri Krishna, also called *Brahman*, *Parmatama* and *Bhagvan*, who was omnipotent, omnipresent, omniscient, self-dependent, and indestructible, and manifested *sat, chit,* and *ananda*. The *jagat* or the universe, Vallabhacharya reiterated, was the revelation of his *sat*, while both *chit* and *ananda* were concealed from it, and *jiva* was the manifestation of *chit*. Asserting that the worship of Shri Krishna was the only way of redemption in *Kaliyug* and that all things dedicated to him ensured divinity, Vallabhacharya claimed that *Bhagvan* had revealed to him that *Brahmasambhanda* (relationship with God) was the only assured path to clean all impurities.

After Vallabhacharya's death in 1531, his sons Gopinath and Vitthalnath and subsequently his grandsons assumed the responsibility of Shri Nathji's temple at Gokul. Charlotte Vaudeville (1996) remarked that the sect founded by Vallabhacharya owed its present body of doctrines, rituals, and organisation to Vitthalnath. *Vallabha Sampradaya* became widespread in Rajasthan and Gujarat, with Nathdwara in Mewar as the premier centre. Later, its influence extended to Braj and other parts of north India. Akbar's *farman* of 1572 recognised the importance of Gokul as a township and patronised Vitthalnath by granting him revenue-free land for the maintenance of the temple and commons for grazing the cows, and enforced the remission of *gau-shumari* (tax on cows). State patronage to the descendants of Gosain Vitthalnath at Gokul was continued during the reigns of Jahangir and Shahjahan. Evidence from Shah Alam's period further corroborate that he had granted Gokul village in *pargana* Mahaban as *altamgha in'am* in perpetuity to Gosain Murlidhar and his descendants.

The *bhakti* movement in Maharashtra that developed as *Varkari Sampradaya* advocated the worship of one God—God Vitthala (also known as Vithoba)—and a regular pilgrimage (*vari*) to his abode, Pandharpur. The earliest reference to Vitthala was found in an inscription of 1209, while a Kannada inscription of 1248 mentioned Vitthala as well as the pilgrimage to Pandharpur. The origins of Vitthala were not firmly established. It was not certain whether the tradition of Vitthala belonged to Karnataka and if it was brought from there. But it was accepted that it reached Hampi through Krishna Deva Raya, a ruler of Vijayanagara, and installed in the temple called Vijaya Vitthala. *Vari* stood for regular visits to Pandharpur and *kari* defined the person who made the visits. The etymology of the term therefore implied that a regular pilgrimage to Pandharpur was imperative for a *varkari* at least twice a year. Vitthala was generally considered a manifestation of Vishnu or his *avatar*, Krishna. The cult of Vitthala as a young cowherd boy merged with the cult of Krishna as cowherd, and that was how Vitthala was identified with Krishna. While the *sant* tradition, particularly in north India, was associated with *nirguna bhakti*, the *varkari*s were, to a certain extent, *saguna bhakta*s, that is, devoted to at least one visible *murti*, that of Vitthala—considered a *swarupa* (manifestation) of God. It was the cult of Vitthala that gave the Maharashtra *sant* tradition a Vaishnava tradition. In the Maharashtra tradition, the *sant*s were referred to as not only Vaishnava *bhakta*s or *bhagavata*s, but were specifically also identified as *varkari*s, that is, the devotees of Lord Vitthala of Pandharpur. Yet it was believed that it was not the icon of Vitthala that granted salvation but devotion to the name of God: the invisible, omniscient God. It was devotion to the divine Name which brought all *sant*s—northern and southern—together. So whatever their religious traditions, the *sant*s pursued the *niranjan* (pure) and absolute, and it was these beliefs that transcended their traditional allegiances. This spiritual attitude blurred the distinction between *nirguna* and *saguna*.

The *varkari*s believed in the succession of almost fifty poet saints over a period of 500 years, all of whose lives were written as hagiographies in the eighteenth century. From amongst these, four known for their significant contributions to the *sampradaya* may be mentioned:

- Jnaneshwar, also called Jnandeva, a Brahmin and exponent of *bhakti* in Maharashtra, is usually credited with the foundation of the *varkari pantha*. Providing an intellectual base to the movement, he prescribed *bhagvata dharma*, equated it with *manava dharma* (humanism), and emphasised the importance of *bhakti*, *guru*, and the *sant*s of God in his Marathi commentary on *Bhagavad Gita*, known as *Jnaneshwari*.

- His contemporary Namadeva (1270–1350), whose verses are mentioned in the *Guru Granth Sahib* and who is seen in the seventeenth-century tradition as a monotheist like Kabir, came from a different social spectrum: he was a dyer and a calico printer. He travelled throughout Maharashtra and to north India, establishing thus a link between the two regional *sant* traditions. Namadeva made the teachings of Jnaneshwar accessible to the masses by the use of a simple local dialect and introduced a new vision by breaking class distinctions and including the low classes in the movement.
- Eknath (1533–99) introduced a new phase in the *varkari* movement. He spoke of the union of worldly life (*prapancha*) and spiritual life (*parmartha*), and believed that God could be realised more easily through *saguna* rather than *nirguna bhakti*. For him, God, the ultimate object of reverence and love, could be realised through *bhakti*, knowledge, renunciation, and meditation. He was convinced of the importance of songs and dance, which ought to be performed with the faith that God alone existed in the world and that there was no duality. He projected himself as a *kunbi-vani* (*kunbi* represented the agricultural caste and *vani* stood for merchant) and a Sudra, and emphasised that caste was irrelevant to salvation. He rejected both idol worship and pilgrimage to holy places and stressed on *bhakti* as the only way to reach God and do penance. He was dedicated to a form of *bhakti* in which God could be perceived in all beings and all beings in God, although he recommended idol worship for the common man who, with his limitations of knowledge, could not comprehend the presence of God in all beings. He composed many devotional lyrics and translated several *bhakti* texts like the *Bhagvata Purana*. His commentary on the eleventh book of the *Bhagvata Purana* acquired scriptural status as *Eknathi Bhagvata*. Acknowledging the debt of his *Guru* Janardhan Swami, he often referred to himself as 'Eka-Janardhani' in his *abhanga*s (a form of devotional poetry sung in praise of Vitthal or Vithoba).
- The movement reached its pinnacle with Tukaram, the fourth important *varkari* saint who lived during 1598–1649. A Maratha by caste, he too represented himself as a *kunbi-vani* and a Sudra and stressed on the irrelevance of caste to attain *nirvana*. Apparently, he had no *Guru*. It seems that the formless Vithoba appeared in his dream and instructed him to compose *abhanga*s in his praise. Like Jnandev's *Jnaneshwari* and Eknath's *Eknathi Bhagvata*, Tukaram's own *Gatha* was a valuable addition to the scriptures of the *varkari*s. He asserted that devotion to Vithoba did not entail the abandonment of the material world, and that God could be realised if His name was repeated several times and through *bhajan*s and *kirtan*s. Like Eknath, he rejected idol worship and the significance of pilgrimage, urging *bhakti* as the only pathway to God and the means to be rid of all sins.

The *varkari* movement that dominated Maharashtra from the thirteenth to the eighteenth centuries represented a protest against *vedic dharma* and the conservative, customary, traditional practices of the Brahmanical priestly class. The *Varkari Sampradaya* practised no caste or gender bias; it was equally accessible, notwithstanding the distinctions. While it was popular among the peasants, craftsmen, and traders, women and low-caste men had as much right to be *varkari* as high-caste men. The *varkari* movement was a spiritual confluence in which all binary oppositions were submerged: men-women, Brahmin-outcaste, poor-wealthy. The leadership of the *varkari pantha* came from the socially marginalised, deviant, unprivileged, and underprivileged. Jnaneshwar and Muktabai were ostracised by their Brahmin community and considered social outcastes; Eknath and Bahinabai were non-conformist Brahmins. Bahinabai was particularly criticised because she adopted a path of spirituality and chose Tukaram, a Sudra, as her *Guru*. Namadeva was a dyer and calico printer; Chokkamela, his wife Soyrabai, and Nirmala were Mahars; Gora Kumbar belonged to the caste of potters; Narahari was from the caste of goldsmiths; Sena was a low-caste gardener; Janabai was a Matanga (similar to Mahars); and Kanhopatra belonged to the *devadasi* caste.

Gender equality was evident from the *kirtan* and *bhajan* tradition of the *varkari pantha*. There were several *varkari* women saints: Janabai, Chakkubai, Muktabai, Premabai, Soyrabai, Nirmala, Kanhopatra, Rajai, and others. The literary achievements of these women were plentiful; their *abhangas* formed a part of the living tradition of Maharashtra and the *varkaris*. The *kirtans* and *bhajans* included the compositions of not only high-caste women like Muktabai, but also low-caste women like Janabai and Soyrabai. However, there was a certain ambivalence in the *varkari pantha*'s ideology on gender. While women were included in the sacred space, their status continued to be countered by patriarchal statements in the *varkari* texts. Jnaneshwar advocated egalitarianism and equality of castes but remained a strong supporter of the custom of Sati. Sati was not just valorised; if a widow dared to live after her husband's demise, she was ostracised and condemned. Regardless of these 'masculinist' patriarchal gender statements by the *varkaris*, whether from Jnaneshwar, Eknath or Tukaram, the social base of the *varkari* movement remained unstinted. Notwithstanding the ideological shifts, the *varkari pantha* continues to be a living tradition in Maharashtra and a significant part of its ethos.

The *bhakti* movement, which represented heterodox cults, stood against social and ritual hierarchy and Brahmanical puritanism, promoted the use of vernacular languages or local dialects against Sanskrit, witnessed the rise of low-caste persons as spiritual leaders, and also saw the emergence and power of women *bhaktas*. The role and contributions of women *bhaktas* can be understood in the social context of the time. Women saints had risen in the environment of social discrimination and social exploitation. While through their writings Kabir and Nanak emphasised a woman's chastity, motherhood, and negative patriarchal perceptions of women's sexuality, some others like Dharanidas focused on removing women from their traditional role. Others like Bahinabai also reinforced a woman's traditional position, but Lalla, Mirabai, and Akka Mahadevi rejected the customary status of women and challenged the patriarchal order. In the medieval-early modern Indian patriarchal society, the birth of a son was celebrated whereas daughters were seen as inferior; the morality and chastity of women were emphasised; a girl was considered an economic drain; and a girl's sexuality was seen as dangerous, which had to be controlled by marriage. Hence pre-pubertal and child marriages were prescribed, sati was upheld, and widowhood was defined as a curse, while non-compliance with these practices was met with ostracisation. Women were socially oppressed because of their lack of education and economic independence, although property rights for women showed some improvement from the twelfth century. As women *bhakta*s challenged these ideas, they flourished as thinkers, scholars, and spiritual human beings. Yet, unlike the male *bhakta*s, information on women *bhakta*s is scarce. This was probably because the women saints did not establish *guru parampara* or monastic traditions with disciples, nor actively maintained accounts of their lives and compositions.

A few women saints, however, had a following, but that developed only by the seventeenth century. In the seventeenth century Venubai, disciple of Samarth Ramadas, became the head of a *math* at Miraj in Maharashtra. Rupa Bhavani (also known as Rwaff), a seventeenth-century Kashmiri saint, had a substantial following, although barely any of her works have survived. She was referred to as Akleshwari Sahiba by her disciples, who called themselves *Sahib Dhar*s. Mirabai attracted substantial supporters known as 'Mirabais', but it remained a minor sect. These women saints received virtually no recognition from their contemporary society, which tended to dismiss them as 'mad' or 'shameless'. Lalla was called *matsar* or mad and Mirabai was referred to as *diwani* or not in her senses, but several saints like Akka Mahadevi or the 'naked saint' and Karaikkal Ammaiyan (called *peyar* or demoness) were respected both by their followers and others. Akka Mahadevi followed the *Virashaiva* philosophy and was an important member of the *Virashaivite* council of saints, and is also known for her contributions to Kannada literature. The *Virashaiva* philosophy believed that *sarana* or a devotee of Shiva was the bride, and the *linga* the bridegroom. The *Shaiva Siddhanta* saints invoked the man-woman relationship to express the God-soul relationship. The 'bride of the Lord' concept may have come naturally to women saints, but it was followed by male saints as well.

Lalla and Mirabai were married, but both were reluctant brides. Lalla was married to a Brahmin at the age of twelve and Mirabai was married to Prince Bhoj Raj of Mewar. Both had abandoned their homes and domesticity and talked of ill-treatment, subordination, and oppression in their marital homes. Challenging social conventions and social norms, Lalla discarded her clothes and danced naked. In her *Vak* (literally meaning 'speech), she related that when her father-in-law objected to her behaviour, she retorted, 'I see no men, I see only sheep'. Lalla was the disciple of priest Srikanta and a companion of Muslim *dervish*es such as Sayyid Ali Hamadani and Sayyid Husain Samnani. For these reasons, she was criticised by her contemporary society; now, however, Lalla is revered equally by both Hindus and Muslims. Muslim chroniclers like Pir Ghulam Hasan referred to her reverentially as Lalla Arifa and *Rabia* (saint). Mirabai, a Rajput queen, was expected to observe *purdah*, but violated conventional social behaviour and danced and sang publicly with abandon with the other devotees, wearing anklets (defying the belief about the association of anklets with only courtesans or *devadasi*s). Her confrontation was widely noticed when she chose the low-caste Raidas as her *Guru*. Unlike Lalla and Mirabai, Bahinabai was a Brahmin and an upholder of traditional customary patriarchal norms. Yet she was denounced when she decided to become the disciple of the low-caste Tukaram. Like Lalla and Mirabai, Akka Mahadevi too was a rebel. Deviant, recalcitrant, and rejecting patriarchy, the issue of Akka Mahadevi's marriage is shrouded in controversy. A source suggested that she went to King Kaushika's palace but never actually married him because he remained unyielding on his faith in Jainism, and refused to abandon it. Another account, however, mentioned her marriage to King Kaushika, although she later renounced it on charges of exploitation and oppression by her husband. Regardless of whether Akka Mahadevi was married or not, it is certain that she did not stay within the system. Forsaking domesticity, it is alleged that she walked out naked from Kaushika's palace with her body covered only by her long hair, demonstrating complete freedom from inhibitions and defiance of patriarchal notions of a woman's sexuality. In her *Vachanas* (words; speech), she narrated that she covered her body not to protect herself, but to protect others from temptation.

It is apparent from the discussion of these women saints that caste rigidities and rituals did not affect them. Most of them were rejected by their contemporary society, which prevented the upper strata from imbibing the spirituality of women *bhaktas* or interacting with them. Nevertheless, women *bhaktas* made significant contributions to the religious and social developments of the period and attracted large audiences from the common masses, artisans, and the low castes.

Embedded within an experiential base, *bhakti* demonstrated a language of aspiration and desire through personal devotion, direct communication, and interaction with a compassionate God. Yet, the hierarchy it had hoped to challenge did not collapse. 'The world,' as Rosalind O'Hanlon and David Washbrook (2011a, 2) observed, 'was not turned upside'; indeed, in certain ways, 'the hierarchy came to be strengthened, as religion collided with other historical forces'. The Brahmin *pandits* spread across the subcontinent asserted themselves with even greater vigour, prescribed moral values, and endorsed the authority of the kings. The rulers, too, were eager to obtain the commendation of priests and clerics so as to secure the approval of the orthodoxy and affirm the divinity of royal power. Ironically, hierarchies grew even within the *bhakti* sects themselves. As hierarchies became widespread, bringing into their fold kings, the courtly elite, and the people, they sought to institutionalise themselves, weakening the radicalism that the *bhakti* movement had inspired. The charismatic leadership of *bhakti* saints was replaced with a routinisation of authority and adherence to rigid rituals. In other words, the profound essence of Sufism and *bhakti* could not 'undo the orders of either this world or the next'. It became enfolded within them.

7

GENDER, ART AND OTHER CULTURAL PATTERNS

HIGHLIGHTS

- Profiles of Mughal royal women: Family, household, the 'private' and the 'public'
- Mughal royal women as *mansabdar*s, in court politics, traders, patrons of arts and aesthetics, as litterateurs
- The harem as a site of etiquette, culture, and influence
- Women other than royal women: *Madad-i-ma'ash* grants, family, household, caste panchayats and the State
- Mughal imperial architecture: Heritage, influence, forms, and contexts
- Mughal culture of gardens
- Mughal painting: Distinctive style, atelier of artists and artisans
- Genres of music

The Mughal State, notwithstanding its political and socio-economic processes to achieve legitimacy and consolidation, was essentially a culture State. Cultural grandeur and magnificence was in itself a source of legitimacy. The assimilative character of the Mughal Empire and its process of adoption, adaptation, and appropriation were remarkable in the construction of a culture that diminished its alien character, providing it phenomenal durability and legitimacy. A keen patron of aesthetics, including architecture, painting, music, language and literature, the Mughal State was a witness to an efflorescence of diverse forms of culture. Folklore as a stratum of culture, whether magic, miracles or faith, has a universalist identity that serves as a significant medium for the percolation of ideas. In this chapter, however, that is not a point of discussion; the focus here is on imperial culture. Yet another important facet of culture in any society is the understanding of gender roles, family, household, the private and the public. There are several scholarly works on eminent women of the royal family, the harem, and family and household that have explained interpersonal relationships—diverse, conflictive, yet relatively smooth—between women who came from varied backgrounds and status, possessing different temperaments and personalities, with only a few select men around them, generally the emperor, who was central to their lives.

GENDER ROLES

Women's active contributions to different spheres indicated a close interplay between the private (family, harem) and public (court) spaces, with virtually no distinction between the two domains. The performance of rituals was as much a requisite in private or family interactions as in the court or public assemblies. The private was never exclusively residential. Many activities took place in the public-private sphere, several of which were of immense political significance. In fact, during the reigns of Babur and Humayun, there was no segregation between the public and the private, in the sense of a physical demarcation between the court and the harem, although rigid distinctions emerged in physical spaces during the reign of Akbar. But even while Akbar's harem was secluded, sacred, and inaccessible to most people, it was not excluded from worldly matters, nor was it unconcerned with politics or power or disinterested in public affairs. The activities of women, the construction of permanent domestic quarters, and the conceptualisation of the harem were attempts to shape the new regime and consolidate its power. If women eventually became *pardeh-giyan* (veiled ones) and were confined to the seclusion of the harem, they did not lose their status or identity but remained crucial in the establishment and concretisation of imperial traditions and grandeur, which were indispensable—rather, critical—in the making of an illustrious monarchy.

Mughal documents attached significant value to gender roles, yet in some sense they represented a biased view, portraying women at the centre of the familial nexus, facilitating connections between different lineages and kingdoms. Even as they mentioned the births and deaths of all important elite women and focused on the role of older women whose age, experience, wisdom, and lineage placed them in a position of respect and deference amongst the other women and all men of the palace, the perception of these documents often undeviatingly reflected, as Manucci observed, that 'all Mughals are very fond of women, who are their principal relaxation and almost their only pleasure'. The harem was represented by many as 'an ordered community with its own decorum and gentility' that ideally provided a respite, a retreat for the nobleman and his closest male relatives—a 'retreat of grace, beauty, and order designed to refresh the males of the household'. Inhabited by a number of women with the sole purpose of providing pleasure to one man, namely the emperor, whose sexual appetite was insatiable, the harem seemed to arouse images of an 'immense fortified playground' for fulfilling a man's sexual fantasies, with hundreds of women at his disposal. Contrary to this imagery, it is pertinently noteworthy that 'harem' is a sacred word, signifying a place of worship, the sanctum sanctorum, where the commitment of sin was considered *haram* (forbidden). In concept, at least, it was a place where restraint was the norm, rather than excesses in sexual amongst other filial relationships. Challenging the stereotyped representation of the harem, that is, as a fixed, sensual, lustful domain of 'sin' and pleasure, devoted to the comfort of men, in which women were like wine—unfeeling, unthinking, and entirely 'material'—Ruby Lal (2005) conceptualised the 'domestic' life and activity of a world that was not fixed, unchanging, or unhistorical. She analysed the nature and meaning of the family, household, marriage, and the role of women in courtly life in the sixteenth century, particularly during the reigns of Babur and Humayun, the peripatetic emperors. Considerable changes occurred, though, in the 'domestic' world as the Mughal power consolidated under Akbar.

The meanings of love, marriage, filial relationships or sexuality were not fixed or frozen during the duration of Mughal rule. These emotions and relationships changed over time and were historically and culturally constituted according to the different needs, experiences, and conditions. Women entered the imperial family or were 'given' by their families to the emperor and princes under different circumstances, that is, to fulfil a political alliance between the emperor and a noble, or in exchange for land, or by capture. But there were also marriages made for love; descriptions of romantic love emerged strongly during the reigns of Jahangir and Shahjahan. It is from then onwards that the power of passion and consort ties became increasingly important, whether between Jahangir and Mihir-un-Nisa (Nurjahan), Shahjahan and Anjuman Banu Begum (Mumtaz Mahal), Dara Shukoh and Nadira Banu, Aurangzeb and Dilras Banu Begum, although romantic sentiments had been depicted even earlier in the *Baburnama*, which described Babur's love for Mahim. Analysing matters of love and the politics of marriage and reproduction during the reigns of Babur and Humayun, Ruby Lal evaluated the personalised accounts of love and marriage that Babur recounted in his memoirs. While Babur apparently did not remember any feelings of affection or passion towards his wife, he vividly recollected his infatuation for a *bazaar* boy, whom he called Baburi. The accounts are rather ambiguous for Humayun's reign, but it is a known fact that he did not leave behind a large harem or a wide range of relatives or kin in Amarkot, and that Hamida Banu Begum, whom he passionately desired, accompanied him in all his wanderings. In this instance, the family appeared to be a close unit, with the focus on a pregnant wife.

The understandings of 'marriage' and 'love', however, as perceived in Babur's time, changed in the different circumstances of Hindustan. Homosexuality, for instance, was a few decades later considered transgressive, with Akbar criticising it as a fundamental contradiction to the ideal of 'self-controlled masculinity'. Rosalind O'Hanlon (2007a) drew attention to the essential gender dimension in the investigation of imperial politics and identity, examined Akbar's self-projection as a universal monarch and the careful construction of imperial masculinity as a previously neglected part of the strategy of governance, and illustrated the development of patriarchal power in the sixteenth–seventeenth centuries. The character of the harem became increasingly diverse under Akbar, with his marriages to women who were Muslim, Hindu, as well as Christian. If Abu'l Fazl is to be believed, more than 5,000 women lived in the *zenana* in Fatehpur Sikri and each maintained a separate household. The concubines were allotted independent houses, the names of which indicated the days when the emperor could visit them; for the sex-workers, Akbar constructed an entire city district called *Shaytanpura* or 'City of Satan', with prescribed regulated hours for visiting them. Nevertheless, Fazl emphasised the necessity of the institution of marriage 'to preserve the stability of human race and progress of the world'. Reproduction within wedlock, he argued, was 'divine', for the emperor needed heirs; it was indisputably important for an empire even if there was no threat to the dynasty becoming extinct.

Expounding the norms of marriage that Akbar considered prudent, *Ain-i-Akbari* related his strong disposition towards arranged marriages and his insistence on the emulation of certain patterns:

- pre-pubertal marriages were strictly discouraged;
- no marriage could be solemnised without the consent of the bride, the groom, and the parents;

- marriages between close relatives were discouraged;
- huge dowries were deterred. Instead, the *tu'i-begi* (master of marriages) was advised to assess and scrutinise the circumstances of the families of the bride and the groom so as to tax them accordingly.

Gulbadan Banu Begum's assertions on marriage in her memoir, *Ahwal-i Humayun Badshah*, complemented those of Akbar. Writing about the marriage of Humayun and Hamida Banu Begum, she emphasised issues of organisation and 'control' in marriages. Women's consent in matrimonial matters, she stressed, reflected not only their concern about whom they married but, more importantly, the significance that they attached to dynasty and lineage. While negotiating a marriage, tradition, protocol, legality, and the minute details of social codes and social interaction were necessarily considered. For instance, the number of times it was *jayiz* (legitimate) for a wife to visit the king, the equal status that a woman could demand in marriage, and determining the importance of marriage (*mahram misazim*, in the words of Humayun) if the king wished to enter into a relationship with a noble woman.

Family, in early modern times, was undefined, with no particular term that could be translated into English as 'family'; the expression most popularly used was a compound of three words—*ahl o ayal* (relatives and dependents)—and that in itself suggested the family's vast dimensions. A non-public structure, the family was prone to several dynamics, like how the members of the royal family, their servants, maids, and others interacted with one another, the tensions in these 'familial' relationships, and the role of 'politics' within the so-called 'private world'. Polygamy was the prevalent predominant norm within the ruling elite. It emerged as a factor that ensured a wide, expansive family, marked by the presence of a number of women in the harem, which added to the power and grandeur of the State. An important occasion for a woman was her entry into the harem through marriage, for the objective of marriage was essentially the procreation of children, particularly sons; special attention was, therefore, focused on the couple's first intercourse and consummation of marriage, distinguished by a public ceremony.

The emperor was the only adult male with unrestricted access to the harem. His mother enjoyed the greatest ascendancy and influence in the harem. Being respectful to one's mother was a *Chingizi* custom (*buzurgdasht*, bestowed by ancestors), a tradition held in high stature by all the Mughal emperors. Abu'l Fazl reported that Akbar was extremely deferential towards his mother, replicating before her the procedure that was due to him as an emperor in the court. Narrating the instance of a meeting between Akbar and his mother in the twenty-third year of his reign, when she visited his camp on the bank of river *Bihat* (Jhelum), Fazl wrote that Akbar first deputed Jahangir to receive her and then, riding a horse of 'lightning and graceful speed', rushed forth to meet her and 'treating the making of reverence to the visible God [his mother] as an act of worship of the true Creator, he at once performed all etiquette, this exalted the level of his knowledge of God'. Jahangir, too, in his *Tuzuk-i Jahangiri*, reverentially mentioned the meeting with his mother in a village called Dahr, when he did obeisance and prostration (*kurnish* and *sajda*) before her and later obtained 'leave to return'. Aunts, that is, the sisters of both parents, were next in hierarchy to the king's mother. Within the family, while the mother and elderly aunts were shown reverential courtesy, there was no standard mode of greeting. Babur, however, mentioned the practice of bending of knees—a reciprocal bending of knees was indicative of a symbolic equality of status, while non-reciprocal bending suggested status hierarchy—as a form of greeting, which he appropriated during the visit to his paternal aunts in Herat in 1507 and later in 1519, when he went to meet his 'honoured elder sister' Sultanam Begum. Emulating the etiquette of her father, when Gulbadan Begum accompanied her family to Agra as a young girl in 1527, she did *mulazimat* or 'presented' herself to Babur. (*Mulazimat* is the term for a courtier presenting himself before the throne.) Her father (Babur) acknowledged the gesture by holding her in his arms and showered her with affection that she allegedly continued to remember even decades later.

For Humayun's reign, Bayazid Bayat reported a reunion of 'his sisters and female relations and everyone among the group related to His Majesty by ties of slavery or *bandagi*, who had the honour of kissing his feet'. (*Bandagi*, literally meaning slavery, is a term of honour, indicating a master-servant relationship vis-à-vis the emperor or his court.) Simulating the mannerisms of his predecessors, Shahjahan, Fray Sebastian Manrique asserted, showed graciousness and reverence to his mother-in-law and addressed her as 'mother' throughout the visit to his father-in-law, Asaf Khan's house for a feast. (Manrique was a Portuguese missionary and traveller from Oporto. He travelled around countries of the East for sixteen years, from 1628–43. He travelled through northern India from Dacca to Qandahar on his way to Europe. He was in India from August 1640 to November 1641.) As the emperor moved towards the inner chamber, Asaf Khan's family and the emperor's family (comprising the emperor, Dara Shukoh, and Jahanara) 'suddenly knelt down' to perform *kurnish*. Manrique described his astonishment 'to see so many polite usages and good order in practice among such barbarians'. Manrique's observation is significant and reflects his pre-conceived notion of a clear division of humanity into 'the polite and civilised Europe' and the 'barbarian others'. Over the years, these customary styles of greeting evolved from the bending of the knee to *mulazimat* and the kissing of the feet, redefining filial relationship between the emperor and his female relatives.

The elder women of the family were esteemed as political advisors to the Mughal court, as supervisors of the *zenana*, and as surrogate mothers of the children in the royal household. A significant customary obligation of the elder women was to incentivise the younger queens to produce heirs to carry forward the lineage. This task was especially crucial during the reigns of the early Timurids, Babur and Humayun, to protect and preserve their dynasty against the scourges of the Uzbeks of Central Asia and the Afghans in Hindustan. This context was vividly described by Gulbadan Banu Begum and noticed in the anxieties and concerns of Mahim Begum (Babur's chief and favourite wife) in her search for wives for Humayun who could conceive and produce a male heir. The elderly women, connected by either maternal or paternal blood, or as wet-nurses, or as 'mothers' through formal or informal adoption, were thus considered competent and valuable in shielding the Timurid–Mughal genealogy. Gulbadan Begum, in her memoirs, provided substantial details of the activities that engaged most Mughal women, whether in times of celebration or grief, comprising marriage, childbirth or adoption; celebration of feasts and festivals; moments of intimacy, strategy, and planning that they shared with the emperor; illness or death. But Gulbadan Begum articulated that certain emotions and sentiments were forbidden to royal women, particularly such intimate relationships and actions that were contrarian and unfavourable to imperial power. Profiling Mughal women, Ellison Findly (2002) observed that 'female townships' were comprehensive in nature, comprising mothers, wet-nurses or foster mothers, aunts, a heterogeneous body of elderly women, wives, concubines, daughters, granddaughters, nieces, women slaves, eunuchs, and several other relatives and friends. As invaluable compatriots, they participated in the working of the imperial court and in the business deals—domestic or foreign—even if from behind the *purdah* or the *jali* (screen), and accompanied the emperor on military expeditions, recreational and hunting activities. Women thus became both the inheritors and transmitters of tradition through these assorted roles.

The pivotal role of women in Mughal India—direct or indirect—in 'public' affairs was evocatively characterised by Babur while alluding to his genealogy in the *Baburnama*. He observed that women could be memorialised either as 'women who remember' or as 'women who are remembered'. The women whom he remembered, he narrated, were those who possessed exceptional ancestry or were married to members of distinguished families. Describing his grandmother, Esan Dawlat Begum, as one of the most commendable women, Babur wrote that 'few amongst women will have been my grandmother's equals for judgment and counsel' or, as an alternative, 'for tactics and strategy ... she was very intelligent and a good planner ... most affairs were done by her counsel'. It was not only her judgement, advice, and wisdom that Babur held in high esteem, but also her marriage to Yunus Khan (his maternal grandfather) and their three daughters (Mihr Nigar Khanum, Qutluq Nigar Khanum, and Khub Nigar Khanum). Reminiscing about his grandmother and expressing intense emotions, Babur described her prominent role in extending and perpetuating the lineage of the Khans and the eminent Timurid family. Babur was the son of her second daughter and, although the birth of noble children (like Babur himself) was a matter of routine, in the case of his lineage, Babur wrote, it had an extraordinary impact by heralding the dynasty, preserving it, and providing it with longevity. In the intensely patriarchal society of the Timurids, women's lives, he expounded, were not their exclusive domains; they were deemed to procreate, and uphold 'hallowed' and 'illustrious' traditions. In case they lacked the requisite ability to fulfil these obligations, they were, in Babur's words, 'sent out'. He cited the example of Ulus Agha, one of the wives of his father, Umar Shaikh Mirza, who was 'sent out' a year-and-a-half after her marriage, when she gave birth to a daughter who could not survive her infancy.

Mughal women had a diverse, complex role that contributed to shaping the political culture of the time. The elite women in Mughal India were not confined to mere subservience; their engagement with politics, trade and commerce, education and the arts was remarkable and valuable. Significantly, the princesses had access to the imperial seal that they could use while issuing *farmans*. The *uzuk* or the round seal, it is noteworthy, was kept in the harem. Although Akbar had attempted to regulate imperial life and therefore domestic life, which led to a distinct separation between 'private' and 'public' spaces, there appeared to be no rigidity in his format, as was apparent from his numerous political decisions that merged the 'private' with the 'public', the harem with the court. He appointed his sister, the wife of Khwaja Hasan of Badakhshan, as Governor of Kabul, a post that she held uninterruptedly for three years.

Elaborating the high profile, power, and authority of the women of the harem, Monserrate made some valuable observations on the role of imperial women in court politics. He observed that while Akbar was on an expedition to Kabul to subdue the rebellion of Mirza Hakim, he appointed his mother, Hamida Banu Begum, in charge of the *suba* of Delhi. In 1578, he supported his aunt, Gulbadan Banu Begum, in organising the pilgrimage for the women of the harem to Mecca. Abu'l Fazl, too, in his *Akbarnama*, narrated the pietistic activities of Akbar and gave an exhaustive account of the *hajj* exclusively undertaken for women and led by Gulbadan Begum. Delving into court politics, the royal women often functioned as interlocutors; for instance, towards the end of Akbar's reign, it was Gulbadan Begum, Maryam Makani (Hamida Banu Begum), and Salima Sultan Begum (Akbar's wife) who succeeded in persuading a reconciliation between Akbar and Jahangir, although they were not as effective in the parleys between Jahangir and Khusrau or in subduing Khusrau's rebellion against Jahangir. Maryam-us-Zamani (the Rajput princess, Harka Bai), Jahangir's mother, owned substantial wealth and was one of only four members of the court (the emperor was another) and the only woman to have enjoyed the rank of 12,000 *sawar*. Notably, she received a jewel annually on the occasion of New Year festivities from every *mansabdar*, determined by the potential value of their *jagir*s. Possessing the right to issue *farman*s, a privilege that usually rested with the emperor, Maryam, like Nurjahan, expended her wealth and influence for public utility—for instance, constructing gardens, wells, and mosques around the countryside. Nurjahan, regardless of her unusual relationship with her second husband, Jahangir, and her depiction by Pelsaert and Ralph Fitch as a 'crafty wife of humble lineage' and 'a very cunning and ambitious woman', was distinguished by her exceptional ambition, courtly endurance, military acumen, and ascent to power, which often saw her involved in strategising the court hierarchy, approving official appointments, and signing the *farman*s or the emperor's decrees.

Equally dominant in court politics were the daughters of Shahjahan: Roshnara Begum and Jahanara Begum. Narrating Jahanara's ascendancy in the court as 'nearly unlimited', Bernier described her as 'passionately beloved by her father'; 'rumour has it that his attachment reached a point which is difficult to believe'. Commenting on the political as well as personal attributes of both princesses, Bernier related Shahjahan's 'unbounded confidence' in his 'favourite child' Jahanara, 'beautiful, learned and statesmanlike', who, on the death of her mother, Anjuman Banu Begum (Mumtaz Mahal), became the head of Shahjahan's household and his companion for the rest of his life. Her renowned status in Shahjahan's court was established when she inherited half of her mother's movable property—the remainder was shared amongst her six siblings—the enhancement of her annual stipend from Rs 600,000 to Rs 1 million, and custody of the royal seal. Her political wisdom kept her close to power, first during her father's reign and then under Aurangzeb. Although Jahanara had supported Dara Shukoh in the struggle for succession, Aurangzeb allegedly admired her greatly and, on Shahjahan's death, nominated her first lady of the empire with the title *Padshah Begum* and raised her stipend to Rs 1.7 million. Roshnara Begum possessed the same vivacity as Jahanara Begum and, like her, influenced the political culture of the Mughal Empire by partaking a significant role in negotiating marriages, welcoming new wives and extended female family members into the *zenana*, and advising the emperors and princes on political matters. More importantly, as a sibling close to Aurangzeb, she remained his major confidante.

A few women of the harem were also engaged in intellectual and artistic pursuits. Keen to promote the education of women, Akbar had established a school for girls in Fatehpur Sikri. Seal imprints in a variety of fine Persian scripts reveal that some princesses, such as Akbar's wife Salima Sultan Begum, had their own individual libraries. Women of the harem, in addition to receiving instructions in reciting the *Quran*, were taught Persian language and literature, especially classical poetry. Many of them were active patrons of litterateurs who wrote in Persian. Zeb-un-Nisa, Aurangzeb's favourite daughter and his first child with Dilras Begum, was a poet herself, celebrated for her literary abilities. A mystic and a Sufi, she imbibed the path of chaste and pure love of God advocated by Rabia, one of the first mystic women of Islam, highly esteemed and admired by fellow male Sufis. Rabia lived in Basra during the eighth century. Notwithstanding the love and affection that Aurangzeb showered on Zeb-un-Nisa, he imprisoned her in the fort of Salimgarh in 1681 on suspicion of supporting the rebellion of his son, Prince Akbar. He even believed that she had plotted with her brother to assassinate him. Profoundly grieved, the emperor stopped her annual pension of Rs 4 lakh, confiscated all her property, and confined her to the prison to languish for twenty-two years until her death at the age of 65.

Jahanara, too, was a deeply religious woman and a disciple of the *Chishti* and *Qadiri* Sufi orders, as well as being a scholar of Islamic mysticism, held in high regard by her Sufi mentor, Mulla Shah. Empowered by her enormous wealth, Jahanara emerged as a major patron of arts and sponsored architectural feats like mosques, *sarai*s, and gardens in Agra, Delhi, Lahore, and Kashmir. There are several depictions of women of the *zenana* playing board games like chess and *chaupasi*; as patrons of music; or engaged in weaving, drawing and painting. Sahifa Banu was one of the noted female artists around the 1620s. She is depicted in a fine drawing from the reign of Shahjahan in the company of other women, capturing her surroundings on a drawing block. She is also known to have painted 'A Portrait of Shah Tahmasp' in the early seventeenth century. Customarily, women were more engaged in calligraphy. Timur's great granddaughter, Shah Mulk Khanum, allegedly presented a copy of the *Quran* to Jahangir, written in fine *rihani* script.

Mughal women actively engaged in determining the quality and types of trade items that could be used in the imperial court. It was during Akbar's reign and later under Jahangir that royal women became involved in domestic and international trade. Generally, trade and commerce were the domains of Muslim merchants along the coast, Hindu *bania*s of Gujarat, Hindu *chetti*s of Coromandel Coast, nobles, and members of the royal family. International trade, more than domestic trade, attracted two important women of Jahangir's reign—his mother Maryam-us-Zamani and wife Nurjahan. Using money from gifts and revenue from lands, women like Nurjahan traded in domestic items and controlled mercantile routes by imposing taxes on the movement of goods. Nurjahan was a party to a significant trading contract with the first English embassy that had approached the Mughal court for an official deal in indigo and cloth. Maryam-us-Zamani owned ships that operated on international shipping lines and carried a variety of items, largely cotton and indigo dyes. These trading ships often transported pilgrims to and from Mocha, 650 miles south of the holy city of Mecca. But regardless of her status, Maryam-us-Zamani was not immune to the risks of business. She often faced trouble in the waters: either she was coerced into paying exorbitantly high prices for a Portuguese *cartaz* or was chased by pirates, or her ships were occasionally hijacked and extraordinary demands placed on Jahangir. *Rahimi*, the largest of the Indian ships trading in the Red Sea, owned and patronised by Maryam-us-Zamani, was seized by the Portuguese and diverted to Goa, although the Queen Mother possessed the necessary safe travel pass. *Rahimi*, like the other ships, was not only trading but also transporting pilgrims to Mecca, a fact that made its capture, as Findly (2010) observed, both illegal and an act of religious persecution by the Portuguese. Being an adventurous trader, Maryam-us-Zamani could survive most of these attempts and carried on her trade activities, organised commercial contacts, consolidated trade networks, and pioneered normative patterns in trade that continued to be influential and imitated later.

Compared to the information on royal women, data on women of the middle and lower classes is scarce. But there is some evidence on the *madad-i ma'ash* grants allotted to women from respectable, educated classes. A different perspective on family and household other than the imperial family was constructed by Dilbagh Singh (2010) on the basis of *hasil farohi* (revenue head) contained in the *arhsatta*s (annual revenue records for *pargana*s), to evaluate the role of the State and its intervention in domestic, caste and community life in order to regulate interpersonal relations in a disciplined manner and in accordance with the prescribed norms and practices. These documents facilitate the study of the crimes, offences, violations of existing social customs, and the social groups that participated in them, in addition to the views of the State and contemporary society for the period 1680–1790. Citing examples from the *pargana*s in the Mughal *sarkar*s of Akbarabad, Rewari, Narnaul, Alwar, Ranthambor, and Ajmer, Singh observed that all castes and communities had their separate caste panchayats which had jurisdiction over the domestic sphere; violation of caste rules, particularly pertaining to marriage; norms for adoption; and customs regarding property rights and inheritance. The jurisdictional rights of the panchayats also extended to resolving intra-caste disputes. It was only when they failed that the State interfered.

Within the family, power belonged to the elders over the young and males over females, which implied that any challenge to their authority or any arguments contrary to their decisions were seen as violations of the code of conduct in a family system. The elders of the family, too, were reprimanded for their discourteous behaviour towards the young. In case of any altercation, the State intervened and took punitive action against the offender, regardless of caste, community or status. The State was also critical of the ill-treatment of women and violence against them. In fact, there were four kinds of family strife that were seen as crimes by the State, namely:

- ill-treatment of wives;
- assault;
- homicide; and
- sexual abuse.

The *hasil farohi* reported homicidal and murderous assaults against women by not only their husbands but also their husbands' families and other relatives; they also contained several examples of *chamchori* (literally meaning 'theft of the body') or sexual misconduct—adultery, rape, sexual abuse. Women's reactions to these kinds of aggressive misbehaviour were varied—sometimes passive when they withdrew from the family and broke all bonds with relatives, but at times they turned violent and even committed suicide. If, in such matters, the *pancha*s acted arbitrarily, the State intervened and ordered action against them. The State also regulated community relations and upheld the integrity and individuality of persons, irrespective of gender, caste, community or status.

MUGHAL IMPERIAL ARCHITECTURE

Scholars in the recent past have been widely engaged in studying the impression of political power on specific works of art, and how power gained legitimacy through art. Comprehending politico-socio-cultural history, it may be worthwhile to locate architecture within its larger realm and remove art forms from the sphere of exotic, and of purely artistic value judgements—themselves historically constituted—and bring them to the centre of history. Architecture is a central referent in attempts to invent collective memories and therefore inseparably linked with notions of heritage and identity. However, any endeavour to place the study of architecture at the juncture of a history of culture, society, and politics must be equally entrenched within the specificities of architecture as a form of artistic-cum-scientific production in which the iconic, the spatial, the functional, and the technical come together. In other words, it is relevant to recognise the centrality of forms and techniques to understand the creations and nuances of Mughal architecture. The architectural heritage of Samarqand, Herat, and other Timurid cities had played an important role in the development of the Mughal architectural tradition. Understanding complex geometrical patterns and proportions, Timurid architects had succeeded in designing innovative spaces that were vertical in nature, using elaborate transverse arches to produce spectacular interiors. Acquiring expertise in Timurid technologies, the Mughals also created structures with complex interior plans, elevations, and arches with *pendentives* (*pendentive* is a concave triangular surface that allows a square structure to support a dome) and *net pendentives* (*net pendentive* is a stucco—a durable finish for exterior walls, applied wet and usually composed of cement, sand and lime, used for wall ornamentation—decoration in vaulting or *pendentives*). Scale, symmetry, and dimension had a crucial role in imperial Mughal architecture; in fact, it became the hallmark of Mughal construction. In the Timurid buildings, brightly glazed tiles were used to enrich the exterior surfaces, whereas in the Mughal buildings juxtaposed inlaid stones and tiles provided colour to the façade. Gardens were another important Timurid tradition that the Mughals emulated. A significant Safavid Persian influence is noticed in the use of the double dome in Humayun's tomb in Delhi and the bulbous domes with constricted necks used by Shahjahan in almost all his buildings.

Mughal architecture was also influenced by pre-Mughal Hindu and Jain structures—forms that were used by the Delhi Sultans, too. The features adopted by the Mughals included *trabeate* (post and lintel) construction, where flat or corbelled roofs were built rather than domes or vaults; curved brackets and deep eaves (an overhang to prevent excessive sunlight from entering a chamber) were also a characteristic of pre-Mughal architecture. Many of the motifs—bell and chain, *chandrasala* (an elaborate niche-like structure topped by an ogee arch: a double curve with the shape of an elongated S), and *torana* (a serpentine lintel often found at the head of a doorway or an entrance)—were used by the Mughals, particularly Akbar, in the ornamentation of buildings. Imbibed from Hindu architecture, these features were also prominently displayed in pre-Mughal Muslim architecture, specifically that of Gujarat and Bengal. In addition, the motif of a bird—a design not sanctioned in Islam—on the borders of the gateways of Akbar's buildings is a representation of his spirit of tolerance. Ornamentation became more Persianised from Jahangir's reign with the appropriation of a new art form, that is, *pietra dura*, or inlay work with gold and precious stones. This style reached further sophistication under Shahjahan who used cuspated, foliated or ingratiated arches and introduced pillars with tapering shafts, voluted brackets and foliated bases—a technique that typified his architecture. As the Mughal power penetrated into regions, there arose specific structures, marked by absorption and assimilation, within imperial styles of regional forms—for instance, brackets taken from civic, domestic, and religious structures in Gujarat, terraced pavilions from the palace complexes of central India, and vaulting systems from Central Asia.

Mughal architecture resolved itself largely in red sandstone and white marble and represented the synthesis and culmination of the *archoate* (arches) and *trabeate* style of construction, marking its debut formally with the reign of Akbar. Babur inaugurated his reign with the proclamation of his Timurid heritage, and then proceeded to Delhi (his capital was Agra) to pay homage at the tombs, gardens, walled suburbs, and mosques of the important kings, including Qutb-ud-din Aibak's *masjid-i-jami*, heralding thus the visiting patterns of the Mughal emperors, particularly Akbar, Jahangir, and Shahjahan, before the latter made Delhi his permanent capital. This clearly showed that even when the early Mughal emperors (Humayun and Akbar stayed briefly in Delhi, but generally the Mughal emperors till Shahjahan lived in Agra or Lahore or, as in Akbar's case, at Fatehpur Sikri or their summer residence in Srinagar) did not reside in *Dar al-Mulk Dehli* (Delhi, seat of the empire), it did not mean that they were unaware of the importance of the old historical capital as a significant political symbol. In fact, during the initial years of consolidation, the early Mughal emperors did not reside in any of the capital cities but moved about; the capital was wherever the imperial camp moved. So whenever the Mughal court came to Delhi, the 'mobile Mughal court' settled here. But perhaps when Babur set about on his tour of Delhi, it was, as Ebba Koch (2001) argued, an attempt at legitimisation by retracing the footsteps of his paternal ancestor, Timur, after he had conquered Delhi in 1398. It was, however, not a mere re-enactment of Timur's actions for, in addition to getting the *khutba* read in his name to promulgate his sovereignty, Babur also made a pious gesture by visiting various Sufi shrines in Delhi, including that of Nizam ud-din Awliya. Babur's relationship with Delhi, then, was not that of a mere 'sightseer', but a symbolic gesture of appropriation of land for his dynasty and to declare his association with the religious and spiritual authority of the Sufi saints.

An aesthete and a biased critic of indigenous Indian architecture, Babur complained about the lack of planning, formality, and symmetry in the Indian buildings. He had hoped to invite the

Ottoman architects to implement his architectural schemes, which apparently did not materialise. His contribution to visual culture lay in the introduction of the Timurid tradition of ordered and regular ornamental gardens, in which the land was divided by water channels and pools. Such gardens, known as *chahar bagh* or four-square, symmetrical, walled gardens (usually considered paradise on earth), were imbued with political meaning, considered visual metaphors to celebrate the Mughal success in bringing order and stable rule to a land and people that Babur had considered chaotic and unruly. Evidence of Babur's gardens came from his memoirs rather than from any extant garden. One of his gardens to have survived in some original sense is located at Dholpur, approximately 50 km south of Agra. Carved from a living rock, the garden consists of a series of terraces linked by water channels and pools or *chahar bagh*, one of them in the form of an open lotus. By the late sixteenth century, the notion of *chahar bagh* in India had evolved into a terrace garden, with the tiers of each divided by straight bisecting water channels into four symmetrical quadrants. Two mosques from Babur's reign that have survived are the Kabuli Bagh mosque at Panipat and *Jami Masjid* (congregational mosque) at Sambhal. Built in 1527–28, both emulated the imperial Timurid mosque style, that is, a large central bay (individual chamber formed by pillars covered by a single dome) flanked on either side by rows of multiple bays with great vaulted entrances. The Kabuli Bagh mosque, built in celebration of Babur's victory at Panipat, was meant as an announcement of his political aspirations and a declaration of the new Mughal hegemony. The Babri *Masjid*, destroyed on 6 December 1992, was built in 1528–29 by one of Babur's nobles, Mir Baqi Beg, in the single-aisled multi-bayed plan following the Lodi style. Later, most non-imperial Mughal mosques adhered to this design.

With the accession of Humayun and his decision to reside in Delhi, there was a brief lull in the imperial visits to the city. In 1533 he built a new capital called *Din Panah* (refuge for religions), which was destroyed by Sher Shah Sur after he ousted the emperor from the throne and built a citadel instead, now known as Purana Qila. Sher Shah had given the name *Sher Manzil* to his *kushak* (palace) within the fortified area. This name continues to be identified with the octagonal pavilion built by Humayun inside the Purana Qila upon his return from Persia in 1555. It represented the 're-Mughalisation' of the fort although, ironically, it was from this pavilion that Humayun fell and died in 1556. The second site in Delhi connected with Humayun was also acquired from the Surs. This was the citadel of Salimgarh built by Islam Shah Sur near river Yamuna—it is from here that Humayun had re-conquered Delhi. Given his brief stay of six months in Delhi after the re-conquest of India till his untimely death, Humayun could hardly make any substantial contribution to the landscape of Delhi. Two mosques of his time—at Agra and Fatehabad—are extant, but in a dilapidated condition. Constructed of ashlar masonry, most of the original features can no longer be clearly identified; it appears, though, that its ornamentation consisted of geometrical patterns sunk in the surface of the plaster.

Sher Shah's patronage of building enterprises and architectural projects is evident from a variety of constructions—roads, *sarais*, mosques, and forts—that he undertook during his short tenure of four years. The massive stone-constructed Purana Qila can be read as a symbol of his enormous military power. Two gateways mark the size and position of this *Qila*. Its bastioned walls constructed of rubble masonry are a testimony to its solidity. The entrances of the citadel, particularly the *Bara Darwaza* or the main gateway, look sturdy but are exceptionally elegant; their design marked the beginnings of a refined, artistic, ornate type of building. The subtle aesthetics are further noticed in the *Qila-i Kuhna Masjid* inside the Purana Qila. Its ornate style is perceptible in the wide use of coloured stones spread throughout the mosque and cusped entrances—the features adapted from the *Alai Darwaza*. The façade of the *masjid* has five archways with a *mihrab* (an arched niche that indicates the direction towards Mecca) at the centre of the western wall. The interior consists of one large hall divided into five bays by lateral arches, but there is only one central dome and the *pendentives* support the wall. The *sahn* (courtyard), a distinctive part of all mosques, has an octagonal tank in the centre, and at the side is a doorway that served as a royal private entrance. Three techniques were used on the roof of the mosque:

- The centre has a *squinch* for the effective construction of a dome (*squinch* is used on the upper part of a square hall, converting its square shape into an octagon. If necessary, this can be transformed in the same manner into a hexagon or cut into sixteen sides. This technique creates a convenient base on which the lower circular rim of the dome rests without any portion being left unsupported);
- In the next bay, the design is in the form of a stalactite. Sher Shah built his own tomb at Sasaram. An enormous octagonal tomb situated in the midst of an artificial lake, it is a visual representation of the abundant waters of paradise described in the *Quran*: the specific *Quranic* verse that makes such a reference is carved on the interior prayer niche of the tomb.
- At the end is an unusual semi-vault pattern.

The other two forts—Rohtas (one in Pakistan and the other in eastern India)—served the needs of the public.

In addition, Sher Shah also built a tomb for his grandfather and father at Narnaul and Sasaram, respectively. These mausoleums, placed within a walled enclosure, resemble the Lodi tombs of the octagonal style. None of these tombs have a plinth; the building touches the ground, depriving it of the stature of tombs built by the Mughal emperors.

Akbar considered Humayun's residence in Delhi a symbol of the establishment of Mughal presence and built Humayun's tomb in Delhi rather than in Agra where he had shifted his capital in 1562. Tomb construction was initiated in the Indian subcontinent as early as the tenth century. Subsequently, with the establishment of the Delhi Sultanate in the thirteenth century, the building of mausoleums for rulers and the elite attracted greater attention. The Mughals, perhaps even more than the contemporary Ottomans and Safavids, were engaged in the construction of tombs, particularly during the late sixteenth and through the seventeenth century. Reflecting on why there are so many extant tombs, Ebba Koch (2001, 2014) has argued that tomb construction may essentially have been a form of estate planning in Mughal India; the tombs during the period were always set in gardens and exempted from the customary norm of land reverting to the State upon the death of the landholder.

The first major Mughal imperial tomb complex was Humayun's tomb that dominates the landscape of southeast Delhi, close to the shrine of the Sufi saint Nizam ud-din Awliya, and

Humayun's capital city, *Din Panah*, now known as Purana Qila. The tomb was completed in 1571 and designed by a father-son team from Bukhara trained in structural and landscape architecture. Surrounded by a park-like enclosure, the tomb is a well-proportioned large domed structure of a Baghdadi octagonal variety. The double dome appeared for the first time, mounted on a high drum, that is, instead of one thickness of masonry, it is composed of two separate shells—an outer and an inner shell with space in between. The outer shell supports the white marble casing of the exterior while the inner shell forms the ceiling of the main hall in the interior. Sitting on a high square plinth of red sandstone in the middle of a *chahar bagh*, it is the first of the monumental garden tombs in India. The garden can be interpreted in two ways—as an earthly paradise and a symbol of political control introduced by Babur. The first impression that the tomb leaves is that of its size; its effect is further enhanced by the use of a red sandstone veneer and a white marble trim that relieves the façade of its monotony. In scale, design, and garden plan, the tomb is an emulation of the Timurid architectural pattern. The interior of the tomb consists of a central chamber surrounded by eight smaller rooms in a plan known as *hasht bihisht* or eight paradises, derived yet again from the Timurid tradition. Emulating Timurid custom, Humayun's tomb was probably designed as a Mughal dynastic tomb, although no other Mughal emperor was buried here; Humayun's cenotaph is in the centre, with smaller ones in each angle for the royal elite.

Situated near Humayun's tomb is that of Atgah Khan, a minister of Akbar killed in 1562. Although similar in character to Humayun's tomb, it appears less refined, even though the use of coloured marble, low relief carving, and free embellishment of the wall surface suggests that the style had evolved into an elegant form. A second structure completed at the same time as Humayun's tomb was the Akbari mosque located at the shrine of the *Chishti* Sufi saint, the *dargah* of Muin ud-din Chishti in Ajmer. Like the earlier mosques at Panipat and Sambhal constructed during the reign of Babur, the multi-bayed prayer chamber with its enormous central entrance arch is not free-standing but, in the Timurid tradition, there are enclosed galleries to the east, north, and south. During the brief tenure (1560–62) of Akbar's stay in Delhi, Mughal Delhi was represented by the area between Purana Qila, the *dargah* of Nizam ud-din Awliya, and the site of the construction of Humayun's tomb. The *madrasa* of Mahamanaga, known as *Khair al-Manazil*, was also constructed during this period. Crediting Humayun with the magnificence of the city of Delhi, Monserrate, who accompanied Akbar on his campaign to Kabul in 1581, wrote that as he passed through '*Delinum*', he was impressed by its broad roads planted with beautiful green trees, parks, gardens, fruits, and flowers, with residences on both sides of river Yamuna (although Abu'l Fazl mentioned that in the 1590s, most parts of Delhi were in ruins and only the cemeteries remained). For Akbar, Delhi remained a place of *ziyarat* (pilgrimage) and entertainment; he visited the shrine of Nizam ud-din Awliya, Humayun's tomb, Salimgarh, and the hunting grounds in Palam.

The buildings of Akbar were chiefly executed in red sandstone with insertions of white marble. The style of construction was *trabeate* and *archoate* in equal proportion, with arches used as decorative arcades. The domes were usually of the Lodi-type, sometimes built hollow; technically, though, they were never a double dome. Carvings or boldly inlaid designs were common, while painted patterns were introduced on the interior walls and ceilings. Making a transition from the forts of Sher Shah which were generally rubble-constructed, Akbar, from 1565, initiated a series of strong stone-built fortified palaces across his kingdom, from Attock to Allahabad. The first was his fort at Agra that replaced the older mud structure. The red sandstone walls of the fort give it a spectacular, impressive appearance; ornamentation on the façade is rich and varied, comprising patterns in white marble inlay on the red sandstone surface. The aesthetics of the fort are enhanced by the arcades, arched recesses, and other decorative features like *cupolas* (rounded dome), kiosks, and pinnacles that surmount the gateways of the fort—one on the southern side for private entry and the other on the west, known as Delhi Gate—and those of other buildings within the fort. Abu'l Fazl informed that there were at least 500 buildings within the fort in the 'fine styles of Bengal and Gujarat'. Today, however, only a few of these remain; they were dismantled, re-modelled, and reconstructed by Shahjahan in white marble. The most notable of the buildings in the Agra Fort is the Jahangiri *Mahal*, a part of the women's quarters. Like Humayun's tomb, its exterior is of red sandstone with insertions of white marble and intricate carving on both the exterior and the interior. The fort, a remarkable example of the combination of beam and bracket, looks splendid, sumptuous, and majestic.

Akbar's most ambitious architectural project was the creation of a new city, 35 km west of Agra at Sikri—the residence of Shaikh Salim Chishti. Akbar began the construction in 1571 allegedly to honour Salim Chishti, who had predicted the birth of his son, Salim, but perhaps more specifically to celebrate his victory over Gujarat. Walled but not fortified, the city was named Fatehabad (city of victory), more popularly known as Fatehpur Sikri. A complex of palatial, residential, official, and religious buildings, Fatehpur Sikri is a solid creation in red sandstone and marks the synthesis of Indian and Persian artistic traditions, in contrast to the Persianised buildings of Shahjahan. The *khanqah* built for Salim Chishti marks the focal point of the city. It is entered on the south through an enormous arched gateway—the *Buland Darwaza*—that rests on a plinth of steps 54 metres high. In the *khanqah*'s inner courtyard is a huge *jami masjid*; its façade and interior reflect a combination of Timurid and indigenous Indian elements. The white marble tomb of Salim Chishti in the *sahn* of the *masjid* is exquisitely designed, showing the influence of fifteenth-century Sufi saints' tombs in Gujarat. The interior square chamber of the tomb that contains the cenotaph of Salim Chishti has an enclosed passage to facilitate the circumambulation of the grave—a practice observed in the shrines of all saints. The outer wall of the tomb looks splendid with a delicately pierced stone screen, and the ornamentation appears even more magnificent with carved brackets.

Several entrances lead to the palace complex of Fatehpur Sikri, but the main one is the *Hathiya Pol* or *Elephant Gate*, intended as a grand ceremonial gate for Akbar. Numerous pillared pavilions, constructed of red sandstone and ornately carved, are spread throughout the complex. The use of post and lintel or the *trabeate* style in the structures of the complex, grouped in clusters and related to the *khanqah* in axial and geometric terms, reflect the indigenous Indian influence, although the carved motifs are derived from both Indian and Timurid traditions. *Diwan-i-Aam*, to the east of *Hathiya Pol*, has the pillared throne of Akbar on the western wall, which implied that when his subjects presented themselves, they were faced towards the *qibla* (direction while performing *namaz*, always facing Mecca), revealing thus the Mughal imperial ideology as it had evolved under Akbar, emphasising the divinity of the king. To the west of the *Diwan-i-Aam* are several ceremonial and administrative structures, while at the southern end is a window through which the emperor gave *jharokha darshan*. Towards the north, moving in a direct line, is the *khwabgah* or Akbar's bedroom and *anup talao*—a square pool in the centre of which was a pavilion (now, only its base remains), allegedly meant for discussions, as Abu'l Fazl reported. Located on the same axis is the *Diwan-i-Khas*, the square *trabeate* structure, with its exterior similar to the other buildings at Fatehpur Sikri; its interior, though, is remarkably unique. In the centre of the hall is an elaborately carved pillar that extends halfway up the hall's total height. Its capital consists of S-shaped brackets, fuller at the top than at the bottom; the brackets support a circular platform, connected to each corner by walkways. This platform supposedly served as Akbar's throne, projecting him as the pillar of the Mughal State. Further west of the ceremonial and administrative structures are the *zenana*s or the harem. Composed of a series of *trabeate* pavilions, they were linked by covered passages to Akbar's *khwabgah*. Among these, a singularly magnificent one was the *panchmahal* or five-storey palace, enclosed (though no longer extant) within aesthetically pierced stone screens. Other buildings in the complex include *hammam*s (baths) where the hot water was brought in through terracotta piping, *baoli*s (deep stepped wells), and small mosques, whereas some others—like the chapel for the Jesuit fathers and the areas specified for gambling and drinking—can no longer be identified.

The cultural synthesis achieved in Fatehpur Sikri reached its culmination in Akbar's tomb on the outskirts of Agra, called *Bihishtabad* or the 'Abode of Paradise' and popularly known as Sikandara. The architectural conception of the tomb exemplifies indigenous effect, but it cannot be wholly ascribed to the personal influence of Akbar for Jahangir redesigned several of its features and completed its construction in 1614. The tomb is a multi-storied structure placed on a high stucco-covered plinth, similar in depiction to the plinth at Humayun's tomb. The arched openings in the plinth were specifically designed as spaces for readers of the *Quran*. The first three stories of the tomb are pillared and constructed of red sandstone, while the top floor, elaborately conceived in white marble, is left open to the sky. The tiered tomb, situated in the midst of a *chahar bagh*, was probably inspired by the 'promised mansions of Paradise' which, according to the *Quran*, would be 'one above the other' and 'beneath them would flow rivers of delight'. The use of white marble on the top floor can be interpreted in a variety of ways. The transition from red sandstone to delicate marble work shows the evolution of the dynasty and its move from basic means to opulent ones; added to this were the exquisite architectural tastes of Jahangir, reflected in the delicate screens in white-grey marble with elevated kiosks on the top floor. More significantly, the use of white marble, associated with the tombs of saints, illustrates the blurring of the distinction between kings and saints, projecting the Mughal concept of divine sovereignty. The reason why the top floor was left open to the sky is given in an inscription on the tomb's southern gate, the final verse of which reads, 'May his (Akbar's) soul shine like the rays of the sun and the moon in the light of God'. This gate, crowned with four towering white marble minarets, one at each corner, looks spectacular, initiating a new Mughal tradition of associating imperial mausoleums with minarets. The entrance, too, looks splendid, beautifully inlaid with coloured stones and white marble.

Yet another valuable architectural contribution of Jahangir's reign is the tomb built by Nurjahan in 1626–28 to memorialise her parents: the tomb of Itimad-ud-Daula in honour of her father's official title. Situated in the centre of a *chahar bagh*, the tomb comprises two stories with turrets on its corner crowned by *chattris* (small domed kiosks). The interior of the ground floor consists of nine chambers in the *hasht bihisht* plan, but unlike Humayun's tomb, which uses a similar arrangement, the central chamber is surrounded by two rooms on each side. The second floor is a single-chambered room, with its walls covered with exquisitely carved marble screens through which the light enters—a metaphor for *farr-i izadi* (divine light). The exterior of the tomb, created in white marble, reflects the emergence of a new art form, *pietra dura* or inlay work with gold and precious stones. The inlay work is generally in floral and geometric designs, but more remarkable are the representations of cypress trees, fruits, and slender-necked vessels for nectar. These symbols are probably an allusion to passages from the *Quran* and Persian poetry that describe paradise. What is even more significant about the exterior is its resemblance to the canopied structures over the graves of saints, emphasising thus the reverential disposition of the royal family, like that of the saints. The tomb, in its elegant and resplendent form, provides an invaluable link between the styles of Akbar and Shahjahan, heralding the emergence of Safavid elements in Mughal architecture and the transition towards the opulent tastes of Shahjahan.

Among the other buildings of Jahangir are palaces, gardens, and hunting pavilions in Kashmir, Shaikhupura near Lahore, and his most preferred palace, *Cheshma-i Nur* (Fountain of Light) in the hills around Ajmer. In addition, the emperor built palace pavilions in the Agra Fort and Lahore Fort (earlier constructed by Akbar), Mandu and Salimgarh in Delhi. One of his palace pavilions, extant and intact, is the *Kala Burj* (Black Tower) inside the Lahore Fort, known for its black stucco and unadorned exterior. Several mosques and *sarais* of Jahangir's time dot the landscapes of Lahore, Allahabad, Agra, and Jullundur.

Under Shahjahan, architecture entered a phase of magnificence, splendour, and perfection. It became 'botanised', as Ebba Koch called it, and made extensive use of balustrade columns, arched roofs, and marble in the buildings. Like in the other Mughal palaces and a few mausoleums, a noteworthy feature in his buildings was that of *jalis* or screens, often constructed from a single block of stone, meant to protect the rooms and corridors from the outside. These latticework windows made of red or yellow sandstone or marble exhibit the extraordinary creativity of Mughal stonemasons. They used a stone tablet that measured approximately 1–1.5 metres in height and a few centimeters in thickness to carve interweaving geometrical patterns or botanical designs, 'in which buds and blooms appeared to be growing naturally out of the stone'. In some *jalis*, the stone gives the appearance of wax moulded into bowed and curved shapes. Other distinguishing characteristics of Shahjahan's buildings included bulbous domes with a constricted neck, ornamentation with *pietra dura* and cuspated, foliated or ingratiated arches, pillars with tapering shafts, voluted brackets and foliated bases.

In the early years of his reign, Shahjahan constructed the tomb for Jahangir, similar in conception to Akbar's tomb at Sikandara and a glittering mausoleum for his wife, Anjuman

Banu Begum, popularly known as Mumtaz Mahal, 'the Chosen One of the Palace'. Jahangir's tomb, set in the midst of a huge *chahar bagh* at Lahore, is marked for its large sandstone platform with arched openings and towering minarets at each corner of the platform. Ornamentation in the tomb is primarily inlay work in marble, while *jali*s made from carved marble surround the cenotaph that was left open to the sky at Jahangir's wish.

The Taj Mahal, a monumental, enormous white marble tomb, is the most splendid, as Ebba Koch (2006) described it, in a series of mausoleums built by the emperors of the Mughal dynasty. No other culture of the medieval or early modern period, she observed, produced mausoleums in such numbers and of such vast proportions. Not even the tombs of the Mamluks in Egypt and of the Mongols and Timurids in Iran and Central Asia can defy the monumentality of the tomb. For Koch, the first Western scholar since India's independence to be granted permission by the Archaeological Survey of India (ASI) to measure the buildings within the Taj complex, the Taj Mahal represents 'the house of the queen in paradise', a monument of 'conjugal love', its perfect aesthetics reflecting the pure sentiment to which it owed its existence. Wayne Begley (1979) argued that the tomb and its garden setting are depictions of Islamic cosmological concepts, whereas for Catherine Asher (2016), the Taj Mahal appears to be a continuation of the paradisiacal theme seen in the earlier Mughal imperial mausoleums. For Francis Robinson (2007), too, every aspect of the tomb was designed to represent paradise, but it was also, he reiterated, a statement of the emperor's profound Islamic belief and of the central place that Islam had in his empire. Situating Taj Mahal amongst the great contributions to world architecture, Ebba Koch stated that the tomb was built with posterity in mind: 'we, the viewers are part of its concept'. The veracity of this statement was seemingly anticipated in the observation of Muhammad Amin Qazwini in his *Padshahnama* (1636) that the building would be 'a masterpiece for ages to come', increasing 'the amazement of all humanity'. The complex of the Taj Mahal, originally part of the urban landscape of Mughal Agra, the core of which consisted of gardens lining river Yamuna on both sides, now stands almost by itself on the bank of the river. In Shahjahan's time, Agra was a riverfront city, described by poets as 'a sweet-smelling garden with new blossoms'. A few of these gardens are extant, at least in part. Conceived as 'an allegory of the Day of Resurrection, when the dead shall rise to be judged beneath the Divine Throne', the complex was built between 1632 and 1647–48 in which skilled men from the eastern Islamic world actively participated. The main architect was Ustad Ahmad of Lahore, also party to the planning of Shahjahanabad, and the primary calligrapher was Amanat Khan of Shiraz. Notwithstanding repairs, restorations, and changes, especially in the plantation of the garden over the last 350 years, the complex continues to reflect the original vision of Shahjahan.

The charismatic entrance or the arched gateway to the Taj complex, situated in the centre of the north wall, faced with red sandstone, is quite similar in conception to the entrance of Akbar's tomb. Unlike the latter, though, the entrance to the Taj Mahal is marked by *chattri*s rather than minarets. The calligraphy, however, on both gateways was designed by Amanat Khan; while the inscription on Akbar's tomb is in Persian, those on the Taj Mahal are in Arabic, derived directly from the *Quran*. The theme is the same on both gateways that propel the believer to enter paradise.

Passing through the gateway, the mausoleum that dominates the skyline stands overlooking river Yamuna at the end of the *chahar bagh*, with the four water channels of the gardens representing the four rivers of paradise. The tomb is placed centrally on a high marble plinth and, like in Jahangir's tomb, each corner of the plinth is marked by a tall slender minaret. The interior of the main hall, a sophisticated statement of the *hasht bihisht* plan as opposed to Humayun's tomb, comprises two stories of arcades over which rises a semi-circular vault forming the inner shell of the double dome—a Baghdadi octagon like Humayun's tomb. The walls are enriched with murals and inlaid patterns distributed with restraint on the surface. The cenotaphs are surrounded by an exquisitely carved octagonal marble screen inlaid with coloured stones, replacing the original enamelled gold one; Shahjahan, as Asher pointed out, probably feared the looting of the gold. Ornamentation of the mausoleum is splendid and varied with white marble on the outer layer or surface. The use of marble can be attributed to a variety of reasons: marble, as noted earlier, was associated with the tombs of saints and later with royalty, blurring the distinction between the two; also, marble has the capacity to absorb light and change colour with each change of the day. In Islamic tradition, light is connected to God's presence, and therefore the tomb acquired spiritual significance. Other decoration motifs included inscriptions embellished on both the exterior and the interior; carved floral motifs designed on the tomb's interior and exterior dado or the lower portion of the wall; and *pietra dura* inlay work elaborately done on the imperial cenotaphs and the screens that enclosed them.

When Shahjahan died in 1666, he was buried in the Taj Mahal next to his wife. The question is: Was this always his intent? Catherine Asher observed that although the texts are silent on the issue, the fact that Taj Mahal was officially referred to as *Rauza-i-Munavvara*, 'the Illumined Tomb', a term shared with Prophet Muhammad's tomb in Medina, suggests that Shahjahan perhaps intended the Taj Mahal to be his tomb as well. He wished history to remember him like Prophet Muhammad, to conform to the Islamic theological concept of a Perfect Man.

The other architectural distinctions of Shahjahan included a palace complex, new capital city, and mosques. In the forts of Agra and Lahore, he dismantled some Akbari and Jahangiri structures—the *Diwan-i-Aam*, *Diwan-i-Khas*, the royal quarters—redesigned them, and replaced red sandstone with white marble; in the Agra Fort, the Moti Masjid or the Pearl Mosque was also refurbished. In the 1640s, Shahjahan concentrated on building a new planned city: Shahjahanabad, north of Humayun's *Din Panah* in Delhi. Its construction was initiated on the advice of imperial astrologers and Ghairat Khan, the *subadar* of Delhi, which transformed Delhi from a historical political symbol (*Dar al-Mulk Dehli*) into the site of new imperial residence and seat of government (*Dar al-Khilafa Shahjahanabad*). Muhammad Salih, an official historian of Shahjahan's reign, described Shahjahanbad as *markaz-i khak* (centre of the earth), and a scholar of the early eighteenth century referred to it as *markaz-i dairah* Islam (centre of the circle of Islam).

The plan of Shahjahanabad was allegedly influenced by ancient Hindu texts, *vastu sastras* (rules for architecture), that laid down the patterns for mechanical and fine arts. The *vastu sastra*s described the layout of buildings (both religious and secular) and settlements, their construction and habitation. For instance, *Manasara*, a *vastu sastra* (400–600 CE), advised that all settlements should have a semi-elliptical shape like a *karmuka* (tortoise), and such a design was particularly suitable for a site in front of the river or sea-shore. In the *karmuka* plan, the most auspicious spot in a village or town was the juncture of the two cross-roads on which ideally the temple of Lord Vishnu or Lord Shiva was situated. Interestingly, in Shahjahanabad the *Lal Qila* or Red Fort is situated at the junction of two streets, that is, the meeting point of Chandni Chowk and Faiz *Bazaar*. Shahjahanabad is enclosed by a huge stone wall—27 feet high, 12 feet thick, and 3.8 miles long. The wall, surmounted by twenty-seven towers, has gates and entrances, large and small, in several places. Joining the northern and southern parts of the city were seven large gates that enclosed the urban parts of Delhi, that is, an area where heavy mounted, vehicular and pedestrian traffic moved. These included the Kashmiri, Mori, Kabuli, Lahori, Ajmeri, Turkman, and Akbarabadi gates. The wall, facing river Yamuna, also had several large gates, namely the *Raj Ghat*, *Qila Ghat* and *Nigambodh Ghat*. These three *ghat*s served as riverside crematoriums for the Hindus. Further, there were small gates that provided pedestrians access to the city. Some of these gates were the *Zinat al-Masjid* gate on river Yamuna, thc *Farrash Khanah* gate, and the gates of *Gazi al-Din Khan* and *Ahmad Baksh Khan*. The two most important topographical features within the area were two hillocks—*Bhujalal Pahari* that became the site of *Jami Masjid* and *Jhujalal Pahari*, near the northwest of the city but hardly of any significance.

The inhabitation plan of Shahjahanabad was diverse. The *haveli*s of the royal princes and nobles of the upper strata contained gardens and water courses and were aesthetically built, whereas the lower ranking nobles and wealthy merchants had smaller houses built with stone, brick or clay, and had roofs of straw. Hindu merchants, who were generally rich and prosperous, lived in houses that had six or seven stories. Ordinary merchants usually lived in quarters behind their shops, but the soldiers, craftsmen, small traders, and generally the common man lived in straw-thatched mud huts. As the population increased and the houses multiplied, they encroached upon the lanes and empty spaces; this often resulted in fires during summers, leading to the collapse of mud houses, especially during monsoons.

The two important thoroughfares in Shahjahanabad were described in the historical sources as *bazaar*s, where the streets on both sides were lined with shops of different kinds. The largest and richest commercial complex extended from Lahori Gate of the *Lal Qila* to *Fatehpuri Masjid*; a canal, the *nahr-i bihisht* (canal of paradise), flowed through the centre of the *bazaar* and on each side of the canal, trees were planted for mulch and to provide a resting place.

- The Urdu *Bazaar* (camp market) in Shahjahanabad catered to the needs of the imperial household—soldiers, clerks, servants, artisans, and others—who lived in the neighbourhood of the palace-fortress and accompanied the emperor when he toured the countryside or resided in a camp.
- The *Asharfi Bazaar* (moneylenders' market) or *Jauhari Bazaar* (jewellers' market) were probably the sections that dealt with finances.
- The other major *bazaar* in Shahjahanabad extended from the *Akbarabadi* gate of the fort to the *Akbarabadi* gate of the city. Built by Nawab Akbarabadi Begum in 1650, this *bazaar* also had a *nahr-i bihisht* at its centre. An imposing structure in the *bazaar* was

a mosque—black, red, and creamy white—and opposite that a *sarai* and a *hammam*. In the early eighteenth century, Raushan al-Daulah, a noble of emperor Mohammad Shah, apparently put strings of lights on both sides of the *nahr*. Originally named *Akbarabadi Bazaar*, its name was subsequently changed to *Faiz Bazaar* (bazaar of plenty).

- Another noteworthy *bazaar* was *Khas Bazaar* that connected the *Jami Masjid* and the *Lal Qila*. The dancing girls, physicians, storytellers, and astrologers dominated this place and the shops here sold a variety of commodities ranging from cloth, medicine, cooked food, weapons, birds, fruits, flowers, wild animals, sugarcane, etc.
- While these markets represented the largest and richest of markets, there were shops and stalls in almost all the lanes and streets of Shahjahanabad. Markets known as *nakhas* were held in several places in the mornings and early hours of the evening. People from the neighbourhood visited these markets to sell their commodities, which were generally perishable goods and meant for daily consumption.
- *Dakakins* or retail outlets were a major medium of exchange—open for long hours, these sold both luxurious items and those for daily consumption—situated in the lower storey of mosques and within *mohallas*. The *dakakins* multiplied with the rise in population; but perhaps the other reason for the expansion of shops was the extension of credit facilities between wholesalers and retailers, and retailers and consumers.

As the population grew, Shahjahanabad emerged as the centre of exchange and the increasing demand for goods led to a high cost of living. Delhi continued to be a centre of exchange in the eighteenth century despite the weakening of the Mughal Empire. In the early nineteenth century, family-run businesses dominated. These families continued to live in Delhi despite the hardships following the collapse of the Mughal Empire. In fact, business transactions were now taken over by manufacturers, merchants, traders, and skilled craftsmen.

The *Lal Qila* or Red Fort or the palace-fortress of Shahjahan called *Qila Mubarak* was constructed of red sandstone and situated above river Yamuna along the eastern wall of the city of Shahjahanabad. Ebba Koch is the only art historian who was allowed to measure the entire *Lal Qila*. According to her, the whole plan of the fortress was based on a mathematically proportioned grid that facilitated Shahjahan to build a palace on the principles of bilateral symmetry. A moat 75 feet wide and 30 feet deep surrounded the fort, filled with water and stocked with fish; it also served as a shelter to the imperial household. Beyond the moat were a number of gardens—*buland* (high), *gulabi* (rose), and *anguri* (grapes). Near the eastern wall of the *Qila* was the sandy beach where people assembled in the morning for the emperor's *darshan*, and later in the day, elephant fights were organised on the beach for the entertainment of the emperor and the royal family. The *Qila* had four large gateways, two small entrances, and twenty-one towers. The gates towards the west and south—the Lahori and Akbarabadi gates—were the main entrances. The gate centrally located to the fort's western side led to a long covered *bazaar* into the *naqqar khana*, which was an entrance to the fort's *Diwan-i-Aam*. Shahjahan's marble throne, embedded in the central bay of the eastern wall of *Diwan-i-Aam*, was designed as a high platform surmounted by a curved roof supported by bulbous baluster columns. These architectural features, exclusive to Shahjahan at this time, emphasised the emperor's paramountcy and majesty. The back wall of the throne is immaculately filled with inlaid patterns of Italian panels of birds, animals, and one of the Greek figure Orpheus (a poet and musician who ventured into Hades to retrieve his wife Eurydice) taming wild animals. These symbols depicted an Islamic understanding of Solomon's throne, that is, the throne of an ideal, just, and wise ruler. This notion is visible in the conceptualisation of both Jahangir and Shahjahan in the Lahore Fort as well.

East of the *Diwan-i-Aam* are royal chambers arranged on a north-south axis—a canal bisects each room, including the royal chambers for Shahjahan and his daughter Jahanara, the *Diwan-i-Khas*, and a *hammam*. Most of these chambers are characterised by bulbous baluster columns, seen most prominently in the *Shah Burj* (used exclusively by Shahjahan and Jahanara). The white marble walls of the chambers are aesthetically inlaid with rare stones, using the technique of *pietra dura*. The southern half of the *Qila* comprised the *harem* and no male had access to it except the emperor, his sons, and the household servants. The largest building in the area exclusively identified for royal gathering and entertainment was the *Imtiaz* or *Mumtaz Mahal*, later known as *Rang Mahal*. It was here that the emperor played with his children, watched music and dance performances by the dancing girls, and listened to poets and storytellers. Near the *Imtiaz Mahal* were the *Aramgah* and *Khwabgah* of the emperor; protruding from the eastern wall of the room was a tower called *Jharokha-i Darshan*, subsequently called *Mussaman Burj*, from where the emperor received petitions and complaints. Leading into Shahjahan's *Khwabgah* is a panel with high relief carving in marble, covered with gold gilt of the scales of justice; this is believed to be a reference to how the emperor perceived his rule. Near this carving is a lengthy inscription in eulogy of Shahjahan that compares the *Qila* to the mansion of paradise. In the *Qila*, each structure is in the form of an open pavilion in one storey; their façades are shaded by wide eaves or *chajja*s, above which rises the parapet and, from each corner, a kiosk.

In the cities of Mughal India, *masjid*s formed a significant part of the religious architecture. Building a mosque was seen as a virtuous task and *waqf* was granted for the construction, maintenance, and payment of salaries to mosque officials. Shahjahan, too, commissioned two mosques in Delhi—an *Idgah* constructed outside the city of Shahjahanabad in 1650 and an enormous *Jami Masjid* near *Qila Mubarak*, completed in 1656 and known as *Masjid-i-Jahannuma* (Mosque of the World). The *Jami Masjid*, constructed with red sandstone, rests on a lofty plinth of steps that adds to its height and dignity, with minarets rising from all corners of the plinth. A black-and-white marble dome further accentuates the beauty of the mosque. The mosque has a huge *sahn* with *liwan*s (cloistered pillared verandahs) on three sides, a tank in the middle for *wuzu* (washing hands), and *mihrab*s on the western wall. An unusual and creative feature marks the three *mihrab*s, which have pierced stone screens that allow the light to come in—a reference to the *Quranic* verse that compares God's presence to a lamp in a niche. The arched effect is continued in the surface decoration of the *masjid* in the form of panels designed with blue and yellow tiles containing ornamental and foliated arches. Aesthetically built, the mosque looks symmetrical and formal, with its architectural treatment and decoration in conformity with its large dimensions.

Building art did not decline with Aurangzeb; distinct from his predecessors, his interests lay not in the creation of palace complexes but in the construction of *sarai*s, baths, gardens, fortified walls, tombs, and mosques. He is known to have introduced new architectural techniques, particularly in the construction of mosques. Aurangzeb built three mosques in the initial years of his reign: *Moti Masjid* or the Pearl Mosque inside the *Lal Qila*, the *Badshahi* Mosque in the precincts of the Lahore Fort, and a mosque in Mathura. *Moti Masjid*, built in 1662 and intended as the emperor's private mosque, is a delicate white marble building with graceful domes, almost Rococo in appearance. The rich organic ornamentation on the *masjid* was interpreted by Ebba Koch as a reflection of Aurangzeb's lack of personal interest in his architectural projects, but Catherine Asher (1992a) argued that forms that were earlier considered appropriate for palace architecture—such as the decoration on Shahjahan's Delhi throne—were now used in palace mosques. Keen on formality and sobriety in architecture, Aurangzeb used fine embellishments on the mosque. The *Badshahi* Mosque built in 1673–74 displays features similar to Shahjahan's *Jami Masjid* in Delhi. Constructed with red sandstone and white marble, the mosque, designed to be both an *idgah* and a *jami masjid*, is enormous in size. It has a large *sahn*, five open *liwan*s, and an elaborately decorated interior with delicately painted stucco. Aurangzeb's distinct architectural style comes across remarkably in the tomb of his wife, Rabia Durrani, that he built in Aurangabad in 1660–61. Contrary to the perfect balance, proportion, and symmetry in Shahjahan's buildings, the tomb reflects new aesthetics, with the emphasis on verticality. The tomb in this new spatial arrangement and its naturalistic fine floral ornamentation—much of it in stucco—renders the style novel. The declining political strength and wealth of the Mughal Empire in the eighteenth century may have caused a shift in the patronage of architecture from the imperial dynasty to wealthy nobles and merchants and the regional states, but building art did not cease; emulations, imitations, technical skills, and the efflorescence of the art continued to be noticed in the regions.

MUGHAL CULTURE OF GARDENS

Gardens are no longer conceived as merely a site or a physical space, but are seen more as a cultural space and an aesthetic form that harmonise the visual with the senses of smell and hearing, a space with light, sound, and fragrance that may engender mystical and ethical experiences or even romantic sentiment. Narratives on gardens and their spatial organisation have often represented them as that which 'epitomize a human urge to shape nature so as to cast it as a space for multifarious human activities'. Travel writings cutting across international boundaries—whether Ibn Batuta's *Rihla*, Babur's impressions of Hindustan, or descriptions and mapping of the gardens in Isfahan or any other—have hailed gardens as conspicuous elements of civilised societies. Gardens were central to the understanding of Mughal life, art, and architecture, providing a valuable historical perspective on the events of the past. Gardens of the Mughal Empire that visibly embody Mughal cultural attitudes greatly influenced the colonial concept of gardens in the Indian subcontinent, probably because the Mughal gardens (and the palaces and mausoleums to which they were generally attached) were better preserved as compared to those of their predecessors. The British anxiety to preserve Mughal legacy was probably motivated by the objective of consolidating their political legitimacy; or perhaps their interest in Mughal gardens was inspired by their metropolitan concerns or to evolve notions of gardens and landscapes in Victorian England.

Mughal gardens and garden architecture in Delhi, Agra, Fatehpur Sikri, and Lahore have inspired specific studies as well as synthetic overviews that had earlier focused on a discussion of classifications or 'typologies' of Mughal gardens, and examined the historical influences upon them. Researches from the 1990s have generally concentrated on the form, function, and meaning of the gardens. A concept much debated in any conversation on gardens in South Asia during early modern times is the notion of the 'Islamic garden'. While Richard Ettinghausen in the introduction to *The Islamic Garden* (1976) hailed the studies of garden traditions of the Islamic realm from Spain to India rather than those of a particular region or people, many others from the mid-1990s contributed to a new perspective and argued for Mughal gardens as representations of a distinct garden tradition, rather than as a subject of Islamic gardens. Some even questioned the generalised concept of 'Islamic garden' and 'Islamic city' in view of the variations in opinions expressed by different Muslim groups, places, and times. The notion of the 'Islamic garden', a construct of the discipline of Art History, has, however, tended to be upheld for two reasons.

- First, it is posited that the Islamic garden is essentially an earthly representation of Paradise as narrated in the *Quran*, even though the *Quran* makes no mention of the layout of the gardens of Paradise. Nevertheless, many have interpreted the description of the four rivers in Paradise as the origin of the geometrical compartmented gardens or four-square symmetrical, walled gardens, known as *chahar bagh*. It is argued that the idea of the Islamic garden and its assumed layout was probably influenced by the existence of the Mughal gardens that have long outlived the empire, and the early study of these gardens in India. While scholarly studies from the 1970s observed that the layout of *chahar bagh* was a legacy of the Persianate tradition, going back to Achaemenid Persia, counter-claims by several others suggested that its roots can be traced to ancient Egypt. The idea that the Islamic garden was a *chahar bagh* has, however, endured.
- This explains the second assumption that has supported the notion of the 'Islamic garden'. It argued that the stable constituent features (roses, tulips, jasmine, and rivers) of the Islamic garden were used as metaphors across the Islamic world by poets to construct a traditional and stylised image of Paradise. Notwithstanding this, it has been asserted that while a few of these characteristics have stimulated historical ideas in the history of West and South Asia, nowhere have they become parts of a coherent entity of the 'Islamic garden'.

Prior to the establishment of Mughal rule in India, the Indo-Persian tradition of creating gardens had flourished. The Sultans of Delhi, Malwa, Jaunpur, Gujarat, the Bahmani kingdom, and others, as well as their nobles built gardens in northern India and Deccan. In cities like Champanir and Ahmadabad, gardens were luxuriant, impressive and profusely spread. The Mughal emperors in the early sixteenth century introduced new intensity and passion to the construction of gardens in north India, making them a hallmark of the elite imperial culture that served a ceremonial purpose—pleasure and entertainment. If the Mughal gardens are considered within the broad framework of landscape research, as suggested by James Wescoat Jr. and Joachim Wolschke-Bulmahn (1996), it entails the understanding of some issues: the scenery or the landscape that these artefacts represented for their designers, users, and patrons; the emotional and aesthetic responses that they evoked amongst those who viewed them and walked among them; the extent to which the designers or creators of each garden fulfilled the aesthetic and cultural needs.

The analysis of these issues necessitates the study of an intertwined aspect in landscape research, that is, the social context of gardens. Laid formally, gardens were seen as an accessible symbol for territorial and social domination. Following the Timurid concept, gardens were generally built at locations that were not only outside of and distinct from the walled towns, but that were also discrete from ordinary cultivated lands or common pastoral lands. Wescoat argued that the gardens were a 'middle landscape—a synthesis of meadow and orchard, which interacted harmoniously or antagonistically with the walled towns of Central Asia'. In the context of Central Asia, it can be observed that in the fifteenth and early sixteenth century, gardens provided a flexible, enclosed, royal space where the rulers could preside over a large gathering of military men. Suburban gardens emerged as the focal point from which walled cities and towns were conquered. Babur, in the early sixteenth century, had used these bounded but open spaces to initiate military campaigns, celebrate triumphs, conduct royal audiences, and pronounce punishments. Subsequent to the conquest of Kabul in 1509, Babur's first act was to construct a garden, the *Bagh-i Wafa*, 'Garden of the Faithful' (see Plate 3).

In 1526, Babur introduced Central Asian traditions of garden design in India, but he also emphasised on gardens as places of territorial expansion and as a medium to proclaim his newly acquired power. Upon conquering India, Babur built gardens along the way, not only in an attempt to capture the beauty of the natural landscape, but also to claim the territory. He sought, as he observed in the *Baburnama*, to make 'that charmless and disorderly Hind more like home'. Consequently, gardens were laid out within fortresses, royal palaces, inside and outside the walled capital cities. Gardens along riverbanks and important routes of travel were used for pleasure, entertainment, convivial parties, and for ceremonial purposes; but whatever the occasion, the intention was clear: to assert the presence of royal power and authority. When he acquired Lahore in 1526—a provincial capital before it became the imperial capital briefly towards the end of the sixteenth century—Babur constructed gardens along its riverbanks, paving the way for two centuries of urban landscape. He expressed the skill of controlling territory by making confederations of military and cultural groups on the one hand, while on the other, he created spaces that were clear, functional, aesthetically defined, and symbolised discipline that could impose, as he believed, order over the 'disorderly, dusty landscape of India'. For Babur, each royal garden symbolised the formal symmetry of imperial rule, as opposed to the 'turbulent, multi-layered social landscape of India'. Metaphorically, perhaps, Babur's message was that just as the physical landscape was disciplined by the emperor, so was the society.

The period following Babur's reign, that of Humayun, has often been ignored by garden historians, regardless of contemporary sources that reveal that despite his inept handling of administration and political misadventures, Humayun was an 'inventive genius' who pioneered significant innovations in the design of the Mughal garden. He introduced extensive experimentation and transformation in the concept of the garden and infused it with mystical significance, marking a difference with Babur, who had hardly stressed on the religious dimension of garden design. Contrary to the pattern under Babur, the gardens were no longer associated with territorial control but became 'places of territorial contraction' or 'places of refuge'. This information on the garden conventions and innovations in Humayun's time, in the absence of any extant garden, is derived from the first paintings of Mughal garden scenes that date to his period. It appears that Humayun had intended the construction of *Din Panah* as a seven-storey palace surrounded by orchards and gardens, but before he could implement his visionary project, he was compelled to seek refuge in Persia, making it difficult to conjecture about the gardens that he might have planned for his new city.

Akbar's reign, which witnessed massive architectural complexes, included gardens as well in his different capital cities—Agra, Fatehpur Sikri, and Lahore. Synthesising garden traditions, Akbar combined Humayun's fascination with mysticism and Babur's link between garden and territorial control with his paternal ancestor Timur's fusion of gardens and urban design. Patronising suburban and riverfront gardens that continued to flourish, Akbar revived the Timurid tradition of constructing gardens within the city and the citadel. The rhetoric of the garden and the emperor as gardener, devised under Babur, was also noticed in Akbar's reign when, in 1586 in his diplomatic letter to Abdullah Khan of Balkh, he invoked the metaphor of garden to refer to his own accomplishments in the thirty years of his rule. The reiteration of the practice of associating gardens with imperial authority was evident during Akbar's tour of Punjab in 1591, when he was ceremoniously weighed against different items to be distributed to the poor, a gesture linked to the annual solar festival. Subsequent to the ceremony, the emperor ordered the local *jagirdar*, Zain Khan Koka, to convert the site where he was weighed into a garden, and named it Zainabad.

While on occasions gardens could be the scene of formal ceremonies, they were remarkably significant in the convivial culture of the imperial court, sensual and pleasantly delightful in the warm Indian climate that touched the aesthetic sensibilities of not only the emperor, but also his nobles and women of the *zenana*. This form of gardens represented the Mughal court in its social mode. Akbar patronised the convivial aristocratic functions in the gardens and emulated the garden festivals that marked the early years of Humayun's reign. In 1582, he revived the celebration of *Nauroz* or the Persian New Year, initiated and organised by Humayun in the Agra *chahar bagh*. Religious symbolism and rituals had defined the celebrations in Humayun's time, but under Akbar, festivities in the gardens became essentially secular—for instance, to signify the spring equinox, which led to several weeks of banquets, merriment, and excursions. The magnificent imperial gardens of Kashmir made by Akbar, Jahangir, and Shahjahan were designed primarily for aesthetic and convivial purposes, in addition to their role as statements of power and domination. In fact, most imperial gardens of Kashmir and elsewhere in the empire had a secular rather than a religious objective. Kashmir was the ideal chosen land for constructing gardens: Akbar built the first Mughal garden, *Nasim Bagh*, in 1597 near Dal Lake; *Nishat Bagh* was laid out by Asaf Khan, and *Shalimar Bagh* by Jahangir in 1619. The Shalimar Garden in Lahore that illustrates the Mughal notion of an ideal garden was named after the one in Kashmir. Jahangir created not only gardens but also hunting complexes that comprised the features of a garden, such as the *Hiran Minar* near Lahore.

The most renowned and enduring projects of Mughal gardens were undertaken by Shahjahan, the women of his harem, his sons and courtiers. Shahjahan rebuilt many of the garden courts in the forts of Agra and Lahore and sponsored the synthesis of garden design and urban design in his capital city Shahjahanabad, in Delhi. The concept of gardens in Shahjahanabad was influenced both by the notion of Paradise as a garden and the West Asian Islamic custom of royal pleasure gardens. Imitating these patterns, the emperor reworked and refined these designs to create gardens. An urban garden during the Mughal period was characteristically rectangular in shape and enclosed by high walls; but the major feature in these gardens was a central pool with a small open structure called *barahdari* (summer house). In Shahjahanabad, in addition to these features, there were also canals, flowers, birds, and fish. The cypress and fruit trees in the gardens had a special significance. The cypress symbolised death and therefore eternity, and the fruit trees, especially mango, plum, and almond, represented life and hope. In other words, cypress and fruit trees in a garden brought together the harmony of life and death, the ephemeral and the eternal, joy and happiness.

In the given Timurid tradition, gardens, whether established by Mughal emperors or the nobles, were situated beyond the city walls; for instance, Shahjahan established a garden called Khizrabad on the west bank of river Yamuna about 5 miles south of the Akbarabadi gate of the city; another garden, Tis Hazari Bagh, was created outside the Kabuli gate of the city. Like Akbar, Shahjahan too linked gardens to an assertion of imperial power, and often demonstrated this by establishing new gardens when on tour or on military expeditions. In 1646, for example, while leading the Qandahar campaign from Kabul, he issued a *farman* to construct a garden at the village of Nimla near Kabul by diverting the stream that flowed through the town. His sons explored and extended different strands of garden tradition: Dara Shukoh was inclined towards the mystical dimensions of design; Shah Shuja leaned towards the riverfront garden tradition; and Aurangzeb towards dynastic tomb-gardens. In 1659, Aurangzeb built a garden southeast of Agra at Fatehabad in celebration of his victory over his brothers in the struggle for succession. The walled garden was a pleasure garden with a brick and sandstone pavilion in the centre.

Gardens were confined, closely bound areas and, like the harem, enclosures were protracted spaces that facilitated their use by women; this symbolised the notion of feminine exclusion. It was during the reign of Akbar that women emerged as prominent patrons and supervisors of garden designs, especially in the case of Humayun's tomb-garden. Like Maryam Makani, many other royal women contributed to garden construction. Nurjahan, along with her father and brothers, became one of the foremost patrons of garden design in the capital cities, caravanserais, and the leading land of gardens, Kashmir. In 1621, she built the Ram Bagh in Agra, wrongly attributed to Babur. In close proximity to this garden, Zahara Bagh, also ascribed to Babur, was constructed under the patronage of Mumtaz Mahal. In 1650, Roshnara Begum laid a large garden near the

Lahori gate of the city of Shahjahanabad, known as *Sabzi Mandi*. Nawab Akbarabadi Begum established yet another garden in Shahjahanabad known as Shalimar, in the same style as the Shalimar gardens of Lahore and Kashmir in 1653–54. The most artistic garden in Shahjahanabad was the one created by Jahanara Begum in 1650, north of Chandni Chowk, called Sahibabad. Built in a rectangular design, the garden covered about 50 acres and comprised canals, waterfalls, fountains, pools, flowers, trees, *barahdaris*, and a *nahr-i-bihisht* for an elaborate water supply. The construction of gardens continued into the eighteenth century. Amongst these, significant is *Qudsiya Bagh* on the bank of river Yamuna, north of Kashmiri gate, constructed in 1748 by Nawab Qudsiya Begum, wife of Mughal Emperor Mohammad Shah.

The royal pleasure gardens of the Mughals stood in sharp contrast to the formal gardens designed for the royal tombs or tombs for the nobles. Royal tomb-gardens represented the emerging royal cult in which the living monarch and his court prayed for his deceased ancestors. Humayun's tomb was the first such shrine; his descendants offered prayers and made a ritual circumambulation of the tomb. Akbar was buried in a monumental garden complex at Sikandara, northwest of Agra. The most harmonious assemblages of Mughal tomb-gardens were the ones constructed for Jahangir, Asaf Khan, and Nurjahan in the Shahdara area outside Lahore, and for Khusrau and his mother at Allahabad. The greatest of the celebrated monumental garden-tombs is the Taj Mahal, an impressive, enduring, ideally planned depiction of a typical Agra garden that best represents the Mughal fascination with the imagery of paradise in a funereal setting. In view of the intellectual spirit of the times, particularly the predisposition of the Taj Mahal towards mysticism, it appears that both the emperor and the architect were conversant with the metaphorical imagery of the literary and visual Islamic Paradise of Ibn al-'Arabi. These imageries, it seems, inspired the architect to place the tomb at one end of the garden rather than in the centre. In this allegorical statement, the garden of the Taj Mahal functions as a symbolic replica of the celestial Paradise: the promised eternal reward of the faithful following the Judgement. In consonance with the traditional Muslim belief that the celestial Paradise would be a place of eternal feasting and banquetry, Shahjahan organised regular feasts in the Taj Mahal complex on the death anniversary of Mumtaz Mahal. The banquet held on the first anniversary of death—known as *'Urs*—was lavish, although the extent of the ceremony, the generosity and largesse was reduced after Shahjahan. The practice was continued nevertheless. Segregated by gender and structured by prayer, homilies, and meditation, these annual ceremonies at the tomb were different in intent and practice from the occurrences and experiences at the pleasure gardens. The orthodox forms of public piety—Muslim and imperial piety—emphasised under Shahjahan were imparted at the tomb site to both the elite and the larger audience.

In 1661, Aurangzeb constructed a tomb-garden that imitated the Taj Mahal for his wife, Rabia Durrani, at Aurangabad in Deccan. Except for this, Aurangzeb built no other large tomb-garden complexes for members of the royal family. Instead, in keeping with his own piety, the emperor reverted to the earlier custom of modestly built open-air tombs and prohibited the formal practice of regular prayers and ceremonies for his ancestors, which he considered a royal cult. Gardens, in fact, were given a new orientation during Aurangzeb's reign. They were either used for religious rituals or for formal imperial ceremonies, or for both events together. The garden festival of *Nauroz* was stopped, and so were the commensally convivial gatherings in the gardens that had characterised elite royal culture. Except for the gardens that the emperor had built adjoining the mosques or those constructed by his daughters or nobles, none others have survived. Even though Aurangzeb abandoned the tradition of monumental garden design for religious architecture in pursuance of his modesty and sobriety, the tradition continued in the regional courts of Rajasthan, Punjab, Awadh, and the Deccan.

MUGHAL IMPERIAL PAINTING

Visuality and the visual medium emerged as central and significant to Mughal court culture, regardless of the fact that any form of figural art was contrary to Islamic orthodoxy and had received no patronage from pre-Mughal dynasties. Timur was the first Muslim ruler to defy *Quranic* injunctions and develop the Timuri school of painting, which evolved as the Safavid style. Subsequently, Persian and Central Asian influences were brought to the Mughal court by Humayun. The Mughals in India were exposed to a variety of indigenous beliefs that regarded images as animate beings, instilled with holy spirits and sacral presence and the power to perform miraculous deeds. Apprehensive that the *'ulama* might react adversely to these concepts, Abu'l Fazl stipulated that the act of creating and viewing a work of art was parallel or similar to a mystical experience. The term *taswir* (image) was defined in the *Ain-i Akbari* as 'drawing the likeness of anything'; or 'a means both of study and amusement'; or a 'magical art through which inanimate objects look as if they had life'. Painted images, with such multilayered meanings, acquired special powers to render visions tangible, to become a chosen space for revealing utopian visions. A utopian ideal, Monica Juneja (2001, 2010) observed, could be realised as present and absolute 'uniquely' in representation.

The Mughal patronage of painting, notwithstanding Islamic instructions, represented the Mughal spirit of tolerance and cultural synthesis that engendered painting as a valuable style of propaganda, a medium for recording and depicting the history of the Mughal Empire. Cognition, adaptation, and adoption of several influences marked the character of the Mughal painting. The Persian impact is visibly evident in the use of bright colours like the tile colours: blue, red or the luminous colours that outrage the eye; to highlight the colours, one colour was placed next to the other. In adherence to Islamic norms, the Persian or Safavid school was a stylised form of painting in which there was no portrayal of real life. Consequently, no human figure or representation of any living being looked natural or realistic; human figures and faces were given a special rock treatment and invariably painted pink; the style was characterised by a calligraphic sweep that gave the figures an elongated torso. It was from the Ajanta school of painting that Mughal painting imbibed its style of fresco painting, and several other stylised forms were adapted from Jain paintings. The Jain paintings were characteristically done on palm leaves, with the face portrayed in profile, a sharp elongated nose with one eye visible while the other jutted out, giving the painting a two-dimensional effect. The drapery in these paintings looked quite unrealistic, stiff and starched. Irrespective of these impressions, Mughal painting displayed a few variations. The character of the court was significantly displayed in Mughal paintings, with an emphasis on dimension, perception, and a realistic view of life. Blended colours provided the softness that made the painting appealing to the eye, and the clothes were represented as solid blocks of colour.

The Mughal style of painting unfolded smoothly and logically during the transitional periods between imperial changeovers. For instance, the earliest examples of historical documentation through painting, attributed to Akbar's patronage, were actually found during Humayun's period. Similarly, the interest in acutely sensitive, highly individualised portraits and technical refinement, that was used to define Jahangir's patronage, appeared in the works created at the end of Akbar's reign. In this context, Milo Beach (1992, 2012) argued that paintings were not simply illustrations of the interests and moods of whichever emperor was in power; rather, paintings and painters had a momentum of their own that was as capable of determining as of responding to imperial interests. The Mughal emperors patronised an atelier of artists and artisans that produced illustrated manuscripts and individual paintings depicting poetic, historical, and religious subjects. The imperial Mughal painters and calligraphers were both Muslims and Hindus from different parts of India, as well as from Persia and Central Asia.

From the sixteenth century, imperial Mughal painters worked in a distinctive style that some scholars have characterised as eclectic. Mughal painting derived its expressive line and decorative polish from Persia; its compositional technique and bright colours from India; and its illusionistic devices were selectively borrowed from Europe. By the late sixteenth century, these diverse components had been skilfully blended into a coherent and highly refined style that was neither Persian nor Indian nor European, but distinctively Mughal. The evolution of the imperial Mughal style was deeply influenced by the personality, preferences, and needs of each Mughal emperor, and even though the emperor could not administer the daily activities of the painters, he supervised them closely. The emperor's tastes invariably influenced the aesthetics of the painter, evident from the dynamic and innovative paintings of Akbar's period and the refined and naturalistic renderings produced under Jahangir and Shahjahan. But while the emperor's choice was important, equally significant were the talents, interests, and personalities of the artists who ultimately strived to earn the appreciation and patronage of the emperor.

Both Babur and Humayun demonstrated keen interest in representing the 'natural' although, in the absence of any of these works, it is difficult to establish their style of painting. Beach observed that Babur patronised painters, even though there is no corroborating evidence from either Kabul, where he had a lively court, or India. It is speculated that Humayun too had established a workshop in the earlier part of his reign before his exile to Persia. There are several illustrations in a 'transplanted' Safavid style that can be dated to roughly after 1550, when Humayun, subsequent to his visit to the Safavid court of Shah Tahmasp, apparently cultivated an interest in painting as a symbol of power. During his stay at the Safavid court, Humayun hired several artists who had earlier worked for Shah Tahmasp: two painters, Mir Sayyid Ali and Abdus Samad, joined Humayun in Kabul in 1550; later, they were joined by Mir Musavvir and Dost Muhammad. These artists brought Persian techniques and styles to the Mughal court, creating thus the earliest known Mughal portraits as well as the first representations of contemporary events and flora and fauna. Some scholars have argued that no homogeneous style of art could develop during Humayun's reign for he hired painters from not only the court of Shah Tahmasp but also from Timurid centres like Bukhara. Nevertheless, the paintings extant from his time clearly reflect Persian style and attributes, affirming that the Safavid style was firmly entrenched as the basic element of Mughal painting once Humayun returned from Persia in 1555.

Inheriting the aesthetic sense of his father and grandfather, Akbar had, by the early 1560s, introduced traditions that became a part of the evolving Mughal court style. Demonstrating a deep inclination for and appreciation of a variety of Indian forms, colours, and techniques that he found different and exciting, Akbar introduced new concepts from local cultural traditions, including the hiring of artists from indigenous Indian workshops, influencing thus the development of the Mughal style in painting and architecture. Akbar presided over the elaboration of distinctive traditions of Mughal painting and expanded the imperial atelier. To accomplish these tasks, he hired the services of Humayun's Persian painters Mir Sayyid Ali and Abdus Samad, who in turn hired local artists and trained them in different styles (see Plate 4). Some of them worked in simplified and/or Indianised versions of the Persian school patronised earlier by the Sultans of Delhi; others painted in indigenous Indian styles that were used to illustrate texts in Indic languages; and still others worked in the Jain styles of Gujarat and Rajasthan. The emperor's encounter with the Europeans in 1572 during the campaign in Gujarat and even later had a tremendous impact on artistic traditions of the time. Akbar was so intrigued and impressed by European prints and paintings that he ordered his artists to undertake their in-depth study and copy them.

However, in the early Akbari period, the Mughal artists remained loyal to their Persian style, although they borrowed many Western techniques as well. They were especially interested in the illusionistic creations of Western pictorial conventions and techniques, that is, the concepts of spatial planes, single point perspective and spatial recession, the use of pictorial elements that diminished in size according to distance, and shading to give figures a sense of volume and weight. The youthful energy and direct narrative of the early Akbari paintings gave way to subtle elegance and a heightened naturalistic effect. By the late 1580s–90s, the imperial Mughal style had evolved into a coherent form and highly controlled works of art that made brilliant use of delicate line, quiet colour, deep spatial recession, and sensitive modelling. Abu'l Fazl observed that the emperor not only gave credit to the artists for their achievements, but also instructed his *darogahs* and clerks to record the contribution of each artist to a picture. The works of all painters were laid weekly before the emperor, who then conferred rewards according to the excellence of the workmanship and even enhanced their monthly salaries. Analysing the nature of workmanship, Milo Beach (2012) observed that certain artists specialised in an art form, such as battle or court scenes, portraits or animal studies. It was in fact a small group of artists who created designs and illustrations in any one volume, although Abu'l Fazl recounted the names of at least eighteen leading painters during Akbar's time and over 100 artists who contributed to the production in the library workshop. The list of names provided by Fazl suggests that there were many Hindu and Muslim artists in Akbar's atelier, pointing also towards the distinctive accomplishment and competence of the Safavid artists in India and their foremost contribution to the fusion of Safavid refinement with Indian vitality and realism.

Meticulous and specific, Akbar's paintings reflected his fondness for the realistic portrayal of not only animals and birds, but also people. Portraits were often filled with energetic figures engaged in some kind of activity that conveyed a sense of the motion, hustle, bustle and restlessness characterised by conquests and territorial expansion, but which did not distract the eye. Walter M. Spink and Deborah Levine (*Akbarnama*: Catalogue, New York, n.d.) observed that the visual narratives marked by aggressive physical action and excitement in the *Akbarnama* illustrate the artists' keenness on a diagonal emphasis, which they considered more vital than a vertical or horizontal one. Akbar's interest in the rational and verifiable led to his obsession, particularly in the latter phase of his reign, with the recording of historical events and the development of portraiture. The latter was different from the earlier Hindu and Islamic portraits in that they moved away from generalised and metaphorical references and instead focused on capturing the specific appearance and personality of the subjects, in complete contrast to traditional Islamic practice. In other words, Akbar's artistic style was 'untraditional' during this period; the Mughal library and workshops were active, productive, and innovative; there was more technical control, brilliance of surface and miniatures, which re-emphasised the Iranian roots of Mughal paintings. Painting under Akbar, largely connected with the art of book illustration, can be described essentially as narrative art that traced its roots to both Persian and Indian art (sculpture as well as painting).

The first output of the library workshop under the charge of Safavid painters Abdus Samad and Mir Saiyid Ali reflected Akbar's interest in tales and fables from Islamic and Indian traditions (see Image 7.1). The simplest mode of the artist's expression in Mughal narratives is portrayed by illustrations of the *Tutinama* (Tales of a Parrot), *c.* 1565–70, characterised by the representation of a single scene from an episode, in which the earlier or latter part of the event does not figure in the artist's description (see Plate 5). The single scene therefore remains isolated with no continuity in the narration of the event, and illustrates only a part of the story. For example, an episode from the 'Thirty-First Night' is represented by a single scene of how the donkey wearing the skin of a tiger revealed his identity by braying, alarming the guards hiding in the foliage of trees with his raucous noise. Such visual narratives lacked the concept of space and time, with limited possibilities of pictorial action. Their purpose appeared to be didactic and purely decorative, and thus tended to disappear gradually from the Mughal school as the art of visual narration evolved from simple to complex.

Contemporaneous with *Tutinama* is *Anwar-i Suhaili* (1570) in which the continuous narration of an event is seen sometimes, although generally this manuscript also comprised one-scene representations. However, in it, within one picture plane, more than one phase of an event or story is represented; usually the end and the climax with no demarcation between the two phases, depicting them in a single visual field facilitating movement in the story. This is indicative of space and time in the painting, as opposed to the portrayals in *Tutinama*. Continuous narration in the Mughal school appeared in the illustrations of *Hamzanama*, *c.* 1565–80, which showed multiple phases of an event portrayed within a single visual field, with greater elaboration and description, revolving around a central theme without any repetition of the main figures. The *Hamzanama*, the first considerable credo to Akbar's enthusiasm for painting, is a comprehensively

Image 7.1: Mir Sayyid Ali: Portrait of a young Indian scholar

Source: https://commons.wikimedia.org/wiki/File:Mir_Sayyid_Ali_-_Portrait_of_a_Young_Indian_Scholar.jpg.

illustrated heroic tale of the adventures of Hamza, the uncle of Prophet Muhammad (see Plate 6). The *Hamzanama* was written on fabric and illustrated with 1,400 pictures divided equally into fourteen volumes. It was painted on one side with the text on the reverse in blocks of nineteen lines, so that they could be recited while holding the corresponding painting for the audience to see. This gigantic task, which began in 1558, took fifteen years to complete, with dozens of artists engaged in it under the supervision of Abdus Samad and Mir Sayyid Ali. Allegedly, fewer than 200 folios of *Hamzanama* have survived. From 1580, Akbar increasingly became conscious that art should serve the purposes of the Mughal regime, that is, symbolise imperial power and sovereignty. One manifestation of this was the *Razmnama*, the translation of the *Mahabharata* from Sanskrit into Persian, copies of which were made for the library so that its knowledge could spread throughout his empire; another was a number of commissions to celebrate the achievements of the Mughal ancestry and project the imperial ideology, evidence of which are the illustrations to the *Baburnama*, *Timurnama*, and *Akbarnama*.

Through the 1590s, a constant community of artists created the mature manuscripts of Akbar's reign. Change set in with the end of Basawan's (master artist of Akbar's period) career after 1600. The young artists could nevertheless respond to Jahangir's passionate interest in painting, his specific aesthetic demands and creativity. The best textual source on Jahangir is the *Jahangirnama*, his autobiography that revealed his multifaceted personality as a sovereign, naturalist, and hunter, but above all as an aesthete, patron of the arts, and collector. Mughal painting reached its zenith with the emperor's fascination for painting, his knowledge and involved patronage. He was particularly impressed by the accomplishments of European art and was keen to transform the production of the imperial library, that is, move from the recording of human activities and events to more reflective work revelatory of the human personality. Even before he ascended to power, Jahangir had commissioned and collected works of art, first when the court was at Lahore from 1586–98, and then after he established his own court at Allahabad from 1660. He continued the practice initiated by Akbar of exposing his artists to European paintings and engravings. Consequently, from the 1580s to the 1620s, motivated by imperial patronage, Mughal artists interacted with European models—a process that facilitated experiments with light and shade and the use of perspective. This was interwoven with a change in style—from the hustle-bustle of events to simpler compositions focusing on the interplay of individuals and the revelation of personality.

The presence of Aqa Riza, an Iranian émigré, his son Abu'l Hasan, and their disciples gave a particular Iranian orientation to Jahangir's workshops, which were quite distinct from the imperial studios. Milo Beach described an important album of Jahangir's period, five pages of which are available in the Freer Gallery of Art, Washington. The album is evidence of the emperor's eclecticism and aesthetic tastes, but more significantly is indicative of the influence of Deccani, Mughal, Persian, and Turkish paintings and drawings and European prints. Like Akbar, Jahangir closely supervised the painters, but he also distinguished himself by his connoisseurship and recognition of artists' personal styles. The painters of Jahangir's reign largely adopted two distinctive modes:

- a simplified and more focused version of the Akbari court style; and

- a precise, flat, and highly decorative style inspired by Safavid Persian paintings, especially those of Aqa Riza.

Although Jahangir patronised both modes, he preferred the refinements of the second. In addition to Jahangir's artistic tastes, his painters focused on realising their own version of the imperial Mughal style. They refined the energetic naturalism of the Akbari period into a calmer and more intensely realistic style capable of revealing not only the outer appearance of physical reality, but also the inner; they could achieve this through their extraordinary technical skills. They generally modelled in light and shade to give weight and volume to the figures, and emphasised the qualities of the human character and psychological interrelationships. In fact, the paintings of Jahangir's time were so probing that they made the contents of Akbari paintings, which were realistically portrayed, appear generic.

Jahangir preferred individual paintings that focused on Mughal themes: the pleasures and pasttimes of court life, birds, animals, and flowers, scenes from European pictorial sources, and studies of holy men (see Plate 7). Jahangir's sense of aesthetics was as remarkable as his involvement with nature; he therefore hired his outstanding artists, specialists in nature studies like *Ustad* Mansur and Abu'l Hasan, to depict nature through their works. As a commendation, the emperor decorated both artists with the titles *Nadir al-Asr* and *Nadir az-Zaman*, respectively (both of which meant 'Wonder of the Age'). The paintings that emerged were exact replications of natural history. These Mughal artists copied the flowers of European herbals and, adapting them, represented a plant native to India according to the European herbal style. *Ustad* Mansur's famous painting of tulips, *c.* 1620, kept at the Maulana Azad Library, Aligarh Muslim University, was perhaps the earliest illustration of *Tulipa Linifolia*. Ebba Koch (2009) identified it as such, though Som Prakash Verma (1999) described it as *Tulipa Dusiana*. Koch observed that a principal image of a Mughal floral painting by *Ustad* Mansur was inserted in Jahangir's magnificent album, a large part of which is preserved under the name *Gulshan Album* in the Gulistan Library at Tehran. *Ustad* Mansur's page, signed *'amal-i Mansur Jahangir Shahi* (work of Mansur, [servant] of King Jahangir) demonstrates a compendium of a different variety of flowers, primarily lilies, copied in reverse from various European works and rendered in colour. Jahangir's interest in birds resulted in the representation of several species, imitating the European style of scientific portrayal.

Equally significant was his passion for and obsession with self-portraits. Jahangir often depicted himself as bedecked with jewels, turban, and clothes with *sanganeri* print. Portraits had been painted in India much before the Mughals, but they were always idealised representations of individuals, distinct from an exact likeness. In a Mughal painting, at the centre of an imagined vision of the perfect kingdom stood the person of the monarch; royal portraiture thus became an important genre where utopian ideals could be located. At first glance, royal portraits in Mughal painting appeared stylised, static, and inexpressive. Nevertheless, they were chosen as a medium, Monica Juneja (2001, 2010) argued, to translate an ideal vision located at an 'intersection of sacrality, fixity and mystical feeling' by 'representing' something that once existed but no longer does; therefore, bridging an absence in time and space, the royal portraits purported both omnipresence and accessibility.

By 1615, a new element had entered portraiture, viz., the portraits now contained allegorical and symbolic references, such as the globe upon which Jahangir placed his feet in a portrait painted by Abu'l Hasan. Mughal allegorical portraits also based their concepts on general British prototypes. The arrival of Sir Thomas Roe, cousin of the leading English miniaturist Isaac Oliver, at the court in 1616 brought this development to its zenith. Roe brought paintings with him which fascinated the emperor, and it is from that time that Mughal portraiture began using striking symbolic imagery. Bichitr's remarkable allegorical portrait of Jahangir paying attention to a Sufi Shaikh rather than to kings is significant to the genre: in the painting, Jahangir sits on an hourglass denoting the passing of time, while the angels at its foot write 'O Shah may your reign last a thousand years' (Image 7.2). The Sufi is probably Shaikh Husain Chishti, the contemporary representative of the shrine of Muin ud-Din Chishti at Ajmer; kingly power is represented by King James I of England and the Ottoman Sultan Selim; and on the bottom left, the artist paints his own figure (description borrowed from Monica Juneja 2001, 2010). The portraits that Jahangir commissioned revealed his deep interest in people and his scientific inclination towards the appearance and character of the natural world. The major manuscript of the period, worked upon from 1612–27, was the *Jahangirnama*, the illustrated version of the emperor's memoirs. According to Milo Beach, only dispersed pages of it are available, and it could even be that ultimately, they were never placed in a bound copy. Prior to 1615, the painters had presented the emperor in a narrative context; after this, however, he is shown as a majestic figure surrounded by symbols of wealth and power. These changes in style that glorify Jahangir also reflect the sacred elements attributed to the emperor. Such a conscious use of paintings to achieve political ends would dominate the imperial paintings of Shahjahan as well.

The Mughal emperors, beginning with Babur, had excelled in and dominated the arts of the empire, but the Mughal court was perhaps never as strictly regulated as it was under Shahjahan. Shahjahan used both architecture and art to represent the emperor and the State to the public and provide an enduring memory of his splendid empire. He, in fact, meticulously used art to convey the imperial ideology. Ebba Koch observed that in his own characteristic perfectionist style, Shahjahan was his own artistic director and supervised his artists as part of his daily routine. His court historians Muhammad Amin Qazwini and Abdul Hamid Lahori have narrated that the emperor daily met with both his architects and the painters in his *daulat khana-i khas* or *diwan-i khas*. Shahjahan's personal involvement with the artists is evident in the pictorial representations of artists illustrating their direct access to the emperor. The artists invariably included their self-portraits in the *darbar* scenes to emphasise their presence and manifest their special relation with the emperor. The paintings of Shahjahan's period reveal an innovative trend, although there were elements of continuity with Jahangir's naturalism, particularly portraiture. For Shahjahan, too, the preference lay in individual paintings done by a single artist and mounted in a *muraqqa*. His artists did not apply realistic techniques like those adopted by Jahangir's artists to define the inner character and outward appearance of a subject; their attempt, instead, was to idealise and glorify it. In other words, Shahjahan's artists wanted to show the Mughal world not as it was, but as the emperor wanted it to be—a harmoniously ordered, sublime, beautiful heaven on earth. The albums of Shahjahan provide evidence of this, especially since the production

Image 7.2: Painting by Bichtr, *c.* 1615–18, shows Emperor Jahangir with a Sufi Shaikh

Source: https://commons.wikimedia.org/wiki/File:Bichtr_Jahangir_preferring_a_Sufi_Sheikh_to_kings.jpg.

of manuscripts had declined during his period. Commenting on the nature and character of Shahjahani albums, Milo Beach asserted that as compared to Akbar and Jahangir, Shahjahan had neither the eclectic tastes nor the intellectual voraciousness, although he was obsessed with imperial splendour. He fostered a style that was technically faultless, highly perceptive, and painted with alarming self-confidence. The *Portrait of Abd al-Rahim Khan Khanan* by Hashim (one of his master artists) is a unique example of this style.

The new aesthetic values of Shahjahan are best seen in many immaculate portraits of himself that he had commissioned. In all his portraits, the emperor appears as a stiff, formal, aloof individual with a halo around his head. He bears fixed symbolic attributes—sword, dagger, turban, ornaments, amulets, and others—that proclaim his superior wisdom, taste, and power. Transient feelings and human emotions were never revealed on his face; his eyes usually stared firmly into the distance. The emphasis was on the impeccable representation of the clothes, particularly the turban, *patka*, *qamarband*, and the *jama*, to divert the eye from the figures. Shahjahan had a passion for grand imagery; this therefore transformed the depictions of his life and court into visions of cosmic splendour. A painting that makes a bold statement of imperial power is Hashim's 'Shahjahan, Master of the Globe' (1629; see Plate 8). This painting was created to impress the audience with the majesty and magnificence of the Mughal dynasty in general, and Shahjahan in particular. The emperor is shown holding a sword and amulet, standing atop a globe inscribed with a panegyric and painted allegorical figures: the scales symbolised justice; the lion lying with the lamb represented the peace brought about by the emperor's just rule; and the delicately drawn holy men were a testimony to the emperor's humility and wisdom. This portrait intended to convey the righteous, fair, and legitimate rule of Shahjahan, protected by the powers of heaven that had caused the creation of a harmoniously ordered world—a place where the lion could lie with the lamb.

Another significant visual of Shahjahan's reign is the *Padshahnama*, an illustrated history of his reign that revealed a special relationship and close collaboration between the emperor, his historians, and his painters. In miniature format, the *Padshahnama* paintings provide the most exhaustive pictorial records of Mughal court culture and are, as Ebba Koch (2001) stated, a congenial visual equivalent to the detailed literary account of the *Ain-i Akbari*. The purpose of the *Padshahnama* paintings was to allegedly create appropriate images in an official style—both in writing and painting—and maintain a uniform standard of quality. The artists of Shahjahan's reign were extremely creative and skilled, and while their artistic freedom was suppressed and their talent strictly controlled, they could produce works marked by high quality and innovation. Several painters who had worked under Jahangir and illustrated the *Jahangirnama* had continued in Shahjahan's reign; the *Padshahnama* paintings emulated many patterns of Jahangiri paintings, but they also systematised and transformed trends initiated by the latter. Shahjahan's paintings were stylistic, had a definite political purpose, and aimed at, as Ebba Koch stipulated, making a statement of order and hierarchy, which was a basic feature of Shahjahan's ideology. The focus of the paintings was to record the main activities of Shahjahan's public life: *darbar* scenes, abstract images of the Shahjahani power structure, court festivals, visits to Muslim shrines, elephants and imperial hunts. The hustle and bustle of military activities of Akbar's paintings, abandoned in

Jahangiri paintings, were revived and reinterpreted to suit the principles of Shahjahani paintings. They no longer portrayed the emperor in action; instead, it was his agents who were shown as capturing fortresses and cities on behalf of the emperor or punishing rebels in his name.

One volume of this splendid art is preserved in the Royal Library, Windsor Castle. Almost one-third of the illustrations in the Windsor manuscript depict the assembly of *jharokha-i khas-u-aam* that represented the focal centre of court events, where the pomp and authority of the 'Great Mogul' was enacted. The paintings of the *jharokha* represent it as an image of the Mughal State. Although the *jharokha* paintings were done by several artists, the *darbar* scenes are based on similar compositional principles, that is, the emperor appeared in a central position in the *jharokha* with a raised seat projected in the back hall of the *diwan-i aam* (audience hall), protected by a *cupola* in front of which was a canopy; below the emperor, his nobles were assembled in two groups facing each other, following the principle of *qarina*, the Shahjahani idea of bilateral symmetry. The nobles appeared as a collection of self-contained, idealised individual portraits that were not unified psychologically; they stared straight ahead into the distance and their eyes appeared to meet only because they were placed opposite to each other. But they were necessarily positioned in subordination to the powerful, overpowering figure of the emperor. These basic parameters had to be followed. The artists of the *Padshahnama* had to be perfect in their style to obtain hierarchically correct representations; within these variables, artistic variations were permitted and the artist could express himself freely.

Such representations were also seen in the *Akbarnama*. Emulating the schematic figure conventions of Persianate paintings, participants in these public *darbar* assemblies were shown as small figures, albeit more realistically as compared to the Persianate style. The figures, in fact, were so small that the artist was unable to depict individual personal traits; they mostly looked alike, and were crammed into the space below the emperor. The emperor was generally presented in a three-quarter profile and always identified by a golden sun nimbus. Side-view portrayals of emperors could be seen from the reign of Akbar, who was generally presented in three-quarter profile. Jahangir adopted the pattern and all portraits of Shahjahan were essentially in profile, although no contemporary sources or modern scholars have provided any explanation for it. Ebba Koch, however, averred that the profile view was probably a way to protect Shahjahan and his courtiers from realistic portrayal. The objective of this standardised, idealised profile was perhaps to emphasise that the king and his State elite were above all that was human, imperfect, and subject to change.

Painting to suit the emperor's aesthetic tastes and political ambitions, the painters of Shahjahan idealised physical reality and were passionate about the use of lush colours and opulent effects, which they depicted in not only the representation of imperial power and glory, but also birds, animals, and flowers. A motif of birds sitting on trees in their natural form, identified with ornithological species, was illustrated in a hard stone inlay in *pietra dura/parchin kari* ornamentation on the wall of Shahjahan's throne in the *Qila Mubarak* at Delhi. In addition, the outdoor scenes of the *Padshahnama* depicted *darbar*s in the imperial encampment, processions, pilgrimages, hunts, elephant fights, sieges, surrender of fortresses and cities, and the punishment of rebels. Like in the portrayal of figures in *darbar*s and court festivals, the principle of hierarchical representation was adapted for images in landscape; the figures were flattened in a two-dimensional arrangement to render the event and the landscape as real and naturalistic as possible.

The momentum of the established practice of art continued under Aurangzeb, but with a difference. With declining patronage to artists, the style became simpler and lacked the visual richness, complexity, and surface opulence basic to the paintings of his predecessors. There was less distinction between the works of his artists and those made for patrons elsewhere in India. In the early years of his reign, Aurangzeb patronised self-portraits, primarily to serve a political purpose, rather than illustrations to represent poetic texts or romantic literature. The idealising tendencies of Shahjahani paintings were continued, as were the concerns with the immaculate representation of clothes and other visual patterns, although in comparison to *Padshahnama* paintings, there was inconsistent modelling and the paintings appeared somewhat simplified and flat. Evaluating the Mughal manuscripts and albums in a broad context, Milo Beach (2012) talked about other related traditions like Deccani and Rajput art, and also the 'subimperial' culture of the smaller courts. Each of these maintained their own cultural identities and interrelationships. Even as the influence of the Mughal court weakened, the artistic traditions initially pioneered and consolidated by the Mughals continued, with the artists often engaged in the copying of earlier imperial images.

With the political weakening of the Mughal Empire, the imperial style of painting did not decline, but merely changed its course. Many artists left Delhi to join the emerging regional kingdoms (for example, Awadh and Bengal) that became flourishing centres of art in the eighteenth and early nineteenth centuries, and the painters of the regions evolved distinct variants of the imperial Mughal style. But not all Mughal painters abandoned Delhi in the eighteenth century: some of them continued to be patronised by the Mughal emperors to paint their portraits, hunting scenes, and festive occasions; some others made opulent paintings for the commercial market; and still others copied seventeenth-century Mughal paintings or refurbished old *muraqqa*s and manuscripts.

GENRES OF MUSIC

Music during the Mughal period represented a gradual synthesis of South Asian with Central and West Asian musical traditions on the one hand, and the gradual indigenisation of Mughal court music and dance on the other. Musical forms like *dhrupad*, *khayal*, and *ghazal* and instruments like the *sitar*, *sarod*, and *tabla* can be traced to the thirteenth century in India. *Dhrupad*, the earliest form of Hindustani music, is difficult to date exactly, but it is alleged that by the time of Amir Khusrau, it had become one of the main forms of classical music in north India. Its beginnings can then be fixed between the twelfth and early thirteenth century. Amir Khusrau is credited with modifying *dhrupad* by adding Persian melody and beat to it, and thus creating another musical style, namely *qawwali*. *Dhrupad* was first introduced to the royal court by Raja Mansingh Tomar of Gwalior (1486–1517) and reached its pinnacle during the reign of Akbar. *Dhrupad* compositions and style were serious and mostly in Sanskrit phraseology. It was during the reign of Humayun that it was adopted as the main style of court music in north India; *dhrupad* singer and composer Nayak Bhakshu was, at the time, in his service. Later, 1,000 of his lyrics were collected by Shahjahan, known as *Sahasras* or *Hazar Dhrupad*. Several prominent *dhrupad* artists flourished in the court of Akbar; of these, Tansen is the most popularly known. Tansen reshaped the entire genre of *dhrupad* by the addition of new Persian ornamentations like *meend* and *gamaka*. *Meend* in Hindustani music refers to a glide from one note to another. It is an essential performance practice and used often in both vocal and instrumental music. *Gamaka*, also known as *gamak*, means 'ornamented note' in Sanskrit. It refers to the ornamentation used in the performance of Indian classical music. *Gamaka* involves a variation in the pitch of a note, using heavy forceful oscillations between adjacent and distant notes. Each *raga* has standard rules on the types of *gamaka*s that might be applied to specific notes, and the types that may not (see Image 7.3).

Tansen also developed the *rabab* (*rudra-veena*) and created several *raga*s (melody patterns with a characteristic rhythm and style that set forth a certain tone or mood to a musical phrase) that remain the foremost *raga*s of north India. Some of these are *darbari kanada*, *darbari todi*, *miyan ki malhar*, and *miyan ki sarang*. Tansen was not seen as belonging to a particular *gharana* (a school of music), but after his death, his work was attributed to the *Senia gharana* from the Gwalior school of music. The tradition of *dhrupad* was continued by Tansen's son Bilas Khan, known for his style *bilas todi*. Swami Haridas, *guru* of Tansen, was also a court musician during Akbar's reign; other musicians of this period included Baiju Bawra, Ramdas, Tanrang, and others (see Plate 6).

Dhrupad continued to dominate, although later, the emphasis shifted more towards beautification and ornamentation. Several disciples of Swami Haridas and Tansen became court musicians in different *subas* (province) and *sarkars* (subdivision of a *suba*) of the Mughal Empire during the reigns of Jahangir and Shahjahan, for instance in Jaipur, Punjab, Gwalior, Lucknow, and others. Akbar's period also witnessed the synthesis of music and devotional literature by poets like Surdas,

Image 7.3: Akbar, Todarmal, Tansen, Abu'l Fazl, Faizi, and Abdur Rahim Khan-i-Khana in a court scene (sixteenth century CE)

Source: https://commons.wikimedia.org/wiki/File:Akbar, Todarmal, Tansen and Abul Fazl, Faizi and Abdur Rahim Khan-i-Khana in a court scene (16th century AD).jpg.

Tulsidas, Kabir, and Mirabai. Their devotional *bhajans* have become immortal and continue to be popular in contemporary times. Aurangzeb was trained in music and while he banned vocal music, he patronised instrumental music in the court, particularly the *veena*. Music continued to be popular with the elite and a number of books on the history and theory of Indo-Islamic music were written during this period. One of the most famous was *Rag-Darpan* (The Mirror of Music) written by Fakirullah (Saif Khan), who was earlier the Governor of Kashmir.

Khayal blended Indian musical theory with Persian musical expression. These were composed in the common spoken language and the theme was mostly romantic. The style of singing was leisurely, ornamental, and improvised. Since it was not a part of religious ritual or sung in places of worship, the *khayal* had an element of physical pleasure. Its origin can be traced to the court of Muhammad Shah Rangila (1720–48). Bahadur Shah Zafar II (1837–57) was himself a patron of music and literature; in his court lived Ghalib and Zauq. *Thumri*, another genre of music, developed in the court of Nawab Wajid Ali Shah of Awadh (1847–56). In contrast to symbolic representations of divine longing, which constituted the theme of earlier forms of music, *thumri* focused on human love and made a sensuous appeal through the repetition of words and musical phrases. *Tappa*, on the other hand, found inspiration in folk music that was earlier ignored by court music.

The political decline of the Mughal Empire did not affect the patronage of music and musicians. Musicians from different regional kingdoms participated in royal competitions, constantly researched and improved their *gayaki* (the style of presenting a song), innovated and studied deeper aspects of music. One such art form that evolved and flourished during the eighteenth–nineteenth centuries was *ghazal*. It was essentially the poetry of romance, introduced in Persia around the tenth century. With its aesthetics derived from Persian–Arabic Islamicate literature, the genre was developed in north India and became popular with the emergence of Urdu as the prominent language of poetry in the Mughal court. *Ghazal* is a form of rhymed verses that comprise couplets, the number of which could vary according to the composition. Each couplet or *she'r* is complete in form and meaning, but the *ghazal* does not always represent a single mood; often the mood of one *she'r* in a *ghazal* differs from, or is opposed to, that of another. It is essentially oriented towards musical rendering; therefore, singing all the couplets (*ash'ar*) of a *ghazal* in the same format is contrary to its nature.

It is pertinent to understand the gender politics of the early modern *ghazal* and appreciate the issues inherent in *rekhta* and *rekhti*. An average enthusiast would know that *ghazal* is a love lyric composed in two-line *she'r*s, and that its main subject is *ishq* (idealised love) and *ashiq* (the lover). But it is equally important to understand that in earlier times, Urdu poetry was called *rekhta* (the 'scattered' idiom) because it was expressed in a combination of Persian and the local vernacular languages of north India. It is a literature narrated in the masculine voice, 'spoken' by a masculine *ashiq* to a grammatically masculine *ma'shuq*; although s/he may in fact be female, any forthright specific reference to the grammatical feminine is avoided. The sub-genre of poetry called *rekhti* was considered *rekhta*'s counterpart; it manifests itself through a feminine narrator and usually a feminine addressee and explains gender politics within the world of Urdu culture. Although it follows a number of classical conventions, it is not considered normative. Composed in the form of a *ghazal*, *rekhti* clearly defined the expression of desire and was associated with the domestic life of the upper strata, socially elite, secluded women during the late eighteenth and nineteenth centuries. It claimed to speak in *begamati zaban*. This would explain the reason for linking *rekhti* with the *zenana*. Its explicit gender and social cosmos distinguish it from *rekhta*'s understanding of the universality of expression and relevance.

Rekhti was introduced in Lucknow by Sa'adat Yar Khan 'Rangin'. 'Rangin' is said to have adapted *rekhti* from the style of the not so well-reputed women, with whom he had consorted in his youth. By the end of the eighteenth century, Lucknow emerged as an important *markaz* (cultural centre), although perhaps second in status to Delhi. Some of Delhi's former aristocrats were involved in 'perfecting' Urdu in Lucknow to nurture an indigenous literary language that would surpass Persian. Although *rekhti* was well-received as a literary genre, twentieth-century critical writings on *rekhti* are characterised by moral judgements and subterfuge.

8

REGIONS AND REGIONAL KINGDOMS

Interactions and Responses

HIGHLIGHTS

- Region and Empire; Regional centralisation
- Rajputana: Internal social structure
- Rajput-Mughal relations: Amber, Marwar, Mewar, and others
- Disintegration of Bahmani and Vijayanagara kingdoms; struggle over Raichur Doab; arrival of *Estado da India*
- The *Nayaka*s: Politics, economy, literature, art, and culture
- Deccan Sultanates: Internal social structure; relations with the Mughals
- Maratha polity: Shivaji and the *Peshwa*s

Regional centralisation, a legacy of the pre-eighteenth century, was stimulated further in the late eighteenth–early nineteenth centuries by the political and military expansion of the English East India Company, and 'when India was the most diverse place on earth, the Mughal throne symbolized the distant potential of that sub-continental empire, that language of power which is authority' (Pinch 2006, 1). The fact that regional centralisation preceded the eighteenth century is amply illustrated by the contours of regional states that showed a shift towards centralisation, and ultimately evolved into state systems much before the coming of the Mughals. Each region had its own peculiarities and a system of governance, responsive to local requirements and changing situations. From the last quarter of the sixteenth century, with the emergence of the Mughal Empire as a powerful political entity, there were attempts at centralisation through the *mansabdari* and the *jagirdari* systems—the two major instruments of Mughal State power—and consolidation of authority over the regions. Keen to integrate political culture and evolve a common social and economic experience out of diversity, the imperial policies were formulated accordingly with the design to include even far-flung territories into the Mughal system. The persistent, continuous endeavour of the Mughals was to transform their tenuous grip into firm control. The centralising pull was felt by all regions; but then, the Mughal administration was markedly flexible and ensured the accommodation of regional eccentricities. Yet there was a limit to which the regions could adapt; unfazed, they often resisted the Mughal State. This chapter studies the particularities of regional polities and the relations between region and empire through the cases of Rajputana, Deccan, and Maharashtra.

RAJPUTANA: INTERNAL SOCIAL STRUCTURE; RELATIONS WITH THE MUGHALS

The centralisation of local authority around *raja*s or chieftains, the *rajas*' control over the lands in their respective kingdoms, and their military valour were some of the characteristic features of the kingdoms in Rajputana. Representing a separate cultural group with their own distinct history, myths, and customs in north Indian politics, the Rajputs enjoyed the added advantage of the strategic location and landscape of their region. Rajputana was spread over a relatively isolated frontier region of marginal agricultural importance, an extension of the geographical and cultural shatter belt extending across central India from Kathiawar to Orissa, an area characterised by internal sub-division. The physiography and topography of Rajwarra (the traditional name for Rajputana or Rajasthan), dominated by the Aravalli ranges, were an obstacle to external attacks, but encouraged the growth of petty kingdoms, fostering a parochial or regional outlook, clan rivalries or jealousies, rather than a political alliance between the princely states. There were three dominant Rajput kingdoms—Amber, Marwar, and Mewar—ruled by the Kachhawahas, Rathors, and Sisodias, respectively. Mewar had acquired regional dominance under Sisodia Rana Kumbha (1433–68) in the mid-fifteenth century, while Marwar acquired regional supremacy in the early sixteenth century under Rao Maldeo Gangavat (1532–62). By the 1540s, Rao Maldeo of Jodhpur controlled not only Marwar, but also Ajmer, Nagaur, Siwana, Bikaner, Didwana, and Sambhar, raided territories in southern and central Rajputana, and expanded as far as Chatsu (south of Amber).

Norman Ziegler (2010) connected the evolution of the Rathor kingdom of Marwar under Rao Maldeo to the use of horses, introduced in the kingdom in the late fifteenth–early sixteenth centuries. Horses, he argued, had played a dominant role in Rajput history, and local sources often related the prominence of clans to their possession of horses and their use in the campaigns. Horses emerged as a central military supply that influenced the structure and organisation of the kingdom. Although the greater use of horses impacted Rajput military behaviour and the technology of warfare, both remained rooted in the ideologies and equipment of the past centuries. Prior to the sixteenth century, the Rajputs had generally functioned without horses either because of their poor quality, which made them unsuitable for battles, or because of their short supply. The situation changed after the construction of stables on the eastern border of Marwar by Rao Ganga Bhagwat to protect his kingdom from the incursions of his brother, Rao Bikram Deo of Sojat. Ziegler argued that with the greater availability of horses, the political order in Marwar stabilised and so did the mobility of the army, facilitating a number of victories for Rao Maldeo between 1532 and 1543. By 1544, Rao Maldeo had touched such zeniths of power that he could even challenge the military supremacy of Sher Shah. With increased requirements of feeding and maintaining the horses, prebendal tenures (lands granted to Rajputs in return for military service) were developed. Changes similar to that of Marwar occurred in other Rajput kingdoms as well, resulting in new patterns of authority and control in Rajputana.

Persistent in their efforts to enhance their individual power and challenge the prestige and authority of their clansmen and kinsmen, the Rajput chieftains yearned for outside support, towards which the Mughal emperors, beginning with Akbar's reign, were favourably disposed.

Notwithstanding their problems with the Mughal notion of integration and control, authority and legitimacy, the Rajputs were inclined to strike a political bond with the Mughals. Consequently, the area that each Rajput clan controlled changed frequently, depending not so much on the power of the respective rulers as on their relations with the Mughal emperors.

In 1560, Rajwarra was inducted as the imperial *suba* of Ajmer. Exemplifying the attributes of an imperialist and pragmatic statesman, Akbar understood the importance of the strategic location of Rajputana, ideal for fulfilling his ambitions of expansionism and defence aggression. Added to this was his recognition of the significance of political traditions and the resources of the region, as well as the value of the Rajputs' military prowess in achieving the objectives of consolidation and power, authority and legitimacy. By 1658, Rajwarra was demarcated in the north by Shahjahanabad (Delhi), in the east by Akbarabad (Agra), in the southeast by Malwa, in the south by Gujarat, and in the west by Multan. Considered to be of utmost financial value, the precise contribution of the Rajput states to the imperial treasury is not known, but Irfan Habib has argued that the *jama* or the assessed land revenue for the *suba* of Ajmer between 1595 and 1709 indicated that it was the wealthiest in the empire. Complementing the land revenue were the rich mineral resources of the region; while *Ain-i Akbari* referred to copper and zinc mines, *Waqaya-i Ajmer*, a contemporary account of Aurangzeb's period, talked of the large reserves of salt and marble. The significance of the *suba* was further enhanced by the connectivity that it provided to commerce between Delhi and Agra and the western seaports.

The commercial utility of Rajwarra was additionally augmented by the western sea route that cut across it. Although it was prone to external raids and heavy transit duties were imposed on this route by the Rajputs, it was preferred to the eastern route that passed through Malwa, which encountered climatic variations and flooding during monsoons, making it impenetrable. So, both commercially and strategically, the Mughals stood to gain from Rajwarra, for it not only facilitated access to Deccan but also linked north India to Cambay and Surat, the two ports connected to Mecca. Aware of the politico-economic potential of Ajmer, the Mughal emperors perceived that control of Rajwarra could be best achieved through this city. It was centrally located to Jodhpur, Udaipur, and Amber, was deemed the most powerful in the plains on either side of the Aravallis, and provided a base for military operations. Akbar annexed it in 1561; thereafter, it continued to be used as a centre for military operations. Moreover, the localism, parochialism, and political disunity amongst the Rajput chieftains assisted the tightening of the Mughal hold over Rajputana.

Clan relationships and land control were the preponderant features of Rajputana, and perhaps a major factor that kept the Rajput chieftains divided and in a constant state of conflict. Understanding the tussle, socialisation, and loyalties, Norman Ziegler (1998) drew evidence from *vamsavaliyam* (genealogies), *khyat-bat* (clan histories), and *vigat* (administrative chronicles) and emphasised the importance of *bhaibandh* (brotherhood) and *saga'i* (marriages), the two primary units of reference and identification for a Rajput. He explained the concepts of *bhai-vamt* or land held or divided among different brothers and *pimda*, that is, brotherhood and land, which were inseparable and mutually supportive and dominated the social and political structure of Rajputana. Since land control was distinctive in the Rajput system, it led James Tod to argue for similarities between Rajput patterns and the European model of landholding and describe the Rajput polity as feudal. However, arguments such as Tod's and the analysis of the Rajput social system entail discretion because, while land control might have been typical of the Rajput polity and made it appear feudal, it had various other unique traits. Clan, a pre-eminent attribute of Rajputana, was generally widely dispersed over different territories within Rajasthan and was not itself, as Ziegler defined it, a corporate group in the sense that it enjoyed joint control over a specific territory. The functionally corporate units or *shakha*s or branches of the wider clan were smaller brotherhoods, comprising between three to six generations, and included members related by close ties of male blood, their wives, sons, and unmarried daughters. While these corporate units or smaller brotherhoods acknowledged their ties to the wider clan and showed deference to the 'senior' or 'ruling' line by descent within the clan, they generally regarded themselves as separate and distinct units, with each claiming equal rights and privileges to the land. Each *shakha* maintained its lineage, connecting its roots to a heroic ancestor to fulfil the standard criteria for claims to the throne. The *shakha* of the ruling family was, however, distinguished by its large landholding, with its chief possessing the title of *raja*.

The political identity of a clan was further impressed upon by its military power, rendering the Rajput state, according to Robert Hallissey (1977), a conquest state, in which each clan could assert military power and the clan that exhibited the maximum military strength could acquire the right of occupation. So a clan could call itself 'Rajput' if it succeeded in establishing its right to rule, that is, initiate a dynasty and trace its genealogy to the Kshatriya or warrior caste of the *Vedic* tradition. To assert the importance of their clan, each maintained a *vanshavali* (genealogy) and traced their clan heritage to antiquity so as to link their descent to some heroic ancestor. The Sisodia clan, for instance, delineated its origins to Rama to 1000 BCE.

Clan consciousness was further ingrained by the Rajput belief that they belonged to an endogamous group, distinct from other Indian castes. So marriages outside one's own caste, that is, Kshatriyas, was not permissible, nor was marriage within one's own clan allowed because of the conviction that members of the same clan had descended from one common ancestor. Polygyny was a general norm of marriage; rather, it was an obligation for a Rajput chief because the number of wives a chief could keep reflected on his economic status and finances. This custom applied to all *shakha*s, small or large. The polygynous system encouraged each wife to promote the lineage of her son, in which the son was identified not only by the name of his father and his brotherhood, but also by the name of his mother's father or brother and his brotherhood. Genealogical entries in particular displayed this feature, listing sons as daughter's son (*dohitro*) or sister's son (*bhanej*) of a certain Rajput clan. Consequently, the sense of identity of the children of such marriages revolved around the entity of the clan and its heritage. This implied that if the *vadi rani* (first or elder wife) and the *lodi rani* (second or the junior wife or wives) extended the cause of their sons and if the latter conceived first and assumed the role of a *patrani* (chief queen or mother of the first son or heir-apparent), the death of the *raja* would inevitably be marked by civil strife, despite him designating his heir (*patvi*) from amongst his many sons and giving the heir-designate greater authority and status as compared to the other sons. The heir was not necessarily the eldest son or chosen on the principle of primogeniture; often, he was the son of the ruler's favourite wife or the *patrani*, who possessed the customary right to provide the successor. Intra-clan rivalry and struggle over succession could turn macabre if a Rajput *raja* did not have a male heir, like in the case of the Rathors of Marwar in 1678–80.

The ruling authority in each Rajput kingdom was vested in a *raja* or a chief, who belonged to a dominant clan and was recognised as a military commander if he undertook the initial conquest. For his security and defence, the *raja* maintained vassals or clients, referred to in the texts as *chakar*, meaning 'servant', although in Marwari usage they were designated 'military retainer'. These terms suggest a subordinate position and do not adequately describe the relationship between the clan chief and his vassals, who were mostly his own kinsmen belonging to different *shakha*s of the clan. Each vassal generally owed both allegiance and service to the *raja*, which he acknowledged through a vow taken before a *devata* in a local temple. In addition, he was obliged to perform certain military, economic, and social obligations. His status was determined by the size of the *jagir* allotted to him, his relationship with the *raja*, his loyalty to the clan, and his military strength. As kinsmen of the *raja*, the vassals considered themselves equal to the *raja* and equivalent partners in the ruling elite; even at the lowest hierarchy and as *jagirdar*s, they maintained their own retinue of kinsmen and could often pose a challenge to the *raja*. Thus, while the *raja* emerged as the most powerful in the Rajput polity, he could not rule without the support and consent of his clansmen and kinsmen, for it was they who elevated him to the *gaddi*. If the *raja* was weak, they could revolt and overthrow him. To counter the enormity of the power of his clansmen and kinsmen, the *raja* sought the support of other Rajput clans, inducted them into his nobility and important administrative and military positions, although, as members of a clan other than that of the *raja*, they could not participate in any decision-making process.

Even as the clansmen and kinsmen exercised a significant vote in determining the political power of the *raja*s, the latter, for their stability and sustenance, also solicited the support of non-Rajput elements—Brahmins, artisans, merchants, and cultivators—and in turn provided them protection and security. These groups were neither the kinsmen nor the blood relatives of the *raja*, but they dominated the administrative organisation of Rajputana and were used as a check by the *raja* on his kinsmen. So while the *raja* enjoyed absolute authority in the internal affairs of his *raj* (kingdom), he was assisted by various non-Rajput officers. The person immediately subordinate to the *raja* was the *Pradhan*, who defined the fiscal and military responsibilities of the vassals and supervised land distribution. The *Diwan* headed the financial and revenue department and supervised the assessment, collection, and payment of revenue to the state. Both the *Pradhan* and the *Diwan* could be recruited from either the Brahmin or the Vaishya (mercantile) caste. The *Bakshi* was the military paymaster who supervised the salaries of nobles and military commanders, while the *Kotwal* was responsible for law and order, weights and measures, and regulated the prices and transit of commercial goods. These officials generally remained strong supporters of the *raja* not only because he appointed them, but also because their economic and social status depended on his discretion. This bureaucratic pattern, as it evolved by the seventeenth century, was similar in most Rajput states, especially in the three major states of Marwar, Mewar, and Amber.

Notwithstanding several efforts to achieve stability, Rajwarra remained at an imminent risk of political flux caused by clan loyalties and clan ties. The Sisodias of Mewar did not witness as much clan factionalism and fissiparous tendencies as in Marwar, they (Sisodias) could mobilise the support of their caste and clan, control the *gaddi*, and consolidate power without Mughal assistance. The Rathors of Marwar, on the other hand, often sought the indulgence of the Mughals to strengthen their position and free themselves of clan hierarchy. It is in the context of this political and social structure of Rajputana that Mughal–Rajput relations were located. By the last quarter of the sixteenth century, the number of Rajputs had gone up significantly in the Mughal imperial service. They acknowledged the sovereignty and authority of the Mughal emperor, acclimatised themselves with imperial customs and patterns, and acquired fluency in Persian language and etiquette. In return for accepting the paramountcy of the emperor, fulfilling revenue obligations, offering *peshkash* or tribute, and providing cavalry contingents and military service, the emperor conferred on the Rajputs the title of *raja*, *rana*, and *rao*, performed the *tilak* ceremony to formalise the legitimacy of Rajput rulers, sanctioned their independent right to rule their territories, but with a condition: their kingdoms (ancestral lands, *watan*) were granted as *jagir*s over which they held hereditary, non-transferable rights. Mughal–Rajput relations, dominated by the principle of paramountcy, matrimonial alliances, the *mansab* system, *watan jagir*s, *nazr*, and *peshkash*, transformed the Rajputs into allies, but not equal partners in the governance of the Mughal Empire. Their kingdoms were not shown as autonomous units but as a part of the Mughal *suba* of Ajmer; they were reduced to the status of zamindars and *jagirdar*s and were obliged to abide by the Mughal institutions and implement them. This weakened the Rajput traditional base, that is, the clan and the importance of *vanshavali*.

Babur had used the tactic of military conquest against Rana Sanga of Mewar, while Humayun had alienated the Rajputs by rejecting Rani Karnavati's appeal for help against Sultan Baz Bahadur of Malwa. Akbar, however, redefined his relationship with the Rajputs by emphasising political alliances, including matrimonial alliances, negotiations and bargaining, although, in case of resistance, he invoked force. He appeared to have had a dual focus—to constitute and control the Mughal bureaucracy and dominate various autonomous *raja*s and zamindars. Akbar's decision to establish links with these chieftains was probably influenced by a plan to implement the *wasiyat* (will) of Humayun. Shaikh Fakhruddin Bhakkari, who wrote the chronicle *Zakhirat-ul-Khawanin* in the mid-seventeenth century, observed that Shah Tahmasp of Persia had enquired of Humayun the reasons for the expulsion of the Mughals from Hindustan. Upon being informed that the two martial *qaum*s (castes) were the Rajputs and Afghans and that these *giroh*s (groups) had cordial relations with each other, the Shah advised Humayun to first strike an alliance with the Rajputs, and that 'efforts should be made to rear them up since without gaining control over the zamindars it is not possible to rule in Hind'. On recovering the throne, Humayun implemented the advice and also passed it on as a *wasiyat* to Akbar. He advised Akbar that 'this *qaum* (Rajputs) should be reared up because they do not have contumacy and disobedience but only obedience and service'. Bhakkari stated that it is 'well known to all and sundry . . . he showed preference to the Kachhawahas, Rathors, Tanwar, Bahai and Baghela (Rajputs) and raised them from zamindari to position of nobility (*bah-amirai*)'.

Bhara Mal of the Kachhawaha clan, ruler of the small principality of Amber in eastern Rajasthan, was the first to seek Akbar's support in 1562 against Mirza Sharafuddin Husain, *hakim* (governor) of Mewat. Kachhawahas were introduced as *alus* (tribe or clan) by Abu'l Fazl in his *Akbarnama*, a term used in Mongolia and Central Asia for a kinship group organised as a military contingent. So as a 'tribal chief' or clan chief, the Kachhawaha ruler derived sustenance from his own kinship group, unlike a 'territorial chief' represented by the Rana of Mewar, whose power-base extended beyond his single kinship and included groups other than his own kinship and military unit, which inhabited his territory. To consolidate his bond with Akbar, Bhara Mal offered a vast booty, his daughter in marriage, and his nephew and grandnephew Bhagwant Das and Man Singh, respectively, as *mansabdar*s in the imperial service. This event was significant for its chronological proximity to the abolition of pilgrimage tax and *jizya* in 1563 and 1564, respectively, and systematised subsequent Mughal–Rajput relations. With matrimonial alliances, as the Rajputs became Mughal kin and imperial *mansabdar*s, they acquired wide exposure and were placed in a wider political arena that rid them of local internecine conflicts.

Akbar, in addition to marrying the daughter of Bhara Mal, married the daughter of Tipu, a *patar* (concubine) of Rao Maldeo. Later, in 1584, kinship with the Kachhawahas was further strengthened when Salim (Jahangir) was married to Man Bai, the daughter of Bhagwant Das. Notwithstanding the insubordination they may have caused, matrimonial alliances appeared significant from the reign of Akbar for the stability and order that they ostensibly engendered in personal and political relations between the Rajputs and the Mughals. The Rajputs did not just become Mughal kinsmen, as mentioned above; more importantly, the Rajput princesses were given the status of *patrani* (chief queen) and their children the opportunity to ascend the throne.

Box 8.1: Inter-faith marriages for political alliance

The practice of marriage to seal a political accord was not unique; marriages had been solemnised even earlier to achieve political ends. For instance,

- Firuz Shah Bahmani married the daughter of Deo Raj of Vijayanagara;
- Yusuf Adil Shah of Bijapur married the sister of Mukund Rao Maratha;
- Muhammad Shah of Gujarat married the daughter of Idar;
- Two daughters of Rao Maldeo—Bai Kanka and Lal Bai—were married to Sultan Mahmud of Gujarat and a Sur ruler, possibly Islam Shah Sur, respectively;
- Haji Khan Pathan, ruler of eastern Rajasthan, married another daughter of Rao Maldeo, namely Ratnavati, as well as the eldest daughter of Raja Bhara Mal subsequent to his invasion of Amber;
- Marriages were also solemnised between the Rajput rulers and the Khans of Nagor.

With the crystallisation of Mughal–Rajput relations that began in 1562, Akbar realised the importance of invoking the already existent feuds amongst the Rajput states. Military expeditions were sent to Jaitaran and Merta in 1558 by the Mughal *subadar* of Ajmer, and when the two forts of Marwar were besieged in 1562, the Kachhawaha contingent played a significant role on the side of the Mughals. Subsequently, in the Mughal conquest of Jodhpur, Ram Rai, the elder brother of Rao Chandrasen, ruler of Marwar, supported Akbar. The acquisition of Marwar was considered inevitable for both political and economic reasons. Trade routes passed through Marwar, but more significantly, the conquest of Gujarat and Deccan could be facilitated if Marwar was conciliated. Rao Chandrasen was compelled to relinquish the fort of Jodhpur; thereafter, only the southern part of Marwar remained with him. Although he had married one of his daughters to Akbar, he soon turned rebellious. Nonetheless, Akbar succeeded in consolidating his relations with Ram Rai and Udai Singh, Rao Chandrasen's two brothers, as well as with Rai Singh of Bikaner. In 1583, Jodhpur, which had been under *khalisa* for long, was restored to Mota Raja Udai Singh, the younger brother of Rao Chandrasen, who incidentally was in the Mughal imperial service. As a step towards cementing the relationship with the Mughals, he had his daughter Jagat Gosain (mother of Khurram [Shahjahan]) married to Salim, putting an end to any further Mughal incursions in Marwar. It may nevertheless be pointed out that a matrimonial alliance was not considered a test of loyalty or submission to the Mughal emperor, apparent from the fact that no marriages were negotiated with the Hadas, Sirohi, Banswara, and others even after their rulers had surrendered to Akbar (Image 8.1).

Mewar, however, had continued to resist Mughal authority and constituted a strong independent political entity at the time of Akbar's accession. Adding to its strength was the fact that the Rana of Mewar, as mentioned above, was a 'territorial chief', which implied that within the territory over which he possessed sovereign rights, the chiefs of the different groups that lived in that territory, namely the Bhils, Rana Punja, Sonigara, chief of Pali, and others, accepted his authority, while he was also chief of the Sisodia clan. The principal support for the Rana, therefore, came not only from his kinsmen, but also other clans like the Bhils. Like the Sisodia Rana, some chiefs were distinctly 'territorial', while lack of evidence makes it difficult to identify whether the others were tribal or territorial. For these reasons, it was imperative for the Mughals from the reign of Akbar to subdue Mewar in order to achieve complete control over Rajputana and the territories in its proximity. Akbar attacked Mewar in 1567 on the pretext that the Rana of Mewar had provided shelter to the Mughal refugees, Baz Bahadur of Malwa and the Uzbek Mirzas. In fact, like the earlier rulers of Delhi, Akbar too sought to expand into Malwa and Gujarat, and this necessitated the conquest of Rajputana since all routes to Malwa and Gujarat traversed through it. Akbar sieged Chittor in 1567 and occupied it in 1568, assimilating it as a Mughal *sarkar*, although the siege was valiantly resisted by Jaimal and Patta and their forces. The protracted siege, which resulted in tremendous loss of life, devastation, and *jauhar*, was hailed by Akbar in a *fathnama* issued to the *Qazi* of Bilgram as *fatah* over the *kafir*s by the *ghazi*s. The language of the *fathnama* was the same as that used by Babur after his victory over Rana Sanga. Iqtidar Alam Khan argued that although Akbar has often been questioned on these grounds, it was political expediency that prompted him to issue the *fathnama*. It was never repeated again. Khan suggested that by 1565, Akbar had successfully conciliated most of the Rajput states; he was compelled to make these pompous announcements in order to win the support of the *'ulama* and fulfil his ideal of neo-imperialism or rule by tacit consent.

Mewar revived its resistance with the accession of Maharana Pratap in 1572. The Rana's opposition implied that western Rajputana and the states dependent on Mewar or ruled by the Sisodia clan—that is, Dungarpur, Banswara, Bundi, Sirohi, and others—would either remain

Image 8.1: Illustration from *Akbarnama* by Miskina, Sarwan, Portraits by Madhav, *c.* 1590–95, depicts a scene from the court of Emperor Akbar, 1577, with the emperor greeting Rajput rulers and other nobles

Source: https://commons.wikimedia.org/wiki/File: 1577-Akbar_greeting_Rajput_rulers_and_other_nobles_at_court-*Akbarnama*.jpg.

beyond the control of the Mughals or be fluctuating allies. Akbar sent a number of embassies to resolve the issue, but the Rana, keen to avenge the defeat at Chittor, refused to offer personal submission to the emperor and prepared for war, leading to the battle of Haldighati in 1576. The battle failed to break the stalemate between the Mughals and Mewar. The Rana retreated to the hills and, with the support of the contingents of his subordinates, continued to resist the Mughals—although this did not affect Mughal relations with the other Rajput states. Military operations against the Rana were slackened by 1585–86; he succeeded in retrieving most parts of Mewar except Chittor and Mandalgarh, and Chawand in south Mewar continued to be his capital until his death.

With the accession of Jahangir, efforts to tighten and deepen the domination of Mewar continued. Jahangir, too, faced the biggest resistance from the Rana of Mewar, whom he had failed to subdue in his earlier assignment during the latter years of Akbar's reign. On acceding to the throne, Jahangir despatched Prince Parvez, accompanied by Rana Sagar, brother of Maharana Pratap, on a military expedition against Mewar. Jahangir focused on conciliating Rana Sagar, hoping that if he became the Rana, Mewar might cease to defy the Mughals; or at least a breach could be created, making possible the conquest of Mewar. He thus demonstrated that the Mughals understood the differences based on clan and kin relationships and took advantage of it to extend the imperial cause, even if it often ignited discord amongst the Rajputs. Prince Parvez, however, could hardly withstand the evasive tactics of Rana Amar Singh; moreover, even before an open battle could take place, he was recalled because of Prince Khusro's rebellion, leaving the task of securing the capitulation of the Rana to Prince Khurram in 1615. Delighted at the Rana's submission, Jahangir wrote in his *Tuzuk-i Jahangiri* that the former 'chose obedience and loyalty' and that he (Jahangir) 'forgave the Rana's offences and gave a gracious *farman* ... impressed with the mark of my auspicious palm'. Pleading old age, the Rana requested exemption from personal appearance at the Mughal court, offering to send his son, Karan Singh, instead and maintain a contingent of 1,500 *sawar*s to serve in the Mughal army. Jahangir agreed to grant the terms, provided the Rana did not fortify Chittor. As a step towards further reconciliation, Karan Singh was given the *mansab* of 5,000 *zat*/5,000 *sawar* and a substantial *jagir*, while all territories captured during the reigns of Akbar and Jahangir, including Chittor, were reinstated to the Rana. None of these imperial concessions appeared to soothe the pride of Rana Amar Singh, who abdicated in favour of Karan Singh (although Jahangir refused to accept it); matters pertaining to the issue were resolved only on the death of the Rana.

Significantly, Jahangir did not insist on matrimonial relations with Mewar, a pattern that continued even subsequently between the Mughals and Mewar. Otherwise, the political strategy of negotiating marriages with the Rajput *raja*s invoked by Akbar was continued by Jahangir. Jahangir married Man Bai, the Kachhawaha princess, and Jagat Gosain/Jodha Bai, daughter of Mota Raja Udai Singh, during the lifetime of his father. Subsequently, he married the princesses from Bikaner and Jaisalmer, the daughter of Ram Chand Bundela, and yet another Kachhawaha princess, the daughter of Jagat Singh Kachhawaha, eldest son of Raja Man Singh. Early in Jahangir's reign, Shahjahan was married to Bai Lilawati, granddaughter of Raja Gaj Singh of

Marwar, and Parvez was married to Bai Manbhawati, daughter of Raja Suraj Singh of Jodhpur; his grandson, Dawar Baksh (son of Khusro), was also married to a Rajput princess. There are no other recorded marriages of Shahjahan or Aurangzeb with Rajput princesses, but Aurangzeb's sons Azam and Muazzam were married to the daughters of Kirat Singh Kachhawaha (son of Mirza Raja Jai Singh) and Raja Rup Singh of Kishangarh (a small principality in Rajputana), respectively, whereas his nephew, Sulaiman Shukoh (Dara Shukoh's son), was married to the granddaughter of Raja Gaj Singh. It is apparent from these examples that matrimonial alliances between Mughals and Rajputs (excluding Mewar) continued to be the tool to achieve political cordiality, although, from the late seventeenth century, they became rare, except in anticipation of an impending struggle for power.

By the seventeenth century, the Mughal emperors had transformed the traditional power base of the Rajputs, that is, the clan ties and clan hierarchy of Rajputs was replaced by the *mansabdari* system that facilitated the enhancement of personal prestige and power amongst the Rajputs. Self-aggrandisement was the main objective of the Rajput rulers; they had earlier used their positions in their respective clans to achieve this and now, as *mansabdar*s, they realised that it was not binding on them to protect or secure imperial interest. The Mughal and Rajput attitude during the reigns of Shahjahan and Aurangzeb can be illustrated through the example of Raja Jaswant Singh, the ruler of Marwar from 1638–78, whose accession marked the importance and dominance of the Mughal emperor in Rajputana. Raja Gaj Singh, the ruler of Marwar, had disinherited his elder son, Amar Singh, and nominated Jaswant Singh as his heir. To strengthen his decision and implement it, Gaj Singh secured Shahjahan's approval recognising Jaswant Singh as his heir in 1638. In this context, it may be observed that to be the heir-designate or ascend the throne, the law of succession or of primogeniture was not a sacred or a defined norm—although legitimacy, or the ability to rule, was an important criterion; perhaps most desirable was imperial approval of the *gaddi*, which both the Mughal emperors and Rajput *raja*s exploited to the maximum.

To legitimise Jaswant Singh's accession, it was necessary that the *tika* ceremony be performed by the emperor. Therefore, after Gaj Singh's death in 1638, while Jaswant Singh made no attempt to gain the approval of his clan for the next two years, he considered it appropriate to go to Agra to secure the *tika* personally from Shahjahan prior to his formal coronation at Jodhpur in 1640. This indicates not only the commanding position of the Mughals over Marwar, but also the declining influence of the clan. More noticeably, it was apparent that Shahjahan held the Marwar alliance in high esteem; he performed the *tika* ceremony for Jaswant Singh (who held a special place in Shahjahan's heart, probably because of his blood relationship with the emperor's mother, Jodha Bai), inducted him as a *mansabdar* of 4,000 *zat*/4,000 *sawar* (which was raised to 7,000 *zat*/7,000 *sawar* by 1657), and presented *khilat*s or robes of honour to all Rathor clansmen in the Mughal court. Jaswant Singh reciprocated by establishing an administration in Marwar independent of clan ties, but supported by the Mughal emperor. Subsequently, he was deputed by Shahjahan to lead the imperial army in the war of succession, but when Aurangzeb defeated the royal army in the battle of Dharmat, Jaswant Singh pleaded for alliance with Aurangzeb, even though he continued to conspire with Shuja, Dara, and Shivaji to defeat Aurangzeb.

Realising that defeating Aurangzeb would be difficult, Jaswant Singh sought Aurangzeb's pardon, to which the latter readily complied. On accession, Aurangzeb reinstated Jaswant Singh as the ruler of Marwar, reconfirmed his *mansab*, and appointed him the *thanadar* of Jamrud, a position that he continued to hold till his death in December 1678. By 1678, Jaswant Singh had been reduced to a mere Mughal vassal; he had compromised his independence and that of his clan, which aroused the resentment of his clansmen. His clansmen realised the futility of any rebellion against Jaswant Singh because he ruled with the consent of the Mughal emperor. They perhaps waited for an opportunity to revolt, which came with the death of Jaswant Singh. Civil rebellion then ensued in Rajputana, especially because he had died without any heir. In Marwar, there were no definite principles that governed succession; the general custom that had evolved was that the prince whose mother was the *raja*'s favourite was nominated as the heir. In Jaswant Singh's case, the issue was further complicated because he had no male heir. According to the norms of escheat that prevailed in the Mughal Empire, the property of heirless nobles was resumed by the Mughal emperor; the noble's property was assessed and restored only after determining the debt that he may have owed the empire. Responding to developments in Marwar, but more significantly to the realisation that Jaswant Singh had died in heavy debt to the empire, Aurangzeb ordered that the state of Marwar, including Jodhpur, be brought under *khalisa* and a detailed inventory be prepared of Jaswant Singh's property. It may be pertinent to note that the emperor's decision to bring Marwar under *khalisa* did not imply its 'annexation' to the empire, but was necessitated by the pending decision on disputed succession in the Rathor kingdom and the Mughal policy of escheat, which entailed inquiry in the event of the death of an indebted noble.

The Rathors rebelled against the Mughal decision to implement escheat and to secure their clan domination. The rebellion took a more definitive turn with the posthumous birth of two sons of Jaswant Singh in February 1679. But even before the birth of the two sons, the situation in Marwar had become explosive. On the request of Jaswant Singh's clansmen at Jamrud, the emperor granted the *pargana*s of Sojat and Jaitaran as *jagir*s to his family for their maintenance. All Rathors, however, were unwilling to accept the leadership of the Rathors of Jamrud. Rani Hadi, the chief queen of Jaswant Singh who was then in residence at Jodhpur, pleaded that since Jodhpur was his *watan* (homeland), it was against customary practice to dispossess his descendants. She further suggested that except for Jodhpur, which should remain in her possession, the whole of Marwar could be placed under *khalisa*. Even as Rani Hadi continued to petition the emperor for her rights over Jodhpur, Indra Singh Rathor, the grandson of Jaswant Singh's elder brother, Amar Singh, demanded the recognition of his rights and the reversal of the injustice meted out to his father upon the death of Gaj Singh. Meanwhile, news arrived of the birth of two posthumous sons to the *rani*s of Jaswant Singh. Their claims were supported by Rao Anup Singh, the ruler of Bikaner and Khan-i-Jahan, the imperial *bakshi*. Given the growing factionalism and divisiveness, Aurangzeb decided to assert imperial authority to resolve the succession issue. In May 1679, he conferred the *tika* on Indra Singh Rathor, who paid a *peshkash* of Rs 36 lakh to the emperor. Towards the end of June 1679, the two sons, along with the *rani*s and Durga Das, reached Delhi, after Aurangzeb's assurance that he would grant the princes a *mansab* if they were brought up in Delhi. One of the sons died, but Ajit Singh survived to continue the contest for the *gaddi*. Defying Aurangzeb's orders to keep the infant prince at the Mughal court, the Rathors, led by Durga Das, hid Ajit Singh in a basket and reached Marwar in July 1679. To resist the authority of Indra Singh Rathor, Durga Das organised the coronation of Ajit Singh as the ruler of Marwar in August 1679. Reacting to the events, Aurangzeb removed Indra Singh Rathor from the *gaddi* for his incompetence in controlling the fissiparous circumstances in Marwar and despatched troops to Marwar in September 1679. He posted himself in Ajmer to control the imperial forces and deputed his son, Akbar, to Jodhpur to crush the Rathor rebellion. For the time being, resistance in Marwar appeared to have been curbed. Jodhpur was occupied and Rani Hadi was pacified with the grant of the *pargana* of Baran as *jagir* for her maintenance. But this did not placate the Rathors who, led by Durga Das, sought the assistance of Mewar.

The traditional rivalry between Marwar and Mewar was characteristic of Rajputana, but when Rana Raj Singh acceded to Durga Das' plea for help, the Rathor–Sisodia alliance transformed the nature of Rajput resistance against the Mughals. The Rana perhaps considered the disputed succession in Marwar an opportunity to reassert the importance of Mewar in the affairs of Rajputana, although he must have known that this would mean open defiance of the Mughal emperor and entail an attack on Mewar. Aurangzeb marched to Mewar from Ajmer in November 1679, deputed his sons Azam and Muazzam to attack Mewar from different directions, and appointed his other son, Akbar, as the administrator of Mewar. The Rana proposed terms of peace to the Mughals and the Rathors swore them loyalty, renewing their plea for the restoration of Ajit Singh as the Maharaja of Marwar. This was the situation when Rana Raj Singh died in September 1680, putting an end to bonds of unity between the Rathors and the Sisodias. In the meantime, Prince Akbar succeeded in suppressing the Rathor rebellion in October 1680 and defeated the Sisodias in November 1680. The Mughal success against Marwar and Mewar undermined the significance of Rajput resistance, but the Rajputs dominated once again when both the Rathors and the Sisodias supported the rebellion of Prince Akbar and his machinations to declare himself emperor at Nadol in January 1681. His recalcitrance failed with the withdrawal of Sisodia support and Rana Jai Singh's offer of peace to Aurangzeb, which resulted in the treaty of Rajasamudra between the Rana and Prince Azam on behalf of Aurangzeb in June 1681. The Rana agreed to cede the *pargana*s of Mandal, Pur, and Bidnur in lieu of *jizya* and assured against any future cooperation with the Rathors. Emulating the pattern set in the sixteenth century by Akbar, Aurangzeb, in return for acceptance of his sovereignty, conferred the title of Rana on Jai Singh, bestowed on him a *mansab* of 5,000 *zat*/5,000 *sawar*, and absorbed his kins as *mansabdar*s. In recognising these terms, the emperor was also motivated by a pragmatic political strategy—after Shivaji's death in 1680, Aurangzeb had become increasingly interested in Deccan and wanted to use Mewar as the northern plank for his Deccan conquest.

The Rana, however, remained dissatisfied. He demanded the restoration of the *pargana*s of Mandal, Pur, and Bidnur as a precondition for the fulfillment of the requirements of his *mansab*. that is, the supply of a contingent of 1,000 *sawar*s for Mughal service. In 1684, Aurangzeb agreed to restore the *pargana*s, but stipulated the payment of a *peshkash* of Rs 1 lakh annually.

This led to further complications and disputes later when Prince Azam entered into a secret pact with Rana Amar Singh, promising to restore the *pargana*s and write off the annual tribute in exchange for his support in the war of succession.

The Rathor rebellion continued intermittently with varying degrees of intensity from 1681–1707, probably because Durga Das was unsuccessful in securing imperial recognition for Ajit Singh. Durga Das and Prince Akbar sought the help of Sambhaji, but Sambhaji was so keenly engaged in his own territorial defence against the Mughals that he provided no substantial support to Prince Akbar. Consequently, in February 1687, Prince Akbar took refuge with Shah Abbas of Persia and Durga Das returned to Marwar in August of the same year. Ajit Singh grew up in a contentious, divisive, faction-ridden Rathor society dominated by Mughal manoeuvres. In 1698, he reluctantly allowed Jodhpur to continue in the possession of the Mughal emperor and offered his services as a *mansabdar*. However, on two occasions—1701 and 1706—he turned defiant against the Mughal occupation of Jodhpur, albeit with little success. Subsequently, with the appointment of Durga Das to the imperial service, the Rathor rebellion came to an end.

Assessing the nature of the Rathor rebellion, Robert Hallissey argued that it was a factional conflict among different Rathor *shakha*s to assert their dominance, rather than being against Mughal imperialism. Aurangzeb initially remained indifferent to clan factionalism; however, once it had deepened into civil war and become a threat to the stability of the Mughal Empire, he intervened, clearly demonstrating his political objectives. The rebellion was not caused by the Rathor need to protect their religion, nor was it against Aurangzeb's orthodoxy or an expression of clan sentiment for the heir of Jaswant Singh, or a people's war in support of Ajit Singh, as argued by Jadunath Sarkar (1972 [1928]), V. S. Bhargava (1966), and S. R. Sharma (1966). The reimposition of *jizya*, which coincided with the Rathor rebellion, has often been subjected to critical assessment by some like Jadunath Sarkar and Faruki, but there was a complete lack of protest following it and a continuation of the friendly alliance between Rajputs and Mughals. G. N. Sharma (1962) has rightly argued that had there been any local protest, it would have been recorded by contemporary scholars. There is, nevertheless, a debate on an anonymous letter of protest against *jizya*, the language of which suggests, as observed by Jadunath Sarkar, that it was probably written by Shivaji rather than any of the Rajputs. In this context, if one examined Aurangzeb's responses, it would be evident that a religious perspective would be an inadequate explanation of his decisions, which were influenced by local conditions and political expediency rather than reactionary orthodoxy. More significantly, the politics of Marwar and Mewar had no impact on Rajput states like Amber, Bikaner, Bundi, Kotah, and others that continued to be in Mughal service even after 1679. The period following Aurangzeb's death was marked by campaigns to crush the resistances led by Ajit Singh and Jai Singh of Marwar and Mewar, respectively, especially during the reign of Bahadur Shah (1707–12), but after Bahadur Shah's death, when power passed into the hands of the *wazir* Zulfiqar Khan, the Rajputs were once again assigned important administrative positions, their *mansab*s raised to 7,000 *zat*/7,000 *sawar*, and marriages solemnised between the Mughals and Rajputs. The first such marriage in over 100 years was celebrated between a daughter of Maharaja Ajit Singh of Marwar and Farrukh Siyar. The Mughal–Rajput alliance, as Satish Chandra (1993) defined it, was *ab inito*—a class alliance of two ruling groups. Their mutual conflicts were largely political, whether for power, *mansabs*, *jagirs* or territory, with recourse to religion whenever convenient.

THE PORTUGUESE, VIJAYANAGARA, *NAYAKAS*, AND DECCAN SULTANATES

In 1526, when Babur had established himself in the Ganga–Yamuna *doab* region, the core of north India, the states of Bengal, Orissa, and Vijayanagara (Karnataka) were considered sovereign political entities. The Deccan Sultanate of Bahmani that had derived its political legitimacy and economic experience from Iran had disintegrated by then. Firishta observed that it was Ahmad Shah Bahmani (r. 1422–36) who imported the disciples of Sufi saint Shah Niamatullah from Kirman, and a merchant, Khalaf Hasan, from Basra. The latter was given the title of *malik ut-tujjar* for promoting trade connections between Deccan and Iran. Khwaja Mahmud Gawan, also a migrant from Iran along with his son, Abdullah, had continued the process of commercial exchange between Bahmani and Iran. Generally, those who migrated to the Bahmani Sultanate did not abandon their links with Iran; instead, they fostered it. By the mid-fifteenth century, the foreigners increasingly monopolised administrative positions, resulting in the exclusion of the Deccanis, who felt deprived of social and political status. To maintain a distinction between the two, noteworthy Iranians like Mahmud Gawan were referred to as *afaqi* (distant) or *ghair mulki* (foreign), as opposed to *dakhni* or Deccani (sons of the soil). Of the established states in 1530, the Vijayanagara kingdom, which at that time spread from Telangana and southern Maharashtra to the Madurai–Tirunelveli area in south India, lasted the longest. In the heydays of Vijayanagara during the early sixteenth century, the southern peninsula experienced increased elite migration. Telugu-speaking warriors had moved into upland sections of the Tamil country. The kingdom surrounded several linguistic regions, encouraging a multilinguistic milieu at the court. This trend was further strengthened after 1565 when the remains of Vijayanagara were concentrated in Tamil south, outside the demarcated core area of the former empire. Vijayanagara was far from being a unitary, centralised state, although there was a regular capital flow between distant regions and the imperial centre. This compels a reconsideration of Burton Stein's proposition that Vijayanagara was a 'segmentary' state, with the regions preserving autonomy and only recognising the ritual superiority of the centre. Vijayanagara's active politics and its alliance with Bijapur in 1560 to defeat Ahmadnagar had alarmed the Mughals. Akbar had watched with apprehension Vijayanagara's extension close to his territory, especially after his annexation of Malwa in 1561. Yet he had no role to play in the decline of Vijayanagara, for which he has been implicated by at least one Telugu text, *Ramarajana Bakhair*, which stipulated that the defeat of Vijayanagara by the Deccan Sultanates was strategised by Akbar, and that the emperor was actually present on the battlefield!

To the contrary, the disintegration of Vijayanagara was the result of a long-engineered process. For several centuries preceding 1520, the Bahmani Sultans to the north of the Raichur Doab (an exceptionally fertile area in Deccan situated between rivers Tungabhadra and Krishna) and the kings of Vijayanagara to the south had battled incessantly for control of the economic resources of the Raichur Doab and the fortified city of Raichur. The Bahmani Sultanate lost

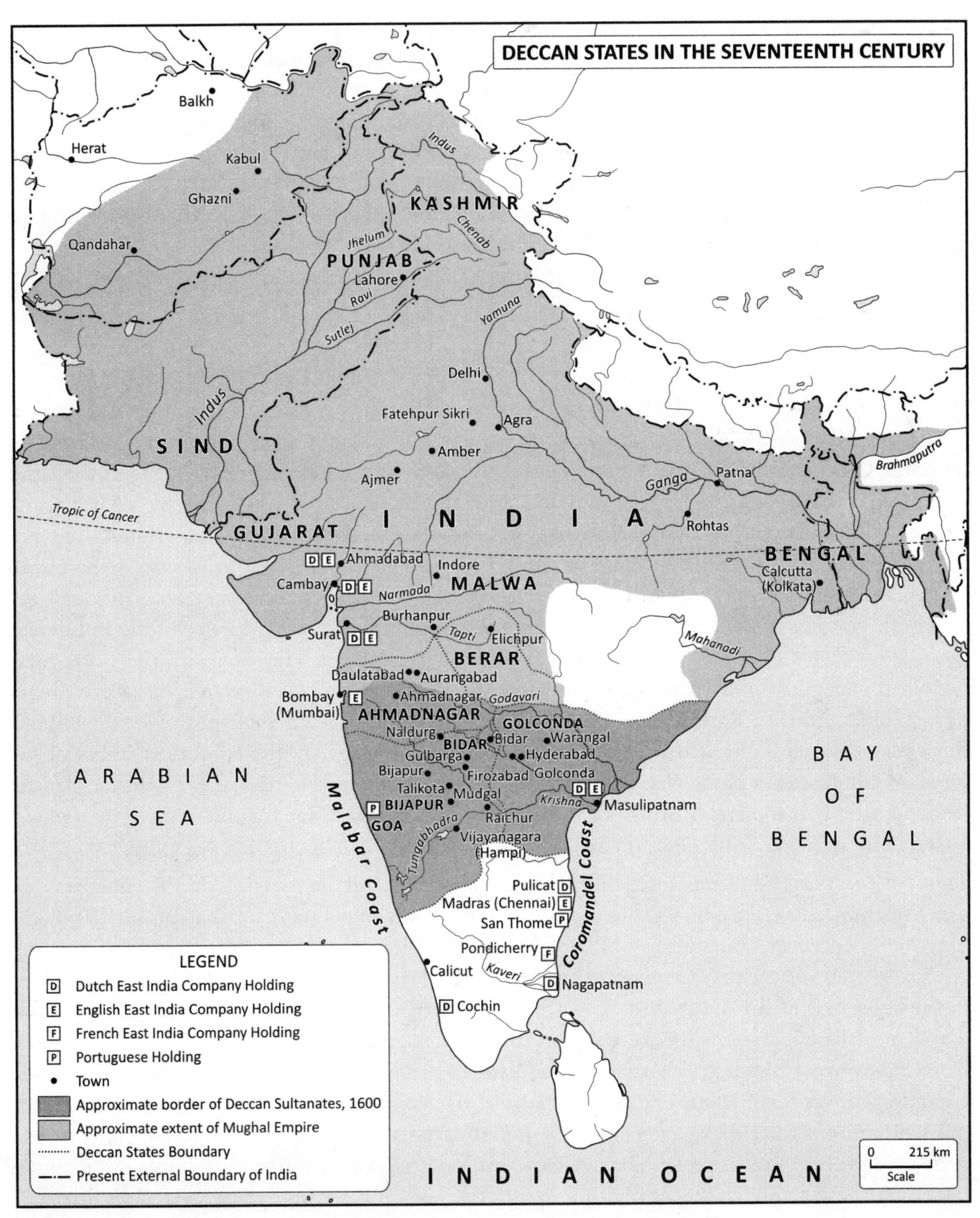

The external boundaries and coastlines of India agree with the Record/Master Copy certified by the Survey of India.

its prolonged hegemony over Raichur Doab by the first decade of the sixteenth century when it disintegrated into five *de facto* successor states—Bijapur, Golconda, Ahmadnagar, Berar, and Bidar—that inherited the quarrel over the Raichur Doab. Taking advantage of the feuds between the five newly created states, Krishna Deva Raya of Vijayanagara conquered and annexed the entire peninsula, from the southern tip of the Raichur Doab to Cape Comorin, between 1509 and 1520, consolidating manpower and accumulating capital resources that boosted his endeavours to recapture Raichur from Bijapur. Krishna Deva Raya defeated Isma'il 'Adil Khan in the contest of 1520 for control over Raichur fort and the Raichur Doab.

The power-tilt in favour of Vijayanagara was facilitated by the arrival of *Estado da India*, a formidable coastal power since 1498 that not only sought to control commerce in the Arabian Sea, but was also keen to end the dominance of the newly founded Sultanate of Bijapur, which controlled the west coast and the Raichur Doab. With these objectives, the Portuguese found an ally in Vijayanagara and in 1510 Albuquerque, assisted by the loyalists of Vijayanagara, captured Goa from Yusuf 'Adil Khan of Bijapur. The Sultans of Bijapur made no serious attempt to reoccupy Goa. This limited the conflict between Bijapur and the Portuguese, but then the latter came into a tussle with the trading settlements of the Kanara coast controlled by Vijayanagara. More significantly, the tolerance towards Vijayanagara practised under Dom Manuel did not persist, apparent from the 1540 order of the Portuguese governor, Martim Afonso de Souza, to launch an attack on the Tirupati temple patronised by the kings of Vijayanagara. Although the attack did not materialise, the fact that it was even contemplated was evidence of the indifferent attitude of *Estado da India* towards the religious sentiments of Vijayanagara. The Portuguese remained quiet in the 1550s and early 1560s with the revival of Vijayanagara as a military power under Aravidu Rama Raya. However, they soon resurrected their position when Rama Raya was defeated and killed in the battle of Talikota in 1565 by the combined forces of the Deccan Sultanates—a battle that had a lasting impact on the geopolitics of the Deccan plateau, reconfiguring it completely. By 1600, the Vijayanagara Empire was fragmented.

Immediately after the defeat of Vijayanagara, the Portuguese, through a series of attacks, acquired the ports of Mangalore, Basrur, and Honawar. But the decline of Vijayanagara had a detrimental effect on Goa's trade economy, which was dependent on the imports from the kingdom. Moreover, the Sultans of Ahmadnagar and Bijapur, taking advantage of the vacuum created by the collapse of Vijayanagara, attacked the Portuguese settlements of Konkan and Goa in the latter part of the 1560s and early 1570s. The situation became increasingly unfavourable for the Portuguese. Meanwhile, subsequent to the defeat, the capital of Vijayanagara was shifted from Hampi to Chandragiri, situated at a distance from the cities of Bijapur and Golconda. Chandragiri was fortified and palaces were built by Aravidu Venkatapati II (1586–1614), the most prominent ruler of Vijayanagara's imperial dynasty, the Aravidu. Although he aimed to revive the greatness of imperial Vijayanagara, his long reign was marked by succession disputes heralding the collapse of the Aravidu dynasty. The last king of the dynasty, Aravidu Sriranga, in an attempt to recover his territories occupied by Bijapur and Golconda from the later years of the 1630s, established contact with the Mughal court during the reign of Shahjahan in the 1650s. The letters of a spy in the Aravidu camp revealed that Sriranga offered huge wealth to the emperor, including jewels and gold from the Vaishnava temple at Tirupati, in return for the emperor's patronage, a subordinate position under him, and the grant of territories around Chandragiri and Velur as his *watan jagir*. While Shahjahan was ostensibly inclined to accept the offer, the Sultan of Golconda reacted sharply and compelled Sriranga to leave the territory. There was, in fact, no respite for the Aravidus after 1565 when the *nayaka*s or warrior nobles assumed the role of kings in the far south. The *nayaka*s of many areas, especially Karnataka, asserted their independence. Although the borderlands between Andhra Pradesh and Tamil Nadu continued to be managed by the Aravidu dynasty, most of the Tamil country was occupied by three Telugu-speaking *nayaka* warrior families, all of whom had been firmly established in the far south since around 1530, regardless of the glory of Vijayanagara's imperial power.

The *nayaka*s, as local military chiefs, were recognised as key political figures in the Vijayanagara state. According to some sixteenth-century European narratives, a part of the resources that the *nayaka*s held was transferred to the imperial capital of Vijayanagara in the form of tribute, although indigenous sources are ambiguous on the issue. Fernao Nuniz, a Portuguese horse-trader who had resided temporarily in Vijayanagara during the 1530s, commented that there were roughly 200 *nayaka*s in the empire, each of whom possessed land rights granted to them by the Vijayanagara king. In Nuniz's opinion, the *nayaka*s were the owners of all lands in the empire. As early as 1946, Nilakanta Sastri had argued that the *nayaka*s were completely dependent on the decisions of the kings of Vijayanagara until 1565, when they achieved a semi-independent status. Later in 1955, in the first edition of *A History of South India*, Sastri reinforced the feudal terminology used by scholars like D. C. Sircar, who characterised Vijayanagara as 'feudal' on the basis of the suggestion that 75 per cent of the villages of the empire were under *amaram* (prebend), and described the *nayaka*s as feudatories with conditional military tenure. Questioning the feudal meaning ascribed to the office of the *nayaka*s and their definition as 'one who holds land from the Vijayanagara king on condition of offering military service', Burton Stein commented that a more prudent understanding of *nayaka* would be that of a powerful warrior who could occasionally be associated with the military ventures of Vijayanagara kings; but in effect, a *nayaka* was a territorial magnate in his own right.

Sastri changed his interpretation yet again in 1964 and observed that Vijayanagara was best defined as a military confederation of many chiefs. Stein, however, argued that the *nayaka* institution marked the modification of the segmentary state of the Cholas; it was a system that had antecedents in the political and military arrangements of the Hoysala kingdom of Karnataka and the Kakatiya kingdom of Andhra. Vijayanagara was, in Stein's opinion, a significant variant form of segmentary organisation in which the chiefs or *nayaka*s of localities (whom 'Abdur Razzaq, in his fifteenth-century account of Vijayanagara, described as the 'powerful men of each province') possessed greater independence from local society than ever before in Tamil country. Velcheru Narayana Rao, David Shulman, and Sanjay Subrahmanyam (1992b) remain sceptical of the characterisation of Vijayanagara as a segmentary state.

The *nayaka* rule in Tamil Nadu extended roughly from the early sixteenth century to the 1730s when Madurai, the last of the 'great' *nayaka* states, declined. The three dominant *nayaka* states based at Senji (Gingee), Tanjavur, and Madurai (Tiruccirappalli) varied in their ruling spans, development plans, and geo-ecological environments and experienced distinct historical encounters, notwithstanding their several common characteristics and cultural patterns. These states were in extent smaller than their contemporary Mughal Empire or the Karnataka (Vijayanagara) kingdom, from which the *nayaka* kingdoms had originated. From amongst the three *nayaka* kingdoms, the richest and largest was based at Madurai, located on Vaigai River; the *nayaka*s from Tanjavur controlled the fertile delta region of Kaveri River; and the most tenuous of the three was situated at Senji, fairly close to Chandragiri, the Aravidu base, and an obstacle to the expansion of Senji. Generally, the *nayaka* rulers had continued with the ceremonial acknowledgement of the Vijayanagara kings even under the Aravidu dynasty, and gave a part of their revenues to Chandragiri till the 1630s. The social groups that fostered the emergence of the *nayaka* rulers comprised not the old landed aristocracy but upwardly mobile entrepreneurs, who represented an amalgam of martial and commercial skills. These warrior-merchants contributed to the growing commercialisation of the *nayaka* political economy. The *nayaka* economy in fact witnessed energetic growth with expanding networks of trade and extension of agriculture into the dryer zones of the Tamil countryside. Both the *nayaka* and Aravidu states stood to gain from the sales tax and custom duties generated from the market towns that had arisen throughout the far south as a result of the increasing domestic trade and exports from the several ports along the Coromandel Coast. Moreover, subscribing to the importance of international trade, imports were mildly charged. Emulating the kings of Vijayanagara, these southern states were particularly anxious about the overseas trade of horses to strengthen their armies. Their eagerness for the import of precious metals facilitated a substantial supply of gold into their territories, which boosted their gold-based currency in contrast to the silver coins that were the primary unit of the northern monetary system under the Mughals. Consequently, the large flow of bullion (gold, silver, and copper) into India from the international market became a remarkable feature of the seventeenth and eighteenth centuries.

The *nayaka* rulers were ardent patrons of literature. The Tanjavur *nayaka*s were especially known for their patronage of Sanskrit and regional literatures, most notably in the genre of dance drama known as *Yakshagana*. One of the *Yakshagana* composed by a Tanjavur prince about his father, Raghunatha Nayaka (r. 1612–34), depicted a scene of accountants speaking and bickering in different languages—Tamil, Telugu, and Kannada—representing thus the tension between the diverse constituents of the kingdom. Regardless of the similarities with the former Vijayanagara Empire, the *nayaka* kingdoms revealed a different trend. They were less militaristic in their disposition, evident from their representations in literature not as warrior-heroes or moral archetypes, but as semi-divine and deeply erotic individuals. The essence of kingship had changed; it was, as Rao, et al. (1992) suggested, 'heroism not of the battlefield but of the bedroom'. With the emphasis on eroticism, the literary works mirrored an element in *nayaka* culture on *bhoga* or consumption (which may imply 'to eat', but the definition may be extended to mean 'to enjoy'). The concept of 'pleasurable consumption' was reflected not only in literature but also in visual representations in the form of sensual sculptural depictions of the kings and courtiers, and their images on calicos, in ivory, and on stucco-decoration on the local temples.

The characteristic of *bhoga* also influenced *nayaka* religious values and attitude; instead of giving land grants or making permanent endowments to temples or other religious institutions, they preferred to host lavish meals in the temples for Brahmins and other religious elite. Adhering to the traditional concept of kingship that implies sheltering the subjects, but more significantly, protecting the religious institutions of the kingdom, Tirumala Nayaka of Madurai, for instance, organised feasts and gifts for the temple priests even as he generously assisted the temples and ensured the maintenance of religious rituals. His foremost contribution was the merging of two separate festivals of Madurai—celebration of the marriage between Shiva and Minakshi at the Minakshi temple, and the festival at the Vishnu temple—thus integrating the different high-caste traditions of worship in Tamil Nadu.

The *nayaka* rulers, in addition to being patrons of literature, emulated the imperial architectural forms of Vijayanagara, a combination of *archoate* and *trabeate* styles. While the palace architecture was generally a combination of arch (*archoate*) and beam (*trabeate*), the temple construction was always a beam structure. An important example of a *nayaka* palace that merged the arch and the beam is a seventeenth-century palace at Madurai with an arched audience hall, embellished with stucco-sculptured figures and mythic animals. The style of large temple-construction typified by massive *gopuras* (gateways) initiated by the rulers of Vijayanagara was further consolidated by the *nayakas*. The most prominent of their temple complexes is the Minakshi temple in Madurai, which dates back to the seventeenth century.

The decline in the power of the *nayaka* kingdoms coincided with the weakening of the Aravidu dynasty, the last of the Vijayanagara dynasty. Neither the Aravidus nor the Senji *nayakas* could effectively resist the Deccan Sultanates of Bijapur and Golconda in 1636, after they had secured their northern boundaries against the Mughals by a treaty that same year. Both the Aravidus and Senji *nayakas* lost their respective kingdoms by 1650, and the Tanjavur *nayakas* were displaced in 1670 by a section of the Maratha Bhonsle clan. The *nayaka* kingdom of Madurai, however, survived till the eighteenth century. Distinct in many ways from the classic Vijayanagara rule, the *nayaka* cultural and artistic legacy had a lasting impact.

The disintegration of the Bahmani and Vijayanagara kingdoms led to the emergence of new Deccan Sultanates in peninsular India roughly by 1500, although these states could reach their culmination only by 1565, subsequent to the battle of Talikota and the defeat of Vijayanagara. Succeeding the Bahmani kingdom, Bijapur, ruled by the Adil Shahi dynasty and situated in the proximity of the capital of Vijayanagara, was a major beneficiary as it acquired the arable lands and mineral resources of the Raichur Doab. The other two noteworthy Sultanates in addition to Berar and Bidar that succeeded the Bahmani kingdom were Ahmadnagar and Golconda, ruled by the Nizam Shahi and Qutb Shahi dynasties, respectively. While Ahmadnagar controlled the present Maharashtra area, Golconda was spread over northern Andhra Pradesh. The remains of Vijayanagara were wiped away from Karnataka after 1565 and reduced considerably in southern Andhra Pradesh, but between 1550 and 1650, many states succeeded Vijayanagara in southern Karnataka and the Tamil country.

The Deccan Sultanates that rose from the debris of Bahmani shared certain common concerns, one of which was the ratio between *afaqi* (foreigners) and *dakhni* in the administration, not quite dissimilar to what had prevailed in the Bahmani kingdom. The *afaqi*s largely comprised Persian-speaking Iranians, although Arabs and Africans were also included amongst them. The *dakhni*, on the other hand, were Muslim migrants and converts from north India. Yet another aspect that separated them was sectarian: the *dakhni*s were Sunni and the *afaqi*s Shi'i. The distinction between the two groups began in mid-fifteenth century Deccan when the *afaqi*s thronged the nobility and civil bureaucracy to the exclusion of the *dakhni*s, who complained about losing their political and social status. Immigration from the Middle East had continued into Deccan till at least 1575 as compared to north India, where migration from Persia and Arabic-speaking countries was revived only in the last decades of the sixteenth century. Consequently, the flow of Persians and Persian culture around 1600 was greater in Deccan than in north India. A demographic estimate based on a Portuguese report of the early sixteenth century suggested that the *afaqi* population in Deccan, comprising scholars, Sufi saints, militarists, and merchants, ranged from 10,000–12,000. The successor states of Bahmani, particularly Bijapur, Golconda, and Ahmadnagar, continued their links with Iran in the sixteenth century and encouraged the migration of the Iranian learned class, warriors, administrators, and merchants. The account of Rafi-ud-din Shirazi revealed that Yusuf Adil Shah (r. 1490–1510), the founder of the Bijapur Sultanate, was brought to Deccan by an Iranian merchant, Khwaja Zainal Abidin Simnani. The Qutb Shahs of Golconda also claimed Iranian descent. The founder of the Qutb Shahi dynasty, Quli Qutb Shah, had fled Hamadan for India in 1478. While Bijapur and Ahmadnagar could not sustain the migrations from Iran beyond the late sixteenth century, Iranian influence maintained its grip over Golconda until the seventeenth century.

With the persistent Iranian migration and influence in Deccan, Shi'ism was actively adopted here. In Bijapur, a few rulers were ardent Shi'i followers; although there was no rigidity, some were Sunni Muslims as well. While the gateway of the tomb of Ali Adil Shah (r. 1558–80) was inscribed with Shi'i inscriptions, there was no building in Bijapur that was assigned for the exclusive use of the Shi'is. Another characteristic that distinguished Bijapur from Golconda, a strictly Shi'i state, was the adherence to both Sufism and Shi'ism by rulers like Ali Adil Shah, who even chose to be buried near Sufi shrines even though Sufism was considered antithetical to Shi'ism. By the seventeenth century, Sufis in Bijapur had diverse affiliations and interests; some of them worked in close association with the court and were recipients of state land grants, while several others remained aloof from state patronage and engaged in propagating their ideas through literary works that they composed in both Persian and *dakhani*. Sufism, in fact, had a tremendous impact in Deccan from the early fourteenth century. The first Sufi order introduced here was that of the *Chishti*s, followed by other orders in the fifteenth and sixteenth centuries from either the Middle East, or other parts of India.

In Golconda, to the contrary, Shi'ism was the declared state religion. The architecture of the region also displayed Shi'i features. For instance, the stucco ornamentation on the interior of the gateway of Char Minar in Hyderabad, situated close to Golconda city, is designed in the shape of *alam*s, that is, standards used by the Shi'is to commemorate the day of Muharram and Husain, the martyred grandson of the Prophet. Later, a royal *Ashur Khana* was constructed with the specific purpose of holding the huge metal *alam*s used during the commemoration of

Ashur, the tenth day of Muharram, when Husain was martyred. In fact, small *alams* in stucco are widely distributed on the religious buildings of Hyderabad, as confirmation perhaps of commitment to Shi'ism.

The economic prosperity and growth of Golconda were linked to its main port city, Masulipatnam. Masulipatnam flourished as compared to any of the port cities in Ahmadnagar or Bijapur, where the Portuguese were strongly entrenched. With bare minimum intervention from the Portuguese, Masulipatnam emerged as a centre for international trade and the redistribution of commodities from other coastal areas such as Bengal. Overland trade between Masulipatnam and Surat via Golconda became a possibility with the construction of a road connecting Masulipatnam to the capital city of Golconda. Initially, Masulipatnam's maritime trade was focused on Southeast Asia, where items from Coromandel Coast were in great demand. But by the last decades of the sixteenth century, Masulipatnam emerged as the first port on the east coast to connect the eastern and western zones of the Indian Ocean trade and commerce. Masulipatnam's maritime trade was largely in cotton textiles, including muslin and chintz. In addition, Golconda was known for its exports in diamonds and high-calibre iron and steel. The Sultans of Golconda could foster the growth of Masulipatnam with the collaborative efforts of Iranian migrants, who made substantial investments in shipbuilding and maritime trade. Strategically located, Masulipatnam provided a direct link to Mecca, establishing itself as a base for pilgrims.

In the early seventeenth century, revenue farming was a popular mode in Golconda like in Chandragiri (the capital of the Aravidus) and the *nayaka* states; the ruling dynasties reflected the influence of the ideology of the Balija Naidus, a semi-commercial, semi-warrior caste group with whom they were closely associated. The method of revenue assessment in the fertile coastal rice fields in these states, including Golconda, was that of crop-sharing, similar to the practice of *batai* or *ghalla-bakshi* in the Mughal Empire. Crop rates were applied to non-food crops and low value crops like millets, but they were not adequately systematised. Around the latter part of the 1670s and early 1680s, a Telugu Brahmin minister of Golconda, Madanna Pandit, and his brother Akkanna attempted to redefine the financial policy of the Sultanate. Recruiting revenue officials from their own caste group, they attempted to redeem the *jama'-i kamil* (perfect assessment) so as to reduce the gap between assessment and collection. Regardless of the resistance mounted by Muslim notables, probably for sectarian reasons, the reform did happen and formed the basis of the revenue settlement of 'province *dar-ul-jihad* Hyderabad'. It was further regulated after the Mughal conquest of Golconda in 1689–90. Alam and Subrahmanyam argued that in the absence of *arazi* statistics for this settlement, it was clear that it was not based on land measurement but had *jama'* (assessment) figures and *muqarrar hasil* (established receipts). It was the Mughal *diwan*, in consultation with local magnates, who decided on the level of increase of assessment in each region, depending on the gap between revenue assessment and revenue receipt. The Mughals emulated the Madanna settlement in Hyderabad after annexing it. The system of revenue farming continued—the Dutch held the revenue farms allotted to them under Abu'l Qutb Shah through the 1690s; more significantly, within a half-century of the Mughal conquest of Golconda, the coastal districts were again brought under revenue farming. Such patterns continued to evolve into the second quarter of the eighteenth century.

Faizi Fayyazi, while on a mission to Deccan during the years 1591–93, provided a valuable account—in appreciation as well as critical—of Ahmadnagar and Burhanpur, perhaps to instigate the conquest of Ahmadnagar that could bring massive economic gains to the Mughals. Providing an exhaustive description of the flora—trees, variety of fruits and flowers—of the city of Ahmadnagar, Faizi also talked of the goldsmiths and the weavers of the city, who in his opinion were 'unparalleled'. Generally appreciative of the high-quality cloth of Deccan, he especially mentioned Patan and Daulatabad as textile centres. Somewhat similar was the description of Burhanpur, which he described as a small town (*baghayat tang*) but full of gardens, greenery (*bustan*), cultivable fields, and plenty of fruits. These elaborate descriptions were obviously attractive to Akbar and his sons, who not only planned military expeditions in the region but also made Burhanpur their residence.

The Sultanates of Bijapur and Golconda were the most prosperous of the Bahmani successor states; the other states located more towards the north of the Deccan frontier were subjected to frequent Mughal aggressions. By the 1630s, though, with the Mughal annexation of northern Maharashtra, Bijapur and Golconda were compelled to sign a treaty with the Mughals. Relieved to have protected their respective kingdoms, particularly their northern sectors, both Sultanates acquired an aggressive tenor towards the territories further south. Bijapur annexed southern Karnataka and the fortress of Senji, putting an end to the *nayaka* states, whereas Golconda occupied southern Andhra, heralding the dissolution of the Aravidus, the last ruling dynasty of Vijayanagara. The respite from Mughal expeditions was brief for both Bijapur and Golconda, for they were annexed by the Mughals in the 1680s.

MUGHAL RELATIONS WITH THE DECCAN SULTANATES

The Deccan frontier in the late sixteenth–seventeenth centuries offered major political largesse to variant power-holders, be it the expanding Mughal Empire from the 1560s or the kingdoms of Bijapur, Ahmadnagar, and Golconda, or the Portuguese *Estado da India* (established in the western Indian Ocean in 1497, with its primary base in Goa and subsidiary ones in Daman and Diu), or even the Safavid dynasty of Persia, which had nurtured political ambitions from its base at Ardabil. The invincibility of Shah Isma'il of Persia weakened with his defeat by the Ottoman Sultan in the battle of Chaldiran in 1514. It is in this context that Mughal relations with Deccan and their control of the region need to be understood.

Babur was the first Mughal emperor to have established diplomatic contacts with the Portuguese. However, his ambitions with regard to the control of two maritime provinces—Gujarat and Bengal—remained unfulfilled. Humayun, too, despite his aspirations and interest in developments in the Deccan, had to abandon his expansionary activities perforce, compelled into exile by Sher Shah Sur. Akbar also had to keep aloof from Deccan politics till he had achieved the much desired conquest of Gujarat and Bengal and other strategic zones like the autonomous kingdom of Sind. With Rajputana and Malwa under his control, Akbar succeeded in conquering Gujarat in 1572, but the rulers of Bengal—whether Afghans or belonging to older local lineages—continued to resist the Mughals for several decades until the early seventeenth century.

The conquest of Gujarat was not without complications; Akbar was apprehensive that Gujarat and Khandesh were on cordial terms although, ironically, Muhammad Shah II of Khandesh had laid claims on Gujarat. Muhammad Shah II had been in conflict with the Mughals from 1562 when the Mughal general, Pir Muhammad Khan, entered Khandesh in search of Baz Bahadur, the former Sultan of Malwa defeated by the Mughals and suspected to have taken refuge in Khandesh. The expedition had, however, failed. Another development of the 1570s that alarmed Akbar and the Sultans of Khandesh, Bijapur, and Golconda was the annexation of Berar by Ahmadnagar in 1574. Meanwhile, the death of Muhammad Shah II in 1577 and the succession of Raja Ali Khan (Adil Shah IV) came as an opportunity for the Mughal emperor, who deputed another military expedition to Khandesh to retrieve the pending tribute to the Mughals from the state. Adil Shah IV surrendered without resistance, although his sympathies lay with the Deccan Sultanates. It appears that in view of the aggression of Ahmadnagar and Bijapur, Adil Shah IV was constrained to align with the Mughal emperor, who by now had emerged as a powerful political force. For the Mughals, Khandesh was of strategic importance. It formed a link between Gujarat and Deccan, and its alliance was therefore of special significance in order to secure the Mughal frontiers in Gujarat and Malwa and serve as a base for further entry into Deccan.

In western India, the Portuguese viewed the Mughal expansion, at least from the 1570s, with apprehension, fearing that with the collapse of the Vijayanagara Empire in southwestern Deccan, the Mughals might enter Goa and threaten their supremacy. In fact, Mughal–Portuguese relations after the conquest of Gujarat in 1572 and during the reign of Akbar had equal potential for conflict as for collaboration. The Mughal ports of Gujarat and Portuguese-controlled ports like Goa and Hurmuz were linked to important trade routes in the last quarter of the sixteenth century, and if the coastal *qafila*s along the west coast and the annual fleets to the Persian Gulf had to continue to ply, both the Mughals and the Portuguese had to reach a consensus. Both were keen on this movement; for the Mughals, Surat was important because it was supplied with silver *reales* and other goods, and the Portuguese *Estado da India* was interested because it received customs revenue, and Gujarat textiles brought to Goa could be sent to Europe. Both were also keen on the *hajj* traffic—the Portuguese as the *cartaz*-issuing authorities and the Mughals, whose ships received the safe conducts, were obliged to enter into contracts similar to those between the Portuguese and the Deccan Sultans for the same purpose. Such contracts were often a source of conflict: the Mughals were hesitant to accept *cartazes* and the Portuguese officials were keen to not lose any opportunity to get the maximum benefits out of this arrangement. Additionally, if the *hajj* from Surat and other ports was to be maintained, an understanding with the maritime power was necessary. Moreover, from the late 1570s, Mughal–Portuguese relations acquired a religious dimension with the presence of the Jesuit fathers in Akbar's court. While the Jesuits hoped to convert the emperor and some of his nobles to Christianity, they were also a conduit between the Portuguese authorities at Goa and the Mughal court. The Jesuits were thus a convenient presence, especially since *Estado da India* and the Mughals did not encourage permanent diplomatic missions in each other's territories. Monserrate gave an exhaustive account of the tensions between the Mughals and the Portuguese in Gujarat and off the coast of Konkan during 1581–82, and so did Abu'l Fazl in his *Akbarnama*. While Mughal–Portuguese relations remained ambiguous and incongruous, Mughal expansion in different directions continued to be a matter of anxiety for the Portuguese.

In addition to Khandesh, Akbar conquered Berar and partially annexed Ahmadnagar; it was the death of Chand Bibi Sultana that precipitated the fall of Ahmadnagar in 1600. In 1601, the imperial army sieged Burhanpur and captured the fort of Asirgarh, thus extending the Mughal southern frontier as far as Bijapur. Although Akbar had personally supervised the campaign, he gave the charge of Deccan to his son Daniyal along with Abdul Rahim *Khana-i-Khanan*, the veteran general. In fact, from the 1520s to the early eighteenth century, the Mughals were engaged in territorial expansion in all directions, from the Ganga–Yamuna *doab* region to the south. If Abu'l Fazl is to be believed, Akbar's objective was not 'a display of mere personal ambition or lust for conquest but an expression of the enlightenment of a great monarch', so that 'various classes of mankind could experience the joys of concord'. After the early 1590s when Sind was captured and the resistance of the Sultans of Gujarat overpowered, the western territory remained largely stable, while the campaigns to the east could stop only in the 1660s with the fall of Chittagong. North and northwest continued to be potential areas for expansion up to the reign of Shahjahan, when the latter led an unsuccessful expedition to Balkh. Following the consolidation of their conquests in Bengal, Gujarat, the north and northwestern frontier, the Mughal emperors remained focused on Deccan and Karnataka.

Jahangir had hoped to consolidate Akbar's conquest in Deccan but for the revival of the Nizamshahi dynasty of Ahmadnagar under Malik Ambar, who caused a hiatus in the Deccan policy of the Mughals. Malik Ambar rose to prominence in Ahmadnagar during 1595–1600. His emergence to power was also supported by the Marathas. In fact, under the direction of Malik Ambar, the Sultanate of Ahmadnagar had effectively become a joint *habshi*-Maratha enterprise. Analysing the career of Malik Ambar, Richard Eaton (2008, 2010) referred to a number of factors related to the social history of Deccan—issues of race, class, gender, and the institution of slavery. Malik Ambar (his original name was Chapu, which suggests his origins in the Kambata region of southern Ethiopia) was a slave from Ethiopia who was sold to a merchant in Baghdad. Recognising Chapu's intellectual abilities, the merchant raised and educated him and converted him to Islam, giving him the name Ambar, before sending him to Ahmadnagar. Both Ahmadnagar and Bijapur had the largest number of *habshi* slaves and Ambar was one of the 1,000 *habshi* slaves purchased by Chingiz Khan (himself a *habshi* and a former slave). Eaton, in this context, explained Afro-Indian relations and more specifically Africa's role in the rise and fall of military slavery in Deccan between the mid-fifteenth and mid-seventeenth centuries. Understanding the large extent of the trafficking of military labour from Africa to India, it is possible to evaluate the commercial system of the basin of the Arabian Sea and the political system of the Deccan Sultanates, and examine why this trade began, why it ended, and what ultimately happened to the military slaves who were imported to Deccan.

Assisted by the Marathas and recruited as *bargir*, Malik Ambar posed a major challenge to the Mughal army in Deccan. In 1610, he succeeded in expelling the Mughal army from the fort of Ahmadnagar. Significantly, he contributed to the economic revival of Ahmadnagar by adopting

Todar Mal's revenue reforms, according to which land under cultivation was measured, revenue collected both in kind and cash, and the State demand fixed at a rate that varied from two-fifth to one-third. To counter Malik Ambar, Jahangir attempted to conciliate the Marathas by recognising them as the *sardars* of their territories. By 1615, many Maratha *sardars* had accepted the sovereignty of Jahangir and consented to assist Prince Khurram in defeating the combined Deccan forces. By 1622, both Bijapur and Golconda had sought Mughal alliance and agreed to pay the annual tribute. To celebrate the victory in Deccan, Khurram was decorated with the title of Shahjahan and his *mansab* was raised to an unprecedented 30,000 *zat* and 20,000 *sawar*.

The accession of Shahjahan in 1627 was marked by new exertions in Mughal–Deccan relations that culminated in the 'Treaty of Submission' for Bijapur and Golconda in 1636. The period also witnessed the declining economic strength of Goa and the death of Malik Ambar. These developments gave Shahjahan an opportunity to be aggressive in Deccan and assert Mughal power by attempting to crush Ahmadnagar and offer Bijapur an offensive-defensive alliance with the objective of partitioning Ahmadnagar. Shahjahan began by capturing the new Nizamshahi capital, Daulatabad, and defeated Husain Shah in 1633. Taking advantage of the declining Ahmadnagar, Bijapur and Golconda joined the tussle to seize it. With the support of Bijapur, Shahji Bhonsle, Shivaji's father, nominated a puppet Nizam Shah and ruled one-fourth of the territory in his name. Shahjahan reacted by separating Daulatabad and Ahmadnagar from the province of Khandesh, placing it under another viceroy in 1634. In 1636, Shahjahan organised to attack Bijapur and Golconda. Golconda responded by tacitly accepting the sovereignty of the Mughal emperor, agreed to pay an annual tribute of 2 lakh *huns*, read the *khutba* in the name of the emperor, and issued *sikkas* in his name. Bijapur, however, resisted. Shahjahan attempted to conciliate Bijapur by granting it one-third of the southern territories of Ahmadnagar, but compelled it to pay a revenue of 20 lakh *huns* or a sum of Rs 80 lakh. The Sultan of Bijapur agreed to pay an indemnity of 20 lakh *huns*, but not an annual tribute. Having demarcated the Mughal frontier in Deccan and established his sovereignty, Shahjahan appointed Aurangzeb as the viceroy of Deccan in July 1636. The accord of 1636, however, proved more beneficial to Bujapur and Golconda. Relieved temporarily of Mughal pressure, the combined forces of both Sultanates engaged in campaigns further south and annexed lands in Karnataka—both to the west on the Kanara coast and in the areas from Senji to Tanjavur. The Mughal emperor consented to maintain neutrality except if Deccan was torn by conflicts, or if it affected the Mughal political interest. Two other gains for Shahjahan in 1636 were the defeat of Shahji Bhonsle and the annexation of Ahmadnagar.

The period 1640s–1650s saw a few changes and new developments in Mughal–Deccan affairs. Aurangzeb was removed as the viceroy of Deccan in 1644 and sent as governor of Gujarat in 1645. Subsequently, in 1647, he was asked to join the military expedition to Balkh as second-in-command. By 1648, the Mughal emperor was becoming increasingly restive with his declared neutrality in Deccan and assurance that he would not woo the subordinates of the Deccan Sultanates. This became apparent when, in 1649, Shahji Bhonsle was granted a *mansab* of 5,000 *zat*/5,000 *sawar*, indicating clearly that the Mughals were keen on intervention in Deccan and the conciliation of the Maratha *sardars*. Aurangzeb was restored as viceroy of Deccan in 1652, notwithstanding his differences with Shahjahan. Aurangzeb objected to his *jagir*, which apparently yielded 17 lakhs less than his previous *jagir* in Sindh. Yet another friction pertained to Bijapur and Golconda. In 1656 and 1657, respectively, Golconda and Bijapur were attacked on the pretext that the Mughals were not satisfied by the size of their tribute, especially after their territorial expansion further south; and also that the Mughals did not approve of the exchange rate between the rupee and the *hun*. While these were cited as causes, Aurangzeb, as viceroy of Deccan, appeared keen on an outright annexation of the two Sultanates. However, before the annexation could take place, Shahjahan ordered the lifting of the siege. Some historians have argued that Shahjahan's decision was perhaps influenced by Dara Shukoh and his bias against Aurangzeb. Satish Chandra (1993) interpreted the situation differently. He saw it as evidence of Shahjahan's 'limited policy'; Shahjahan, persuaded by financial crisis, the growing gap between *jama* and *hasil*, adoption of *mahwar*s, and crisis in the *jagirdari* system, was not in favour of a complete annexation of the Deccan states. By the treaty of 1657, Bijapur was forced to surrender all Nizamshahi territories granted to it by the treaty of 1636. Golconda too was compelled to abandon its hold over the Coromandel Coast, which had emerged as a vibrant commercial centre for foreign trade and the export of textiles and indigo. By the end of Shahjahan's reign, it was evident that the treaty of 1636 was dead, even as the Deccan states remained un-annexed and Mughal ambitions in Deccan became infinite.

Regardless of his aggressive goals in Deccan as its viceroy, Aurangzeb the emperor was more cautious in his engagements with Deccan. His accession coincided with the rise of the Marathas under Shivaji and Maratha claims over former Nizamshahi territories, on which the Mughals too asserted their rights. In addition, Shivaji also demanded the forts and palaces of Bijapur. Another issue that irked Aurangzeb was that even though Bijapur had not implemented the treaty of 1657, it exhibited its eagerness to control the former Nizamshahi territories. Such a situation created a dilemma—on the one hand, Aurangzeb wanted to compel Adil Shah of Bijapur to implement the treaty of 1657, surrender Parenda, its dependencies and Nizamshahi Konkan, while on the other, he sought his support to oust Shivaji from the Mughal frontier and the former Nizamshahi territories. The emperor, however, was unwilling to compromise on the treaty of 1657. In these circumstances of 'Mughal political bankruptcy', as Satish Chandra called it, political tensions aggravated in Deccan. Even as Aurangzeb prepared to resolve issues with Bijapur, Shivaji attacked Shaista Khan in 1660. To counter the rising scuffles in Deccan, Aurangzeb appointed Jai Singh as the viceroy of Deccan, who advocated a policy vexed with contradictions and complexities. Jai Singh advised the annexation of Deccan on the one hand and consolidation of Mughal–Maratha relations on the other to achieve a successful conquest. Simultaneously, he suggested a strategy of divide and rule to keep the Deccanis divided, without conceding anything in return for their support against the Marathas. Pursuing his objective of building Mughal–Maratha relations, Jai Singh signed the treaty of Purandhar with Shivaji in 1664. Shivaji was forced to surrender twenty-three of the thirty-five forts he had occupied in Mughal territory; he was instead compensated with equivalent territory at the expense of Bijapur. Notwithstanding these developments, Aurangzeb did not quite agree with Jai Singh that alliance with Shivaji was necessary for the conquest of Bijapur. For Aurangzeb, the expedition against

Bijapur and alliance with Shivaji were two independent issues. Persistent in his efforts to recover the territories that Bijapur and Golconda had been expected to cede to the Mughals in 1657, Aurangzeb was triumphant to an extent when he recaptured Sholapur, the last Nizamshahi settlement, from Bijapur (see Plate 9).

Bijapur experienced internal decline with the death of Ali Adil Shah in 1672, which coincided with the growing ambitions of Shivaji. To curtail the Marathas, Aurangzeb had hoped to use Bijapur and, if necessary, Golconda against Shivaji, but neither Bijapur nor Golconda (nor, indeed, any of the Deccan states) was willing to join the Mughals against the Marathas. By 1684, the Marathas had established themselves in Karnataka and developed guerilla tactics, which Bhimsen (in the *Nushka-i-Dilkusha*) described as *bargiri*, that is, surrounding the field from all four sides before launching an attack, a system prevalent in most parts of Deccan. More importantly, Shivaji was no longer considered a rebel by the Deccan states, including Bijapur, despite him usurping some of its territories; in fact, they looked forward to his alliance. From 1684, therefore, Aurangzeb resorted to the annexation of Deccan states, beginning with Bijapur, Golconda, and then Karnataka, achieving some success between 1684 and 1689. He put the Marathas on the defensive by sealing the routes they could have used to provide assistance to Bijapur and Golconda. Sambhaji's preoccupation with the Sidis and the Portuguese at this time came as an opportunity for Aurangzeb, who could now pursue his tactic of isolating the Deccan states and dealing with them separately. Sambhaji was captured and executed in 1689, causing widespread Maratha resistance.

Aurangzeb's move to bring Bijapur, Golconda, and Karnataka under direct Mughal administration was not trouble-free either; it brought him into conflict with the local landed magnates: Nayakas, Valemas, Berads, and Reddis. These non-Maratha zamindars had close relations with the Marathas, particularly the *mirasdar*s and zamindars of Maharashtra. None of these adverse circumstances affected Aurangzeb's consistent determination to capture Maratha forts or the forts in the possession of Bijapur and Golconda. He was probably instigated by the economic prosperity of the Coromandel Coast, rich in handicraft production and foreign trade, which could compensate for the famine in Gujarat and Malwa and the stagnation of trade in Surat caused by Maratha raids. The emperor may have also felt the need to counter the European companies engaged in their consolidation, and demanded licenses of trade from the weak, semi-independent Deccan Sultanates.

Analysing Aurangzeb's relations with the Deccan Sultanates and finding reasons as to why he could not achieve his objectives, Satish Chandra blamed the *jagirdari* crisis, which coincided with Aurangzeb's expeditions to Bijapur and Golconda, as well as Maratha activities. The peculiar feature of Deccan politics, he argued, was the overlapping of two crises:

- the political crisis caused by the internal decline of the Deccan Sultanates, and
- the rise of the Marathas and the *jagirdari* crisis, which affected the entire empire and administration.

Satish Chandra, along with Athar Ali, also ascribed the growing factionalism in the nobility to Aurangzeb's Deccan policy. In his urge to annex Bijapur, Golconda, and the Maratha kingdom,

Aurangzeb allocated high positions to Deccani nobles—Muslim or non-Muslim—provided they agreed to defect from their original states. The rising number of Deccanis in the imperial nobility caused widespread resentment amongst the *khanazads*, whose productive *sair-hasil jagirs* were allotted to the newly-recruited Deccani nobles; the latter refused to accept 'unsettled' lands, even while all 'settled' lands of Deccan were brought under *khalisa*.

John F. Richards (2014), in his interpretation of the imperial crisis in Deccan, accepted the suggestion of factional conflict among the nobles promoted by Satish Chandra and Athar Ali, but saw a certain 'sense of inevitability' implicit in their hypothesis. That is to say, it seemed to suggest that as soon as Deccan was conquered and Deccanis absorbed as *mansabdars*, the *jagir* shortage began, leading to the crisis. Regardless of this, Richards accepted two other assumptions put forward by Chandra and Ali: first, for a Mughal noble, his economic and monetary status was very important, and second, the strength of the empire depended on the efficiency and loyalty of the nobles. He added to this argument by stating that the Mughal imperial system comprised not merely the civil and military elite but several other groups in the empire as well, whose loyalty was equally important. He further observed that even though Bijapur and Golconda were annexed in 1686 and 1687, respectively, leading to an increase in the number of *mansabdars*, the empire need not have collapsed due to a shortage of funds. The problem, Richards said, lay in the decisions of the emperor, who failed to secure his southern frontiers and exploit the resources of Bijapur and Golconda to supplement his additional expenditure. Moreover, Richards averred that Aurangzeb, in his urge to subjugate Deccan, annexed areas that had never been subordinated, and thus failed to utilise the warrior traditions of the Marathas, Bidar, Gond or Telugu. Nor could he create effective political ties with the local zamindars, that is, the Nayakas, Valemas, Reddis, and Berads.

Yet another decision of Aurangzeb that went wrong, argued Richards, concerned the allocation and utilisation of *jagirs* in Deccan. If utilised properly, Bijapur and Golconda could have enhanced the revenue by 23 per cent. In addition, annual revenue from the districts of Hyderabad had increased revenue by 26 per cent in the *khalisa* of the empire. But Aurangzeb transferred the potential areas under *khalisa* and put the least promising lands in *paibaqi*. According to Richards, the shortage of *jagirs* was thus 'artificial'; it was not a scarcity of *paibaqi* or *be-jagiri* as suggested by Chandra and Athar Ali, respectively. Richards believed that the imperial crisis in Deccan could have been avoided had the emperor granted *jagirs* from *khalisa*; instead, he kept converting fertile *paibaqi* into *khalisa* and imposed restrictions on the allotment of *jagirs* in Deccan, that is, they could be given only to the Deccanis. In such a situation, it became difficult for Aurangzeb to resolve the problem of the northern *mansabdars*. These factors, Richards stipulated, along with the emperor's failure to mobilise lineage and caste networks of rural aristocracy, made his stay in Deccan burdensome.

THE MARATHA POLITY AND SHIVAJI

The emergence of the Marathas in the seventeenth century and their consolidation as an important political force by the end of the 1720s represents a social and political phenomenon. Different hypotheses have been suggested to explain the rise of the Marathas. S. R. Sharma, Jadunath Sarkar, and G. S. Sardesai considered the Maratha movement a counter to the religious orthodoxy of Aurangzeb, and saw it as a Hindu reaction against the emperor's communal policies; R. P. Tripathi talked of it as a regional reaction against the process of absorption into the Mughal Empire, and M. G. Ranade and V. V. Joshi explained the rise of Shivaji as heralding the Maratha nationalist movement. Satish Chandra rejected these theories on grounds of historical validity. He argued that the description of the Maratha movement as a nationalist movement presumed the existence of a foreign power, and if this implied that the Mughals, being Muslims, were foreigners in Deccan, then the same principle should have applied to the Sultans of Bijapur, Golconda, and Ahmadnagar. The evidence, to the contrary, shows that the Marathas had no hesitation in accepting the rule of the Deccan Sultans, and so if they resisted the Mughals, the reasons lay not in religion, but elsewhere. Chandra further argued that the expansion of Maratha power, first under Shahji Bhonsle and then under Shivaji, coincided with Shahjahan's reign, which was considered one of religious toleration. The struggle during this period was between the Marathas and the Deccan Sultanate of Bijapur, and was not directed towards the Mughals. In fact, many Maratha families prior to Shivaji were the recipients of grants and political favours from the Deccan Sultans. Shahji Bhonsle, for instance, owed his prominence to Malik Ambar of Ahmadnagar. Explaining the rise of Shahji from a 'minor commander of Bijapur and Ahmadnagar to kingmaker', Stewart Gordon (1993) applied the theory of warfare and invasion, that is, in the context of the Deccan Sultanates, he talked of the relationship between *wazir* and Sultan and the evolution of *dar wajh-i-istiqamat* or 'integrity fiefs' and forts as power structures.

Shivaji may have been projected as a 'rebel' for his resistance against the Deccan states and for asserting his dominance, but this was hardly connected to the issue of the religion of the Deccan states. Shivaji was not concerned with the welfare of 'Hindus' outside Maharashtra, nor did he introduce any social reform in the 'Hindu' society of Maharashtra. While he assumed the title of *haindeva-dharamodharak* at the time of his coronation, it can only be considered an emulation of a customary tradition, similar to that in Rajput states. It is apparent, observed Chandra, that religion—whether of Aurangzeb or Shivaji—had no role in establishing the power of the Marathas. Both Shahji and Shivaji were military strategists interested in carving out kingdoms for themselves; they were fortunate in the sense that their military adventurism was facilitated by the disintegration of Ahmadnagar and the gradual expansion of the Mughals in Deccan following the death of Akbar. Their military expertise and qualities as military commanders could thus be one way of explaining the rising prominence of the Marathas.

S. N. Sen (2002 [1925]), on the other hand, ascribed Shivaji's success to the support of the peasants, with whom he had established direct contact. He had also allegedly discontinued the zamindari and *jagirdari* systems. Sen's arguments, however, do not seem to be in line with the narrative of the Maratha chronicles, *Sabhasad* and *Ajnapatra*. *Sabhasad* does not talk about the abolition of zamindari rights or the *mokasa* grants (*mokasa* was a proprietary right in land, whether rent-free or at low quit-rent or revenue farming on conditions of service); in fact, it mentioned the grant of *mokasa* by Shivaji. *Ajnapatra*, on the other hand, emphasised the importance of *watandar*s and reprimanded the resumption of *watans*. In view of this evidence, it would appear that instead of abolishing these institutions, Shivaji perhaps regulated and systematised them. In this regard, it may be surmised that responding to Shivaji's attempts, *deshmukh*s of Maval, who were petty landholders at the mercy of big *deshmukh*s like the Morays and Nimbalkars and closely associated with the Sultan of Bijapur, were the first to align with Shivaji. Shivaji overpowered the big *deshmukh*s with the support of his army and compelled them to either surrender or cede their land. The crumbling of the big *deshmukh*s proved advantageous to both the small and middle-level *watandar*s, who were instead given the responsibility of improving and extending cultivation, and assessing and collecting land revenue.

To understand the making of Maratha polity under Shivaji, it is pertinent to mention his social motivations in addition to his military attributes, and the upward or downward social mobility of certain groups and families. Shivaji attempted to knit together the Marathas and the *kunbi*s (a cultivating caste) and convinced the latter that by aligning with the Marathas, they could raise their social status. Similarly, the *koli*s and other tribal groups were made to believe that by becoming a Maratha *kunbi* and opting for sedentary cultivation, they too could rise in the social hierarchy. Such efforts clearly demonstrate that the Maratha movement was far from being a political movement aimed at overthrowing 'foreign governments' or establishing independent states; it was visibly inspired by the objective of land control and control over big and small *deshmukh*s, *mirasi*s (*khudkasht*s), and *upari*s (*pahikasht*s). The Maratha movement illustrated how, within the framework of a traditional Hindu society, some groups and communities could rise up the social ladder, improve their *varna* status, and legitimise their right to exercise political power. An analysis of the composition of the Maratha ruling class revealed that it retained its regional character, and hardly any non-Maratha rose to a prominent position in the Maratha state during the eighteenth century. Shivaji's social strategies were simultaneously combined with his efforts to raise the status of his family in the social hierarchy by soliciting matrimonial alliances with the *deshmukh* families. This dual process of combating the big *deshmukh*s at the political and military level and then marrying them to seek social equality emboldened Shivaji to crown himself the sovereign of the Maratha state in 1674.

It is in this context that Stewart Gordon (1993) explained the etymology of the term Maratha, which, he observed, had developed as a caste category on the basis of its martial ideology, kinship and marriage restrictions. Coronation raised Shivaji's status from that of an ordinary *deshmukh*—he could no longer be dismissed as a 'rebel' and, more importantly, he could now relate to the Sultans of Bijapur and Golconda on a fairly even footing. To consolidate his position further, Shivaji prepared a genealogy linking him with the *suryavanshi* Kshatriya families of India, assumed the title of Kshatriya *kulavatamsa*, and claimed exclusive *sardesmukhi* rights over Deccan, setting aside the tradition of these rights being granted by the Sultans of Bijapur and Ahmadnagar to other Maratha families. However, Shivaji's claim of being a high-status Kshatriya and tracing his *vanshavali* to *suryavanshi* Kshatriyas raised the issue of the *varna* status of Marathas when the Brahmins of the time, who considered the Marathas low caste, refused to recognise them as Kshatriyas. Despite the Brahmin reactions, Shivaji was looked upon as a religious saviour by Maratha sources, mostly available for the late seventeenth–early eighteenth centuries. *Sabhasad*, written in 1697, declared Shivaji an incarnation of Mahadeva and attributed his victory over

Afzal Khan and Shaista Khan to the advice and miracle of Goddess Bhawani. *Sabhasad* may have attributed these characteristics to Shivaji for his learned, knowledgeable scholarship of the scriptures, but then Shivaji never relied on the scriptures to guide him in matters of state; he, in fact, rooted his administration in the ideas and institutions of both the Deccan Sultanates and the Mughal State.

The early Maratha historians derived their arguments from *Sabhasad*, *Ajnapatra*, and *91-Kalami Bakhar* and idealised Shivaji as a divine representation, a proto-nationalist, a 'glorious rebel', and an ideal Hindu ruler who resisted Mughal domination and struggled against the Muslims. Recent scholarship, however, has explored different themes for both seventeenth and eighteenth-century Maharashtra and not indulged in a mere eulogy of Shivaji. Andre Wink (1986) argued that Maratha *swarajya* was established and consolidated within the political and socio-economic context of Mughal polity; that *swarajya* as a political structure represented that 'intermediary gentry' or zamindars which the universalist Islamic ideology of empire had dismissed as illegitimate, and which the theory of despotism had excluded as non-existent. In this context, he explained the emergence of Maratha *swarajya* through the *fitna* tradition, that is, shifting alliances, and *fasad*, disturbances, sedition, rebellion, defection. Wink talked of the 'inward process' of *fitna*, which contributed to the expanding powers of Maratha zamindars; and that the institutionalisation of this power had resulted in a new agrarian order while the Mughal Empire was dissolving. It was through the process of *fitna*, Wink argued, that various local structures had emerged within the Mughal system, setting aside the notion of the despotic, unmitigated sovereignty of the Mughals. The Mughal Empire may have appeared centralised and despotic, but these were not its characteristics. Had the empire been despotic, the mechanics of Mughal politics would have been different; despotism does not permit the incorporative, assimilative methods of expansion as practised by the Mughal emperors. The empire demonstrated flexibility and fluidity and a loose structure which encouraged the growth of local power within its polity. The Marathas, therefore, were not an exclusive force that rose against the Mughals or because of the weak structure of the Mughals; it was within the context of Mughal polity that the Marathas could, without much effort, intensify and exploit factionalism in Mughal Deccan. Hiroshi Fukazawa (1968) emphasised state, caste, and rural labour relations to understand the eighteenth-century Maratha state, while Frank Perlin (1978) focused on the 'great families' pre-eminent in Maratha history in the same period and explained the processes of money, use, and credit; Stewart Gordon (1994), on the other hand, stressed on the nature of conquest, the military practices, and intra-state relations. Narrating the experiences of the Marathas and Brahmins in the Deccan Sultanates, Gordon explained the culmination of the Maratha state that ultimately replaced the Deccan Sultanates. Understanding the complexities of the eighteenth-century Maratha state, he talked of the taxation and credit structure, problems of loyalty and legitimacy, military and technological change, and the impact of Maratha polity on the society and economy of central India, Gujarat, and Maharashtra.

Interpreting the seventeenth century in Maratha affairs, Gordon argued for social mobility and continuity in Shivaji's administrative and social structure with the Sultanates of Bijapur and Ahmadnagar, whether with regard to his important officials comprising *ashtapradhan*—such as *peshwa, majumdar, dabir*, and others—or the administrative divisions—*prant* or *suba, taraf* or *mauza*—or the rights of the *deshmukh*s. Describing the *deshmukh* rights as 'nested rights' 'interpenetrated with other family rights', Gordon observed that Shivaji permitted the *deshmukh*s to 'live in peace', realising that without them, it would be impossible to collect taxes or govern. The *deshmukh*s enjoyed a variety of rights in addition to their land rights. They held forts, were headmen of villages (sometimes of more than one), and possessed hereditary rights to *inam* lands as well as orchards in the villages. Defining the rights and privileges of the primary zamindars, Shivaji reduced the *peshkashi* zamindars to the position of *khiraji*, that is, instead of being autonomous, they were now subject to government rules and regulations and compelled to abide by the orders of the revenue collectors. The *Sabhasad* suggested that this system was largely applied to *desh* or regions conquered from the Mughals or Bijapur and Golconda; it was not implemented in the scattered districts or the southern Maratha region. It is difficult to ascertain the actual revenue demand under Shivaji, although *Sabhasad* stated that it was two-fifth of the produce in grain; if the customary cesses were added to this, the state demand would compare considerably with the Mughal State demand of one-half, based on the same set of revenue ideals. Income from trade formed a substantially small portion of the revenue, with trade and handicraft production confined largely to the coastal areas.

Shivaji generally paid his officials through *iqta*s, held on revenue-farming terms. Revenue farming did not entail hereditary rights (although, on the frontiers where the authority of the Sultans or Shivaji was weak, the revenue farmers tended to assert their position). The other mode of payment to civil and military officials was *tankhwa* by means of *barat*, which was paid either on the treasury of the capital or the district. Soldiers from the cavalry and infantry were usually not assigned entire villages as *mokasa mahal*s, for there was always the fear of *mokasa* holders aligning with the zamindars and becoming rebellious. However, *Sabhasad*'s statement regarding refraining from granting *mokasa mahal*s appeared to be only an ideal rather than a practice under Shivaji, for *Sabhasad* itself mentioned the assignment of *mokasa mahal*s; two prominent occasions were the grant of it to many subsequent to the defeat of Afzal Khan, and its allocation to invoke Goddess Tulja Bhawani. In addition to the payment of cash salaries through *barat* to soldiers and *havaldar*s, they were paid through the assignment of lands known as *saranjam*. *Saranjam* was an assignment of revenue from villages or lands for the support of troops or personal military service, usually for life, to the grantee. It appeared to be a conditional grant that was neither transferable nor hereditary, but held at the discretion of the sovereign. *Mirasdar*s (*khudkasht*s) formed a large part of Shivaji's civil administration as well as the armed forces. They were assessed like ordinary peasants and the revenue due from them was set off against their salaries. An important aspect of Shivaji's military administration was the concept of plunder that he associated with the notion of *mulkgiri*. He systematised plundering and justified it as necessary to maintain large armed forces as a protective defence against the incursions of the Mughal Empire. Shivaji's army comprised infantry and cavalry, directly recruited and paid (by Shivaji), unlike the feudal armed retainers of the big *deshmukh*s and the *bargir*s controlled by their *sardar*s. The *bargir*s were paid irregularly but compensated through plunder during the war, a significant tool of Shivaji's military strategy. Ultimately, however, it resulted in the ruination of the peasantry of Deccan, both in and outside Maharashtra, undermining the Maratha state of Shivaji.

Having considered the rise of the Marathas and the contributions of Shivaji to the consolidation of Maratha polity, the question that arises is: Was Shivaji a potent factor in the decline of the Mughal Empire? M. N. Pearson (2014) analysed this and observed that although the Marathas had consistently gained power from the middle of the 1660s, what sustained them were the concept of Maratha *swarajya* and the tactical and strategic expertise of Shivaji, the Maratha fort-ability or *bargiri* tactics, the weakening of Bijapur, Aurangzeb's involvement in the quadrangular struggle for succession, and also perhaps, at least initially, the geographical location of the Maratha territories. The terrain of the Maratha kingdom posed physiographical difficulties for both Bijapur and the Mughals, especially the latter, who were not trained, or were unused to *bargiri* or guerilla tactics. By 1680, at the time of his death, Shivaji had created tremendous political and military strength for the Marathas, secured the support of the Deccan states, and was no longer considered a 'rebel' by them. He controlled 50,000 square miles or 4.1 per cent of the area of the entire subcontinent, and his revenue calculated up to one-fifth or one-sixth of that of Aurangzeb's. These factors, Pearson said, established his dominance as compared to the other 'rebel' groups, namely Jats, Sikhs, Yusufzais, and Afridis, who were not as effective in organising their regions. Shivaji's significance lay in the fact that he resisted being a 'rebel' and worked towards establishing himself as the head of a rival state.

Pearson discussed three events related to Shivaji and Aurangzeb which, in his opinion, may have contributed to the weakening of the Mughal Empire. By 1666, the unremitting escalation in Shivaji's power compelled Aurangzeb to interfere in Deccan politics, heralding thus the decline of the Mughal Empire. Aurangzeb deputed Shaista Khan, the viceroy of Deccan, to deal with Shivaji, but the latter defeated Shaista Khan in 1663, much to Aurangzeb's alarm. Shivaji's second attack on Mughal prestige was the sack of Surat in 1664. Surat, in the seventeenth century, represented an important trade centre; more significantly, it was a port from where the ships left for *hajj* to Mecca. Shivaji's plunder amounted to a loss of more than Rs 1 crore, leaving Surat unsettled; losses notwithstanding, what irked the Mughals was the fact that the attack was derogatory to Mughal military renown. Shivaji, nevertheless, remained adamant and reinforced his authority by demanding *chauth*. By 1670, Shivaji had overpowered Surat and weakened the Mughal resistance even further. To counter the Maratha attack on Shaista Khan and the raid on Surat, Aurangzeb deputed Jai Singh in 1665. Shivaji was defeated and compelled to sign the treaty of Purandhar, which led him to cede twenty-three of the thirty-five forts and 80 per cent of their revenue. But the treaty failed to eradicate the Marathas. Shivaji continued to hold a few forts; his son, Sambhaji, was granted a *mansab* of 5,000 *zat*/5,000 *sawar*, and Aurangzeb allowed Shivaji a share in the spoils of Bijapur and excused him from personal presence at the imperial court. Notwithstanding these concessions, the treaty was hardly a gain for the Mughals. Pearson argued that some success might have been possible had Shivaji been inducted into the *mansab* system and 'bonded to the empire'. But Aurangzeb did not offer a *mansab* acceptable to Shivaji, fearing the alienation of the Rajput and Persian *mansabdars*. None of Aurangzeb's attempts at conciliation or subjugation appeared to succeed, perhaps because by 1666, Shivaji had become so strong that Aurangzeb could find no means of 'buying' him. The third blow to the Mughal emperor was Shivaji's escape from imprisonment in August 1666.

The issue that needs to be considered is: Were these events so explosive as to weaken the Mughal Empire? Despite the raids on Surat, it had survived as an important trade centre in the eighteenth century; irrespective of the political manoeuvres of Shivaji, the Marathas desisted from attacking the centre of the Mughal Empire, nor did they adversely affect the interests of the Mughal nobility. So Aurangzeb could have protected his empire without interference in Deccan. But, as Pearson observed, Shivaji's activities aroused a very different kind of response. In Robert Berkhofer's (1971, 46) words, 'Behaviour is not a direct reaction to the stimuli but a response made in accordance with ideational mediation.' An analysis in the context of this definition would suggest that when Aurangzeb and his empire were openly challenged and Mughal invincibility broken, there was no alternative left except that of military response and an expedition to Deccan.

THE MARATHA STATE, 1680–1740, AND THE MAKINGS OF THE *PESHWA*

Following the death of Shivaji, that is, between 1680 and 1818 (the year when the British formally removed the *Peshwa*), the Maratha state was torn by factionalism; it nevertheless displayed certain continuities with the Mughal State, both in terminology and function, whether in legal institutions, court rituals, or rural and urban patterns. One faction supported Sambhaji, Shivaji's son, and the other group was loyal to Shivaji's 8-year-old son, Rajaram. Immediately after Shivaji's death, one of his wives and his ministers crowned Rajaram. It took Sambhaji eight months to crush the opposition and he could ascend to power only by December 1680. Involved in a number of campaigns with Mysore, Madurai, Golconda, and Karnataka, Sambhaji realised that he lacked the knowledge of the technology of sapping, mining or artillery to capture the forts. He thus persuaded the British stationed at Bombay to sign a defensive treaty in 1684 to procure quality guns and ammunitions. With the assistance of the British, Sambhaji made his first capture: the fort of Pratapgad and then several others along the Western Ghats. Despite his military success, Sambhaji could rarely ensure the loyalty of all Maratha families; instead, he was overwhelmed with defections towards the end of his reign. For instance, after a prolonged battle with the Portuguese, Sambhaji alienated the *deshmukh* families of south Konkan when he ordered the burning of their villages to stop supplies to Goa. Political activities of this kind often caused a dilemma for the Maratha families: Should they choose loyalty towards Sambhaji or align with the Mughals? The Shirke, relatives of Sambhaji, for example, had allied with the Mughals, but Sambhaji attacked and persecuted them in 1688. Sambhaji's tenure did not last long; while moving from Panhala to Raigad fort with a small contingent, he was captured by the Mughal army and then subsequently executed. Analysing the growing defections and factionalism during Sambhaji's rule, Marathi dramas and ballads have related these to Sambhaji's moral ineptitude, his alcoholism, consumption of drugs, and dalliances in the harem. Gordon, however, argued to the contrary. He suggested that the evidence of administrative orders till the month of his execution indicated that the reasons for his political decline lay not in his deficient moral character, but in the strategy of conquest.

The political situation continued to deteriorate after Sambhaji's death. The other surviving son of Shivaji, Rajaram, and his mother were besieged in Raigad fort, even as the Marathas continued to resist outside the fort. Rajaram could ultimately crown himself in November 1689, but was soon besieged by the Mughals in the fort of Gingee, a siege that continued for nine years. By 1697, as he faced financial stringency, Rajaram sued for peace. In 1698, although Aurangzeb deputed a military commander with reinforcements and cash, the siege of Gingee was pushed ahead; meanwhile, Rajaram escaped to Vellore fort and, within a few days, the Mughal army scaled the walls and captured the fort, ending the nine-year siege. Throughout the 1690s, it appeared as if the Maratha polity had ceased to exist, for the Mughals controlled almost all the major forts in Maharashtra and much of its countryside, feeling empowered thereby to assign *jagir*s to their troops as they had done in Bijapur and Golconda. Both Rajaram and Aurangzeb offered rights, privileges, and recognition to large *deshmukh* families and competed for their loyalty. Regardless of the large army stationed in Maharashtra, the Mughals failed to secure the loyalty of the *deshmukh*s, who continued to resist Mughal control. Rajaram, on the other hand, attempted to raid Berar and Surat in 1699 and managed to collect *chauth* and *sardesmukhi* in Khandesh, but his success was short-lived. He was forced out of the region and central *desh* by the Mughals. Following the raid on Berar and Surat, Rajaram died at Singhgad.

Rajaram's death signalled a tussle for succession. The obvious choice fell on Shahu, Sambhaji's son, who had been a Mughal captive for long. Rajaram's survivors were complex: three sons, one of whom was illegitimate, four widowed queens and a concubine (of these, one queen committed sati, one died a natural death, and the other two had minor sons). In brief, succession was bound to be conflictive, with no substantial strong claims to the throne and two minor sons. Each of them was ambitious, leading to the emergence of three factions—two of these supported the two queens and their infant sons, respectively, and the other favoured Shahu. Tarabai, the elder queen, emerged victorious and ruled for a decade in the name of her infant son, Shivaji II. Maratha factionalism provided an opportune moment for Aurangzeb, who continued to capture fort after fort, beginning with Satara fort and the neighbouring Parli fort. Instead of retaliating, the Maratha strategy throughout was to hold on to a fort till it became difficult to sustain, then escape with as much treasure and as many men as possible, while independent Maratha bands continued to raid the settled Mughal areas of Khandesh and Malwa.

By late 1705, as Aurangzeb faced political tensions in the north, his army in Maharashtra was exhausted and anxious to leave; it seemed, Gordon (1993) argued, as if both the Mughals and the Marathas were waiting for Aurangzeb to die. Factions and alliances were formed and re-formed and Maratha raids on Mughal-occupied territories in Deccan continued. In 1706–07, Baroda and the city of Burhanpur were sacked. After nearly forty years of campaigning in Deccan, Aurangzeb died at Aurangabad in March 1707, leaving the Marathas and Maharashtra unvanquished. Taking advantage of Aurangzeb's death and the war of succession that ensued, Shahu's release was organised at Malwa, putting an end to his eighteen years of captivity in the

Mughal camp. Losing no opportunity, Shahu proceeded further south in Maharashtra to assert his claim to the Maratha throne. The next eight years witnessed intense civil war between the two groups, led respectively by Shahu and queen Tarabai, who was ruling Maharashtra in the name of her son, Shivaji II. The situation was further complicated when the Mughals joined the conflict. All three—Shahu, Tarabai, and the Mughals—rivalled each other to obtain the support and loyalty of the *deshmukh* families and the Maratha bands. The Mughals, despite their inconsistencies during the period, countered the Maratha raids successfully and continued the strategy devised in the last year of Aurangzeb's reign, that is, win over important Maratha leaders into the Mughal military system. Nimaji Shinde, for instance, who was engaged in raiding Malwa and Khandesh, was offered a *mansab* of 7,000 and his sons and grandsons were admitted into the imperial service. Despite this, politics in Maharashtra remained chaotic, with the incessant resistance of the Maratha bands and the constant warfare between Shahu and Tarabai. Both of them sought grants of the Mughal share of the revenue of Deccan, which included rights to *chauth* and *sardesmukhi*. The Mughals eventually confirmed these rights to Shahu, but that hardly improved his control over Deccan; he remained confined to the area in the vicinity of Pune, while Tarabai's base in Konkan continued to be equally ineffective.

The year 1715 saw a different beginning when Shahu initiated a process of consolidation of power and monarchy in Maharashtra with the support of his military elite. While discussing the military elite of Shahu in 1715, it needs to be noted that few of the families associated with Shivaji survived in the eighteenth century. Many had died in protracted wars and dislocations, while several others had collapsed as a result of Maratha factional politics. Sambhaji had ordered the execution of at least twenty-five members of important Maratha families, including highly positioned cabinet members of the government, when the plot to poison him was discovered in 1683. Two decades later, as a consequence of the factional conflict between Tarabai and Shahu, other Maratha families declined. The inner coterie of Shahu, however, which comprised 'new' Brahmins, was sheltered. Of these, one of them was Parushram Pant Pratinidhi, a *deshasta* Brahmin, whose family originally belonged to Karhad; the other was the Bhat family of *chitpavan* Brahmins, who functioned as *Peshwa*s of the Maratha rulers and were set to exercise de facto power in the Maratha state for the next sixty years. They were basically hereditary *deshmukh*s of Danda Rajpuri on the Konkan coast, roughly 60 miles south of Bombay. It is in the context of the importance of the *Peshwa* family and the significance of the office of *Peshwa* that the rise of Balaji Vishwanath ought to be considered.

Balaji Vishwanath, a clerk in the salt works of the Siddis of Janjira (in Konkan), recruited first as *subadar* of Pune in 1700 and then of the district of Daulatabad, emerged as Shahu's main supporter. In 1713, he was appointed *Peshwa* by Shahu. His first assignment as *Peshwa* was his negotiations in Konkan with Kanoji Angria, the loyalist of Tarabai, whom he persuaded to ally with Shahu, weakening Tarabai's support base and leading to her subsequent imprisonment. He also commanded Shahu's army against the Mughal forces led by the Nizam in 1713–15. Balaji thus made a definite mark in the early part of Shahu's reign, which witnessed the disappearance of *deshmukh* families and the rise of 'new' Maratha and Brahmin families, even as Tarabai and Shahu remained engaged in civil war. Taking advantage of the Mughal failings in Maharashtra and their inability to win against the Maratha bands, Balaji in 1716 demanded from the Mughals the recognition of Maratha rights in Maharashtra—that is, he urged the Mughal emperor to issue a *sanad* granting Shahu the right to *chauth* and *sardesmukhi* from the government revenue throughout the six Mughal *suba*s of Deccan, namely Aurangabad, Berar, Bidar, Golconda, and Bijapur, including entire Karnataka and Khandesh. The demand also included the *chauth* of Malwa and Gujarat and the recognition of *swarajya* in Maharashtra, stipulating that the Mughals should withdraw from all forts. In return, the *Peshwa*, on behalf of Shahu, promised to maintain 15,000 troops for the Mughal *subadar* of Deccan, preserve law and order, and return 10 per cent of *sardesmukhi* to the Mughals. In addition, Shahu agreed to pay an annual tribute of Rs 100,000.

The Mughal *subadar* agreed to the proposed terms but Farrukhsiyar, the Mughal emperor, was hesitant to issue such a *sanad*, fearing that it might lead to the complete dissolution of Mughal power in Deccan. Rejecting the proposal, he prepared for war. Within a year, Balaji Vishwanath mobilised the Maratha army and proceeded to Delhi, where they were recruited as the troops of the Sayyid brothers, one of the factions competing for the Mughal throne. With Maratha support, the Sayyid brothers placed a puppet on the Mughal throne, which added to the political confusion. However, the melee facilitated the ratification of the treaty between the Mughals and the Marathas and the release of Shahu's family, who had been in Mughal captivity from 1708 (even though Shahu had been released earlier). A triumphant Balaji returned to Deccan in May 1719 with the Mughal grant that recognised Shahu's legal rights of revenue collection in the territory south of river Narmada. No other faction or Maratha band had enjoyed this privilege earlier. The significance of the grant of 1719 lay in Shahu's acquisition of various assets that could now be distributed to his loyalists, while the disloyal could be dislodged. The grant of 1719 matured only by 1740; nevertheless, the *Peshwa*, in the name of Shahu and the central Maratha government, controlled the grants in Maharashtra—*saranjam*, *deshmukhi*, *patil*, *inam*, and others—whether for new allotment or continuation.

Tarabai's son, Shivaji II, was eventually conciliated by Balaji by the treaty of Warna in 1731, which gave his family independent authority over the state of Kolapur. A separate power base was created for Tarabai in Karnataka and she was empowered to distribute small maintenance grants to her supporters. Kolapur survived as a separate, rarely threatening state into the eighteenth century, and then later as a princely state in the nineteenth and twentieth centuries. While Shahu lacked the charisma of a ruler, his alliance with Balaji Vishwanath proved beneficial for the consolidation of his kingdom. Balaji, as the *Peshwa*, demonstrated extraordinary acumen as a leader and statesman. The Maratha state was further strengthened when the *Peshwa* offered patronage to other *chitpavan* Brahmins, the core of the rapidly expanding literate elite, and inducted them as tax collectors and administrators, who introduced regularised record-keeping in the state. This performance-oriented Brahmin elite soon enhanced the powers of the Maratha state, serving as its civil and military officials and remaining loyal to the *Peshwa* and intermarrying into his family. Balaji also exclusively mobilised Brahmin banking families to facilitate banking and credit schemes for Shahu's government. Notwithstanding a systematic plan for consolidation, like the refined finance system and political or military order, Shahu's kingdom was beset with inherent problems. Shahu was completely marginalised by the *Peshwa* who wielded de facto power with overpowering control over the *saranjams*, the Brahmin administrative and banking elite. Further, the creation of Thanjavur and Kolapur states encouraged the belief that the conquests could be shared and divided between the king and the military leaders—a perception that became apparent in 1729 when the Maratha leaders demanded the division of the new conquests in Malwa and Gujarat.

Balaji Vishwanath died in 1720. The Maratha resistance to Shahu's decision to elevate Balaji's son, Baji Rao, as the next *Peshwa* had no impact. Baji Rao had impressed Shahu with his strategic assessment while on an expedition to Delhi in 1719. He convinced Shahu that since the Mughal Empire had collapsed, its energies to resist the Marathas in the north, in Malwa, and even further were completely sapped. For the next two decades, this premise overwhelmed the military and administrative activities of Baji Rao. Reiterating that the Mughal Empire had lost its political and military strength, Baji Rao urged the invasion of Gujarat and Malwa but advised restraint in the southern region and the Nizam's territories, for the Nizam too was interested in the weakening of the Mughal Empire. Baji Rao gave himself the charge of leading the expedition to the north. In the course of these campaigns, he was joined by the Holkars, who had been deputed in 1723–24 to the state of Bhopal in eastern Malwa to settle affairs. The Maratha efforts succeeded against the Mughals only in 1728 when the Holkars cut off Mughal supplies and communications in the battle of Palkhed (20 miles west of Aurangabad). In the next four years, the Holkars created a contingent of several thousand cavalry loyal to the *Peshwa*, and was rewarded with a substantial portion of western Malwa following the technique of 'division' announced by the *Peshwa* in 1732.

In Deccan, Baji Rao consolidated the Maratha position with the assistance of his cavalry when he defeated the Mughal army and the Nizam, an ally of the Mughals, in 1723 near Aurangabad in northern Maharashtra. (The Nizam's capital during this period was located at Aurangabad. It was shifted to Hyderabad only in the nineteenth century.) This defeat transformed the Nizam into an arch-rival of the Marathas, not only in his home territory of Hyderabad but also in Karnataka where both claimed revenue rights; in Khandesh, where revenue was divided between the Mughals and the Marathas by the treaty of 1717; and in Gujarat, where the Nizam's relatives were briefly in power. The reactions of the Marathas and the Nizam indicated, Gordon argued, that neither state followed the notion of 'boundaries'. The rights of the Marathas and the Nizam not only overlapped, but they often collected revenue from the same *pargana* or village. With their rights virtually intermixed, both the Nizam and the *Peshwa* tried to use, subvert, and destroy the other. The Nizam, as the Mughal representative in Deccan, resisted the payment of *chauth* and *sardesmukhi* to the Marathas. To counter his oft-repeated challenges, Baji Rao, supported by Shinde, Holkar, and the Pawar brothers, attacked the territories of the Nizam in Khandesh; the Nizam retaliated by attacking the Marathas in Pune. Baji Rao finally besieged the Nizam at Palkhed, cut off his supplies, and compelled him to surrender in March 1728. The Nizam was coerced into recognising Shahu as the sole Maratha sovereign, conceding to him the rights of *chauth* and *sardesmukhi* in Deccan; reinstating the Maratha tax collectors who had been driven out; and paying the outstanding arrears of *chauth* and *sardesmukhi*.

The implications of these concessions were far-reaching. Baji Rao claimed military superiority, having defeated the best-equipped army of those days in the subcontinent: the Mughal army and the superior artillery of the Nizam. More importantly, the Maratha victory at Palkhed settled the issue of Shahu's legitimacy and authority. The grant of the state of Kolapur in 1731 had reduced Tarabai's faction to a junior status and rendered non-threatening the holder of estates and rights in southern Maharashtra. The defeat of Gaekwad, Dabhade, and the Kadam Badam faction in 1731 heralded the end of factional conflicts. These developments once again established the *Peshwa* as the de facto ruler of the Maratha state. In addition, as was apparent from political and military events till 1740, it appeared that the Marathas and the English East India Company were the only surviving competing powers for supremacy in coastal Maharashtra.

By the middle of the 1730s, the Mughal emperor had begun vacillating between a 'peace' party that wanted to appease the Marathas and a 'war' party. The Mughal plan for campaign against the Marathas coincided with suggestions for a friendly meeting between the emperor and Baji Rao. In 1735–36, Baji Rao sought intermediation to negotiate with the Mughals on several issues. But such were the enormous and unending nature of Baji Rao's demands that they yielded no results. Baji Rao claimed a hereditary state for himself, allotment of *jagir*s for his loyalists, immediate cash payments, complete control over Malwa, including absolute management of the Rajput and Afghan zamindars, the right to nominate the Mughal officials to be posted in Deccan, and personal rights to 5 per cent of the revenue of Deccan. Wary of these demands, the Mughal emperor accepted none of them. Baji Rao thus prepared for war, although the campaign of 1737 proved indecisive. Delhi was attacked and the Mughal emperor was temporarily held to ransom. He sought the support of the Nizam and, in return, provided him with zamindars from Malwa, a few troops from Rajasthan, and an army from Delhi. As this huge Mughal contingent moved from Delhi to Bhopal, the Marathas reacted by cutting supplies; the zamindars from Malwa and troops from Rajasthan deserted the Nizam's camp as it was overcome by famine and starvation, leading to the treaty of Bhopal in January 1739. The Nizam agreed to grant the entire *suba* of Malwa to the *Peshwa*, surrendered all sovereign rights over the territories between rivers Narmada and Chambal, and promised to obtain a large cash tribute from the Mughal emperor. These concessions, however, did not satisfy Baji Rao's demand for an independent kingdom for himself and large *jagir*s for his loyalists.

Nadir Shah's invasion in 1739 further weakened the Mughal Empire. The *Peshwa*, on the other hand, persistently accumulated power and strengthened his control over the military, administrative, and banking families. As a further step towards aggrandisement of power, Baji Rao centralised the rights-granting authority in his person, setting aside the other Maratha families or alternative authority. Moving strategically, the *Peshwa* scattered and intermixed the grants so that no leader could use a compact territory as a base for rebellion, and consented to share power in the newly conquered regions of Malwa and Gujarat; most significant in this regard was the 'division' of Malwa in 1732 between the *Peshwa*, Holkar, and Shinde, with a small share to the Pawar brothers. Baji Rao maintained his invincibility by retaining the right as grant-giver of this devolution, insisting that all those who were party to the sharing of power or included in the 'division' were obliged to be loyal to the *Peshwa*. He deliberately kept the settlement, collection, and division of revenue complicated so as to facilitate high administrative posts for his relatives, the *chitpavan* Brahmins. By these means, he could continue to hold the august position as arbitrator of disputes. To maintain his monopoly over military services, he regularly sanctioned *inam* grants, that is, hereditary merit grants of villages in Maharashtra, to military commanders and others with extraordinary distinction in service. The *inam* grants were coveted but conditional; while they represented a stable personal income in Maharashtra, the grantees could be divested of it if found to be disloyal. Relentless in empowering the *Peshwa*, Baji Rao centralised banking in Maharashtra so that bank administrators had to perforce visit the capital annually, pay their advance, and receive personal audience with the *Peshwa* before proceeding to their respective districts. To further consolidate his relations with the banking and administrative communities and move up in the social hierarchy, he intermarried into these families. Such patterns of centralisation of power made the *Peshwa* powerful and a de facto sovereign of the Maratha kingdom.

With such immense powers arrogated to the *Peshwa*, Baji Rao's death in 1740 was a repetition of the time after Balaji Vishwanath's demise, of claims and counter-claims and a scramble for the office of the *Peshwa*. As on the previous occasion, Shahu set all conflict to rest by appointing Baji Rao's son, Balaji Baji Rao, popularly known as Nana Sahib, as the *Peshwa*. The story of politics as witnessed under the earlier *Peshwa*s continued.

9

THE EIGHTEENTH CENTURY

HIGHLIGHTS

- Interpreting the eighteenth century
- Debate on the decline of the Mughal Empire: Core issues examined:
  - personality and religion of the Mughal emperors
  - the assignment system
  - role of bankers and merchants
  - cultural and scientific trends
  - regional elites

The debate on the decline of the Mughal Empire and the interpretations pertaining to the eighteenth century have been exhaustively studied in two separate volumes of *Debates in Indian History and Society* by Seema Alavi (2007b) and Meena Bhargava (2014), in addition to the edited volumes by P. J. Marshall (2003), an anthology by R. B. Barnett (2002), and several other scholarly works. A few observations, however, may be considered. Different paradigms and assumptions have shaped interpretations of the decline of the Mughal Empire; yet it is no longer plausible, in view of new research and data, to accept the concept of decline or of a decadent, stagnant economy, or that the economy did not have sufficient initiative and potential to grow, or that the eighteenth century was a mere story of 'reckless rapine, anarchy and foreign conquest'. Even if the collapse of the Mughal Empire overwhelmed a large part of the eighteenth century, it was not the only phenomenon of the period, although the process may have engendered a phase of political flux. The eighteenth century was a period of transition, marked by the emergence, consolidation, and social and economic dynamism of regional political configurations virtually independent of Mughal imperial control. In some of these regions, Mughal idioms and institutions generally continued. Yet the fortune or misfortune of the Mughal Empire cannot be considered the sole determining factor in understanding the historical processes in the regions.

Regional centralisation and social change in the transition period was not an index of collapse of the social order; the changes that happened were constituents of state formation at diverse levels, so that the formation of a regional system was largely a movement from within. By the mid-eighteenth century, the power of the Mughals had shifted to the regional successor states.

In fact, the eighteenth century has been quite appropriately described as a 'time of new states'. The most 'unlikely adventurers', William Pinch (2006) argued, built on the ruins of the Mughal Empire, and many of them maintained their new polities quite successfully, either through military strategies, political astuteness, or through social mobility. 'New men of consequence' ruled from capitals like Lucknow, Jaipur, Calcutta, and Mysore, some of whom were former *subadars* of the Mughal emperors whose families had served the Mughal State for generations. Others were the heirs of rebel chieftains who had challenged the Mughal power; some were a little of both, while others were men of trade from Europe who had brought silver from the New World, as well as new forms of military organisation and new ways of perceiving governance and the state. Some, like Hyderabad, moved beyond Mughal patterns of governance, even as it maintained the fiction that it was a Mughal dependency. Ultimately, Munis Faruqui (2009) argued, Hyderabad emerged as neither a poor imitation nor a miniature version of the Mughal Empire.

These developments are a clear indication that the disintegration of the Mughal Empire did not mean the eclipse of political authority and the economic stagnation of the entire society. The economy showed a shift, a new direction, leading to decentralisation and economic density at the local level. These local centres remained integrated by a network of trade and monetary transactions. The period also acquired added historical significance as it coincided with the rising power of the English East India Company. Regional centralisation, which had begun before the eighteenth century, was stimulated in the late eighteenth and early nineteenth centuries by the political and military expansion of the East India Company. As the European influence grew, the regions came into contact with a variety of institutions that threatened to erode the foundations of the erstwhile social order and heralded the unmistakable rise of a new one as an *inqilab*, a world turned upside down.

In an attempt to understand the diverse opinions and discussions that surround the withering of, in R. B. Barnett's (2002) words, the 'mammoth imperial banyan tree' (see Plate 10), a few core issues can be identified to examine the decline of the Mughal Empire:

- the personality and religion of the Mughal emperors, in particular the religious policy of Aurangzeb;
- the assignment system or the nature of the *jagirdari* system;
- the role of bankers and merchants and their failure to support the empire fiscally or commercially;
- cultural and scientific trends or other larger forces at work, especially in view of the fact that three large empires (Mughal, Safavid, and Ottoman) faced their decline at roughly the same time;
- the regional elites and the failure of the centre to retain their loyalty.

PERSONALITY AND RELIGION OF THE MUGHAL EMPERORS

Writing the political history of the Mughal Empire after the death of Aurangzeb, William Irvine (1922) put forward a few questions that were personality-oriented to explain the decline of the Mughal Empire. Asserting that it was the degenerative character of the emperors and the nobles that was responsible for the decline, he held Aurangzeb accountable for alienating the Hindus and the Shi'is. In some ways, Irvine became the harbinger of the hypothesis proferred by Jadunath Sarkar (1972 [1928]), who characterised the eighteenth century as crisis-ridden and chaotic—both politically and economically—and affirmed Aurangzeb's religious policy and Deccan campaigns as the prime factors in the decline of the Mughal Empire. Unrelenting towards Aurangzeb, Sarkar argued that his ideology and religious practices made a radical shift from Akbar's syncretism, leading to fanaticism and alienation of the Hindus—the Rathor, Bundela, Maratha, and the Sikh—who organised resistances to challenge the orthodoxy of the Mughal emperor. For Sarkar (1972 [1928], 1–2), Aurangzeb's reign depicted 'the first rudimentary beginnings of that political, economic and cultural breakdown ... rightly given the name of the "Great Anarchy" to the eighteenth century in northern India'. The analyses of Irvine and Sarkar barely moved beyond the perspective of the seventeenth and eighteenth-century Persian chroniclers. There was a difference, though, as pointed out by Muzaffar Alam (2013 [1986]). While both Irvine and Sarkar saw evidence of a 'Hindu reaction' in the revolts of Rathor, Bundela, Maratha, and Sikh against the Mughals, Alam provided a contrary view and argued that the rebels and 'disturbers' mentioned in contemporary sources were identified either by their class, namely as zamindars, or by their caste, clan, or region.

Providing legitimacy to the William Irvine–Jadunath Sarkar interpretation, Ishwari Prasad (1974), S. R. Sharma (1988), and Jagdish Narayan Sarkar (1976) argued that the theocratic elements in Aurangzeb's administration, his bigotry and forcible conversion to Islam aroused the wrath and defiance of the Hindus. Aurangzeb may have attempted to associate the Mughal State with Islamic orthodoxy, but to suggest that this alienated only the Hindus, or that the Hindus alone were the troublemakers, or that the 'Hindu reaction' was the primary cause of the decline is untenable. There is enough evidence to prove, Alam observed, that Muslim officials and nobles also resisted such policies of the emperor, and that the Muslim *madad-i ma'ash* holders created problems of equivalent stature for the empire.

Interpretations such as these, which emphasise the personality, religious ideology, and religious practices of the Mughal emperors, particularly Aurangzeb, were influenced by colonial understandings and Orientalist definitions of Indian history. The notion that the 'Muslim' (medieval) period was marked by Muslim tyranny and suffering of the Hindus was a colonial construct to justify British rule, so that it could then be projected as having liberated the Hindus from severities and persecution. Further, the depiction of Hindus and Muslims as warring communities was a colonial ploy to legitimise the British presence in India and prevent the two communities from uniting against the British.

THE ASSIGNMENT SYSTEM

The debate on the decline of the Mughal Empire veered from the personality-based, ideology-prone analysis towards the left with a series of publications in the late 1950s and early 1960s from Aligarh Muslim University, which reiterated—albeit with different formulations—that the eighteenth century was politically chaotic and crisis-ridden. These included Satish Chandra's

Parties and Politics at the Mughal Court, 1707–1740 (1959), Irfan Habib's *The Agrarian System of Mughal India, 1556–1707* (1963), M. Athar Ali's *The Mughal Nobility under Aurangzeb* (1966), and Noman Ahmad Siddiqui's *Land Revenue Administration under the Mughals, 1700–1750* (1970), which provided, as Alam and Subrahmanyam have argued, a 'systemic' perspective on the Mughal Empire, focused on the State as a 'revenue sponge or fiscal mechanism', and explained the decline of the empire by linking it to the Mughal assignment system. Satish Chandra spoke of the '*jagirdari* crisis' while Irfan Habib talked of an 'agrarian crisis', that is, a crisis in the distribution of *jagirs*, decline in production and revenue, and Mughal exploitation. Moving away from individuals and personalities, these historians stressed on institutions, identified social groups with certain material interests, and linked the rationale of the rise and decline of empire with tensions arising from systemic rather than psychological contradictions. Another line of argument associated with historians like Sayyid Nurul Hasan emphasised the tensions between the State and the rural 'gentry' or zamindars, or the symbiotic and contradictory relationship between the State and zamindars to understand the mechanism of the Mughal State, particularly during the period of decline, roughly after 1700.

The significance and implications of the Mughal revenue assignment system were first noted by Francois Bernier, a French physician who visited the court of Aurangzeb in the seventeenth century. He asserted that the frequent transfers of *jagirs* were a disincentive to *jagirdars*/*mansabdars* to improve the land or its production; unconcerned about the peasants, they appropriated large amounts for themselves, leading to complete depletion and exhaustion of the land and agricultural production. His proposition of the 'crisis' in the Mughal revenue assignment system first impressed W. H. Moreland who, through his several works (*From Akbar to Aurangzeb*; *India at the Death of Akbar*; and *The Agrarian System of Moslem India*) published in the 1920s, talked of the exploitative nature of the Mughal assignment system and, like Jadunath Sarkar, held Aurangzeb responsible for the calamities faced by the empire. Also influenced by the narrative of William Hawkins, a visitor to the court of Jahangir, he stipulated that the assignment system was so exploitative, particularly during Aurangzeb's reign, that it left the peasants impoverished while also exhausting agricultural production to such an extent that it led to the collapse of the Mughal Empire. Moreland's writings, in addition to being influenced by the hypotheses of Bernier, Hawkins, and other foreign travellers, were also affected by the controversy between the apologists and critics of British colonial rule. His major concerns were to compare the national wealth and income in India at the death of Akbar with early twentieth-century British India to refute the notion of a pre-colonial 'golden age', and affirm that the economy of India under British rule was an improvement, however slight, in terms of per capita output and consumption.

Satish Chandra's *Parties and Politics at the Mughal Court* was the first serious attempt to explain the decline of the Mughal Empire by studying the structural flaws in its system. He argued that the stability of the empire as a centralised State depended on the efficient working of the *mansab* and the *jagirdari* system. It may be recalled that the status and position of nobles was designated by the *mansabs*, and they were paid by *jagirs* or the assignments of land revenue. This implied that the *jama'* of a *jagir* had to be necessarily equal to the pay-claim of a *mansabdar* because *hasil* formed the income of a *mansabdar*. In other words, availability of the revenues to be assigned and the ability to collect revenue were the two crucial pre-requisites for an efficient *jagirdari* system. But these institutions had failed to function effectively by the reign of Aurangzeb. Aurangzeb's political problems were accompanied and accentuated by a crisis in the *jagirdari* system. The crisis had in fact appeared as early as the sixteenth century, and Akbar had attempted to resolve it through territorial expansion and land revenue organisation so as to ensure that the benefits reached both peasants and zamindars. Since then, the Mughal emperors had evolved several administrative devices to facilitate the proper functioning of the *mansabdari* system. However, these practices failed to assist the emperors in overcoming the basic administrative problems, that is, the available social surplus continued to be insufficient to meet the cost of administration, or pay for wars and military expeditions, or fulfil the extravagant needs of the ruling class. Chandra argued that while the demands of the ruling class became exorbitantly large, there was no corresponding increase in agricultural production—despite the continuing expansion in cultivated area during the seventeenth century—which led to growing economic pressure on the producing class. Thus, the crisis of the *jagirdari* system re-surfaced during the later years of Jahangir's reign. *Zat* and *sawar* ranks that in principle were expected to correspond to a *jagirdar*'s required cavalry contingents failed to reflect the total number of horsemen or horses that *jagirdar*s actually maintained.

Shahjahan tried to mitigate the crisis by introducing certain reforms: he re-fixed salaries and ordered that not more than one-third the size of the contingent indicated by the *sawar* rank could be maintained by a noble. The *mansabdars*' salaries were scaled down proportionately and fixed at *dashmah*, *ashtmah*, *shastmah*, that is, ten, eight, six, or even four months in a year. Most of the nobles evidently received salaries for *ashtmah* or *shastmah*. And yet Shahjahan could not resolve the financial crisis; the gap widened between the resources available and growing expenses and demands, worsening the crisis under Aurangzeb and leading to a revenue deficit in the thirteenth year of his reign. He urged cuts in expenditure, emphasised simplicity, imposed fresh taxes, and advised his nobles to extend and improve cultivation. He, too, failed to reverse the financial crisis. There were inordinate delays in the grant of *jagirs*, and when ultimately granted, the *jagirdars* could realise only a fraction of their sanctioned pay. Many *mansabdars* resisted the maintenance of notified *sawars* or kept a much smaller number, whereas several others—especially in the lower cadre—demanded salaries in *naqd* instead of *jagirs*, or often farmed out their *jagirs* to different middlemen. The abandonment of lands by peasants, later accompanied by violence and armed uprisings, heralded the growing crisis. By the end of Aurangzeb's reign, the *jagirdari* system had reached a state of acute crisis, leading to a complete breakdown. Chandra argued that the *jagirdari* system was, at its root, a social problem, which no mere reduction in expenditures or administrative strategies for expanding cultivation could solve. In fact, he observed that a basic improvement in the situation was beyond the competence of any one king.

As Chandra discovered new archival sources, he argued in his *Medieval India: Society, the Jagirdari Crisis and the Village* (1982) that with the growth of a central authority, there developed a system of checks and balances to prevent one group of people from encroaching upon the functions and duties of another. Consequently, various sections of society, including the cultivators, looked to the central government (rather than the local government or zamindars) to redress their grievances. This led to the development of a triad or a triangular or tripolar relationship between the *jagirdars* (representing the central government), the zamindars, and the *khudkasht*. This relationship—a marked feature of the first half of the seventeenth century—was a principal factor that contributed to the stability of the Mughal Empire; but, Chandra argued, it could last, as long as the central government could convince the zamindars and the peasants that it was more beneficial for them to be loyal to the centre and look to it for support in resolving their grievances, rather than resist it or be in conflict with it. But this delicate social balance could be disturbed by a variety of factors: the effects of the scramble for power at the centre, disenchantment in the nobility, resistance by the regional chiefs, tensions at the village or local level on matters of caste, religion, ethnicity, or local migrations.

Social and economic crisis, Chandra reiterated, appeared during the first half of the seventeenth century—the so-called period of stability—and manifested itself in the form of a financial and administrative crisis, that is, a growing gap between the revenue required for assignment (*jama*) to the *mansabdars* and its availability (*hasil*). The situation had worsened to such an extent by the reign of Shahjahan that he was compelled to introduce the rule of one-third/one-fourth and *mahwar* in order to reduce the emoluments and obligations of *mansabdars* and bridge the gap between the required and available revenue. By the twenty-seventh year of Shahjahan's reign, a *mansabdar*'s cash salary could never exceed eight-monthly; sometimes it was even less than four-monthly. In this context, Chandra argued that the lowering of the effective shares of nobles in the agricultural surplus indicated a social and economic crisis which the Mughal ruling class attempted to redress through different administrative tactics. Regardless of these endeavours, the basic problem of the growing inadequacy of available revenue persisted. The gap between *jama* and *hasil* grew wider, owing to the inability—or perhaps the unwillingness—of the central government to make any drastic changes in existing agrarian relations, which were based on the triad between *jagirdars*, zamindars, and the *khudkasht*. The government's decision was probably influenced by its absolute dependence on the zamindars and dominant landowning castes at the village level.

Chandra further argued that there was no shortage of *paibaqi* or land reserved for assignment as *jagirs* to the *mansabdars*; instead, it was a shortage of *sair-hasil* (productive) *jagirs*. The imperial *mutassadis* demanded *sair-hasil jagirs*, leaving the *mansabdars* to manage the less productive *jagirs*, especially in the *zortalab* areas, where realisation was made difficult by the recalcitrance of the zamindars. In addition, while many of the *jagirs* lay *viran* (waste), and the realisation of revenue from them was virtually nil, the *mutassadis* demanded payment of *khurak-i dawab* from the *jagirdars*. If the latter resisted, they were imprisoned. Chandra thus observed that the struggle for *sair-hasil jagirs* became 'a matter of life and death' for the *mansabdars* and gave the imperial *mutassadis* an opportunity to indulge in corrupt practices, including frequent transfers of the *jagirdars*. So it was not the shortage of *paibaqi* but the scarcity of *sair-hasil jagirs* and delay in the grant of *jagirs* that affected the *khanazads* and the new recruits, especially the small *mansabdars*. He thus suggested a clear distinction between *be-jagiri*, which affected the new entrants rather than the existing incumbents, and the crisis in the *jagirdari* system. Central to the growth of crisis in the *jagirdari* system was its non-functionality, that is, its inability to assist in the maintenance of law and order and collection of the government's share of land revenue over large parts of the empire. These developments, Chandra observed, had repercussions for the rest of the empire. The *jagirdari* system, in his view, was a complex phenomenon linked to the structure and working of village society, and to the Mughal system of administration at both the central and local levels. Thus, the crisis in the *jagirdari* system—a consequence of a complex interplay between social and administrative factors—led to a breakdown in the eighteenth century.

Providing yet another 'fresh look' on the *jagirdari* crisis in his *State, Society and Culture in Indian History* (2012), Satish Chandra stated that some studies like those of Athar Ali and John F. Richards have viewed the *jagirdari* crisis as merely a financial-cum-administrative crisis, rather than as a manifestation of a deep-seated social crisis. The *jagirdari* crisis, Chandra stipulated, grew rapidly during the first half of the eighteenth century when the struggle between centripetal and centrifugal forces reached a new phase; it therefore has to be necessarily studied in the larger socio-cultural context. The *jagirdari* system failed to sustain a rapidly changing social-political situation during the eighteenth century. This implied that as long as the system worked, it could keep in check the centrifugal forces represented by zamindars and preserve administrative centralisation. Satish Chandra thus averred that his main thesis on the *jagirdari* crisis continues to be valid: 'the linking of the crisis of the *jagirdari* system with a deepening social crisis and increased factionalism in the ruling class leading to a break-up of central polity remains at the core of the Mughal crisis of empire'.

It is pertinent to note that the issue of 'tripolar' relationships, as argued by Satish Chandra, was further investigated by Muzaffar Alam (1986, 2013). He added a fourth dimension in the form of *madad-i ma'ash* holders and a large number of indigenous elements such as *Shaikhzada*s in Awadh and *Khatri*s in Punjab, who derived their sustenance from the imperial treasury and contributed significantly to defining the nature of the struggle for control over resources during this period.

Irfan Habib's seminal work, *The Agrarian System of Mughal India*, derived widely from Persian sources, reflects a Marxist perspective; yet it betrays the significant influence of the Bernier and W. H. Moreland model. What Moreland categorised as Oriental Despotism, Habib saw as class-based exploitation, to explain the decline of the Mughal Empire and the political and social unrest that followed it in fiscal terms. Pointing to the regressive nature of *kharaj* and its impact on the peasants, Habib observed that while on the one hand the revenue demand was fixed at exorbitantly high rates to ensure the military strength of the empire, on the other, the frequent transfers of *jagir*s kept the *jagirdar*s insecure in their assignments. Reinforcing Bernier's thesis, Habib suggested that the nature of the *jagir* system was such that it prompted *jagirdar*s to appropriate the maximum from their *jagir*s, even if this proved detrimental and ruinous to agricultural production and impoverished the peasantry, divesting them of their ability to pay the revenue. To escape exploitation and oppression, the peasants resisted the payment of land revenue and fled the fields—a feature that led to 'agrarian crisis' in the eighteenth century and the ultimate collapse of the empire. The zamindars were yet another class that threatened the law and order of the State by refusing to pay the land revenue or the State's share of the produce, and had to be subjugated by either the *faujdar*s or the *jagirdar*s. The peasants and zamindars frequently collaborated in the struggle against the Mughal State, although this was not a universal feature, for the zamindar leadership was not accepted uniformly across all peasant uprisings, nor did the peasants support all the zamindars' rebellious actions. Nevertheless, the two most successful revolts—those of the Marathas and the Jats—were led by men who aspired to be zamindars.

These issues were first raised by Irfan Habib in his article, 'The Agrarian Causes of the Fall of the Mughal Empire' (1959–60, 2014). The Mughal Empire was thus destroyed and, like most systems of oppression, became its own 'grave-digger', dissolving the administrative unity that it had formerly fostered. As the crisis developed, it engulfed the entire Indian economy, which was largely parasitical and depended upon a system of direct agrarian exploitation by a small ruling class; practically no rural market existed for urban crafts and rural monetisation was almost entirely the result of the need to transfer surplus agricultural produce to the towns. The empire, Habib further reiterated, had restricted capitalistic development, which became apparent when merchant capital was denied access to the large market in the eighteenth century; significant capitalistic tendencies noticed during the earlier prosperous days of the empire receded, and the empire, deprived of all alternatives, had no choice but to 'atrophy'.

Athar Ali (1997 [1966]) accepted Irfan Habib's model of a fiscally centralised State, although he did not attribute the decline to excessive *kharaj* but to *be-jagiri*. The *jagirdari* system, which had worked fairly efficiently till the middle of Aurangzeb's reign, lost its efficacy because of the increasing pressure of the Deccan wars on the financial resources of the empire, and the dislocation of the administration caused by the absence of the emperor and his court from northern India. The crisis was felt in the form of *be-jagiri*, that is, there were no areas left for assignment in *jagir.* Quoting Mamuri, Athar Ali said, 'A world became *jagirless* and there was no *paibaqi* left'. The scarcity of *paibaqi* compelled the emperor to resume the *jagirs* of few nobles to allot to the others. Aurangzeb granted *mansab*s on a large scale to Deccani nobles to attract them to the Mughal camp and prevent them from turning recalcitrant. The shortage of *paibaqi* adversely affected the working of the *jagirdari* system and made it difficult for new *mansabdar*s to get *jagir*s, leading to resentment and growing factionalism amongst the nobility, and thereby to the weakening, and ultimately the collapse, of the Mughal Empire.

The hypotheses of Satish Chandra, Irfan Habib, and Athar Ali dominated the debate on the decline of the Mughal Empire for almost fifteen years until 1975, when, at a symposium, Michael N. Pearson, John F. Richards, and Peter Hardy provided an alternative understanding on the issue. Hardy argued that the works of the three Aligarh historians were like simple formulae that provided an understanding of the growing weakness of the empire, which was 'almost Newtonian in their force and simplicity'. From the works of these historians, he observed, it was possible to draw 'a diagram of tensions' between the emperor, the *mansabdars/jagirdars*, the zamindars and the *raiyat*, which, if maintained in equilibrium, could bring order and stability; however, if control over them was loosened, the consequences could be detrimental. Critical of the argument of these historians, Hardy proposed a greater attempt at reintegration of ideological with other economic and institutional considerations, but not in the old simplistic terms of Aurangzeb's bigotry and his deliberate undoing of the efforts of Akbar as argued by Jadunath Sarkar.

Both Richards and Pearson, in their respective articles 'The Imperial Crisis in Deccan' (2014 [1976]) and 'Shivaji and the Decline of the Mughal Empire' (2014 [1976]), raised questions of ideology and accepted the 'diagram of tensions' sketched by the Aligarh historians, but proposed important modifications to the direction and reading of the tensions at work.

John F. Richards re-examined the reasons for the decline of imperial authority in Deccan during the two decades following the conquests of Bijapur and Golconda in 1686 and 1687, respectively. Based on Mughal archival records and comprehensive research on Mughal rule in Golconda between 1687 and 1724, Richards offered an alternative interpretation for the failure of the Mughal Empire in Deccan. He accepted the arguments of Satish Chandra and Athar Ali on the 'economic squeeze' following Aurangzeb's Deccan conquest between 1686 and 1689 and the shortage of *paibaqi* that contributed to factional conflict within the nobility, but he was critical of the 'sense of inevitability' implicit in their analysis that seemed to suggest that as soon as Deccan was conquered and the Deccanis absorbed as *mansabdars*, the *jagir* shortage became imminent, leading to the crisis. Instead, Richards demonstrated that there was no scarcity of funds and the empire need not have collapsed, despite the increase in the size of the Mughal nobility. The fault lay in the decision of Aurangzeb, who failed to secure his southern frontiers and exploit the resources of Bijapur and Golconda that could have supplemented his additional expenditure. Arguing against the shortage of *jagirs*, Richards held the strategic objectives of Aurangzeb responsible for the disorder in Deccan and suggested that the shortage of *jagirs* in the 1690s was partly 'artificial', caused by the emperor's decision to put the *sair-hasil* lands under *khalisa* and the least promising areas in *paibaqi*. Had the emperor used discretion, Richards stipulated, in the allocation and utilisation of *jagirs*, the annexation of Bijapur and Golconda could have enhanced the annual imperial revenue by at least 23 per cent and Hyderabad could have added another 26 per cent to the annual revenue in the *khalisa* areas. In his keenness for territorial expansion, Aurangzeb attacked such regions in Deccan that had until now remained sheltered from any external assault. The emperor thus proved ineffective in assimilating the Maratha, Bedar, Gond, or Telugu warrior chiefs into the imperial elite, nor could he establish political bonds with them as tributary chiefs or zamindars. Such circumstances demoralised the *mansabdars* and zamindars in Deccan, who not only challenged imperial *farmans* subsequent to 1700, but also took recourse to open rebellion by 1711–12.

Michael N. Pearson concurred with Athar Ali's argument of *be-jagiri* but disagreed with his calculation of the rate of increase in Aurangzeb's nobility, and also with his division of Aurangzeb's reign into periods of unequal length. Pearson suggested that even if Athar Ali's calculations were corrected, there would still remain a large increase in the number of nobles in the late seventeenth century. Regardless, Pearson argued that trouble for the empire began in the last few years of Aurangzeb's reign when he shifted to the south—a decision that revealed a central weakness in the empire—in the final desperate bid to defeat his formidable Maratha rival who had inflicted humiliating defeat on the empire. Stationed in Deccan, the emperor carried out protracted wars against the Marathas but failed to triumph over them, endangering Mughal invincibility. It was these prolonged wars that caused an imbalance between the number of *jagirdars* and the *jagirs* available, engendered peasant revolts, and beget disloyalty and factionalism within the nobility, thus heralding the decline of the empire. Analysing the Mughal failure to vanquish the Marathas, Pearson argued that the emperor had no choice but to respond to the military challenges of Shivaji, his escape from Mughal custody, his attack on Shaista Khan, and his rout of the valuable, strategic Mughal port of Surat; all these made the 'tragedy' of Aurangzeb inevitable. For Pearson, the Mughal Empire owed its decline to its military orientation and its failure to evolve a more impersonal political system.

Peter Hardy, in his commentary and critique of the interpretations provided by Richards and Pearson, raised some valuable points. Emphasising the importance of the study of military technology and military ethos, Hardy asserted their relevance to explain the decline of the Mughal Empire. He stipulated on the necessity of an evaluation of the military history of the period to confirm whether the deficiency in mere numbers of cavalry contingents against the Marathas was of decisive importance, or if the possibility that lightly armed cavalry would have been of greater value against the Marathas than the traditional Mughal heavy cavalry had been considered. Or was the preference for the use of heavy cavalry attributable more to social than to military conservatism? Or, if the Maratha light cavalry was the main tactical threat to the Mughal armies, what steps were taken to resist it, or what was the state of musket technology in Mughal India? To this, he added the value of a study of the science of gerontology for, while a historian of military technology may contribute to a new insight into the subject (which many of them have since the time of Hardy's writing), a gerontologist could provide a fresh glimpse into the behaviour of Aurangzeb, who was in extreme old age when the empire witnessed its decline.

Hardy also disagreed with Pearson's proposition that the Mughal Empire declined because it failed to evolve a more impersonal structure. Muzaffar Alam, too, argued that while the personal achievements and failures of the emperors affected the nobles, the absence of an impersonalised Mughal bureaucracy cannot be accepted on the basis of contemporary evidence as a viable factor for failure. It was not just the small group of nobles or *umara*, but also the zamindars, the village and *qasba*-based *madad-i ma'ash* holders, and a large number of lower-level officials from different regional and local communities who were integrated intimately into the framework of the empire. It was the balancing of these diverse interests that ensured the stability of the empire. But then political integration remained inherently defective in the Mughal Empire. It was conditional and rested on the coordination of the interests and political activities of different social groups.

BANKERS AND MERCHANTS

In addition to these theories, scholars have pointed to the critical role of the bankers and merchants—*sahukars*, *shroffs*, *mahajans*—in the Mughal political system, particularly those in the 'great firms', to understand the decline of the Mughal Empire. Focusing on their significant involvement in the Mughal Empire, Karen Leonard, in her essay 'The "Great Firm" Theory of the Decline of the Mughal Empire' (2014), analysed the organisation and volume of economic activities of the great indigenous banking firms and their participation in politics during the

Mughal and early British period. She used the term 'great firms' to describe a business firm engaged in a variety of enterprises, with several branches, often based on one 'household'. The banking firms, she observed, were crucial to the financial functioning of the central government as well as its governing class, comprising *mansabdars*, *jagirdars*, zamindars, and *ta'alluqdars*. When the 'great firms'—the 'indispensable allies' of the Mughal State—began diverting their resources, both credit and trade, from the Mughal Empire to the regions, the empire weakened. During 1650–1750, Leonard asserted, as the banking firms became increasingly engaged in revenue collection at regional and local levels, transcending their credit to the centre, the centre was adversely affected, even as the banking firms and merchants continued to expand and diversify. Philip Calkins (1970) and Michael N. Pearson (1972), too, studied the political participation of the merchants in Bengal and Gujarat, respectively, but neither suggested that the Mughal financial system depended on the merchants' credit or that the stability of the empire was derived from merchant participation. Similarly, Muzaffar Alam, on the basis of Persian sources, doubted the extent of the political participation of merchants, although there were some references to *khatris* as 'nobles' (*umara*) and 'notables' (*a'yan*). He conceded, though, that the *sahukars* and some artisans had supported the Mughals against the Sikhs in the early eighteenth century. This would indicate that the trading community was possibly active in the politics of some parts of the Mughal Empire; it could also mean that the interests of the merchants were connected to the prosperity and stability of the ruling class and the markets that they fostered; also, they may have shown keen interest in politics when they felt threatened by the impending imperial decline.

John F. Richards (1981), in contravention of Leonard's argument, which he dismissed as lacking in documentation and implausible when it came to explaining the 'puzzling aspects' of the Mughal decline, conceded that the various private banking firms contributed significantly to the restructuring of the imperial system by the regional states in the eighteenth century, and that these firms acquired power and importance through their ties with European trading companies. He stressed on the absence of any available data that could substantiate a similar role of the 'great firms' for the Mughal imperial system in the sixteenth and seventeenth centuries. He acknowledged, however, that in the seventeenth century there may have been occasional cases of merchants with enormous wealth; but even the wealthiest of these men were not direct participants in the imperial system, nor were they 'indispensable allies of the Mughal state'. Their services were limited and dispensable. The private bankers or moneychangers did not control or manage the imperial treasuries and mints, nor did the private entrepreneurs collect imperial revenues. Instead, in the large commercial centres, the Mughal emperors imposed limits on indigenous markets, appointed traders or headmen for each specialised market, and recruited an officer from the local commercial community, who, alongside the imperial officials, collected urban taxes. In other words, unlike Leonard, he attributed the development and significant role of the 'great firms' to the eighteenth century; for Richards, economic decentralisation was a consequence and not a cause of political disintegration.

Sanjay Subrahmanyam and C. A. Bayly (1990) disagreed with Richards' proposition of 'centralization through state power', which seemed to suggest that fiscal integration under

Aurangzeb was mediated by the Mughal treasury and the 'great households' rather than by bankers. Richards assumed the existence of a huge interregional commodity trade and an agro-based trade that balanced the flows of treasure, while the provinces were deprived of it. If such were the case, Subrahmanyam and Bayly argued, then there must have been merchants who controlled the trade. Where were such merchants, they asked, and how did they finance their trade? Further, if it is assumed that the change came early in the eighteenth century, where did great merchant corporations with vast resources, influence, and a well-developed culture of book-keeping and subcontinental credit come from? Probing such questions, Subrahmanyam and Bayly emphasised the important role of 'portfolio capitalists' or merchants who were 'able to straddle the worlds of commerce and political participation'. These large-scale entrepreneurs and great merchant families emerged as significant in northern India over the first half of the eighteenth century. They utilised not only their own capital, but also that of the small-scale operators who served as conduits for indirect investment. These men had good control over the military labour market and could comfortably engage in political matters without relenting on their credit. These 'great houses', Subrahmanyam and Bayly argued, were already firmly entrenched in the administration of the *jagir*s of the *mansabdar*s even before the beginning of the eighteenth century, and the disintegration of the Mughal system in the early eighteenth century further facilitated the consolidation of their power. This would suggest that the portfolio capitalists had begun to intervene in agricultural production and controlled labour and trade. This led to the rise of many 'new' zamindars of the eighteenth century. In these specific ways, merchant capital made a significant contribution to state and military finance, which subsequently supported the rise of the English East India Company.

CULTURAL AND SCIENTIFIC TRENDS

Interpreting the early eighteenth century, Athar Ali (2006d) expressed his dismay at the understanding of the decline of the Mughal Empire in insular terms that ignored wider historical contexts. He argued that this period witnessed the disintegration of not only the Mughal Empire, but also that of the three other Islamic Empires—the Safavid, Uzbek Khanate, and the Ottoman. This was no mere coincidence, he argued. There were factors common to these empires that led to their decline. Their disintegration probably preceded the military impact of colonial powers like Britain and Russia. Even before the effects of colonial military coercion were felt by these empires, Europe had emerged as the centre of world commerce during the period 1500–1700, dominated the New World, and monopolised commerce surrounding the Cape of Good Hope, and thus subverted the states and societies of Asia. Further, as Europe became a dominant market for luxury items and high-value products from Asia, Iran was divested of its position as the principal market for Indian commodities; India and Iran could thus no longer maintain their hold over Chinese exports. These developments, Athar Ali argued, severely disrupted the economies of the Asian states, leading to their decline. Moreover, the financial difficulties of the ruling classes intensified with the rise in the costs of luxury items; as the income of the ruling elite became increasingly inadequate, they indulged in agrarian exploitation; and when this failed or was counter-productive, they took recourse to factionalism for personal gains, which resulted in endless civil wars. Such circumstances, Athar Ali asserted, sounded the death knell of the Asian empires.

Also, unlike Europe, progress in science and technology was slow and limited in Asia. Mughal India, for instance, made no effort to advance the technique and design of its artillery weapons along the lines of new science and technology. The manufacture of guns and muskets remained a mere craft. By 1700, the empire had become outdated in the pursuit of not only science and technology, but also intellectual activities; the towns could not emerge as 'safety-valves' that could grapple with the agrarian crisis; the Indian urban population remained 'parasitical' and dependent on the appropriation of agrarian surplus; the zamindars and peasants incessantly resisted the expropriation, notwithstanding the professional Mughal army. The disintegration of the Mughal Empire, Athar Ali averred, was an outcome of a 'cultural' failure that it shared with the other Asian states. Even as the empires became increasingly incompetent to deal with the agrarian crisis, the economic balance tilted in favour of Europe and contributed to political and military disasters. All these, Athar Ali believed, emanated from the 'intellectual stagnation' that had gripped the Asian world.

Marshall G. S. Hodgson (1974) stated that while one can talk of the cultural and social stalemate in the Islamic Empires during the eighteenth century, there was no absolute credence in the argument that there was a decline in Islamic culture. He insisted on the necessity of understanding the evolution of Islamic culture in a larger global context, in which the Islamic Empires were confronted with 'modernity' during the period 1600–1800. The internal workings of the Asian societies and state systems, he argued, were affected by the commercial expansion of Europe, its search for new markets, introduction of new military and economic systems, and its innovations in science and technology.

Rejecting the argument concerning the 'cultural' failure and intellectual and technical barrenness of the Mughal elites, I. G. Khan (2002) focused on the training of Mughal *mansabdars* as technocrats and the patronage that they received from the Mughal emperors to accomplish the task. This aspect is sufficiently covered in the chapters in *Ain-i Akbari* on metal purification, alloying, canon casting, handgun boring devices, and geared wagons that ground grain as they moved. In addition, *Ain-i Akbari* described the syllabus for school-going boys, introduced in 1580, which comprised not only general subjects that were usually taught, like logic, prosody, disputation, and recitation of the *Quran*, but also disciplines such as agriculture, land measurement, medicine, mathematics, algebra, and household management, which included a variety of managerial and pragmatic skills. The study of these subjects, Khan argued, provided a foundational basis for the careers of nobles who joined the Mughal bureaucracy as military, civil, and revenue officials. In this context, Khan cited Aurangzeb's emotional outburst in 1661 against his teacher, Mulla Saleh, for training him in the specialised theological-scholastic syllabus. Later, in the seventeenth century, the emperor expressed great satisfaction when the technical and *falsafi* (reason-based) syllabus for elite education was revised and strengthened by the *Dars-i Nizamiyya* of Mulla Nizamuddin Sahalvi at Firangi Mahal in Lucknow. Elite youth in the Mughal Empire thus had access to more technical roles than was evident in their *madrasa* syllabi. This reflected, Khan asserted, that within the Mughal system, there were opportunities, avenues, and resources for technical intervention and innovation. In consonance with Khan and critical of Athar Ali, Richard Barnett (2002) observed that as in the 'high Mughal period', the courtiers of Muhammad Shah 'Rangila' (r. 1719–48) and other regional courts patronised disciplines of technology, even if it was not strictly science, namely metallurgy, chemistry, agrarian management, cost-accounting, mathematics, astronomy, craft-related sciences, and hydrology. Warning against the Whig interpretation of history, Barnett argued that the characterisation of the eighteenth century as a 'cultural failure of the Islamic World' amounted to a 'prefiguring of modernity' and judging historical societies by contemporary standards; it also legitimised British opinion on the pre-colonial period.

Rejecting arguments on cultural stagnation, military decline, and elite debauchery in the Mughal, Safavid, and Ottoman Empires, Christopher A. Bayly (1989) attributed the weakening of these empires to a variety of internal political factors. He argued that the peace and stability provided by the imperial authorities in these states contributed to the deepening of commercial networks, expansion of urbanisation, and dominance of the landed class. These different interests emerged and consolidated into a new economic and social order that later weakened the empire. Bayly emphasised that a combination of 'accommodating indigenous capitalism' and fiscal weakness unsettled these centralised bureaucracies. This resulted in structural changes, and the new commercial and landed classes merged into vibrant regional and provincial formations.

John F. Richards (1990), on the other hand, argued that a 'general crisis', which overcame several parts of the world like Western Europe, the Ottoman Empire, China, and Japan in the first half of the seventeenth century, was not apparent at any point in India in the seventeenth century. During this period, these regions were marked by political instability, war, population decline, urban stagnation, economic crises, falling prices, depleted stocks of precious metals, and climatic changes, while most of the Indian subcontinent under Mughal rule could boast of peace and order, territorial expansion, smooth flow of resources, diffusion of imperial culture, and an overarching imperial sovereignty throughout South Asia. It was a period of moderate but steady population growth and rising productivity. It was only at the turn of the seventeenth century, Richards argued, that India encountered political crises, warfare, disease, and economic disruption, which accompanied the Mughal imperial decline. Recovery, nonetheless, was possible. Had Bahadur Shah lived longer, had the empire not been subjected to two wars of succession in 1712–13, and had Farrukhsiyar (1713–19) succeeded in controlling his king-makers—the Sayyid brothers—revenues could have been restituted. Instead, all the reserves of the empire were squandered in Farrukhsiyar's rebellion. The six-year hiatus spent in political struggle ended with the execution of Farrukhsiyar, which empowered the Marathas to consolidate their power over large parts of Deccan. Between 1711 and 1719, as power passed from the centre to its constituent regional units, the centralised polity of earlier centuries could not be sustained and the emperor ceased to be the sole arbiter and dispenser of legitimate authority. By the mid-eighteenth century, while the process of political reconstruction had begun, the Mughal Empire continued to decline and displayed symptoms of a 'general crisis', noticed during the Deccan famines of 1703–04. The eighteenth-century crisis, Richards suggested, was the product of the new forces and new connections to which the Indian subcontinent was subjected.

An interesting perspective on the decline of the Mughal Empire was added by Rosalind O'Hanlon (1999), who provided a gendered dimension to the disintegration of Mughal service morale, beginning later in the seventeenth century. Studying gender identity and norms of manhood in the political and religious discourses of Mughal north India, O'Hanlon argued that a concern with the meanings of ideal manhood cut through these discourses and through medieval Perso-Islamic political culture that served to connect kingship, norms of statecraft, and imperial service. These connections were noticed in the traditions of moral and political theory of the Delhi Sultanate as well. But from the late sixteenth century, gendered idioms of kingship were developed in significantly different ways. Akbar and his courtiers attempted to strengthen the associations between imperial service and ideal manhood, making these a more public and explicit part of court culture. Bodily and sexual codes for imperial servants were reworked to emphasise the possibilities for moral and human perfection in the 'homologous worlds'—the worlds of the kingdom, the household, and the body—that men occupied as governors. These eclectic norms for ideal manhood were expected to cut across all differences of law, religion, caste, and region, with imperial service being the best (and perhaps the sole) way for its realisation. This Mughal strategy sought to create a new north Indian model of patriarchal and heterosexual male virtue, different from the Iranian-influenced courts of Deccan. O'Hanlon argued that Mughal officials negotiated these bodily codes and used wider idioms of sexual difference in their understanding of imperial authority and imperial service. These codes and idioms changed between the early seventeenth century and the first decades of the eighteenth century—a period that witnessed the high point of Mughal power as well as its crisis and disintegration. During Aurangzeb's prolonged stay in Deccan and absence from the north, important implications emerged for the wider cultural authority of Mughal imperial service, that is, existing loyalties and salaries were put under strain, the older ethic of service, obligation, and reward lost much of its meaning, and the older model of the imperial servant as an embodiment of ideal manliness was fractured. Some of its fragments became a part of the new and powerful notion of man as 'sophisticated gentleman connoisseur', although it did not gel with the ethic of absolute personal subordination to the emperor. To the contrary, the inner dynamic that connected body, moral self, and environment in this thought suggested a strong concern with the individual and with 'self-cultivation as both ambition and reward'. Such ideas, O'Hanlon asserted, gained prominence in the first half of the eighteenth century as the emperor's personal authority diminished. The decline of the emperor's power and authority 'coincided with the remarkable flowering of a wider and overtly celebratory urban culture of pleasure at the imperial capital'.

REGION AND REGIONAL IDENTITIES

While some debates point towards 'cataclysmic change' in the eighteenth century, or state that the period was marked by gloom and despondency, it is germane to warn against generalisations and exaggerations. In the first half of the eighteenth century, Delhi confronted considerable political turmoil, dissipation of resources, court politics, factionalism amongst the nobility, invasions of Nadir Shah and Ahmad Shah Abdali, and persistent challenges by the Marathas. The city and its people must surely have felt 'a sense of being under permanent siege', but then such feelings were not necessarily shared beyond the capital. Political decentralisation at the centre was accompanied by economic reorientation in the regions, which followed their own formats and trajectories to carve their own autonomy, leaving Delhi with mere ceremonial powers. It is for this reason that the experiences of the centre or that of Delhi and Agra cannot be generalised or projected onto India as a whole for the eighteenth century. It is worth pondering whether the Mughal administration had ever performed effectively even in its prime, or the extent to which the Mughal traditions and institutions survived the collapse of Mughal imperial power in the eighteenth century.

In this context, it is worth noting the observations of Alam and Subrahmanyam on the nature of the Mughal Empire. They have argued that the Mughal State continuously evolved during the period 1530–1750, and yet it failed to reach perfection by 1600. Moreover, the incorporation of new regions in the Mughal Empire entailed the accommodation of several local factors, implying that imperial control over the regions was uneven rather than uniform. If such were the political configurations, then the emergence of regional states and kingdoms in the eighteenth century was not necessarily the 'political revolution' that has often been argued. Regional identities were the consequence of a complex interaction between region and empire, in the process of which both were redefined. Regional centralisation, Jos Gommans (2002) argued, was already 'pre-cooked' in the late seventeenth-century process of 'zamindarisation', that is, the roots of several new regional rulers of the eighteenth century lay in the families of zamindars who had either suppressed, or cooperated with, their local gentry in order to resist imperial authorities. The two processes of zamindarisation and regional centralisation were further stimulated with the political and military expansion of the East India Company in the late eighteenth and early nineteenth centuries.

Historians writing since the 1980s have rarely concerned themselves with issues around the decline of the Mughal Empire, a matter that has aroused more dispute than consensus. Engaged in the understanding of economic processes, political transformations or social changes in the eighteenth and early nineteenth centuries, they have focused on the phenomenon of change and continuity, growth and development, and the transition to colonialism. While they acknowledge the 'immortality' of Mughal achievements, they are not obsessed by the loss of empire. Recent scholarly research on the eighteenth and early nineteenth centuries is prolific in the understanding of historical problems of the period, provides a heterogeneous vision with multiple discourses, relates more to indigenous Indian pragmatism and realism, and is free from Eurocentric, Mughal-centric, and essentialist viewpoints. In brief, the fortune or misfortune of the Mughal Empire cannot be considered the sole determining factor in an understanding of historical processes in the eighteenth century. Nor is it possible, in view of the sources and newly analysed data, to accept the concept of decline or of a decadent, stagnant economy, or that the economy did not have sufficient initiative and potential to grow. In other words, the eighteenth century no longer appears like a 'dark age'. In fact, the politics of the eighteenth century was more noteworthy for its decentralisation rather than decline. It demonstrated a stimulating, buoyant economy, and in effect, it was the pulsating, throbbing, and 'tributary commercialism' of the period, as David Ludden (1990) has argued, that made India attractive to the European companies.

These patterns, widely displayed in works on eighteenth and nineteenth-century South Asia, were first mentioned by Bernard Cohn in his study of the Banaras region in the first half of the 1960s. Later, investigations shifted into other regions, namely Bengal, Maharashtra, parts of peninsular India, Awadh, and others. Inquiries into the economy, polity, and society of the period have contributed to a different theoretical and ideological perspective and set aside the notion of a static, stagnant, traditional India in the eighteenth century. The discourses, instead, are focused on the establishment of secure power bases, their agrarian and commercial dynamism, the growth of towns, proliferation of markets, and urban development; and the East India Company's interaction with the indigenous military labour market and its negotiations with 'native' sepoys to acquire strength and sustenance. In the sphere of law, the Company adapted the existing prescribed systems of rule, rank, status, and gender and redefined them to accommodate its political purpose; in writing medical histories, particularly relating to *Unani* medicine, some have focused on understanding medicine as science, while others have explored the ideas of healing in the specific tradition of *Unani* and seen it as a cultural process that shaped social change. Even as these developments took place, the Mughal Empire continued to disintegrate, a process that began much before the consolidation of power by the East India Company. These arguments attest to the flexibility and adaptability of India's society and economy, demonstrating the stability and commercial growth of the period.

Muzaffar Alam (2013 [1986]) talked of economic stability and a rather unusual growth in the regions in the earlier half of the eighteenth century, regardless of the political crisis during the period. The period witnessed a growing regional identity that propelled political and economic decentralisation; and the regions were not divested of economic prosperity. While the centre collapsed, the 'restabilisation' of the regions was achieved almost wholly within the Mughal institutional framework. Although the symptoms of political disintegration had become apparent by the 1720s, no regions remained isolated but were integrated through trade and monetary transactions. Consequently, the economic and monetary institutions of the seventeenth century that had contributed to the expanded network of commerce and credit markets survived the collapse of the Mughal Empire, and kept the 'erstwhile' empire interconnected even through the political turmoil in the eighteenth century. Alam argued that despite the shift from the control of peripheries by the centre in the seventeenth century to the control of the centre by the peripheries in the eighteenth, the 'myth and influence' of Delhi remained unfazed. No region could match or replace the symbolic power of Delhi in this period.

Chetan Singh (1991), in his study of seventeenth-century Punjab, was sceptical of whether the Mughal Empire was ever centralised. He observed that the region had acquired local roots and displayed administrative peculiarities in the seventeenth century, which was apparent from its revenue administration and the functioning of the bureaucratic system that comprised *subadar*s, *diwan*s, *bakhshi*s, *faujdar*s, and several other officials at the local level. Singh substantiated his argument by taking up the Mughal policy of transferring imperial officials periodically so as to prevent them from becoming locally entrenched, and argued that even though medieval chronicles created the impression that the Mughal 'bureaucracy' could not develop a regional power base, this was far from the truth. The appearance of certain names as appointees to various positions in

Punjab suggest that while transfers occurred frequently, officials either remained within the region or were transferred back often. This was considered a way to utilise the regional experience of these officials, although such appointments may also have been caused by political considerations. Moreover, the system of transfers could not prevent officials from building strong regional ties, especially in the case of influential *mansabdars*. Such patterns, particularly towards the latter part of the seventeenth century, led to friction between officials in the *suba* as imperial supervision was relaxed. Further, the hierarchy, designations, and functions of subordinate officials in the local administration did not remain constant throughout the seventeenth century, thus suggesting flexibility in the system.

A considerable amount of flexibility was also noticed in the creation and functions of the *faujdars*. Often, the reorganisation of the *faujdari* was affected by the personal influence of the *mansabdars*. This regionalisation of administrative functionaries indicated, Singh observed, that while the Mughal Empire outwardly appeared highly centralised, it actually was not. Had it been a rigid, centralised bureaucratic structure, it would have been unable to accommodate the regional diversity of the empire. In fact, for its survival, it was essential for the empire to incorporate the regional landed elite into the administration. Dismissing the notion of the 'high degree of Mughal centralisation' as an illusion, Singh argued that the developments in eighteenth-century Punjab can be traced back to the seventeenth century and to the emergence and long-term survival of regional administrative elites.

Christopher A. Bayly (2012 [1983]) advanced the notion of 'unity' in the political economy of north India from about 1740 to 1830. He argued that the political turbulence of the eighteenth century did not herald the ultimate dissolution of Mughal polity or the collapse of a political culture; instead, it was the emergence of regional dynastic rulers that pioneered processes of growth and regeneration. Indeed, the Mughal Empire did not fall: 'it was simply swallowed by a larger political organism'. Political decentralisation boosted the growing economic vitality of the regional and local powers that gained autonomy between 1735 and 1762, and encouraged the growth of a service gentry and homogeneous mercantile class that operated around small towns, situated at a distance from the imperial capitals. India's so-called 'Black Century' was in fact witness to the redeployment of merchant capital, rather than its destruction. India's merchants and service gentry continued to flourish in the nineteenth century and dominated the commercial and political life of the later colonial period. Similar arguments were made by David Ludden, Burton Stein, Nicholas Dirks, David Washbrook, Sanjay Subrahmanyam, Andre Wink, and Stewart Gordon, among others.

This vast body of literature seeks to identify continuities rather than ruptures in the transition to colonialism, and suggests that the critical changes that Bayly located in the 1830s, the 'age of reforms', had been anticipated in the eighteenth century itself. The East India Company continued to borrow from indigenous structures, even as it reinvented and reformulated them to legitimise its political sovereignty. The impact of the colonial State was felt not in the mid-eighteenth century but much later, in the second quarter of the nineteenth century. By the mid-nineteenth century, when prices showed an upward trend and economic expansion had resumed, it was evident that India was being governed in ways different from those of the eighteenth century, and that it was moving in new directions. Such changes may or may not have initiated something that could be called a 'revolution' or the beginning of 'modernity', but they certainly heralded a break with the continuities prevalent throughout the eighteenth century.

The eighteenth century was complex, perhaps even 'unfortunate', sandwiched, as Alam argued, between the political glory of the great Mughals and the humiliation of colonial rule. Colonial writers, in their urge to legitimise British rule in India, had portrayed the period as 'bleak' and sought justification from the writings of those Persian chroniclers who had presented the period as one of total chaos and failure. These chroniclers, Alam warned, were the protégés of the nobles who, as beneficiaries of the Mughal State, had felt deprived of privileges as the regions resisted Mughal central authority and became increasingly autonomous. They viewed their decline as the 'decline and decay of the entire society'. Obsessed with the fortunes of the Mughal throne and the person of the emperor, they tended to equate the decline of the imperial structure with the 'total collapse of all society'. It is apposite, therefore, to guard against the prejudiced perspective of a 'crisis' following the weakening of the Mughal Empire. Perhaps the best way to evaluate the fate of the Mughal Empire is to consider the local and regional ties of the Mughal elites and focus on the study of regions for, despite the decline of the centre, the Indian economy and polity showed resilience and patterns of growth and development; it was not static, stagnant, or in decay.

GLOSSARY

Abwab	cess or tax or exactions imposed by local officials.
Adab	social etiquette, decorum, behaviour.
Akhbar	news report.
Akhlaq	political and ethical theory.
Alim	one of the names of God in Islam, meaning 'All-Knowing'; also a scholar or Muslim learned in religious matters.
Al-tamgha	permanent revenue assignment to an assignee's family in his native place.
Amil	revenue collector.
Amir	noble.
'aql	rationality, reason.
Arazi	taxable land.
Arbab-i-zamin	owner of the land.
Arhsatta	account of revenue receipts and expenditure for each harvest.
Asnad/isnad	original or primary source.
Ataliq	regent.
Azaan	call for Muslims to prayers.
Bait-ul mal	public treasury.
Bakshi	minister or official who supervised the maintenance of military contingents and postings of military commanders.
Baoli	deep stepped well.
Banth	one-fourth of a landowner's land held revenue-free.
Baraka	inner essence or radiance.
Barat	cash salary.
Beopari	merchant.
Bigha	measure of area.
Buyutat	central department of the household.
Chapparbandi	setting up of huts; also used for settling a village.
Chaudhuri	revenue collector.
Chauth	one-fourth of revenue claimed by chiefs or landowners.
Daftar	volume.
Dagh	brand on horse for identification at inspection.
Dalal	agent.

Dasturu'l 'amals	revenue rate in cash; also used for administrative or financial regulations, administrative manual
Deshmukh	landholder; also revenue collector.
Desai	landholder; also used for revenue collector.
Doab	literally means two waters; generally used for land between two waters; land between rivers Ganga and Yamuna.
Dhimmi/zimmi	literally meaning 'protected person'; also used for non-Muslims living in an Islamic state with legal protection.
Fana	Sufi term for 'passing away' or 'annihilation', or 'to die before one dies'.
Farman	written royal order or edict, attested by the emperor's personal seal.
Farzand	in Persian language, this means son; also used affectionately for son-in-law.
Fatah	victory in military conquest.
Fathnama/Fatahnama	edict issued after military victory; it usually emulates a format where victory is attributed to Islam's glory.
Faujdar	*pargana*-level administrator or military commander.
Filasafa	an appeal to the tradition of the philosophers.
Ghazi	a Muslim soldier fighting against non-Muslims.
Ghusl khana	emperor's consultation room or tent.
*Gumashta*s	agents or revenue collectors of *jagirdar*s, or revenue assignees or any other official.
Hadis	traditions of the Prophet.
Hasil	actual revenue collection.
Hasil farohi	revenue head.
Hukama	scientists.
Hundi	bill of exchange.
Ijara	revenue farming, lease.
Ijtihad	reason.
Ilm	knowledge.
Imarat	statecraft.
Inam	*jagir* assigned as 'reward' in excess of *mansab* pay claim; also revenue-free land granted in reward for service.
Iqta	territorial revenue assignment; synonym of *jagir*.
*Jagir*s	land revenue assignment.
Jahiliyya	an Islamic concept of the period of time and state of affairs in Arabia before the advent of Islam. It is often translated as the 'Age of Ignorance'.
Jama'	total revenue assessed.
Jama'bandi	the work of determining *jama'*.

Jami	caste.
Jarib	measuring rope or bamboo rod; measurement; unit of length.
Jins-i kamil	high value crops.
Jizya	poll tax on non-Muslims.
Jnana	knowledge.
Karamat	magical powers.
Khalisa	territories and sources of revenue assigned to yield revenue for imperial treasury.
Khanqah	Sufi hospice or monastery.
Khansama	household servant.
Khatib	preacher.
Khatima	conclusion.
Khilat	a ceremonial robe or robe of honour.
Khurak-i dawwab	feed for the animals of the imperial stables.
Khutba	sermon by the *'ulama* read in the name of the King at the Friday *namaz*.
Kufr	in Arabic, it literally means covering or concealing something; in a religious context, it refers to hiding or denying religious truth, or disbelief in *Allah* and His Messenger, Prophet Muhammad.
Kurnish	form of court etiquette performed before the emperor by bending one's torso.
Madad-i ma'ash	revenue-free land grant.
Mahal	unit for revenue purposes; when territorial, it corresponded to a *pargana*, but it could also be non-territorial, for example, market dues, customs house, mint.
Mahsul	revenue collected.
Ma'jun	in Arabic, it means 'kneaded', but the medical books call it an 'electuary', that is, a compound of medicines kneaded with syrup into a soft mass (although it was sold in the bazaars as an intoxicating confection of *ganja* [hemp] leaves). The main ingredient for making *ma'jun* were *ganja* leaves, milk, ghee, poppy seeds, flowers of the thorn-apple (*dhatura*), the powder of *nux vomica*, and sugar.
Maktab khana	bureau of translation.
Malik	proprietor; used for zamindar or owner of the land.
Malik-i zamin	owner of the land.
Mir bakhshi	minister in charge of paying salaries to the army.
Muchalka	bond; written undertaking.
Mufti	theologian deemed qualified to interpret Muslim law.
Mulk-i marusi	ancestral domain.

Muqaddam village headman.
Muraqqa album.
Muezzin cleric who gives the call for prayers to Muslims from the minaret of a mosque.
Muhtasib official who enforces public compliance with Muslim law.
Mujtahid spiritual guide, or one who can or has the right to interpret the law.
Mulkgirliq imperialist ambitions.
Murid disciple, especially of a Sufi saint.
Mushrib a philosophical or scientific temper.
Murshid spiritual guide.
Mutalaba the imperial treasury's claim against *mansabdars*.
Mutassadi clerk; generally used for official.
Mutawalli administrator of a trust (*waqf*); also used for official at the *pargana* level entrusted with the supervision of revenue grants.
Nawisindagan scribes.
Nazr an expensive gift, usually gold or silver coins.
Nishan order.
Pabos the ceremony of kissing the emperor's feet.
Parasang an ancient Persian unit of distance, equal to about 3.5 miles (5.6 km).
Pargana smallest administrative unit delimited by Mughal administration for revenue and administrative purposes.
Parwana order.
Patta written document stating the revenue demand assessed upon a village or an individual.
Peshkash offering, present, tribute.
Phutkal miscellaneous.
Qabuliyat written document giving acceptance of the revenue assessed, and an undertaking for its payment.
Qanungo semi-hereditary *pargana* official responsible for revenue assessment and maintaining revenue records.
Qarar-dad agreement; paper prescribing procedure for revenue realisation.
Qasba small town.
Qaul-qarar document setting out the amount or rate of revenue demand.
Qaum clan; caste; community.
Qazi Muslim judge with jurisdiction generally within the limits of a *pargana*.
Qilacha/garhi small fort.
Rai' yield of crop per *bigha*; revenue rate in kind.
Ra'iyat/ri'aya subjects; peasants.

Ra'iyati	land or village held by the peasants.
Ruba'i	a quatrain, a poem or a verse of a poem consisting of four lines. It refers specifically to a form of Persian poetry or its derivative form in English and other languages.
Rusum	customary cesses or taxes.
Sadr	minister or officer in charge of revenue grants.
Sadru-s sudur	central minister in charge of revenue grants.
Sahukar	big merchant.
Sajda	prostration.
Sama	literally means 'listening'. It is a Sufi ceremony performed as *dhikr* (remembrance). The rituals include singing, playing instruments, dancing, recitation of poetry, prayers, wearing symbolic attire, etc.
Sara'i	inn.
Sarkar	subdivision of *suba* comprising a group of usually contiguous *pargana*s.
Sarraf/shroff	money-changer; banker.
Shahbandar	official of the port.
Shahid	martyr.
Shari'at	source of Islamic jurisprudence.
Sir	land on which peasants are directly assessed and revenue collected from them without intermediaries.
Suba	province.
Subadar	provincial governor.
Tadbhava	vernacular derivative.
Takhullas	title.
Tamassuk	bond.
Tankhwa	salary.
Taqavi	loan given to a peasant for agricultural purposes.
Taslim	a variation on *kurnish*.
Tatsama	pure Sanskrit word.
Tauhid	monotheism.
Tijarat	trade.
Tuyul	revenue assignment.
'Ulama/ulema	Islamic theologians, plural of *alim*, literally meaning scholar.
Ulus/jama'iyat	tribe or clan; troops, armed contingent.
Umara	nobles, plural of *amir*.
Ummi	illiterate, as the *Sura* 7:15 of the *Quran* defines it.
Vilayet-i marusi	hereditary territories.

Wajh	territorial revenue assignment.
Wajhdar	holder of *wajh*.
Waqf/auqaf	trust for religious purposes.
Waqia	news, report.
Waqi'a-navis	official news-writer.
Wasiyat	will.
Watan	hereditary principality of chief (held in *jagir* permanently against whole or part of *mansab*).
Yad-dasht	memoranda.
Zabitana	cess per *bigha* to meet the expenses of the measuring party.
Zabti	cash rents varying with crops.
Zawabit	new or special regulations.
Zenana	harem.
Zil Allah	shadow of God.
Zor-talab	not paying revenue unless force was used.

BIBLIOGRAPHY

Adle, Chahryar, and Irfan Habib (eds). *History of Civilizations of Central Asia, Development in Contrast: From the Sixteenth to the Mid-Nineteenth Century*, Vol. V. Paris: UNESCO, 2003.

Ahmad, Aziz. *Studies in Islamic Culture in the Indian Environment.* New Delhi: Oxford University Press, 1999.

Alam, Muzaffar. 'The Zamindars and Mughal Power in the Deccan, 1685–1712'. *The Indian Economic and Social History Review* 11 (1), 1974, 74–91.

———. 'Aspects of Agrarian Uprising in North India in the Early Eighteenth Century'. In Sabyasachi Bhattacharya and Romila Thapar (eds), *Situating Indian History: For Sarvepalli Gopal*, 146–70. New Delhi: Oxford University Press, 1986.

———. 'Eastern India in the Early Eighteenth Century "Crisis": Some Evidence from Bihar'. *The Indian Economic and Social History Review* 28 (1), 1991, 43–71.

———. 'Trade, State Policy and Regional Change: Aspects of Mughal-Uzbek Commercial Relations, *c.* 1550–1750'. *Journal of the Economic and Social History of the Orient* 37 (3), 1994, 202–27.

———. 'Assimilation from a Distance: Confrontation and Sufi Accommodation in Awadh Society'. In R. Champaklakshmi and S. Gopal (eds), *Tradition, Dissent and Ideology: Essays in Honour of Romila Thapar.* New Delhi: Oxford University Press, 1996.

———. 'Politics under the Later Mughals'. In Indu Banga (ed.), *Five Punjabi Centuries: Polity, Economy, Society and Culture, c. 1500–1900*, Essays for J. S. Grewal, 61–83. New Delhi: Manohar, 1997.

———. '*Akhlaqi* Norms and Mughal Governance', In Muzaffar Alam, Francoise 'Nalini' Delvoye, and Marc Gaborieau (eds), *The Making of Indo-Persian Culture*, 67–95. New Delhi: Manohar, 2000.

———. 'The Culture and Politics of Persian in Pre-colonial Hindustan'. In Sheldon Pollock (ed.), *Literary Cultures in History: Reconstructions from South Asia*, 159–71. Berkeley: University of California Press, 2003.

———. *The Languages of Political Islam in India c. 1200–1800.* New Delhi: Permanent Black, 2004.

———. 'The Mughals, the Sufi Shaikhs and the Formation of the Akbari Dispensation'. *Modern Asian Studies* 43 (1), 2009, 135–74.

———. 'Strategy and Imagination in a Mughal Sufi Story of Creation'. *The Indian Economic and Social History Review* 49 (2), 2012, 151–95.

———. *The Crisis of Empire in Mughal North India: Awadh and the Punjab, 1707–1748*, Oxford India Perennials Series. New Delhi: Oxford University Press, 2013 [1986].

Alam, Muzaffar, and Seema Alavi. *A European Experience of the Mughal Orient, The I'jaz-i Arsalani (Persian Letters, 1773–1779) of Antoine-Louis Henri Polier.* New Delhi: Oxford University Press, 2001.

Alam, Muzaffar, Francoise 'Nalini' Delvoye, and Marc Gaborieau (eds). *The Making of Indo-Persian Culture*. New Delhi: Manohar, 2000.

Alam, Muzaffar, and Sanjay Subrahmanyam. 'Discovering the Familiar: Notes on the Travel Accounts of Anand Ram Mukhlis, 1745'. *South Asia Research* 16 (2), Autumn 1996, 130–54.

———. *The Mughal State, 1526–1750*. New Delhi: Oxford University Press, 1998.

———. 'Empiricism of the Heart: Close Encounters in an Eighteenth Century Indo-Persian Text'. *Studies in History* 15 (2), 1999, 261–91.

———. 'The Deccan Frontier and the Mughal Expansion, ca. 1600: Contemporary Perspectives'. *Journal of the Economic and Social History of the Orient* 47 (3), 2004a, 357–89.

———. 'The Making of a Munshi'. *Comparative Studies of South Asia, Africa and the Middle East* 24 (2), 2004b, 61–72.

———. *Indo-Persian Travels: In the Age of Discoveries, 1400–1800*. Cambridge: Cambridge University Press, 2008 (first South Asian edition).

———. 'Witnesses and Agents of Empire: Eighteenth Century Historiography and the World of the Mughal *Munshi*'. *Journal of the Economic and Social History of the Orient* 53, 2010, 393–423.

———. *Writing the Mughal World, Studies in Political Culture*. Ranikhet: Permanent Black, 2011.

Alavi, Seema. 'The Company Army and Rural Society: The Invalid *Thanah*, 1780–1830'. *Modern Asian Studies* 27 (1), February 1992, 147–78.

———. *The Sepoys and the Company: Tradition and Transition in Northern India, 1770–1830*. New Delhi: Oxford University Press, 1998.

———. *Islam and Healing: Loss and Recovery of an Indo-Muslim Medical Tradition, 1600–1900*. New Delhi: Permanent Black, 2007a.

——— (ed.). *The Eighteenth Century in India*, Debates in Indian History and Society. New Delhi: Oxford University Press, 2007b.

———. 'Medical Culture in Transition: Mughal Gentleman Physician and the Native Doctor in Early Colonial India'. *Modern Asian Studies* 42 (5), 2008, 853–97.

———. *Muslim Cosmopolitanism in the Age of Empire*. Cambridge and London: Harvard University Press, 2015.

Al-Badaoni, Abdul Qadir Ibn-i Muluk Shah. *Muntakhabu't-Tawarikh*, Vol. I, George S. A. Ranking (trans.). New Delhi: Idarah-i Adabiyat-i Delli, 1973a.

———. *Muntakhabu't-Tawarikh*, Vol. II, W. H. Lowe (trans.). New Delhi: Idarah-i Adabiyat-i Delli, 1973b.

———. *Muntakhabu't-Tawarikh*, Vol. III, Wolsley Haig (trans.). New Delhi: Idarah-i Adabiyat-i Delli, 1973c.

Ali, Daud. *Courtly Culture and Political Life in Early Medieval India*. Cambridge: Cambridge University Press, 2006 (first South Asian edition).

———. 'The Historiography of the Medieval in South Asia'. *Journal of the Royal Asiatic Society*, Third Series, 22 (1), January 2012, 7–12.

Ali, Daud, and Emma J. Flatt (eds). *Garden and Landscape Practices in Pre-Colonial India, Histories from the Deccan*, Visual and Media Histories. New Delhi: Routledge, 2012.

Allami, Abul Fazl. *The Akbar Nama*, Vol. I, H. Beveridge (trans.). New Delhi: Rare Books, 1972a.

———. *The Akbar Nama*, Vol. II, H. Beveridge (trans.). New Delhi: Rare Books, 1972b.

———. *The Akbar Nama*, Vol. III, H. Beveridge (trans.). New Delhi: Rare Books, 1973.

———. *The Ain-i Akbari*, Vol. I, H. Blochmann (trans.), D. C. Phillot (ed.). New Delhi: Low Price Publications, 1997.

———. *The Ain-i Akbari*, Vols II and III, Col. H. S. Jarrett (trans.), Jadunath Sarkar (corrected and annotated). New Delhi: Low Price Publications, 1997, 2e.

Alvi, M. A., and A. Rahman. *Jahangir, the Naturalist*. New Delhi: National Institute of Sciences of India, 1968.

Alvi, Sajida Sultana. 'Religion and State during the Reign of the Mughal Emperor Jahangir (1605–1627)'. *Studia Islamica* 69, 1989, 95–119.

———. *Perspectives on Mughal India, Rulers, Historians, 'Ulama and Sufis*. Karachi: Oxford University Press, 2012.

Anderson, Benedict. *Imagined Communities: Reflections on the Origin and Spread of Nationalism*. London: Verso, 1991, 2e.

Anooshahr, Ali. 'Mughal Historians and the Memory of the Islamic Conquest of India'. *The Indian Economic and Social History Review* 43 (3), 2006, 275–300.

———. 'The King Who Would Be Man: The Gender Roles of the Warrior King in Early Mughal History'. *Journal of the Royal Asiatic Society*, Third Series 18 (3), July 2008, 327–40.

———. 'Author of One's Fate: Fatalism and Agency in Indo-Persian Histories'. *The Indian Economic and Social History Review* 49 (2), 2012a, 197–224.

———. 'Dialogue and Territoriality in a Mughal History of the Millennium'. *Journal of the Economic and Social History of the Orient* 55 (2–3), 2012b, 220–54.

Ansari, Mohammad Azhar. *European Travellers under the Mughals, 1580–1627*. New Delhi: Idarah-i Adabiyat-i Delli, 1975.

Aquil, Raziuddin. 'Reconsidering Sovereignty and Governance under the Afghans: North India in the Late Fifteenth and Early Sixteenth Centuries'. *South Asia* 26 (1), April 2003, 5–21.

———. 'Salvaging a Fractured Past: Reflections on Norms of Governance and Afghan-Rajput Relations in North India in the Late Fifteenth and Early Sixteenth Centuries'. *Studies in History* 20 (1), 2004, 1–29.

———. *Sufism, Culture and Politics: Afghans and Islam in Medieval North India*. New Delhi: Oxford University Press, 2007.

——— (ed.). *Sufism and Society in Medieval India*, Debates in Indian History and Society. New Delhi: Oxford University Press, 2011.

Aquil, Raziuddin, and Kaushik Roy (eds). *Warfare, Religion, and Society in Indian History*. New Delhi: Manohar, 2012.

Aquil, Raziuddin, and Partha Chatterjee (eds). *History in the Vernacular*. Ranikhet and New Delhi: Permanent Black, 2008.

Arasaratnam, S. 'Weavers, Merchants and Company: The Handloom Industry in South-eastern India, 1750–1790'. In Sanjay Subrahmanyam (ed.), *Merchants, Markets and the State in Early Modern India*, 190–214. New Delhi: Oxford University Press, 1990.

Arasaratnam, S. *Maritime India in the Seventeenth Century*. New Delhi: Oxford University Press, 1994.

Asher, Catherine B. *Architecture of Mughal India*. Cambridge: Cambridge University Press, 1992a.

———. 'The Architecture of Raja Man Singh: A Study in sub-imperial Patronage'. In Barbara Stoler Miller (ed.), *The Powers of Art: Patronage in Indian Culture*, 183–201. New Delhi: Oxford University Press, 1992b.

———. 'Architecture'. In Zeenut Ziad (ed.), *The Magnificent Mughals*, 184–228. Oxford: Oxford University Press, 2002.

———. 'Multiple Memories: Lives of the Taj Mahal'. In Jaynie Anderson (ed.), *Crossing Cultures: Conflict/Migration/Convergence*, 614–20. Melbourne: University of Melbourne Press, 2008.

———. 'Mapping Hindu-Muslim Identities through the Architecture of Shahjahanabad and Jaipur'. In Meena Bhargava (ed.), *Exploring Medieval India, Sixteenth to Eighteenth Centuries: Culture, Gender, Regional Patterns*, Vol. II, 141–68. New Delhi: Orient BlackSwan, 2010.

———. 'An Introduction to Taj Mahal'. *Sahapedia*, Open Online Resource Journal, 2016. Available at https://www.sahapedia.org/introduction-the-taj-mahal.

Asher, Catherine B., and Cynthia Talbot. *India Before Europe*. Cambridge: Cambridge University Press, 2008.

Ashrafyan, K. F. *The Agrarian System of North India in the Thirteenth–Mid-Eighteenth Centuries*. Moscow, 1965.

Athar Ali, M. 'Akbar and Islam'. In Milton Israel and N. K. Wagle (eds), *Islamic Society and Culture: Essays in Honour of Professor Aziz Ahmad*, 123–34. New Delhi: Manohar, 1983.

———. *The Apparatus of Empire: Awards of Ranks, Offices and Titles to the Mughal Nobility, 1573–1658*. New Delhi: Oxford University Press, 1985.

———. *The Mughal Nobility under Aurangzeb*. New Delhi: Oxford University Press, 1997 [1966], rev. edn.

———. 'Pursuing an Elusive Seeker of Universal Truth: The Identity and Environment of the *Dabistan-i Mazahib*'. *Journal of the Royal Asiatic Society*, Third Series 9 (3), November 1999, 365–73.

———. *Mughal India: Studies in Polity, Ideas, Society and Culture*. New Delhi: Oxford University Press, 2006a.

———. 'The Islamic Background to Indian History: An Interpretation of the Islamic Past'. In M. Athar Ali, *Mughal India: Studies in Polity, Ideas, Society and Culture*, 3–11. New Delhi: Oxford University Press, 2006b.

———. 'The Perception of India in Akbar and Abu'l Fazl'. In Irfan Habib (ed.), *Akbar and His India*, 215–24. New Delhi: Oxford University Press, 2006c.

———. 'The Passing of the Empire: The Mughal Case'. In Athar Ali, *Mughal India: Studies in Polity, Ideas, Society and Culture*, 337–49. New Delhi: Oxford University Press, 2006d.

Babur, Zahir-ud-din Muhammad. *The Baburnama: Memoirs of Babur, Prince and Emperor*. Wheeler M. Thackston (trans.). New York: Oxford University Press, 2002.

Balabanlilar, Lisa. 'Lords of the Auspicious Conjunction: Turco-Mongol Imperial Identity on the Subcontinent'. *Journal of World History* 18 (1), March 2007, 1–39.

Balabanlilar, Lisa. *Imperial Identity in the Mughal Empire: Memory and Dynastic Politics in Early Modern South and Central Asia.* New Delhi: Viva Books, 2013.

Banga, Indu. (ed.). *The City in Indian History*. New Delhi: Manohar and Urban History Association of India, 1994, reprint.

———. *Five Punjabi Centuries: Polity, Economy, Society and Culture, c. 1500–1900*, Essays for J. S. Grewal. New Delhi: Manohar, 1997.

———. 'Gender Relations in Medieval India'. In J. S. Grewal (ed.), *The State and Society in Medieval India*, History of Science, Philosophy and Culture in Indian Civilization, Vol. VII, Part I. New Delhi: Oxford University Press, 2005.

Barnett, R. B. *North India Between Empires: Awadh, the Mughals and the British, 1720–1801.* New Delhi: Manohar, 1987.

———. 'Embattled Begams: Women as Power Brokers in Early Modern India'. In Gavin Hambly (ed.), *Women in the Medieval Islamic World*, 521–36. New York: St. Martin's Press, 1998.

——— (ed.). *Rethinking Early Modern India.* New Delhi: Manohar, 2002.

Bayly, Christopher A. 'Town-Building in North India, 1780–1830'. *Modern Asian Studies* 9 (3), 1975, 483–503.

———. *Rulers, Townsmen and Bazaars: North Indian Society in the Age of British Expansion, 1770–1870.* New Delhi: Oxford India Perennials Series, 2012 [1983], 3e.

———. 'The Pre-History of Communalism? Religious Conflict in India, 1700–1860'. *Modern Asian Studies* 19 (2), 1985a, 177–203.

———. 'State and Economy in India over Seven Hundred Years', *The Economic History Review* 38 (4), 1985b, 583–96.

———. *Indian Society and the Making of the British Empire*, The New Cambridge History of India, II.2. Cambridge: Cambridge University Press, 1988.

———. *Imperial Meridian: The British Empire and the World, 1780–1830.* London: Longman, 1989.

———. 'Knowing the Country: Empire and Information in India'. *Modern Asian Studies*, Special Issue: How Social, Political and Cultural Information is Collected, Defined, Used and Analysed 27 (1), February 1993, 3–43.

———. 'British Orientalism and the Indian "Rational Tradition" c. 1780–1820'. *South Asia Research* 14 (1), April 1994, 1–9.

———. *Empire and Information: Intelligence Gathering and Social Communication in India, 1780–1870.* Cambridge: Cambridge University Press, 1996.

———. *Origins of Nationality in South Asia: Patriotism and Ethical Government in the Making of Modern India.* New Delhi: Oxford University Press, 1998.

Beach, Milo Cleveland. *Early Mughal Painting.* Cambridge MA: Harvard University Press, 1987.

———. *Mughal and Rajput Painting*, The New Cambridge History of India. I.3. Cambridge: Cambridge University Press, 1992.

———. *The Imperial Image, Paintings for the Mughal Court.* Washington, D.C.: Smithsonian Institution, Freer Gallery of Art, Arthur M. Sackler Gallery, Mapin Publishing, 2012, revised and expanded edition.

Beach, Milo Cleveland, and Ebba Koch (with new translations by Wheeler M. Thackston). *King of the World: The Padshshnama, an Imperial Mughal Manuscript from the Royal Library, Windsor Castle*. London and Washington, D.C.: Azimuth Editions and Smithsonian Institution, 1997.

Begley, Wayne E. 'The Myth of the Taj Mahal and a New Theory of its Symbolic Meaning'. *The Art Bulletin* 61, 1979, 7–37.

Begley, Wayne E., and Z. A. Desai. *Taj Mahal: The Illumined Tomb. An Anthology of Seventeenth-Century Mughal and European Documentary Sources*. Cambridge, MA and Seattle: Aga Khan Program for Islamic Architecture and University of Washington Press, 1989.

Behl, Aditya. 'Presence and Absence in Bhakti: An Afterword'. *International Journal of Hindu Studies* 11 (3), December 2007, 319–24.

Behl, Aditya, and Simon Weightman. *Madhumalati: An Indian Sufi Romance*. Oxford: Oxford University Press, 2000.

Berkhofer Jr., Robert F. *Behavioral Approach to Historical Analysis*. New York: Free Press, 1971.

Bernier, Francois. *Travels in the Mogul Empire, A.D. 1656–1668*, Trans. on the basis of Irving Brock's version, Archibald Constable (annotated). New Delhi: Low Price Publication, 2008, 2e [Vincent A. Smith rev.). Also published by Forgotten Books, 2014.

Beveridge, Henry, and Alexander Rogers (trans. and ed.). *The Tuzuk-i-Jahangiri or Memoirs of Jahangir*, Vol. I. New Delhi: Munshiram Manoharlal Oriental Publishers & Booksellers, 1968, 2e.

Bhadani, B. L. (ed.). *Medieval India 3, Researches in the History of India*. New Delhi: Manohar, 2012.

Bhargava, Meena. '*Madad-i Maash* and *Ma'afi* Grants in Gorakhpur during the Late Eighteenth–Early Nineteenth Century'. *Proceedings Indian History Congress*, 52nd session, 1992.

———. 'Perception and Classification of the Rights of the Social Classes: Gorakhpur and the East India Company in the Late Eighteenth–Early Nineteenth Century'. *The Indian Economic and Social History Review* 30 (2), 1993, 215–37.

———. 'Growth of Mughal Empire, 1526–1556'. In *EHI-04: India from 16th to Mid 18th Century*, Unit 5, 5–17. New Delhi: Indira Gandhi National Open University, 1994a.

———. 'Expansion and Consolidation, 1556–1707'. In *EHI-04: India from 16th to Mid 18th Century*. Unit 6, 18–31. New Delhi: Indira Gandhi National Open University, 1994b.

———. 'Landed Property Rights in Transition: A Note on Cultivators and Agricultural Labourers in Gorakhpur in the Late Eighteenth and Nineteenth Centuries'. *Studies in History* 12 (2), 1996, 243–53.

———. *State, Society and Ecology: Gorakhpur in Transition, 1750–1830*. New Delhi: Primus Books, 2014 [1999], rev. edn.

———. 'Agricultural Technology and Patterns of Exchange: A Study of Central Asia and its Interaction with India, 10th–18th Centuries'. In A. Rahman (ed.), *India's Interaction with China, Central and West Asia*, 392–408, History of Science, Philosophy and Culture in Indian Civilization, Vol. III, Part 2. New Delhi: Oxford University Press, 2002.

———. 'Nomadic or Semi-Nomadic: *Banjaras* and the Indian Economy, Sixteenth to Nineteenth Centuries'. In Biswamoy Pati, Bhairabi Sahu, and T. K. Venkatasubramanian (eds), *Negotiating India's Past: Essays in Memory of Partha Sarathi Gupta*. New Delhi: Tulika, 2003, 153–73.

Bhargava, Meena. 'Re-Visiting Medieval Indian History'. *The Book Review*, Education Special 29 (10), 2005, 35–36.

——— (ed.). *Exploring Medieval India: Sixteenth to Eighteenth Centuries: Politics, Economy, Religion*, Vol. I. New Delhi: Orient BlackSwan, 2010a.

——— (ed.). *Exploring Medieval India, Sixteenth to Eighteenth Centuries: Culture, Gender, Regional Patterns*, Vol. II. New Delhi: Orient BlackSwan, 2010b.

———. 'Delhi Under The Mughals'. In Swapna Liddle and Annabel Lopez (eds), *Delhi, A Living Heritage*, 34–45. New Delhi: IGNCA and INTACH, 2010c.

——— (ed.). *The Decline of the Mughal Empire*, Debates in Indian History and Society. New Delhi: Oxford University Press, 2014.

———. '*Akbarnama*, a Sixteenth Century Chronicle of India'. *Indian Horizons* (ICCR Publication) 62 (4), 2015/2016, 20–29.

——— (ed.). *Frontiers of Environment: Issues in Medieval and Early Modern India*. Hyderabad: Orient BlackSwan, 2017.

Bhattacharya, Neeladri. 'Colonial State and Agrarian Society'. In Burton Stein (ed.), *The Making of Agrarian Policy in British India, 1770–1900*. New Delhi: Oxford University Press, 1986.

———. 'Introduction. Special Issue: "Forests, Fields and Pastures"'. *Studies in History* 14 (2), July–December 1998, 165–71.

Blake, Stephen P. 'Courtly Culture under Babur and the Early Mughals'. *Journal of Asian History* 20, 1986a, 193–214.

———. 'Cityscape of an Imperial Capital: Shahjahanabad in 1739'. In R. E. Frykenberg (ed.), *Delhi Through the Ages: Essays in Urban History, Culture and Society*, 152–91. New Delhi: Oxford University Press, 1986b.

———. 'The Urban Economy in Premodern Muslim India: Shahjahanabad, 1639–1739'. *Modern Asian Studies* 21 (3), 1987, 447–71.

———. *Shahjahanabad: The Sovereign City in Mughal India, 1639–1739*. Cambridge: Cambridge University Press, 2002 [1991].

———. 'The Patrimonial-Bureaucratic Empire of the Mughals'. In Hermann Kulke (ed.), *The State in India, 1000–1700*, 278–303, Themes in Indian History. New Delhi: Oxford University Press, 1995.

Bose, Sugata. *A Hundred Horizons: The Indian Ocean in the Age of Global Empire*. Cambridge, MA: Harvard University Press, 2006.

Bose, Sugata, and Ayesha Jalal. *Modern South Asia: History, Culture, Political Economy*. New Delhi: Oxford University Press, 1998.

Brittlebank, Kate. *Tipu Sultan's Search for Legitimacy: Islam and Kinship in a Hindu Domain*. New Delhi: Oxford University Press, 1997.

Bronner, Yigal, and David Shulman. 'A Cloud Turned Goose: Sanskrit in the Vernacular Millennium'. *The Indian Economic and Social History Review* 43 (1), 2006, 1–30.

Brown, Katherine Butler. 'Did Aurangzeb Ban Music? Questions for the Historiography of his Reign'. *Modern Asian Studies* 41 (1), 2007, 77–120.

Busch, Allison. 'Literary Responses to the Mughal Imperium: The Historical Poems of Kesavdas'. *South Asia Research* I, 2005, 31–54.

———. 'Hidden in Plain View: *Braj Bhasha* Poets at the Mughal Court'. *Modern Asian Studies* 44 (2), 2010, 267–309.

———. '*Riti* and *Register*: Lexical Variation in Courtly *Braj Bhasha* Texts'. In Francesca Orsini (ed.), *Before the Divide: Hindi and Urdu Literary Culture*, 84–120. New Delhi: Orient BlackSwan, 2011a.

———. *Poetry of Kings: The Classical Hindi Literature of Mughal India*. Oxford: Oxford University Press, 2011b.

———. 'The Anxiety of Innovation: The Practice of Literary Science in the Hindi *Riti* Tradition'. In Sheldon Pollock (ed.), *Forms of Knowledge in Early Modern Asia: Explorations in the Intellectual History of India and Tibet, 1500–1800*, 115–39. New Delhi: Manohar, 2011b.

Calkins, Philip. 'Formation of a Regionally Oriented Ruling Group in Bengal, 1700–1740'. *Journal of Asian Studies* 29 (4), August 1970, 799–806.

Chandra, Satish. *Parties and Politics at the Mughal Court, 1707–1740*. New Delhi: Oxford University Press, 2002 [1959], 4e.

———. *Medieval India: Society, the Jagirdari Crisis and the Village*. New Delhi: Macmillan, 1982.

——— (ed.). *The Indian Ocean: Explorations in History, Commerce and Politics*. New Delhi: Sage Publications, 1987.

———. *The Eighteenth Century in India: Its Economy and the Role of the Marathas, the Jats, the Sikhs and the Afghans*. Calcutta: Centre for Studies in Social Sciences, 1991, 2e.

———. *Mughal Religious Policies, The Rajputs and the Deccan*. New Delhi: Vikas Publishing House Pvt. Ltd, 1993.

———. *Historiography, Religion and State in Medieval India*. New Delhi: Har-Anand Publications, 1996a.

———. 'Historical Background to the Rise of the Bhakti Movement in Northern India'. In Satish Chandra, *Historiography, Religion and State in Medieval India*, 110–31. New Delhi: Har-Anand Publications, 1996b.

———. *Essays on Medieval Indian History*. New Delhi: Oxford University Press, 2003.

———. *History of Medieval India*. New Delhi: Orient Longman, 2007.

———. *State, Pluralism and the Indian Historical Tradition*. New Delhi: Oxford University Press, 2008.

———. 'Social and Attitudinal Change in Medieval India: Thirteenth–Seventeenth Century'. *The Indian Historical Review* 34 (1), 2009, 23–35.

———. 'Religious Policy of Aurangzeb during the Later Part of his Reign: Some Considerations'. In Meena Bhargava (ed.), *Exploring Medieval India, Sixteenth to Eighteenth Centuries: Politics, Economy, Religion*, Vol. I, 461–79. New Delhi: Orient BlackSwan, 2010.

———. *State, Society and Culture in Indian History*. New Delhi: Oxford University Press, 2012.

Chatterjee, Kumkum. 'History as Self-Representation: The Recasting of a Political Tradition in Late Eighteenth Century Eastern India'. *Modern Asian Studies* 32 (4), October 1998, 913–48.

Chatterjee, Kumkum. 'The Persianization of *Itihasa*'. *Journal of Asian Studies* 67 (2), May 2008, 513–43.

———. 'Scribal Elites in Sultanate and Mughal Bengal'. *The Indian Economic and Social History Review* 47 (4), 2010, 445–72.

Chatterjee, Prasun. 'Gender and Travel Writing in India, c. 1650–1700'. *Social Scientist* 40 (3 & 4), March–April 2012, 59–80.

Chattopadhyaya, B. D. *Representing the Other? Sanskrit Sources and the Muslims (Eighth to the Fourteenth Century)*. New Delhi: Manohar, 1998.

———. *The Making of Early Medieval India*. New Delhi: Oxford University Press, 2005.

Chaudhuri, K. N. *The Trading World of Asia and the East India Company, 1660–1760*. Cambridge: Cambridge University Press, 1978.

———. *Trade and Civilization in the Indian Ocean: An Economic History from the Rise of Islam to 1750*. Cambridge: Cambridge University Press, 1985.

Chaudhury, Sushil. *From Prosperity to Decline: Eighteenth Century Bengal*. New Delhi: Manohar, 1995.

Chicherov, A. I. *India: Economic Development in the 16th–18th Centuries, Outline History of Crafts and Trade*. Moscow, 1971 [1965].

Cohn, Norman. *The Pursuit of the Millennium: Revolutionary Messianism in Medieval and Reformation Europe and its Bearing on Modern Totalitarian Movements*. New York: Oxford University Press, 1961, 2e.

Copland, Ian, Ian Mabbett, Asim Roy, Kate Brittlebank, and Adam Bowles. *A History of State and Religion in India*. London and New York: Routledge, 2012.

Dale, Stephen Frederic. 'Steppe Humanism: The Autobiographical Writings of Zahir al-Din Muhammad Babur, 1483–1530'. *International Journal of Middle East Studies* 22 (1), February 1990, 37–58.

———. 'The Poetry and Autobiography of the *Baburnama*'. *The Journal of Asian Studies* 55 (3), August 1996, 635–64.

———. 'The Legacy of the Timurids'. *Journal of the Royal Asiatic Society*, Third Series 8 (1), April 1998, 43–58.

———. *Indian Merchants and Eurasian Trade, 1600–1750*. Cambridge: Cambridge University Press, 2002.

———. *The Garden of the Eight Paradises: Babur and the Culture of Empire in Central Asia, Afghanistan and India (1483–1530)*. Leiden and Boston: Brill. 2004.

———. *Babur: Timurid Prince and Mughal Emperor, 1483–1530*. Cambridge: Cambridge University Press, 2018.

Dalmia, Vasudha. 'Mosques, Temples and Fields of Disputations in a Late Eighteenth Century Chronicle'. In Meena Bhargava (ed.), *Exploring Medieval India, Sixteenth to Eighteenth Centuries: Politics, Economy, Religion*, Vol. I, 480–96. New Delhi: Orient BlackSwan, 2010.

Dalmia, Vasudha, and Munis D. Faruqui (eds). *Religious Interactions in Mughal India*. New Delhi: Oxford University Press, 2014.

Damrel, David W. 'The "*Naqshbandi* Reaction" Reconsidered'. In David Gilmartin and Bruce Lawrence (eds), *Beyond Turk and Hindu: Rethinking Religious Identities in Islamicate South Asia*, 176–98. New Delhi: India Research Press, 2002.

Darling, Linda T. '"Do Justice, Do Justice, For That is Paradise": Middle Eastern Advice for Indian Muslim Rulers'. *Comparative Studies of South Asia, Africa and the Middle East* 22 (1 & 2), 2002, 3–19.

Das Gupta, Ashin. 'Trade and Politics in Eighteenth Century India'. In D. S. Richards (ed.), *Islam and the Trade of Asia: A Colloquium*, 181–214. Oxford: Bruno Cassircr; Philadelphia: University of Pennsylvania Press, 1970. •

———. Review of Holden Furber, *Rival Empires of Trade in the Orient, 1600–1800*, Vol. II: *Europe and the World in the Age of Expansion* (Minneapolis: University of Minnesota Press, 1976), in *The Journal of Asian Studies* 38 (2), February 1979.

———. 'Indian Merchants and the Trade in the Indian Ocean'. In Tapan Raychaudhuri and Irfan Habib (eds), *The Cambridge Economic History of India*, Vol. I, 407–33. New Delhi: Orient Longman, 1984.

———. *India and the Indian Ocean World, Trade and Politics*. New Delhi: Oxford University Press, 2004.

Das Gupta, Ashin, and M. N. Pearson. *India and the Indian Ocean, 1500–1800*. Calcutta: Oxford University Press, 1987.

Datta, Rajat (ed.). *Society, Economy and the Market: Commercialization in Rural Bengal, c. 1760–1800*. New Delhi: Manohar, 2000.

———. *Rethinking a Millennium: Perspectives on Indian History, from the Eighth to the Eighteenth Century*, Essays for Harbans Mukhia. New Delhi: Aakar Books, 2008.

Day, U. N. 'Religious Policy of Aurangzeb'. In U. N. Day, *Some Aspects of Medieval Indian History*, 199–234. New Delhi: Low Price Publications, 2004.

Derrett, J. Duncan. *Religion, Law and the State in India*. London: Faber & Faber, 1968.

Digby, Simon. 'Beyond the Ocean: Perceptions of Overseas in Indo-Persian Sources of the Mughal Period'. *Studies in History* 15 (2), 1999, 247–59.

———. *Sufis and Soldiers in Aurangzeb's Deccan*. New Delhi: Oxford University Press, 2001.

Duby, Georges. 'Land and Labour'. In Maurice Aymard and Harbans Mukhia (eds), *French Studies in History*, 141–67, Vol. I, New Delhi: Orient Longman, 1988.

Eaton, Richard M. *Sufis of Bijapur: Social Roles of Sufis in Medieval India*. Princeton: Princeton University Press, 1978.

———. *The Rise of Islam and the Bengal Frontier, 1204–1760*. New Delhi: Oxford University Press, 1994.

———. *Essays on Islam and Indian History*. New Delhi: Oxford University Press, 2001.

——— (ed.). *India's Islamic Traditions, 711–1750*, Oxford in India Readings, Themes in Indian History. New Delhi: Oxford University Press, 2003.

———. *A Social History of the Deccan, 1300–1761, Eight Indian Lives*, The New Cambridge History of India. I.8. Cambridge: Cambridge University Press, 2008.

Eaton, Richard M. 'Malik Ambar (1548–1626): The Rise and Fall of Military Slavery'. In Meena Bhargava (ed.), *Exploring Medieval India, Sixteenth to Eighteenth Centuries: Politics, Economy, Religion*, 121–47. New Delhi: Orient BlackSwan, 2010.

———. 'India's Military Revolution: The View from Early Sixteenth Century Deccan'. In Raziuddin Aquil and Kaushik Roy (eds), *Warfare, Religion, and Society in Indian History*. New Delhi: Manohar, 2012.

Eaton, Richard M., Munis D. Faruqui, David Gilmartin, and Sunil Kumar (eds). *Expanding Frontiers in South Asian and World History*, Essays in Honour of John F. Richards. New York: Cambridge University Press, 2013.

Elias, Norbert. *The Court Society*, Edmund Jephcott (trans.). Oxford: Blackwell, 1983.

———. *The Civilizing Process: Sociogenetic and Psychogenetic Investigations*: Vol. I, *The History of Manners*; Vol. II, *State Formation and Civilization*, Norman Jephcott (trans.). Oxford: Blackwell, 1994.

Elliot, H. M., and J. Dowson (eds). *The History of India as Told by its Own Historians*, 8 volumes. London: Trubner, 1867–77.

Eraly, Abraham. *The Mughal World: Life in India's Last Golden Age*. New Delhi: Penguin Books India, 2007.

Ernst, Carl W. 'Lives of Sufi Saints'. In Donald S. Lopez Jr. (ed.), *Religions of India in Practice*, 495–512. Princeton: Princeton University Press, 1995.

———. 'Persecution and Circumspection in *Shattari* Sufism'. In Fred De Jong and Berndt Radtke (eds), *Islamic Mysticism Contested: Thirteen Centuries of Debate and Conflict*, 1–14. Leiden: E. J. Brill, 1999.

———. 'Muslim Studies of Hinduism? A Reconsideration of Arabic and Persian Translations from Indian Languages'. *Iranian Studies* 36 (2), June 2003, 173–95.

———. *Eternal Garden, Mysticism, History, and Politics at a South Asian Sufi Center*. New Delhi: Oxford University Press, 2004, 2e.

Esty, Daniel, and Marian Chertow (eds). *Thinking Ecologically: The Next Generation of Environmental Policy*. New Haven: Yale University Press, 1997.

Faruqi, Shamsur Rahman. *Early Urdu Literary Culture and History*. New Delhi: Oxford University Press, 2001.

Faruqui, Munis D. 'The Forgotten Prince: Mirza Hakim and the Formation of the Mughal Empire in India'. *Journal of the Economic and Social History of the Orient* 48 (4), 2005, 487–523.

———. 'At Empire's End: The Nizam, Hyderabad and Eighteenth Century India'. In *Modern Asian Studies* 43 (1), 2009.

———. *The Princes of the Mughal Empire, 1504–1719*. Cambridge: Cambridge University Press, 2012.

———. 'Dara Shukoh, *Vedanta*, and Imperial Succession in Mughal India'. In Vasudha Dalmia and Munis D. Faruqui (eds), *Religious Interactions in Mughal India*, 30–64. New Delhi: Oxford University Press, 2014.

Findly, Ellison B. 'Nur Jahan and the Exercise of Power'. *Manushi* 84, September–October 1994, 14–21.

———. *Nur Jahan: Empress of Mughal India.* New Delhi: Oxford University Press, 2000.

———. 'The Lives and Contributions of Mughal Women'. In Zeenut Ziad (ed.), *The Magnificent* Mughals, 26–58. Oxford: Oxford University Press, 2002.

———. 'The Capture of Maryam-uz-Zamani's Ship: Mughal Women and European Traders'. In Meena Bhargava (ed.), *Exploring Medieval India, Sixteenth to Eighteenth Centuries: Culture, Gender, Regional Patterns*, Vol. II, 261–84. New Delhi: Orient BlackSwan, 2010.

Fischel, Walter J. 'Jews and Judaism at the Court of the Moghul Emperors in Medieval India', *Islamic Culture* 25, 1951.

Fisher, Michael H. *A Clash of Cultures: Awadh, the British, and the Mughals.* New Delhi: Manohar, 1987.

———. 'The Office of the *Akhbar Nawis*: The Transition from Mughal to British Forms'. *Modern Asian Studies* 27 (1), February 1993, 45–82.

———. *Counterflows to Colonialism: Indian Travellers and Settlers in Britain, 1600–1857.* New Delhi: Permanent Black, 2004.

——— (ed.). *Beyond the Three Seas: Travellers' Tales of Mughal India.* New Delhi: Random House, 2007a.

———. 'From India to England and Back: Early Indian Travel Narratives for Indian Readers'. *Huntington Library Quarterly* 70 (1), 2007b, 153–72.

———. *A Short History of the Mughal Empire.* London and New York: I. B. Tauris, 2016.

Flood, Finbarr B. *Objects of Translation: Material Culture and Medieval 'Hindu-Muslim' Encounter.* New Delhi: Permanent Black, 2009.

Foltz, Richard. 'Two Seventeenth Century Central Asian Travellers to Mughal India'. *Journal of the Royal Asiatic Society,* Third Series 6 (3), November 1996, 367–77.

Foster, William. *The Embassy of Sir Thomas Roe to India, 1615–1619 as narrated in his Journal and Correspondence.* New Delhi: Munshiram Manoharlal Pvt. Ltd, 1990 [1926].

Friedmann, Yohanan. *Shaykh Ahmad Sirhindi: An Outline of his Thought and Study of his Image in the Eyes of Posterity.* New Delhi: Oxford University Press, 2001 [1971].

———. 'The Origins and Significance of the *Chachnama*'. In Yohanan Friedmann (ed.), *Islam in South Asia*, 23–37. Jerusalem and Boulder, CO: Magnes Press and Westview, 1985.

Frykenberg, R. E. (ed.), *Delhi Through the Ages.* New Delhi: Oxford University Press, 1986.

Gascoigne, Bamber. *The Great Moghuls.* London: Jonathan Cape Ltd, 1976.

Ghosh, Pika. 'Krishna's Dance and Devotion in the Temples of Seventeenth Century Bengal'. In Meena Bhargava (ed.), *Exploring Medieval India, Sixteenth to Eighteenth Centuries: Politics, Economy, Religion*, 434–60, Vol. I. New Delhi: Orient BlackSwan, 2010.

Gilmartin, David, and Bruce B. Lawrence (eds). *Beyond Turk and Hindu: Rethinking Religious Identities in Islamicate South Asia.* New Delhi: India Research Press, 2002.

Gommans, Jos J. L. *The Rise of the Indo-Afghan Empire, 1710–1780.* Leiden: E. J. Brill, 1995.

Gommans, Jos J. L. *Mughal Warfare: Indian Frontiers and High Roads to Empire, 1500–1700*, Warfare and History Series. London and New York: Routledge, 2002.

Gommans, Jos J. L., and Dirk H. K. Kolff (eds). *Warfare and Weaponry in South Asia, 1000–1800*. New Delhi: Oxford University Press, 2001.

Gordon, Stewart. *The Marathas*, The New Cambridge History of India, II.4. Cambridge: Cambridge University Press, 1993.

———. *Marathas, Marauders and State Formation in Eighteenth Century India*. New Delhi: Oxford University Press, 1994.

———. 'Legitimacy and Loyalty in Some Successor States of the Eighteenth Century'. In John F. Richards (ed.), *Kingship and Authority in South Asia*, 327–47. New Delhi: Oxford University Press, 1998.

——— (ed.), *Robes of Honour: Khil'at in Pre-Colonial and Colonial India*. New Delhi: Oxford University Press, 2003.

———. 'Epistemologies Concerning the Past in Maharashtra'. In D. N. Jha and Eugenia Vanina (eds), *Mind Over Matter: Essays on Mentalities in Medieval India*, 57–70. New Delhi: Tulika Books, 2009.

Green, Nile. 'Tribe, Diaspora and Sainthood in Afghan History'. *The Journal of Asian Studies* 67 (1), February 2008, 171–211.

———. 'The Uses of Books in a Late Mughal *Takiyya*: Persianate Knowledge between Person and Paper'. *Modern Asian Studies* 44 (2), 2010, 241–65.

Grewal, J. S. *The State and Society in Medieval India*, History of Science, Philosophy and Culture in Indian Civilization, Vol. VII, Part I. New Delhi: Oxford University Press, 2005.

———. (ed.). *Religious Movements and Institutions in Medieval India*, History of Science, Philosophy and Culture in Indian Civilization, Vol. VII, Part II. New Delhi: Oxford University Press, 2006.

Grover, B. R. 'Nature of Land Rights in Mughal India'. *The Indian Economic and Social History Review* 1 (1), 1964, 1–23.

Guha, Sumit. 'Transitions and Translations: Regional Power and Vernacular Identity in the Dakhan, 1500–1800'. *Comparative Studies of South Asia, Africa and the Middle East* 24 (2), 2004a, 23–31.

———. 'Speaking Historically: The Changing Voices of Historical Narration in Western India'. *American Historical Review* 109 (4), October 2004b, 1084–1103.

Gulbadan Begum. *Humayun-Nama*, Annette S. Beveridge (trans.). New Delhi: Idarah-i Adabiyat-i Delli, 1972.

Habib, Irfan. 'The Political Role of Shaikh Ahmad Sirhindi and Shah Waliullah'. *Proceedings of the Indian History Congress* 1960, Aligarh, 41–52.

———. *The Agrarian System of Mughal India, 1556–1707*. New Delhi: Oxford University Press, 1999 [1963], 2e, rev.

———. 'The Mansab System, 1595–1637'. *Proceedings of the Indian History Congress* 1967, Patiala, 221–42.

———. 'Technology and Barriers to Technological Changes in Mughal India'. *The Indian Historical Review* 5 (1 & 2), 1978–79, 152–74.

Habib, Irfan. 'Cartography in Mughal India'. *The Indian Archives* 28, 1980, 88–105.

———. *An Atlas of the Mughal Empire: Political and Economic Maps with Detailed Notes, Bibliography and Index*. Aligarh: Centre of Advanced Study in History, Aligarh Muslim University, and New Delhi: Oxford University Press, 1982, 2e, rev.

———. 'Capacity of Technological Change in Mughal India'. In Aniruddha Ray and S. K. Bagchi (eds), *Technology in Ancient and Medieval India*, 1–23. New Delhi: Sundeep Prakashan, 1986.

———. 'Merchant Communities in Pre-Colonial India'. In James D. Tracy (ed.), *The Rise of Merchant Empires: Long-Distance Trade in the Early Modern World, 1350–1750*, 371–99. Cambridge: Cambridge University Press, 1990.

——— (ed.). *Medieval India I: Researches in the History of India, 1200–1750*. New Delhi: Oxford University Press, 1992.

———. 'Reason and Science in Medieval India'. In D. N. Jha (ed.), *Society and Ideology in India: Essays in Honour of Professor R. S. Sharma*, 163–74. New Delhi: Munshiram Manoharlal Publishers, 1996.

———. 'A Political Theory for the Mughal Empire: A Study of the Ideas of Abul Fazl'. *Proceedings of the Indian History Congress* 1999, 329–40.

———. *Essays in Indian History: Towards a Marxist Perception*. New Delhi: Tulika, 2001a.

———. *The Economic History of Medieval India: A Survey*. New Delhi: Tulika, 2001b.

———. 'Potentialities of Capitalistic Development in the Economy of Mughal India'. In Irfan Habib, *Essays in Indian History: Towards a Marxist Perception*, 180–232. New Delhi: Tulika, 2001c.

———. *India—Studies in the History of an Idea*. New Delhi: Munshiram Manoharlal Publishers Pvt. Ltd, 2005.

——— (ed.). *Akbar and His India*. New Delhi: Oxford India Paperbacks, 2006a.

———. 'Persian Book Writing and Book Use in the Pre-Printing Age'. *Proceedings of the Indian History Congress* 2006b, 514–37.

——— (ed.). *Religion in Indian History*. New Delhi: Tulika, 2007.

———. 'Two Indian Theorists of the State: Barani and Abu'l Fazl'. In D. N. Jha and Eugenia Vanina (eds), *Mind Over Matter: Essays on Mentalities in Medieval India*, 15–39. New Delhi: Tulika, 2009.

———. *Technology in Medieval India, c. 650–1750*, A People's History of India. New Delhi: Tulika, 2012, 3e.

———. 'The Agrarian Causes of the Fall of the Mughal Empire'. In Meena Bhargava (ed.), *The Decline of the Mughal Empire*, Debates in Indian History and Society, 23–52. New Delhi: Oxford University Press, 2014.

Hardy, Peter. 'Force and Violence in Indo-Persian Writing on History and Government in Medieval South Asia'. In Milton Israel and N. K. Wagle (eds), *Islamic Society and Culture: Essays in Honour of Professor Aziz Ahmad*, 165–208. New Delhi: Manohar, 1983.

———. 'Abul Fazl's Portrait of the Perfect *Padshah*: A Political Philosophy for Mughal India—or A Personal Puff for a Pal?' In Christian W. Troll (ed.), *Islam in India, Studies and Commentaries:*

Religion and Religious Education, 114–37, Vol. II. New Delhi: Vikas Publishing House Pvt. Ltd, 1985.

———. 'Approaches to Pre-Modern Indo-Muslim Historical Writing: Some Reconsiderations in 1990–1991'. In Peter Robb (ed.), *Society and Ideology: Essays in South Asian History Presented to Professor K. A. Ballhatchet*. New Delhi: Oxford University Press, 1993.

———. *Historians of Medieval India: Studies in Indo-Muslim Historical Writing*. New Delhi: Munshiram Manoharlal, 1997.

Hasan, Farhat. *State and Locality in Mughal India: Power Relations in Western India, c. 1572–1730*. Cambridge: Cambridge University Press, 2004.

———. 'Forms of Civility and Publicness in Pre-British India'. In Rajeev Bhargava and Helmut Reifeld (eds), *Civil Society, Public Sphere and Citizenship: Dialogues and Perceptions*, 84–105. New Delhi: Sage Publications, 2005.

Hasan, Mohibul (ed.). *Historians of Medieval India*. New Delhi: Aakar Books, 2018 [1968].

Hasan, S. Nurul. *Religion, State, and Society in Medieval India* (edited, and with an Introduction by Satish Chandra). New Delhi: Oxford University Press, 2005.

Hawley, John Stratton. 'Author and Authority in the Bhakti Poetry of North India'. *The Journal of Asian Studies* 47 (2), May 1988, 269–90.

———. *Three Bhakti Voices: Mirabai, Surdas and Kabir in their Times and Ours*. New Delhi: Oxford University Press, 2005.

Hawley, John Stratton, and Mark Juergensmeyer. *Songs of the Saints of India*. New York: Oxford University Press, 1988.

Heesterman, J. C. *The Inner Conflict of Tradition: Essays in Indian Ritual, Kingship and Society*. Chicago: University of Chicago Press, 1985.

Hegel, G. W. Friedrich. *The Philosophy of History*, J. Sibree (trans.). New York: Dover Publications, 1956.

Hobsbawm, E. J. 'The Social Function of the Past: Some Questions'. *Past and Present* 52, 1972, 3–17.

Hodgson, Marshall. *The Venture of Islam: Conscience and History in a World Civilization*, 3 volumes. Chicago: University of Chicago Press, 1974.

Inden, Ronald. *Imagining India*. Oxford: Blackwell, 1990.

———. 'Orientalist Constructions of India'. In Ronald Inden, *Text and Practice: Essays on South Asian History*, 13–60, SOAS Studies on South Asia. New Delhi: Oxford University Press, 2006.

Iraqi, Shahabuddin (ed.). *Medieval India 2: Essays in Medieval Indian History and Culture*. New Delhi: Manohar, 2008.

Irvine, William. *The Army of the Indian Moghuls: Its Organization and Administration*. New Delhi: Low Price Publications, 1998 [1903].

Jha, D. N., and Eugenia Vanina (eds). *Mind over Matter: Essays on Mentalities in Medieval India*. New Delhi: Tulika, 2009.

Jones, William. 'On the Chronology of the Hindus'. *Asiatic Researches* 2, 1779, 111–47.

Juneja, Monica (ed.). *Architecture in Medieval India: Forms, Contexts, Histories*. New Delhi: Permanent Black, 2001.

Juneja, Monica (ed.). 'On the Margins of Utopia: One more Look at Mughal Painting'. In Meena Bhargava (ed.), *Exploring Medieval India, Sixteenth to Eighteenth Centuries: Culture, Gender, Regional Patterns*, 113–40, Vol. II. New Delhi: Orient BlackSwan, 2010.

Khalidi, Rashid. 'Is There a Future for Middle East Studies?' *Middle East Studies Association Bulletin* 29 (1), 1995, 1–6.

Khalidi, Tarif. *Arabic Historical Thought in the Classical Period.* Cambridge: Cambridge University Press, 1994.

Khan, Ahsan Raza. *Chieftains of the Mughal Empire during the Reign of Akbar*. Shimla: Indian Institute of Advanced Study, 1977.

———. 'Abul Fazl's Account of Akbar's Expansionism: Ambit of Reason and Tolerance?' In Meena Bhargava (ed.), *Exploring Medieval India, Sixteenth to Eighteenth Centuries: Culture, Gender, Regional Patterns*, 486–508, Vol. II. New Delhi: Orient BlackSwan, 2010.

Khan, Hafiz A. Ghaffar. 'Shah Wali Allah: On the Nature, Origin, Definition and Classification of Knowledge'. *Journal of Islamic Studies* 3 (2), 1992, 203–13.

Khan, Iqtidar Alam. *Mirza Kamran: A Biographical Study*. Bombay: Asia Publishing House, 1964.

———. 'The Nobility under Akbar and the Development of his Religious Policy, 1560–80'. *The Journal of the Royal Asiatic Society of Great Britain and Ireland* 1 & 2, April 1968, 29–36.

———. 'The Mughal Court Politics during Bairam Khan's Regency'. *Medieval India: A Miscellany*, 21–39, Vol. I. Bombay: Asia Publishing House, 1969.

———. 'The Turko-Mongol Theory of Kingship'. *Medieval India: A Miscellany*, 8–18, Vol. II. Bombay: Asia Publishing House, 1972.

———. *The Political Biography of a Mughal Noble: Munim Khan Khan-i Khanan, 1497–1575*. New Delhi: Orient Longman, 1973.

———. 'A Note on the Conception of Akbar's Religious Policy'. In Debiprasad Chattopadhaya (ed.), *History and Society: Essays in Honour of Professor Niharranjan Ray*. Calcutta: K. P. Bagchi, 1978.

——— (ed.). *Akbar and His Age*. New Delhi: Oxford University Press, 1999a.

———. 'Nature of Gunpowder Artillery in India during the Sixteenth Century—A Reappraisal of the Impact of European Gunnery'. *Journal of the Royal Asiatic Society*, Series 3 9 (1), 1999b, 27–34.

———. *Gunpowder and Firearms: Warfare in Medieval India*, Aligarh Historians Society Series. New York: Oxford University Press, 2004.

———. 'Gunpowder and Empire: Indian Case'. *Social Scientist* 33 (3–4), March–April 2005, 54–65.

———. *Historical Dictionary of Medieval India*. Lanham, Maryland: The Scarecrow Press, Inc., 2008.

———. 'Tracing Sources of Principles of Mughal Governance: A Critique of Recent Historiography'. *Social Scientist* 37 (5 & 6), May–June 2009, 45–54.

———. *India's Polity in the Age of Akbar*. Ranikhet: Permanent Black, 2016.

Khan, I. G. 'Technology and the Question of Elite Intervention in Eighteenth Century North India'. In Richard B. Barnett (ed.), *Rethinking Early Modern India*, 257–88. New Delhi: Manohar, 2002.

Khan, Saqi Must'ad. *Maasir-i Alamgiri*. Jadunath Sarkar (trans.), *Maasir-i Alamgiri: A History of the Emperor Aurangzeb Alamgir*. Lahore: Suhail Academy, 1981.

Kinra, Rajeev. 'Infantalizing Baba Dara: The Cultural Memory of Dara Shekuh and the Mughal Public Sphere'. *Journal of Persianate Studies* 2, 2009, 165–93.

———. 'Master and Munshi: A Brahman Secretary's Guide to Mughal Governance'. *The Indian Economic and Social History Review* 47 (4), 2010, 527–61.

———. 'Handling Diversity with Absolute Civility: The Global Historical Legacy of Mughal *Sulh-i Kull*'. *The Medieval History Journal* 16 (2), 2013, 251–95.

———. *Writing Self, Writing Empire: Chandar Bhan Brahman and the Cultural World of the Indo-Persian State Secretary*, South Asia: The Disciplines. New Delhi: Primus Books, 2015.

Koch, Ebba. 'Mughal Palace Gardens from Babur to Shah Jahan (1526–1648)'. *Muqarnas* 14, 1997, 143–65.

———. *Mughal Art and Imperial Ideology: Collected Essays*. New Delhi: Oxford University Press, 2001.

———. 'The Taj Mahal: Architecture, Symbolism and Urban Significance'. *Muqarnas* 22, 2005, 138–49.

———. *The Complete Taj Mahal: And the Riverfront Gardens of Agra*. New York: Thames & Hudson, 2006.

———. 'Jahangir as Francis Bacon's Ideal of the King as an Observer and Investigator of Nature'. *Journal of the Royal Asiatic Society*, Series 3 19 (3). 2009, 293–338.

———. 'The Mughal Emperor as Solomon, Majnun and Orpheus, or the Album as a Think Tank for Allegory'. *Muqarnas* 27, 2010, 277–311.

———. 'The Symbolic Possession of the World: European Cartography in Mughal Allegory and History Painting'. *Journal of the Economic and Social History of the Orient* 55, 2012, 547–80.

———. *Mughal Architecture: An Outline of its History and Development (1526–1858)*. New Delhi: Primus Books, 2014, rev. edn.

Kolff, Dirk H. A. *Naukar, Rajput and Sepoy: The Ethnohistory of the Military Labour Market in Hindustan, 1450–1850*. Cambridge: Cambridge University Press, 1990.

Krynicki, Annie Krieger. *Captive Princess: Zebunissa, Daughter of Emperor Aurangzeb*. Oxford: Oxford University Press, 2005.

Kulke, Hermann. 'The Early and the Imperial Kingdom: A Processural Model of Integrative State Formation in Early Medieval India'. In Hermann Kulke (ed.), *The State in India, 1000–1700*, 233–62, Themes in Indian History. New Delhi: Oxford University Press, 1995.

Kumar, Mayank. *Monsoon Ecologies: Irrigation, Agriculture and Settlement Patterns in Rajasthan during the Pre-Colonial Period*. New Delhi: Manohar, 2013.

Kumar, Sunil. *Demolishing Myths or Mosques and Temples? Readings of History and Temple Desecration in Medieval India*. New Delhi: Three Essays Collective, 2008.

Lal, K. S. *The Mughal Harem*. New Delhi: Aditya Prakashan, 1988.

Lal, Ruby. 'Settled, Sacred and All-Powerful: Making of New Genealogies and Traditions of Empire under Akbar'. *Economic and Political Weekly* 36 (11), 17–23 March 2001, 941–58.

———. 'Rethinking Mughal India: Challenge of a Princess' Memoir'. *Economic and Political Weekly* 38 (1), 4–10 January, 2003, 53–65.

———. 'Historicizing the Harem: The Challenge of a Princess's Memoir'. *Feminist Studies* 30 (3), 2004, 590–616.

———. *Domesticity and Power in the Early Mughal World*. Cambridge: Cambridge University Press, 2005.

———. 'The 'Domestic World' of Peripatetic Kings: Babur and Humayun, c. 1494–1556'. In Meena Bhargava (ed.), *Exploring Medieval India, Sixteenth to Eighteenth Centuries: Culture, Gender, Regional Patterns*, 221–60, Vol. II. New Delhi: Orient BlackSwan, 2010.

———. *Empress, The Astonishing Reign of Nur Jahan*. Penguin Viking, 2018.

Lal, Vinay. 'Walking with the Subalterns, Riding with the Academy: The Curious Ascendancy of Indian History'. *Studies in History* 17 (1), 2001, 101–33.

Lefevre, Corinne. 'Recovering a Missing Voice from Mughal India: The Imperial Discourse of Jahangir (*r.* 1605–1627) in his Memoirs'. *Journal of the Economic and Social History of the Orient* 50 (4), 2007, 452–89.

———. 'The *Majalis-i Jahangiri* (1608–11): Dialogue and Asiatic Otherness at the Mughal Court'. *Journal of the Economic and Social History of the Orient* 55, 2012, 255–86.

Leonard, Karen Isaksen. 'The Hyderabad Political System and its Participants'. *Journal of Asian Studies* 30 (2), May 1971, 569–82.

———. 'Family Firms in Hyderabad: Gujarati, Goswami, and Marwari Patterns of Adoption, Marriage, and Inheritance'. *Comparative Studies in Society and History* 53 (4), 2011, 827–54.

———. 'The "Great Firm" Theory of the Decline of the Mughal Empire'. In Meena Bhargava (ed.), *The Decline of the Mughal Empire*, 107–27, Debates in Indian History and Society. New Delhi: Oxford University Press, 2014.

Lorenzen, David (ed.). *Bhakti Religion in North India: Community, Identity and Political Action*. New Delhi: Manohar, 1996.

———. *Religious Movements in South Asia, 600–1800*, Debates in Indian History and Society. New Delhi: Oxford University Press, 2006.

Lowry, Glenn D. 'Humayun's Tomb: Form, Function and Meaning in Early Mughal Architecture'. *Muqarnas* 4, 1987, 133–48.

Ludden, David. 'World Economy and Village India, 1600–1900: Exploring the Agrarian History of Capitalism'. In Sugata Bose (ed.), *South Asia and World Capitalism*, 159–77. New Delhi: Oxford University Press, 1990.

———. *Peasant History in South India*. New Delhi: Oxford University Press, 1993, 2e.

———. *An Agrarian History of South Asia*, The New Cambridge History of India, Vol. 4, No. 4. Cambridge: Cambridge University Press, 1999.

———. *India and South Asia: A Short History*. Oxford: Oneworld, 2002.

Majeed, Javed. *Ungoverned Imaginings: James Mill's The History of British India and Orientalism.* Oxford: Clarendon Press, 1992.

Malekandathil, Pius. *The Mughals, The Portuguese and the Indian Ocean: Changing Imageries of Maritime India*. New Delhi: Primus Books, 2013.

Manucci, Niccolao. *Storia do Mogor.* William Irvine (trans.), *Mogul India or Storia do Mogor*, 4 volumes. New Delhi: Low Price Publications, 1990 [1907–08].

Marshall, P. J. 'Economic and Political Expansion: The Case of Oudh, 1765–1804'. *Modern Asian Studies* 11 (4), 1975, 465–82.

———. *East Indian Fortunes: The British in Bengal in the Eighteenth Century*. Oxford: Clarendon Press, 1976.

———. *Bengal: The British Bridgehead, Eastern India, 1740–1828*. Cambridge: Cambridge University Press, 1987.

——— (ed.). *The Eighteenth Century in Indian History, Evolution or Revolution*, Themes in Indian History. New Delhi: Oxford University Press, 2003.

McDougall, Elizabeth B., and Richard Ettinghausen (eds). *The Islamic Garden*. Washington: Dumbarton Oaks, 1976.

McNeill, William H. *The Pursuit of Power: Technology, Armed Force and Society since* AD *1000.* Chicago: University of Chicago Press, 1982.

Metcalf, Barbara Daly (ed.). *Moral Conduct and Authority: The Place of Adab in South Asian Islam.* Berkeley: University of California Press, 1984.

———. 'Too Little and Too Much: Reflections on Muslims in the History of India'. Presidential Address, *The Journal of Asian Studies* 54 (4), November 1995, 951–67.

———. 'A Historical Overview of Islam in South Asia'. In Barbara D. Metcalf (ed.), *Islam in South Asia in Practice*, 1–39. Princeton: Princeton University Press, 2009.

Mill, James. *The History of British India*, H. H. Wilson (ed.), 10 vols. London: James Madden, 1858.

———. *The History of British India*, (abridged). Chicago: University of Chicago Press, 1975.

Mill, John S., and Henry Maine. 'Memorandum of the improvements in the administration of India during the last thirty years, 1858'. In John M. Robinson, Martin Moir, and Zawahir Moir (eds), *Writings on India by John Stuart Mill.* Toronto: University of Toronto Press, 1990.

Miller, Barbara Stoler (ed.). *The Powers of Art: Patronage in Indian Culture*. New Delhi: Oxford University Press, 1992.

Mitchell, George (ed.). *Architecture of the Islamic World: Its History and Social Meaning.* New York: Thames & Hudson, 1995.

Moin, A. Azfar. *The Millennial Sovereign: Sacred Kingship and Sainthood.* New Delhi: Primus Books, 2017.

Momin, Mohiuddin. *The Chancellery and Persian Epistolography under the Mughals (Babur to Shahjahan)*. Calcutta: Iran Society, 1971.

Moosvi, Shireen. *The Economy of the Mughal Empire c. 1595: A Statistical Study*. New Delhi: Oxford University Press, 1987.

Moosvi, Shireen. 'Man and Nature in Mughal Era'. Symposia Paper 5, Thematic Symposium: 'Man and Environment in Indian History', 5–33. Mysore: Indian History Congress, 1993.

———. 'The Road to Sulh-i Kul, Akbar's Alienation from Theological Islam'. In Irfan Habib (ed.), *Religion in Indian History*, 167–76. New Delhi: Tulika Books, 2007.

———. *People, Taxation and Trade in Mughal India*. New Delhi: Oxford India Paperbacks, 2010.

Moreland, W. H. *India at the Death of Akbar: An Economic Study*. London: Macmillan, 1993 [1920].

———. *From Akbar to Aurangzeb: A Study in Indian Economic History*. London: Macmillan, 1992 [1923].

———. 'Rank (*mansab*) in the Mogul State Service'. *Journal of the Royal Asiatic Society*, 1936.

———. *The Agrarian System of Moslem India*. New Delhi: Oriental Books Reprint Corporation, 1995 [1929].

Moreland, W. H., and P. Geyl (trans.). *Jahangir's India: The Remonstrantie of Francisco Pelsaert*. New Delhi: Idarah-i Adabiyat-i Delli, 1972.

Morris, Morris D. 'Towards a Reinterpretation of Nineteenth Century Indian Economic History'. *The Journal of Economic History* 23 (4), 1963, 606–18.

———. 'Values as an Obstacle to Economic Growth in South Asia: An Historical Survey'. *The Journal of Economic History* 27 (4), The Tasks of Economic History, December 1967, 588–607.

Mukherjee, Tilottama. 'The Co-ordinating State and the Economy: The *Nizamat* in Eighteenth-Century Bengal'. *Modern Asian Studies* 43 (2), 2009, 389–436.

Mukherjee, Tarapada, and Irfan Habib. 'Akbar and the Temples, Mathura and its Environs'. *Proceedings of the Indian History Congress*, 234–50. Panajim, Goa, 1988.

———. 'The Mughal Administration and the Temples of Vrindavan during the Reigns of Jahangir and Shahjahan'. *Proceedings of the Indian History Congress*, 287–99. Dharwad, 1989.

Mukhia, Harbans. *Historians and Historiography during the Reign of Akbar*. New Delhi: Aakar Books, 2017 [1976].

———. 'Agricultural Technology in Medieval India'. In Aniruddha Ray and S. K. Bagchi (eds), *Technology in Ancient and Medieval India*, 107–27. New Delhi: Sundeep Prakashan, 1986.

———. *Perspectives on Medieval History*. New Delhi: Vikas Publishing House, 1993.

———. '"Medieval India": An Alien Conceptual Hegemony?' *The Medieval History Journal* 1 (1), January–June 1998, 91–105.

———. *The Mughals of India*. London: Blackwell Publishing, 2005.

———. *Exploring India's Medieval Centuries: Essays in History, Society, Culture and Technology*. New Delhi: Aakar Books, 2010.

———. *Subjective Modernities*. NMML Occasional Paper, History and Society, New Series 13. New Delhi: Nehru Memorial Museum and Library, 2013.

Mukhoty, Ira. *Daughters of the Sun: Empresses, Queens and Begums of the Mughal Empire*. New Delhi: Aleph, 2018.

Nair, Janaki. 'Tipu Sultan, History Painting and the Battle for "Perspective"'. *Studies in History* 22 (1), 2006, 97–143.

Nath, Pratyay. 'Rethinking Early Mughal Warfare: Babur's Pitched Battles, 1499–1529'. In Raziuddin Aquil and Kaushik Roy (eds), *Warfare, Religion and Society in Indian History*, 109–46. New Delhi: Manohar 2012.

———. *Climate of Conquest: War, Environment and Empire in Mughal North India*. New Delhi: Oxford University Press, 2019.

Nath, Ram. *Private Life of the Mughals of India (1526–1803 AD)*. New Delhi: Rupa & Co., 2005.

Nizami, Khaliq Ahmad. '*Naqshbandi* Influence on Mughal Rulers and Politics'. *Islamic Culture* 39, 1965, 41–52.

———. *Politics and Society during the Early Medieval Period*, Vol. II. New Delhi: People's Publishing House, 1981.

———. *On History and Historians of India*. New Delhi: Munshiram Manoharlal, 1983.

———. *Akbar and Religion*. New Delhi: Idarah-i Adabiyat-i Delli, 1989.

———. *On Sources and Source Material*. Historical Studies: Indian and Islamic, Vol. I. New Delhi: Idarah-i Adabiyat-i Delli, 1995.

O'Hanlon, Rosalind. 'Manliness and Imperial Service in Mughal North India'. *Journal of the Economic and Social History of the Orient* 42 (1), 1999, 47–93.

———. 'Kingdom, Household and Body History, Gender and Imperial Service Under Akbar'. *Modern Asian Studies* 41 (5), 2007a, 889–923.

———. 'Cultural Pluralism, Empire and the State in Early Modern South Asia—A Review Essay'. *The Indian Economic and Social History Review* 44 (3), 2007b, 363–81.

———. 'Letters Home: Banaras *Pandits* and the Maratha Regions in Early Modern India'. *Modern Asian Studies* 44 (2), 2010a, 201–40.

———. 'The Social Worth of Scribes: Brahmins, *Kayasthas* and the Social Order in Early Modern India'. *The Indian Economic and Social History Review* 47 (4), 2010b, 563–95.

———. 'Speaking from Siva's temple: Banaras scholar households and the Brahman "ecumene" of Mughal India'. In Rosalind O' Hanlon and David Washbrook (eds), *Religious Cultures in Early Modern India: New Perspectives*, 174–211, South Asian History and Culture Series 7. London, New York, New Delhi: Routledge, 2011.

O'Hanlon, Rosalind, and Christopher Minkowski. 'What makes people who they are? *Pandit* networks and the problem of livelihoods in early modern Western India'. *The Indian Economic and Social History Review* 45 (3), 2008, 381–416.

O'Hanlon, Rosalind, and David Washbrook. 'Introduction: Religious Cultures in an Imperial Landscape'. In Rosalind O' Hanlon and David Washbrook (eds), *Religious Cultures in Early Modern India: New Perspectives*, South Asian History and Culture Series 7. London, New York, New Delhi: Routledge, 2011a.

——— (eds). *Religious Cultures in Early Modern India: New Perspectives*, South Asian History and Culture Series 7. London, New York, New Delhi: Routledge, 2011b.

Orsini, Francesca (ed.). *Before the Divide: Hindi and Urdu Literary Culture*. New Delhi: Orient BlackSwan, 2011.

Orsini, Francesca (ed.). 'How to do multilingual literary history? Lessons from fifteenth and sixteenth century north India'. *The Indian Economic and Social History Review* 49 (2), 2012, 225–46.

Orsini, Francesca, and Samira Sheikh (eds). *After Timur Left: Culture and Circulation in Fifteenth Century North India*. New Delhi: Oxford University Press, 2014.

Panikkar, K. N., Terence J. Byres, and Utsa Patnaik (eds). *The Making of History: Essays Presented to Irfan Habib*. New Delhi: Tulika, 2011, 3e.

Pavlov, V. I. *The Indian Capitalist Class: A Historical Study*. New Delhi: Aakar Books, 2016 [1964].

Pearson, Michael N. 'Political Participation in Mughal India'. *The Indian Economic and Social History Review* 9 (2), June 1972, 113–31.

———. *The Portuguese in India*, The New Cambridge History of India. Cambridge: Cambridge University Press, 1987.

———. *The Indian Ocean*. London and New York: Routledge, 2003.

———. 'Brokers in Western Indian Port Cities: Their Role in Servicing Foreign Merchants'. In Meena Bhargava (ed.), *Exploring Medieval India, Sixteenth to Eighteenth Centuries: Politics, Economy, Religion*, 307–26, Vol. I. New Delhi: Orient BlackSwan, 2010.

———. 'Shivaji and the Decline of the Mughal Empire'. In Meena Bhargava (ed.), *The Decline of the Mughal Empire*, Debates in Indian History and Society, 84–106. New Delhi: Oxford University Press, 2014.

——— (ed.). *Legitimacy and Symbols: The South Asian Writings of F.W. Buckler*, Michigan Papers on South and Southeast Asian Studies. The University of Michigan, No. 26, 1985.

Petievich, Carla. 'Gender Politics and the Urdu Ghazal: Exploratory Observations on *Rekhta* versus *Rekhti*'. In Meena Bhargava (ed.), *Exploring Medieval India, Sixteenth to Eighteenth Centuries: Culture, Gender, Regional Patterns*, 186–217, Vol. II. New Delhi: Orient BlackSwan. 2010.

Philips, C. H. *Historians of India, Pakistan and Ceylon*. New York, Toronto, London: Oxford University Press, 1961.

Phukan, Shantanu. '"Through Throats Where Many Rivers Meet": The Ecology of Hindi in the World of Persian'. *The Indian Economic and Social History Review* 38 (1), 2001, 33–58.

Pinch, William. 'Same Difference in India and Europe'. *History and Theory* 38 (3), October 1999, 389–407.

———. *Warrior, Ascetics and Indian Empires*. Cambridge: Cambridge University Press, 2006.

Pollock, Sheldon. 'Ramayana and Political Imagination in India'. *The Journal of Asian Studies* 52 (2), May 1993, 261–97.

———. 'The Cosmopolitan Vernacular'. *The Journal of Asian Studies* 57 (1), February 1998, 6–37.

——— (ed.). *Literary Cultures in History: Reconstructions from South Asia*. Berkeley: University of California Press, 2003.

———. *The Language of the Gods in the World of Men: Sanskrit, Culture and Power in Pre-Modern India*. Berkeley: University of California Press, 2006.

Pollock, Sheldon. 'Pre-textures of Time'. *History and Theory* 46 (3), October 2007a, 366–83.

———. 'Literary Culture and Manuscript Culture in Pre-Colonial India'. In Simon Eliot, Andrew Nash, and Jan Willison (eds), *Literary Cultures and the Material Book*, 77–94. London: The British Library, 2007b.

———. 'Is There an Indian Intellectual History? Introduction to "Theory and Method in Indian Intellectual History"'. *Journal of Indian Philosophy* 36, 2008, 533–42.

——— (ed.). *Forms of Knowledge in Early Modern Asia: Explorations in the Intellectual History of India and Tibet, 1500–1800*. New Delhi: Manohar, 2011.

Powell, Baden. *The Land Systems of British India*. Oxford: Clarendon Press, 1892.

Prakash, Om. *European Commercial Enterprise in Pre-Colonial India*, The New Cambridge History of India. Cambridge: Cambridge University Press, 2000.

Prakash, Om, and Denys Lombard (eds). *Commerce and Culture in the Bay of Bengal, 1500–1800*. New Delhi: Manohar and Indian Council of Historical Research, 1999.

———. 'Cooperation and Conflict among European Traders in the Indian Ocean in the Late Eighteenth Century'. In Meena Bhargava (ed.), *Exploring Medieval India, Sixteenth to Eighteenth Centuries: Politics, Economy, Religion*, 327–49, Vol. I. New Delhi: Orient BlackSwan, 2010.

Qaisar, Ahsan Jan. 'The Role of Brokers in Medieval India'. *The Indian Historical Review* I (2), September 1974, 220–46.

Qaisar, Ahsan Jan, and Som Prakash Verma (eds). *Art and Culture: Felicitation Volume in Honour of Professor S. Nurul Hasan*. Jaipur: Publication Scheme, 1993.

———. (eds). *Art and Culture, Painting and Perspective*. New Delhi: Abhinav Publications, 2002.

Qureshi, Ishtiyaq Husain. *The Muslim Community of the Indo-Pakistan Subcontinent (610–1947)*, The Hague: Mouton & Co., 1962.

———. *Ulema in Politics: A Study Relating to the Political Activities of the Ulema in the South-Asian Subcontinent from 1556–1947*. New Delhi: Renaissance Publishing House, 1985, 2e.

Rahman, A. (ed.). *India's Interaction with China, Central and West Asia*, History of Science, Philosophy and Culture in Indian Civilization, Vol. III, Part 2. New Delhi: Oxford University Press, 2002.

Ramaswamy, Sumathi. 'Sanskrit for the Nation'. *Modern Asian Studies* 33 (2), May 1999, 339–81.

———. 'Conceit of the Globe in Mughal Visual Practice'. *Comparative Studies in Society and History* 49 (4), 2007, 751–82.

Rao, Velcheru Narayana, and Sanjay Subrahmanyam. 'Notes on Political Thought in Medieval and Early Modern South India'. In Richard M. Eaton, Munis D. Faruqui, David Gilmartin, and Sunil Kumar (eds), *Expanding Frontiers in South Asian and World History: Essays in Honour of John F. Richards*, 164–99. New York: Cambridge University Press, 2013.

Rao, Velcheru Narayana, David Shulman, and Sanjay Subrahmanyam. *Symbols of Substance: Court and State in Nayaka Period, Tamilnadu*. New Delhi: Oxford University Press, 1992.

———. *Textures of Time: Writing History in South India, 1600–1800*. Ranikhet: Permanent Black, 2001.

———. 'A Pragmatic Response'. *History and Theory* 46 (3), October 2007, 409–27.

Raychaudhuri, Tapan. 'The Mid-Eighteenth Century'. In Dharma Kumar and Meghnad Desai (eds), *The Cambridge Economic History of India*, Vol. II. New Delhi: Orient Longman, 1984.

Raychaudhuri, Tapan, and Irfan Habib (eds). *The Cambridge Economic History of India*, Vol. I. New Delhi: Orient Longman, 1984.

Ray, Nihar Ranjan. 'The Medieval Factor in Indian History', General President's Address. *Proceedings of the Indian History Congress*, 1–29, Patiala, 1967.

Richards, John F. 'Mughal State Finance and the Pre-modern World Economy'. *Comparative Studies in Society and History* 23 (2), April 1981, 285–308.

———. 'Norms of Comportment among Imperial Mughal Officers'. In Barbara Daly Metcalf (ed.), *Moral Conduct and Authority: The Place of Adab in South Asian Islam*, 255–89. Berkeley: University of California Press, 1984.

——— (ed.). *The Imperial Monetary System of Mughal India*. New Delhi: Oxford University Press, 1987.

———. 'The Seventeenth Century Crisis in South Asia'. *Modern Asian Studies* 24 (4), 1990, 625–38.

———. *The Mughal Empire*, The New Cambridge History of India, I.5. Cambridge: Cambridge University Press, 2007 [1993].

———. 'Early Modern India and World History'. *Journal of World History* 8 (2), 1997, 197–209.

———. 'The Formulation of Imperial Authority under Akbar and Jahangir'. In Meena Bhargava (ed.), *Exploring Medieval India*, 183–224, Vol. I. New Delhi: Orient BlackSwan, 2010.

———. 'The Imperial Crisis in the Deccan'. In Meena Bhargava (ed.), *The Decline of the Mughal Empire*, Debates in Indian History and Society, 53–83. New Delhi: Oxford University Press, 2014.

——— (ed.). *Kingship and Authority in South Asia*. New Delhi: Oxford University Press, 1998.

Rizvi, S. A. A. *Muslim Revivalist Movements in Northern India in the Sixteenth and Seventeenth Centuries*. New Delhi: Munshiram Manoharlal, 1965.

———. *Religious and Intellectual History of the Muslims in Akbar's Reign, with Special Reference to Abu'l Fazl, 1556–1605*. New Delhi: Munshiram Manoharlal, 1975.

———. *A History of Sufism in India*, 2 vols. New Delhi: Munshiram Manoharlal, 1983.

Robb, Peter. (ed.). *Society and Ideology: Essays in South Asian History Presented to Professor K. A. Ballhatchet*. New Delhi: Oxford University Press, 1993.

———. *A History of India*. New York: Palgrave, 2002.

Robinson, Francis. *The Mughal Emperors and the Islamic Dynasties of India, Iran and Central Asia*. London: Thames and Hudson Ltd, 2007.

Rosenthal, Franz. *A History of Muslim Historiography*. Leiden: E. J. Brill, 1952.

Rudolph, Lloyd I., and Susanne Hoeber Rudolph. 'Writing and Reading Tod's *Rajasthan*: Interpreting the Text and its Historiography'. In Jos Gommans and Om Prakash (eds), *Circumambulations in South Asian Histories: Essays in Honour of Dirk H.A. Kolff*, 251–82. Leiden and Boston: Brill, 2003.

Ruggles, D. Fairchild. 'Humayun's Tomb and Garden: Typologies and Visual Order'. In Attilio Petruccioli (ed.), *Gardens in the Time of the Great Mughal Empires: Theory and Vision*, 173–86. Leiden: Brill, 1997.

Russell, Ralph. *The Pursuit of Urdu Literature: A Select History*. New Delhi: Oxford University Press, 1992.

——— (ed.). *Ghalib, the Poet and his Age*. London: George Allen & Unwin Ltd, 1972.

Russell, Ralph, and Khurshidul Islam. *Three Mughal Poets: Mir, Sauda, Mir Hasan*. Cambridge, MA: Harvard University Press, 1968.

——— (eds and trans.). *Ghalib, 1797–1869: Life and Letters*, Vol. I. London: George Allen & Unwin, 1969.

Sangari, Kumkum. 'Mirabai and the Spiritual Economy of Bhakti'. *Economic and Political Weekly* 25 (28), 14 July 1990, 1537–52.

———. 'Tracing Akbar: Hagiographies, Popular Narrative, Traditions and the Subject of Conversion'. In Neera Chandhoke (ed.), *Mapping Histories: Essays Presented to Ravinder Kumar*, 61–103. New Delhi: Tulika, 2000.

———. 'Mirabai: The Female Voice and Oral Compositions'. In J. S. Grewal (ed.), *Religious Movements and Institutions in Medieval India*, 228–62, History of Science, Philosophy and Culture in Indian Civilization, Vol. VII, Part II. New Delhi: Oxford University Press, 2006.

Saran, Parmatama. *The Provincial Government of the Mughals, 1526–1658*. Bombay: Asia Publishing House, 1974 [1941].

Sarkar, J. N. *A History of the Emperor Aurangzib (r. 1658–1707 A.D.* Translated edition of Saqi Mustaid Khan, *Ma'asir-i Alamgiri*. Calcutta: Royal Society of Bengal, 1947.

———. *Military History of India*. Calcutta: M. C. Sarkar and Sons, 1960.

———. *History of Aurangzib, Northern India, 1658–1681*, Vol. III. New Delhi: Orient Longman Ltd., 1972 [1928].

———. *History of Aurangzeb*, Vols. I and II. New Delhi: Orient Longman Ltd., 1975 [1912].

———. *History of Aurangzeb*, Vol. IV. New Delhi: Orient Longman Ltd, 1972.

———. *Fall of the Mughal Empire*, 4 vols. Bombay: Orient Longman, 1988.

Sastri, Nilakanta. *A History of South India: From Pre-Historic Times to the Fall of Vijaynagar*. New Delhi: Oxford University Press, 1955.

Schacht, Joseph. *An Introduction to Islamic Law*. Oxford: Oxford University Press, 1964.

Schimmel, Annemarie. *A History of Classical Urdu Literature from the Beginning to Iqbal*. Weisbaden: Otto Harrassowitz, 1975a.

———. *Mystical Dimensions of Islam*. Carolina: University of North Carolina Press, 1975b.

———. 'A Dervish in the Guise of a Prince: Khan-i-Khanan Abdur Rahim as a Patron'. In Barbara Stoler Miller (ed.), *The Powers of Art: Patronage in Indian Culture*, 202–23. New Delhi: Oxford University Press, 1992.

———. *The Empire of the Great Mughals: History, Art and Culture*. New Delhi: Oxford University Press, 2005.

Schwartzberg, Joseph E. (ed.). *A Historical Atlas of South Asia*, Association for Asian Studies Reference Studies, No. 2. New York and Oxford: Oxford University Press, 1992.

Sen, Geeti. *Paintings from the Akbar Nama*. Calcutta and Varanasi: Lustre Press under arrangement with Rupa & Co., 1984.

Seyller, John. 'The Inspection and Valuation of Manuscripts in the Imperial Mughal Library'. *Artibus Asiae* 8 (2), 1997, 197–209.

Sharma, G. D. *Rajput Polity: A Study of Politics and Administration of the State of Marwar, 1638–1749*. New Delhi: Manohar, 1977.

Sharma, Krishna. *Bhakti and the Bhakti Movement: A New Perspective*. New Delhi: Munshiram Manoharlal Publishers, 1987.

———. 'Towards a New Perspective'. In David Lorenzen (ed.), *Religious Movements in South Asia, 600–1800*, Debates in Indian History and Society. New Delhi: Oxford University Press, 2006.

Sharma, R. S. 'Problem of Transition from Ancient to Medieval in Indian History'. *The Indian Historical Review* I (1), 1974, 1–9.

Sharma, S. R. *The Religious Policy of the Mughal Emperors*. Jaipur: Book Enclave, 2001 [1940].

Sharma, Yogesh, and Pius Malekandathil (eds). *Cities in Medieval India*. New Delhi: Primus Books, 2014.

Shulman, David. *The King and the Clown in South Indian Myth and Poetry*. Princeton: Princeton University Press, 1985.

Siddiqi, Asiya. *Agrarian Change in a Northern Indian State: Uttar Pradesh, 1819–1833*. Oxford: Clarendon Press, 1973.

Siddiqui, Iqtidar Husain. '*Nuqtavi* Thinkers at the Mughal Court: A Study of their Impact on Akbar's Religious and Political Ideas'. *Islamic Culture* 72, 1998, 65–84.

———. *Medieval India: Essays in Intellectual Thought and Culture*, Vol. I. New Delhi: Manohar, 2003.

Siddiqui, Noman Ahmed. *Land Revenue Administration under the Mughals, 1700–1750*. Aligarh: Centre of Advanced Study, Department of History, 1970.

Silver, Brian. 'The *Adab* of Musicians'. In Barbara D. Metcalf (ed.), *Moral Conduct and Authority: The Place of Adab in South Asian Islam*, 315–29. Berkeley: University of California Press, 1984.

Singh, Chetan. 'Centre and Periphery in the Mughal State: The Case of the Seventeenth Century Panjab'. *Modern Asian Studies* 22 (2), 1988, 299–318.

———. *Region and Empire: Punjab in the Seventeenth Century*. New Delhi: Oxford University Press, 1991.

———. 'Polity, Economy and Society under the Mughals'. In Indu Banga (ed.), *Five Punjabi Centuries: Polity, Economy, Society and Culture, c. 1500–1900*, Essays for J. S. Grewal, 42–60. New Delhi: Manohar, 1997.

———. 'Conformity and Conflict: Tribes and the "Agrarian System" of Mughal India'. In Meena Bhargava (ed.), *Exploring Medieval India, Sixteenth to Eighteenth Centuries: Politics, Economy, Religion*, 259–86, Vol. I. New Delhi: Orient BlackSwan, 2010.

Singh, Chetan. 'Forests, Pastoralists and Agrarian Society in Mughal India'. In Meena Bhargava (ed.), *Frontiers of Environment: Issues in Medieval and Early Modern India*, 71–97. Hyderabad: Orient BlackSwan, 2017.

Singh, Dilbagh. *The Peasant and the State: Eastern Rajasthan in the Eighteenth Century*. New Delhi: Manohar, 1990.

———. 'Regulating the Domestic: Notes on the Pre-colonial State and the Family'. In Meena Bhargava (ed.), *Exploring Medieval India, Sixteenth to Eighteenth Centuries: Culture, Gender, Regional Patterns*, 285–306. New Delhi: Orient BlackSwan, 2010.

Singha, Radhika. *A Despotism of Law: Crime and Justice in Early Colonial India*. New Delhi: Oxford University Press, 1998.

Soucek, Priscilla P. 'Persian Artists in Mughal India: Influences and Transformations'. *Muqarnas* 4, 1987, 166–81.

Spear, Percival. 'The Mughal Mansabdari System'. In Edmund Leach and S. N. Mukherjee (eds), *Elites in South Asia*, 1–15. Cambridge: Cambridge University Press, 1970.

Spence, Jonathan D. *God's Chinese Son: The Taiping Heavenly Kingdom of Hong Xiuquan*. London: W. W. Norton & Co., 1996.

Spink, Walter M., and Deborah Levine. *Akbarnama: Catalogue*. New York, n.d.

Stein, Burton. 'State Formation and Economy Reconsidered'. *Modern Asian Studies* 19 (3), July 1985, 387–413.

———. *Thomas Munro: The Origins of the Colonial State and His Vision of Empire*. New Delhi: Oxford University Press, 1989.

———. *A History of India*, David Arnold (ed.). Chichester: Wiley-Blackwell, 2010a, 2e.

———. 'Eighteenth Century India. Another View'. In Meena Bhargava (ed.), *Exploring Medieval India, Sixteenth to Eighteenth Centuries: Culture, Gender, Regional Patterns*, 337–66, Vol. II. New Delhi: Orient BlackSwan, 2010b.

Streusand, Douglas. *The Formation of the Mughal Empire*. New Delhi: Oxford University Press, 2001, 2e.

———. *Islamic Gunpowder Empires: Ottomans, Safavids and Mughals*. Boulder, Colorado: Westview Press, 2011.

Subrahmanyam, Sanjay. *The Political Economy of Commerce: Southern India, 1500–1650*. Cambridge: Cambridge University Press, 1990a.

———. *Improvising Empire: Portuguese Trade and Settlement in the Bay of Bengal, 1500–1700*. New Delhi: Oxford University Press, 1990b.

———. 'Iranians Abroad: Intra-Asian Elite Migration and Early Modern State Formation'. *Journal of Asian Studies* 51 (2), 1992a, 340–63.

———. 'The Mughal State—Structure or Process? Reflections on Recent Western Historiography'. *The Indian Economic and Social History Review* 29 (3), 1992b, 291–321.

———. 'Of *Imarat* and *Tijarat*: Asian Merchants and State Power in the Western Indian Ocean, 1400–1750'. *Comparative Studies in Society and History* 37 (4), October 1995, 750–80.

Subrahmanyam, Sanjay. 'Connected Histories: Notes towards a Reconfiguration of Early Modern Eurasia'. *Modern Asian Studies* 31 (3), 1997, 735–62.

———. 'Hearing Voices: Vignettes of Early Modernity in South Asia, 1400–1750'. *Daedalus* 127 (3), Summer 1998, 75–104.

———. *Penumbral Visions: Making Politics in Early Modern South Asia*. Ann Arbor: University of Michigan Press, 2001.

———. *Explorations in Connected History: From the Tagus to the Ganges*. New Delhi: Oxford University Press, 2005a.

———. *Explorations in Connected History: Mughals and Franks*. New Delhi: Oxford University Press, 2005b.

———. 'On World Historians in the Sixteenth Century'. *Representations* 91 (1), Summer 2005c, 26–57.

———. 'Taking Stock of the Franks: South Asian Views of Europeans and Europe, 1500–1800', *The Indian Economic and Social History Review* 42 (1), 2005d, 69–100.

———. 'Further thoughts on an enigma: The tortuous life of Nicolo Manucci, 1638–c. 1720'. *The Indian Economic and Social History Review* 45 (1), 2008, 35–76.

———. 'Turning the Stones Over: Sixteenth Century Millenarianism from the Tagus to the Ganges'. In Meena Bhargava (ed.), *Exploring Medieval India, Sixteenth to Eighteenth Centuries: Politics, Economy, Religion*, 370–410, Vol. I. New Delhi: Orient BlackSwan, 2010.

——— (ed.). *Merchants, Markets and the State in Early Modern India*. New Delhi: Oxford University Press, 1990.

——— (ed.). *Money and Market in India, 1100–1700*, Themes in Indian History. New Delhi: Oxford University Press, 1994.

——— (ed.). *Sinners and Saints: The Successors of Vasco Da Gama*. New Delhi: Oxford University Press, 2000.

Subrahmanyam, Sanjay, and C. A. Bayly, 'Portfolio Capitalists and the Political Economy of Early Modern India'. In Sanjay Subrahmanyam (ed.), *Merchants, Markets and the State in Early Modern India*, 242–65. New Delhi: Oxford University Press, 1990.

Subrahmanyam, Sanjay, and David Shulman. 'The Men Who Would be King? The Politics of Expansion in Early Seventeenth Century Northern Tamilnadu'. *Modern Asian Studies* 24, 1990, 225–48.

Subrahmanyam, Sanjay, and Luis Filipe F. R. Thomaz. 'Evolution of Empire: The Portuguese in the Indian Ocean during the Sixteenth Century'. In James D. Tracy (ed.), *The Political Economy of Merchant Empires, State, Power and World Trade, 1350–1750*. Cambridge: Cambridge University Press, 1991.

Talbot, Cynthia. 'Inscribing the Other, Inscribing the Self: Hindu-Muslim Identities in Pre-Colonial India'. *Comparative Studies in Society and History* 37 (4), October 1995, 692–722.

———. 'The *Nayakas* of Vijayanagara Andhra: A Preliminary Prosopography'. In Kenneth R. Hall (ed.), *Structure and Society in Early South India: Essays in Honour of Noboru Karashima*, 251–75. New Delhi: Oxford University Press, 2001.

Talbot, Cynthia (ed.), *Knowing India: Colonial and Modern Constructions of the Past*, New Perspectives on Indian Pasts, Essays in Honor of Thomas R. Trautmann. New Delhi: Yoda Press, 2011.

Tambiah, Stanley J. 'What did Bernier actually say? Profiling the Mughal Empire'. *Contributions to Indian Sociology* 32 (2), 1998, 361–86.

Tavernier, Jean-Baptiste. *Travels in India*, V. Ball (trans.), William Crooke (ed.), Vol. I. New Delhi: Munshiram Manoharlal Publishers, 2001.

Teltscher, Kate. *India Inscribed: European and British Writing on India, 1600–1800*. New Delhi: Oxford University Press, 1997.

Thackston, W. M. (trans. and ed.). *The Jahangirnama: Memoirs of Jahangir, Emperor of India*. New York: Oxford University Press, 1999.

Thapar, Romila. 'Imagined Religious Communities? Ancient History and the Modern Search for a Hindu Identity'. *Modern Asian Studies* 23 (2), 1989, 209–31.

———. 'The Tyranny of Labels'. *Social Scientist* 24 (9 & 10), September–October 1996, 3–33.

———. 'Reporting History: Early India'. *Social Scientist* 40 (7–8), July–August 2012, 31–42.

Thompson, Edward. *The Other Side of the Medal*. London: The Hogarth Press, 1925.

Thompson, Edward, and G. T. Garrett. *The Rise and Fulfilment of British Rule in India*. London: Macmillan, 1934.

Tilly, Lousie A. 'Connections'. *The American Historical Review*. 99 (1), February 1994, 1–20.

Torri, Michelguglielmo. 'For a New Periodization of Indian History: The History of India as Part of the History of the World'. *Studies in History* 30 (1), 2014, 89–108.

Trautmann, Thomas. *Aryans and British India: New Perspectives on India's Pasts*. New Delhi: Yoda Press, 2004.

Trivedi, Madhu. 'Hindustani Music and Dance: An Examination of Some Texts in the Indo-Persian Tradition'. In Muzaffar Alam, Francoise 'Nalini' Delvoye, and Marc Gaborieau (eds), *The Making of Indo-Persian Culture*, 281–306. New Delhi: Manohar, 2000.

———. 'Images of Women from the Fourteenth to the Sixteenth Century: A Study of Sufi *Premakhyans*'. In Rajat Datta (ed.), *Rethinking A Millennium: Perspectives on Indian History from the Eighth to the Eighteenth Century*. New Delhi: Aakar Books, 2008.

Truschke, Audrey. 'Cosmopolitan Encounters: Sanskrit and Persian at the Mughal Court'. Ph.D. Thesis, Columbia University, 2012a.

———. 'Defining the Other: An Intellectual History of Sanskrit Lexicons and Grammars of Persian'. *Journal of Indian Philosophy* 40 (6), 2012b, 635–68.

———. 'Contested History: Brahmanical Memories of Relations with the Mughals'. *Journal of the Economic and Social History of the Orient* 58, 2015a, 415–52.

———. 'Regional Perceptions: Writing to the Mughal Court in Sanskrit'. *Purusartha* 33, 2015b, 251–74.

———. *Culture of Encounters: Sanskrit at the Mughal Court*. New York: Columbia University Press, 2016.

———. *Aurangzeb: The Life and Legacy of India's Most Controversial King*. Redwood City. CA: Stanford University Press, 2017.

Vanina, Eugenia. *Ideas and Society: India between the Sixteenth and Eighteenth Centuries*. New Delhi: Oxford University Press, 2004, 2e.

———. 'Roads of (Mis)Understanding: European Travellers in India (Fifteenth to Seventeenth Century)'. *The Indian Historical Review* 40 (2), 2013, 267–84.

Verma, Som Prakash. *Art and Material Culture in the Paintings of Akbar's Court*. New Delhi: Vikas Publishing House, 1978.

———. 'Elements of Historicity in the Portraits of the Mughal School'. *The Indian Historical Review* 9 (1–2), 1982–83, 63–73.

———. *Mughal Painters and their Work: A Biographical Survey and Comprehensive Catalogue*. New Delhi: Oxford University Press, 1994.

———. *Mughal Painter of Flora and Fauna, Ustad Mansur*. New Delhi: Abhinav Publications, 1999.

———. *Interpreting Mughal Painting: Essays on Art, Society and Culture*. New Delhi: Oxford University Press, 2009.

———. *Ordinary Life in Mughal India: The Evidence from Painting*. New Delhi: Aryan Books International, 2012.

———. *Mughal Painting*, Oxford India Short Introduction. New Delhi: Oxford University Press, 2014.

Wagoner, Philip B. '"Sultan Among Hindu Kings": Dress, Titles and the Islamicization of Hindu Culture at Vijayanagara'. *The Journal of Asian Studies* 55 (4), November 1996, 851–80.

———. 'Pre-Colonial Intellectuals and the Production of Colonial Knowledge'. *Comparative Studies in Society and History* 45 (4), 2003, 783–814.

Weber, Max. *The Religion of India*, H. H. Gerth and D. Martindale (ed. and trans.). Glencoe III: The Free Press, 1958.

Wescoat Jr., James L. 'Gardens of Invention and Exile: The Precarious Context of Mughal Garden Design during the Reign of Humayun (1530–1556)'. *Journal of Garden History* 10 (2), 1990, 106–16.

———. 'Mughal Gardens and Geographic Sciences, Then and Now'. In Attilio Petruccioli (ed.), *Gardens in the Time of Great Muslim Empires: Theory and Design*, 187–202. Leiden, New York: E. J. Brill, 1997.

Wescoat Jr., James L., and Joachim Wolschke-Bulmahn (eds). *Mughal Gardens: Sources, Places, Representations, Prospects*. Washington, D.C.: Dumbarton Oaks, Trustees for Harvard University Press, 1996.

Wink, Andre. *Land and Sovereignty in India: Agrarian Society and Politics under the Eighteenth Century Maratha Svarajya*. Cambridge: Cambridge University Press, 1986.

———. *Al-Hind, The Making of the Indo-Islamic World: Early Medieval India and the Expansion of Islam, 7th–11th Centuries*, Vol. I. New Delhi: Oxford University Press, 1990.

———. *Al Hind, The Making of the Indo-Islamic World: Indo-Islamic Society, 14th–15th Centuries*, Vol. III. Leiden and Boston: Brill, 2004.

Zaman, Taymiya R. 'Instructive Memory: An Analysis of Auto/Biographical Writing in Early Mughal India'. *Journal of the Economic and Social History of the Orient* 54, 2011, 677–700.

Ziad, Zeenut. *The Magnificent Mughals*. Oxford: Oxford University Press, 2002.

Ziegler, Norman P. 'Some Notes on Rajput Loyalties During the Mughal Period'. In Muzaffar Alam and Sanjay Subrahmanyam (eds), *The Mughal State, 1526–1750*, 168–210, Themes in Indian History, Oxford in India Readings. New Delhi: Oxford University Press, 1998.

———. 'Evolution of the Rathor State of Marvar: Horses, Structural Change and Warfare'. In Meena Bhargava (ed.). *Exploring Medieval India, Sixteenth to Eighteenth Centuries: Culture, Gender, Regional Patterns*, 463–85, Vol. II. New Delhi: Orient BlackSwan, 2010.